GNOSTICISM IN CORINTH

GNOSTICISM IN CORINTH

AN INVESTIGATION OF THE LETTERS TO THE CORINTHIANS

Walter Schmithals

Translated by
John E. Steely

ABINGDON PRESS

Nashville   New York

GNOSTICISM IN CORINTH

Copyright © 1971 by Abingdon Press

Translation from the German language with the approval
of the Publishing House Vandenhoeck and Ruprecht, Göttingen.
© Vandenhoeck & Ruprecht, Göttingen

ISBN: 06-687-14887-1
Library of Congress Catalog Card Number: 70-158670

SET UP, PRINTED, AND BOUND BY THE
PARTHENON PRESS, AT NASHVILLE,
TENNESSEE, UNITED STATES OF AMERICA

Dedicated to
PROFESSOR RUDOLF BULTMANN
with gratitude

TRANSLATOR'S PREFACE

The work of translating Professor Schmithals' stimulating book has been both enjoyable and instructive. No introduction to the book by the translator is necessary. The work speaks for itself. I only hope that in the English form it has lost none of the vigor, clarity, and close-knit reasoning which marked the German original.

I am grateful to Professor Schmithals for his generous cooperation and encouragement in this undertaking. Thanks must be expressed to Mrs. Norma Owens Hash for her skilled and diligent work in preparing the typescript from my handwritten copy. The Southeastern Seminary Alumni Fund provided generous assistance with the costs of typing. Once again, my largest debt is owed to my family for their sharing with me the delights and discouragements involved in presenting this book to a new circle of readers.

JOHN E. STEELY
Wake Forest, N. C.
November, 1970

FOREWORD TO THE SECOND EDITION

The first edition of this study came into being far from any library, during free evening hours after heavy factory labor. I thank the reviewers for having treated with indulgence the obvious deficiencies which have their explanation in those conditions. I ask for the same indulgence for this new edition, which developed in the infrequent and oft-interrupted hours which a large rural parish left me for scholarly labors.

A reworking, which those who own the first edition will forgive, was required not only because of many deficiencies of the old edition. There was also the fact that I have done further work on the same topic and, I hope, have learned something more. A number of essays, which have appeared together under the title *Paulus und die Gnostiker* (English translation in preparation), and a study of *Paul and James* (English translation by Dorothea M. Barton, 1965), cited in the following as Vol. 2 and Vol. 3, form the immediate continuation of the present work. Moreover, in the meantime much important literature on our topic requiring consideration has appeared. I am grateful to the favorable and unfavorable reviewers for many a helpful criticism.

In order to keep the price of the book within tolerable limits, we have refrained from resetting the entire work. This made it necessary to append supplementary materials in the form of postscripts. These postscripts, to which reference is made throughout the body of the book by the numbers in the margins, are found on pages 326 ff.

Those who have used the first edition will note, moreover, that Excursus II has been omitted and replaced with Introduction A, and that in the main part of the book there is a new section: VIII. The Functions of the Community.

Nothing has been changed in the aim and the conclusion of the work, so the remarks in the foreword of the first edition still retain their relevance.

The present study was accepted in 1954 as a dissertation by the theological faculty of the Philipps-Universität in Marburg, on the basis of the report of Prof. D. Rudolf Bultmann. I now dedicate it in gratitude to my honored teacher, whose lectures on the Corinthian epistles awakened in me an interest in "Gnosticism in Corinth," in the hope that this is not only a newly reworked but also an improved edition.

FOREWORD TO THE THIRD EDITION

The text of the second edition has been reviewed, corrected, and occasionally modified. The supplementary notes on pages 326 ff. have been expanded by some 35 pages and again refer to the section which first appeared in the second edition of the book.

Since my suggestions in the foreword to the first edition were not always heeded, I take this occasion once again to say that the concern of this book is not the theology of Paul but rather that of his opponents.

CONTENTS

LIST OF SCRIPTURE PASSAGES

The various individual passages in the Corinthian epistles are treated in the pages indicated below:

I Corinthians

II Corinthians

BIBLIOGRAPHY

My own works are cited in the following way:

1st ed.=*Die Gnosis in Korinth,* FRLANT NF 48 (1956, 1st ed.).

The Office of Apostle=The Office of Apostle in the Early Church (Abingdon Press, 1969), ET by John E. Steely of *Das kirchliche Apostelamt,* FRLANT NF 61 (1961).

Vol. 2=*Paulus und die Gnostiker, Theologische Forschung* 35 (1965). ET by John E. Steely to be published by Abingdon Press, 1971.

Vol. 3=*Paul and James, Studies in Biblical Theology* No. 46 (Alec R. Allenson, 1965), ET by Dorothea M. Barton of *Paulus und Jakobus,* FRLANT 85 (1963).

Works used only occasionally are identified fully in the notes.

Acta Archelai, ed. Beeson, GCS 16 (1906).

C. R. C. Allberry: *A Manichaean Psalm-Book,* Part II (1938).

E. B. Allo: *Saint Paul: Première Épître aux Corinthiens,* 1956, 2nd ed.

W. Anz: *Zur Frage nach dem Ursprung des Gnostizismus,* 1897.

P. Bachmann [1]: *Der erste Brief des Paulus an die Korinther,* mit Nachträgen von E. Stauffer, 1936, 4th ed.

————[2]: *Der zweite Brief des Paulus an die Korinther,* 1918, 3rd ed.

C. K. Barrett: "Christianity at Corinth," BJRL 46 (1964): 269-97.

H. W. Bartsch: "Der korinthische Missbrauch des Abendmahls," DtPfrBl, 1949.

W. Bauer: *Rechtgläubigkeit und Ketzerei im ältesten Christentum,* 1934, 2nd ed., with supplement by Georg Strecker, BhTh 10 (1964). ET *Orthodoxy and Heresy in Earliest Christianity,* ed. by Robert A. Kraft and Gerhard Krodel, Fortress Press, 1971.

R. Baumann: *Mitte und Norm des Christlichen,* NtAbh NF 5 (1968).

A. Bentzen: *Messias—Moses redivivus—Menschensohn,* 1948.

U. Bianchi: *Le Origine dello Gnosticismo, Studies in the History of Religions* (Supplements to *Numen*) XII (1967).

W. Bieder: "Paulus und seine Gegner in Korinth," ThZ 17 (1961): 319 ff.

P. Billerbeck: *Kommentar zum Neuen Testament aus Talmud und Midrasch,* 1956, 2nd ed.

A. Böhlig and P. Labib: *Koptisch-gnostische Apokalypsen aus Codex V von Nag Hammadi, Wissenschaftliche Zeitschrift der Martin Luther Universität Halle-Wittenberg,* 1963, Sonderband 3.

15

G. Bornkamm [1]: *Die Vorgeschichte des sogenannten Zweiten Korintherbriefes*, SAH, 1961, 2.

———— [2]: "Herrenmahl und Kirche bei Paulus," ZThK 53 (1956) : 312 ff.

W. Bousset [1]: *Hauptprobleme der Gnosis*, 1907.

———— [2]: *Die Religion des Judentums im späthellenistischen Zeitalter*, 1926, 3rd ed., ed. H. Gressmann.

———— [3]: "Die Himmelsreise der Seele," ARW, 1901, Sonderdruck 1960.

E. Brandenburger: *Adam und Christus*, WMANT 7 (1962).

W. Brandt: *Elchasai, ein Religionsstifter und sein Werk*, 1912.

———— *Die mandäische Religion*, 1889.

———— "Das Schicksal der Seele nach dem Tode nach mandäischen und parsischen Vorstellungen," *Jahrbücher für protestantische Theologie* 18 (1892) : 405 ff., 575 ff.

F. Büchsel: *Der Geist im Neuen Testament*, 1926, pp. 367-95.

R. Bultmann [1]: *Exegetische Probleme des zweiten Korintherbriefes*, Uppsala, 1947.

———— [2]: *Theology of the New Testament*, ET by Kendrick Grobel of *Theologie des Neuen Testaments*, 1953.

———— [3]: "Die Bedeutung der neuerschlossenen mandäischen Quellen für die Erforschung des Neuen Testaments," ZNW 24 (1925).

———— [4]: *Der Stil der paulinischen Predigt und die kynisch-stoische Diatribe*, 1910.

———— [5]: *Das Evangelium des Johannes*, Meyer *Kommentar* II (1952, 12th ed.).

H. v. Campenhausen: *Die Askese im Urchristentum*, 1949.

Clemens Alexandrinus: *Opera*, ed. Stählin, GCS.

C. Colpe: *Die religionsgeschichtliche Schule, Darstellung und Kritik ihres Bildes vom gnostischen Erlösermythos*, FRLANT NF 60 (1961).

H. Conzelmann: *Der erste Brief an die Korinther*, Meyer *Kommentar* V (1969, 11th ed.).

Corpus Hermeticum, ed. A. D. Nock and A.-J. Festugière, 1945, 1954.

O. Cullmann [1]: *The Christology of the New Testament*, ET by Shirley C. Guthrie and Charles A. M. Hall, 1959, of *Die Christologie des Neuen Testaments*, 1957.

———— [2]: *Peter: Disciple, Apostle, Martyr*, ET by Floyd V. Filson, 1962, of *Petrus*, 1960, 2nd ed.

P. Dalbert: *Die Theologie der hellenistisch-jüdischen Missionsliteratur . . .* , ThF 4 (1954).

K. Deissner: *Auferstehungshoffnung und Pneumagedanke bei Paulus*, 1912.

G. Delling: *Paulus Stellung zu Frau und Ehe*, 1931.

A. Dieterich: *Eine Mithrasliturgie*, 1903, or 3rd ed., 1923.

E. S. Drower: *The Secret Adam*, 1960.

J. Dupont: *Gnosis. La connaissance religieuse dans les épîtres de Saint Paul*, 1949.

P. Feine: *Einleitung in das Neue Testament*, 1935, 7th ed.; 14th rev. ed. of Feine-Behm-Kümmel, ET by A. J. Mattill, Jr. as *Introduction to the New Testament*, 1966.

W. Frankenberg: *Die syrischen Clementinen mit griechischem Paralleltext*, 1937.

M. Friedländer [1]: *Die religiösen Bewegungen innerhalb des Judentums im Zeitalter Jesu*, 1905.

────── [2]: *Geschichte der jüdischen Apologetik*, 1903.

────── [3]: *Der vorchristliche jüdische Gnostizismus*, 1897.

A. v. Gall: *Basileia tou Theou*, 1926.

O. Gebhardt, A. Harnack, and T. Zahn: *Patrum Apostolicorum Opera*, 1877.

D. Georgi [1]: *Die Gegner des Paulus im zweiten Korintherbrief*, WMANT 11 (1964).

────── [2]: Review of the 1st ed. of the present work in VuF, 1960, pp. 90 ff.

────── [3]: *Die Geschichte der Kollekte des Paulus für Jerusalem*, ThF 38 (1965).

F. Godet: *Der erste Brief an die Korinther*, 1886.

E. J. Goodspeed: *Die ältesten Apologeten*, 1915.

L. Goppelt: *Christentum und Judentum im ersten und zweiten Jahrhundert*, 1954.

H. Grass: *Ostergeschehen und Osterberichte*, 1962, 2nd ed.

H. Gressmann: *Der Messias*, 1929.

H. Greeven: "Propheten, Lehrer, Vorsteher bei Paulus," ZNW 44 (1952/53): 1 ff.

E. Güttgemanns: *Der leidende Apostel und sein Herr*, FRLANT 90 (1966).

E. Haenchen [1]: "Gab es eine vorchristliche Gnosis?" ZThK 49 (1952): 316 ff.

────── [2]: *Die Apostelgeschichte*, Meyer *Kommentar* III (1961, 13th ed.).

F. Hahn: *Das Verständnis der Mission im Neuen Testament*, WMANT 13, (1963).

S. Hanson: *The Unity of the Church in the New Testament*, 1946.

W. Hartke: *Die Sammlung und die ältesten Ausgaben der Paulusbriefe*, Diss. Bonn, 1917.

G. Heinrici: *Der zweite Brief des Paulus an die Korinther*, Meyer *Kommentar* VI (1900, 8th ed.).

E. Hennecke: *Neutestamentliche Apokryphen*, 1924, 2nd ed.

E. Hennecke and W. Schneemelcher: *New Testament Apocrypha* I, ET ed. by R. McL. Wilson, 1963, from *Neutestamentliche Apokryphen* I (1959), 3rd ed.

J. Héring [1]: *The First Epistle of Saint Paul to the Corinthians*, 1962, ET by A. W. Heathcote and P. J. Allcock of *La première Épître de Saint Paul aux Corinthiens*, 1959, 2nd ed.

────── [2]: *The Second Epistle of Saint Paul to the Corinthians*, 1967, ET by A. W. Heathcote and P. J. Allcock from the 1st French ed. of *La seconde Épître de Saint Paul aux Corinthiens*, 1958.

J. Hermann: *Kyrios und Pneuma*, 1961.

A. Hilgenfeld: *Die Ketzergeschichte des Urchristentums*, 1884.

Hippolytus: *Philosophumena* (*Refutatio omnium haeresium*), ed. Wendland, GCS 26 (1916).

P. Hoffmann: *Die Toten in Christus*, NtAbh NF 2 (1966).

Irenaeus: *Adversus haereses,* ed. Harvey, 1857.

H. L. Jansen: *Die Henochgestalt,* 1939.

J. Jeremias: *The Eucharistic Words of Jesus,* ET by A. Ehrhardt, 1955, from the 2nd ed., 1949; by Norman Perrin, 1966, from the 3rd ed., 1960, of *Die Abendmahlsworte Jesu.*

J. Jervell: *Imago Dei,* FRLANT 58 (1960).

H. Jonas [1]: *Gnosis und spätantiker Geist* I (1954, 2nd ed.).

———— [2]: *Gnosis und spätantiker Geist* II, 1 (1954).

———— [3]: *The Gnostic Religion,* 1958.

E. Kähler: *Die Frau in den paulinischen Briefen,* 1960.

E. Käsemann [1]: "Die Legitimität des Apostels," ZNW 41 (1942).

———— [2]: *Leib und Leib Christi,* 1933.

———— [3]: *Das wandernde Gottesvolk,* FRLANT 55 (1957, 2nd ed.).

G. Klebba: *Des heiligen Irenäus fünf Bücher gegen die Häresien, übersetzt,* BKV, 1912.

G. Klein: *Die zwölf Apostel,* FRLANT NF 59 (1961).

C. H. Kraeling: *Anthropos and Son of Man,* 1927.

G. Kretschmar: "Zur religionsgeschichtlichen Einordnung der Gnosis," Ev-Theol 13 (1953) : 354 ff.

J. Leipoldt and H. M. Schenke: *Koptisch-gnostische Schriften aus den Papyrus-Codices von Nag-Hammadi,* ThF 20 (1960).

H. Leisegang: *Die Gnosis,* 1955, 4th ed.

M. Lidzbarski: *Mandäische Liturgien,* 1920.

———— *Ginza,* 1925.

———— *Das Johannesbuch der Mandäer,* 1915.

R. Liechtenhahn: *Die Offenbarung im Gnostizismus,* 1901.

H. Lietzmann: *An die Korinther* I, II, HNT 9 (1949, 4th ed.), with supplements by W. G. Kümmel.

G. Lindeskog: *Studien zum neutestamentlichen Schöpfungsgedanken* I (1952).

R. A. Lipsius and M. Bonnet: *Acta Apostolorum apocrypha,* 1891.

D. Lührmann: *Das Offenbarungsverständnis bei Paulus und in paulinischen Gemeinden,* WMANT 16 (1965).

W. Lütgert: *Freiheitspredigt und Schwarmgeister in Korinth,* 1908.

W. Marxsen: *Introduction to the New Testament: An Approach to Its Problems,* 1968, ET by G. Buswell of *Einleitung in das Neue Testament,* 1963.

A. Merx: *Der Messias oder Ta'eb der Samaritaner,* 1909.

W. Michaelis [1]: *Einleitung in das Neue Testament,* 1954, 2nd ed.

———— [2]: *Ergänzungsheft* to the preceding, 1961.

———— [3]: *Die Gefangenschaft des Paulus in Ephesus,* 1925.

O. Michel: *Abraham unser Vater: Festschrift für O. Michel zum 60. Geburtstag,* 1963.

J. A. Montgomery: *The Samaritans,* 1907.

L. Morris: *The First Epistle of Paul to the Corinthians,* 1958.

S. Mowinckel: "Urmensch und Königsideologie," StTh II (1949) : 71 ff.

J. Müller-Bardorff: "Zur Frage der literarischen Einheit des Philipperbriefes," WZUJ 7 (1957/58) : 591-604.

J. Munck: *Paul and the Salvation of Mankind*, 1959, ET by Frank Clarke of *Paulus und die Heilsgeschichte*, 1954.

B. Murmelstein: "Adam, ein Beitrag zur Messiaslehre," WZKM, 1928, pp. 242 ff.; 1929, pp. 51 ff.

F. Neugebauer: *In Christus*, 1961.

K. Niederwimmer: *Der Begriff der Freiheit im Neuen Testament*, 1966.

H. Noetzel: *Christus und Dionysos*, 1960.

E. Norden: *Agnostos Theos*, 1956, 4th ed.

D. W. Oostendorp: *Another Jesus*, Kampen, 1967.

E. Osty: *Les Épîtres de Saint Paul aux Corinthiens*, 1959, 3rd ed.

E. Percy [1]: *Untersuchungen über den Ursprung der johanneischen Theologie*, Lund, 1939.

—— [2]: *Die Probleme der Kolosser- und Epheserbriefe*, Lund, 1946.

E. Peterson: *Frühkirche, Judentum und Gnosis*, 1959.

Philastrius: *Adversus haereses*, CSEL 38 (1898).

A. Plummer: *A Critical and Exegetical Commentary on the First Epistle of St. Paul to the Corinthians*, 1914, 2nd ed.

—— *A Critical and Exegetical Commentary on the Second Epistle of St. Paul to the Corinthians*, 1915.

P. Pokorný: *Der Epheserbrief und die Gnosis*, 1965.

H. Preisker: "Zur Komposition des Zweiten Korintherbriefes," ThBl 5 (1926): 154 ff.

K. Preysing: Hippolyt, *Philosophumena*, übersetzt, BKV, n. d.

K. Prümm: *Diakonia Pneumatos*, Vol. I (1967); Vol. II, 1 (1960); II, 2 (1962).

Pseudo-Clementines: *Homilien*, ed. B. Rehm, GCS 42 (1953).

G. Quispel [1]: "Der gnostische Anthropos und die jüdische Tradition," *Eranos-Jahrbuch* 22 (1953): 195-234.

—— [2]: "Christliche Gnosis und jüdische Heterodoxie," EvTheol 14 (1954): 474 ff.

B. Reicke: *Diakonie, Festfreude und Zelos*, 1951.

R. Reitzenstein [1]: *Die hellenistischen Mysterienreligionen*, 1956, 4th ed.

—— [2]: *Poimandres*, 1904.

—— [3]: *Das iranische Erlösungsmysterium*, 1921.

—— [4]: "Zur Mandäerfrage," ZNW 26 (1927): 39 ff.

R. Reitzenstein and H. H. Schaeder: *Studien zum antiken Synkretismus*, 1926.

P. Riessler: *Altjüdisches Schrifttum ausserhalb der Bibel*, 1928.

J. Rohr: "Christuspartei und Schwarmgeister in Korinth," TheolQuart, 1911, pp. 165 ff.

J. Roloff: *Apostolat—Verkündigung—Kirche*, 1965.

E. Rose: *Die Christologie des Manichäismus*, Diss. Marburg, 1941.

K. Rudolph [1]: *Die Mandäer I, Das Mandäerproblem*, FRLANT NF 56 (1960).

—— [2]: *Die Mandäer II, Der Kult*, FRLANT NF 57 (1961).

—— [3]: "Ein Grundtyp gnostischer Urmensch-Adam-Spekulation," ZRGG 9 (1957): 1 ff.

H. M. Schenke [1]: *Die Herkunft des sogenannten Evangelium Veritatis*, 1959.

—— [2]: *Der Gott "Mensch" in der Gnosis*, Berlin, 1962.

D. Schenkel: *Ecclesia Corinthia primaeva factionibus turbata*, 1838.

A. Schlatter [1]: *Die korinthische Theologie*, 1914.

—— [2]: *Paulus, der Bote Jesu*, 1934.

H. Schlier [1]: *Christus und die Kirche im Epheserbrief*, 1930.

—— [2]: *Religionsgeschichtliche Untersuchungen zu den Ignatiusbriefen*, 1929.

—— [3]: *Der Brief an die Epheser*, 1958.

—— [4]: *Die Kirche im Epheserbrief*, 1949.

C. Schmidt: *Gespräche Jesu mit seinen Jüngern (Epistula Apostolorum)*, TU III, 13 (1919).

C. Schmidt and W. Till: *Koptisch-gnostische Schriften*, 1959, 3rd ed.

P. Schmiedel: *Die Briefe an die Corinther*, Hand-Commentar zum Neuen Testament, 1893.

H. J. Schoeps [1]: *Theologie und Geschichte des Judenchristentums*, 1949.

—— [2]: *Aus frühchristlicher Zeit*, 1950.

—— [3]: *Paul*, 1961, ET by Harold Knight of *Paulus*, 1959.

—— [4]: *Urgemeinde, Judenchristentum, Gnosis*, 1956.

G. Scholem: *Die jüdische Mystik in ihren Hauptströmungen*, 1957.

M. Schrage: *Die konkreten Einzelgebote in der paulinischen Paränese*, 1961.

K. Schubert: *Die Religion des nachbiblischen Judentums*, 1955.

S. Schulz [1]: *Untersuchungen zur Menschensohnchristologie im Johannesevangelium*, 1957.

—— [2]: *Komposition und Herkunft der johanneischen Reden*, 1960.

W. Schultz: *Dokumente der Gnosis*, 1910.

H. Schwantes: *Schöpfung der Endzeit*, 1962.

A. Schweitzer: *The Mysticism of Paul the Apostle*, 1931, ET by William Montgomery of *Die Mystik des Apostels Paulus*, 1930.

E. Schweizer [1]: *Erniedrigung und Erhöhung bei Jesus und seinen Nachfolgern*, 1955.

—— [2]: "Die Kirche als Leib Christi in den paulinischen Homologumena," TLZ 86 (1961), cols. 161 ff.

—— [3]: "Die Kirche als Leib Christi in den paulinischen Antilegomena," TLZ 86 (1961), cols. 241 ff.

E. Sjöberg: *Der Menschensohn im äthiopischen Henochbuch*, 1946.

J. S. Semler: *Paraphrasis II epistulae ad Corinth.*, 1776.

H. v. Soden: *Sakrament und Ethik bei Paulus*, 1931.

W. Staerk [1]: *Soter* I (1933).

—— [2]: *Die Erlösererwartung in den östlichen Religionen, Soter* II (1938).

E. Stauffer: *New Testament Theology*, 1955, ET by John Marsh of the 5th ed. of *Die Theologie des Neuen Testaments*.

H. L. Strack: *Jesus, die Häretiker und die Christen*, 1910.

G. Strecker: *Das Judenchristentum in den Pseudoclementinen*, TU 70 (1958).

K. Stürmer [1]: "Judentum, Griechentum und Gnosis," TLZ, 1948, cols. 581 ff.

—— [2]: *Auferstehung und Erwählung*, 1953.

R. C. Tannehill: *Dying and Rising with Christ*, BZNW 32 (1967).

R. V. G. Tasker: *The Second Epistle of Paul to the Corinthians*, 1958.

H. E. Tödt: *The Son of Man in the Synoptic Tradition*, 1965, ET by Dorothea

M. Barton of *Der Menschensohn in der synoptischen Überlieferung*, 1959.

J. Thomas: *Le mouvement baptiste en Palestine et Syrie*, 1935.

W. C. Till: *Die gnostischen Schriften des koptischen Papyrus Berolinensis 8502*, TU 60 (1955).

H. Weinel: "Die Echtheit der paulinischen Hauptbriefe im Lichte des anti-gnostischen Kampfes," *Festgabe für J. Kaftan*, 1920, pp. 376 ff.

J. Weiss [1]: *Der erste Korintherbrief*, Meyer *Kommentar* V (1910, 9th ed.).

———— [2]: *Earliest Christianity*, 1959, reprint in two vols. of ET (originally published in 1937 under the title *The History of Primitive Christianity*) by Frederick C. Grant and others of *Das Urchristentum*, 1917.

H. D. Wendland: *Die Briefe an die Korinther*, NTD 7 (1938, 3rd ed.).

G. P. Wetter: *Der Sohn Gottes*, 1916.

G. Widengren: *Iranische Geisteswelt*, 1961.

R. McL. Wilson [1]: "Some Recent Studies in Gnosticism," NTS 6 (1960): 32 ff.

———— [2]: *The Gnostic Problem*, 1958.

U. Wilckens [1]: *Weisheit und Torheit*, 1959.

———— [2]: "Kreuz und Weisheit," KuD 3 (1957): 77 ff.

H. Windisch: *Der zweite Korintherbrief*, Meyer *Kommentar* VI (1924, 9th ed.).

T. Zahn: *Introduction to the New Testament*, ET by John Moore Trout and others from the 3rd ed. of *Einleitung in das Neue Testament*.

L. Zscharnack: *Der Dienst der Frau in den ersten Jahrhunderten der christlichen Kirche*, 1902.

ABBREVIATIONS

ARW	Archiv für Religionswissenschaft
AThANT	Abhandlungen zur Theologie des Alten und Neuen Testaments
BhTh	Beiträge zur historischen Theologie
BiblZ	Biblische Zeitschrift
BJRL	Bulletin of the John Rylands Library
BKV	Bibliothek der Kirchenväter
BZAW	Beihefte zur Zeitschrift für die alttestamentliche Wissenschaft
BZNW	Beihefte zur Zeitschrift für die neutestamentliche Wissenschaft
CBQ	Catholic Biblical Quarterly
CD	The Cairo Document (Damascus Document)
Comm. Viat.	Communio Viatorum
CSEL	Corpus Scriptorum Ecclesiasticorum Latinorum
DtPfrBl	Deutches Pfarrerblatt
ET	English translation
EvTheol	Evangelische Theologie
FRLANT	Forschungen zur Religion und Literatur des Alten und Neuen Testaments
GCS	Die griechischen christlichen Schriftsteller
HNT	Handbuch zum Neuen Testament
HTR	Harvard Theological Review
JBL	Journal of Biblical Literature
KuD	Kerygma und Dogma
LXX	Septuagint
NF	Neue Folge
NtAbh	Neutestamentliche Abhandlungen
NTD	Das Neue Testament Deutsch
NTS	New Testament Studies
OLZ	Orientalistische Literaturzeitung
PSG	Patrologia, Series Graeca
PSL	Patrologia, Series Latina
1QS	Manual of Discipline from Qumran 1
RAC	Reallexikon für Antike und Christentum
Rech. Bibl.	Recherches Bibliques
RGG	Die Religion in Geschichte und Gegenwart
SAH	Sitzungsberichte der Heidelberger Akademie der Wissenschaften
SJT	Scottish Journal of Theology

StTh	Studia Theologica
TDNT	Theological Dictionary of the New Testament, ET by G. W. Bromiley of G. Kittel's Theologisches Wörterbuch zum Neuen Testament
ThBl	Theologische Blätter
Theol. Jb.	Theologische Jahrbücher
Theol. Quart.	Theologische Quartalschrift
Theol. Viat.	Theologia Viatorum
ThF	Theologische Forschung
ThRs	Theologische Rundschau
ThStKr	Theologische Studien und Kritiken
ThZ	Theologische Zeitschrift
TLZ	Theologische Literaturzeitung
TSanh	Tosefta Sanhedrin
TU	Texte und Untersuchungen
TWNT	Theologisches Wörterbuch zum Neuen Testament, ed. G. Kittel
VC	Vigiliae Christianae
VuF	Verkündigung und Forschung
WMANT	Wissenschaftliche Monographien zum Alten und Neuen Testament
WUNT	Wissenschaftliche Untersuchungen zum Neuen Testament
WZKM	Wiener Zeitschrift für die Kunde des Morgenlandes
WZUJ	Wissenschaftliche Zeitschrift der Universität Jena
ZKG	Zeitschrift für Kirchengeschichte
ZNW	Zeitschrift für die neutestamentliche Wissenschaft und die Kunde der älteren Kirche
ZRGG	Zeitschrift für Religions- und Geistesgeschichte
ZThK	Zeitschrift für Theologie und Kirche

INTRODUCTION A: GNOSTICISM

A study which, like the following, does not have Gnosticism itself as its subject but employs the phenomenon of "Gnosticism" as a key in order to unlock what is still hidden, the nature and character of Paul's opponents in Corinth, must first say what it means by the term "Gnosticism." This is to be done in the following under the first division (I). The more general statements made there are then, under division II, to proceed into the description of a definite theological system which, in view of the Gnosticism in Corinth, deserves our special attention.

I. General and Methodological Remarks   1

The interest of Christian theology in the complex known as Gnosticism is still increasing; for more than ever, questions are being asked about the connections particularly of the New Testament with the Gnostic movement. This increasing interest is matched by a growing uncertainty about what is after all to be understood by "Gnosticism," and this uncertainty is heightened in recent times by discussions as to the proper method of comprehending the phenomenon "Gnosticism."

The church fathers saw in the Gnostic movement in general an apostasy, staged by the devil and standing under the influence of Greek philosophy, from the true and original teaching of Christianity. Even Harnack's famous definition of Gnosticism as the "acute hellenizing of Christianity" said nothing essentially different. The fact that already long before Harnack some were speaking more correctly of "orientalizing" rather than "hellenizing" still did not decisively alter this judgment.

It was only at the beginning of the present century that the recognition prevailed that Gnosticism does not represent a Christian heresy but an independent "pagan" religion which could appear as a Christian heresy only through its penetration into Christian circles and its association with Christian thought-material, as in the same way it appeared as Jewish, Iranian, or Islamic heresy, among others. Under the impact of this awareness, the historians of religion (Anz, Reitzenstein, Bousset, and many others) asked anew about the origin of Gnosticism. People recognized in it some motifs—mostly mythological ones—of Babylonian, Iranian, Greek, and Jewish, yes, and even of Indian and Egyptian beliefs. Gnosticism thus was shown to scholarship to be a phenomenon of the syncretism which was widespread in the period around the birth of Christ. It was not always seen or noted that Gnosticism was *more* than the sum of diverse mythologoumena, and thus it was found difficult to determine the specifically Gnostic as such. Anyone who saw this "more," that is, the actually Gnostic element, tried to explain it in terms of the adding together of the individual elements.

Over against this, H. Jonas showed convincingly in a number of examples that what was distinctive in the Gnostic religion could not be explained in terms of the combination of diverse mythological motifs.[1] For this distinctive element is in fact more than a new myth; it is a new understanding of God, man, and world, and Jonas is concerned in his study above all to lift this Gnostic understanding out of the Gnostic myth by means of the methods of existential interpretation. Even though the Gnostic myth may be compounded of mythological motifs of various origins, yet the Gnostic self-understanding cannot possibly be. When, for example, the Gnostic imagines himself to be imprisoned in this world as in an evil and alien world, such a feeling cannot be derived from Hellenism nor from Iranian religion, and therefore naturally not from the two together,[2] even if the representation of such a self-understanding—the body as prison of the soul —has as its presupposition the anthropological dualism of Hellenism *and* the cosmological dualism of the religion of Zarathustra. Thus Gnosticism as an understanding of human existence is older than the religio-historical phenomenon of "Gnosticism."

The question as to what then Gnosticism really is has been at first complicated by Jonas' new methodological beginning; for today one can see, in the peculiar misunderstanding of what Jonas meant, Jonas' existence-analytical method played off against the motif-historical method of study.[3] Jonas' demonstration that the latter is "inadequate" [4] indeed does not mean that it can be *replaced* by the method of existential interpretation. For if one attempted to grasp and to describe the phenomenon "Gnosticism" by means of this latter method alone,

---

[1] H. Jonas, [1], pp. 25 ff.

[2] *Contra*, again most recently, G. Quispel, [1], pp. 223-24: "That there is a rupture in the deity or even that the life-will is to be denied may not be classified as Hellenistic or Jewish. And yet the Jewish conceptual world and the Hellenistic popular philosophy and astrology are sufficient to clarify the question of origin" (*scil.*, of Gnosticism) !

[3] E.g., C. Colpe, *Die religionsgeschichtliche Schule*, p. 64.

[4] D. Georgi, [2], p. 93.

the concept "Gnosticism" would become unusable for all religio-historical labors.

The unitary fundamental attitude of Gnosticism, as Jonas ([1], pp. 140-251) describes it, is the feeling of man that he lives in a world that is alien to him, in which he must be afraid. True life is beyond. Hence the Gnostic yearns for a redemption which frees him from the world and the body. Therefore typically Gnostic concepts are, for example: anxiety, lostness, homesickness; stupor, sleep, drunkenness; fall, sinking, imprisonment; darkness, alienation, mixing. It is clear that such a basic attitude is found in many places and in many times, in various religions and in the most diverse forms of expression ("Objekti- 2 vationen"). With these concepts important formulations of the Christian understanding of existence also are to be described. In the Western world alone, then, the following, for example, would be Gnostic: the mystery cults and Pauline theology, Marcion's doctrine and that of the Bogomils, monasticism and branches of Jewish apocalyptic, the heretics and heresy fighters of the early church, Albigenses and modern anthroposophy.[5]

Now of course one may attempt to criticize Jonas' interpretation of the Gnostic self-understanding. Such criticism would be justified. Jonas' interpretation is one-sided. This is probably to be attributed to the fact that he leans too much on the Mandaean and Manichaean texts,[6] which indeed, because of their scope, provide a relatively comfortable basis for an investigation of the Gnostic attitude toward existence, but represent a late Gnosticism for which essential elements of the genuine Gnostic self-consciousness have already been lost. Thus Jonas sets forth with emphasis the feeling of anxiety, the homesickness, the yearning for redemption, and the "thrownness" of the Gnostic. This last-named feature is centrally present particularly in the Mandaean texts, for which the concept of sin is again current in a thoroughly un-Gnostic manner. But the tremendous sense of freedom and victory on the part of the pneumatic person, who has overcome the hostile world, who is free from anxiety and care, who is satisfied and full of self-glorying, all this is treated much too lightly. And yet these latter features are really the self-consciousness of the genuine Gnostic, who knows himself as φύσει σωζόμενος to be already perfect and complete (see pp. 179 ff.), while the cosmic dread with its consequences of various magical-mysterious assurances against the demons is a sign of the late period

---

[5] Opinions like the following then are not surprising: ". . . the question as to a definite place and a definite time of the emergence of Gnosticism probably is wrongly posed. . . . In any case it appears justified in the history of religion to reckon with various times of emergence as well as with various places of emergence of Gnosticism" (C. Colpe, pp. 7-8). Cf. Vol. 2, p. 45.

[6] Cf. C. Colpe, p. 191.

and of the decay of Gnosticism. Where this is observed, Paul for example can no longer appear as a Gnostic, and it becomes doubtful whether Origen and Plotinus are representatives of genuinely Gnostic self-understanding.

But even the correctness of this criticism[7] and the consideration of it in interpretation would change nothing in the fact that following the way of existential interpretation *alone* one does not arrive at a religio-historically usable concept of "Gnosticism"; for the number and the kind of the possible objectivations of the "Gnostic" self-understanding are *in principle* unlimited.[8]

Nothing is said therewith against Jonas' brilliant and epochal investigation. Only its mistaken application is rejected, and Jonas himself is quite innocent of such. Jonas does not intend to suppress motif-historical research; he intends to supplement it. Where it reaches its goal, there he begins, at the same time consigning it to its limits.[9] To

---

[7] The necessity of such criticism is shown, e.g., in C. Colpe, who, following the one-sided categories of H. Jonas, states that in view of the Gnostic assertion of the essential divinity of the human self or of the substantial unity of redeemer and redeemed, "the two major problems with which Gnosticism is concerned" lose "their ultimate sharpness": "the depravation of the light becomes merely accidental, since its substance remains in essence the same as that which it will redeem; and since light remains light and presses toward the light, the redemption must take place with an almost mechanical necessity—ultimate obligation then no longer befits the efforts for it" (*ibid.*, p. 186). Indeed! But may we accuse Gnosticism here of illogic and inconsistency? Certainly not! Colpe's argument rather shows that Jonas' categories are inadequate. They mislead one into seeking the major problems of Gnosticism in the wrong place, for they are not able adequately to grasp the "predestinationist" basic structure of Gnostic existence: the knowledge of the inalienability of the pneumatic substance and the inevitability of the redemption which is in God's interest. Just to recognize this inalienability is Gnosticism!

[8] Thus, correctly, Colpe in *ibid.*, pp. 190-91.

[9] "Traditional dualism, traditional astrological fatalism, traditional monotheism were all drawn into it, yet with such a peculiarly new twist to them that in the present setting they subserved the representation of a novel spiritual principle; and the same is true of the use of Greek philosophical terms. . . . They all do in fact appear in the new stream: symbols of old oriental thought, indeed its whole mythological heritage; ideas and figures from biblical lore; doctrinal and terminological elements from Greek philosophy, particularly Platonism. It is in the nature of the syncretistic situation that all these different elements were available and could be combined at will. But syncretism itself provides only the outer aspect and not the essence of the phenomenon. The outer aspect is confusing by its compositeness, and even more so by the associations of the old names. However, though these associations are by no means irrelevant, we can discern a new spiritual center around which the elements of tradition now crystallize, the unity behind their multiplicity; and this rather than the syncretistic means of expression is the true entity with which we are confronted. If we acknowledge this center as an autonomous force, then we must say that it makes use of those elements rather than that it is constituted by their confluence; and the whole which thus originated will in spite of its manifestly synthetic character have to be understood not as the product of an uncommitted eclecticism but as an original and determinate system of ideas" (H. Jonas, [3], pp. 23-24).

define and delimit the concept "Gnosticism" in such a way that it becomes religio-historically usable, one cannot avoid motif-historical research. But this teaches us to reserve the concept "Gnosticism" for that objectivation of the Gnostic understanding of existence which Jonas calls "mythological Gnosticism."

Of course the problematic of this phenomenological definition of "Gnosticism" consists in the fact that one is in danger of speaking of Gnosticism wherever a motif of the Gnostic myth emerges, even when, as for example in Paul or John, it expresses an understanding of existence wholly different from the genuinely Gnostic. R. Reitzenstein, for example, succumbed to this danger; he made Paul out to be a Gnostic, not because of his understanding of existence but because of the Gnostic ideas and concepts which occur in him. Here the method of existential interpretation, which Jonas has so splendidly demonstrated with the late Gnostic texts, proves itself to be a useful and necessary corrective.

Thus for the determination of what Gnosticism is, the phenomenological method of the historian of religion and the religio-philosophical method of existential interpretation are to be used *together*.[10] Then Gnosticism, however much it is drawn into the syncretism of its time and could not even emerge without it, still is exhibited as a religious phenomenon *sui generis*, for which two essential features are characteristic and distinctive: a pronounced understanding of the world and of self, and a distinctive mythology as the expression of that understanding. There is a Gnostic understanding of being which is just as clearly distinguished from that of the pure mystery cults as from the Pauline consciousness of existence. And there is a Gnostic myth which in spite of its demonstrable origin in the diverse oriental mythology is a precise and substantial expression exactly and only of the Gnostic picture of the world and man. Only where the two coincide may one speak of genuine Gnosticism, and within this Gnosticism the two are always indissolubly joined together, sometimes one component, sometimes the other being preponderant. In general one may say that an excess of mythological speculation is always a sign of diminishing exis-

3

---

[10] Of course in so doing one runs the danger of being reproached by one reviewer "that the author works with the religio-historically unusable Gnosis-concept of H. Jonas" (*Literaturanzeiger* 1 [1957]) , and from a second, on the other hand: "Thus on the whole Schmithals pursues the motif-historical method which Jonas has shown to be unsatisfactory" (D. Georgi, [2], p. 93) ; and from a third, that an investigation with "an intention sometimes aimed at historical reconstruction, sometimes at grasping human historical atttiudes" is "far from being a scientific comprehension of the subject" (C. Colpe, p. 64) .

tential tension—and conversely, as one can study in the later Gnostic systems.[11]

Under this presupposition, we shall use in the following the name "Gnosticism" for that religious movement which teaches man to understand himself as a piece of divine substance. Although he has fallen, through a disastrous fate, into captivity to an alien world and its demonic rulers, he may be certain of liberation from that captivity because he possesses the awareness of his inalienable divine being.

4   The major motifs in which this Gnosticism is objectified are:

1. a cosmological dualism, whether of an original or of a derived kind;
2. the myth of the fall of the light-substance into the power of the evil forces, i.e., the primal man myth;
3. the presence of the knowledge of this human essence and destiny,
5   i.e., the redemption.[12]

The following concepts, among others, through which the mythological motifs are shown to be related to the existence of man, correspond to these major motifs:

1. Light-darkness; good-evil; life-death; from above-from below; spirit-flesh; God-world;
2. Anxiety; wandering; "thrownness"; captivity; sleep; drunkenness;
3. Call; wisdom; illumination; knowledge; salvation; redemption; resurrection; ἤδη τέλειος; freedom.

The mythological motifs named above as such are not originally

---

[11] This paragraph is taken verbatim from the first edition. In view of this fact, a criticism like the following rebounds on its author himself: Schmithals has "fallen into a historical pan-Gnosticism which no longer recognizes any distinctions, not only between Gnosticism with and without the redeemer myth, but also between these two types on the one hand and syncretism, the Stoa, and Hellenistic Judaism on the other" (Colpe, p. 64). The problem of pre-Christian Gnosticism is too important for one to replace substantive discussion with irritated polemics which refrain from actually taking note of the other person's meaning.

[12] A redeemer myth is *not* included among these motifs. Phenomenological research has already seen that indeed redemption itself, but not a redeemer myth, is constitutive for Gnosticism (see *The Office of Apostle*, pp. 115-16) ; Jonas' existence-analytical method allows us fully to understand this fact. C. Colpe, who correctly recognizes this state of affairs (pp. 30, 198, *et passim*) nevertheless writes on p. 200 concerning the Gnostic redeemer myth: "But it is this after all that first holds the above-named motifs (*scil.,* of the Gnostic understanding of existence) together and gives to Gnosticism its typical character as doctrine and system." He proposes therefore to define the essence of Gnosticism by inquiring, in a book that has not yet appeared, after the Gnostic redeemer myth. Such a study certainly is necessary and promises new information. Nevertheless the key to the determination of the essence of Gnosticism does not lie here. For even if one disregards the fact that the *essence* of Gnosticism is not at all derived from the study of mythological motifs, still there is the fact that the genuine mythological objectivation of Gnosticism is not the redeemer myth but the myth of "man," of which the redeemer myth is only a reflection.

Gnostic. They have their pre-Gnostic history which can be traced out more or less extensively and certainly.

The cosmological dualism of Gnosticism has without question the dualistic world outlook of Iranian religion as its presupposition. On the other hand, the anthropological dualism of Gnosticism, by which man is pulled in both ways in this cosmological dualism in such a way that he himself is seen dualistically, is hardly to be explained without reference to the religious and philosophical traditions of Greece. As far as we know, the oriental religions did not afford Gnosticism the possibility of objectifying its self-understanding in the form of anthropological dualism.[13] But this was done by that stream of Greek dualism as it confronts us in Plato's *Phaedo* as the earliest explicit source.[14] It made possible the Gnostic conceptions of the otherworldly home of the self and the return to the heavenly home after death.[15]

What is common to Plato's doctrine of the soul in *Phaedo* and the Gnostic self-expressions (ἐγώ εἰμι . . .) may be limited altogether to the formal aspect. But precisely this *form* which was originally alien to the Orient, to be able to divide man in dualistic fashion, made possible the mythological representation of that self-understanding which we know as the Gnostic self-understanding by means of just this mythology. All this does not dispute that Gnosticism did not develop out of Greek dualism but made use of it; it is, on the contrary, explicitly affirmed. But with all the recognition of the fact that there was a "gnosticism" before "Gnosticism," we still must ask seriously about the historically conditioned origin of the anthropological dualism of Gnosticism. This is not to deny that the Gnostic understanding of existence, especially the negative attitude toward the world, to a great extent stands in opposition to the Greek understanding of existence of all shades. However, at least the *possibility* of a derivation of the anthropological dualism of Gnosticism from the Greek spirit is not affected, at least not if one understands the concept "derivation" with the limitation with which it can only be reasonably understood in general in the context of the phenomena of intellectual history.

[13] Rather, they taught Judaism to confess the specifically undualistic view of the resurrection of the body; cf., e.g., A. v. Gall, *Basileia tou Theou*, pp. 245-46.

[14] On the obscure origins of this dualism, see, e.g., H. Jonas, [1], pp. 251 ff.; K. Prümm, "Die Orphik im Spiegel der neueren Forschung," *Zeitschrift für katholische Theologie*, 1956, pp. 1 ff.; G. Pfannmüller, *Tod, Jenseits und Unsterblichkeit* (1953), pp. 25 ff., 30-31, 167, 171 ff.; U. v. Wilamowitz-Moellendorf, *Der Glaube der Hellenen* (1959, 3rd ed.), I: 368 ff.; II: 56, 185 ff., 249 ff.; F. Cumont, *Die orientalischen Religionen* (1959), 4th ed., pp. 192 ff.; R. Bultmann in ThRs 23 (1955): 214, 222; H. Noetzel, *Christus und Dionysos* (1960), p. 12; W. Jaeger, *Die Theologie der frühen griechischen Denker* (1953), pp. 69 ff., 88 ff.; E. Frank, *Wissen, Wollen, Glauben* (1955), pp. 51-85.

[15] A. Dieterich (*Eine Mithrasliturgie*, pp. 185 ff.) shows with complete accuracy that the conception of the heavenly journey of the soul can be explained neither from Iranian nor from Babylonian religion.

6

7

It will also be impossible to understand the third of the above-named Gnostic motifs without the presuppositions which were given through the Greek concept of knowledge; on this, see pp. 141 ff.

In the following we are interested above all in the second named motif, the primal man myth. The basic expression of the Gnostic understanding of existence is the mythological conception that the selves of individual men are parts of *one* heavenly figure, which were overpowered by lower powers hostile toward God, torn away and fettered in individual material bodies, after they had been robbed of the recollection of their heavenly origin. This figure of the "primal man" was early recognized as pre-Gnostic,[16] and following the lead of others, above all W. Bousset, R. Reitzenstein and H. Schaeder traced it back into the sphere of Indo-Iranian mythology.[17] According to Indo-Iranian cosmogony, as it is best seen in the Rig-Veda (X, 90), the universe emerged when the gods sacrificed Purusha and from the parts of the body made earth and heaven, moon and sun. Still more wide-spread is the conception of the primal beast from the body of which the gods formed the universe. These views are best known to us from the Germanic mythology in which the giant Ymir corresponds to Purusha, the cow Audhumba to the primal beast. Thus the entire myth may ultimately be of Aryan origin. In this form it still contains nothing Gnostic but, if one does not reject religio-historical derivations in general, there can be no doubt that the Gnostic primal man is related to the Aryan cosmogony. It is impossible to mark out the path from there to here in detail. Yet two great turning points of the primitive myth of a cosmic primal creature as the substance of the universe are to be postulated: a dualistic and an anthropological. The two could run parallel in time; both can be demonstrated in Iranian religion.

On this, Schaeder has set forth a splendid investigation in which happily he has printed his sources—above all the cosmogonic sections of the Great Bundahisn—in full.[18] In these sources the primal beast and primal man, here called Gayōmart, "mortal life," always stand side by side, though this duplication would not be necessary. The original cosmogonic function of the two figures is still presupposed when it is said that eight metals came forth from the slain Gayōmart. One new

---

[16] Cf. R. Bultmann, [5], p. 12.

[17] In the more recent literature, cf.: C. H. Kraeling, *Anthropos and Son of Man*, pp. 85 ff.; S. Mowinckel, "Urmensch und Königsideologie," StTh II (1948/49) : 72 ff.; K. Kerényi, *Mythologie und Gnosis* (1942), pp. 69 ff.; S. S. Hartman, *Gayōmart* (Uppsala, 1953) ; C. Colpe, *Die religionsgeschichtliche Schule*, pp. 140-70 (Literature) ; G. Widengren, *Iranische Geisteswelt*.

[18] Reitzenstein-Schaeder, *Studien zum antiken Synkretismus*, pp. 205 ff. Cf. also A. v. Gall, *Basileia tou Theou*, pp. 108-9, 124-25, 138-39; C. Colpe, *Die religions-geschichtliche Schule*, pp. 153 ff.; G. Widengren, *Iranische Geisteswelt*, pp. 56 ff. *passim*.

thing is that the primal man (as also the primal beast) is slain by powers hostile to the deity; another is that the emergence of the first human pair is placed in connection with Gayōmart. At his death Gayōmart lets seed fall on the earth, and men come forth from the seed. Therewith the dualistic and the anthropological turning points of the Indo-Iranian myth are already accomplished, the latter of course still in a pre-Gnostic form. There is no thought of a substantial connection between primal man and individual men. Only after the bones of Gayōmart have been once again awakened to life at the end of time do men also have hope of being resurrected in his train in glory. Here certainly is the point of beginning for the most ancient, pre-Gnostic mystery cults for which in fact the primal beast also still played a central role: through magical means mortal man intended to secure participation in the destiny of the dead and rising god.

The decisive turn to Gnosticism lay in the fact that man recognized his real self, his soul, as a part of the god "Man." [19] Now he no longer understood himself as merely bound up in fate, but as substantially and personally identical with the primal man who has fallen into the power of darkness;[20] he is φύσει, by nature, god.[21]

Underlying this change is an original Gnostic "fundamental experience" which is not to be derived from any previous mythical motifs. However, just as Gnosticism apparently made use of the anthropological schema which the Greek world placed at its disposal without it thereby becoming possible to explain Gnosticism in terms of the Greek understanding of existence, so also it made use of motifs of oriental

---

[19] But this heavenly being appears also in Gnosticism occasionally still as a bull; cf. C. R. C. Allberry, *A Manichaean Psalm-Book*, II: 226.15 ff.

[20] It cannot be often enough emphasized that the Gnostic conception of man's being, which by its very nature is divine since its origin, is strictly to be distinguished from the much older mystery piety of all shades, according to which the natural man is deified by means of mysteries in the course of which the god or a divine Dynamis takes up its abode in him or bestows upon him a share in the destiny of the god. Even if the differences between an ecstatic mystery gathering and Gnostic ecstatics appear to be minimal, still it may not be overlooked that *there* the primitive, generally diffused ecstatic religiousness, which always was already aware of being possessed by a god, laid hold upon the primal man myth for the (creative) interpretation of itself, while *here* a fundamentally different human self-understanding, which was always alien to the Orient, is connected with this very same myth. 8

Until late the distinction between mystery cults and Gnosticism is evident in the fact that the mystery communities remain individual communities, while the Gnostic (and the Christian) communities represent the whole ecclesia, which exists before the member communities as σῶμα Χριστοῦ or σῶμα τοῦ ἀνθρώπου. The individualistic aspect, which shaped the eschatology of the mystery cults, also explains the fact that they did not conduct organized missions and send out apostles as did Gnosticism.

Cf. further G. Kretschmar in RGG (3rd ed.), II, col. 1658; H. Jonas, [2], pp. 53 ff.; G. Pfannmüller (see p. 31, n. 14), pp. 18-19.

[21] On the Gnostic Anthropos myth, cf. now E. S. Drower, *The Secret Adam* (1960).

primal man myths in order mythologically to objectify its understanding of existence without thereby being derivable from the Iranian primal man speculation.[22]

The Gnostic consciousness found its apparently simplest mythological expression in the trinity of Father-Mother-Son or God-Sophia-Anthropos: the ineffable primal Father emanates Sophia who together with the primal Father brings forth Anthropos, who then falls into the power of the dark forces. This simple myth forms the basis of almost all the later speculative Gnostic systems.

C. Colpe (pp. 140-70) has recently attempted to present proof "that the Iranian primal man Gayōmart did not have a subsequent history in Gnosticism or in late Judaism" (p. 169), that his figure "did not have a further influence in Gnosticism, either directly or indirectly, or in any kind of transformations" (p. 205). This judgment, set forth with great assurance, forms the actual conclusion of his work. He comes to this conclusion by way of the "typological investigation" (p. 154). I give an example of this: "Gayōmart's role as warrior. The role has had various formulations: he is slain by Ahriman or is tortured with a thousand tortures; he lives thirty years more after Ahriman's attack; on the other hand he is said to destroy Ahriman, and the latter does not venture to rebel for fear of Gayōmart.

The conceptions which may most readily be compared with this one, the Manichaean conceptions, have altogether different presuppositions. The invasion of the king of darkness takes place in the pre-existent world of light; that of Ahriman in the already created world which in itself is good. Correspondingly, the battle of Gayōmart takes place on this concrete earth, not in the world of darkness into which he had to descend. Consequently his death also only has anthropogonic, not cosmogonic, significance. It is not a redemption of his Self in the pre-existent world, but of his entire corporeal person at the end of time. With the Manichaeans the redemption consists of his entrance into the realm of light, over against which the darkness, again separated from the light, stands. Among the Zoroastrians it consists of the entrance into a naturalistically conceived Paradise which is all in all" (p. 159).

Let us grant that all this is correctly seen. What then follows from this? Only that Gnosticism is something other than the religion of Zarathustra! But no one questions that. Of course, in the history-of-religions school, which Colpe is criticizing, it was occasionally attempted to explain the emergence of Gnosticism as a modification of Iranian (or Babylonian or Egyptian or other) conceptions which on their part were already essentially Gnostic. But this happened only occasionally, and at least since Hans Jonas' book [1], that is, in the past twenty-five years, has not happened at all in any way that is to be taken seriously. If Colpe intends to prove that the primal man myth in Gnosticism expresses something other than the primal man myth of the Pahlavi writings, this proof is indeed successful, but at the same time then Colpe's investigation appears as a hardly understandable anachronism.

[22] Cf. K. Rudolph, art. "Urmensch," 2c, in RGG (3rd ed.), VI, col. 1196.

But now Colpe intends more than this. He intends to show that the one has nothing to do with the other. But how does this judgment proceed from the knowledge that the primal man myth in Gnosticism expresses something other than in Iran? Here we have a hasty conclusion which overshadows everything which Colpe—often rightly—criticizes in the historians of religion by way of erroneous conclusions. The faulty and outdated method of deriving an essentially new understanding of existence from an adding together of objectivations, and thus the naïve identification of conception and content, is now simply elevated by Colpe to the rank of a methodological law, even though it is a law of criticism, in that he considers a migration of motifs possible only when therein the continuity of what is expressed by means of such a motif continues to be preserved. But this method actually means the end of all religio-historical work.

Actually the motifs migrate in such a way that they are also fitted in their entirety into the wholly different presuppositions of their new surroundings.[23] An example may make clear what is meant: a typological investigation in the style of Colpe certainly will not be able to establish any sort of agreement between the Old Testament Messiah, the Jews' earthly king of the end-time, and the New Testament Christ, the heavenly redeemer of the world. But to conclude from this that the two figures had nothing to do with each other, as Colpe's method demands, obviously would be absurd.

Further, H. M. Schenke ([2], esp. pp. 16 ff., 108 ff., and 155) has recently denied that the Anthropos myth of Gnosticism is related to the oriental myths of the primal man; it is in Manichaeism that the figure of Gayōmart is first connected with the Gnostic myth. Schenke's criticism of the prevailing thesis that the Gnostic primal man presupposes pre-Gnostic myths of the Orient is strained and not convincing. It becomes understandable only when one keeps in mind that in his book Schenke is attempting to derive the Gnostic Anthropos myth "from Gnostic speculation on the Scripture passage

[23] ". . . as in the New Testament, one will be obliged to determine, with the help of the religio-historical comparative method, the dependence of Gnostic expressions upon earlier conceptions, in which case then it would be inappropriate to speak of Gnosticism in the Iranian, Qumran-Essene, and Greek-Orphic perspective circle and the semi-Jewish baptist sects' region. Rather, in this primitive oriental and Asiatic 'quarry' there are the building stones, concepts, and motifs; in short, the themes which then passed through the medium of the typically Mandaean-Gnostic understanding of existence, the Gnostic consciousness. Only after this appropriation, critical revision, and refocusing can we speak of Gnostic views" (S. Schulz in ThRs 26 (1960/61) : 333). In essence this is excellently seen and described.

C. Colpe also, in his essay "Zur Leib-Christi-Vorstellung im Epheserbrief" in the Festschrift for J. Jeremias ([1960], pp. 172 ff., esp. 182 ff.) , works with this correct method, even though, as it seems to me, quite awkwardly (see below, p. 66), in that he ultimately traces the Pauline body-of-Christ conception back to the Stoic Logos doctrine, which is supposed to have come to Paul in a metamorphosed form as it is found in Philo. Whatever truth this theory may possess, at any rate one must affirm that the typological differences between the Gayōmart myth and the Manichaean primal man conception are minor in comparison with the differences between the Stoic Logos doctrine and the Pauline σῶμα Χριστοῦ idea.

K. Rudolph also takes a position against Colpe, correctly, in TLZ 88 (1963), esp. col. 30.

Gen. 1:26-27" (p. 155). Since this attempt is untenable (see below, pp. 77-78),
the old, recognized, even though unprovable derivation of the Gnostic primal
man from mythological speculations of the Orient remains the only sensible
religio-historical explanation of this central Gnostic figure.[24]

But our interest here is directed less to the *motif-historical* problems
of the primal man myth than to this mythological motif itself; or, more
exactly stated, to a definite systematic formulation of the Gnostic
primal man myth. Therefore in the following we shall investigate—
primarily phenomenologically—a system of pre-Christian Christ Gnosticism.

II. A System of Pre-Christian Christ Gnosticism

Our attention thus is drawn to a Gnostic *system,* not to individual
features of Gnostic mythology or of Gnostic self-understanding. This
system is a *pre-Christian* system. This is to be understood in terms of
substance as well as temporally: The system to be set forth is not only
uninfluenced by Christian ideas, but is also older than the beginnings
of the Christian proclamation. Nevertheless what is involved is the
system of a *Christ Gnosticism.* The figure or the name of the Messiah
thus plays a central role in this system. It necessarily follows that in
the pre-Christian Christ Gnosticism we have to do with a system of
Jewish Gnosticism.

In Book VI, 9-18 of his *Refutatio,* Hippolytus discusses the contents
of a Simonian writing which bears the title ἡ μεγάλη ἀπόφασις, "Great
Proclamation," or "Great Revelation." The discussion contains only
three apparently literal quotations from the Ἀπόφασις, two short ones[25]
and one longer one, the limits of which cannot be precisely determined.[26] We do not know to what extent Hippolytus follows the
arrangement of his copy of the work in his treatment of it; to what
extent he reproduces his source correctly, or how much he abridges
it without understanding it, or understanding it amiss; whether and

---

[24] E. Brandenburger, *Adam und Christus,* p. 133, also regards it as unsatisfactory
to see the *cosmological* figure of the Iranian primal man as prototype for the
anthropological figure of the Gnostic Anthropos. Since on the other hand the points
of affinity between the two types are not to be overlooked, he reckons with later
influences of the cosmological primal man idea or its conceptualization on the
Gnostic Anthropos myth (p. 153). But this means the renunciation of a religio-
historical understanding of the origin of just this Anthropos myth, a renunciation to
which the considerable differences between the primal man conception in Iranian
dualism and the Anthropos myth in Gnosticism would give occasion only if the
concept of derivation should presuppose that what is derived has taken over its
model without alteration.

[25] VI, 9.4 = Wendland, p. 136.16 ff.; VI, 14.4 = 139.25-26.

[26] VI, 18.2 ff. = 144.10 ff.

where he allows other accounts of the Simonians to enter into his discussion; whether he shifts the sense of his source, either consciously or unwittingly. This makes it impossible for us to reconstruct his source as it lay before him, even with only a measure of probability.

Thus it also remains uncertain whether this source itself formed an original unity or already exhibited traces of a more or less extensive reworking and expansion. There is much to suggest that the 'Απόφασις did not lie before Hippolytus in its original integrity (see below).

In any case it is impossible to fit together into one simple clear scheme all the concepts, notions, figures, allegories, etc., which occur in Hippolytus' treatment. Breaks of various kinds are inescapable. Nevertheless the Gnostic thought underlying all of Hippolytus' statements may be clearly recognized.

The key word is the designation appearing in Hippolytus' discussion in various connections: ὁ ἑστώς, στάς, στησόμενος.[27] In this name for the central figure of the Gnostic myth, who in the 'Απόφασις is usually called ἡ μεγάλη δύναμις or ἡ ἀπέραντος δύναμις, there is also reflected the destiny of this figure and thus the destiny of God, of man, and of the world.

As ἑστώς the "unbegotten, incomparable and infinite Power"[28] rests in itself "above."[29] But it derived no pleasure from it, so it set in motion the process of becoming. As source of becoming, the unbegotten δύναμις is compared with the fire[30] which is the "root of the universe."[31] The "world thus begotten"[32] has a "twofold nature";[33] it is partly concealed, partly visible. The visible part of the world can be compared to the trunk of a tree, the invisible part to its fruit.[34] Thus the visible part exists not for its own sake but for the sake of the invisible part.

The invisible part, however, is nothing other than the δύναμις itself, which as στάς stands "below," "in the stream of waters, begotten in the

[27] On this formula, see E. Haenchen, [1], p. 330, n.

[28] VI, 12.3 = 138.19.

[29] VI, 17.1 = 142.28.

[30] VI, 9.5 = 136.22 ff.; VI, 12.1 = 138.7.

[31] VI, 9.4 = 136.18 ff. In VI, 18, Sigē appears as the root of the universe. Presumably this is an indication of an expansion of the writing which underlies the "Apophasis"; this expansion then is found elsewhere also in chap. 18, e.g. in the bestowal of the name "Father" upon the "Dynamis," and appears already to have left traces in chaps. 13-14.

[32] VI, 12.1 = 138.8-9.

[33] VI, 9.5 = 136.24-25; VI, 14.5-6. = 139.30 ff.

[34] VI, 9.8 ff. =137.4 ff. As is known, a man named Elchesai is acknowledged as founder of the Jewish-Gnostic sect of the Elchesaites. This name means "hidden power" (see G. Strecker in RAC, s.v. Elkesai) and originally certainly does not have reference to any individual person, but rather the power which is concealed in all Gnostics, which redeems itself: the στάς (see below, p. 50). Widespread in Gnosticism also is the allusion to the "hidden treasure" or something similar.

image." [35] "In the stream of waters" means "in man," for in the Ἀπόφασις Paradise with its four streams[36] is interpreted allegorically as the womb with two veins and two arteries surrounding it.[37] Thus according to Simon "this man begotten of blood" is "a house, and in it dwells the unlimited Dynamis which he calls the root of the universe." [38] That this δύναμις as στάς is "begotten in the image" expresses the identity of begotten and unbegotten Dynamis.[39] Of course the ἑστώς lives in the στάς, as is repeatedly emphasized, only δυνάμει, i.e., potentially, not ἐνεργείᾳ, actually.[40] However, when the "Logos," [41] which here is promulgated in the form of the Apophasis (ἀπόφασις φωνῆς καὶ ὀνόματος),[42] reaches the understanding of man, the unlimited power which is present as potentiality is "ἐξεικονίσθη," stamped as an εἰκών,[43] that is, it now "is one and the same in essence, power, greatness, and perfection with the unbegotten and infinite Power and in no way is inferior to that unbegotten, incomparable, and unlimited Power." [44] The δύναμις of the στάς which is stamped as an εἰκών thus will stand "above" as στησόμενος "with the blessed, unlimited Power." [45]

This is apparently the meaning of the entire world process, that in the process of becoming, the *one* Power, "divided above and below," "enlarges itself" (αὔξουσα), in that it "begets itself," "seeks itself, finds itself, its own mother, its own father, its own sister, its own spouse, its own daughter, its own son, mother, father, one, root of the All." [46]

Hence the unlimited Dynamis is placed in *every* man as potentiality;[47] this system knows nothing of a distinction of Pneumatics and hylics.

[35] VI, 17.1 = 142.28-29.
[36] Cf. Hipp. V, 9.15 (Naassene Preaching) = 101.4 ff.
[37] VI, 14.7 = 140.7 ff.
[38] VI, 9.5 = 136.19 ff.
[39] VI, 14.5 = 139.31.
[40] VI, 12.2 = 138.14-15; VI, 14.6 = 140.2; VI, 16.5 = 142.16-17; VI, 17.1 = 142.27.
[41] VI, 16.5 = 142.17; VI, 17.7 = 143.29-30; VI, 10.2 = 137.24 ff.
[42] VI, 9.4 = 136.16.
[43] In VI, 12 = 138.7 ff., the world's coming to be is grounded in three pairs of roots: νοῦς and ἐπίνοια; φωνή and ὄνομα; λογισμός and ἐπιθύμησις. In these six roots the whole infinite "Dynamis" (as potentiality) is present. The pairs named stem, as to form, from the biblical creation story (LXX; cf. H. Leisegang, *Die Gnosis,* pp. 72-73). In the "Apophasis" the first pair apparently designates the Dynamis as such, perhaps in its doubling as ἑστώς and στάς; cf. VI, 13.1 = 138.25-26; VI, 18.3 = 144. 13 ff., where of course there can also be a later interpretation of VI, 12. The second pair refers to the summons which comes to man to actualize himself, thus the Gnostic "call," "Gnosis" itself. The third pair denotes then the insight, the thought, the will of the man who accepts the call and follows it. Only through this threefold rooting does the created world find its way through to the uncreated Dynamis.
[44] VI, 12.3 = 138.16 ff.
[45] VI, 17.1 = 143.2.
[46] VI, 17.3 = 143.7 ff.
[47] VI, 13 = 139.9 ff.

For this reason also an end of becoming apparently is not foreseen. The Logos, which alone can change the στάς into the actuality of the στησόμενος, abides to eternity,[48] and begetting may not and will not cease, as is shown in an allegorical exposition of Gen. 3:24, since otherwise even the μεγάλη δύναμις residing in man as potentiality would be destroyed.[49]

Important for us is the fact that in this Gnostic system a redeemer apparently does not appear. I deliberately say "apparently." It is clear that this system knows nothing of a heavenly redeemer who comes down in order to instruct ignorant men. There is not even the suggestion of such a mythological redeemer figure. Indeed one cannot really speak even of a redemption which takes place within this system. For redemption presupposes a catastrophe in the course of which the Pneuma falls into the hands of evil forces. Nothing is said of such a catastrophe in our system. The Pneuma—the "unlimited Dynamis"— is, by virtue of its own will, in the dual nature of the cosmos as potentiality. But *enlightenment* about the *meaning of becoming,* in which man is actively to participate, is needed. This enlightenment comes about by means of the Word, which emerges ἐν τόπῳ κυρίου[50] = ἐν στόματι[51] = ἐξ ἐπινοίας τῆς μεγάλης δυνάμεως.[52, 53]

The one who speaks this word is Simon as actual or alleged author of the Ἀπόφασις. He speaks with divine authority: Ὑμῖν οὖν λέγω ἃ λέγω καὶ γράφω ἃ γράφω. Τὸ γράμμα τοῦτο.[54] His authority is that of the μεγάλη δύναμις in general, which he himself is as well. Beginning with the earliest report about Simon in Acts 8:9 ff., it is unanimously related in all the accounts about him that he claims to be ἡ μεγάλη δύναμις. No doubt is possible as to the actuality of this claim. In the framework of the system of the Apophasis, of course, this claim cannot be meant in an exclusive sense. Nevertheless one must describe the Simon of the Ἀπόφασις, using the traditional concepts, as redeemer or, better, as revealer, even if his self-consciousness is not different from that of men in general who have stamped their δύναμις into an εἰκών.

[48] VI, 10.2 = 137.22 ff.

[49] VI, 17:4-7 = 143.12 ff. Only those who do not realize their potentiality are permanently annihilated together with their potentiality: VI, 9.9-10 = 137.10 ff.; VI, 12.4 = 138.19 ff.; VI, 16.6 = 142.22 ff. Cf. Saying 71 of the Coptic Gospel of Thomas: "Jesus said: When you beget in yourselves him whom you have, he will save you. If you do not have him within yourselves, he whom you do not have within yourselves will kill you" (Robert M. Grant with David Noel Freedman, *The Secret Sayings of Jesus,* p. 174.)

[50] VI, 17.7 = 143.29.

[51] VI, 10.2 = 137.24 ff.

[52] VI, 9.4 = 136.16-17.

[53] Cf. Hipp. V, 9.5 = 98.16 ff.

[54] VI, 18.2 = 144.10-11; cf. John 3:11!

There is no higher being than the δύναμις, and even the latter is placed in every man as potentiality,[55] thus also in Simon. If a man by virtue of his Dynamis leads other men to the actualization of their Dynamis-Self, this one man is thus the typically Gnostic "redeemed redeemer" who, in that he "redeems" the δύναμις of which he also is a part, is himself "redeemed." Thus it is also said of the δύναμις that it "seeks itself, finds itself." [56] Moreover, it therefore is not accidental that in the traditions about him Simon does not appear alone but in a circle of so-called pupils who make the same claim without thereby competing with him.[57]

Is the system of the 'Απόφασις—that the concept of "system" is appropriate here is beyond question—a system of pre-Christian Gnosticism? Certainly so as far as substance is concerned. The fact that Hippolytus' treatment contains two or three New Testament quotations[58] changes nothing of the fact that the construction of the system of the 'Απόφασις at no point presupposes the Christian proclamation.[59] But in point of *time* also? In other words: does the system of the 'Απόφασις exhibit the features of the original Simonian Gnosticism, or is it the outcome of a long development of this Gnosticism?

If the question were only whether the 'Απόφασις, so far as we can determine from Hippolytus' treatment, was an original work of Simon and as such pre-Christian, it would be easy to answer. Obviously the 'Απόφασις is not an original work of Simon. The New Testament quotations argue against that. Further, in VI, 14.8 [60] Galienus (2nd cent. A.D.) perhaps is used. Finally, as we have seen, the 'Απόφασις appears not to have been a unitary work in all respects.

But we are not asking about the age of the 'Απόφασις as a literary document, but about the age of the system portrayed in it, a system which in all its terminology betrays its closeness to the other[61] representations of the Simonian Gnosticism which have been handed down, but in other respects differs so significantly from the latter that one must decide for the priority of the one system or the other.[62]

[55] It is well known that in late Judaism δύναμις has become a name of God, as is shown in the New Testament in Mark 14:62 and parallels. The designation δύναμις is used with this import in the "Apophasis."

[56] VI, 17.3 = 143.9.

[57] Cf. *The Office of Apostle*, pp. 162-63.

[58] VI, 9.10 = 137.11 ff.; VI, 14.6 = 140.3-4; VI, 16.6 = 142.23 ff.

[59] Cf. E. Haenchen, [1], p. 336.

[60] = 140.15 ff.; cf. Wendland, *in loc.*

[61] E.g. Philastrius, Haer. 29; Const. Ap. VI, 7 ff.; Iren. I, 23; Hipp. VI, 19; Justin, Apol. I, 26.1-3; Epiph. Haer. XXI; Tert., de anima 34; the sources rather fully in A. Hilgenfeld, *Die Ketzergeschichte des Urchristentums*, pp. 163 ff.

[62] The attempt of H. Jonas ([1], pp. 353 ff.) to combine the two streams of tradition is impermissible and futile.

According to Iren. I, 23.2-3, Simon propounded the following false teaching:

"He leads about with him a certain Helena whom he himself bought in Tyre, a city of Phoenicia, as a prostitute, and says that she is the first conception of his mind, the mother of all, through whom he determined at the beginning to create angels and archangels. This Ennoia went forth from him, recognized what her father intended, descended, and gave birth to the angels and powers by whom this world is said to have been made. But after she had borne them, she was seized by them out of jealousy, because they did not wish to be regarded as the children of any other.

"He himself was wholly unknown to them. But his Ennoia was held fast by the powers and angels which she herself had brought forth. She had to suffer all sorts of indignity at their hands so that she might not return again to her father, until she was even put into a human body and in the course of time migrated, as from vessel to vessel, into ever new female bodies.

"Thus she was also in that Helen on whose account the Trojan War was fought, because of whom also Stesichorus, who composed insulting songs to her, was blinded and received his sight again only when he apologized and wrote odes in which he praised her. Thus she wandered from one body to another, in every one always suffering humiliation anew, until she finally landed in a brothel: she is, in other words, the lost sheep.

"On her account he himself came, in order first to raise her herself and to liberate her from her fetters, but then also to bring salvation to men through his Gnosis."

In comparison with this portrayal, E. Haenchen ([1], 337-38, 349) holds the system of the Ἀπόφασις to be the later formulation of Simonian Gnosticism. What reasons are determinative for this judgment?

First, "it is *philosophical*, no longer actually mythological *Gnosticism* that is visible here." [63] Indeed, in the system of the Ἀπόφασις the myth is sharply broken. There is no genuine dualism, which of course holds true also for the Simonian system as found in Irenaeus. The dual character of the world is willed by the δύναμις so that in the world that is becoming manifest the δύναμις which is hidden there as potentiality might be actualized. Angelic powers hostile to God and the devilish demiurge are lacking.

More important is the fact that the purely substantial basic attitude of Gnosticism is relaxed. Nothing is said of the Pneumatic who is saved in any case, or of the Hylic, for whom there *can* be no salvation. Rather, in *every* man the Pneuma, the δύναμις, is placed potentially, and it requires no human activity to actualize the potentiality of the

[63] [1], p. 337.

δύναμις into the imperishable being of the στησόμενος. Of course this conversion is only imperfectly achieved. It is not an act of the will or of obedience that leads to such actualization, but in good Gnostic tradition the mere acceptance of the illuminating word.

This already suggests that the understanding of existence which is expressed in the system of the "Great Proclamation" is the genuinely Gnostic one: man is not a creation but divine nature, divine Dynamis. Earth and flesh are his temporary dwelling. Like all that is visible they will be destroyed by fire (VI, 9.8 ff. = 137.4 ff.). Man himself returns to his heavenly home if he follows the word of redemption which Simon addresses to him.

This allows us to recognize that the system of the "Great Proclamation" does not represent a premythological form of Gnosticism but one that has been demythologized to a certain degree. The μεγάλη 'Από-φασις presupposes the Gnostic mythology.[64] Is this demythologizing accomplished by philosophical interests or does it issue in a philosophical figure, that is, is it done from motives which we can only with difficulty attribute to the Samaritan Simon in the pre-Christian era? Hardly! The outward character of the 'Απόφασις points in every way to another influence, namely Judaism. The elimination of the cosmological dualism and the softening of the anthropological as well as the transformation of the pneumatic *being* into a *possibility* is in my judgment characteristic of Jewish influence. In this connection one must certainly take into account the fact that already at the time of the birth of Christ many an encounter between Judaism and philosophy had taken place. But the typical problem of later philosophical "Gnosticism" of how the emanation of the lower world from the deity is conceivable still does not interest the author of the "Great Proclamation." One is rather disposed to recall Philo, who was, in his own way, a "philosophical Gnostic," and this precisely as a younger contemporary of Simon. Thus the "philosophical" character of the 'Απόφασις says nothing about the time of its emergence and gives no occasion to deny the system described in it to Simon.

Naturally it is possible that the demythologizing in the system of the 'Απόφασις belongs to a later stratum of tradition; perhaps the system of Simon himself was still more mythological. Yet a reintroduction of the substantial Gnostic concept of the Pneuma into the discussion of the 'Απόφασις which we have before us would not alter the structure of its peculiar system. It would instead only let it all the more clearly emerge—precisely also in comparison with the Simonian system in Irenaeus. This mythological structure, however, draws our interest. However and whenever the shape of this

64 E. Haenchen, [1], p. 349.

system which confronts us in the "Great Proclamation" arose, the—philosophical or Jewish—formulation of the system cannot itself establish a late dating of the basic structure of the system.[65] The strong Jewish influence and the absence of Christian influence argue on the contrary for the great antiquity of the system underlying the "Great Proclamation."

Of course Haenchen particularly misses the redeemer figure of Simon. "The historical figure of Simon has disappeared; he now is only the revealer of the 'Απόφασις." [66] Nevertheless this fact, which Haenchen employs as an argument against the antiquity of the system of the 'Απόφασις, now argues decisively *for* its originality. In that early Christian era there are, especially in Gnosticism, more than a few examples of the proclaimer becoming the one proclaimed. On the other hand, for the proclaimed one to be demoted to a mere proclaimer, for the heavenly emissary to become an ordinary Gnostic, is without example.

We must note also that the later the period, the more securely is the figure of a heavenly redeemer-emissary appearing in historical form established in Gnosticism, while early Gnosticism, especially pre-Christian Gnosticism, was not yet acquainted with this figure.[67]

In addition, the following observation should be made: the Simon of the Irenaean system is a highly mythological figure. The claim to be the most high God in person, who has descended to earth in order to seek and to lead back above the Ennoia, the first emanation of his very self, is inconceivable as the claim of a rational historical being. The Simon of the 'Απόφασις, on the other hand, is one of those numerous prophetic apostles who appear in the Near East around the beginning of the Christian era and are also characteristic of early Gnosticism.[68] G. P. Wetter has made a study of these figures in his book *Der Sohn Gottes,* and H. Leisegang[69] also rightly classes Simon in the series of those earthly apostles who announce their truth with the

[65] Of course one should also refrain from turning the argument around, as J. Jervell (*Imago Dei,* p. 132, n. 50) does: "The Gnosticism of Simon Magus, which is so important for our presentation, is early Gnosticism, as is shown by the thought that makes use of conceptual categories and the reduction in the use of mythology." The "philosophical" form of a Gnostic system can *in no wise* be adduced for a dating of this system.

[66] [1], p. 349.

[67] Cf. J. Jervell, p. 145, n. 91; p. 137, n. 63; W. Schultz, *Dokumente der Gnosis,* pp. XIII, 125, 130; M. Dibelius in *Botschaft und Geschichte* II (1956) : 69; 78; *The Office of Apostle,* pp. 115 ff.

Above all, concerning the Anthropos figure which is identical with the Dynamis of Simon, one can say at the outset only that it "is identical with the inner man." "Only as Christian influences began to have their effect did the Anthropos become primal man *and* redeemer" (J. Jervell, p. 138, n. 63) .

[68] Cf. *The Office of Apostle,* pp. 159 ff.

[69] *Die Gnosis,* pp. 83 ff.

claim of immediate divine revelation or of their own divine authority.[70]

E. Haenchen himself sees a further difficulty which results from placing the Irenaean system earlier than that of the 'Απόφασις. The personification of the Ennoia in the figure of Helena is already a stage of development of the myth, since the Ennoia must originally have been thought of as scattered in *all* Pneumatics, as then also the redemption by Simon originally can have applied only to the Pneumatics in general, not to the individual Helena.[71] Thus undoubtedly the system of Irenaeus, in which the redemption of the Pneumatics is portrayed in the form of the Simon-Helena legend, was preceded by a more original system, in which Simon appears in direct contact with concrete individual men. This system of Simon that is to be presupposed was, according to Haenchen, based upon Simon's self-understanding that "in him the most high deity, the father of the Ennoia, the 'Great Power,' has come down in order to redeem men and therewith to set the Ennoia free." [72] That such a redeemer myth underlies the Simon-Helena legend may still be clearly seen from the presentation given by Irenaeus and reproduced above. But, as we have already said, such a mythological self-understanding cannot have been that of the historical Simon. So we are directed still further back to that original system of Simonianism which is present in the 'Απόφασις—possibly in a sharply demythologized form—and which knows Simon only as proclaimer.

We should observe further that the system of the 'Απόφασις, in spite of two or three New Testament quotations, which will hardly have belonged to the original form of the writing, exhibits no Christian influences of any kind. It is a different story with the system portrayed by Irenaeus. Already the figure of Simon as a heavenly emissary appearing in a historical man may betray a Christian influence.[73] This is certainly true of the distinct stamp of this figure: "Now this man, who was revered by many as a god, taught concerning himself that he had appeared among the Jews as Son, descended in Samaria as Father and among the other peoples had come as Holy Spirit." [74] Simon came in such a form "that he looked like a man and yet was not one, appeared to have suffered in Judea and yet had not suffered." [75] The formal Christianization appearing here of a pre-Christian system is typical of the development of the Gnostic systems generally and is a symbol of

<hr>

[70] Herein the "Apophasis" is essentially distinguished from the productions of actual philosophical Gnosticism.

[71] E. Haenchen, [1], p. 341.

[72] [1], p. 348.

[73] See *The Office of Apostle*, pp. 132 ff.

[74] Iren. I, 23.1; cf. Hipp. VI, 19.6.

[75] Iren. I, 23.3.

the church's superiority in the struggle with Gnosticism during the second and third centuries. The reverse development would be unexampled and in the second and third centuries unthinkable, so on the basis of this consideration also the system of the Ἀπόφασις is indicated as the original one.

Further, it will presently be shown that Gnostic systems without a redeemer myth of the same kind as the Simonian system discussed by Hippolytus appear frequently among the early accounts of Jewish and Christian Gnosticism; among them are the original systems of the Naassenes, the Valentinians, and the Marcosians, which we cannot consider in detail in the following, but cf. pp. 53-54 and *The Office of Apostle*, pp. 168 ff.

Finally, it is worthy of note that the so-called Naassene Preaching in Hippolytus, which appeals to numerous passages of biblical and poetic tradition, contains in V, 9 (= 98.17 ff.) a detailed quotation from the Ἀπόφασις, which—in whatever form—accordingly already qualified as Holy Scripture for the author of the "Naassene Preaching." This also proves the relatively high antiquity of the system of the Ἀπόφασις, which according to all these considerations is to be regarded even *temporally* as a system of pre-Christian Gnosticism.   12

Now it is no longer a very long step to the identification of this system as "pre-Christian Christ Gnosticism." When Simon identifies himself as the "Great Power," he therewith makes the claim, not to be a definite divine emanation, but an emanated part of the one original God himself. We have seen that the Ἀπόφασις developed just this Simonian claim and how it developed it. It is immediately understandable that all the divine predicates can be claimed by Simon or can be attributed to him. Thus, following Irenaeus, Hippolytus rightly says that Simon tolerated "being called by any name with which people wished to name him." [76] Hence he is called not only Great Power[77] or The Standing One,[78] but also God,[79] Son of God,[80] Father,[81] Holy Spirit,[82] Kyrios,[83] Savior,[84] and so on.

The title "Christ" however also belongs to these titles used by him

[76] Hipp. VI, 19.6 = 147.8-9; cf. Iren. I, 23.1.
[77] Hipp. VI, 19.4; Epiph. Haer. XXI, 1; Origen Cels. V, 62; VI, 11; Iren. I, 23.1; Ps.-Cl. Hom. II, 22; Acts 8:10; Acta Petri 4; Ps.-Cl. Rec. III, 47.1.
[78] Clem. Alex. Strom. II, 11.52; Ps.-Cl. Hom. II, 22; Rec. III, 46-47; Mart. Petri II = Lipsius-Bonnet I, 80.37.
[79] Ps.-Cl. Hom. II, 22; Rec. II, 9; III, 63; Iren. I, 23.1; Acta Petri 4, 10; Justin Apol. I, 26.1-2; Jerome on Matt. 24:5; Justin Dial. 120.6.
[80] Hipp. VI, 19.6; Iren. I, 23.1; Epiph. Haer. XXI, 1; Mart. Petri et Pauli 15.
[81] Hipp. VI, 19.6; Epiph. Haer. XXI, 1; Iren. I, 23.1-2.
[82] Hipp. VI, 19.6; Iren. I, 23.1.
[83] Hipp. VI, 20.1.
[84] Acta Petri 4.

or ascribed to him.[85] In the pre-Christian system of Simonianism as it underlies the ᾿Απόφασις this title of Christ is not taken from the Christian conception of the redeemer but from the religious terminology of Judaism. In essence, it is only the *title* which is appropriated, not a conception originally bound up with it (see p. 53). When it is said in Hipp. VI, 19.6[86] that Simon had appeared as a man although he was not a man, and had *apparently* suffered in Judea, had appeared to the Jews as Son, and to the other peoples as Pneuma Hagion, it is still clear in this late report that Simon is the Christ not as the *one* Christ who has appeared in Jesus but as the Pneuma who has appeared in all, and only thus also in Jesus.

Did Simon himself also call that divine figure, as a part of which he was on earth, by the name of Christ? In that case the system of Simon would actually be the system of a pre-Christian *Christ* Gnosticism. Unfortunately it cannot be *proved* that Simon himself used this name. It is true that it is told even of Dositheus,[87] who serves as Simon's teacher and also as ἑστώς[88] and who doubtless was a—presumably earlier—representative of the "Simonian" system, that he represented himself as "Christ," [89] a claim which naturally did not compete with that of Simon; still the Simonian system which has been presented is not meant to serve as *proof* of the existence of a pre-Christian *Christ* Gnosticism. It is sufficient that in the foregoing investigation we have become acquainted with the *structure* of such a system:

A heavenly being (ἑστώς) —whether God himself or a divine emanation—

enters into matter (στάς) —which was always there or (in good Jewish tradition) is first created by him—

and there concerns himself with the return upwards (στησόμενος) — which means the liberation from captivity in matter or the transfer of the "Dynamis," which has been actualized out of potentiality into substance, into the heavenly treasury.

Every man or every pneumatic is part of the descended heavenly being and is responsible for his "redemption" or self-realization, which has as its presupposition the "redemption" also of the other parts of the

---

[85] Hipp. VI, 9.1; 20.3; Ps.-Cl. Hom. II, 22; Rec. III, 47.3 (Jesus); cf. Hom. XVI, 16.5; Acta Petri 4. R. Eisler, *Jesus Basileus* . . . , I: 133; II: 708, surmises that the disturbances which led to the expulsion of the Jews from Rome by Claudius and which according to Suetonius (*Vita Claudii* 25) went back to followers of a certain Chrestus/Christus were set in motion by Simon.

[86] = 147.5-6; cf. Epiph. Haer. XXI, 1; Ps.-Tert. Haer. 1.

[87] Cf. W. Bousset, [1], pp. 382 ff.; K. Rudolph, [1], pp. 33-34.

[88] Ps.-Cl. Rec. II, 8-9, 11; Hom. II, 24.

[89] Origen Cels. I, 57 = Koetschau I, 108.25 ff.; cf. VI, 11 = II, 81.17 ff.

"Dynamis." This system knows nothing of a special redeemer figure or a real redeemer myth.

The Ἐγώ εἰμι formula, which stems from the oriental sacral style and is widespread in Gnosticism, gives simple and clear expression to the divine claim of these Pneumatics—"Dynamics" would better correspond to the terminology of the Ἀπόφασις. Precisely for Simon this formula is characteristic: ἐγώ εἰμι ὁ υἱὸς τοῦ θεοῦ.[90] The occasional occurrence of the genitive is a sign of a precise formulation; Simon claims εἶναι δύναμις καὶ αὐτοῦ τοῦ τὸν κόσμον κτίσαντος θεοῦ,[91] i.e., to be *part* of God, or εἶναι τῆς τελείας δυνάμεως καὶ μετέχειν τῆς ἀνεννοήτου ἐξουσίας.[92] Insofar as they are active as "redeemers," the individuals who share in the δύναμις, the κοινωνία τοῦ πνεύματος, often bear the title of apostle while on their missionary journeys.[93] It will be shown that this aspect of the described system—like many another—also is of significance for the presentation of Gnosticism in Corinth; however, in the following our attention will be devoted above all to the title "Christ" which occurs in this system.

The title "man" or a similar title does *not* occur in the "Great Proclamation" as a designation for the ἐστώς-στάς-στησόμενος. That is of course of no importance. It is familiar to us, for example, from the Naassene Preaching which, however diverse the material used by it may be, as a whole is to be classified with the system discussed here of a redeemerless Gnosticism.

The Naassenes venerate the ἄνθρωπος or the υἱὸς τοῦ ἀνθρώπου, whom they also call Ἀδάμας.[94] He is the central figure of their system[95] and corresponds to the "Dynamis" in the "Great Proclamation." The three stages in the destiny of the "Dynamis"—ἐστώς-στάς-στησόμενος —appropriately occur in the Naassene Preaching as teaching concerning the φύσις τῶν γεγονότων καὶ γινομένων καὶ ἐσομένων.[96] One finds this doctrine allegorically in Isa. 28:10: Οὗτοί εἰσιν οἱ τρεῖς ὑπέρογκοι λόγοι. καυλακαῦ, σαυλασαῦ, ζεησάρ. Καυλακαῦ τοῦ ἄνω τοῦ Ἀδάμαντος, σαυλασαῦ τοῦ κάτω θνητοῦ, ζεησὰρ τοῦ ἐπὶ τὰ ἄνω ρεύσαντος Ἰορδάνου.[97] Then is added: Οὗτος ἐστί, φησίν, ὁ ἐν πᾶσιν ἀρσενόθηλυς ἄνθρωπος.[98] Thus men stem ἀπὸ τοῦ μακαρίου ἄνωθεν ἀνθρώπου ἢ ἀρχανθρώπου ἢ

13

---

[90] Mart. Petri et Pauli 15 = Lipsius-Bonnet I, 132.10. Cf. Jerome on Matt. 24:15: *"ego sum speciosus, ego paracletus, ego omnipotens, ego omnia Dei."*

[91] Ps.-Cl. Hom. II, 22.3.

[92] Hipp. VI, 41.1 = 172.20-21 as a description of the Marcosians, whose system is similar to that of the Apophasis.

[93] See *The Office of Apostle*, pp. 159 ff.

[94] Hipp. VI, 6.4-5 = 78.5 ff.

[95] V, 7.2 = 79.6 ff.

[96] V, 7.20 = 83.9 ff.; cf. V, 7.29 = 85.18 ff.

[97] V, 8.4 = 89.20 ff.

[98] V, 8.4 = 89.22 ff.

Ἀδάμαντος.[99] They are fettered εἰς πλάσμα τὸ πήλινον, ἵνα δουλεύσωσι τῷ ταύτης τῆς κτίσεως δημιουργῷ Ἰαλδαβαώθ, θεῷ πυρίνῳ, ἀριθμὸν τετάρτῳ.[100] For "anyone who says that all consists of one thing errs; anyone who says 'of three things'[101] speaks the truth and gives the explanation of the universe. Μία γάρ ἐστι, φησίν, ἡ μακαρία φύσις τοῦ μακαρίου ἀνθρώπου τοῦ ἄνω, τοῦ Ἀδάμαντος. μία δὲ ἡ θνητὴ κάτω. μία δὲ ἡ ἀβασίλευτος γενεὰ ἡ ἄνω γενομένη."[102]

Here the mythological character of the system emerges more strongly than in the "Great Proclamation."[103]

Now in the middle of the portrayal of this happening "πότε ἄνω πότε κάτω"[104] is found the well-known passage: "About this one (scil. the Logos), they say, it is written: awake, thou that sleepest, and arise, and Christ will illumine thee. Οὗτός ἐστιν ὁ χριστός, ὁ ἐν πᾶσι, φησί, τοῖς γενητοῖς υἱὸς ἀνθρώπου κεχαρακτηρισμένος ἀπὸ τοῦ ἀχαρακτηρίστου λόγου."[105] The κεχαρακτηρισμένος corresponds to the ἐξεικονισμένος in the "Great Proclamation." The υἱὸς ἀνθρώπου κεχαρακτηρισμένος is the γινόμενος or στάς, namely the ἀρχάνθρωπος ἄνωθεν Ἀδάμας who is now to be found as ἔσω ἄνθρωπος[106] in all men.[107] In our quotation he is called "Christ," which clearly means not the one person of the church's redeemer but the "primal man." Of course the church's redeemer also appears in isolated passages of the Naassene Preaching, but he is always called "Jesus" and is "Christ" only insofar as he is also the τέλειος ἄνθρωπος: "Διὰ τοῦτο, φησί, λέγει ὁ Ἰησοῦς. Ἐγώ εἰμι ἡ πύλη ἡ ἀληθινή. Ἔστι δὲ ὁ ταῦτα λέγων ὁ ἀπὸ τοῦ ἀχαρακτηρίστου, φησίν, ἄνωθεν κεχαρακτηρισμένος τέλειος ἄνθρωπος. Οὐ δύναται οὖν, φησί, σωθῆναι ὁ τέλειος ἄνθρωπος, ἐὰν μὴ ἀναγεννηθῇ διὰ ταύτης εἰσελθὼν τῆς πύλης."[108] For the Christ-Anthropos has flowed down into all pneumatic men, and everyone can become the redeemer of another. The Naassene Preaching likewise still knows nothing of an actual 15 redeemer figure.[109] The "perfect man" saves himself. "Christ" is not

99 V, 7.30 = 86.7-8.
100 V, 7.30 = 86.8 ff.
14   101 This triad is not to be confused with the threefold division of man or of humanity, also occurring in the Naassene Preaching, as νοερός, ψυχικός, and χοϊκός.
102 V, 8.2 = 89.10 ff.
103 Cf. as a parallel from the Mandaean writings: "The man who is seated there above is hidden far below" (Lidzbarski, Mandäische Liturgien, p. 12.6).
104 V, 7.38 = 88.13.
105 V, 7.33-34 = 87.3 ff.
106 V, 7.36 = 87.22.
107 V, 7.36 = 88.1.
108 V, 8. 20-21 = 93.1 ff.
109 Thus Jesus only plays the role of the exemplary Gnostic as in the system of Carpocrates described by Iren. I, 25.1-3; Hipp. VII, 32; Epiph. Haer. XXVII, 2 ff.: "Jesus, however, is Joseph's son and is like other men. He was distinguished from others in that his soul, since it was strong and pure, had remembered what it had

the Christian redeemer but one of the varying designations for the "primal man." This designation betrays Jewish but no Christian influences, even if the quotation in V, 7.33-34 should stem from Eph. 5:14—which in view of the difference in wording is by no means certain—and not rather from a common Gnostic source.

Before we trace out the extant evidences of the pre-Christian Christ Gnosticism now adequately identified as a *system*, we must explain how the transferral of the Jewish title of Christ to the Gnostic primal man could come about. The setting of this transferral is not hard to discover: it must have involved a Jewish Gnosticism in which the traditional figure of Jewish eschatology was terminologically joined with the Gnostic chief figure. This process is typical of Gnosticism. It could combine all the motifs at hand with the conceptions that had come down to it, if it was a matter of securing admittance for its own understanding of existence in the sphere of already present religions. The terminological introduction of the Jewish figure of the Messiah into the Gnostic mythology was therefore unavoidable in the Jewish territory. This association between Messiah and the Gnostic primal man was, moreover, not entirely unmotivated. Most of all, the significance of both was in essence eschatological. In addition, there was the fact that according to the schema of primordial time–end-time, the Messiah also—as David's son—was seen in a primordial-time relation. But it is just this generally oriental schema that also dominates the primal man myth. The unexampled ability of Gnosticism to amalgamate to itself alien conceptions therefore was not at all strained in the equation of "primal man = Christ."

Conversely, for a Judaism which was exposed to Gnosticism in the

---

seen in the presence of the unbegotten Father. The Father had sent him a 'Dynamis' so that he might escape the creators of the world, and he ascended to him through all and set free from all. Those who are like him have the same experience . . . . For anyone who, like Jesus' soul, holds the Archons, the creators, in contempt will likewise receive δυνάμεις to bring about the same effect. Hence some also became so arrogant that they said they were equal to Jesus; others even said that in a certain sense they preceded him. These also held themselves to be better than Jesus' disciples like Paul, Peter, and the other apostles, who on their own part had not been inferior to Jesus in any respect. For their souls came from the same circle and hence they likewise despised the creators of the world; they possessed the same δύναμις and would again return thither. But if anyone scorned what is here more than that one did, he could also be more than that one" (Iren. I, 25.1-2).

The original Christology of Cerinthus (cf. Iren. I, 26.1; Ps.-Tert. Haer. 3.2; Epiph. Haer. XXVII, 1), whom the heresiologists connect closely with Carpocrates (Ps.-Tert. Haer. 3.2; Philastrius Haer. 36; Epiph. Haer. XXVIII, 1.1), is probably to be understood in the same way, even though already in Irenaeus the early form of Cerinthus' system has been altered in the direction of the church's Christology (but cf. Epiph. Haer. XXVIII, 6; see below, p. 57).

Whether the figure of Jesus in the Naassene Preaching is literally secondary can remain open here. It is beyond question that it is secondary in a substantive sense.

Diaspora, there was no occasion to reject such interpretation of the conception of the Messiah; for doubtless certain circles in Judaism, especially among the folk who after the exile had intentionally remained in Babylonia, had long since abandoned the Jewish hope which was connected with the land of Canaan and the Messiah-king in Jerusalem.[110] Mesopotamia however may also have been the homeland of Gnosticism. A reinterpretation of the messianic idea did not discomfit Jewish circles here.

If we look now for further traces of the system described, it becomes evident that we must turn our attention to Jewish Gnosticism. We find a presentation of this system distinguished by brevity and clarity, even though for the most part not correctly interpreted, in Hippolytus in connection with the mention of Elchasai (X, 29).

The Jewish Gnostics pictured here confess, to be sure like Simon in good Jewish fashion, that the origins of the universe lie in God alone; nevertheless they do not confess *one* Christ, i.e., as Hippolytus corrects himself, there is indeed, according to their opinion, *one* Christ, but only *in the heavens;* he has, however, ofttimes changed into many different bodies, and hereafter he will continue to enter into bodies and will show himself temporarily in many. Reference is made to the same people by Hippolytus' comment in IX, 14 that "Christ" is said to have been an ordinary man like everyone else, that he had not now for the first time been born (of a virgin) , but also previously, and also thereafter had appeared and emerged as one who was born and still is being born, since he changes his ways of coming and the bodies he occupies.

Thus Christ appears on earth only in the form of the ordinary man. Nevertheless he is or was here below not as a *particular* man, but at all times is divided up among many men. On earth, this phenomenon is the "hidden power," ἡ κρυπτὴ δύναμις of the "Great Proclamation," namely "Elkesai," which in all the various forms of the name surely means "hidden power" [111] and originally hardly denoted an individual person but rather that "Dynamis" also called "Christ," which is found on earth in all Pneumatics and can be active as redeemer in each of its parts.

There is *one* Christ only ἄνω as ἑστώς or στησόμενος. On earth Christ is found as the στάς at all times in many ordinary men. It is clear that this Christ has nothing in common with the church's Christ; he is after all not a mythological redeemer figure but "man" himself.

---

[110] It is well known that Philo and Josephus, e.g., completely ignore the messianic hope.

[111] See G. Strecker in RAC, *s.v.* Elkesai; E. S. Drower, *The Secret Adam*, p. 93, n. 1.

The Christ Gnosticism before us here is thus a purely Jewish Gnos- 16 ticism.

What Hippolytus tells in VII, 34 about the Ebionites, who "like Cerinthus and Carpocrates"—i.e., in Gnostic fashion—"tell fables," is to be understood only in the light of this Christ myth: "εἰ γὰρ καὶ ἕτερός τις πεποιήκει τὰ ἐν νόμῳ προστεταγμένα ἦν ἂν ἐκεῖνος ὁ χριστός. Δύνασθαι δὲ καὶ ἑαυτοὺς ὁμοίως ποιήσαντος χριστοὺς γενέσθαι. καὶ γὰρ καὶ αὐτὸν ὁμοίως ἄνθρωπον εἶναι πᾶσι λέγουσιν."

A reshaping of this system which presumably took place under Christian influence is present when in certain Jewish-Christian circles in which the church's Christ was venerated as the prophet promised by Moses (Deut. 18:15-18) [112] it is explained concerning this prophet that he has already appeared earlier in *individual figures*—Ps. Clem. Hom. XVIII, 13.6 enumerates seven such incarnations.[113, 114] The passages quoted from Hippolytus' *Refutatio* still know nothing of this conception. For them Christ is found on earth generally not as *one*, but only in the form diffused among many ordinary men at any and all times.

G. Strecker writes (*Das Judenchristentum . . . ,* p. 149) about Ps.-Clem. Rec. VIII, 59-62:[115] "According to this the true prophet is said to fill the world and to inhabit the *mens* of every single man; he sleeps in the unbelievers, but in those who seek him he ignites the light of knowledge. In this conception only a little is preserved of the change in form." Just the opposite is true! The conception of the light-sparks of the true prophet Christ present in all men was *later* transposed into the view that the prophet as redeemer has appeared only in individual outstanding figures. This tendency toward hypostatizing can most clearly be detected in the later passages of the Pseudo-Clementines, while it is still largely absent from the earlier passages, according to which the true prophet Christ is, rather, present *at all times*, that is, in men themselves, and is revealed to those who are willing to hear.[116] The view according to which Christ appears as an individual figure and as redeemer is in the Christian sphere more clearly delineated and therefore later than the purely anthropological Christ myth, against which Judaism naturally also protested. Od. Sol. 41.15 may contain such a protest: "The anointed one is in truth *one*, and he was known before the foundation of the world."

[112] W. Staerk, [2], pp. 99 ff.; H. J. Schoeps, [1], pp. 87 ff.
[113] Cf. Epiph. Haer. XXX, 3.2 ff.; Ps.-Cl. Rec. II, 47; Hom. II, 52; XVII, 4; W. Staerk, [2], pp. 105 ff.
[114] As is well known, this conception is also found elsewhere in Gnosticism, esp. in Manichaeism; cf. G. Strecker, *Das Judenchristentum,* . . . p. 151; 1st ed., pp. 113-14.
[115] Cf. Epiph. Haer. XXX, 3.3 ff.; Ps.-Cl. Hom. II, 15, 17.
[116] Cf. H. J. Schoeps, [4], p. 51; G. Strecker, pp. 149-50.

The remark of Epiphanius (Haer. LIII, 1.8) that Christ is for the Sampsaeans a "κτίσμα καὶ ἀεί ποτε (= at all times, from eternity) φαινόμενον καὶ πρῶτον μὲν πεπλᾶσθαι αὐτὸν τὸ σῶμα τοῦ ᾽Αδάμ, καὶ πάλιν ἐνδύεσθαι ὅτε βούλεται is also to be understood in the sense of the still pre-Christian Christ myth; cf. XXIX, 6. Also Ps.-Clem. Rec. I, 52.3: "Christus, qui ab initio et semper erat, per singulas quasque generationes piis, latenter licet, semper tamen aderat"; and Rec. II, 22.4-5 (cf. Hom. III, 20.2) : "Nam et ipse verus propheta ab initio mundi per saeculum currens festinat ad requiem." The altogether more dependable Syrian lets us recognize the anthropological components of this statement even better: "ἐπεὶ καὶ ὁ ἀληθὴς προφήτης ἀπ᾽ ἀρχῆς τοῦ κόσμου εἰς τὴν ἀνάπαυσιν ἐπείγει ἡμᾶς ἀεὶ μεθ᾽ ἡμῶν τρέχων. ὥστε ἐστὶν μεθ᾽ ἡμῶν πάσας τὰς ἡμέρας." The rest mentioned is in the sense of the Gnostic myth the eschatological rest[117] of the στησόμενος that embraces all individual souls, of which we read in Hippolytus (VI, 12.3 = 138.16 ff.) that he "will be one and the same in essence, might, greatness, and perfection with the unbegotten and infinite Power . . . ."

The well-known passage from j Taan 2.1:[118] "If a man says 'I am God,' he lies; 'I am the Son of Man,' he will regret it; 'I ascend to heaven,' he will not achieve it" should be mentioned here also. It is impossible to take this as a polemic against Jesus Christ as is everywhere done; for in addition to the fact that the saying obviously does not have in view one certain man or an *individual* man at all, the third part of the saying makes sense only if it is directed against the assertion of *presently* living men that they would ascend to heaven. Against the church's proclamation of the already accomplished ascension of Christ, the assertion "he will not achieve it" would be an uncalled-for and wholly misconceived polemic. People like the Jewish Gnostics such as we have become acquainted with are rather meant here.[119] They represent themselves to be God or the Christ = Son of Man; they would ascend to heaven as the Pneuma in ecstasy or after their death.[120]

Irenaeus tells us, as we have already seen, of the sect of the Carpocratians that according to their teaching Jesus was an ordinary man. He

---

[117] ἀνάπαυσις is one of the most widespread Gnostic terms; it is an indication of the decisive eschatological interest of Gnosticism.

[118] Cf. H. L. Strack, Jesus, die Häretiker und die Christen, p. 37.

[119] Thus, correctly, G. P. Wetter, Der Sohn Gottes, pp. 17, 85, 104; cf. M. Friedländer, [1], *passim*, who also correctly finds polemics against Jewish sects elsewhere in the Talmud; K. Schubert, Die Religion des nachbiblischen Judentums, pp. 94 ff.

[120] For example, Simon undertakes to fly into the heavens: Mart. Petri II = Lipsius-Bonnet I, 80.33; Mart. Petri et Pauli 30 = 144.8 ff.; cf. 162.2 ff.; 164.10 ff.; 209.14 ff.; cf. Ps.-Cl. Rec. II, 61-62. After all the description of j Taan 2.1 in all respects fits in with the way in which Simon and the Simonians appear according to the ecclesiastical reports; cf. The Office of Apostle, pp. 216 ff.

had preserved undimmed the recollection of his stay in the upper world and therefore had received a "Dynamis" with which he ascended. But they said the same thing also about themselves, for their souls had descended from the same circle and for this reason had similarly scorned the creator of the world; they are blessed with the same "Dynamis" and would return again to the same goal.[121]

Again we encounter the same redeemer-less system as we have come to know it in the Ἀπόφασις. To be sure the "Dynamis," which all Gnostics possess and ascend with, is not called "Christ," but the "Dynamis" dwelling in Jesus, in the context of the familiar schema of the dualistic Gnostic Christology, can only have been the "Christ" who then, however, as "Dynamis" lived in *all* Gnostics and ascended.[122]

Even the Gnosticism of Marcus, of which Irenaeus gives us a detailed account, belongs here as to its contents. We do not encounter *one* redeemer; instead, all Gnostics are parts τῆς τελείας δυνάμεως (Hipp. VI, 41.1). They go about as redeemer apostles and attempt, by means of ecstatic productions which the church fathers scornfully called magic, to awaken the "Dynamis" hidden in other men, "so that you may become what I am, and I what you are" (Iren. I, 13.3), as Marcus says to his medium. It is true that in the reports about Marcus, "Christ" does not occur directly as a title for the "Dynamis." The Marcosian says "ἐγὼ υἱὸς ἀπὸ πατρός" (Iren. I, 21.5).[123] But he could of course just as

---

[121] Iren. I, 25.1-2; Hipp. VII, 32.1 ff.

[122] The same conception of the exemplary character of Jesus the Christ, which presupposes the equation "Pneumatic = Christ," may stand behind Saying 116 of the Coptic Gospel of Philip from the Nag Hammadi find; on this, see H. M. Schenke, [2], p. 12. The peculiar μίμησις conception as it is found in Paul will also have to be understood from this perspective; on this, cf. *The Office of Apostle*, pp. 216 ff.

The third (earthly) Christ of the Valentinians presumably goes back to the Christ who is understood in this Gnostic fashion as an example, while the first (heavenly) Christ apparently represents the original Christ-primal man figure (ἑστώς) and the second (redeemer) Christ takes on the basic conception of the church's Christology.

[123] To be compared with this is the Gnostic speculation which is offered by the pagan alchemist Zosimus, who may have written about the end of the 3rd or the beginning of the 4th cent. (on him personally, see R. Reitzenstein, [2], pp. 8-9), in one of his writings on the origin and destiny of man. (The text in question in Reitzenstein, [2], pp. 102 ff., following M. Bertholet, *Alchimistes grecs* II, [1888]: 229 ff.; recently translated by H. M. Schenke, [2], pp. 52 ff.) Adam, so we learn from Zosimus, is a being of two parts, Light-Adam and Heimarmene-Adam, thus soul and body, Prometheus and Epimetheus, inner man and outer man. It goes on to say: "In other words, our Νοῦς says: But the Son of God, who can do all things and becomes all that he will, appears to everyone as he will. And to the present and until the end of the world he will come and will be with his own, secretly and openly, in order to counsel them secretly and through their understanding . . . ." Still more is said of this Son of God whom his own "have received," and it is understandable that this section in Zosimus exhibits many Christian interpolations, which are relatively easy to recognize (see in Reitzenstein, [2], pp. 103 ff.). But Reitzenstein's comment ([2], p. 106) also applies to the presumably original text of Zosimus:

well have said, if the external proximity to Christianity had not hindered him, "ἐγώ εἰμι ὁ χριστός," as Gnostics resembling the Marcosians do after the performance of their "magical" rites, according to the report of Epiphanius (Haer. XXVI, 9.9). This is indeed late but clear documentation for that pre-Christian Gnostic "Christology" in which Christ is not the heavenly emissary but the "man" to be found in all Pneumatics. The self-movement of this Christ as the ἑστώς or στησόμενος ἄνω and the στὰς κάτω apparently is expressed among these Gnostics portrayed by Epiphanius in the form of a distinction between the χριστὸς ἄλλος αὐτολόχευτος and the χριστὸς οὗτος ὁ κατελθών (Haer. XXVI, 10.4).

Most of the later witnesses for the collective significance of the Christ appear in a context in which Christ appears as the *one* redeemer *also*. Attempts are frequently made to reconcile the two Christologies; frequently they stand in close conjunction. It is certain that the two conceptions are basically in competition with each other. Now it is inconceivable that the Christ of Christian Gnosticism was later anthropologized. It is rather the tendency of Gnosticism, the later it is, the more to approximate the church's Christology, that is, to place Christ as the *one* redeemer over against men. So at the beginning there stands the conception of Christ as the sum of all Pneumatics. Christ as the *one* redeemer then makes his way into Gnosticism from ecclesiastical Christianity, yet without being able ever completely to suppress the title of "Christ" for "man"; indeed, the *one* Christ frequently appears still to be altogether expendable even in his redeeming function.

Let me offer some examples:

Eclogae ex proph. 23 could belong to a Gnostic source of Clement. Here indeed the σωτήρ is spoken of, but he actually is identical with the ἐκκλησία and is at work in her: "ὥσπερ διὰ τοῦ σώματος ὁ σωτὴρ ἐλάλει καὶ ἰᾶτο, οὕτως καὶ πρότερον μὲν διὰ τῶν προφητῶν, νῦν δὲ διὰ τῶν ἀποστόλων καὶ τῶν διδασκάλων. ἡ ἐκκλησία γὰρ ὑπηρετεῖ τῇ τοῦ κυρίου ἐνεργείᾳ ἔνθεν καὶ τότε ἄνθρωπον ἀνέλαβεν, ἵνα δι' αὐτοῦ ὑπηρετήσῃ τῷ θελήματι τοῦ πατρός. καὶ πάντοτε ἄνθρωπον ὁ φιλάνθρωπος ἐνδύεται θεὸς εἰς τὴν ἀνθρώπων σωτηρίαν, πρότερον μὲν τοὺς προφήτας, νῦν δὲ τὴν ἐκκλησίαν."

Within the account of the ascension of the Christ redeemer that is customary in Christian Gnosticism, it is said in Iren. I, 30.14 that the

---

". . . Christianity probably also has exerted its influence, even though in my judgment half unconsciously." It is obvious that the strange emergence of the "Son of God" who is always present to all ἔσω ἄνθρωποι can easily be explained, as in Marcus, from the basic conception of the Jewish Christian Gnosticism in connection with the Christian equation of Christ and Son of God. More than this of course cannot be said.

ascended Christ *"post depositionem mundialis carnis recipiat in se"* the souls of the Gnostics; he enriches himself with these souls, while the world loses ever more of the heavenly power until at last all the "droplets of light" are again gathered above, i.e., until the perfect Christ-Anthropos is reconstituted. Here people clearly have combined the original Christ-primal man conception with the church's picture of Christ, without making clear how then Christ as a person acts, redeems, and lives in the celestial world when the same Christ at the same time is still diffused in the world.

According to Exc. ex Theod. 26 the adjustment of the two christological conceptions was made in such a way that a distinction was made between the visible and invisible aspects of "Jesus." There also occurs the explicit equation of Christ and church: "τὸ ὁρατὸν τοῦ Ἰησοῦ ἡ Σοφία καὶ ἡ Ἐκκλησία ἦν τῶν σπερμάτων τῶν διαφερόντων . . . ." Cf. also § 41 of the Exc. ex Theod., important in this connection; and on this also W. Foerster, *Von Valentin zu Herakleon* (BZNW 7 [1928]), p. 86.

In Act. Thom. 10 Christ is praised as the one "who is in all and permeates all and inhabits all his works and is visible through all activity," a passage which indeed has a pantheistic ring but may be originally Gnostic.[124] Cf. also Peter's address to Christ before his own martyrdom: "σὺ τὸ πᾶν καὶ τὸ πᾶν ἐν σοί. καὶ τὸ ὂν σύ, καὶ οὐκ ἔστιν ἄλλο ὃ ἔστιν εἰ μὴ μόνος σύ." [125] Closer to the myth is a comment of the Rhetor Victorinus, who gives as an assertion of the Symmachians (!) about Jesus: *"Dicunt enim eum ipsum Adam esse et esse animam generalem."* [126] Here the anthropological function of the "Christ" clearly comes out. Cf. further Aphraates (TU III, 3: 103) : "Christ . . . he dwells with many, since he is only one, and with the believers here and there, because they stem from him; and he is not thereby diminished, as it stands written (Isa. 53:12?) : He has divided him among many. And although he is divided among many . . . ."

It is generally known how strongly, especially in the Acts of Thomas but also in other acts of apostles, the figure of the apostle stands in equal significance *alongside* the figure of Christ. When in the Acts of Thomas the apostle is represented as Christ's twin brother,[127] this is only a superficial concealing of what is constantly expressed in the entire writing, that Thomas himself and thus the pneumatic person generally is "Christ." 17

---

[124] Cf. Oxyrhynchus Papyrus 1, Logion 5 = *Kleine Texte* 8: 19; Ephraem in Resch, *Agrapha*, TU NF XV, Heft 3/4 (1906) : 201.

[125] Mart. Petri 10 = Lipsius-Bonnet I, 98.4-5.

[126] Comm. in Gal. 1:15 = Migne, PSL VIII, col. 1155.

[127] Acta Thom. 39, *et passim;* cf. *The Office of Apostle*, pp. 187 ff. (Lit.) .

In Act. Joh. 100 Christ says, ". . . not yet has every member of the one who descended been gathered together . . . so long as you are not called my own, I am not what I am. But if you listen to me, you will be as I am and I shall again be what I was, when I have you with me as I myself am." This is originally not the utterance of *one* emissary as it now appears, but the utterance of the στάς, the "descended one," that "Christ" who, divided among all, seeks himself and finds himself (Hipp. VI, 17.3). Cf. also Epiph. Haer. XXVI, 13.2: "I have recognized myself and have gathered myself from everywhere . . . καὶ συνέλεξα τὰ μέλη τὰ διεσκορπισμένα, and I know who you are. ἐγὼ γὰρ τῶν ἄνωθέν εἰμι" (from the Gospel of Philip).[128] Further, Haer. XXVI, 3.1: "I am you and you are I, and where you are I am, and I am diffused in all. And where you will, you gather me; in gathering me you are gathering yourself" (from the Gospel of Eve). To be understood in this sense also is the song of Christ which is taken up in Act. Joh. 95:

> Saved shall I be, and I shall save.
> Delivered shall I be, and I shall deliver.
> Wounded shall I be, and I shall wound.
>
> . . .
>
> I shall hear, and I shall be heard.
>
> . . .
>
> I shall be united, and I shall unite.
>
> . . .
>
> A door am I to you, on me you knock.
> A way am I to you, the wandering one.

The identity of Christ with the Christians can also find the following expression: "See me in yourselves as one of you sees himself in the water or in a mirror," [129] or "Behold, our mirror is the Lord. Open your eyes and look at them therein, and learn the nature of your countenance." [130]

In *Pistis Sophia* 96 (= Schmidt-Till, p. 148.6-7, 18-19, 29), Christ says of the Gnostics: "These men are I and I am they." This relationship can be expressed in imagery in the following way: Jesus says, "I am as near to you as the clothing on your body" (C. R. C. Allberry, *A Manichaean Psalm-Book,* II: 39.23-24).

In the recently discovered Coptic Gospel of Thomas we read in Logion 108 (Leipoldt-Schenke, p. 25): "Jesus said, whoever will drink from my mouth will be drunk. And I shall become he. . . ." In the

18

---

[128] Cf. Hennecke-Schneemelcher-Wilson, I: 273 ff.; E. Norden, *Agnostos Theos,* pp. 183 ff.; M. Dibelius, *Botschaft und Geschichte,* II: 156; A. Dieterich, *Eine Mithrasliturgie,* p. 97; H. Jonas, [1], pp. 125, 318-19.

[129] Ps.-Cyprian, De montibus Sina et Sion 13.

[130] Od. Sol. 13.1-2.

Gospel of Philip from the same find, there is in Logion 44 this sentence, "You (saw) Christ and became Christ," and in Logion 67 it is said of the perfected Gnostic that he "is no longer a Christian but a Christ" (Leipoldt-Schenke, p. 46.50).

Tertullian tells (de praescr. haer. 30.12 ff.) of Gnostics who represent themselves as "new apostles" and are still circulating in his day, that they had asserted that Christ had descended again, had again taught the same things, was crucified again, died again, rose again; thus of course he created apostles and gave them power also to perform the same signs which he performed. These people hardly asserted that the Christ-event of the church's proclamation had been repeated only *once,* as Tertullian apparently understands it. Where and how would this have been? The meaning of the Gnostic apostles rather seems to be that Christ is present in themselves, who, as apostles, are also redeemers; they are Christ and Christ is identical with them.

In this connection these χριστοί may have spoken of being crucified, dying, and rising, for we know, for example,[131] from the Pauline terminology of Gnostic origin how one could interpret the concepts of the church's Christology anthropologically in Gnosticism.[132]

The notice of Epiphanius (Haer. XXVIII, 6.1; cf. Philastrius, Haer. 36.2) also is probably to be understood similarly: "οὗτος δὲ ὁ Κήρινθος, ἀνόητος καὶ ἀνοήτων διδάσκαλος, φάσκει πάλιν τολμήσας χριστὸν πεπονθέναι καὶ ἐσταυρῶσθαι, μήπω δὲ ἐγηγέρθαι, μᾶλλον δὲ ἀνίστασθαι, ὅταν ἡ καθόλου γένηται νεκρῶν ἀνάστασις. Since Cerinthus made a distinction between Jesus and Christ,[133] the "Christ" mentioned here is the "inner man," τὸ πνεῦμα τὸ ἅγιον or the ἄνωθεν δύναμις (Epiph., Haer. XXVI, 1.5-6), which suffers in all men and experiences its "resurrection" in the final gathering together of all its scattered parts.   19

The identification of the Christians with Christ has been preserved, not accidentally, in Origen: "For Christ is likewise found in every saint, and because of the one Christ many χριστοί, his imitators, arose."[134] "If anyone wishes to see many bodies which are filled with the divine Spirit and like the one Christ are everywhere concerned to serve the salvation of men, he should consider those who everywhere teach the word of Jesus rightly and with pious lives and also themselves are called χριστοί by the divine Scriptures. . . . For as we have heard that

131 Cf. the Manichaean passages in H. Jonas, [1], pp. 310-11.

132 One who participates in the crucifixion slays the σῶμα τῆς ἁμαρτίας; gnostically interpreted, this means the anti-godly body (Rom. 6:6). One who shares in the burial puts off the σῶμα τῆς σαρκός; gnostically interpreted, this means the body as prison of the soul. In Gnosticism, however, "resurrection" is a favorite and widely used metaphor for the reception of Gnosis or the ascension of the soul (see p. 177).

133 Iren. I, 26.1; Epiph. Haer. XXVIII, 1.5 ff.

134 Comm. in Joh. VI, 42; cf. X, 92-93.

an antichrist will come, so also we know that Christ has come down and we see that on account of him many χριστοί have been in the world." [135] Examples of this kind could be multiplied and are found also in Cyril, Methodius, and others.[136]

Perhaps the quotation of Maximilla also belongs in this connection. It is reported to us by Epiphanius in Haer. XLVIII, 12.4: ἐμοῦ μὴ ἀκούσητε, ἀλλὰ χριστοῦ ἀκούσατε. He interprets it ironically: she is right when she says not to listen to her but to Christ. This is doubtless a misunderstanding of Maximilla, who according to Haer. XLVIII, 13.1 asserts concerning herself: ἀπέστειλέ με κύριος. Thus she means to say: anyone who hears me is not hearing me but Christ. Naturally Maximilla could be directly dependent on Luke 10:16. But Luke 10:16 on its own part goes back to an early tradition which exhibits "Johannine" peculiarities, i.e., bears gnosticizing features, and in the framework of this tradition [137] is found in Mark 9:41 the ὅτι χριστοῦ ἐστε (otherwise unknown in the Synoptic tradition); in my judgment this likewise is a dislocated fragment from the circle of the christological tradition of a Jewish Gnosticism (see p. 65) which is of interest to us.

The identification of Christ with the Pneuma, the light-substance to be found in all men, also goes back to the pre-Christian Gnostic Christology. Cf., e.g., Ign. Magn. 15: "Farewell in God's harmony, you who possess the unshakable Pneuma which is Jesus Christ." Underlying this salutation is the Gnostic conception that Christ as Pneuma dwells in all Pneumatics.[138] "The Spirit, which is the Christ, came upon him," it is said in Epiphanius (Haer. XXX, 3.6 = Ebionites). This equation has been preserved terminologically on into the speculative systems of Gnosticism: Hipp. VI, 36; 49.5; X, 21.3; Iren. I, 2.5-6; 30.12. It is found also in Hermas: Sim. V, 6-7; Mand. III, 1. Cf. also the well-known speech of the prophets who travel around in Phoenicia and Palestine of whom Celsus reports (Origen, Contra Cels. VII, 8-9): Ἐγὼ ὁ θεός εἰμι ἢ θεοῦ παῖς ἢ πνεῦμα θεῖον, ἥκω δε. The identification of Christ and Ecclesia, as it appears for example in Exc. ex Theod. 58.1, has the same origin: "The great warrior Jesus, who with power assimilates to him-

---

[135] Orig. Cels. VI, 79 = Koetschau II, 150.18 ff.

[136] Cf. W. Völker, *Das Vollkommenheitsideal des Origenes*, BhTh 7 (1931) : 99-100, 191-92, 226; A. v. Harnack, TU 42.3: 134-35; E. Peterson, *Frühkirche, Judentum und Gnosis*, pp. 63-64; J. Jervell, *Imago Dei*, p. 248, n. 272; cf. Barn. 16.8 ff.—χριστόφορος, formed on the analogy of θεόφορος, occurs, e.g., in Ign. Eph. 9.2; Eus. CH VIII, 10.3; cf. II Cor. 4:10; similarly πνευματόφορος in Herm. Mand. XI, 16; cf. XI, 9; see the Ergänzungsband to HNT, *in loc.* Cf. also II, 10:7 in the version of P[46].

[137] Cf. R. Bultmann, *History of the Synoptic Tradition*, pp. 142-43.

[138] Other terminology of Ignatius also stems from the sphere of pre-Christian Christ Gnosticism, e.g., Philad. 5.2: the prophets are saved ἐν ἑνότητι Ἰησοῦ Χριστοῦ ὄντες.

self the church." [139] The double equation Pneuma = Ecclesia = Christ
is found in Hermas, if one compares Sim. IX, 1.1 with Vis. III, 3.3
(see below, pp. 61 ff.) .[140]

According to Eusebius (CH IV, 22.6), Hegesippus enumerates the
various Gnostic sects and then remarks: "Out of these came forth the
false Christs, the false prophets, and the false apostles." In the undoubtedly Gnostic teachers of his time Justin also sees the fulfillment
of Jesus' prediction[141] that false Christs and false prophets would come
(Dial. 82.2). Thus both authors are acquainted with the claim of
definite and apparently numerous Gnostics to be χριστοί, just as their
emergence as apostles and prophets is typically Gnostic (see below,
pp. 275 ff.). We may then ask whether in Mark 13:6 and parallels[142]
also the apostrophe was not originally addressed, not to figures of
political messianism, but to apostles of a Jewish Christ Gnosticism,
whatever connection Mark and even his source may have made with
this passage.

In many of the later Gnostic systems there appears a "Christ" as a
heavenly hypotasis who has no redemptive function, shows no points
of contact with the church's Christ figure, and is more securely and
more originally anchored in the system than the revealer Christ who
frequently appears simultaneously. The position of the first-named
"Christ" can be explained only as a late formulation of the old Jewish-
Gnostic Christ myth.

As an example I take the Apocryphon of John from the Coptic
Papyrus Berolinensis 8502 (ed. Till, 1955).

Barbelo, the first Ennoia of the ineffable Primal Father, gives birth
to the "Christ" in devotion to this Father. In the Apocryphon of John
and in the corresponding systems this Christ originally has nothing
to do with that revealer Christ as the earthly disciple of whom John
receives the revelation. The latter Christ always speaks of the former
in the third person, just as generally the entire revelation of the
Apocryphon of John only subsequently has been put in the mouth of
the church's redeemer Christ. The system itself does not require this
redeemer, since the redemption of man has already occurred in primor-

---

[139] "ἐν ἑαυτῷ δυνάμει τὴν ἐκκλησίαν ἀναλαβών."

[140] Ignatius' peculiar affirmation (Smyrn. 1.2) that Christ has risen "εἰς τοὺς
ἁγίους καὶ πιστοὺς αὐτοῦ εἴτε ἐν 'Ιουδαίοις, εἴτε ἐν ἔθνεσιν ἐν ἑνὶ σώματι τῆς ἐκκλησίας αὐτοῦ" finds its explanation only in terms of the Gnostic equation of Christ
= church. Here the church's Easter event is reinterpreted to mean the re-establish-
ment of the body of Christ, wherein Ignatius naturally applies this body of Christ
to the church and to this extent demythologizes it.

[141] Matt. 24:5, 11, 24.

[142] The logion in Mark 9:41 could also be considered from this perspective; cf.
E. Klostermann in HNT 3 (4th ed.) : in loc; see below, p. 65.

dial times, indeed through the ἔννοια of light which "illumines" man "concerning the origin of his fault and shows him his ascent." [143] This "ἔννοια of the first light is in him [man] and awakens his thought," [144] so that all attempts of the darkness to cast over man an incapacity for knowledge fail.[145] Thus it is inconsistent that the book of revelation is put in the mouth of the historical redeemer Christ.

The original identity of the latter with the heavenly hypostasis "Christ" is also ruled out because a descent of this exalted light-being into darkness in the context of thought which is determinative for the system of the Apocryphon appears utterly inconceivable; this Christ is not a redeemer.

Of course he moreover is no longer identical with "man." Rather, as has been said, the fall of such an exalted light-being into darkness is inconceivable for the thought of the Apocryphon, and the difficult problem as to how light-substance could fall into the power of darkness *in the first place* is acute. The Apocryphon of John solves this problem by setting forth an abundance of descending aeons and groups of aeons, the last of which, "Sophia," emanated a "thought" from herself but without the approval of the "spirit" and her own "counterpart." Therefore this emanation, named "Jaldabaoth," was a hateful being, although it bore within itself light-substance from its mother "Sophia." This light-substance is now transported through many further stages downward until at last it is found within dark matter, in the fetters of the body (55.3 ff.) .

The origin of the entire chain of descending emanations, however, is the "πρωτογενέτωρ, who also is called 'the Christ.' " [146] This fact and other names of "Christ" such as σπινθήρ, ἀόρατον πνεῦμα, τέλειος, νοῦς, etc.—in other systems also "Anthropos" or "Church"—show that the whole system goes back to an original myth in which the "only begotten" (μονογενής) " [147] of the primal father and primal mother, the "Christ," *himself* as "man" falls into the power of darkness from which he is again freed in all "perfect men." Only later was the system ecclesiasticized by the quite superficial introduction of the church's redeemer figure as the revealer of this system.[148]

21

---

[143] 53.15 ff. = Till, 147.
[144] 55.15 ff. = Till, 151.
[145] 55.18-62.
[146] 99.14 = Sophia of Jesus Christ = Till, 239.
[147] 30.4-5 = Till, 101.
[148] How this could occur is shown, e.g., by Heracleon in Fragment 35 (Orig. Comm. in Joh. 13.49; see in W. Völker, *Quellen zur Geschichte der christlichen Gnosis* [1932], pp. 78-79; W. Foerster, *Von Valentin zu Herakleon*, BZNW 7 [1928]: 37 ff.) . The proverb quoted in John 4:37, "One sows, another reaps," is interpreted in the following fashion: "The higher Son of Man sows. But the redeemer, himself also Son of Man, reaps." Thus the Pneumatics are seed of the Christ-Son-of-Man, the

The same original equation of Christ = "Man" in which a redemptive function of the Christ figure is not presupposed can also be inferred from many others of the later Gnostic systems.[149] This points to the fundamental significance of the pre-Christian Christ myth for Jewish Gnosticism and its Christian offshoots. The example cited may be sufficient.

In this connection it is rewarding to take a more careful look than has previously (pp. 58-59) been done at the Shepherd of Hermas, whose otherwise quite confused Christology has preserved for us surprisingly clear documentation of the fact that the Gnostic who held the myth which we have examined in principle set himself *beside* Christ. In one of the interpretations of the fifth Similitude it is said, among other things, "The preterrestrial Holy Pneuma, who formed the whole creation (!), God caused to take up residence in a Sarx which he had chosen. Now this Sarx in which the Holy Pneuma dwelt served the Pneuma splendidly . . . . Since it aided the Holy Pneuma and cooperated with it in every deed, God chose it as companion of the Holy Pneuma" (Sim. V, 6). So much for Christology, which in addition to the Gnostic elements exhibits strong adoptionist elements also. Then immediately there follows the surprising anthropological expression, which however is not exactly a genuine *expression:* "For every Sarx which is found unspotted and free of fault, in which the Holy Pneuma dwelt, receives a reward . . . . Keep this your flesh pure and unspotted, so that the Holy Pneuma who dwells in it may give it a good testimony and you may be justified" (Sim. V, 6-7). The basically similar estima-

---

primal man, who is found (ἐστὼς) ὑπὲρ τὸν τόπον, that is, they are part of him. The Christ redeemer is not identical with this higher Son of Man, nevertheless he bears the same name: he is later inserted as a special figure into the system which originally had no acquaintance with a redeemer myth.

[149] In place of the *one* figure, which can be called Christ and Anthropos, Holy Spirit and Church, Teletos, Monogenes, Zoe, Logos, Soter, Adam, and so on, there appears a host of aeons of the most diverse position and function, who fill the Pleroma and to whom the various designations for the one primal man are applied as special proper names at times. But remnants of the original myth are still shown in the close connection of Anthropos and Ecclesia on the one hand (Iren. II, 13.10), and of Christ and Pneuma on the other hand (I, 2.5) in the Valentinian system, in the interpretation of the leaven that is mixed into everything to mean Christ (Iren. I, 8.3), and in many other individual features. When Irenaeus (I, 2) tells that the aeons through the activity of the Holy Spirit, which takes away all distinctions among them, have become inwardly and outwardly all alike, i.e., they all have become Nous, Logos, Anthropos, Christ, etc. (I, 2.6), this is probably also to be traced to a recollection of that original myth.

In his presentation of the system of Marcus (I, 15.3), Irenaeus writes: "Thus Jesus now is a name for the man of the dispensation of salvation, and it is used after the image and likeness of the man who descends upon him," and he reports concerning Valentinus that the latter once asserted that Jesus descended from the Christ, *qui recucurrit sursum in pleroma,* and another time that he was brought forth by Man and Church (I, 11.1).

tion of Christ and man here becomes just as clear as the identification of Christ and Pneuma, which Hermas of course does not hold consistently.

In general, in terminology and conception the Shepherd of Hermas indicates a strong influence of the Jewish Christ myth. Here should be mentioned the equation of Pneuma and Kyrios, as it is made in Mand. III, 1 terminologically as something self-evident: "Love the truth . . . so that the πνεῦμα which God causes to dwell in this flesh may be found true in all men and thus the κύριος who dwells in you shall be glorified."

Still more emphatic and, without reference to the purely anthropological Christ myth, utterly puzzling, is Sim. IX, 1.1: "θέλω σοι δεῖξαι ὅσα σοι ἔδειξε τὸ πνεῦμα τὸ ἅγιον τὸ λαλῆσαν μετὰ σοῦ ἐν μορφῇ τῆς Ἐκκλησίας (cf. Vis. III, 3.3, where the Pneuma says ἐγώ εἰμι ἡ Ἐκκλησία) . ἐκεῖνο γὰρ τὸ πνεῦμα ὁ υἱὸς τοῦ θεοῦ ἐστίν." Thus Pneuma = Ecclesia = Christ.[150]

It has long been known that the figure of the cosmic primal man which is identical with the ἐκκλησία underlies the tower in the vision of the building of the tower and in the parallel parable of the building of the tower (Vis. III; Sim. IX).[151] But even in details all essential features of the mythological equation "man" = Christ can be identified in the parable of the building of the tower. One may note for example Sim. IX, 13.1, where Hermas asks the Shepherd what the tower represents and receives the answer, "ὁ πύργος . . . ἡ ἐκκλησία ἐστίν." A little earlier (IX, 12.1), in answer to the question about the meaning of the rock and the gate, the foundations of the tower which has grown with them into *one* stone (Sim. IX, 9.7; cf. Matt. 16:18!?) , he receives the explanation: "This rock and the gate are the Son of God." With the unity of rock and tower, the personal unity of church and Christ is established. Also gnosticizing is Sim. IX, 13.5 (cf. 13.7; 17.5; 18.3) where expression is given in the familiar mythological terminology to what is very vividly set forth in the parable (: the tower was built ὡσὰν ἐξ ἑνὸς λίθου, μὴ ἔχων μίαν ἁρμογὴν ἐν ἑαυτῷ, Sim. IX, 9.7) . The believers will become εἰς ἓν πνεῦμα, εἰς ἓν σῶμα, καὶ μία χρόα τῶν ἱματισμῶν αὐτῶν.

By far the best source from which the presence of a Gnosticism can be demonstrated in which the individual soul is identified with Christ is the New Testament. A large part of the terms taken over from Gnosticism into New Testament language, particularly in Paul and the Deutero-Paulines, presupposed this special mythological background. Unfortunately this set of concepts has not yet been studied

---

[150] Cf. H. Schlier, [1], p. 54.

[151] Cf. H. Schlier, [1], pp. 51-52, 120-21; M. Dibelius in HNT 12 (3rd ed.) : *in loc.*

in context. Such an omission cannot and will not be made up for here. I shall mention only the most characteristic expressions without striving for any sort of completeness. It probably does not need to be said that the conception which Paul connects with the individual appropriated expressions is not the original mythological one at all. But what interests us is not the Pauline theology, but the Gnostic mythology which stands behind his terminology.

In II Cor. 3:17 the unity of the pneuma-self and Christ is directly and programmatically announced with the "ὁ κύριος τὸ πνεῦμά ἐστιν." [152] In Rom. 8 Paul sets forth precisely the same idea. I quote Rom. 8:9-10: "ὑμεῖς δὲ οὐκ ἐστὲ ἐν σαρκὶ ἀλλὰ ἐν πνεύματι, εἴπερ πνεῦμα θεοῦ οἰκεῖ ἐν ὑμῖν. εἰ δέ τις πνεῦμα Χριστοῦ οὐκ ἔχει, οὗτος οὐκ ἔστιν αὐτοῦ. εἰ δὲ Χριστὸς ἐν ὑμῖν, τὸ μὲν . . ." "To possess the Pneuma of Christ" thus is the same as "to have Christ in you"; i.e., Christ is the Pneuma. Χριστὸς ἔν τινι is here the most compact expression of the Jewish-Gnostic Christ myth.[153] One should note the splendid passage in Gal. 2:20: "ζῶ δὲ οὐκέτι ἐγώ, ζῇ δὲ ἐν ἐμοὶ Χριστός" [154] or II Cor. 13:5: "οὐκ ἐπιγινώσκετε ἑαυτοὺς ὅτι 'Ιησοῦς Χριστὸς ἐν ὑμῖν" (cf. Gal. 4:19) .

As in Rom. 8:9 the πνεῦμα ἔν τινι alternates with the equivalent ἐν πνεύματι εἶναι, so also the "we in Christ" corresponds to the "Christ in us." [155] The conception of the cosmic figure of the primal man = Christ

---

[152] On this verse, cf. below, pp. 315 ff. On the identification of Christ and Pneuma in Paul, see also G. Friedrich, "Amt und Geist," in *Wort und Dienst*, 1952, pp. 63-64; cf. also above, pp. 58-59.

[153] Cf. H. Schlier, [2], p. 143.

[154] On this, cf. J. Weiss in ZNW 19 (1919/20) : 139 ff.

[155] The formula ἐν Χριστῷ in Paul has been frequently investigated as to its use and its origin, most recently among others by F. Büchsel in ZNW, 1949, pp. 141-58: " 'In Christus' bei Paulus." Of course Büchsel knows only to say whence the formula does *not* stem, namely not from the Septuagint, which translates the ב with ἐν (κυρίῳ) . This view has increasingly prevailed since A. Deissmann's book, *Die neutestamentliche Formel "in Christo Jesu"* (1892) . But I do not know of anyone yet who has consistently interpreted the formula in terms of the Gnostic Christ myth. B. Murmelstein may possibly have come closest to the correct explanation in "Adam, ein Beitrag zur Messiaslehre," WZKM 35 (1928) : 242-75; 36 (1929) : 51-86. Following him, A. Oepke in TDNT II: 542, refers quite generally to the oriental primal man speculation (on p. 537 also a listing of the literature on this entire problem) .
The occasional indication that the ἐν Χριστῷ must be seen in connection with the Gnostic conception of the σῶμα Χριστοῦ (R. Bultmann, E. Käsemann, H. Schlier, *et al.*; see A. Oepke in TDNT II) is a correct one.
This is already suggested by the fact that Paul can say ἐν Χριστῷ, then ἐν Χριστῷ 'Ιησοῦ, and further (following the Old Testament usage) ἐν κυρίῳ, but never ἐν 'Ιησοῦ. Further, σῶμα 'Ιησοῦ does not occur alongside σῶμα Χριστοῦ.
Of the more recent literature, one should consult also: W. Schmauch, *In Christus* (1935) ; M. Dibelius, "Paulus und die Mystik," in *Botschaft und Geschichte* II: 134 ff.; H. L. Parisius in ZNW 49 (1958) : 285 ff.; J. A. Allan in NTS 5 (1958) : 54 ff.; F. Neugebauer, *In Christus* (1961) ; W. Schrage, *Die konkreten Einzelgebote in der paulinischen Paränese*, pp. 80 ff. Important also is A. Dieterich, *Eine Mithrasliturgie*, pp. 109 ff. 22

admits of either form of expression. One speaks as it were analytically of "Christ in us"; we think of the splitting-up of the Christ into the many individual pneumata. "We in Christ" is then synthetically said with a view to the physical unity of the scattered light-substance. Thus Gal. 3:28: "πάντες ὑμεῖς εἷς ἐστε ἐν Χριστῷ ᾿Ιησοῦ," and Rom. 12:5: "οὕτως οἱ πολλοὶ ἓν σῶμά ἐσμεν ἐν Χριστῷ, τὸ δὲ καθ᾽ εἷς ἀλλήλων μέλη." For Paul the believers are "in Christ." Thus there were already before Paul's conversion those who were ἐν Χριστῷ (Rom. 16:7). All are sanctified ἐν Χριστῷ (Phil. 1:1; I Cor. 1:2), of course occasionally also νήπιοι ἐν Χριστῷ (I Cor. 3:1), that is to say, when they consider themselves to be φρόνιμοι ἐν Χριστῷ (I Cor. 4:10). Nevertheless it is basically true that "εἴ τις ἐν Χριστῷ καινὴ κτίσις. τὰ ἀρχαῖα παρῆλθεν, ἰδοὺ γέγονεν καινά" (II Cor. 5:17). To those who are ἐν Χριστῷ there is no longer any condemnation (Rom. 8:1). They have eternal life ἐν Χριστῷ (Rom. 6:23; cf. Iren. I, 21.5 and Eth. Enoch 49.3), though they must always remain conscious of the admonition: "στήκετε ἐν κυρίῳ" (Phil. 4:1; I Thess. 3:8). Paul regards his whole existence κατὰ σάρκα as refuse, ἵνα Χριστὸν κερδήσω καὶ εὑρεθῶ ἐν αὐτῷ (Phil. 3:8).

In Paul this set of concepts is already so polished that its mythological origin oftentimes is hardly any longer noticeable. I add here some documentation from Gnosticism in which the "christological" ἐν occurs:

". . . (are) beloved ones in the beloved one
and such as are preserved in the one who lives
and redeemed in the one who is redeemed" (Od. Sol. 8.22).

"I thank thee, Lord, who wast proclaimed by the alien man and art found in us" (Act. Thom. 15 = 120.14-15; 10 = 114.15 ff.).

". . . ἐν αὐτῷ συνεσταλκέναι" (scil. the church; Iren. I, 8.3).

"Οὗτος (Marcus) ἔλεγεν ἐν αὐτῷ τὴν μεγίστην . . . εἶναι δύναμιν" (Hipp. VI, 39; cf. Iren. I, 13.3: "ὁ δὲ τόπος τοῦ μεγέθους ἐν ἡμῖν ἐστιν").

"ἐμὲ ὁ ζητῶν εὑρήσει ἐν παιδίοις ἀπὸ ἐτῶν ἑπτά . . ." (Hipp. V, 7.20 = 83.14-15).

According to Iren. I, 21.3, the Gnostics speak in the name of Jao of the redemption "ἐν τῷ χριστῷ τῷ ζῶντι."

In Eth. Enoch 49.3 it is said: "In him (scil. the Son of Man) . . . dwells the spirit of those who have fallen asleep in righteousness."

Cf. further the passages already cited on pp. 48 and 58 from Exc. ex Theod. 58.1 and Hipp. V, 7.33 = 87.5. These examples could be multiplied.

Let us turn back to Paul. Paul prefers the ἐν with the dative, perhaps because it is close to the language of the Old Testament. Occasionally, however, there also appears the simple genitive which as *genitivus partitivus* gave expression in his mythological understanding to the point that every Gnostic is *part* of Christ: "ὑμεῖς δὲ χριστοῦ" (I Cor. 3:23; cf. 1:12; II Cor. 10:7) is a proper expression of being a Christian (cf. Rom. 8:9). "οἱ τοῦ χριστοῦ" crucify their flesh with its passions and lusts (Gal. 5:24): "οἱ τοῦ χριστοῦ" follow Christ in the resurrection (I Cor. 15:23). In this connection a comparison of Gal. 3:29 with 3:16 is interesting. After Paul had affirmed in Gal. 3:16 that by the promised "seed of Abraham" was meant not a number of persons but no one other than Christ himself, he concludes in 3:29: "εἰ δὲ ὑμεῖς χριστοῦ, ἄρα τοῦ Ἀβραὰμ σπέρμα ἐστέ." This course of thought, although naturally meant by Paul unmythologically, yet allows us clearly to recognize the original mythological conception of the Pneumatics' participation in the cosmic Christ. Cf. also Mark 9:41!

How little Paul thinks in Gnostic fashion becomes just as clear in these passages as does the mythological background of the whole style of speech. For in the Gnostics' view, whoever is really in Christ the light-being and thus is himself a part of Christ, has life. They conceived of the Christ-primal man as a cosmic σῶμα whose members are formed of the individual souls.[156] "καθάπερ γὰρ τὸ σῶμα ἕν ἐστιν καὶ

[156] This Gnostic origin of the σῶμα Χριστοῦ conception is still disputed, as it has been. Of the more recent literature on the problem, I mention: H. Schlier, *Der Brief an die Epheser* (1958), pp. 90 ff.; E. Schweizer, *Erniedrigung und Erhöhung bei Jesus und seinen Nachfolgern*, AThANT 28 (1955): 156 ff.; (1962, 2nd ed.): 184 (Literature): *ibid.*, "Die Kirche als Leib Christi in den paulinischen Antilegomena," TLZ, 1961, cols. 241 ff.; *ibid.*, "Die Kirche als Leib Christi in den paulinischen Homologumena," TLZ, 1961, cols. 161 ff.; H. Hegermann, "Zur Ableitung der Leib-Christi-Vorstellung," TLZ, 1960, cols. 893 ff.; J. Reuss, "Die Kirche als Leib Christi," BiblZ, 1958, pp. 103-27; A. Oepke, "Leib Christi oder Volk Gottes bei Paulus," TLZ, 1954, cols. 363 ff.; J. A. T. Robinson, *The Body* (1952); C. Colpe, "Zur Leib-Christi-Vorstellung im Epheserbrief," in *Judentum, Urchristentum, Kirche*, BZNW 26: 172 ff. (Literature); J. J. Meuzelaar, *Der Leib des Messias* (1961); R. Schnackenburg, *Die Kirche im Neuen Testament* (1961), pp. 146 ff.; J. Hermann, *Kyrios und Pneuma*, pp. 79 ff.; H. W. Robinson, *The Hebrew Conception of Corporate Personality*, BZAW 66 (1936).

The impossibility of deriving the σῶμα Χριστοῦ conception from the Stoics and similar pantheistic ideas is shown by E. Schweizer, *Erniedrigung und Erhöhung bei Jesus und seinen Nachfolgern*, and H. Schlier, [3]. Cf. also E. Brandenburger, *Adam und Christus*, pp. 151 ff. Schlier rightly interprets the σῶμα Χριστοῦ conception in terms of Gnosticism. Schweizer proposes (in EvTheol, 1959, p. 66) for the TWNT *s.v.* σῶμα a derivation from Jewish patterns of thought. The body of Christ is supposed to be "the 'historical' body of Jesus in its continuing effect in the community." The article has now appeared in TWNT VII: 1024 ff. Schweizer (pp. 1069-70) derives the Pauline σῶμα Χριστοῦ conception from the late Jewish speculations about Adam. A striking parallel is indeed present here. That Paul developed the one out of the other is of course an assertion which has nothing to document it. The parallelism mentioned may rather rest upon a common (Gnostic) background of both conceptions. I regard as exegetically untenable and theologically very dubious Schweizer's further attempt (p. 1066) to equate the "crucifixion body in its con-

μέλη πολλὰ ἔχει, πάντα δὲ τὰ μέλη τοῦ σώματος πολλὰ ὄντα ἕν ἐστιν σῶμα, οὕτως καὶ ὁ Χριστός" (I Cor. 12:12) . The surprising thing in this formulation is the matter-of-fact way in which Paul says Christ when he means the church, and indeed *without* mythically-mystically identifying it with him. This has always confused the exegetes.[157] But the sentence affords a perfectly classic illustration of the fact that somewhere in Paul's environment the individual was regarded as a part of the σῶμα Χριστοῦ, or the church was identified with Christ. One should compare with this also I Cor. 12:27: "ὑμεῖς δέ ἐστε σῶμα Χριστοῦ καὶ μέλη ἐκ μέρους" and I Cor. 6:15: "οὐκ οἴδατε ὅτι τὰ σώματα ὑμῶν μέλη Χριστοῦ ἐστιν";[158]

It is true that for Paul one is not in this body φύσει, by nature, as the true Gnostic thinks, but the apostle still can conceive of the way to being in Christ after the analogy of the mystery cults: by means of

---

tinuing effects" with the "sphere of the church" (*sic*). "The crucified and resurrected body of Christ is for Paul a present sphere into which the community is placed" (p. 1069). But the community is not, for Paul, *in* the body of Christ, but *is* the body of Christ; hence an identification of this conception of the body with Paul's theology of the cross is not possible.

The following passage from the new Coptic texts from Nag Hammadi ("On the Three Natures," quoted following G. Quispel, [1], p. 227, who however apparently misinterprets the passage) also shows that the σῶμα Χριστοῦ conception has as its presupposition the equation Christ = primal man: "When the redemption was proclaimed, the perfect man received the Gnosis in himself, so that he hastened to return to his unity, to the place from which he came, to the place from which he descended. But his members receive training . . . until the members of the body of the church form a unity, so that together they receive the restoration, the restoration into the Pleroma, manifesting itself as an integral (?) body." This conception, in which the church's Christ does not appear, is not an extension but a basis or a parallel of that σῶμα Χριστοῦ conception in which the "perfect man" in all his members bears the name "Christ."

C. Colpe (see pp. 176 ff.) acknowledges that the Pauline and deutero-Pauline σῶμα Χριστοῦ conception is conceived spatially or cosmically. Nevertheless he disputes the Gnostic derivation because in the passages of the deutero-Pauline epistles in question the Gnostic redeemer myth is lacking. This latter point may be true, but it is only one more indication of the Gnostic background of the conception mentioned, since it is not the Gnostic redeemer myth but the primal man-Christ myth that underlies this conception. Colpe wishes to derive the σῶμα Χριστοῦ conception from σῶμα speculations of Stoic origin, such as are found in Philo. In so doing he does not—to say nothing of all others—consider the Gnostic components of the Philonic Anthropos conception.

E. Brandenburger (*Adam und Christus*, pp. 151 ff.) also correctly traces the σῶμα Χριστοῦ conception back to the Gnostic Adam-Anthropos myth. When he nevertheless purports to have found in this myth the conception "of the redeemer *soma* embracing in itself redeemed humanity" "which in the Christian sphere naturally is the σῶμα Χριστοῦ" (*ibid.*, p. 152), he allows himself to be misled by the Christ concept to the same mistake which I too, among others, made in the first edition of this book, namely, to be concerned for the explanation of the σῶμα Χριστοῦ conception with the redeemer myth.

[157] Cf. the literature in H. Lietzmann, HNT 9: 187 on p. 63, l. 4.

[158] Cf. further Eph. 3:21; II Clem. 14.2; Ign. Smyrn. 1.2; Trall. 11.2; Eph. 4.2; Smyrn. 8.2; see H. Schlier, [2], p. 100, n. 2; cf. *ibid.*, pp. 88 ff.

the sacraments the individual becomes a part of the σῶμα Χριστοῦ. It is in these terms that I Cor. 10:16 is to be understood: "τὸν ἄρτον ὃν κλῶμεν, οὐχὶ κοινωνία τοῦ σώματος τοῦ Χριστοῦ ἐστιν"; and correspondingly, for baptism the same holds: "καὶ γὰρ ἐν ἑνὶ πνεύματι ἡμεῖς πάντες εἰς ἓν σῶμα ἐβαπτίσθημεν" (I Cor. 12:13). Gal. 3:27 shows that the σῶμα mentioned here is actually the body of Christ, and thus Christ himself: "ὅσοι γὰρ εἰς Χριστὸν ἐβαπτίσθητε, Χριστὸν ἐνδύσασθε" (cf. Rom. 6:3).

Christ is "τὸ πλήρωμα τοῦ τὰ πάντα ἐν πᾶσιν πληρουμένου" (Eph. 1:23).[159] With this we may compare, for example, Col. 3:11: "πάντα καὶ ἐν πᾶσιν Χριστός." As the individual souls find their way to Christ, the scattered body of Christ is built up again; for this reason the ministries are placed in the community εἰς οἰκοδομὴν τοῦ σώματος τοῦ Χριστοῦ (Eph. 4:12).[160]

Out of this circle of conceptions also comes the concept of the ἕνωσις or the ἑνότης or the ἑνοῦσθαι of the community with Christ, as it frequently appears in the Ignatian epistles (cf., e.g., "ἐν ἑνότητι Ἰησοῦ Χριστοῦ" in Philad. 5.2), and in the Exc. ex Theod. and already in the New Testament, Eph. 4:13 (cf. 4:3; also John 11:52).[161] The background of this conception is formed by the Gnostic *identification* of Christ and church, as still may be seen relatively clearly, for example, in Ign. Trall. 11.2; Magn. 7.2; Exc. ex Theod. 26 and 42.

If the individual is a part of Christ, it is understandable when in certain Christian-Gnostic circles the teaching is propounded that the suffering of Christ is complete only when the individual bearers of souls have suffered just as he did.[162] Col. 1:24 is to be understood against this background: "Νῦν χαίρω ἐν τοῖς παθήμασιν ὑπὲρ ὑμῶν, καὶ ἀνταναπληρῶ τὰ ὑστερήματα τῶν θλίψεων τοῦ Χριστοῦ ἐν τῇ σαρκί μου ὑπὲρ τοῦ σώματος αὐτοῦ, ὅ ἐστιν ἡ ἐκκλησία," and Paul's "passion theology" is a demythologized but nonetheless clear reminiscence of this mythic basic outlook. The suffering of the community is a suffering ὑπὲρ Χριστοῦ (Phil. 1:29), i.e., (for mythology) a suffering of a

[159] Cf. Col. 2:9; G. Delling in TDNT VI: 300 ff.; Evangelium Veritatis 36.1 = H. M. Schenke, p. 50; H. Schlier, [3], pp. 96 ff.

[160] Cf. Eph. 4:15-16; Col. 2:19; I Peter 2:5 ff.; H. Schlier, [2], pp. 120-21; [1], pp. 37 ff.

[161] Cf. S. Hanson, *The Unity of the Church in the New Testament*, p. 158; H. Schlier, [2], pp. 97 ff.; Od. Sol. 41.15; Gospel of Thomas, Saying 3; Saying 24; O. Hosius in EvTheol, 1960, pp. 32-33.

[162] In this Gnosticism is thinking of suffering in the power of the demons and in the prison cell of the body, and thus of the "incarnation" in general, not specifically of the crucifixion, which can occasionally rather be understood even as liberation from suffering.

part of Christ and therefore a *charis*. Indeed Paul can directly label
the sufferings of the Corinthians as παθήματα τοῦ Χριστοῦ.[163]

Like the individual, so also naturally the totality of the believers are,
as the sum of individual souls, i.e., the "ἐκκλησία," "in Christ." Paul
was unknown by face ταῖς ἐκκλησίαις τῆς Ἰουδαίας ταῖς ἐν Χριστῷ (Gal.
1:22; cf. I Thess. 2:14). The church is the σῶμα Χριστοῦ: "καὶ αὐτός
ἐστιν ἡ κεφαλὴ τοῦ σώματος, τῆς ἐκκλησίας" (Col. 1:18). The same expression is found in Col. 1:24*b*.[164]

To this connection also belongs the question of I Cor. 1:13: "μεμέρισται ὁ Χριστός"; which is posed in view of the divisions in the *congregation*.

Worthy of mention also is Gal. 3:27: "ὅσοι γὰρ εἰς Χριστὸν ἐβαπτίσθητε, Χριστὸν ἐνδύσασθε." We may compare with this Act. Thom. 112:
"Suddenly, when I saw the garment, it resembled me, as I looked in a
mirror, and I saw myself entire in it, and I recognized and saw myself
wholly through it; for we, being of the same essence, were in part
distinguished, and yet one, in one figure . . . ," and we shall recognize
that for the myth standing back of Gal. 3:27, Christ, into whom one is
baptized or whom one puts on, is the sum of the individual selves (cf.
Rom. 6:3; Col. 3:9 ff.).

Of special clarity and purity is Col. 1:26-27. Here Paul is introduced
as the servant of Christ who is called to proclaim the word of God,
namely "the mystery which was hidden from the aeons and the genera-
tions, but now was revealed to his saints to whom God has willed to
make known how rich among the Gentiles is the glory of this mystery,
which is 'Christ is *in you.*'" Thus first he speaks in purely Gnostic
fashion of the mystery which formerly was concealed from the *Gentiles*
(and thus stems from Judaism!? see pp. 71 ff.), but now is *recognized,*
and then the content of this Gnosis is summed up in the phrase
"Χριστὸς ἐν ὑμῖν." [165] The proclamation of Christ as the Pneuma-Self
dwelling in man and guaranteeing redemption is the content in a word
of the Gnosis which stands back of Colossians.

Here I shall add some Gnostic parallels:

"For the Son of Man is within you. Follow after him! Those who
seek him shall find him" (Gospel according to Mary, from Papyrus
Berol. 8502; quoted from Hennecke-Schneemelcher-Wilson, *New Testament Apocrypha,* I: 341).

---

[163] II, 1:5; later examples in H. Schlier, [2], pp. 158 ff.; cf. *The Office of Apostle,*
pp. 47 ff., 222 ff.; J. Kremer, *Was an den Leiden Christi noch mangelt* (Bonn, 1956);
E. Percy, [2], pp. 128 ff.

[164] Cf. Hermas, Sim. IX; H. Schlier, [1], pp. 60 ff.

[165] Cf. Iren. I, 13.3; Hipp. VI, 34.7: ἵνα δῴη ὑμῖν ὁ θεὸς κατοικῆσαι τὸν Χριστὸν
εἰς τὸν ἔσω ἄνθρωπον (Valentinians).

"His disciples said: Show us the place where you are; for it is necessary for us that we seek after him. He said to us: He that has ears, let him hear! Light is within a light-man" (Logion 25 of the Coptic Gospel of Thomas = Leipoldt-Schenke, p. 15).

"Jesus said: if you beget in you that one whom you have, he will save you. If you do not have that one in you, the one whom you do not have within you will slay you" (Logion 71 = L.-S., p. 21).[166]

Further, Gal. 4:19 should be compared here: ". . . μέχρις οὗ μορφωθῇ Χριστὸς ἐν ὑμῖν."[167]

In addition a piece of the Ephesian epistle, which has a strong Gnostic tinge in its concepts to which H. Schlier[168] has called attention, may be cited here. There (4:11-12) it is said that Christ established various ministries for the building-up of his body, μέχρι καταντήσωμεν οἱ πάντες εἰς τὴν ἑνότητα τῆς πίστεως καὶ τῆς ἐπιγνώσεως τοῦ υἱοῦ τοῦ θεοῦ, εἰς ἄνδρα τέλειον, εἰς μέτρον ἡλικίας τοῦ πληρώματος τοῦ Χριστοῦ. Thus we all attain the knowledge of the Son of God, mature manhood, the measure of the Pleroma of Christ. The three expressions naturally stand in parallel, if one does not do violence to the text, and this means that the perfect or mature man,[169] i.e., the primal man who himself is redeemed to completeness, is identical with Christ. A similar note is sounded by the utterance of the Ebionites about Jesus according to Epiph. Haer. XVIII, 6: "αὐτὸν δὲ μόνον (in contrast to the Old Testament prophets) θέλουσιν εἶναι καὶ προφήτην καὶ ἄνθρωπον καὶ υἱὸν θεοῦ καὶ Χριστόν." One may compare also Ign. Smyrn. 4.2, where Christ is described as ἄνθρωπος τέλειος.

---

[166] These logia—others could be added, e.g., the Coptic Gospel of Thomas 112 (see p. 149, n. 49) —appear to be reinterpreting Luke 17:21. Of course in view of the Gnostic passages it should be asked whether the clause in Luke 17:21b, "for behold, the kingdom of heaven is in you," which has never yet been satisfactorily explained in terms of the situation of the primitive community or of the historical Jesus, did not rather, conversely, make its way out of a Gnostic tradition into the Gospel of Luke.

[167] Cf. Koptisch-gnostische Schriften 1, GCS 45; 355.26. On μορφωθῆναι, cf. E. Käsemann, [3], p. 63; J. Behm in TDNT IV: 752 ff. It involves a formulation which could presuppose the influence of mystery thought on the Gnostic myth, insofar as the fashioning of Christ in man is the goal of a development, and as this goal, but not as a fact existent since primordial times, represents the content of Gnosis. Of course μορφωθῆναι then could also have the sense of the ἐξεικονισθῆναι of Simonian Gnosticism: the Christ who is present as potentiality is to be formed as actuality. Or here Christ signifies the sum of all individual selves and as the one Christ is again to take shape in and through the individuals. What Paul himself is expressing with the terminology which in any case is traditional is a question in itself. On this, cf., e.g., R. Hermann in TLZ, 1955, cols. 713 ff.

[168] [1], pp. 27-28.

[169] Cf. Hipp. VI, 8.37; Acta Archelai 8.7, and H. Schlier, [1], pp. 29, 31-32, who of course equates the ἀνὴρ τέλειος with the κεφαλή of the σῶμα, the "highest pinnacle of his own Pleroma" (p. 28) , while yet the ἀνὴρ τ έ λ ε ι ο ς is the whole Pleroma, body and head.

Finally, we should recall Phil. 1:20 ff. Paul has the firm hope that in imprisonment and under persecution he *himself* will not come to naught because καὶ νῦν μεγαλυνθήσεται Χριστὸς ἐν τῷ σώματί μου, εἴτε διὰ ζωῆς εἴτε διὰ θανάτου. This terminology too is purely Gnostic. This becomes even clearer in the following sentence, in which possibly a direct quotation is found: "ἐμοὶ γὰρ τὸ ζῆν Χριστὸς καὶ τὸ ἀποθανεῖν κέρδος." Christ himself is, as the *self of man*, the life of man, and the ἀποθανεῖν as the ἀνάλυσις (vs. 23) of the σάρξ with the goal of ἐν Χριστῷ εἶναι signifies the ultimate achievement of this life. The broader context also has a strong Gnostic tinge in its conceptions. It is interesting that in vs. 23 Paul says σὺν Χριστῷ[170] and in vs. 24 ἐπιμένειν τῇ σαρκί instead of the really Gnostic μένειν ἐν σαρκί. In such small and certainly unconscious alterations of the appropriated terminology is shown the wholly different orientation of Pauline theology.

Here we pause for a moment. I have intentionally given preference to the documentation from the Pauline literature, although the Deutero-Pauline letters, especially Ephesians and Colossians, let the basic Gnostic conceptions become even clearer. Paul however is doubtless the earliest witness for such a source. It is not possible to determine this more precisely. We can say with certainty only that it was not Paul himself who united the Gnostic concepts and thought-world with the message of Jesus as the earthly manifestation of the redeemer. He rather found the two already combined and, before he began his so-called missionary journeys, appropriated them in combination.[171] Otherwise his traditional Jewish-rabbinical manner of expression could not have remained so completely free of Gnostic features as is the case with the midrash in II Cor. 3:7 ff. Moreover, he then would have to show personal and direct acquaintance with the pure Gnostic myth. Nevertheless he knows only christianized concepts and conceptions, and when he encounters genuine Gnostics in Corinth, he not only has no understanding of their myth and self-understanding but also, as we shall see, makes the surely unhappy attempt to oppose the myth by taking the myth as his own standpoint (cf. I Cor. 2:6–3:3; see below, pp. 151 ff.). Though in regard to Paul's intention this happens only terminologically, still the Gnostics could understand this manner of speaking only in their mythological original sense, and not in the Christian reinterpretation which in many cases lies quite far removed

[170] Cf. E. Käsemann, [2], pp. 167-68.

[171] This is also shown clearly in the gnosticizing Christ hymn which Paul takes over in Phil. 2:6-11 (*cf.* E. Lohmeyer in Meyer *Kommentar* 9 [1953, 9th ed.]: *in loc.*). It is true that it stems from another circle of Christian Gnosticism than that to which the terminology which we are investigating is native, but it allows the Gnostic character of the *redeemer myth* clearly to emerge. Thus before Paul this myth has been connected with Jesus of Nazareth.

from the former. Further, it can be shown that there were quite diverse Gnostic systems from which stems the Gnostic interpretation of Paul, and that the apostle thus certainly already draws from a common supply. A demonstration of this would however lead us too far afield here.[172]

But above all the natural and unreflecting way in which Paul uses the Gnostic terminology shows that its original significance was not familiar to him. When J. Schierse[173] poses the question of how it was possible for Paul to understand his own theology when he did not perceive the mythological background of his terminology, the answer is this: If Paul had known the actual meaning of his Gnostic terminology, he would not at all have been able to use this to express his own proclamation, at any rate not in the way in which it was actually done; for the mythological meaning of this set of concepts is often radically different from the Pauline meaning. For this reason, the anti-Gnostic Pastoral Epistles in an extensive imitation of Pauline language consistently eliminate its Gnostic components.

Since Paul was not directly acquainted with the Jewish Christ Gnosticism, he can have acquired the Gnostic elements of his theological set of concepts only during the fifteen-year stay in Arabia, Syria, and Cilicia mentioned in Gal. 1:18 ff. This means, however, that at the latest around the year 40 Jesus was already being proclaimed in the terminology of the Jewish Christ Gnosticism as the Messiah, so that the Jewish-Gnostic terminology, on the circuit of the Christian communities in the wider environs of Antioch, could find entrance into the theological language of Paul. For, as has been said, it is impossible that this entire set of concepts was taken over by Paul directly from a Jewish Gnosticism.

Here now we need to mention a unique, diverse, and often investigated christological conception of late Judaism and of early Christianity. Distinctive features of this conception are, above all:

The Christ becomes a heavenly being.
He bears as such the titles Man, Primal Man, and Son of Man.[174]

---

[172] Of course in this period in which he was developing his theology, Paul took over not only large parts of his reasoning from Gnosticism, but also Gnostic conceptions, particularly important parts of his Christ-redeemer conception. On the Gnostic origin of his consciousness of his apostolic office, see *The Office of Apostle*, pp. 198 ff.

[173] *Scholastik*, 1958, p. 117.

[174] Dan. 7:9 ff.; Eth. Enoch 46 ff., 70-71; IV Ezra 13; the Synoptic Gospels *passim;* John 1:51, *et passim;* Acts 7:56; Hegesippus in Eus. CH II, 23.13; Justin, Apol. I, 51, *et passim;* Acta Joh. 109; Ign. Smyrn. 4.2; Epiph., Haer. XXX, 18.6; Ps.-Clem. Rec. I, 60.3; III, 61.2; Od. Sol. 36.3; fragment of the Gospel of the Hebrews in

He becomes the "express image of God";[175]
occasionally even a collective being.[176]
He serves as mediator of creation[177]
and as Sophia.[178]
He is identified with the biblical Adam[179]

---

28   Jerome, vir. inl. 2 = Hennecke-Schneemelcher-Wilson I: 165; the Gospel of Mary
        from Pap. Berol. 8502, pp. 8, 12 ff., et passim.
            Cf. 1st ed. of this work, pp. 100 ff., 105; E. Sjöberg, Der Menschensohn im äthiopi-
        schen Henochbuch; P. Vielhauer, "Gottesreich und Menschensohn in der Verkündi-
        gung Jesu," in Festschrift für Günther Dehn (1957) pp. 71 ff.; W. Baumgartner in
        ThRs 11 (1939) : 217 ff.; E. Schweizer, [1], pp. 154 ff., 88 ff.; W. Staerk, [2],
        pp. 421 ff.; S. Schulz, [1], pp. 96 ff.; H. J. Schoeps, [1], pp. 78 ff.; A. v. Gall, Basileia
        tou Theou, pp. 126, 268 ff., 385, 409 ff., 441; C. H. Kraeling, Anthropos and Son of
        Man, pp. 128 ff., 166 ff.; H. Gressmann, Der Messias, pp. 343 ff.; H. E. Tödt, The
        Son of Man in the Synoptic Tradition, pp. 22 ff., 319 ff., 329 ff.; O. Cullmann, [1],
        pp. 137 ff.; H. L. Jansen, Die Henochgestalt (1939), pp. 86-111; W. Schultz, Unter-
        suchungen zur Menschensohnchristologie im Johannesevangelium, p. X; W. Grund-
        mann, Die Geschichte Jesu Christi (1956), pp. 278 ff.; E. Schweizer, "Der Men-
        schensohn," in ZNW 50 (1959) : 185ff.; L. Rost, "Zur Deutung des Menschen-
        sohnes in Dan. 7," in Gott und die Götter, Festgabe für E. Fascher, pp. 41 ff.; O.
        Moe, "Der Menschensohn und der Urmensch," StTh XIV (1960) : 119 ff.; G. Dupont,
        Le Fils de l'homme (1924); R. Otto, Reich Gottes und Menschensohn (1940, 2nd
        ed.), esp. pp. 314 ff.; T. W. Manson, "The Son of Man in Daniel, Enoch and the
        Gospels," BJRL 32 (1950) : 171-93; R. Schnackenburg, Gottes Herrschaft und Reich
        (1959), pp. 110 ff.; E. Lohmeyer, Gottesknecht und Davidssohn, FRLANT NF 43
        (1953, 2nd ed.) : 110 ff.; J. Jeremias in TDNT, s.v. Ἀδάμ; ἄνθρωπος; υἱὸς τοῦ ἀνθρώ-
        που; H. M. Schenke, [2], pp. 144 ff.; F. Hahn, Titles of Jesus in Christology, pp.
        17 ff.; E. Jüngel, Paulus und Jesus (1962), pp. 246 ff.; P. Vielhauer in ZThK 60
29   (1963) : 169-70; L. Goppelt, "Zum Problem des Menschensohns," in Mensch und
        Menschensohn, Festschrift für Karl Witte (1963), pp. 20 ff.
            [175] E.g., II Cor. 4:4; Col. 1:15; Heb. 1:3.
            Cf. J. Jervell, Imago Dei, pp. 46 ff., 52 ff., 96 ff., 197 ff.; F. W. Eltester, Eikon im
        Neuen Testament, BZNW 23 (1959); U. Wilckens, [1], pp. 189-90; M. Dibelius/
        H. Conzelmann in HNT 12 (3rd ed.), on Col. 1:15.
            [176] Eth. Enoch 39.8; 49.3; 71.14 ff. Cf. H. Gressmann, Der Messias, pp. 409-10;
        E. Sjöberg, Der Menschensohn, . . . pp. 98 ff.; E. Brandenburger, Adam und Christus,
        pp. 115 ff.; cf. Herm. Vis. II, 4.1.
            [177] I Cor. 8:6; Col. 1:15-16; John 1:2-3; Heb. 1:2 ff.; Herm. Sim. IX, 12; Const.
        Ap. VII, 34; VIII, 12.7 ff.
            Cf. A. v. Gall, Basileia tou Theou, p. 422; O. Michel, Der Brief an die Hebräer,
        Meyer Kommentar XIII (8th ed.) : 36, n. 2; R. Bultmann, [5], on John 1:1-3, esp.
        p. 12; M. Dibelius/H. Conzelmann in HNT 12 (3rd ed.) : 10 ff.; H. Hegermann,
        Die Vorstellung vom Schöpfungsmittler im hellenistischen Judentum und Urchris-
        tentum, TU 82 (1961) passim; G. Lindeskog, Studien zum nt. Schöpfungsgedanken
        I: 207 ff.; G. Widengren, Muhammad, the Apostle of God, and his Ascension (1955);
30   H. Schlier, [3], p. 160; G. Quispel, [2], pp. 475 ff.; 1st ed. of this work, p. 97; E. Percy,
        [2], pp. 68 ff.
            [178] Cf. H. Schlier, [3], pp. 161-62; E. Schweizer, "Aufnahme und Korrektur jüdi-
        scher Sophiatheologie im Neuen Testament," in Hören und Handeln, Festschrift
        für E. Wolf (1962), pp. 330 ff.
            [179] Epiph. Haer. XXX, 3.5; Ps.-Cl. Rec. I, 45; 47 (Syr.). Here also to a greater
        or lesser degree belong those passages in which the Messiah is set in contrast as the
        last man to the first man, as second Adam to the first Adam, as new man to the
        old man, e.g., I Cor. 15:21, 45 ff.; Rom. 5:12, 15, 18; Iren. I, 14.7; Gr. Bar. 9; Gen.

or placed in parallel with him.[180]
Primordial era and end-time then correspond.[181]
Adam appears in such connections as a heavenly, sinless figure.[182]
All these ideas obviously hang together and are related as to origin.
They cannot be derived from Jewish presuppositions. The equation
Messiah = primal man shows that its common origin apparently lies
in the influencing of Jewish messianology by some kind of primal man
conceptions fitted into the schema primordial era = end-time.[183]

Rabba 12.6; late rabbinical passages in Billerbeck, III: 477-78; Josephus, Ant. 1.82; 8.62; passages from Philo in Gfrörer, *Philo*, I: 267-68, 407-8; Rom. 6:6 ff.; Col. 3:9-10; Eph. 2:15; 4:13, 22 ff.; Herm. Sim. IX, 9; Ign. Smyrn. 1.2; Ign. Eph. 20.1; Diog. 2.1; Hipp. V, 7.15; VI, 35.4; Od. Sol. 36.5; Ps.-Cl. Hom. III, 22.
Cf. W. D. Davies, *Paul and Rabbinic Judaism* (1955, 2nd ed.), pp. 36 ff.; E. S. Drower, *The Secret Adam* (1960); J. Jervell, *Imago Dei*, pp. 104, 240 ff.; H. Schlier, [3], pp. 134-35, 200 ff., 220 ff.; C. H. Kraeling, *Anthropos and Son of Man*, pp. 174 ff.; S. Hanson, *The Unity of the Church in the New Testament*, p. 141; V. Stegemann, *Die Gestalt Christi in den koptischen Zaubertexten* (1934); G. Lindeskog, *Studien zum nt. Schöpfungsgedanken*, pp. 220 ff.; G. Strecker, *Das Judenchristentum in den Pseudoclementinen*, pp. 147 ff.; W. Staerk, [2], pp. 21 ff.; B. Murmelstein, "Adam, ein Beitrag zur Messiaslehre," 35 (1928) : 268 ff.; A. Bentzen, *Messias—Moses red.— Menschensohn;* H. J. Schoeps, [2], pp. 7 ff.; 1st ed. of this work, p. 113; P. Riessler, *Altjüdisches Schrifttum ausserhalb der Bibel* (1928), p. 946.

[180] Ps.-Clem. Rec. I, 45.2 ff.–47; Hom. III, 17–19; 22.1; cf. Hom. II, 15.3; VIII, 10.2; Rom. 5:12 ff.; I Cor. 15:21-22, 45 ff.; Test. Levi 18; Test. of Adam 3 = Riessler, 1086 ff.; Book of the Cave of Treasures 6.17-18; 48 ff. = Riessler, 950, 1002-3, *et passim.*
Cf. G. Strecker, *Das Judenchristentum*, . . . pp. 147 ff.; W. Staerk, [2], pp. 21 ff.; E. Brandenburger, *Adam und Christus, passim.*

[181] Barn. 6.13; Coptic Gospel of Thomas 18 = Leipoldt-Schenke, p. 13; Book of the Cave of Treasures 48-49 = Riessler, 1002 ff.; Test. of Adam 3 = Riessler, 1086 ff.
Cf. H. J. Schoeps, [1], p. 99, n. 3; B. Murmelstein, 36 (1929) : 51 ff.; W. Staerk, [2], pp. 21 ff.; G. Quispel, [1], pp. 225 ff.

[182] Ps.-Clem. Hom. III, 17 ff.; II, 52.2; XX, 2 ff.; Rec. III, 52, *et passim;* Vita Adae 12 ff.; Sirach 49.16; Book of the Cave of Treasures 2.12, 18-25; 4.1; 48.29; 49.1; 1 QS IV, 23; Slav. Enoch 30.8 ff.; Wisd. of Sol. 10.1-2; IV Ezra 6.54; Ep. Ap. 39; Apoc. Sedr. 5.2; Apoc. Mos. 39; Philo *passim,* e.g., de opif. mund. 136-39; Christian passages (esp. Ephraem) in abundance, see in B. Murmelstein, 35 (1928) : 247 ff.; rabbinical passages, *ibid.,* and in TDNT I. 143, n. 12.
Cf. E. Sjöberg, pp. 190 ff.; E. Schweizer, [2], cols. 163 ff.; W. Bousset, [2], pp. 408-9; G. Quispel [1], pp. 215 ff., 226, n. 57; O. Cullmann, [1], pp. 140-41; G. Strecker, pp. 145 ff.; H. J. Schoeps, [2], pp. 7 ff., 68, n. 2; J. Jervell, pp. 37 ff.; E. Schweizer, [1], pp. 154 ff.; W. Staerk, [1], pp. 158 ff.; [2], pp. 7 ff., 98 ff., 125 ff.; H. J. Schoeps, [4], pp. 48 ff.; E. Preuschen, *Die apokryphen gnostischen Adamschriften* (Giessen, 1900); K. Rudolph, [3]; R. McL. Wilson, [2], pp. 206, 209-10; E. S. Drower, *The Secret Adam* (1960); G. Scholem, *Die jüdische Mystik in ihren Haupströmungen* (1957), Index *s.v.* Adam; E. Brandenburger, pp. 39 ff., 78, n. 2; 110 ff., 136 ff. H. Hegermann (*Die Vorstellung vom Schöpfungsmittler im hellenistischen Judentum und Urchristentum,* TU 82 [1961]: 68-69) takes a critical position on the evidence from Philo.
The fall is shifted to Gen. 6:1 ff.! Cf. Eth. Enoch 6–16, *et passim;* A. v. Gall, pp. 281-82, 411; E. Brandenburger, pp. 20 ff.

[183] This fact is indeed still occasionally disputed, but without reason; cf. W. Bousset, [2], pp. 267-68; E. Sjöberg, pp. 190 ff.; A. v. Gall, pp. 411 ff.; H. Gressmann, p. 347; J. Jervell, pp. 38 (Literature), 133; F. Hahn, *Titles of Jesus in Christology,* pp. 19 ff.

31

32

33

But the primal man is a non-Jewish figure. How is it possible that this high mythological figure of the primal man could be connected with the earthly figure of the Jewish Messiah? The two figures are so different that a *direct* identification appears to be ruled out.[184] The identification must have been mediated by a religious group between Iranian primal man religion and late Judaism in which the figure of the primal man and the Messiah were already joined.[185] Now since the assimilation of the Son-of-Man conception into late Jewish Christology is bound up with the appropriation of comprehensive Gnostic or Gnosticizing features, a Jewish Gnosticism must have measurably participated in this mediation, a Gnosticism in which this identification was already present.

But just this is the case in the pre-Christian Christ Gnosticism which we have investigated. In it the central figure bears the features of the oriental primal man in the Gnostic metamorphosis of a collective being *and* the name of the Christ. Where this system of a pre-Christian Christ Gnosticism influenced certain circles of late Judaism, the earthly Messiah was logically displaced by the celestial Son of Man; the equating of Messiah and primal man then leads to the equation Adam = Christ; this in turn has as its consequence the well-known glorification of Adam. That the anthropological significance which the Messiah-Son of Man possessed in Gnosticism had only a relatively slight impact on Judaism is to be expected in view of the Jewish conception of the Messiah.

If this development is correctly seen, then the above-mentioned features of late Judaism point back to the system of a pre-Christian Christ Gnosticism which we have explored, in which the earthly "Christ" appears not as an individual figure but as a collective person —expressed in the Simonian way as στάς. (The derivation of those

[184] Cf. A. v. Gall, p. 441; A. Bentzen, p. 37; J. Duchesne-Guillemin, *The Western Response to Zoroaster* (1958), p. 89; E. Brandenburger, pp. 131 ff.

[185] E. Brandenburger (p. 131) does not take into account this possibility when he properly stresses how little affinity there is between the Iranian primal man conception and the late Jewish Son of Man, and therefore rejects any connection between the two. He proposes to derive the Son of Man speculation from primitive forms of the late Jewish Adam speculation. This is undoubtedly correct: late Jewish primal man speculations and Adam speculations come from the same roots. Only one still has not answered the question as to the source of the Son of Man speculation, which is Brandenburger's concern, when one explains that the Adam speculation has the same origin! Brandenburger does not ask of what sort this common origin is and whether Iranian primal man speculations were not perhaps incorporated in it. This apparently is connected with the fact that in spite of the emphasis upon the affinity of the aforementioned late Jewish theologoumena with Gnosticism—he can label individual features "clearly Gnostic" (p. 135)—he apparently does not wish to *presuppose* a Jewish Gnosticism for these features.

special views of late Judaism from a Jewish Gnosticism thus does not presuppose the individual figure of a pre-Christian redeemer!)

What is suggested here is a hypothesis, nothing more—but also nothing less. A hypothesis has its value in that it explains the observed phenomena. Since 34 the cited features of late Jewish theology and speculation find their adequate explanation from the influencing by the described Jewish Christ Gnosticism, I regard our thesis as a *good* hypothesis.

It rests upon the knowledge that the affinity between Gnostic motifs and certain motifs of late Jewish theology is indisputable.[186] This affinity is not limited to the above-named motifs of late Jewish speculation.

For example, it also concerns the "guf"-conception: Adam is the Universal Man, in whom all individual men are included; he is the "treasure-house of souls."[187] To be connected with this is the idea that all men have sinned in Adam.[188] This idea is alien to the Old Testament canon. It is found in the Apocrypha and is obviously a historicizing, undertaken in the interest of orthodoxy, of the Gnostic myth of the unity of substance of men in the fallen Adam=primal man. Perhaps this sphere of motifs also belongs in the complex of motifs mentioned, which find their explanation in the equation Messiah = primal man. Still it is just as possible that a direct equation primal man = Adam underlies the "guf"-conception. The cosmogonic figure of the pre-Gnostic oriental primal man and the conception of the *first* man as the father of the human race are of course different figures *in origin*. A *direct* influence is hardly conceivable. The Gnostic formulation of the primal man myth with the anthropogonic metamorphosis of the old myth, on the other hand, already possessed a strong point of contact with the doctrine of the Archanthropos Adam as the father of the human race.[189]

The affinity of late Judaism with Gnosticism also concerns the Wisdom of God, which appears as a personal hypostasis, which existed before all time, assisted in the creation of the world, and then was sent to men to teach them. It has long been recognized that we have here a faithful reflection of that

[186] On this, cf. K. Rudolph, [1], pp. 153 ff.; [2], pp. 382-83 (Literature); S. Schulz, 35 [2], pp. 161, 166 ff.; E. Brandenburger, pp. 20 ff. *passim*.

[187] Eth. Enoch 49.3; Ps.-Clem. Rec. VIII, 59-62; III, 26.4-5; Lidzbarski, *Ginza*, 426.15-16; Victorinus Rhetor, ad Gal. 1:15 = Migne, PSL VIII, col. 1155; Apoc. Abr. 23.8; 1 QS 4.23; CD III, 20; Hebr. Enoch 43.1 ff. = ed. Odeberg (1928), pp. 132 ff.; Ex. Rabba 40.3; Gen. Rabba 24.2; Qoheleth Rabba 3.21; Tos. Sanh. 8.4-5; Targum Jon. on Gen. 2:7; Philo, de conf. ling. 41; perhaps also in the interpretation of the Danielic Son of Man to mean the people of Israel there emerges the collective interpretation of the primal man (Dan. 7:27). Syr. Bar. 23.4.

Cf. W. D. Davies, *Paul and Rabbinic Judaism* (1955, 2nd ed.), pp. 36 ff.; H. J. Schoeps, [1], p. 99; E. Schweizer, [1], pp. 159-60; [2], cols. 164-65; J. Jervell, pp. 105 ff.; H. Gressmann, pp. 409 ff.; W. Staerk, [2], pp. 125 ff.; B. Murmelstein, 35 (1928): 261 ff.; E. Peterson, pp. 107 ff.; E. Brandenburger, pp. 141 ff.; H. M. Schenke, [2], pp. 127 ff.; E. Sjöberg, pp. 98 ff., 149, 177 ff., 188 f., 190 ff.

[188] Rom. 5:12 ff.; Vita Adae 11, *et passim*; IV Ezra 3.7, *et passim*; Apoc. Mos. 11; Apoc. Abr. 23; Syr. Bar. 78.4, *et passim*. Philo, Vita Mos. II, 147.

Cf. E. Schweizer, [2], cols. 164-65; A. v. Gall, p. 282; E. Brandenburger, pp. 20 ff. *passim*. R. Bultmann, [2], I: 174, 251.

[189] On this, cf. S. Mowinckel, pp. 71 ff.; J. Jervell, p. 38, n. 64.

Gnostic motif according to which the redeeming Gnosis is brought or given to men by their celestial mother, the Sophia.[190] In general, the late Jewish hypostasis speculation, insofar as it inserts mediate beings between God and world, between creator and creation and thus removes the world far from God, betrays foreign influences which can most readily be derived from Gnostic or pre-Gnostic ideas.

Further, the anthropological dualism of late Judaism is immediately related to the corresponding Gnostic conceptions. This holds true above all for the passages in which, in radical contrast to Old Testament as well as to Greek thought, the conception of evil is connected with the concept "flesh." [191]

[190] Prov. 1:20-33; 8:1-36; Wisd. of Sol. 9.1 ff.; 10.1 ff.; Sirach 24.1-31; Eth. Enoch 42.1; 84.3; Slav. Enoch 30.8; 33.3-4; Od. Sol. 12; 33; Philo *passim;* etc.
G. Lindeskog, pp. 118-19; W. Schenke, *Die Chokma (Sophia) in der jüdischen Hypostasenspekulation* (Christiania, 1913) ; H. Windisch, "Die göttliche Weisheit der Juden und die paulinische Christologie," in *Neutestamentliche Studien für Georg Heinrici* (1914) , pp. 220 ff.; S. Schulz, [2], pp. 31 ff.; P. Dalbert, pp. 77 ff., 133; C. Colpe, p. 51; U. Wilckens, [1], pp. 97-213; H. Schlier, [3], pp. 158 ff.; J. Jervell, pp. 46 ff.; H. Becker, *Die Reden des Johannesevangeliums,* FRLANT NF 50 (1956) : 41 ff.; W. Staerk, [2], pp. 71-85; A. Adam, *Die Psalmen des Thomas,* BZNW 24 (1959) : 31 ff., 79-83; E. Schweizer, [2], cols. 166-67; M. Dibelius/H. Conzelmann, in HNT 12 (3rd ed.) : 16-17; U. Wilckens in TWNT VII: 498 ff., 508 ff., *et passim;* H. Hegermann (see above, n. 182) , pp. 70 ff.; W. Vischer, "Der Hymnus der Weisheit in den Sprüchen Salomos 8,22-31," EvTheol 22 (1962) : 309 ff.; H. Jaeger, "The Patristic Conception of Wisdom in the Light of Biblical and Rabbinical Research," *Studia Patristica* IV, TU 79 (1961) : 90 ff.; G. Pfeifer, *Ursprung und Wesen der Hypostasenvorstellungen im Judentum* (Stuttgart, 1967) .

The alien character of the hypostatic Sophia conception in late Judaism becomes particularly obvious in Sirach 24, since the author assimilates the adopted conception to orthodox thought by identifying the pre-existent Sophia with the Torah (24.33) . The doctrine of the Torah as God's instrument of creation is subsequently found not infrequently in rabbinical literature (Pirqe Aboth III, 14; Gen. Rabba 1) .

[191] Noteworthy above all are the new presumably Essene texts from the Dead Sea, which also in other aspects of their concepts and manner of presentation betray a closeness to Gnosticism. Do we have to do here with pseudo-Gnostic features (H. J. Schoeps) ? Or with pre-Gnostic motifs (B. Reicke, K. G. Kuhn, *et al.*) ? Or do the new texts presuppose a fully developed Gnosticism in their environment (R. Bultmann, E. Käsemann, *et al.*) ? I consider the last-named view to be correct; but in view of the present attitude toward the problem of Gnosticism in general, this question will continue to be in dispute. It is generally acknowledged only that the texts themselves are not Gnostic.

Here I should mention some literature on the problem of the Gnosticism in the new texts: M. Burrows, *The Dead Sea Scrolls* (1955) , pp. 251-60; R. McL. Wilson, "Gnostic Origins," VC 9 (1955) : 193-211; also, "Gnostic Origins Again," VC 11 (1957) : 93-110; and, *The Gnostic Problem* (1958) , pp. 73 ff.; B. Reicke, "Traces of Gnosticism in the Dead Sea Scrolls?" NTS 1 (1954) : 137-41; B. Gärtner, "Nazareth, Nazoräer und das Mandäertum," in *Horae Soderblomianae* IV (1957) : 5-36; F. Nötscher, *Zur theologischen Terminologie der Qumran-Texte* (1956) ; S. Schulz, [2], pp. 152 ff.; also, in ThRs 26 (1960/61) : 325 ff. (Literature) ; H. W. Huppenbauer, *Der Mensch zwischen zwei Welten* (1959) ; also, in ThZ 13 (1957) : 298 ff.; K. G. Kuhn, "Die in Palästina gefundenen hebräischen Texte und das Neue Testament," ZThK 47 (1950) : 192 ff.; also, "Die Sektenschrift und die iranische Religion," ZThK 49 (1952) : 296 ff.; and, "Der Epheserbrief im Lichte der Qumrantexte," NTS 7 (1960/ 61) : 334-46; E. Käsemann in *Beiträge zur Evangelischen Theologie* 15 (1952) : 139;

We also recall the ecstatic practices on down to the rabbinical times and groups.[192]

Finally, there appears in late Judaism a large number of typically Gnostic concepts in a manner not characteristic of the Old Testament: γνῶσις, μυστήριον, ἀποκάλυψις, πνεῦμα, etc.

The affinity of the Gnostic and late Jewish motifs referred to is not accidental and cannot be accidental.[193] Anyone who does not wish to explain it in terms of Gnostic influences in late Judaism must go in the opposite way and derive Gnosticism in essence from late Jewish conceptions.[194] But that is a poor way and a poor hypothesis.

It leaves those new—and indeed in part *significantly* new—views in late Judaism unexplained. Whence come then Son of Man and sinless Adam, Wisdom myth and "guf"-conception, dualism and the equation Adam = Christ, and much else besides? The Old Testament hardly afforded even material for these conceptions, let alone an occasion for them.[195]

Further, this hypothesis makes the impossible attempt to derive Gnosticism from Judaism.[196] But apart from the fact that Gnosticism is not at all "derivable," there exists a simply unbridgeable chasm between the understanding of existence of Judaism, even of late Judaism, and that of Gnosticism; for whatever is found of gnosticizing motifs in late Judaism, it has been fitted

---

H. Braun, *Spätjüdisch-häretischer und frühchristlicher Radikalismus* (1957), e.g., I: 21, n. 1; 23, n. 3; 44, n. 2; also, "Röm. 7,7-25 und das Selbstverständnis des Qumran-Frommen," ZThK 56 (1959): 1 ff.; E. Baumbach, *Qumran und das Johannesevangelium* (1957), pp. 29 ff., 46 ff.; S. Wibbing, *Die Tugend- und Lasterkataloge im Neuen Testament*, BZNW 25 (1959): 51, 64 ff.; K. Schubert, *Die Religion des nachbiblischen Judentums* (1955), pp. 80 ff.; also in TLZ 78 (1953), cols. 495 ff.; E. Schweizer, "Die hellenistische Komponente im neutestamentlichen σάρξ Begriff," ZNW 48 (1957): 237 ff.; O. Cullmann, "Die neuentdeckten Qumrantexte und das Judenchristentum," in *Neutestamentliche Studien für R. Bultmann* (1954), pp. 37-38; O. Betz, *Offenbarung und Schriftforschung in der Qumransekte*, WUNT 6 (1960), e.g., pp. 150 ff.; J. Duchesne-Guillemin, *The Western Response to Zoroaster* (1958), pp. 91 ff.   38

[192] Cf. W. Bousset, [3], pp. 14 ff.

[193] This is, however, the opinion of H. J. Schoeps, [4], pp. 44 ff.; similarly C. Colpe; see above, p. 66.

Some—but only a little—could be accounted for by a common source for late Judaism and Gnosticism, such as Iran, e.g., affords.

[194] Thus recently above all G. Quispel, [1], pp. 195-234; [2], pp. 474 ff.; further works by Quispel in ThRs 26 (1960/61): 239; further, C. Colpe, p. 57; E. Schweizer, [2], pp. 161 ff.; cf. [3], pp. 241 ff.; R. M. Grant, *Gnosticism and Early Christianity* (1959); W. D. Davies, *Paul and Rabbinic Judaism* (1955, 2nd ed.), esp. pp. 36 ff. L. Goppelt, *Die Kirche in ihrer Geschichte*, I A: 66-67, holds Old Testament-Jewish influences to be "a necessary presupposition for the emergence of Gnosticism" in general. If one proceeds from the general understanding of "Old Testament" and "Gnosticism," Goppelt's sentence is incomprehensible. What can he mean by "Old   39 Testament" and "Gnosticism"?

[195] Cf. K. Rudolph, [1], p. 92, n. 2; [3], pp. 17 ff. E. Brandenburger rightly suggests "that certain motifs have an illuminating and well-grounded setting in heretical-Gnostic speculations, while on the other hand in 'orthodox'-Jewish literature they appear only isolated, disconnected, and more or less poorly motivated" (p. 139).

[196] G. Quispel moreover reckons with Hellenistic influences, while he completely denies Iranian motifs.

to Jewish thinking, as also conversely Jewish influences in Gnosticism are there subordinated to Gnostic thinking.[197]

In addition, there is the fact that Judaism hardly provided, and could hardly have provided, material for the mythological objectivation of the Gnostic self-understanding in the myths of Gnosticism, even when Jewish Gnosticism rediscovered the myth, by means of various exegetical artifices, above all in the primeval biblical story.[198] It is also excluded because Gnosticism developed, if not *out* of Judaism, yet *within* Judaism.[199] Jewish Gnosticism is an early offshoot of Gnosticism.

So it is a better hypothesis if one explains the gnosticizing conceptions of late Judaism from Jewish Gnosticism.[200] Then however the equation Christ =

[197] Therefore to speak of "Jewish Gnosticism" does not mean to assert a *mixtum compositum* of Judaism and Gnosticism. "Jewish Gnosticism"—how else should one put it—like "Christian Gnosticism" and "pagan Gnosticism" designates a Gnosticism which clothes itself in the garments of Jewish concepts and conceptions, as does the described system of pre-Christian Christ Gnosticism, in order in this clothing to be *Gnosticism*.

[198] H. M. Schenke ([2]) has traced the considerable influence which Gen. 1:26-27 has exerted upon Gnosticism, and therein and elsewhere he has pointed to the strong influence of the Old Testament as a whole upon many branches of Gnosticism. In this respect his investigation is extremely instructive. Of course he thinks that from the frequent use of Gen. 1:26-27 in Gnostic literature he can conclude that the Gnostic myth of the primal man grew out of speculation on this biblical passage (see above, pp. 35-36). The fact that such a derivation is an assumption for which no evidence can be adduced is not an unconditional argument against Schenke's thesis; the traditional derivation of the Gnostic Anthropos myth from oriental primal man speculations is also unprovable. Nevertheless Schenke's explanation fails on the point that it has the Gnostic movement as such actually developing out of a speculation on Gen. 1:26-27; for the primal man myth, i.e., the anthropogonic doctrine of the fall of a light-figure into the material realm, is—under whatever labels— constitutive for Gnosticism. But to make a speculation on Gen. 1:26-27 responsible for the rise of Gnosticism as such is curious.

Of course Schenke sees the problem indicated here and denies that his hypothesis represents "a contribution to the understanding of the development of the Gnostic world view in general" (p. 69). Rather "the Gnostic world view with its interpretation of the identity in nature between God and the innermost core of man" is the presupposition for the process of speculation which he reconstructs (p. 69). But that Gnostic world outlook, which certainly is "more original" than the Gnostic myth, is discernible only in the form of the myth of the fall of light into matter and its reascent into the Pleroma. The myth of the "Man" indeed does not indicate the source but rather the beginning of Gnosticism, which therefore according to Schenke and in spite of his denial of this fact still found this its beginning in a speculation on Gen. 1:26-27.

Actually the Gnostic myth found in Gen. 1:26-27 a substantively and terminologically desirable point of contact with Judaism in the missionary movement. This fact, which explains the frequent use of Gen. 1:26-27 as well as of the early biblical stories in general, and to a certain extent also the use of the ἄνθρωπος title in Gnosticism, is evident and is the actual positive result of Schenke's study.

[199] The question whether Gnosticism can be derived from Judaism has most recently been answered correctly in the negative by W. C. van Unnik, among others. See his "Die jüdische Komponente in der Entstehung der Gnosis," VC 15 (1961): 65 ff., esp. p. 72.

[200] That Gnosticism and Judaism had already met in pre-Christian times is obvious to us, among other reasons, from the fact that not a few Gnostic writings

primal man-Son of Man and the views bound up with it presupposes the Jewish Christ Gnosticism which we have described.

We must still ask how it happens that practically no *direct* literary witnesses to this pre-Christian Christ Gnosticism have been preserved for us, and that even the ecclesiastical heresy fighters deal with it in its pure form only seldom. There is for example hardly any evidence for the σῶμα concept employed in this system outside the indirect documentation in the New Testament and in other ecclesiastical writings.

The answer to the first question would be that almost nothing but indirect witnesses to Jewish Gnosticism have been preserved at all. The soil of Syria and Mesopotamia has not preserved any writings for us, and the early christianizing of Syria put an end to the tradition of Jewish-Gnostic literature. But above all, apart from hymnic fragments such as are preserved for us, for example, in the Odes of Solomon, there was Gnostic literature only where the doctrine of the *one* redeemer had to be handed down. A Gnosticism which knew no redeemer because the Pneuma spoke in ecstasy out of all Pneumatics, thus a Gnosticism which sought "Christ" in men themselves, required no revelational literature and did not have it. On this, cf. pp. 275 ff. below. 43

With respect to the second question, we must recall that the heresy fighters carried on their dispute with *Christian* Gnosticism. The Gnostic system considered by us, however, represents a Jewish Gnosticism which was not able to maintain itself as such for long into the Christian era. The described system was very early christianized, i.e., the figure of the heavenly emissary, Christ, the *one* redeemer, was fitted into the system, and as a consequence the title of Christ then must also be reserved for him. The anthropological Christ myth of Jewish Gnosticism was also intolerable for *pure* Gnosticism if it wanted to gain access to Christian circles or to appear as Christian. Thus we have found a whole series of witnesses for our system as terminological remnants in writings of already christianized Gnosticism or in accounts of such.

This christianizing can be observed best in a comparison between the language of Paul himself and that of the Deutero-Pauline Ephesians and Colossians.[201] The Jewish Christ myth, to which Paul owes his

---

are indeed strongly marked by Old Testament conceptions, but are not influenced by the New Testament, or are only subsequently thus influenced. A good example of this is the "Untitled Work" from Codex II from Nag Hammadi, which in considerable measure is shaped by Jewish and late Jewish ideas, and yet apparently betrays no sort of direct knowledge of the New Testament. Cf. also O. Betz, "Was am Anfang geschah," in Festschrift für O. Michel, pp. 24 ff.; G. Kretschmar, "Zur religionsgeschichtlichen Einordnung der Gnosis," *passim.* 42

[201] The anti-Gnostic Pastoral Epistles deliberately avoid the "mystical" terminology of Paul.

"mystical" language, identifies the Christ simply with the church. The concept σῶμα Χριστοῦ therefore even in Paul designates the whole Christ; as a whole the σῶμα is the church. The Christ of this myth exists only in the individual parts of his body.

In Ephesians and Colossians this picture has been displaced.[202] The myth employed here differentiates between σῶμα and κεφαλή.[203] The Christ consists of head *and* body. The church is no longer identified with the *whole* Christ but only with the σῶμα part of the Christ, who is moreover the κεφαλή τοῦ σώματος, the head of the church.[204] Here we see how the pre-Christian myth was christianized in a first step. To be sure, the personal identity of Christ with the Pneumatics is not yet eliminated. Every Pneumatic is still τοῦ Χριστοῦ. But by making a distinction in the primal man-Christ between head and body, one could build into this Gnostic system the Christian Christ. He is the distinguished and determinative head of the church, which is his body, and as this head he can also be redeemer κατ' ἐξοχήν.[205]

Since the ascension of the Christ-Pneuma took place gradually, a part of the Christ is always risen already. This mythological state of affairs provided a convenient occasion for introducing the "ecclesiastical" Christ into the system by hypostatizing the higher part of the Christ-primal man and identifying this with the "ecclesiastical"

[202] Although the old conception does not completely disappear; cf., e.g., Eph. 4:11-12.

[203] Cf. also Ign. Eph. 4.2; Trall. 11.2; Hipp. V, 7,34 ff.; Lidzbarski, *Ginza*, pp. 522.1 ff., *et passim;* Od. Sol. 17.15; 23.16; 24.1; Acta Joh. 93; 100; Exc. ex Theod. 42.2-3; II Clem. 14.2; Parth. Hymn. AR VI, 53 ff. = C. Colpe, p. 84; cf. pp. 94-95; Theodore bar Khonai, pp. 128.7 ff. Pognon; Exc. ex Theod. 33; Parth. Turfan Fragment M 33, 1. 86.

Cf. J. Jervell, p. 137, n. 63; K. Rudolph, [1], pp. 153-54; H. Schlier, [2], pp. 88 ff.; [3], p. 202; E. Schweizer, [3], col. 245, n. 14; P. Pokorný, *Der Epheserbrief und die Gnosis*, pp. 63 ff., 69 ff.

The schema thus may be older than its use in the expansion, which stands behind Eph./Col., of the originally redeemer-less Christ Gnosticism (see below).

[204] Eph. 1:22-23; 4:15-16; 5:23, 29-30; Col. 1:18; 2:19; 3:5.

Cf., e.g., Eph. 1:22: αὐτὸν ἔδωκεν κεφαλὴν ὑπὲρ πάντα τῇ ἐκκλησίᾳ, ἥτις ἐστὶν τὸ σῶμα αὐτοῦ. Here the ἀνακεφαλαιοῦσθαι in Eph. 1:10 also probably belongs. The word may not be originally Gnostic but may indeed have been used in a technical sense in Gnosticism. It is hardly ever found in profane Greek, but on the other hand more frequently in early Christian writers (cf. Rom. 13:9), particularly among those who show some connections with Gnosticism (cf. H. Schlier on ἀνακεφαλαιόομαι in TDNT III: 681-82). In the language of the myth it literally means "to provide with a head again," and Schlier is certainly correct when he interprets the ἀνακεφαλαιώσασθαι τὰ πάντα . . . ἐν τῷ Χριστῷ in 1:10 by means of 1:22: "He made him head over the whole *ecclesia*." Here then there clearly emerges in language and conception the Gnostic myth, according to which the uniting of head and members of the primal man is the goal of all that happens. (Cf. C. Maurer in EvTheol, 1951, pp. 154 ff.)

[205] Eph. 5:23.

Christ.[206] One may compare for example Exc. ex Theod. 26: "τὸ ὁρατὸν τοῦ 'Ιησοῦ ἡ Σοφία καὶ ἡ 'Εκκλησία ἦν τῶν σπερμάτων τῶν διαφερόντων, ἣν ἐστολίσατο διὰ τοῦ σαρκίου, . . . τὸ δὲ ἀόρατον (τὸ) ὄνομα, ὅπερ ἐστὶν ὁ υἱὸς ὁ μονογενής. ὅθεν ὅταν εἴπῃ 'ἐγώ εἰμι ἡ θύρα', τοῦτο λέγει, ὅτι μέχρι τοῦ ὅρου οὗ εἰμι ἐγὼ ἐλεύσεσθε οἱ τοῦ διαφέροντος σπέρματος. ὅταν δὲ καὶ αὐτὸς εἰσέρχηται, καὶ τὸ σπέρμα συνεισέρχεται αὐτῷ εἰς τὸ πλήρωμα διὰ τῆς θύρας συναχθὲν καὶ εἰσαχθέν."

The higher Christ thus waits at the ὅρος until all his parts scattered below have found their way upward. Then the *whole* Christ, who is nothing other than the sum of the parts of the "primal man" which were dispersed in the flesh, betakes himself into the Pleroma.

From here it is only a short step then to a more thoroughgoing personal separation of church and Christ which resulted everywhere in the Christian-Gnostic systems. Of course even then the special correlation of the redeemer and the community was maintained, not only in remnants of earlier terminology, as we have already observed, but also in various images and conceptions; the transitions from personal unity to separation of persons are especially fluid. The two figures now distinguished in the mythological conception but by no means always separated are paired

> as body and clothing or armor,[207]
> as bride and bridegroom or as husband and wife,[208]
> as tree and fruit or branches,[209]
> as prototype and copy,[210]
> as brother and sister or as twins,[211]

[206] Therefore the members still on earth could appeal for help to their parts that were already once again dwelling above. This may be the case, e.g., in the Naassene Preaching (Hipp. V, 8.15) and in the Jewish prayer in Preisendanz, *Pap. gr. mag.* I: 12-13; 112 ff., where Adam calls on Adam for help.

[207] Acta Arch. 7.3-5; Od. Sol. 33.12; Lidzbarski, *Ginza*, 374.15 ff.; 363.25; Acta Thom. 112; Copt. Psalmbook, C. R. Allberry, p. 39.23-24; Parth. Hymn. AR VI, 9; 21 = C. Colpe, p. 83. Cf. E. Brandenburger, pp. 147-48.

[208] II Clem. 14.2; Exc. ex Theod. 21.1; 26.1-2; 27.5; 64; 68; Eph. 5:29-32; Iren. I, 13.3; 6; 30.12; Hipp. VI, 34.4; Od. Sol. 3.7; 7.1; 38.11; 42.8; Acta Thom. 4 ff., 11; Ps.-Cl. Hom. III, 22.1; 27.3; Coptic Gospel of Philip, Saying 71; 78; the common conception of the bridal chamber and of marriage belongs here; cf. further J. Jervell, pp. 162-63, 170; H. Schlier, [3], pp. 264 ff.; G. Strecker, pp. 161-62; R. Reitzenstein, [1], pp. 245 ff.; W. Völker (see p. 60, n. 148), pp. 100-114, 226; E. Percy, [2], pp. 327-28.

[209] Hipp. V, 9.1; Od. Sol. 11.1-2, *et passim;* Coptic Gospel of Thomas, Saying 44; John 15.1 ff. and R. Bultmann, [5], *in loc.;* Exc. ex Theod. 33.2.

[210] *Pap. gr. mag.* VIII, 37-38 (Preisendanz); Acta Thom. 112; Od. Sol. 34.4; Lidzbarski, *Ginza*, 91.13-14; 331 ff.; 559.29 ff.; this way of speaking is not the source of the Gnostic Anthropos Christology (thus J. Jervell, p. 248), but one of its forms; cf. further E. Käsemann, [2], pp. 81 ff., 147 ff.; R. Bultmann, [5], p. 108, n. 4; K. Rudolph, [1], p. 127; 1st ed. of the present work, pp. 93-94; E. Brandenburger, pp. 147 ff.

[211] Acta Thom. 11, 39; Iren. I, 30.12; Epiph. Haer. LIII, 1.9.

as mother or father and child or seed,[212]
as building and cornerstone,[213]
as higher man and lower man,[214]
as Christ and Jesus,[215]
as Elohim and Edem (Pneuma) ,[216]
as "Jesus the effulgence" and "Jesus patibilis,"
46   his "self thrown into everything" in Manichaeism,[217] etc.

Of course these images are not in their totality an efflux of a Gnosticism in which the unity of *person* of redeemer and redeemed found its clearest expression, because a special redeemer figure did not occur at all. In many cases there is expressed in it simply the widespread Gnostic idea that redeemer and redeemed are closely *related* figures of the Pleroma or that they are identical in *substance*.[218] Even the image of head and members could in individual instances express only this latter idea. Moreover, the original redeemer-less Gnosticism, insofar as it stands in the background of these syzygies mentioned, was not necessarily, either always or even most of the time, the Jewish Christ Gnosticism which we have investigated. Finally, the reason for the division of the *one* basic mythological figure of "man" into a heavenly redeemer and his earthly parts is not to be sought only or even primarily in the influence of the church's Christ.[219]

[212] Cf. Rev. 12; Iren. I, 8.4; 11.1; 30.12; Exc. ex Theod. 23, 32; Od. Sol. 3.7; Acta Petri 39; Acta Thom. 108 ff.; Parth. Turfan Fragment M 42; Coptic Gospel of Philip 102; Heracleon in Orig. Comm. in Joh. 13.49 = Preuschen, p. 276.18 ff.; cf. 1st ed. of this work, p. 90.

[213] Eph. 2:20 ff.; cf. I Peter 2:5; Hipp. V, 7.34 ff.; Coptic Gospel of Thomas, Saying 67.

[214] Iren. I, 29-30; Hipp. V, 6-7; Philo, Leg. all. I, 3 ff.; De opif. mund. 134; Billerbeck, III: 477-78.

This conception is found relatively unretouched in Eph. 2:15: ἵνα τοὺς δύο κτίσῃ ἐν αὐτῷ (Christ) εἰς ἕνα καινὸν ἄνθρωπον . . . καὶ ἀποκαταλλάξῃ τοὺς ἀμφοτέρους ἐν ἑνὶ σώματι τῷ θεῷ. In Christ, Jews and Gentiles become *one* Soma, in other words, the "new man," the σῶμα Χριστοῦ (cf. Eph. 4:13; also Ign. Smyrn. 1.2). The myth appears still more unretouched in the source itself which the author of Ephesians apparently is using in this passage. For this source οἱ δύο are not Jews and Gentiles, but the head which dwells in heaven and the mass of the members of Christ that are captive on earth. The two are separated by τὸ μεσότοιχον τοῦ φραγμοῦ. The head, Christ, by his descending ἐν τῇ σαρκί breaks down (λύσας) this dividing wall, so that now both stand before God ἐν ἑνὶ σώματι or ἐν ἑνὶ πνεύματι (vs. 18; cf. I, 6:17) as καινὸς ἄνθρωπος.

[215] Exc. ex Theod. 42.2; cf. 26.1.

[216] Hipp. V, 26.17 ff.

[217] H. Jonas, [1], pp. 310-11; E. Rose, *Die Christologie des Manichäismus*, p. 52, *et passim*.

[218] ". . . the life found its own" (Lidzbarski, *Ginza*, 567.22, *et passim*).

[219] The Babylonian myth of Marduk unquestionably exerted such an influence in apparently pre-Christian times; cf. 1st ed. of the present work, pp. 90 ff.; C. H. Kraeling, pp. 100 ff.; C. Colpe, pp. 54 ff. (Literature). The mystery cults as also the entire Kyrios cult in general are bound to have tended in this direction.

It would take us too far aside to sift, on the strength of the foregoing, all the material, to see to what extent late formulations of the original Jewish Christ Gnosticism are certainly to be found in it. I offer only a few examples:

II Clem. 14 and Eph. 5:29-32 are interesting as examples of Gnostic exegesis. In both cases the same tradition is in the background.[220] In II Clem. 14.2 it is said: "λέγει γὰρ ἡ γραφή. Ἐποίησεν ὁ θεὸς τὸν ἄνθρωπον ἄρσεν καὶ θῆλυ. τὸ ἄρσεν ἐστὶν ὁ Χριστός, τὸ θῆλυ ἡ ἐκκλησία." The Anthropos of the quotation from Gen. 1:27 is for Gnosticism the primal man. He consists of Christ as his celestial part, the "male," and the church on earth, the "female," which however can also serve as his body (Gen. 2:24): "ἐκκλησία ζῶσα σῶμά ἐστι Χριστοῦ" (ibid.; cf. p. 62). This shows that the entire body of speculation grew out of an original equation primal man = Christ. The eschatological goal is: "ἔσονται οἱ δύο εἰς σάρκα μίαν" (Eph. 5:32), that is, Christ and the church again become the one Anthropos; for "τὸ μυστήριον τοῦτο μέγα ἐστίν, ἐγὼ δὲ λέγω εἰς Χριστὸν καὶ εἰς τὴν ἐκκλησίαν" (ibid.).[221] This tradition is likely to stand in some way also behind I Cor. 6:15.

One may compare further Logion 106 from the Coptic Gospel of Thomas: "Jesus said, 'If you make the two to become one, you will become Sons of man' " (Leipoldt-Schenke, p. 24).

"And at that time he called and said, "My children, whom I bear, until Christ takes form in you,' and he cries moreover, 'I am ready to put a single spouse, Christ, beside a holy virgin' " (Koptisch-gnostische Schriften I, Schmidt-Till [GCS 45], p. 355.26 ff.). The "inner Christ," i.e., the sum of the "ἔσω ἄνθρωποι," is the spouse of the celestial virgin.

We shall conclude this introduction with some remarks about the concept of the "redeemed redeemer," since the material of this introduction was presented in the first edition under just this heading. I have this time avoided the concept whenever possible, since it apparently gives added occasion for misunderstanding.[222]

The concept "redeemed redeemer" is a catchword of modern studies of Gnosticism. In the form salvator salvandus it can be derived from Augustine's Contra Faustum II, 5.[223] That it is used in the form "redeemed redeemer"= salvator salvatus is not materially decisive. For the salvator salvatus is the salvator salvandus himself after the completed redemption. Further, it is not

---

[220] On this, cf. H. Schulte, p. 71; H. Schlier, [1], pp. 67 ff.; [2], pp. 91-92.

[221] Cf. Hipp. IX, 13 (Elchasaites): καὶ τὸν μὲν ἄρσενα υἱὸν εἶναι τοῦ θεοῦ, τὴν δὲ θήλειαν καλεῖσθαι ἅγιον πνεῦμα.

[222] Even C. Colpe (pp. 171 ff.), in spite of many a correct observation, has obscured rather than illumined what clarity the concept still possessed, since he does not take into account the original content of the formula, but connects it in essence with the redeemer myth. Unsatisfactory also is H. M. Schenke's remark, [2], p. 30, n. 120.

[223] CSEL XXV: 258.14-15.

important that the concept does not occur in Gnosticism as an abstract phrase or catchword. How should it?! Nevertheless it is drawn from Gnosticism both as to substance *and* as to terminology.

On terminology one may compare, for example:
". . . (are) beloved in the beloved
and such as are preserved in the one who lives
and redeemed in the one who is redeemed!" (Od. Sol. 8.22).
"We too desire to be redeemed with you,
for you are our redeemer" (Od. Sol. 42.18).
"Saved shall I be, and I shall save.
Delivered shall I be, and I shall deliver.
Wounded shall I be, and I shall wound. . ." (Acta Joh. 95; see p. 56).
"Be thou my effulgence, and I will be thy effulgence;
be thou my light, and I will be thy light" (Lidzbarski, *Liturgien,* p. 128).
On the contents one may compare, for example:
". . . so long as you are not called my own, I am not what I am. But if you listen to me, you will be as I am and I shall again be what I was" (Acta Joh. 100; see p. 56).

"I have recognized myself and gathered myself from everywhere . . . and I have gathered the scattered parts and I know who you are. That is to say, I come from the world above" (Gospel of Philip according to Epiph. Haer. XXVI, 13.2).

"I desire to make you a partaker of my grace, since the Father of all sees your angel before his face continually. But the place of greatness is in us; we must become one. First of all, receive grace from me and through me. Prepare yourself, as the bride awaits her bridegroom, that you may become what I am and I may become what you are. Let the seed of light sink down into your bridal chamber. Receive from me the bridegroom and make a place for him and take your place in him. Lo, grace has come down upon you. Open your mouth and prophesy" (Iren. I, 13.3).

"This is *one* power divided above and below, which begets itself, enlarges itself, seeks itself, finds itself, its own mother, its own father" (Hipp. VI, 17.3 = 143.7 ff.).

These examples, which could be multiplied, anchor the concept "redeemed redeemer," not in just any *substantial* unity of redeemer and redeemed, nor in a commonality *of fate,* but in a—mythologically conceived—*personal,* hypostatic unity of the two figures.[224] In the first case it would be wholly unusable as the designation of a *special* redeemer figure, since for Gnosticism redeemer and redeemed are *always* identical in substance. In the second case the concept would not be covered by the Gnostic terminology. Therefore one should use it only for the special conception of that redeemer who is identical *in*

[224] C. Colpe (p. 175, n. 1 and p. 186, n. 2) criticizes the use of the concept "personally" in this sense. On p. 190, n. 1, he himself correctly uses the concept in just this sense.

person with those whom he redeems, so that in his redeeming others he himself is redeemed as a person.

47

Then, however, the concept belongs above all to that Gnosticism which knows no redeemer myth. Simon, as we have earlier come to know him, and Marcus, as the quotation from Iren. I, 13.3 shows him, are representatives of a Gnosticism *without* a redeemer myth. They are Gnostics who were already redeemed by other Gnostics and now concern themselves with redeeming others also similarly.[225] The sum of all these "redeemed redeemers" forms the one person of the "man" who in the system investigated by us also bears the title "Christ." Since every individual Gnostic understands himself in possession of Gnosis as *already redeemed,* the concept *salvator salvatus* is here more appropriate than *salvator salvandus;* for the ἤδη σωζόμενος (see pp. 179 ff.) is determinative for the Gnostic self-consciousness of these circles, even if the redemption is completed only when all parts of the "man" have been combined into the τέλειος ἄνθρωπος.

The unity of person is still preserved when the primal man = Christ appears divided into head and members, into heavenly and earthly parts. We followed this development on the basis of the Pauline and Deutero-Pauline literature. It may also be traced in the Odes of Solomon, whose christianizing possibly coincides with this development, and elsewhere as well. One may compare:

> "And they received my blessing and became alive,
> and they were gathered to me and were redeemed.
> For they became members to me
> And I became head to them.
> Praise to thee, our head, Lord, Anointed One!"
> (Od. Sol. 17.14 ff.) .

Here too the redemption of the individual members through the reuniting with the head signifies the restoration of the original person, which includes head and members, redeemer and redeemed. Insofar as therein the head appears as redeemer—the members thereafter also mutually redeem themselves—the designation *salvator salvandus* is proper, since the redemption of the head is completed only when the whole person is again complete. Only in this case is the formula "redeemed redeemer" connected with a redeemer myth.

A use of the term "redeemed redeemer" going beyond this even for a redeemer figure personally separated from the ones to be redeemed [226] is not in harmony with the Gnostic set of concepts, and with good reason.

[225] This aspect, which is of great importance for the understanding of early Gnosticism, in particular also of the system of Jewish Christ Gnosticism, is only occasionally touched in the present study. I have examined it in detail in *The Office of Apostle,* pp. 159 ff.; cf. also below, pp. 275 ff.

[226] Cf., e.g., E. Käsemann, *Das wandernde Gottesvolk,* pp. 90 ff. R. Bultmann ([3], p. 104; cf. ThRs, 1932, p. 8) writes: "Now since the figure of the emissary is assimilated to that of the primal man, the emissary in his earthly manifestation also appeared as captive and oppressed, and his ascent is also his own redemption;

he is the redeemed redeemer." Such an assimilation certainly took place. The Mandaean texts above all show that descent of the redeemer was adorned with the features which were also well known from the conception of the descent of the primal man. Thus there can often be doubt as to which descent is meant (cf. also W. Bousset, [1], pp. 242 ff.). If, however, one follows the Gnostic terminology, the distinctive thing about the redeemed redeemer is not that during his soteriological activity he himself falls into distress and is liberated from it, but that he is *identical* with the individual sparks of light which he was sent to set free, and, through them, with the cosmic figure of the primal man; thus that by redeeming those imprisoned πνεύματα he redeems himself. One will do well to limit the expression "redeemed redeemer" strictly to *this* mythological conception, which was its original meaning.

R. Reitzenstein fails to do this when ([3], p. 116) he explains the term "redeemed redeemer" by referring to the fact that the part of the primal man which already at the beginning of the world had returned to the light above required redeeming assistance for this return.

E. Käsemann asks ([2], p. 68): "How is this identity of primal man and redeemer, . . . how is the unity of the company of souls in the heavenly redeemer *Physis* possible?" The answer which Käsemann gives to his own question is: "Of fundamental importance is the . . . statement, that for Gnosticism substance and power are identical. This holds true even for the heavenly 'nature.' Thus the fallen primal man, because the same in substance, is also the same in power with the redeemer. And since only the power is decisive as to the substance, not its individual formation, the identity of primal man and redeemer is absolute. Of course the same is true of the identity with the company of souls, indeed, even with the individual soul."

Apparently following this passage, C. Maurer (in EvTheol, 1951) speaks of the "identity in substance" of redeemer and community: "The ones to be redeemed are redeemed because as regards substance they belong to the redeemer" (p. 168). This is certainly correct, but it still does not justify the use of the title "redeemed redeemer."

INTRODUCTION B:
THE CORINTHIAN EPISTLES

I. Literary-Critical Analysis

1. General

An investigation which, like the present one, constantly has in view the varied and complicated relations of Paul to the community in Corinth must first draw a reasonable and fairly complete picture of these relations, at least so long as there does not exist a certain unanimity in the studies on this problem.

Fundamental here is the question as to the literary composition of our epistles. After Semler[1] first called in question the unity of II Corinthians, the attempts to demonstrate in our canonical epistles three or more originally independent writings have not ceased. While at the beginning only II Corinthians was under discussion, I Corinthians also was later drawn into the debate. It cannot be surprising that up to now an agreement among the various attempts at division has not been reached, even though a certain agreement appears to be in the making in recent research. Nevertheless it is incomprehensible that the necessity of a literary-critical analysis of the Corinthian epistles is still widely disputed. The diversity of the hypotheses about the division and the farcical character of many of the same[2] could of course bring the efforts in general into discredit. Their necessity however can be denied only if one refuses actually to weigh the epistles as *epistles*. Already in 1894 J. Weiss[3] spoke of the "now audacious-appearing hypothesis of the unity" of II Corinthians. This judgment has maintained its full validity. Not only that it is rather unlikely that in Corinth people preserved[4] or published only a portion of the apostle's letters: The arrangement of the letters itself forces us to recognize that Paul cannot possibly have written them thus. This is to be shown

---

[1] Paraphrasis II, ep. ad Cor. (1776), Praefatio b; pp. 238-39, 309-10.

[2] Cf., e.g., C. Clemen, *Die Einheitlichkeit der paulinischen Briefe an Hand der bisher mit Bezug auf sie aufgestellten Interpolations- und Kompilationshypothesen* (Göttingen, 1894).

[3] TLZ, 1894, p. 513.

[4] It is generally recognized today that Paul wrote at least *four* epistles to Corinth. The remarks in I, 5:9 and II, 2:3, 9 admit no other interpretation.

presently in the analysis in detail. Of course Lietzmann[5] thinks: "Paul is not a letter-writer to whom one may apply the usual standards, and for this reason the problem of the exegesis of his epistles is not so much a literary-critical one (as was thought earlier), but a psychological one." This remark appears in connection with II, 10:1. If one wishes to explain psychologically that Paul wrote II, 10–13 at the same time as II, 1–9, then of course Paul's psychical anomie must have reached a high degree—in spite of a "sleeplessly watched-through night" (ibid.).[6] But the opposite is the case. Rom. 1–15 is a literary masterpiece.[7] The Thessalonian epistles display a clear course of thought as well as a strict arrangement. The same holds true for Galatians, which in its plan shows no abnormally changeable temperament (cf. ibid.), but a conscious pastoral responsibility, bound up with thoughtful regard for the psyche of the Galatians. Thus the psyche of Paul is such that precisely a psychological explanation of the Corinthian letters must establish that Paul could not have written them in their present outward form. Lietzmann himself directs us back basically to the literary criticism which is now to follow in detail.

We must, however, strive for the greatest possible brevity and above all refrain from any direct debate with other hypotheses. For the present purpose it suffices to occupy ourselves with a reasonable new arrangement of the epistles according to their division, which then is basic for the presentation of the course of events in and around Corinth at the time of the extant correspondence. In the course of the later investigation the justification will be strengthened in details. The ultimate proof for the analysis which in some respects always remains hypothetical must be its confirmation in exegesis.[8]

To begin with, if we ask about the occasion which led to the combining of various smaller letters into two larger Corpora, we can probably disregard any effort to form pieces more suited for reading in worship, for why should the smaller but by no means always minute epistles have been less suited for this purpose? I should rather assume that the publication of a larger collection of Paul's letters in Corinth was the primary occasion for that editing. The assertion that in the pre-Marcionite period an ecclesiastical collection of Paul's letters was circulated[9] is not a mere supposition but a well-founded statement. It

---

[5] Lietzmann, p. 139.

[6] Cf. Windisch, p. 16.

[7] See G. Schrenk, Studien zu Paulus (1954), pp. 121-22.

[8] J. Héring has offered (The First Epistle of St. Paul to the Corinthians; cf. W. Michaelis, TLZ, 1950, cols. 343 ff.) a new attempt at dividing the epistle which, to be sure, in my judgment is based on astoundingly narrow observation and is correspondingly superficial.

[9] Zahn, Geschichte des neutestamentlichen Kanons, II: 59-60, 344-54.

is indisputable[10] that already in the first century people were collecting the writings of the apostle, and our present arrangement is in any case more recent than that of the Muratorian canon (ad Corinthios prima . . .), which is also known to Tertullian.[11] The placing of the Corinthian epistles at the beginning points to Corinth as the place of origin of such a collection,[12] and this placing was for its own part well founded only if the various writings of varying scope were assembled into larger Corpora that appeared more important than a number of smaller letters. People then had the favorable opportunity of handing down only with the Corpus some very brief letters whose setting in relation to their theologically significant contents was disproportionately large. What the special occasion was that called forth this collection is stated in Vol. 2, pp. 197 ff.[13] Perhaps one may think of the disputes, attested by I Clement, which agitated the Corinthian community at the close of the first century, especially if W. Bauer (Rechtgläubigkeit und Ketzerei im ältesten Christentum [1934], pp. 104 ff., ET Orthodoxy and Heresy in Earliest Christianity [1971], pp. 100 ff.) should be correct in his attractive conjecture (cf. p. 298, n. 32) that here it was a matter of discussions between anti-Pauline Gnostics and representatives of the Pauline-orthodox tradition.[14] What happened

[10] Cf. P. Feine, Einleitung in das Neue Testament (1936), p. 288.

[11] Even Marcion presupposes it (cf. A. v. Harnack, Die Briefsammlung . . . p. 9). Lietzmann has assembled at the beginning of his commentary on Romans the various arrangements in a form easy to survey. Cf. Vol. 2, pp. 185 ff.

[12] A. v. Harnack already saw this (Die Briefsammlung des Apostels Paulus [1926], pp. 8-9) and convincingly demonstrated it.

[13] In any case this collection was intended from the first for a larger group of communities. This is evident from the editorial comments in the introductions to the two epistles as they now stand. J. Weiss rightly excises I, 1:2b: σὺν πᾶσιν τοῖς ἐπικαλουμένοις τὸ ὄνομα τοῦ κυρίου ἡμῶν Ἰησοῦ Χριστοῦ ἐν παντὶ τόπῳ αὐτῶν καὶ ἡμῶν.

(Leipoldt in ZNW 44: 143: "An impossible wording: First Corinthians is prompted by a specific occasion and is directed to one single community.")

Similarly, in II, 1:1 "σὺν τοῖς ἁγίοις πᾶσιν τοῖς οὖσιν ἐν ὅλῃ τῇ Ἀχαΐᾳ" may have been inserted, of course from an epistolary introduction not preserved for us (cf. p. 97, n. 27), which explains the diverse form of the two catholicizing remarks, a feature which Lietzmann (Commentary on I, 1:2) incorrectly adduces as an argument against their interpolation. If the editor did not provide the other epistles of his collection with similar additions, this would have been because in epistles which were sent to him from other communities, such an insertion could not have gone unnoticed by those who sent them. Besides, the addition of I, 1:2 must have seemed necessary for the entire collection which it introduced. In II, 1:1 what we have in fact is not an editorial addition, but one of compilation. The further comments in I Cor. which according to J. Weiss are added to express the same tendency, namely 4:17; 7:17; 11:16; 14:33, are, on the contrary, original and, in the context, either necessary or at least easily accounted for (see p. 244, n. 169).

[14] Anyone who is convinced (properly, in my judgment) that Philippians also consists of two (or three) original epistles of Paul will, if he holds the σὺν ἐπισκόποις καὶ διακόνοις in Phil. 1:1 to be a later addition, reasonably consider whether this

50

later in the formation of the canon on a large scale thus has already
been anticipated here on a small scale: a collection of writings of
apostolic tradition to which one could appeal in the battle with Gnosticism as to the bearers of pure doctrine.

2. Analysis of I Corinthians

One will do well first to enumerate the component parts of I Corinthians. The following parts complete in themselves may be set forth:

a) 1:1-9 Heading and Proem
b) 1:10–4:21 The discussion with the parties and partisans in Corinth
c) 5:1-13 Incest
d) 6:1-11 Action at law
e) 6:12-20 Warning against unchastity
f) 7:1-40 The question of marriage
g) 8:1-13 The eating of meat sacrificed to idols
h) 9:1-23 The example of the apostle
i) 9:24-27 Exhortation to a good warfare
j) 10:1-22 Warning against participation in idol worship
k) 10:23–11:1 The eating of meat sacrificed to idols
l) 11:2-34 Proper behavior in the congregational meeting[15]
m) 12:1–14:40 On the gifts of the Spirit
n) 15:1-58 The resurrection of the dead
o) 16:1-24 Epistolary conclusion (unitary?)

In any case 1:1-9 and 1:10–4:21 may originally have belonged together. One naturally may not expect a close transition between the two
pieces, yet in 1:10 Paul obviously refers back to the κοινωνία 'Ιησοῦ
Χριστοῦ which was mentioned in 1:9.

The decisive observation for the fact that our canonical I Corinthians contains pieces from various Pauline letters is to be made
at I, 11:18 ff. Paul hears of schisms in the community. He believes in
the correctness of this rumor μέρος τι; δεῖ καὶ αἱρέσεις ἐν ὑμῖν εἶναι, ἵνα
καὶ οἱ δόκιμοι φανεροὶ γένωνται. If one compares this passage with Paul's
statements in I, 1–4, it is simply inconceivable that both attitudes
toward disputes could come from the same epistle. In I, 11:18-19 it is
51 obviously a case of a *first* reference to disputes within the community.

---

remark was not meant to give support to the battle of the protectors of the tradition,
namely the bishops and deacons, against the reaction of the Gnostic Pneumatics.

[15] The two major parts of this section, 11:2-16 and 11:17-34, belong together, since
vs. 17 refers back to vs. 2. Because of 11:22*b*, the theory of J. Weiss (Commentary,
in loc.) that vs. 17 is an editorial comment which is supposed to join the two
separated parts of the same Epistle A appears to me very unlikely.

Apparently Paul does not know of what special sort these are. He has "heard" (ἀκούω, 11:18) of them and to some extent believes this report. He touches on them only quite briefly and even knows how to derive a positive aspect from them. It cannot be a question of the mention of other disputes than those discussed in I, 1–4 in the same letter, because with the scantiness with which he is informed about these schismata, Paul would have had to identify them at once with those previously mentioned. But if he had had a concrete conception of them, after the long statements at the beginning of the letter, he would have had to go into more detail, particularly since the opinion that controversies must occur utterly contradicts what was set forth earlier. The possibility that by the σχίσματα and αἱρέσεις he could have been designating disorder in connection with the Lord's Supper is completely ruled out.

Most likely is the well-known explanation that what we have here is a reference to the ἔριδες mentioned in I, 1:11, and in fact a reference which comes from a time when Paul was still less well informed on these conflicts in the community than in I, 1:11. Arguing for this is the fact that the conception which is expressed in the ἀκούω (vs. 18) fits nicely with the report that has come through Stephanas (see p. 101), while the ἐδηλώθη μοι in I, 1:1 which has a significantly different nuance appropriately characterizes reports which Paul received from the official delegates of the congregation (see *ibid*.). Thus one may assign I, 11:18 ff., and with it the entire section 11:2-34, to the apostle's earlier letter mentioned in I, 5:9. If we designate this letter as Epistle A, then I, 1–4 belongs to Epistle B.

Now the observation that from I, 7:1 on to the end of the epistle Paul makes reference in various ways to written inquiries addressed to him by the Corinthians is an important one. The sections introduced with περὶ δέ undoubtedly belong to the same letter of Paul (7:1, 25; 8:1; 12:1; 16:1; 16:12), and it is in fact Epistle B, to which 16:1-12 surely also belongs. It is to be expected that Paul carries through the answering of the letter without any major digressions. That he had this in mind is clear from the περὶ δὲ ὧν ἐγράψατε in 7:1, which not only heads the following statements down to 7:24 but, as distinguished from the later περὶ δέ superscriptions, has in view the whole set of inquiries of the congregation's letter. Thus also the section 11:2-34, which divides the statements περὶ τῶν εἰδωλοθύτων in 8:1 from those περὶ τῶν πνευματικῶν in 12:1, could be extracted as belonging to Epistle A. But in the same way chap. 15 also breaks the connection of 16:1 (περὶ τῆς λογείας) with the statements περὶ τῶν πνευματικῶν in chaps. 12-14. For this reason I should assign chap. 15 also to the apostle's first Corinthian epistle (A). Moreover, arguing for this is not only the fact that 15:1 follows well after 11:34—Paul intends to make more specific arrangements about order in the Supper only when he comes, but on the other hand wishes to call the message of salvation back to the recollection of the Corinthians now—but also the observation that chap. 15 in many respects displays an earlier stage in Paul's relations to Corinth than do parts of Epistle B.[16] One should only compare 15:9, for example, with 9:1 ff. In 9:1 ff. Paul must defend his apostolate against attacks from Corinth with self-commendation, while in 15:9 he still quite innocently calls himself the ἐλάχιστος τῶν ἀποσ-

53   τόλων. It is not conceivable that at the same time in which he writes I, 9 Paul declares that he is not ἱκανὸς καλεῖσθαι ἀπόστολος, thus precisely what people in Corinth are charging. Further, this misunderstanding about the resurrection of the dead is explained only (see pp. 155 ff.) if the cautious ἀκούω of I, 11:18 also holds true for the reports which Paul takes as a basis in I, 15, but not if he has already received a letter and an official embassy from Corinth.[17]

Further, the unity of the section introduced with the περὶ δὲ τῶν εἰδωλοθύτων, 8:1–11:1, is to be contested. Of the five individual pieces of this section of the letter as enumerated above, a continuous train of thought is formed by three: 8:1-13, 9:1-23, and 10:23–11:1. At first Paul speaks in principle about the occasionally necessary renunciation of the freedom to eat meat sacrificed to idols and of Christian freedom in general, then he presents himself as example and model, and finally he gives concrete instructions for the attitude of the Corinthians toward the problem of eating meat sacrificed to idols, for which in fact they had asked him by letter. The statements about the *worship* of idols (10:1-22) by no means fit into this connection. They concern a basically different theme. In the treatment of the profane eating of meat sacrificed to idols there is nothing to indicate that at the same time some in Corinth had the inclination to take part in the pagan wor-

54   ship. Conversely, 10:1-22 treats only of *cultic* meals. Therefore, with J. Weiss, I assign 10:1-22 also to Epistle A.[18]

---

[16] Cf. further below on chap. 16.

[17] Against the attribution of chap. 11 and chap. 15 to the same epistle one might object that chap. 15 does not agree with the Corinthians' faithfulness toward the tradition which is boasted of in 11:2. But this objection cannot be allowed, even though it is in itself correct, because it could be applied with equal force to the deviations from the παράδοσις which are reproved in chap. 11. The tension between 11:2 and 11:17 is still more obvious than that between 11:2 and chap. 15. In this connection we cannot concern ourselves with the question of how to resolve this tension.

[18] One may also consult Hans Freiherr von Soden, *Sakrament und Ethik, Marb. Theol. Studien*, Heft 1, p. 17, where important differences between the two parts are indicated. Von Soden places value upon the fact that in 10:1-22 apparently

Now 9:24-27, however, is also connected with 10:1-22. The metaphorical assertion that, of those who contend for the prize, only one is awarded the prize is illustrated by Paul in 10:1 ff. by means of a historical example: the fathers were all under the cloud, all received the same spiritual gifts. Nevertheless God was not pleased with most of them. If the internal connection of 9:24-27 with the following is thus assured, then this brief section also belongs to Epistle A. Now 56 if one removes 9:24–10:22 from the context of I Cor., then the original order of Epistle B is restored; for the principle of 10:23 can sensibly be joined only with 9:19-23, where it moreover fits *very well*, while in connection with 10:14-22 it is simply impossible.

This now leaves only the arrangement of the sections cited above under c)–e) to be settled. Chapter 5 belongs to Epistle B, because in 5:9 is found the reference to Epistle A. But I, 6:1-11 is closely connected with chap. 5. Apparently Paul deliberately chose a key-word association. In the section 5:12–6:3 the word κρίνειν is found seven times! In view of the fact that the community does not judge outsiders, it is for her a matter of particular shame that she should allow herself to be judged by unbelievers. Thus 6:1-11 is also to be assigned to Epistle B. 57

The placing of 6:12-20 creates some difficulties. I do not venture here to pass *definitive* judgment. Nevertheless it would be strange if Paul should immediately have taken up again in 6:12 the theme "πορνεία" which he has just left in 5:13, particularly when one notes, 58 in accepting the foregoing analysis, that the arrangement of Epistle B is explicitly precise. The doubled reference to the catchphrase "πάντα μοι ἔξεστιν" in the same letter, especially on different themes (cf. 6:12 with 10:23), would moreover be not exactly apt. Finally, J. Weiss (*Kommentar,* pp. 156-57) has pointed to the various substantive and formal parallels which exist between our passage and 10:1-22, while in this respect significant differences with 5:1–6:11 are present. Hence with J. Weiss I also assign the section 6:12-20 to Epistle A and place it before 9:24, where it has good continuity with what follows and, as we shall see, with what precedes it. 59

Finally, however, the unity of chap. 16 is to be disputed. A clear division lies between vs. 12 and vs. 13. It is true that in Paul admonitions are customary before the closing salutations, but they always

---

rights are conceded to the weak without limitation, while elsewhere in principle the strong have the theological right on their side. This is an undoubtedly correct observation, which of course must be supplemented and explained so as to point out that in 10:1-22 Paul is not thinking of the strong and the weak at all. At the time in which he is warning the Corinthians against participation in the *worship* of idols, this problem is utterly remote from his mind—one more indication that the vss. 10:1-22 stem from another situation than that of the other statements. 55

begin with an address.[19] In comparison with that practice, vs. 13 begins much too abruptly for it to have its original connection here. But it fits in well as the continuation of I, 15:58. Here we find the usual transition to the concluding admonitions: ὥστε, ἀδελφοί μου ἀγαπητοί . . . , which are followed then by the closing salutations. Thus in I, 15:58 + 16:13-24 the conclusion of Epistle A would be preserved for us, while Epistle B has been handed down to us only so far as the concluding response to the community's letter (περὶ δὲ Ἀπολλῶ in 16:12). Under this presupposition also is clarified the question which has caused the exegetes much racking of the brain, as to how Paul could be silent in I, 1:11 about Stephanas and his companions but in I, 16 about the people of Chloe—a puzzle that is in fact insoluble if one holds to the unity of I Corinthians. Rather, Epistle A is delivered by Stephanas, and Epistle B has been prompted by those of Chloe. It would indeed be most strange if Paul had only belatedly recalled in I, 1:16 Stephanas who was *present with him.*

The often-posed question as to whether parts of II Corinthians also are to be assigned to Epistles A or B is to be answered in the affirmative for the section II, 6:14–7:1. Even exegetes who otherwise are not very critical affirm that this paraenesis is not original in its present place.[20] On the other hand, it cannot be demonstrated that this piece is non-Pauline,[21] and it is even unlikely, because the canonizing compiler of the epistles would hardly have gone back to a non-Pauline fragment, but a later, "post-canonical" interpolation would have had to be identified in the text tradition. A warning against the heathen however fits only into our Epistle A, from a time when Paul still did not see through the position of his opponents. The best place in it appears to me to be directly before I, 6:12, so that the section II, 6:14–7:1 would be the beginning of the part of Epistle A that has been preserved. Paul would then have joined with a general warning against

[19] Rom. 15:30; 16:17; II Cor. 13:11; I Thess. 5:14 ff.; 5:25, cf. Vol. 2, pp. 122 ff.; Phil. 3:1—if our canonical Philippians contains more than one epistle of Paul to Philippi; cf. Vol. 2, pp. 48 ff.

[20] E.g., Bachmann in Zahn's *Kommentar* (1918, 3rd ed.). The literary arrangement and the contents *must* convince any unprejudiced person of this.

[21] The ideas in detail are not un-Pauline; only, in the present connection they are ill-fitting. It is generally acknowledged that the *hapax legomena* are no argument against the Pauline authorship. And the expression μολυσμοῦ σαρκὸς καὶ πνεύματος indeed does not presuppose the genuinely Pauline usage of σάρξ and πνεῦμα, but neither does it presuppose a genuinely non-Pauline usage, as is shown, e.g., by I, 7:34; I, 16:18; II, 2:13; I Thess. 5:23 for πνεῦμα and by I, 1:26, 29; 5:5; 7:28; 10:18, etc., for σάρξ. If, as we assume (see p. 96), II, 7:5 follows II, 2:13, we have here the same juxtaposition of σάρξ and πνεῦμα as in II, 7:1; in Troas Paul was disturbed τῷ πνεύματι because he did not find Titus; in Macedonia his σάρξ had no rest because he was also oppressed from without.

paganism the treatment of some specific problems—an unchastity and pagan cult. These themes already are suggested in II, 6:14–7:1 (cf. II, 6:16 with I, 10:14 ff. and I, 6:19). I, 5:9 will refer back to II, 6:17! The internal connection of II, 6:14–7:1 is just as prominent directly with I, 6:12 ff. as indirectly with the entire Epistle A. It is understandable that the redactor wanted to have a warning against mixing with paganism in the second epistle also, especially since in his time it certainly was more necessary than in the early period of the community.[22]

Thus the first two letters of Paul to Corinth may be reconstructed in the following way. Epistle A consists of: II, 6:14–7:1; I, 6:12-20; 9:24–10:22; 11:2-34; 15; 16:13-24. It is likely that this first epistle has been preserved for us in its entirety except for the prescript, proem, and perhaps some isolated remarks which had to be eliminated in the editing. In any case the individual pieces follow one another well in the proposed arrangement, and it is not to be supposed that the compiler has excised any important statements of the apostle. Already by that time these would have been much too valuable for such to have been done. And whoever published I, 5 or II, 11 could hardly have taken offense at other statements.

For Epistle B then there remain: I, 1:1–6:11; 7:1–9:23; 10:23–11:1; 12:1–14:40;[23] and 16:1-12. This epistle has certainly been preserved in

61

62

[22] It was early, and has often been, presumed (see Windisch, p. 18) that II, 6:14–7:1 stems from the epistle mentioned in I, 5:9, though, curiously, for the most part without the obvious inference being drawn that other parts of Epistle A must then also have been preserved. Lietzmann's scorn (*Kommentar, in loc.*) at "the 'flying leaves' stirred up by criticism, which have sought out such odd resting places for themselves in various places in the New Testament," is for this reason understandable.

[23] J. Weiss appears to me moreover to have provided convincing proof (in Meyer's *Kommentar, in loc.*) that originally I, 14:1c followed immediately after 12:31a, but that 14:1ab is a redactional gloss which ties 12:31b–13:13 into the present context more by sheer force than with insight. Of course the only sensible place for the undoubtedly not un-Pauline chap. 13 is not "somewhere" beside chap. 8, as J. Weiss thinks because of certain formal points of connection, but immediately after chap. 14. Paul concludes his statements about spiritual gifts with the summary: "Therefore, my brethren, strive for the gifts of prophecy, and do not hinder speaking in tongues; but everything is to be done with decency and order," and then continues logically: "But I show you a still better way. . . ." Thus chap. 13, which clearly represents a climax, has a proper place in conjunction with the statements περὶ τῶν πνευματικῶν, which now move in a sensible progression. Thus however there is also an inner connection between the ἀγάπη in 13:13 and the immediately following recommendation of the collection in 16:1. It is not very likely that the pious editor, whose only personal comment we have, in my judgment, in I, 1:2b, has intentionally undertaken this senseless rearrangement, even though it is not impossible that some reason or reasons invisible to us may have prompted him or someone else to do this (and to insert 14:1ab). One may rather assume that a copyist before him or just after him by mistake skipped chap. 14 and then

full up to the closing salutations, with which a recommendation of the
bearer of the writing surely was connected. It is splendidly arranged.
At the beginning Paul refers to oral reports and in the first four chapters treats the party divisions in Corinth, in the next, two cases of
unchristian conduct. From chap. 7 on, he answers the letter he has
received from Corinth without turning aside from it. The brief closing
salutations, which will have followed immediately after 16:12, have
fallen victim to the editing which at this point inserted the close of
Epistle A. It is interesting that the editor has formed the structure of
I Cor. out of two different letters, a method which he also employs in
the canonical II Cor., surely not without deliberate intent.

3. Analysis of II Corinthians

In II Cor. are found the following sections complete in themselves:

a) 1:1–2:13 + 7:5-16;   d) 8:1-24;
b) 2:14–6:13 + 7:2-4;[24]   e) 9:1-15;
c) 6:14–7:1;   f) 10:1–13:13.

The paraenesis 6:14–7:1 has already found its place in Epistle A. Of the
remaining pieces, a) and f) in no case belong together. Even if one
thinks that it is possible to explain the contradictory character of these
sections by sleepless nights or new reports from Corinth, still it is
simply inconceivable that Paul sent both of them at the same time.
And there is nothing to support the assertion that the last four chapters address another group of Corinthians than does the rest of the
epistle.[25] In view of the special character of the last chapters, the
thesis first proposed by A. Hausrath[26] that in this part of the letter we
have to do with the so-called sorrowful epistle mentioned in II, 2:3 ff.
and II, 7:12 is simply compelling. Reservations about this identification, so far as they are raised even by scholars who separate chaps.
10–13 from the context of II Cor. (e.g., Windisch), rest upon prejudiced opinions of the conditions in Corinth, especially with reference
to the ἀδικήσας of II, 7:12 (cf. pp. 108 ff.). It may be doubted whether
the sorrowful epistle has been preserved for us in reasonably complete
form. Of course it is not necessary to assume that major parts are

---

added it following chap. 13.—Jean Héring in his commentary also has adopted
the theory that chap. 13 is the interpolation of a Pauline piece.

[24] J. Weiss (TLZ, 1894, pp. 512 ff.; cf. also Preisker in ThBl 5 [1926]: 154 ff.)
first noted the fact that this section meaninglessly breaks the thread of the narrative which is interrupted in 2:13 and taken up again in 7:5. It must be conceded
to the redactor that this insertion has been achieved with consummate skill.

[25] Cf. Windisch, p. 15.

[26] Der Vier-Kapitelbrief des Paulus an die Korinther (Heidelberg, 1870).

missing, especially not if one does not presuppose a thorough treatment of the case of the ἀδικήσας known from II, 2:5 ff. and II, 7:11-12 as obligatory in the sorrowful epistle (see below) .   65

II, 1:1–2:13 + 7:5-16 is a coherent piece of the "letter of joy" which Paul writes from Macedonia not long before his arrival in Corinth. Whether still other pieces are preserved from this letter must be shown in the following investigation.

Semler (pp. 238 ff.) had already recognized that chap. 9 is a doublet of chap. 8. Both chapters stem essentially from the same situation, to be sure with one distinctive difference: in chap. 8 Paul can already speak of a successful collection among the Macedonians and can set these before the Corinthians as an example, while in chap. 9 he still speaks of boasting to the Macedonians of the good intention of the Corinthians. Thus chap. 9 appears to be earlier than chap. 8 and will   66 have been written at the beginning of the apostle's Macedonian tour. I regard the chapter as the body of a letter of recommendation with which Paul sends Titus and the two brethren mentioned in chap. 8 back to Corinth[27] just after the meeting reported in II, 7:6, so that the business of the collection, in which the apostle had undertaken nothing more since sending the sorrowful letter, is again pushed. That such a mission must have preceded the letter of joy is proved also by II, 1:8 ff., where it is presupposed that people in Corinth were already informed about the nature of the trouble most recently suffered by Paul in Asia. And II, 8:16 ff. shows that Titus was in a hurry to return soon. In the further course of his journey then the apostle writes the letter of joy, II, 1:1–2:13 + 7:5-16, to which the eighth chapter, composed a short time after chap. 9, is also to be assigned. II, 8:1 follows   70 7:16 well—and better than 9:1—in every respect. Indeed the theme "Collections" basically already begins in 7:13, since Titus' presence in Corinth which is mentioned there served this purpose.[28] If it were not preserved for us, one would simply have to postulate such a recommendation of the collection for Paul's last letter before his arrival in

[27] It should be considered whether chap. 9 is not a letter of recommendation to *all* the communities in Achaia. Achaia is mentioned only in II, 9:2! If this is the case, then the address "σὺν τοῖς ἁγίοις πᾶσιν τοῖς οὖσιν ἐν ὅλῃ τῇ ᾿Αχαΐᾳ" in II, 1:1 would have been inserted there out of the context of this letter of recommendation. In view of the joyful epistle, which pertains to the Corinthians exclusively, it appears to me beyond doubt that in these verses we have to do with an interpolation.   72

[28] H. Greeven ("Propheten, Lehrer, Vorsteher bei Paulus," ZNW 44, n. 75) conjectures, possibly correctly, that in II, 7:11 Paul is already thinking of the collection when he uses the word σπουδή. In any case it is striking—and it certainly argues for the connection of 7:5-16 with chap. 8 as well as for the separation of chaps. 8 and 9—that σπουδή and σπουδαῖος are frequent in chap. 8 (vss. 7, 8, 16, 17, and 22) , but are lacking in chap. 9.

Corinth. The flattering praise of the messengers, which would have
been highly improper in a letter conveyed by them personally, is now
quite in place in chap. 8.

71

The arrangement of the section 2:14–6:13 + 7:2-4 is difficult. Many
have left it in its present position, and others have attached it to the
sorrowful epistle. If one observes the special character of this part of
the letter, it appears that it fits neither of the two known epistles. In
the epistle of joy Paul is zealously concerned with removing the last
misunderstandings which still existed between himself and the community. So he avoids making any charge, even where there are unedifying matters. Above all, not a word more is said about the alien opponents in Corinth. If only this epistle were at hand, one would never
get the idea that *theological* differences existed between Paul and the
Corinthians.

The inserted section displays a fundamentally different character.
Not only that it frequently refers to still existing conflicts (II, 2:17;
3:1; 4:2-3; 5:12), which apparently are nourished by Christians who
have come in (3:1). Rather, the entire part of the epistle, with the
exception of the generally framed midrash in chap. 3, contains in run-
ning form a more or less hidden polemic against the schismatic views
represented in Corinth. That this is the case will be shown in detail
in the course of this work. The tendency of this section thus utterly
contradicts that of the joyful epistle, which refrains from any allusion
to theological differences. This holds true also for the closing vss. 6:11-
13 + 7:2-4, in which Paul requests, in a form that is no less urgent for
being mild, the ὑπακοή which in 7:15 is already *confirmed!* If one considers also that II, 7:5 surely originally followed II, 2:13, and that it
is unlikely that the editor separated parts of the same epistle in order
to combine them in a different way, then it is ruled out that the vss.
2:14–6:13 + 7:2-4 belong to the epistle of joy.

But they are also distinctively different from the sorrowful epistle.
As already mentioned, the theological polemic is pursued in them in
such a veiled fashion that the polemical aim of the individual sections
has often escaped the exegetes. Where the dispute becomes obvious
(2:17 ff.; 4:2 ff.), Paul consistently only refutes the charges which are
raised against his person, without himself becoming sharply polemical.
Instead, the only direct charge which he makes, namely in 5:12*b*, is
surprisingly mild in expression. The character of chaps. 10–13 with its
biting attacks on his opponents in Corinth and the vigorous tone of its
statements is fundamentally different. One may compare also 7:2-4
with 13:1 ff. Further, in chaps. 10–13 it is the community as a whole
which is assailed by Paul. It puts up with the alien teaching (11:4),
it apparently makes no defense against the many charges made against

Paul, demands of him the proof of his apostolate (13:3), must as a *whole* submit to the fact that its Christian position is doubted (13:5), and so on, and when τινές are especially mentioned, they appear as a part of the community. Quite different is the attitude toward the community in 3:2 ff. or in 5:11 ff., where Paul still sees the Corinthians as basically on his side and helps them in the defense against those who are "puffed up." The thesis which is occasionally heard in defense of the unity of the entire II Cor., that chaps. 10–13 are directed to another group of addressees, has its own basis in this difference in the attitude of the apostle to the addressees, even though it is in itself untenable. The fact that in both fragments the same theme stands at the center of the statements, namely the defense of Paul's apostolic authority, may not mislead us to the conclusion that they therefore belonged together in a *single* writing. On the contrary. Precisely the fact that Paul lays hold of the same problematic in such different ways shows that we have to do with two separate treatments. If one wishes to assign both parts of the epistle to *one* letter, one must, in the last analysis, base this upon the same inadequate and often fanciful arguments which are brought forward by those who defend the place of chaps. 10–13 in the entire II Cor., without thereby having explained the special peculiarity of the section being treated here.   73

But now it is precisely this special peculiarity that allows us to arrange the statements distinguished by it with some probability in the sequence of the apostle's other correspondence with Corinth. The cautious polemic cannot be without reason. It fits into a time in which Paul was compromised by recent prejudiced utterances in Corinth and had received information about this exposure. However, both Epistle A and Epistle B contained inaccurate or misinformed statements of the apostle on the situation in Corinth, as is already widely recognized by the exegetes and will also be shown in this work. Paul probably already received reports of it from the returning Timotheus (I, 16:11), but at the latest during his brief interim visit (see pp. 103-4).

Now II, 1:13, which is explained by vs. 17, presupposes that Paul had communicated to the Corinthians in writing the travel plans set forth in vs. 15. This must have been after Epistle B and even after   74 the interim visit, which was the first *charis* (vs. 15). But at the same time it is prior to the sorrowful letter, in which indeed the plan of I, 16 (tacitly?) is again taken up, that something happened which resulted in the ironic charge by Paul's enemies in Corinth that they read something different from what he wrote, i.e., from what he had had in mind in writing as they had to infer from his later conduct. Paul indeed excuses himself on this point by saying that he stands by what he has written, but has changed his plan which was communicated in writing, out of love for the Corinthians (II, 1:17 ff.). Thus there must have been a letter between the interim visit and the sorrowful letter, one in which Paul had communicated the plan mentioned in II, 1:15 ff. I regard II, 2:14–6:13 + 7:2-4 as the body of this letter, which was sent soon after Paul's return from the interim visit, yet before the occurrence of the event which occasioned the sorrowful letter. Here then we have to do with Epistle C, while the sorrowful letter would be Epistle D, the letter of recommendation in chap. 9 Epistle E, and the joyful letter Epistle F.

Thus the editor has preserved for us six letters of Paul to Corinth— Paul can hardly have written more at that time to Corinth—and indeed, as we probably may assume without further ado, in their essential elements. Outside of some epistolary introductions and conclusions as well as contradictory indications of the situation he may have reproduced the correspondence that lay before him with fidelity. The supposed reasons for this redaction have already been mentioned. The composition of II Cor. resulted even more simply than did Cor. Epistle C was very skillfully inserted into the epistle of joy (F), and into the former was fitted, to be sure less skillfully, the brief paraenesis from Epistle A (II, 6:14–7:1). The letter of recommendation (E) and the sorrowful epistle (D) then were simply appended with their major parts to this complex. The fact that this work of compilation was performed neither awkwardly nor with scientific pedantry, but makes a quite natural impression, may strengthen the confidence in the correctness of our analysis.[29] At any rate, all those efforts at division which reckon with a misplacing of leaves or detailed work of the editor (cf. in Clemen, *Die Einheitlichkeit der paulinischen Briefe* . . . , *passim*) appear to me unlikely from the outset. *After* the editing, which certainly was connected with a wider distribution of the epistles, more serious alterations in the state of the text were no longer possible unless they could be demonstrated in the tradition. And since the redactor approached his texts, according to all appearance, with the greatest fidelity, I regard *more serious* interpolations of non-Pauline fragments into our canonical epistles, such as Dutch scholarship in particular has suspected, as inconceivable.

The six letters of Paul to Corinth in the form and order which we have just reconstructed[30] are now the source for a presentation of the

[29] Cf. A. Schweitzer, *Die Mystik des Apostels Paulus* (1930), pp. 51-52. The other composite Pauline letters also show the same method; cf. Vol. 2, pp. 48 ff., 91 ff., 138 ff.

[30] To summarize, the following division emerges:
Epistle A: II, 6:14–7:1; I, 6:12-20; 9:24–10:22; 11:2-34; 15; 16:13-24.
Epistle B: I, 1:1–6:11; 7:1–9:23; 10:23–11:1; 12:1–14:40; 16:1-12.
Epistle C: II, 2:14–6:13; 7:2-4.

events which preceded Paul's last appearance in Corinth and which are decisively affected by the appearance of strange teachers in Corinth.

II. The Course of Events 76

Paul, probably tarrying in the *vicinity* of Ephesus (because of I, 77
15:32; cf. Acts 19:22), receives a visit from Stephanas, Fortunatus, and Achaicus (I, 16:17). The latter two may have belonged to the household of Stephanas (I, 1:16), but were in any case his close fellow-laborers; in other words, Paul is surely thinking of them in the allusion to the συνεργοῦντες and the κοπιῶντες (I, 16:16). Since Stephanas is the first convert in Achaia (I, 16:15) and was also baptized by Paul himself (I, 1:16), he cannot have been a resident of Corinth. In that case, the trustworthy note in Acts 17:34 would have to be a freely invented bit.[31] Of course that does not necessarily mean that he was an Athenian. He may have lived in a part of Achaia north of Athens. Because of I, 1:16 (οἶκον) and Acts 18:1-3, it is rather unlikely that he as a Corinthian resident had already early been converted by Paul outside Corinth. He placed himself with his house at the service of the churches and for this reason appears to have been frequently away on journeys. In any case he claims that people are subordinate to him by reason of his distinction as ἀπαρχὴ τῆς Ἀχαίας, and Paul fully recognizes this demand (I, 16:15 ff.). Of course, in Corinth, where he most recently stopped, his claim had been disputed. Paul must urgently recommend him and demand that the Corinthians acknowledge his authority (I, 16:16 ff.). If we relate this state of things with the total contents of Epistle A, it follows that Stephanas, having arrived at Corinth, finds there conditions deserving reproof, but does not succeed in the effort to eliminate these.[32] He betakes himself to Ephesus in order to stir Paul to intervene. This is the occasion which calls forth Epistle A. The fact that Paul owes his information about the situation in Corinth to people who themselves were present in Corinth only temporarily well accounts for the peculiarity of this epistle. That is 79

Epistle D: II, 10:1–13:13.
Epistle E: II, 9:1-15.
Epistle F: II, 1:1–2:13; 7:5–8:24. 78

[31] Acts 17:34: τινὲς δὲ . . . ἐπίστευσαν, ἐν οἶς καὶ Διονύσιος ὁ Ἀρεοπαγίτης καὶ γυνὴ ὀνόματι Δαμαρὶς καὶ ἔτεροι σὺν αὐτοῖς.

[32] In I, 16:17*b* one could understand the ὑμέτερον subjectively: "These have supplied what you lacked." Of course it is better to translate it, with most commentaries, "*These* have supplied what was lacking to me *from you*." Then the οὗτοι, stressed in contrast with the ὑμέτερον, could mean that Paul does not count the οὗτοι among the ὑμέτεροι.—In any case vs. 18*a* yields the best sense if Paul means to say that the three messengers have refreshed him by their visit just as they refreshed the Corinthians by their visit in Corinth.

to say, Paul shows himself well informed on the conditions in the congregational assemblies (I, 11) as well as on isolated details of the views
represented in Corinth (6:12; 15:12, 29). On the other hand, the
actual character of the σχίσματα in Corinth on their theological side
has not become clear to him. Thus not only are these σχίσματα, which
in truth were the cause of the whole trouble in Corinth, mentioned
only quite briefly (I, 11:18 ff.), but there also are some misunderstandings, particularly with reference to the question of the resurrection. In
II 5:1 ff. Paul shows himself obviously otherwise and better informed
about the eschatological heresy in Corinth than in I, 15, since now he
no longer takes issue with those who deny the resurrection but with a
spiritualistic expectation of the hereafter (cf. pp. 259 ff.).

Stephanas personally brought the first Corinthian epistle (A) which
contained the recommendation of himself to Corinth, for a little later
Paul presupposes his presence there (I, 1:16). At about the same time
he sends Timotheus to Corinth, ὃς ὑμᾶς ἀναμνήσει τὰς ὁδούς μου τὰς
ἐν Χριστῷ (I, 4:17). Of course Timotheus takes the roundabout way
by Macedonia (cf. Phil. 2:19 ff.),[33] so that at the time of Epistle B
Paul still does not reckon on his presence in Corinth (I, 16:10).

Possibly already before the arrival of Stephanas in Corinth, but
more probably soon after it, and influenced by Epistle A, the community directs a letter to Paul in which it asks the apostle for advice
in some questions that are disputed in Corinth, awaits instructions for
the organization of the collection in Corinth, and requests the return
of Apollos. This letter was delivered by Chloe's people (I, 1:11), from
whom Paul also learns more details about the party divisions in
Corinth and other occurrences which the letter itself does not mention.
Chloe's people might just as likely have returned from a visit in
Corinth and thus be residents of Ephesus as the other way around. I
should assume the former, since in the other case they surely would
have delivered Paul's answer and Paul then would have found a more
polite and more personal word than the blunt "ὑπὸ τῶν Χλόης" (cf.
I, 16:15 ff.; Phil. 2:25-26). Besides, as temporary guests in Corinth they
will have been better known under the designation "οἱ Χλόης" than
under their own names which Paul otherwise would have had to name.
Thus it is easily explained that Paul at the time of Epistle B still
possessed only relatively scanty oral reports about the actual conditions
80   in Corinth.

In an answering letter, Epistle B, the apostle at first comes to deal
explicitly with the ἔριδες, in order then to reprove two cases of moral

---

[33] Cf. W. Michaelis, *Die Datierung des Philipperbriefes* (Gütersloh, 1933), pp.
50 ff.; Vol. 2, pp. 183-84.

delinquency. The second part of the epistle serves to answer the letter of the Corinthian community. The fact that Paul is first and explicitly concerned with the disputes in Corinth shows that he indeed has recognized a certain seriousness in the situation. His authority as an apostle was already being attacked (I, 9:1 ff.). In other respects, however, Paul appears not to be afraid that someone will contradict his instructions. The community's letter indeed is a clear sign that the community is altogether subject to the apostle. One may think of the inquiry regarding the collection, of the request for the return of Apollos, who certainly should have supported the community in its defensive struggle against the schismatics, of the fact that the community clearly dissociates itself from the opponents (on I, 12:1, cf. pp. 171-72), and of the obedience with reference to the problems of idol worship (see p. 229) and of sexual life (see pp. 233-34) which the community's letter presupposes.

According to 16:11 Paul expects Timotheus back. He urges his early return, probably not least in order to be informed by his closest colleague about the situation in Corinth and the effect of his letter. At the same time he states his travel plans (I, 16:5-9), according to which he intends to remain in Ephesus until Pentecost and then to travel to Corinth by way of Macedonia.

After his return Timotheus informed Paul about the situation in Corinth and the effect of his letter there. This will have prompted the apostle to make the famous interim visit which is presupposed in II, 2:1; 12:14, and 13:1. It is almost unanimously acknowledged by modern exegetes that this visit took place between "I Cor." and "II Cor.," that is, between Epistle B and the epistle of joy, so I can pass over the discussion of this problem. Under this presupposition the passages in the epistle referring thereto are easily understandable, and furthermore the picture of the sequence of events is illumined at a decisive point, while the other explanations are unsatisfactory in both respects. Whether Paul had planned and announced his visit, whether new reports *suddenly* prompted him to make it, whether he only availed himself of a favorable opportunity to make the trip—all this is unknown. It can be said with certainty only that this visit was brief,[34] that it was made ἐν λύπῃ, and that in it or after it Paul had

---

[34] Since the community at large in Corinth consisted of the most diverse house churches, which moreover had various founders (Paul, Apollos, and Peter are named in I, 1:12; there are also the Gnostics; it may be that there were others unknown to us) and therefore lived in great diversity, it was impossible for Paul on one short visit to come to know the situation in the entire community with any thoroughness, at least that in the Gnostic conventicles. Nevertheless, from Epistle C onward, Paul shows himself *significantly* better informed about the situation in Corinth and the Gnostic theology.

altered his travel plans. All this may have occurred in combination of one element with another. Paul finds disturbing conditions present (II, 2:1), but departs without having taken decisive action (II, 13:2). While even at that time he surely had the will to set conditions in order, he can only have been prevented from doing so by a lack of time or by serious bodily infirmity. He had the hope, however, that the immoral members of the community would repent as a result of his visit (II, 12:21), and therefore only threatened that, if this did not happen, on his return he would not again spare them (II, 13:2). He intends this return to be soon, since he now again explicitly (II, 1:15 ff.) takes up the travel plans which he had given up in I, 16:7a. Thus he had found no time for a conclusive pacification of the community.[35]

The fanciful assertion that Paul left Corinth abruptly in anger has no basis in the text. Above all it is inconceivable that in consequence of the mysterious intervening event (see pp. 105 ff.) that plays such a great role for scholarship Paul should have left Corinth in great haste and then written the sorrowful epistle from a safe distance. Not only would this conduct not even remotely correspond to the same Paul who wrote II, 11:23-33; it would also be assuming that Paul, who allegedly withdrew himself from the events in rather inglorious retreat and was in no way hindered in doing so by the Corinthians, by means of a letter has wrought such σπουδή, ζῆλος, etc. (II, 7:11) among these people who personally drove him out, that all at once all tensions are eliminated! This construction is completely ruled out if the conciliatory Epistle C was written *after* the interim visit (see below) and II, 10–13 belongs to the sorrowful letter, as we suppose. For this angry Epistle D to Corinth is written immediately *before* the final trip to Corinth by way of Macedonia (II, 13:1), but not already on the return trip to Ephesus following his interim visit. And what kind of unique light would it shed on the character of Paul if he should have written II, 13:10 after he had left Corinth in flight! One who would let his fancy have free rein may assume that Paul could not extend the visit because of ship connections and perhaps was in Corinth only for the time of unloading and loading.

Probably just after his return to Ephesus Paul sends Titus[36] to Corinth, so that he might set in motion again the work of the collec-

---

[35] If I Thess. was not written until during the so-called third missionary journey, as W. Michaelis, e.g., with good reasons assumes, Paul had taken Timotheus along on the journey to Corinth and had sent him from Athens to Thessalonica (I Thess. 3:1-2), apparently in concern for this community, which certainly had not been spared the appearance of the Gnostics.

[36] Presumably Timotheus was on the way to Thessalonica (see the preceding note) and therefore was not available to Paul.

tion which certainly had been neglected in the course of the controversies (II, 8:6); for at the time of Epistle B his mission was not yet scheduled (I, 16:1 ff.), while he must already have left Corinth again at about the same time as Paul finally left Ephesus (II, 1:12-13; 7:5).[37] Apparently it was necessary for Paul to give Titus some encouragement to travel to Corinth (II, 7:14). However, not only the fact that he is sending him on such a delicate mission at all, but also that he even boasts of the Corinthians before Titus shows that, in spite of all the λύπη (II, 2:1), the apostle's connections with the community as a whole have not reached a level of excessive strain. Otherwise he would not have been able even in II, 1:15 indirectly to call the interim visit a πρώτη χάρις. It must have been *individuals* who troubled him.

Titus may have taken Epistle C along with him. Since no part of the setting of this letter has been preserved for us, it can hardly be placed in time and identified as to its special intention. It is true that it fits best into this point of time, especially since II, 1:13 presupposes a letter in this situation (cf. p. 99). The setting together with the recommendation of the collection naturally had to be dropped. The extant corpus contains a predominantly cautious polemic against Paul's opponents and shows now a much better acquaintance with their actual position than the earlier writings. The present text closes with the very fervent request: χωρήσατε ἡμᾶς . . . . The announcement which the redactor has excised (II, 1:13 ff.), of the forthcoming visit which Paul obviously regarded as necessary without however regarding the situation as in any way desperate, fits well into a connection with this plea. Nevertheless the letter clearly shows that the opposing side in Corinth has in large measure proceeded, in place of a substantive discussion, toward an attack upon the apostolic authority of Paul.

The further relations between Paul and Corinth are essentially determined by the intervening event which we can infer from the epistle of joy (II, 2:5 ff.; 7:12). It is hard to say what was involved here. The only sure thing is that Paul returns to the travel plans sketched in I, 16:5 ff., and immediately before setting off on the journey writes a bitterly angry letter, the sorrowful epistle. The anticipated second interim visit thus is dropped (II, 1:15 ff.), simply because Paul does not wish to come to Corinth again ἐν λύπη (II, 2:1). The tension between Paul and the Corinthians must have been significantly heightened since the interim visit, if this explanation by the apostle is supposed to be adequate. For during or just after the interim visit,

85

[37] I do not understand why, as W. G. Kümmel remarks (in Lietzmann, *Kommentar*, on p. 139, l. 34), "according to 7:14, at the time of the composition of the interim letter [*scil.*, the sorrowful epistle D] Titus cannot yet have been in Corinth."

which was *also* made in sorrow, Paul indeed had in mind his forthcoming visit. Thus the sorrowful letter in fact is sharply contrasted in
tone with that of the preceding letters. Paul does not recall the collection directly with a single word, not even when he mentions Titus
(II, 12:18).

If one inquires as to the reasons which created this changed situation,
it is advisable at first to leave out of consideration the intervening event
already mentioned, especially since the theme of the sorrowful epistle is
too evident from the first word to the last to require any long search
after the actual motives which evoked Paul's change in attitude: the
apostolic authority of Paul has been disputed in an extreme fashion,
and Paul now attempts to make clear to the community the unjustified
character of these accusations, not, of course, without strongly deplor-
ing the fact that this is necessary at all. While Paul presupposes that
individuals or a small group are the driving force in the movement
which is directed against him (II, 10:7; 10:10; 11:4-5, 20), yet the
accusing letter is aimed at the *entire* community, because it has not
placed itself decisively on his side (11:4). Paul already had been obliged
occasionally in Epistle B to refute similar attacks against himself (I,
9:1 ff.), then in Epistle C quite explicitly, even though cautiously, to
defend his rights. From II, 2:14 to 4:15 Paul speaks more or less emphatically of himself as an *apostle,* and in II, 5:11 ff. he comes back
again to the same theme, not to leave it entirely down to II, 7:4.

Of course at the time of the sorrowful epistle the discussion had
acquired a sharpness and a significance going far beyond the preceding.
The outward occasion for this new and vigorous campaign directed
against Paul personally may still be detectible. On the basis of the
βαρεῖαι and ἰσχυραὶ ἐπιστολαί of the apostle, some from the side of his
opponents who had come in had formed a quite definite picture of him
which was shattered when they discovered, upon his visit, that his
παρουσία τοῦ σώματος was ἀσθενὴς καὶ ὁ λόγος ἐξουθενημένος (II, 10:10).
It will be shown below (pp. 176 ff.) that these judgments do not
refer to Paul's physical weakness or awkwardness of speech but to his
deficiency in pneumatic gifts (see p. 177) which in the view of the
Corinthian schismatics are the most eminent and indispensable sign
of the apostle (see p. 182). In the first letters Paul had emphatically
claimed for himself a possession of the Pneuma in pure Gnostic *terminology* (I, 2:6–3:3; 6:19; 7:40; 9:1, *et passim*), without his having
demonstrated it in Corinth in a Gnostic fashion (I, 14:19). The knowledge, obvious after the interim visit, that according to *Gnostic* standards Paul could not qualify at all as a pneumatic and therefore even
less as an apostle, necessarily had as a result an intensified propaganda

campaign against him personally which is reflected step by step in the sorrowful epistle.

The consequences which this changed situation in Corinth had for Paul and his relationship with the community there are these: Not long after his return from the interim visit he learns that some are attempting to set the community against him with strong arguments and vigorous accusations which the sorrowful epistle allows us still to recognize in part. He is reluctant to come to Corinth at such an unpleasant time, and therefore changes his travel plans (II, 1:15).[38] But immediately before his departure he writes a sharp letter in the hope that this might save him a personal unsparing appearance (II, 12:19 ff.; cf. 2:3). Further, he now has the fear that his boasting before   86 Titus about the Corinthians, which has only recently resulted from the interim visit, has come to naught (II, 7:14). He will at the same time have asked Titus to meet him at Troas and to report on the situation in Corinth following his letter. Thus at the time of the sorrowful epistle Titus is still with the one brother on the collection affair in Corinth (II, 12:18). The widely held but groundless assumption that he had already returned to Ephesus, had informed Paul about the new situation in Corinth, and now delivers the sorrowful letter, is ruled out by II, 7:13-14. Paul cannot brag on the Corinthians to the Titus   87 who comes with most disturbing reports from Corinth, especially not if he places in his hand the sorrowful epistle.   88

The effect of the sorrowful epistle is simply striking. The change in mood in the joyful epistle is a total one. If the situation in Corinth was in fact as serious as Paul regards it at the time of the sorrowful epistle, then this epistle must have wrought a small miracle. I should assume that Paul saw the situation in too dark a color in the sorrowful epistle. Undoubtedly something had happened in Corinth which made Paul fear the worst. Undoubtedly the community had not placed itself on the side of the apostle without reservation. But just as undoubtedly, Paul was in error when now in his letter he made the charge against the *whole* community of insubordination. The joyful epistle makes this clearly evident. The reaction in Corinth to the sorrowful epistle consisted in σπουδή (II, 7:11), but this zeal apparently is expressed in the first place as ἀπολογία (7:11). At any rate Paul places the latter first, in order then explicitly to give the testimony to the community: ἐν παντὶ συνεστήσατε ἑαυτοὺς ἁγνοὺς εἶναι τῷ πράγματι (*ibid.*). Thus some in Corinth have defended themselves against the apostle's charges,

---

[38] It is only natural that in II, 1:15 Paul does not think of the founding visit, which he just as naturally does take into account in the solemn adjurations in 13:1 ff.

and Paul ascertains that this is done rightly. The ὀδυρμός (7:7) and the λύπη (7:8-9) of the Corinthians also may have been evoked as much by unjustified accusations by the apostle as by the insight into their own failures. Even Titus can report only good news from Corinth (II, 7:13-16). Not only had he been well received when he came to Corinth on the matter of the collection (vs. 15), but the whole time he had been treated with friendliness (vs. 13), so that Paul had unjustly feared that his boasting to Titus had come to naught (vs. 14). Thus everything had been only "half as bad" as was thought; in this way, but only in this way, is the sudden change from the sorrowful epistle to the joyful epistle explained satisfactorily.

What role was played in all this by the famed intervening event will never be fully clarified. I should *certainly* assert that Paul himself was the person of the ἀδικηθείς (II, 7:12). For if it had been a matter of someone else, this person would have had to be named in II, 2:5 instead of, or at least along with, Paul.

Since Paul himself was *directly* affected by the ἀδικία (II, 2:5-11), it cannot have been a question of just any case of moral lapse, especially since such cases were not at all so rare in Corinth (II, 12:21; cf. I, 5:6). Since the intervening event moreover must have been closely connected with the sorrowful epistle, one will also have to connect it with the contents of that epistle. So then someone has disputed the apostolic rights of the apostle in an especially injurious way. Such a direct accusation in fact comes to light in II, 12:16. The assertion, ὑπάρχων πανοῦργος δόλῳ ὑμᾶς ἔλαβον, presupposes that someone held Paul to be a sorcerer who of course did his business with special fraudulent cunning, in that he indeed refused all financial support by the community, but only in order to be able all the better to exploit the community by the roundabout way of the collection—anything other than this hardly comes into question.[39] If the ἀδικία mentioned in the joyful epistle consisted in this insinuation, of course Paul cannot have gone into this case more fully in a lost portion of the sorrowful epistle, as is very often naïvely assumed. Under this latter presupposition it would be idle to try to characterize the offense of the ἀδικήσας more precisely. But there is no compelling reason for the assumption that Paul had handled the ἀδικία thoroughly in the sorrowful epistle and even demanded the punishment of the evildoers. The passages involved, II, 2:5 ff. and 7:11-12, are just as well if not better understood if one disregards this assumption (see below). For of course if the sorrowful epistle is fairly fully preserved, hardly any other injury than the one

---

[39] Thus also H. Preisker, ThBl 5 (1926) : 154 ff.

mentioned in II, 12:16 can have been castigated in the epistle.

At any rate this possibility appears to me to be by far the most likely. Paul then had heard of sharp attacks against him within the community, without a decisive stand against these attacks being taken. He feared that the community, which indeed already during the not long past visit in Corinth had made an impression on the apostle which was not altogether pleasant, could be lost to his influence or was even already lost. In the face of this situation the individual case retreats wholly into the background. Paul rather writes in fact: οὐχ ἕνεκεν τοῦ ἀδικήσαντος οὐδὲ ἕνεκεν τοῦ ἀδικηθέντος, ἀλλ' ἕνεκεν τοῦ φανερωθῆναι τοῦ σπουδὴν ὑμῶν (7:12). The community in Corinth receives this letter with the awareness that it has not come out for Paul with the needed decisiveness, and now belatedly punishes a case of especially crass disobedience, probably the one which Paul expressly mentions (II, 12: 16) ;[40] for the rest, however, it defends itself rightly against the charge of having abandoned the authority of the apostle and having joined the "superlative apostles" (II, 11:5). That it now, more decisively than before, places itself on the side of Paul is surely an important achievement of the sorrowful epistle.

Paul learns of this reaction through Titus. He grants to the community the right of the ἀπολογία (II, 7:11), at the same time rejoices over the μετάνοια that has occurred, and also mentions the episode, 91 of course so as to indicate that theretofore nothing definite about it had been known to him, and this only in order to ask pardon for the culprit. The indefinite εἰ δέ τις λελύπηκεν, οὐκ ἐμὲ λελύπηκεν (II, 2:5) appears to me impossible if Paul had treated the disturbing event explicitly in the sorrowful epistle and had even demanded a punishment, but on the other hand it makes sense if one can insert the intervening idea, ". . . as I now have to assume." Besides, the request that the culprit be forgiven would have had to be framed differently if Paul himself had specified the punishment. It is particularly inconceivable that in the reference to the δοκιμή (vs. 9) demanded in the letter he is requesting that this should be confirmed in ἀγάπη (vs. 8) and χάρις (vs. 7), if precisely this δοκιμή signified exactly the opposite, punishment, in the sorrowful letter itself. 92

Of course in view of its relative innocence the community had assumed that Paul had written primarily on account of the ἀδικήσας and

---

[40] It can reasonably be doubted that Paul himself had already connected this complaint with the collection, which certainly would have corresponded to the actual situation. Vss. 17-18 rather give the impression that he suspects the charge that he had enriched himself by means of exaggerated demands for support of his companions.

had acted accordingly. To this Paul responds by correctly stating that
he had not written at all on account of the ἀδικήσας or for *his own*
sake, but had been thinking only of the community and their zeal for
him instead of for the false teachers (II, 7:12).

Immediately after he reached Paul, Titus is sent back—probably not
least at his own insistence (II, 8:17)—with a letter of recommendation
(E) on the matter of the collection to Corinth or to all Achaia. A little
later Paul writes the joyful epistle.[41] The occasion for it may have been
the recommendation of the collection in Corinth which had become
especially urgent through the success of the collection among the
Macedonians (8:1 ff.). Perhaps Paul also announced his coming and
wished to remove any still existing confusion, particularly with reference to the altered travel plans (II, 1:12-13). Besides, he surely felt
a compulsion to take a position on the question of the ἀδικήσας and
to ask pardon for him, whom the community, out of an understandable
misunderstanding of the sorrowful epistle, had punished so sharply.
If one considers also the happily lightened attitude of the apostle
since the arrival of Titus, the composition of the joyful epistle is adequately accounted for in terms of motive.

Only through the book of Acts are we informed about the further
connections of Paul with the Corinthian community. This gives the
stay of Paul in "Hellas" as three months long (Acts 20:3), a note
which seems trustworthy and also is confirmed by the "we"-source
which soon sets in. Paul spends Easter week in Philippi or—more likely
—in Troas (Acts 20:5 ff.). This exact indication of time allows us to
determine the span of time over which the extant correspondence is
distributed.

[41] Here the following may be noted: the redactor wishes II Cor. to be understood as a joyful epistle. But at the time of the joyful epistle Titus was already
again in Corinth. Therefore for the redactor, in the unified II Cor., Titus' stay mentioned in II, 12:18 can refer only to this last visit which is presupposed in II, 8:16 ff.,
while the one cited in II, 2:13 and 7:13 ff. is meant. The name which originally
stood in II, 12:18 instead of ἀδελφός was, however, not identical with any of the
names which Paul has named in chap. 8, for there Paul introduces the two brethren
as previously unknown to the Corinthians. Hence the redactor had to strike out
the names. Thus editorial reasons led to this manipulation, about the motivation
for which there has been much puzzling, and with little success. The redactor in II,
12:18 did not simply insert one of the names from II, 8; indeed, he did not even
write ἀδελφοί, as one would expect. This shows how reverently he handled the text,
and thus how little we have to reckon with interference in the wording of the
epistles from his hand.—In similar fashion the μετὰ τῶν ἀδελφῶν in I, 16:12, which
conflicts intolerably with the same expression in vs. 11, will have appeared for the
names of the bearers of Epistle B, since according to the intention of the redactor,
Stephanas and his people, who were the bearers of Epistle A, are supposed to have
returned to Corinth with I Corinthians.

III. Chronology

If Paul, as he intended (I, 16:8), left Ephesus just after Pentecost (II, 13:1) and celebrated the *following* Passover in Troas (Acts 20: 4 ff.), about ten months have elapsed in the intervening time (6th Sivan to 14th Nisan). If one reckons three months for the collection trip by way of Troas through Macedonia to Corinth, three months for the stay in Hellas (Acts 20:3), and one month for the journey from Corinth to Troas (or Philippi), there still remain three months which can of course be divided among the above-mentioned events without difficulty, if one does not wish to assume that Paul departed from Ephesus only after a longer time after Pentecost (see below). However that may be, it is in any case beyond comprehension that a majority of interpreters does not let the Pentecost observance mentioned in I, 16:8 be Paul's last one in Ephesus, because in the time that follows the many events could not be fitted in. But since Paul wrote the sorrowful epistle while still in Ephesus, the following time has only to account for the meeting with Titus and the two letters connected with that meeting, and there certainly was time enough for all this on the collection trip to Corinth, which could have lasted up to six months.

The question is only how much time lies between Epistle B and the sorrowful epistle. In this span of time in fact many events took place:

1. Delivery of Epistle B.
2. Timotheus' trip from Corinth to Ephesus.
3. Interim visit with connected sending of Titus and of Epistle C.
4. Arrival in Ephesus of the reports which prompted the sorrowful epistle.

If one counts five to ten days for the voyage from Ephesus to Corinth,[42] one could find a place within sixty days for these events if they followed close upon one another. It is unlikely that *significant* intervals lay between the separate events. Thus if one calculates that some four to five months separate the sorrowful epistle from Epistle B, one will hardly have set the figure too low.[43]

[42] According to Heinrici (Meyer *Kommentar* on II Cor., p. 48), in good weather one could travel from Ephesus to Corinth in five days. For purposes of comparison one can adduce the indication given in Acts 20:6, according to which the voyage from Philippi to Troas lasted four to five days.

[43] One could even make the following calculation: Timotheus returns sooner than Paul had expected, and arrives in Ephesus one day after Epistle B has been sent. The next day, prompted by Timotheus, Paul sets out for the interim visit. Thus he is in Corinth seven days after sending Epistle B. One day's stay there and five days for the return make a total of twelve days. On the thirteenth day he sends

That Paul cannot have written ἕως τῆς πεντεκοστῆς (I, 16:8) if the
Jewish church year had not already begun, i.e., until after 1st Nisan,
is an unfounded assertion of T. Zahn (*Introduction to the New Testament* I:268-69). Nevertheless, on the other hand he could be correct
with his conjecture that Paul because of I, 5:7 ff. wrote I Cor.
(= Epistle B) around Passover time. Then Epistle B would be composed some six to eight weeks before Pentecost, and we would have
to assume that Paul remained in Ephesus some two to three months
after Pentecost, until the composition of the sorrowful epistle. There
is nothing in the way of such an assumption, especially not if one notes
the changing situations and the often-changed travel plans of Paul.
Arguing *for* it is the fact that the ἄρτι in I, 16:7 surely must be related
to an early departure of Paul.

If we assume a time span of one to two months between Epistle A
and Epistle B, then some six months lie between Paul's first reaction to
the conflicts in Corinth and the sorrowful epistle. The joyful epistle can
hardly have followed the sorrowful epistle more than two months later,
since the latter was written at the departure from Ephesus, so that the
entire span of time from Epistle A to the end of the tensions between
Paul and the Corinthians stretched over about eight months, say
96   from February till October.

This calculation is called for by the text. Anyone who reckons with
significantly greater periods of time would have to support this with
good reasons. But he can in no case employ the twice-occurring ἀπὸ
πέρυσι (II, 8:10; 9:2) unless he presumes, against all probability, that
the activity of Titus in Corinth mentioned in 8:6 signifies the beginning of the collection for Corinth in general. I, 16:1-2 rather shows
that long before the writing of Epistle B the Corinthians had resolved
οὐ μόνον τὸ ποιῆσαι ἀλλὰ καὶ τὸ θέλειν (II, 8:10), without having received more specific instructions from Paul or through Titus. Thus
Titus must have wrought τὴν χάριν ταύτην (II, 8:6) only later. Even if
one assumes that Paul first called attention to the collection at the
time of Epistle A, and then in a passage of this epistle that was excised
because of I, 16:1-2, or orally through Stephanas, about eight months
lie between the mention of the ἀπὸ πέρυσι and the time indicated
therewith. In view of this fact, the ἀπὸ πέρυσι is quite in place in the
joyful epistle, especially since in these eight months occurred all the
beginnings of the year customarily noted at that time except for the
Roman new year (see Windisch, p. 255). If one presupposes for Paul

---

Titus, who carries Epistle C with him, while on the fourteenth day the reports
arrive which prompt the sorrowful epistle. This calculation, which is altogether
possible in practice, may show that it is mistaken to reckon from the outset with
year-long intervals.

the Roman calendar with January 1 as the beginning of the year, as is generally done, then one must assume that already some time before Epistle A and independent of it Paul had initiated the collection, which of course is likely anyway, because he canvassed for the collection generally in Macedonia and Achaia, while Epistle A had as its occasion a quite specific matter which concerned only the Corinthians.

This connection appears to me the most probable one. If on the other hand one inserts another whole year, thus having Paul refer with the ἀπὸ πέρυσι to a point in time lying almost two years back which then is separated from the present by two changes in the year, the expression would be most unnatural.[44] Thus our calculation of the time given above is confirmed here as well.

97

IV. Paul's Opponents in Corinth

In the foregoing presentation we have deliberately refrained from going into detail on the question of Paul's opponents in Corinth. Here three important complexes of questions are to be suggested: 1. The number of opposing fronts; 2. Source and emergence of the opponents; and 3. The heretical theology in Corinth.

1. The Number of Opposing Fronts

The opinions of the exegetes are widely divergent on the question of whether Paul was battling against one, two, or even three different opposing groups. On this issue every opinion appeals to the passage I, 1:12: ἐγὼ μέν εἰμι Παύλου, ἐγὼ δὲ ᾿Απολλῶ, ἐγὼ δὲ Κηφᾶ, ἐγὼ δὲ Χριστοῦ. μεμέρισται ὁ Χριστός; It is regrettable that this verse stands right at the beginning of the Corinthian epistles, so that the exegetes for the most part are accustomed to deciding already here how many parties are actually to be assumed in Corinth; for this statement of the apostle not only *is* used as a basis for all the various theses, but it *can* be used as a basis for them all. In the context of the existing theses its interpretation is unrestricted. For this reason one must on principle leave I, 1:12 out of consideration in answering the question now being propounded. The meaning of this verse is rather to be determined conversely when the exegesis of the whole epistle has clarified the state of affairs underlying this passage also.

A provisional answer to our question, however, appears to me to be possible even now, before any detailed exegesis. According to our reckoning of the time set forth above, eight months lie between Paul's first intervention in the disputes in Corinth and the conclusion of them, i.e., about one year between their beginning and their end. It

is quite clear that Paul hears of σχίσματα in Corinth for the first time
at the time of Epistle A (I, 11:18), although during his stay in
Ephesus he certainly was not without occasional contact with Corinth.
It is equally clear that at the time of the joyful epistle the situation
was restored to his satisfaction. Thus the emergence of the false teachers
in Corinth forms an episode in the history of the community there
which can be set within narrow limits of time. It would be most unusual if two completely different heresies had been able to secure admission in the community at about the same time, and then similarly
had disappeared again at the same time. Thus Windisch (pp. 25-26)
distinguishes between "a pneumatic-Gnostic tendency which had
already developed in Corinth before the writing of I Cor. and an agitation by Jewish itinerant preachers which perhaps began before the
98   writing of I Cor. but first took an upsurge after I Cor." Such a remarkable coincidence naturally would be theoretically possible, but
it is obvious that it would be a more than rare accident. One could
arrive at such an assumption only if Paul's polemic were clearly directed against *two* opposing fronts. Whether this is the case can be
99   shown only by the further course of the work. At any rate such a
doubled battlefront is not *obvious*. In this point one may definitely
follow F. C. Baur. With his sure historical perception he recognized
that only *one* decisive conflict pervades the epistles, and he defended
this view even against his own pupils. Hence it must serve as a provisional assumption, and the most likely one, that Paul was fighting
100   and forcing into a retreat *one* opponent. The assertion that at the same
time three different groups took up a position against Paul and were
overthrown by him appears to me simply impossible. It is almost
comical when for example we read in Zahn:[45] "Throughout the entire
polemic against the followers of Peter (xi:1–xii:18) there are inter-
spersed apologetic remarks directed to the Christ party (xi:1, 16-21,
30; xii:1, 5-6, 11, 19). Hints of a defensive character directed against
the Apollos followers occur only incidentally (xi:6)" (!). Here as
elsewhere during the painstaking exegetical detailed work Zahn overlooks the larger context, and in the light of all that has heretofore
been developed this context makes it appear inconceivable that three
different parties emerged and disappeared in Corinth simultaneously.
Yet it is natural if the individual members of the community in the
face of the invading opponents should have appealed to their respective
teachers, that is, to Paul, Apollos, and Peter. Therewith the single
101   character of the line of battle by no means needs to be obliterated.

[45] *Introduction*, p. 302.

2. Source and Emergence of the Opponents

If we summarize what we can deduce from the epistles about the origin and the outward emergence of the opponents, the result can be related to only *one* group. This of course is hardly ever contested. A second or even a third group would not even have been mentioned by Paul in any of these respects.

The opponents are of Jewish origin. Ἑβραῖοί εἰσιν; κἀγώ. Ἰσραηλῖταί εἰσιν; κἀγώ. σπέρμα Ἀβραάμ εἰσιν; κἀγώ (II, 11:22). Whether each of these designations is supposed to express a special nuance may be left undecided.[46] It is much more noteworthy that Paul does not say Ἰουδαῖοι. For him the Ἰουδαῖος is the Jew who holds to the patriarchal principles, who is diligent about his conduct ἐν τῷ Ἰουδαϊσμῷ (Gal. 1:14). Thus the opponents in Corinth appear not to have made a special boast of this conduct. When they call themselves Ἑβραῖοι with emphasis, they identify themselves thereby (in the broadest sense) as Palestinian Jews.[47] They may already have resided among the Diaspora, as was also the case with Paul, without having lost the inward and outward connection with the Palestinian homeland.

These Israelites have come into the community from without. Of course we learn this explicitly first in Epistle C, and even here quite incidentally from the remark that some have presented letters of recommendation to the community.[48] Thus we have to do here with "apostles," who, like Paul, traveled on missionary work but now of course did not (or at least not only) begin their preaching in synagogues (as did Peter) or among the Gentiles (as did Paul), but also in the Christian communities. In doing this they took along letters   102
of recommendation on their respective further travels (II, 3:1). If they have success, they boast ἐν ἀλλοτρίοις κόποις (II, 10:15). They ap-   103
parently do not let themselves be supported by the communities (II, 11:20; cf. 11:7; 12:13), and naturally they stress their apostolate (II, 11:5, 13; 12:11). These same opponents are certainly in mind in Epistle B also. For already here the apostle must defend his apostolate precisely as later against the superlative apostles (I, 9:1); already here the right to support is problematical (cf. I, 9:12 with II, 11:7, 20). The fact that in Epistle B he does not attack the new arrivals personally is explained by the fact that he himself does not know them in

[46] Cf. Windisch, pp. 350 ff.

[47] Cf. Lietzmann, *in loc.*; Kuhn in TDNT III: 365 ff.; W. Gutbrod, TDNT III: 104
390.

[48] That they came with very official letters of recommendation from the original community, as lately Käsemann again asserts ([1], pp. 44-45), is impossible, because in II, 3:1 Paul equates the letters given to them in Corinth with those which they had brought along.

any way and has only had an oral report about them from Chloe's people. The letter from Corinth appears not to have mentioned them explicitly. In this case it was requisite and sufficient to let the opponents note, by means of polemic on the issues, that they were meant. It is not surprising that at the time of Epistle A Paul obviously knows nothing of alien teachers in Corinth. In fact he is only superficially informed about the σχίσματα themselves, knows nothing about their background, and addresses himself only to the apparently paganizing disturbances which are visible from without.

The course of the debate between Paul and his opponents is, in brief, that Paul opposes their innovations in cultus and doctrine. Some in Corinth will not yield to him in this but very skillfully pass over to the attack by denying to Paul the office of apostle. Hesitantly and reluctantly Paul must also take his position on this level of discussion and prove that he fulfills all the conditions which the Corinthian schismatics propound for an apostle. Therewith his peculiar concern recedes altogether into the background. In the sorrowful epistle no specific problem of doctrine and of life is any longer treated. The presupposition for such is lacking, according to Paul's opinion. II, 12:20 ff. shows that he is indeed only thinking of creating this presupposition. The struggle ends with the community staying on the apostle's side. The opponents are suppressed. From II, 2:6 (ὑπὸ τῶν πλειόνων) one may perhaps infer that the opponents have not remained entirely unsuccessful. A small part of the community may have followed them, but then has already brought about a separation, since in the remaining joyful epistle and in Epistle E Paul bestows on the *whole* community his praise for obedience and for zeal for him.[49] Of course the "ὑπὸ τῶν πλειόνων" can also be connected with a special form of punishment for the evildoers, so that its interpretation must remain an open question.

---

[49] II, 9:15; cf. Schenkel, *Ecclesia Corinthia primaeva factionibus turbata*, p. 139.

THE HERETICAL THEOLOGY
IN CORINTH

I. The History of the Research

1. *The Various Theses*

It was the great F. C. Baur who evoked the more recent discussion about the character of Paul's opponents and also dominated in a sovereign way this discussion down to the beginning of our present century. In the setting of his *Tendenz* criticism, which, following Hegel's dialectical schema, represented the emergence of Catholicism as a synthesis of Jewish Christianity and Gentile Christianity, he attempted in various essays to prove the Jewish attitude of the Corin-   105 thian schismatics. Most of his pupils and successors recognized that individual features in Paul's characterization of the opponents are simply irreconcilable with an extremely Judaistic attitude on their part. For this reason they frequently assumed that there was in Corinth a second, moderated Jewish-Christian tendency against which also Paul was contending. To this second party then occasionally a more or less rationalizing or gnosticising tendency was attributed, unless one chose to make a third group responsible for this tendency. In an amazingly extensive body of literature this expanded Baurian thesis has been proposed in numerous modifications. Common to all the individual hypotheses of this tendency in interpretation is the assertion that the predominant current in opposition to Paul in Corinth bears explicitly Judaistic features.

In the face of this assertion supported by Baur's authority, the thesis first propounded with decisiveness by Schenkel, that Paul was arguing   106 with non-Judaistic Pneumatics, was not able to prevail, although de Wette, Godet, and others associated themselves with it.[1] It was not   107 until the labors of Lütgert and Schlatter (see Bibliography) that Baur's thesis was effectively assailed. These two scholars recognize in Corinth only *one* opponent, and that in fact, following Schenkel, a pneumatic-libertine Gnosticism.

---

[1] Cf. the presentation and criticism of this tendency of the research in Lütgert, *Freiheitspredigt und Schwarmgeister in Korinth*, pp. 41-47, along with the indication of the literature given there. A brief earlier summary in Godet's commentary, pp. 33 ff. Cf. also D. Georgi, [1], pp. 1 ff.

While around the turn of the century most scholars still regarded
Baur's assertion as convincing (cf. Heinrici, p. 18) and even as late
as 1924 Windisch could describe this opinion as "until quite recently
predominant" (p. 24), the picture has been greatly changed in the
meantime, largely through the work of the two scholars mentioned.
Today it is characterized by an indecisive alternation between the individual extremes or by corresponding compromise solutions. Windisch's solution of the problem which was quoted earlier (p. 114)
may serve as typical of this situation. To it, however, must be added
the distinctive point: "Now . . . a closer connection of the two tendencies, thus a judaizing Gnosticism or a Gnostic Judaism, is not an
impossibility. Thus it would be possible that in Corinth also in the
course of time a certain assimilation of the two groups emerged . . . ."
This solution (like Wendland's, Lietzmann's, and others), which obviously represents more of a synthesis of the existing results of research
which leaves open all the possibilities than the results of a careful
exegesis, is not satisfactory. As has already been stated, it would be
more than strange if the Corinthian correspondence did not, like
Colossians, Galatians, I John, etc., exhibit a single polemical battlefront. Now if Paul is fighting only *one* opponent in Corinth—and we
presuppose this so long as the exegesis does not force us to the contrary
view—then the brief outline given here of the studies on our theme
can show that either a judaizing heresy akin to the Galatian stream or
a group of Pneumatics who somehow are to be described more precisely, possibly of Jewish (not judaizing; cf. p. 294) observance, has
invaded the Corinthian community.

2. The Untenability of Baur's Thesis

Now there is probably no assertion in theological-critical research
that has been defended with greater certainty and wider distribution
and at the same time with less evidence[2] than the assertion that in
the Corinthian epistles Paul is dealing with Judaizers. The heretics in
Corinth are supposed to have been Judaizers *although* Paul does not
slip into anti-Judaistic polemics with a single word; *although* not a
single passage in the epistles allows us to conclude with certainty or
even with some probability a Judaistic attitude of those who have invaded Corinth;[3] *although* it is conceded that these false teachers have

[2] Cf. in particular on the criticism Lütgert, pp. 49 ff., 65-66.

[3] On II, 11:22 see below; II, 3:1 could say something in favor of the theory about
Judaizers only if there were letters among Judaizers only. On II, 11:4 it must be
said that Paul in no way indicates that the other Jesus, the other Spirit, and the
other gospel are marked with a Judaistic stamp; that in II, 11:5, 13, Paul should
have abused the Jerusalem apostles is utterly impossible, especially since at the

even neglected the proclamation of their false teaching in the decisive points,[4] *although* they would have had every reason—especially after the experiences in Galatia—to win the community for their views *before* Paul's intervention; *although* Paul nonetheless polemicizes in several letters (A–E) against their false teaching, which must therefore have been well enough known to him; *although* this polemic exhibits features which certainly rule out the Judaistic character of the opponents; *although* one then would have to regard Paul simply as obtuse if even after his personal sojourn in Corinth he did not perceive the actual intentions of his enemies; *although* it has long been recognized that in Jesus' time Judaism was a religion so much caught up in syncretism that "Hebrews" could also disseminate all sorts of other tendencies than purely Pharisaic, "Judaizing" (II, 11:22). Although one has to wonder then how anyone could even get the idea that Judaizers *could* have emerged in Corinth, there is nevertheless no doubt in many minds that there *were* Judaizers.

Still it is possible to elicit a certain understanding for the fact that the "Judaists" theory was held within the Tübingen school. Here the studies from the first stood under the sign of Baur's construction of history. And since this construction ruled out other significant phenomena in primitive Christianity besides Gentile Christianity and Jewish Christianity, one was simply compelled to characterize the Corinthian heresy as Judaistic. It is true that this necessity became a virtue for the Tübingen school, since the Judaizers in Corinth now could be adduced conversely as evidence of the wide distribution of Jewish Christianity.

But to me it is utterly incomprehensible that also outside the Tübingen school, where the presuppositions of Baur's *Tendenz* criticism were not given, people have not dissented from this theory, for unprejudiced exegesis cannot at all lead in this direction, which has no sort of support in the text. One wonders whether the great advantage in Baur's hypothesis, that the events in Corinth did not need to be considered in isolation but could be placed in the context of the judaizing agitation known elsewhere, was the real reason that the

---

same time he is gathering an offering for them in Corinth with the greatest personal involvement. II, 10:7 also proves nothing. It is not true that the midrash in II, 3:7 ff. is a polemic against the righteousness that is of the law; in details it is not at all polemical. Finally, in II, 11:15, "servants of righteousness" is a title of honor which Paul never could have given in this way to Judaizers who sought to produce righteousness by the fulfilling of the law.

[4] "There is actually nothing in them [the Corinthian epistles] from which it could be concluded that the major difference between Paul and his opponents was related to the extreme dependence of the latter on the Mosaic law, as one . . . should expect" (Baur, "Die Christuspartei in der korinthischen Gemeinde," *Tübinger Zeitschrift*, 1831, 4. Heft, p. 78).

thesis was held. Hardly, for it was also held by other scholars, for example by Reitzenstein,[5] who recognized and described other forms of manifestation of early Christianity besides Paulinism and Judaism. Was it the authority of Baur which extended beyond all boundaries of a school? It could hardly still be that *today*.

The question may be left open. In conclusion, however, I should like here to affirm one point: The thesis that in his letters to Corinth Paul is dealing with Judaizers is to be abandoned without reservation, in whatever form and with whatever dilution it may be proposed. For this reason I shall not consider it in the further course of the work, even though in the most recent research this assertion encounters not inconsiderable resistance. In Lietzmann,[6] Kümmel remarks: "The conclusion is . . . that Paul's opponents in Corinth were Palestinian Jews, . . . thus (*sic*) Judaists." [7] Käsemann[8] also considers them to be emissaries of the original community, even if with a pneumatic—not Gnostic—tendency. They come to Corinth under an official commission in order to test the legitimacy of the Pauline apostolate on the basic of a standard issued in Jerusalem, whose exact contents even Käsemann is not able to specify. He can base his thesis only on II, 10–13 and must refrain from trying to prove that it is confirmed also in the rest of the correspondence.[9] Furthermore, his assertion stands on the slenderest exegetical basis even in II, 10–13, and Bultmann[10] has shown the untenability of that basis. And what the text itself does not cover can be demonstrated neither with Gal. 1–2, Acts 15, and views of contemporary Judaism, nor with a reference to the verse II, 5:16, which has always been used to support all the various theories. Precisely the thesis of the Pneumatics *kat' exochen* as official envoys of the original community (!) shows that it cannot succeed exegetically to justify the assertion that somehow Paul's opponents in Corinth are Judaizers.

3. Lütgert and Schlatter

An exegetical foundation is not however to be denied the counterthesis. Libertine pneumatic spirituality and gnosticizing perfectionism can be demonstrated for Corinth in numerous passages in the Corinthian epistles. This is not even disputed any longer. If, in spite of

---

[5] [1] (3rd ed.) , pp. 368-69, *et passim*.

[6] Lietzmann, Commentary (4th ed.) , p. 211 on II, 11:22*a*.

[7] Similarly Schoeps, *Theologie und Geschichte des Judenchristentums*, p. 449.

[8] "Die Legitimität des Apostels," ZNW, 1942.

[9] Cf. e.g., on I Cor.: "Nowhere in the New Testament is the practice and thought of Gnostic Pneumatics more thoroughly and more clearly portrayed for us than in I Cor., which can be grasped only in terms of the debate with them" (E. Käsemann, "Der Anteil der Frau an der Wortverkündigung nach dem Neuen Testament," 1941; lecture, duplicated in typescript) . Also, Käsemann in ZThK 54 (1957) : 18-19.

[10] [1], pp. 20-30. Cf. G. Bornkamm, [1], p. 15; D. Georgi, [1], *passim*.

that, the Lütgert-Schlatter construction found little unrestrained applause, the reason is not in the last analysis because of the deficiencies of this thesis, which are presently to be set forth.

Lütgert's study of the *Freiheitspredigt und Schwarmgeister in* 108 *Korinth* (The Preaching of Liberty and the Enthusiasts in Corinth) is distinguished by an excellent critique of Baur's thesis. Its inner contradictions are as convincingly set forth as is its defective foundation. The fact that this critique generally received no recognition, or only a divided recognition, is due to the fact that Lütgert's positive assertions exhibit deficiencies which forbid the recognition of it as a solution of the problem under discussion. One must acknowledge that Lütgert did not seriously misrepresent the position of the Corinthian heretics. His mistake is that he has failed in the necessary *sharpness* in characterizing Paul's opponents. He regards them as Pneumatics without making it clear how they proclaim *another* Pneuma than does Paul (II, 11:4). They are "Christ people," but Lütgert is not able to explain with what right and with what justification they appeal as Pneumatics to Christ in an exclusive and *so* emphatic a manner that they receive thence their party name (I, 1:12; II, 10:7; II, 11:23). They are Gnostics who reject the "folly of the cross" and in its place proclaim a wisdom which is strictly in contradiction with the preaching of Paul's gospel. But what is the content of this Gnosis, and how it is a gospel that saves, even if it is "another gospel" (II, 11:4), or in what connection the "boasting" of the Pneumatics stands with the stressing of the Gnosis—these are questions to which Lütgert is not able to give a satisfactory answer.

Thus the Corinthian heresy appears as a hyper-Pauline enthusiasm which lacks any system, as a product of disintegration of the Pauline kerygma in the Hellenistic setting and under Hellenistic influence. To be sure we must acknowledge that the phenomenon of Gnosticism in Corinth *as Lütgert sees it* can be made comprehensible throughout as a deteriorating Paulinism; but it is incomprehensible that such a product of disintegration could assume a shape so compact, forceful, and persuasive as was the case in Corinth. Further, Lütgert must wholly suppress the fact that the heresy took its rise in Corinth from a movement which came, organized, and conducted its missionary work from without. And above all, his failure is that his description of the "Gnostics" in Corinth is not adequate. If Lütgert had made the effort to grasp the pneuma, the gospel, the Gnosis, the Jesus, etc., of the Corinthian schismatics in their *opposition* to the Pauline proclamation which was strongly sensed by Paul himself, and not only in their special hyper-Pauline tendency, then he would have realized the impossibility of understanding the heresy of the Corinthians as a

109   distortion, developed *ad hoc,* of the message preached by Paul. More
than anything else it was probably Lütgert's disregard of the fundamentally different character of the Gnostic preaching in Corinth and
therewith the lack of an explanation for its origin and its abode,
thus the failure to place it in context in the historical phenomena of
the early Christian period, that caused his thesis to receive little
unrestrained recognition.

Schlatter's characterization of the Corinthian heresy is correct on
the essential points and above all is more thorough than that of
Lütgert. It is true that in his basic essay, *Die korinthische Theologie,*
he neglects to account for the outward relationship between Paul
and the Corinthian community and thereby is misled into regarding
the Corinthians simply as heretics, so that he sees polemical comments
even where Paul does not at all have his opponents in view. Also
mistaken, but not decisive for the total picture, is the attempt to see
in the cry "ὑπὲρ ἃ γέγραπται" (I, 4:6) the basic thesis of the Corin-
110   thian schismatics. For the most part it has a very awkward effect when
Schlatter subsumes the various false teachings and manners of conduct
of the Corinthians under this slogan. An unobjectionable pertinent
understanding of I, 4:6 is hardly ever to be found,[11] and against
Schlatter's exposition (explicitly argued by Stauffer in Zahn's *Kommentar* [1936], *in loc.*) there is the decisive argument that nowhere else
does Paul know anything of his opponents' denying the authority of
the Old Testament by disregarding it, but his natural handling of
scriptural proof rather rules this out. What is decisive, however, is
that Schlatter demonstrates no sort of concession to Baur's thesis. The
heretics in Corinth are libertine Pneumatics. The position of Lütgert
is deliberately adopted. At the same time, however, Schlatter also
acknowledges its basic weakness: "When Lütgert's presentation of the
Corinthian 'enthusiasts' evoked scorn from H. Holtzmann and his
friends, this was not to be attributed solely to a dogmatic reinforce-
ment of Baur's picture of the history, which knew only the Pharisaic

---

[11] P. Wallis has recently set forth (in TLZ, 1950, p. 506) an attempt at interpretation, as interesting as it is untenable, which in its punctuation acrobatics
would have done honor to K. v. Hofmann.

111   The only real solution of the *crux* in I, 4:6 is that original proposal of Baljon
to excise τὸ μή ὑπὲρ ἃ γέγραπται as a copyist's remark. The copyist found in his
copy the μή of the second ἵνα clause added above the εἷς (= α) or above the α of
the ἵνα and made a note of this in the margin of the copy he was making. This
comment then made its way into the text. In this way in fact the text is splendidly
restored and its distortion is sensibly explained. All other conjectures fail to satisfy
in at least one of these respects. Of course J. Weiss (*in loc.*) thinks that such
attempts would "never be taken seriously by the critics," but to me it is questionable
whether the assertion that the corrupted text has accidentally acquired the striking
form discovered by Baljon has any more right to be taken seriously.

Jews and reduced the richly diverse movement of primitive Christian history to the only poorly comprehended opposition of Pharisaic Judaism to Paul, but to the gaps which Lütgert's presentation left open. His 'enthusiasts' proceed from Paul and go beyond him in such a way that Pauline liberty degenerates into licentiousness, and, parallel with that, in the place of Pauline faith, Gnosis appears. But Paul's opponents in Corinth are Jews, convinced of the advantage which is possessed by the seed of Abraham. This much is sure, that the opposition to Paul in Corinth did not develop out of Paulinism, does not represent a continuation or extension of the Pauline community, but has been brought into it from without by those whose religious history followed a course independent of Paul and was moved by Jewish motives" ([1], pp. 35-36) .

Now of course Schlatter himself derives the heretical theology from Palestinian Judaism in an untenable way. It would take us too far afield and would not be at all rewarding to subject his statements to a detailed criticism here. It is surely an attempt that is hopeless from the outset to demonstrate that the sexual libertinism and the eating of meat sacrificed to idols, the pneumatic endowment as well as the stressing of Gnosis, are much more readily to be derived from Palestinian Judaism than from any religious manifestation of Hellenism. To a considerable extent Schlatter is able to offer nothing but hypothetical constructions. In this connection it is interesting that he refrains from adducing parallels from Alexandrianism or any gnosticizing Judaism. He wishes to derive the Gnostic theology directly from the Pharisaic theology. Here his often fruitful but basically narrow one-sidedness in New Testament exegesis goes head over heels in its denial of all Hellenistic influences. The fact that even for Schlatter the Corinthian heresy exists in isolation and not only developed through a masterly leap of Palestinian Judaism across a vast abyss into pneumatic-libertine Gnosticism but also disappeared again without a trace does not trouble Schlatter in his "derivation." Basically his solution of the problem signifies a backward step from Lütgert, who had indeed recognized the essentially non-Jewish spirit of the theologians in Corinth. It is no wonder that his thesis has encountered general rejection. But it is regrettable that with it people have also rejected his presentation of the heretical theology in large measure and have stayed with Baur's construction, which indeed on sober reflection is not to be reconciled with the Corinthian heresy, but instead does possess the advantage of being self-contained and complete in itself.[12]

---

[12] *Contra* J. Schniewind (*Nachgelassene Reden und Aufsätze* [1952], p. 114) : Paul's opponents in Corinth are Gnostics. Everything which Paul is fighting in the

In the following now we give an independent, exegetically based answer to the question of what theology the opponents of Paul in Corinth represented. In this undertaking we presuppose, on the basis of what has already been said, that Paul faces a *single* battlefront. But we also presuppose that the contents of the epistles in the broadest scope somehow stand in connection with the discussion, *certainly* recognizable in numerous passages, between Paul and his opponents. In any case it would be arbitrary to exclude from our study at the outset certain parts of our epistles. Since Paul only begins writing on the occasion of conflicts in Corinth and after their settlement, in the joyful letter, no longer treats concrete conditions in Corinth, it is rather to be assumed that all the problems discussed by Paul also are connected with those conflicts, especially since this fact is evident in the sorrowful epistle. If this presupposition should be inappropriate in particular instances, that would have to be shown from case to case.

II. The Corinthian Christology

1. I, 12:1-3

We begin with an investigation of a brief section, I, 12:1-3, and in fact especially vs. 3. The conception of the pneuma in Corinth in general will be considered only later. Our section stands in Epistle B, in the larger context in which Paul answers the community's letter, and indeed Paul begins here with περὶ δὲ τῶν πνευματικῶν the treatment of a new theme. Thus what follows has reference to events in the Corinthian community.[13] Here some obviously in pneumatic speech, and thus surely in the assembly of the community, must have said "ἀνάθεμα 'Ιησοῦς." The community is not sure as to whether such an expression could occur ἐν πνεύματι θεοῦ and requests Paul to give information on the matter.

So much for the outward course of events. It is almost universally acknowledged that this is the way matters stood, so that we need no

---

Corinthian epistles may be understood in unitary fashion in terms of the battle against Gnosticism. Gnosticism is "older than Christianity." Similarly now for a long time R. Bultmann in his lectures (see TDNT I: 709), E. Fuchs, and others, though heretofore the Gnosticism in Corinth has not been consistently investigated under the presupposition that Gnosticism is pre-Pauline and pre-Christian.

[13] It would be the height of banality to say that Paul of his own accord arrives at the idea of telling the Corinthians, who had asked only quite generally for information about the gifts of the Spirit in the community, that in their assemblies no one who wishes to speak in the πνεῦμα θεοῦ may say ἀνάθεμα 'Ιησοῦς. Even if such an inquiry had in mind the pneumatic phenomena in general, and thus also the pagan ones, this distinguishing mark would be as obvious as superfluous, quite apart from the fact that chaps. 12-14 are thinking *exclusively* of the assembled congregation, not at all of the phenomenon of spiritual endowment.

longer tarry at this point. Indeed the text allows us no other interpretation at all. At the most one can ask whether the community's letter also somewhere mentioned the term κύριος 'Ιησοῦς. I should not assume so, since this primitive Christian confession appears in no way problematical. Paul will rather have set forth more sharply the negation in the first part in itself by means of a positive statement in the latter part of the verse.

Who, we now may ask, can have cried out "ἀνάθεμα 'Ιησοῦς" in the assembly of the community? The most obvious answer is: some non-Christian who takes part in the worship, also falls into ecstasy, but in this condition gives powerful expression to his rejection of the Christian faith by means of the ἀνάθεμα 'Ιησοῦς. It is attested in I, 14:23 that ἄπιστοι took part in pneumatically stimulated gatherings. Since ἀνάθεμα in the sense appearing here is only Jewish usage,[14] we should assume that Jews are involved. Schlatter thinks accordingly that here Paul is referring to the synagogue's denunciation of Jesus.[15] But the cursing must have occurred in the Christian service of worship. Then the reaction of the community to these incidents nevertheless is most unusual, indeed is in essence incomprehensible. It is considered possible in the very community which is founded upon the confession κύριος 'Ιησοῦς that an unbaptized Jew curses Jesus ἐν πνεύματι θεοῦ, and Paul is asked in the most official way how this is the case. If this actually did develop in this way, the community in Corinth must in a real sense have consisted of νήπιοι (I, 3:1), not only of νήπιοι ἐν Χριστῷ. I consider such an occurrence to be ruled out as a possibility.

Now of course some explain that for the Corinthians ecstasy as such appeared to prove an utterance ἐν πνεύματι θεοῦ and that for this reason their inquiry of Paul is understandable. But we must answer that such pneumatic manifestations as emerge in the community in Corinth are throughout not specifically Christian. They were widespread in the Hellenistic-syncretistic religions of the primitive Christian era and from that source only temporarily found admittance into the early church. This can be abundantly documented.[16] Precisely Corinth was a converging point of all possible kinds of cults, among them those of Isis, of Serapis, and of Melikertes (Paus. II, 1.3; 2.3; 4.7). The consciousness that heaven and earth are filled with θεοί and κύριοι which dwell in men as πνεύματα or impersonally as πνεῦμα was common not only to the *uneducated* men of that time and is

[14] J. Behm in TDNT I: 354; Lietzmann on Rom. 9:3; Kümmel in Lietzmann's Commentary on Corinthians, p. 61, l. 12.

[15] For other mistaken attempts at explanation, see Kümmel in Lietzmann's Commentary on Corinthians, p. 61, l. 12.

[16] Cf. in Lietzmann's Commentary the excursus on speaking in tongues and the bibliography given there.

presupposed even by Paul (I, 8:5). Admonitions to test the spirits
and to distinguish among them emerge everywhere. I recall only
I John 4:1: 'Αγαπητοί, μὴ παντὶ πνεύματι πιστεύετε, ἀλλὰ δοκιμάζετε
τὰ πνεύματα εἰ ἐκ τοῦ θεοῦ ἐστιν. Here in I John what we have is not
a late development; for Paul also presupposes "the gift of recognizing
whether it is the divine or the human or a demonic spirit that speaks
forth from the enraptured one" (Lietzmann, *An die Korinther,* p. 61)
as something self-evident and well known to the Corinthians, when
he speaks of the διακρίσεις πνευμάτων (I, 12:10) .[17] Even if some naïve
Corinthians out of amazement over the unaccustomed pneumatic manifestations had regarded these *eo ipso* and thus unconditionally Christian, so that to them even the ἀνάθεμα 'Ιησοῦς of unbaptized Jews
could appear as the cry of the Christ speaking in them (II, 13:3),
still it is utterly inconceivable that the community in all seriousness
wrote to Paul in this sense.

But in any case the situation is such that the community has
reservations about denying the Christianity of the ecstatics, even
though they curse Jesus. Thus they must with good reason have appeared to her as Christians. Since the pneumatic endowment as such
did not assure their Christianity even in the eyes of the Corinthians,
one is compelled to admit that we are dealing here with people whose
confession of Christ, in spite of the curses pronounced against Jesus,
could not be flatly denied. Only under this assumption does the com-
116   munity's question make sense at all.

But how could a good Christian curse Jesus? Some have indeed
thought that during the ecstasy, conceptions from the pre-Christian
period which had been suppressed were released from the subconscious.
But this appears to me to be a somewhat questionable use of modern
psychoanalysis. Yet even granting that a member of the community
in ecstasy cries out ἀνάθεμα 'Ιησοῦς from some sort of complexes of
the subconscious, still nothing is gained thereby for the solution of our
problem. For if the Jesus who was cursed was the preached and cul-
tically venerated Kyrios, the question as to whether such a curse can
be spoken in the πνεῦμα θεοῦ is incomprehensible in *any* case. As little
as a congregation of today whose preacher entered the pulpit and spoke
against Christ in the worst terms and cursed him would inquire at the
meeting of the synod whether this preacher had indeed spoken in a
Christian way, just so little could Jesus at that time be cursed, even
in the highest ecstatic excitement, and the hearers still regard it as
possible that this curse is spoken in the name of God, the Father of

---

[17] Cf. I, 14:37. Otherwise, of course, Did. 11.7.

the one cursed, even according to however profound a set of theological and psychoanalytical reflections.

This, since in no case could ecstasy excuse a cursing of Jesus on the part of baptized people, it is to be presumed that one certain understanding of Christianity—precisely the one disputed in Corinth—did not rule out an ἀνάθεμα 'Ιησοῦς. But since on the other hand no one at that time could have been called a Christian or could have appeared as such to the Corinthians without a confession of the proclaimed Christ, there results the paradoxical fact that there were in Corinth people for whom it was not a contradiction to confess the Χριστός and to cry ἀνάθεμα 'Ιησοῦς.

Now such "Christians" are in fact not unknown to us. They also appeared in the communities to which I John is addressed, and asserted ὅτι 'Ιησοῦς οὐκ ἔστιν ὁ χριστός (I John 2:22). Naturally a Jew could also make this assertion, but the pseudo-prophets (I John 4:1) against whom I John is directed did not at all deny that the Messiah had already appeared. When they denied Jesus, they were only disputing that the Messiah had come "in the flesh" (4:2). Thus they were Gnostics who rejected a close connection between the heavenly Pneuma-Christ and the man Jesus. They apparently held the teaching that Christ had taken up residence in Jesus at the baptism, yet without thereby having been bound up with the flesh of the latter. This emerges in I John 5:6. Thus they confessed Christ, but not Jesus as the Christ, and must have given this a sharp emphasis over against the church's teaching.

But now it is Gnostics of a similar sort *also* who cry out ἀνάθεμα 'Ιησοῦς in Corinth in the congregational gatherings. Since because of the ἀνάθεμα (see p. 50) it probably was a group of Jews involved here, these were surely the Hebrews of II, 11:22 whom Paul later so personally fought. They qualify as Christians, i.e., they confess "Christ," whom Paul proclaims as the Son of God. But that this Christ is born ἐκ γυναικός (Gal. 4:4), that he thus is ὁ 'Ιησοῦς—this they deny, and in ecstasy they express this denial in the harsh words ἀνάθεμα 'Ιησοῦς.

That the community asks Paul for information in *this* case is understandable. Still it appears on this question to have been a matter only of a doctrinal dispute within the church. Perhaps people in Corinth would have taken no offense at all at the Gnostic thesis if it had been propounded only ἐν νοΐ; for the distinction of Χριστός κατὰ σάρκα and Χριστός κατὰ πνεῦμα is familiar to Paul also,[18] and for this reason is

[18] Rom. 1:3; 9:5; cf. also the following Excursus. In making this distinction Paul undoubtedly stands in the Gnostic tradition. Of course he was guarded against any ἀνάθεμα 'Ιησοῦς by the fact that the cross of Christ stood at the very center of

to be presupposed for the Corinthian community. Only the ecstatic ἀνάθεμα Ἰησοῦς, which made a sharp separation out of the distinction and with the radical rejection of the cross contained therein overturned the base of the Pauline theology, will have appeared to them doubtful. We do not know how the inquiry of the Corinthians was framed. We cannot even say whether Paul understood that the cursing of Jesus applied only to the Χριστὸς κατὰ σάρκα, although I should assume that he did. In any case it is to be assumed that the question was also discussed in Corinth ἐν νοΐ, so that there people quite correctly understood the curse as an anathematizing of the earthly manifestation of the redeemer. Otherwise the inquiry to Paul would still be incom-

119   prehensible. The evidence for such a doctrinal treatment of the problem is not difficult to produce.

120   But first let us present still another interesting parallel to the ἀνάθεμα Ἰησοῦς from later Gnosticism. In his debate with Celsus, Origen tells (*Contra Celsum* VI, 28 = Koetschau II, 98.19) of Gnostics who "admit no one to their fellowship who has not first cursed Jesus." [19] He wants to prove that these people (the ones involved are the Ophites, whose doctrines Celsus was citing as Christian in his polemic against Christianity) in no case can be Christians since in fact they curse Jesus. But in this he is undoubtedly incorrect. The Ophites of course regarded themselves as Christians, and consequently one cannot make any accusation against Celsus when he adduces their speculations in the presentation of Christianity. Since he was personally acquainted with the Gnostics, there can be no doubt on this point. Thus the curse did not apply to the heavenly Pneuma-Christ but to his earthly dwelling, the *man Jesus*. It was the custom in one Ophite sect to admit no one who had not first cursed this Jesus, probably with the intention—and to this extent Origen was correct in his protest against Celsus—of erecting a clear barrier to the catholic church. One does not need to assume that there were direct connections between the Ophites of Celsus and the Corinthian Gnostics. But this much may

121   be certain, that *both* cases of cursing are to be ascribed to the basic tendency of Gnostic Christology, sharply to separate the man Jesus and the heavenly spiritual being Christ, and to regard the former as without significance.[20]

Irenaeus I, 31.1 offers a convenient parallel *in substance* to the Gnos-

---

his theology. But for the rest the Pauline Christology makes use of the Gnostic schema.

[19] "ἐὰν μὴ ἀρὰς θῆται κατὰ τοῦ Ἰησοῦ."

[20] People may have appealed here to a passage like Deut. 21:23 as an exegetical basis for such anathematizing: κεκατηραμένος ὑπὸ θεοῦ πᾶς κρεμάμενος ἐπὶ ξύλου. The Corinthian Gnostics could even refer with some justification to utterances of Paul such as Gal. 3:13.

tic ἀνάθεμα in a note about the Cainites. These confess Esau, Korah, 122
the Sodomites, and others in whom the creator God, in spite of his
hatred, could not find any weakness, since the Sophia took to herself
the celestial part which stemmed from her. The betrayer Judas also
knew this, they teach, "*et solum prae ceteris cognoscentem veritatem,
perfecisse proditionis mysterium; per quem et terrena et caelestia
omnia dissoluta dicunt.*" Thus here the betrayal of Jesus as the sarkic
part of the redeemer is glorified similarly to the cursing of him.
Parallels of this kind can be brought forward in abundance. The rejection of the Χριστὸς κατὰ σάρκα was expressed in various ways, some
stronger, some weaker. But it should be unnecessary here to adduce
further quotations for the presentation of the generally familiar Gnostic Christology.

The fact that in later Gnosticism people frequently were concerned
also somehow to make a positive evaluation of the man Jesus is to be
traced back to the influence of the Great Church. The essential distinction between Jesus and Christ was steadily maintained, even if the
conceptual distinction was occasionally erased. Thus Irenaeus (III,
16.1) relates of the Valentinians: "They indeed confess with their
tongues one Christ Jesus, but they divide him in their teaching." But
these later developments do not alter the fact that the man Jesus who
was born of Mary and into whom the celestial Christ, without flesh
and impassible (cf. Iren. III, 16.8), has descended, is for the genuine
Gnostic deserving of scorn and therefore can be cursed confidently. A
positive attitude toward him would be a sign that the person making
such a judgment still is living under the power of the evil world (cf.
Iren. I, 24.4). Thus the Christology of the Corinthian "Christians"
which is expressed in the ἀνάθεμα Ἰησοῦς in I, 12:3 is the genuinely
Gnostic Christology.[21]

[21] I was somewhat surprised when, long after completing the present work, I
found in the old commentary by F. Godet (1886) an exposition of I, 12.3 which
corresponds to that given above even down to details. After lengthy consideration
of the passage, Godet asks: "Must we therefore assume that Paul regarded it as
possible that such talk was being uttered in the community itself?" (p. 110). He
answers this question in the affirmative, asks further: "But how could this happen
in a Christian community?" and then points out "how strong was the ferment of
religious ideas which was produced at that time by Christianity." This means Gnosticism, even though the expression is not used. One "must remember that from the
first century on there were people who could not tolerate the idea of the shameful
death on the cross and the unheard-of humiliation of the Son of God and who
therefore thought it necessary to make a distinction between the man Jesus and
the true Christ." It is true that here we have in Godet a historically very defective
picture of Gnosticism, but his argument remains unaffected thereby: "We can
understand how in such views it was possible to curse the crucified one, who indeed
appeared to have been cursed by God himself on the cross, without one's intending
thereby to curse the real Christ and the real redeemer, and without one's having

In conclusion it may be pointed out that the Jesus of the Gnostics in Corinth was the same historical person who was venerated by the primitive church as Lord. A pure Docetism is ruled out by the personal execration just as it is by the general consideration that in a time when there still were numerous people living who had known Jesus personally, the reality of his earthly appearing could not be denied. And the statement of Valentinus that Jesus was a being of the psychical world of aeons which exists between *Sarx* and *Pneuma* is a late attempt to evade the ἀνάθεμα ᾿Ιησοῦς without however coming into conflict with the basic Gnostic dogma, the rejection of the sarkical sphere.

Excursus: Paul's Use of the Name "Jesus"

For the continuation of our work, clarity as to the use of the bare name "Jesus" in Paul's works is essential. Since I do not know of an adequate investigation of this subject, the aspects necessary for our purposes are to be set down here briefly.

124

In the undoubtedly genuine Pauline epistles (Romans, I and II Corinthians, Galatians, Philippians, Philemon, I Thessalonians) I count twenty-eight passages in which the name "Jesus" is found without the appositive "Christ." From these we exclude, for a determination of Paul's personal usage, the passages in which he is quoting formulas handed down to him verbatim. To these belong above all the combinations of ᾿Ιησοῦς with κύριος, thus κύριος ᾿Ιησοῦς, ᾿Ιησοῦς ὁ κύριος ἡμῶν, and similar forms. κύριος ᾿Ιησοῦς is a pre-Pauline confessional formula, as Rom. 10:9 and I, 12:3 show. Correspondingly, they are also found in sections which Paul has taken over as traditional material, for example in the account of the Lord's Supper in I, 11:23 and Rom. 4:24, where a confession of faith is reworked. After eliminat-

125

---

therefore any doubts as to whether one belonged to the Christian community." Godet also refers to the passage cited above from Origen's *Contra Celsum* and very perceptively observes: "Above all one must note the name Jesus, which denotes the Lord in his historical, earthly existence" (on this, cf. the following Excursus).

It is surprising that this "out-of-season" exegesis of Godet was noted by only very few of the later expositors but nowhere, so far as I can see, adopted (Schniewind appears to be an exception; see below). Of course this is due not least of all to Godet himself, who on the whole could not rid himself of the traditional evaluation of the partisan situation in Corinth, did not use his knowledge of I, 12:3 for the exegesis of the other sections of the epistles, and therefore understandably was not convincing even with his interpretation of this one verse. Godet's exposition, pursued entirely independently and proceeding from essentially different presuppositions, was for me a confirmation of the exegesis attempted above. Schniewind (*Nachgelassene Reden*, p. 115) remarks, with reference to I, 12:3, that Gnosticism in Corinth "apparently makes a distinction between the ἄνω Χριστός, the Spirit-Christ, and the κάτω ᾿Ιησοῦς, the earthly Jesus; it scorns Jesus' lowliness, the cross, the Lord's Supper."

123

ing these passages, there still remain thirteen, of which four more drop out as pre-Pauline. Phil. 2:10 belongs to the famous "Gnostic" Christ 126 hymn which Paul is quoting (cf. E. Lohmeyer, *Kommentar* on Phil., *in loc.*). In I Thess. 1:10 and 4:14 Ἰησοῦς occurs in traditional confessional formulas which appear similarly also in Rom. 4:24; 10:9; and I, 15:3-4. The fourth passage of this kind is I, 12:3*a*, where Paul is quoting his Gnostic opponents. Of the remaining nine passages, seven are found in II Cor. 4:5, 10-11, 14 (twice each in vss. 10 and 11), and 11:4. The occurrence of the bare name Jesus in these verses appears to me not to be accidental [22] but to be connected with the apostle's polemic against Corinthian opponents. In order to demonstrate this we must now first deduce from the two remaining passages—Gal. 6:17 and Rom. 8:11—in what special sense Paul uses the name Ἰησοῦς in isolation. The prefixed article shows that in both cases "Jesus" is not merely a proper name but a designation.

In the passage in Galatians Paul obviously is thinking of the appearing of Jesus in the flesh when he speaks of the στίγματα τοῦ Ἰησοῦ which he bears in his body. Thus Ἰησοῦς here is the Χριστὸς κατὰ σάρκα of Rom. 9:5 or Rom. 1:3, who as such stands in a certain contrast to the heavenly being who, ἐν μορφῇ θεοῦ ὑπάρχων, humbled himself in earthly form.

The same specified use of "Jesus" however is present also in Rom. 8:11. The entire beginning of Rom. 8 speaks thoroughly gnostically of σάρξ and πνεῦμα. Any Gnostic would gladly accept at least vss. 5-10 as a precise exposition of his self-understanding. But for him even with vs. 10 everything would be said. The σῶμα is dead; *this* is his gospel. That Paul can add vs. 11 shows how little the preceding may be understood in a Gnostic sense. For the aim and climax of his whole presentation is indeed precisely this, that the θνητὸν σῶμα will live. The basis of this is the fact that τὸ πνεῦμα τοῦ ἐγείραντος τὸν Ἰησοῦν ἐκ νεκρῶν dwells in the believers. It is not the Pneuma as such that guarantees life but the fact that it is the Pneuma of the one who raised τὸν Ἰησοῦν from the dead. The resurrection of this Jesus allows the Pneumatic to have the certainty that even his θνητὸν σῶμα also is raised. The miracle which happened to Jesus will be repeated in him who already possesses the pledge of the Spirit. The direct parallel which exists in vs. 11 between ὁ Ἰησοῦς and τὰ θνητὰ σώματα is not to be overlooked. Paul puts the anticipated *bodily* resurrection of the believers in parallel with the resurrection of the *bodily* Christ, that is, of Jesus.

Thus we maintain as a conclusion that Paul just as much as the

[22] Cf. p. 163.

Gnostics in Corinth distinguished the Christ *kata sarka* as "Jesus" from the heavenly spiritual being. When he says Jesus, he means emphatically the earthly manifestation of the redeemer.[23] Of course this distinction is only one rudiment of the originally Gnostic conception. Paul is interested, in and for himself, only in the Christ *ensarkos*, whom he calls Jesus Christ, Christ, or, in traditional language, also 127 Kyrios Jesus. The influence of Gnosticism emerges only in that Paul in original statements never calls this God-man Jesus, but reserves this personal name for the designation of the earthly figure of the redeemer. Naturally this usage in no wise intends the Gnostic estimate of the same. No ἀνάθεμα is aimed at the Pauline Jesus. He is rather the one who, with his στίγματα (Gal. 6:17) and his ἀνάστασις (Rom. 8:11) is the ground of the apostle's faith and hope.

2. II, 11:4

We now must present the evidence that the Christology which is expressed in the ἀνάθεμα Ἰησοῦς was also discussed in Corinth ἐν νοΐ. In doing this we begin with II, 11:4. Because of the reading ἀνείχεσθε or ἠνείχεσθε beside the present ἀνέχεσθε, this verse causes great difficulties for the exegetes. The question is whether Paul is speaking here hypothetically or not. Textual criticism does not provide a conclusion. The context however can leave no doubt that people were actually tolerating the preaching of another Jesus, a strange Spirit, and a strange gospel. Verse 4 again takes up the figure of vs. 3, and in vs. 3 Paul is afraid that the Corinthians in actuality have already turned aside from their loyalty to Christ. He fears this for the very reason that they have been very well pleased (καλῶς) that another Jesus, et cetera, had been preached to them, but of course not because they *would* have been pleased, according to his opinion, *if* such alien doctrines had been proclaimed among them. We cannot see how Paul could come to such a suspicion and express it if no false doctrines were being disseminated in Corinth. If the Corinthians were pleased at personal attacks against Paul's apostolic authority, this in no way means that they would also

[23] This of course does not mean that Paul always, when he thought of the Christ κατὰ σάρκα, *had* to say Ἰησοῦς. Normally Paul did not distinguish at all in the figure of the incarnate Son of God, which for him was indivisible, between his pneumatic and his sarkic substance or person. Thus in Rom. 8:11, in the same verse "Jesus" can appear again as "Christ Jesus," without further ado, for Jesus of Nazareth of course is the Christ. Similarly in II, 4:5 Ἰησοῦς alternates with Χριστός (see p. 82). The Gnostic usage has an influence on Paul only to the extent that the divine-human figure of the redeemer never is given the human personal name "Jesus," which with Paul emphatically denotes only Jesus' earthly manifestation. Cf. also Foerster in TDNT III: 289, whose statement that with "Jesus" Paul is thinking in "special measure" of the "historical One" of course still says too little.

accept a non-Pauline gospel. If on the other hand a non-Pauline gospel was proclaimed, Paul would never have been able here to speak in terms of an unreal condition. But it is beyond all doubt that false teachings *were* being propounded in Corinth (cf. I, 15). That Paul here does not take a more definite stance with regard to them is explained by the whole thrust of the sorrowful epistle, which was first to produce the presuppositions for such a procedure (cf. pp. 221-22).

Thus our verse is meant in a real sense. When one disputed this, it was done contrary to the context of the passage usually because one was not able to reconcile the proclamation which the context presupposes with the sometimes prejudiced picture of the proclamation of the ἐρχόμενοι. Thus for example Windisch (p. 328), who however for philological reasons rightly holds to a realist understanding of the sentence, does not know exactly what to do with the passage, for "there is nowhere in Galatians (!!) a polemic against 'another Jesus' or even against 'another spirit.'"

If we ask first who represented the false teachings, it can only be the superlative apostles of vs. 5, behind whom Paul does not intend to take an inferior place, and who appear equally impersonally personified in the ἐρχόμενος in vs. 4 [24] (cf. 10:11. ὁ τοιοῦτος; 10:7. τις; 5:12. οἱ καυχώμενοι, and so on). They are the Ἑβραῖοι of 11:22 and thus also those who utter the ἀνάθεμα Ἰησοῦς. In short, they are *the* opponents of Paul in Corinth. They proclaim an ἄλλον Ἰησοῦν, a ἕτερον πνεῦμα, a ἕτερον εὐαγγέλιον. Even though ἄλλος and ἕτερος can be used interchangeably (Windisch, p. 327; cf. I, 12:9), still ἄλλος is throughout weaker than ἕτερος, which signifies a total strangeness and difference in character (cf. *ibid.*). Here the change in expression in this sense is well in place, since Spirit and gospel of the opponents according to Paul's opinion have nothing in common with *his* understanding of these words, but are totally alien, while the Jesus who is preached in

[24] Käsemann ([1], p. 42) disputes this: "How can Paul open up an unbridgeable gulf with respect to the false teachers by charging them . . . in 11:4 with having a different gospel, an alien Jesus and Spirit, only then to conclude that he is not less than they . . . . There can be no comparison with servants of Satan." But one cannot argue thus. Paul indeed is contending—under compulsion—with the Gnostics for the community, and in our passage he simply asserts that he has full right to call himself an apostle, and as regards Gnosis he is not inferior to the opponents. They have contested this. Thus Paul first quite generally places himself as an apostle *beside* them. This is the aim of all the forced (II, 12:11) boasting in II, 10–12. The question whether he did not actually stand above them could only be answered by an investigation of the actual content of the Gnosis, which however was not under discussion for him here. Only if Paul first at least qualifies for the community as an apostle on an equal footing *alongside* the Gnostics, and thus meets the Gnostic standard as he understands it—and it is precisely for this that he is concerned in the sorrowful epistle—can the question as to the authenticity of the apostolic *proclamation* rightly be answered (cf. R. Bultmann, [1], pp. 26-27).

Corinth naturally is the same Jesus of Nazareth whom Paul also proclaims, only that these proclaim this same Jesus as a different one.[25] If the expression is supposed to be exact, that cannot merely mean that people in Corinth preach something different *about* this Jesus. But what is the distinctive element in the proclamation of this "other Jesus"? [26]

The exegetes evade the understanding of the expression when they constantly without hesitation insert the name Christ for Jesus and then seek parallels in II, 10:7, 11:23, 5:16, etc. According to Schenkel, the ἄλλος ᾽Ιησοῦς is supposed to be precisely the *Christus spiritualis!* [27] But Paul indeed uses "Jesus" in a quite specific sense. For him Jesus is the Χριστὸς κατὰ σάρκα, and there must have been in Corinth such a teaching about this Jesus that he could appear to Paul as an ἄλλος ᾽Ιησοῦς. But this was the case if the Jesus who for Paul was one side, the physical side, of the Χριστὸς ἔνσαρκος which is encountered in the world, was regarded in Corinth as the execrable dwelling of the heavenly spiritual being. Then in the apostle's eyes Jesus is in fact being taught as an ἄλλος ᾽Ιησοῦς.[28]

[25] Anyone who thinks that in Paul's enumeration the three items are supposed simply to indicate completeness (Windisch, p. 327, among others, since under the presupposition that in II, 11:4 Judaizers are being characterized, one could not understand the three expressions as specific), so that in II, 11:4 the apostle meant to point out the whole of the perverted proclamation of his opponents, without reflecting on any particular content of the three parts, makes the exposition of the passage too easy for himself and in addition closes his mind to essential points of information about the nature of the Corinthian heretics. Such a simplification is impermissible because, as I, 12:3 and II, 4:7 ff. (see pp. 124 ff.; 163) show, ὁ ᾽Ιησοῦς, like the πνεῦμα (see pp. 167 ff.), was quite specifically under discussion, and it certainly is no accident that Paul speaks, as in Gal. 1:6, of the ἕτερον εὐαγγέλιον (see pp. 141 ff.).

[26] We shall speak later of the "other gospel" and the "other Spirit."

[27] Similarly Lütgert, pp. 62 ff. But then Paul would have been obliged to say, as elsewhere, "Christ," without any condition.

[28] R. Bultmann ([1], p. 25) writes: "That these gnosticizing Christ apostles are proclaiming an ἄλλος ᾽Ιησοῦς (11:4) is explained from the correlative relationship between gospel and apostolate. If Paul's apostolate is wrongly understood, then another, a false, Jesus is also proclaimed; for Jesus is rightly understood only when one sees that his ζωή is realized in θάνατος (4:7 ff.), his δύναμις in ἀσθένεια." The basic thought in this argument is certainly correct, but it contributes nothing to the explanation of 11:4. For it is impossible that the Corinthians were prompted by the mention in 11:4 of the "other Jesus" to reason things out as above, and then from this to recognize that a false Jesus was actually being proclaimed among them, especially if at the same time they held the false view of the apostolate to be the correct one. It must have been clear at once to the Corinthians that another Jesus, another gospel, and another Spirit were being proclaimed in Corinth. At any rate Paul assumes this as self-evident. But then it is true, conversely, that from the preaching of another Jesus a false understanding of the apostolate necessarily had to develop, namely from the elimination of the ἀσθένεια and the θάνατος ᾽Ιησοῦ the exclusive assertion of the δύναμις and the ζωή of the apostle. And this was actually

It follows then that at the time of the sorrowful epistle Paul has heard of the proclaiming of the Gnostic interpretation of Jesus in Corinth and mentions it first in the enumeration of the Gnostic heresies. This shows that the Gnostic Christology must also have been discussed in Corinth ἐν νοΐ. For if one notes that "Jesus" is not simply = Christ, but = Christ *kata sarka*, any other explanation of the ἄλλος   129 ʼΙησοῦς can hardly be offered. Even with the false assumption that by the "Jesus" in 11:4 the *Christus ensarkos* in general or even only the *Christus spiritualis* is to be understood, up to the present the effort to characterize the special nature of the "other Jesus" has not been successful; for indeed it is not to be overlooked that wherever Paul comes to speak of the belief in Christ of his opponents, he does not utter a polemic against that belief, but emphatically claims precisely the same as his own. One may compare from the same epistle II, 10:7; 11:23; and 13:3 ff. In the preaching of Christ, i.e. of the Χριστὸς κατὰ πνεῦμα, Paul obviously sensed *no* divisive difference. Whether he was correct in this remains to be seen.

It is difficult to say to what extent Paul had penetrated into the actual understanding of Gnostic Christology with its rejection of the man Jesus when he engaged in his polemic against the "other Jesus." At any rate he had not yet seen through it at the time of Epistle B, since otherwise in I, 12:3 he would not have been satisfied with the basically very banal answer to the question of the Corinthians, which of course was equally banally understood. A glance at II, 4:5-15 can show that later he was somewhat better informed. This section now would require precise investigation. In it are found the six passages not yet considered from the total of nine in which Paul uses the name "Jesus" alone in original language! This is certainly no accident but is grounded in the polemical aim of these verses. Of course it is possible to prove this in detail only when the anthropology of the Corinthian schismatics is recognized, since in the section in question the reference to the Χριστὸς κατὰ σάρκα is only the other side of the polemical statements of Paul about the ἔξω ἄνθρωπος, that is, the ἄνθρωπος κατὰ σάρκα.

3. The Cross

Therefore we pass over at once to a new problem which is closely connected with the preceding. The rejection of the fleshly exterior of the Χριστὸς ἔνσαρκος necessarily signifies the rejection of the σταυρός as a fact of salvation-history. The two cannot be separated and were never separated in Gnosticism. So far as the Gnostics held to a theologi-

---

Paul's opinion, as II, 13:4 shows. Thus Christology determines the understanding of the apostolate as well as of the Pauline theology in general, not vice versa.

cal significance of the cross,[29] an anathema was never aimed at the man
Jesus—no matter how thoroughgoing the dualism was. Conversely, a
disdain for his passion always ran parallel to the rejection of the man
Jesus. In this connection I refer again to I John, where the polemic
has preserved for us reports which are among the earliest that we
possess about Christian Gnosticism. This polemic is directed not only
against the rejection of the Χριστὸς κατὰ σάρκα but also against the
depreciation of his cross and suffering: οὗτός ἐστιν ὁ ἐλθὼν δι' ὕδατος καὶ
αἵματος, 'Ιησοῦς Χριστός. οὐκ ἐν τῷ ὕδατι μόνον, ἀλλ' ἐν τῷ ὕδατι καὶ
ἐν τῷ αἵματι (I John 5:6); that is, that Christ not only was connected
with Jesus in baptism but also suffered in flesh and blood. The opposite
view was held by Gnostics who, like Cerinthus, taught that "at the
end Christ left Jesus. Jesus suffered; Christ was impassible, since he
was the Pneuma of the Lord" (Hipp. X, 21 = Iren. I, 26.1). Polycarp
in his letter to the Philippians offers another clear documentation of
the common rejection of the incarnation and the cross. There, following I John 4:2-3, it is said: "Anyone who does not confess that Jesus
Christ has come in the flesh is an antichrist, and whoever does not
confess the testimony of the cross is of the devil" (7.1). The following
words also show that this is a polemic against the Gnostics: "And whoever twists the words of the Lord according to his own desires and
asserts that there is neither resurrection nor judgment, he is the firstborn of Satan." If in the Corinthian epistles Paul is addressing himself
to a Christology of the kind which is familiar to us from the anti-
Gnostic polemic of I John and of Polycarp, among other places, then
for his opponents who utter the ἀνάθεμα 'Ιησοῦς the proclamation of
the crucified Christ must have been offensive. And it was offensive to
them. The most comprehensive individual polemic of the apostle in
the two canonical Corinthian epistles is directed against the emptying
of the σταυρὸς Χριστοῦ. We are speaking of the section I, 1:17–2:5,
which is among the most important pieces of Pauline literature in
general. The polemical intention of these theological propositions becomes visible already in the fact that Paul does not proclaim the
λόγος τοῦ σταυροῦ simply as the message of salvation, but this stressing of the cross is connected with an explicit rejection of earthly wisdom as a way to salvation. Moreover, Paul in no way gives a more
specific exposition of the word of the cross. He rather presupposes a
knowledge of it. Therefore he is concerned with proving to the Corinthians that and why just this word which he has proclaimed to them

---

[29] There were such Gnostics in peculiar proximity to the Great Church from
the beginning on (cf. pp. 67-68; 299). According to Iren. I, 6.2 the Valentinians
teach that the death of Christ has significance for the Psychics, while the Pneumatics have no need of it.

and which is familiar to them is God's power εἰς σωτηρίαν, but not the Sophia which some are most recently preaching to them as the true gospel.   130

The apostle's statements on this theme begin very abruptly in I, 1:17.   131 The connection with what precedes is purely external. The actual connection with the preceding consists in the fact that in both passages Paul is censuring grievances in Corinth. He was conscious of the fact that with the statements about wisdom and the cross as foolishness he was speaking about the *motive* behind the previously treated conflicts in Corinth. Therefore in 3:3 he can again take up the earlier theme, once again of course with a very superficial transition which does not make clear the actual connection between the two themes. This is explained by the imperfect knowledge of the situation in Corinth which compels Paul to be cautious in writing. The *material* concern of the apostle nevertheless comes fully into play. In I, 1:17 it is almost thematically set forth. Paul proclaims the good news οὐκ ἐν σοφίᾳ λόγου, ἵνα μὴ κενωθῇ ὁ σταυρὸς τοῦ Χριστοῦ. The passage in 2:1-2 fully corresponds to this: Κἀγὼ ἐλθὼν πρὸς ὑμᾶς, ἀδελφοί, ἦλθον οὐ καθ' ὑπεροχὴν λόγου ἢ σοφίας καταγγέλλων ὑμῖν τὸ μαρτύριον τοῦ θεοῦ. οὐ γὰρ ἔκρινά τι εἰδέναι ἐν ὑμῖν εἰ μὴ 'Ιησοῦν Χριστὸν καὶ τοῦτον ἐσταυρωμένον, only that here in addition the prefixed κἀγώ makes clear the polemical aim of the whole set of statements against those who, ἐλθόντες εἰς Κόρινθον, do the opposite. These indeed also preach Christ, but not as the crucified one. The word of the cross is foolishness to them (1:18). This is consistent with their rejection of the Christ κατὰ σάρκα. As a Gnostic example one may compare also the classic passage   132 from Irenaeus' report about Basilides (I, 24.4): *"Et non oportere confiteri eum, qui sit crucifixus, sed eum qui in hominis forma venerit, et putatus sit crucifixus, . . . uti per dispositionem hanc opera mundi fabricatorum dissolveret. Si quis igitur, ait, confitetur crucifixum, adhuc hic servus est et sub potestate eorum qui corpora fecerunt; qui autem negaverit, liberatus est quidem ab iis, cognoscit autem dispositionem innati Patris."* This passage, which makes it clear wherein the foolishness of the cross of which Paul speaks consists for the Gnostics, also points to the cosmic background of the Gnostic Christology which will occupy us further in the course of the work. *Instead* of the cross the Corinthians know a wisdom which according to Paul's understanding has nothing more in common with the σοφία θεοῦ incarnate in Jesus Christ. He regards it as a wisdom of this world and of its demonic rulers (I, 2:6). This accounts for the apostle's heavy emphasis that among the Corinthians he has proclaimed *only* Jesus Christ, and him precisely—and this is *Paul's* wisdom—as the crucified one.

Some in Corinth were putting *in the place* of the cross a doctrine of

133 wisdom; they were not preaching the crucified Christ merely with special Sophia. Otherwise Paul would not have been able to say that to the others the cross was foolishness. Furthermore, he then would have been obliged to say that *he* had *not* proclaimed the cross καθ' ὑπεροχὴν λόγου ἤ σοφίας, but in more seemly fashion, while he still places value on the affirmation that with him the proclamation of the
134 cross occupies the *place* of the words of wisdom (I, 2:2). It is not uninteresting that in his letter to the Ephesians Ignatius quotes I, 1:20 ff., in part verbatim, when he conducts a polemic against the Gnostics (Ign. Eph. 18-19). He may have had the battlefront of I, 1 correctly identified.[30]

The Christology of the Corinthian schismatics thus shows itself upon closer examination to have been genuinely Gnostic. Jesus Christ is bluntly regarded dualistically. While people appeal with emphasis to Christ (e.g., in II, 10:7; 13:3), they are not interested in the man Jesus and can even curse him while in ecstasy. Thus however the saving significance of the cross also automatically comes to naught, "the cross is emptied" (I, 1:17) and replaced by a wisdom the nature of which
135 we must now investigate. All in all, the picture emerges of a pure
136 "Christian" Gnosis which has not yet been influenced by "ecclesiastical" Christianity. What significance the appeal to Christ has for this Gnosis can, for reasons yet to be set forth, be shown only in the investigation of the Gnostic anthropology; for the Gnosticism in Corinth—this much may be asserted here—*does not know Christ as a heavenly*
137 *redeemer figure.*

Of course this is contradicted decisively by the detailed investigation undertaken by U. Wilckens [1] of the concept σοφία in I, 1-2. According to him, in Corinth σοφία was a designation for the heavenly redeemer Christ. Wilckens correctly explains the fact that I have treated the section I, 1:17-3:3 more briefly than did he by the fact I have "not recognized the christological meaning of the concept 'Sophia'" (p. 213). Nevertheless I still am unable even now to recognize it.

At any rate *no* basis is offered for Wilckens' far-reaching thesis by the following sentence (on 1:18 ff.) : "Where (*sic!* When? While?) Paul so pointedly places the proclamation of the Χριστὸς ἐσταυρωμένος in opposition to the Sophia proclaimed in Corinth, there Sophia must have been a christological title of the exalted Christ" (p. 68). But in opposition to the σοφία Paul places, in I, 1:18, the *"word of the cross,"* in 1:21 "the *foolishness* of preaching," in 1:23 the *"foolishness* of the crucified Christ." By these concepts the σοφία of the Corinthians is clearly defined as an impersonal concept. Moreover, the paralleling of σημεῖα and σοφία in 1:22 rules out the personal interpretation of σοφία.

[30] Cf. Ign. Magn. 9.1; Trall. 9-10.

Nevertheless Wilckens attempts to prove his thesis explicitly on the basis of I, 2:6 ff.: in vss. 6 ff. σοφία signifies the eschatological blessing of salvation which God has prepared for the righteous. "This clearly follows from the text.[31] In 2:7 'wisdom' is proclaimed as a hidden mystery, as which God has predestined it for the glory of the perfect" ([1], p. 70). The *archons* of this world have not recognized this wisdom. For if they had recognized it, they would not have crucified the Lord of glory. "How are we to understand the relationship of θεοῦ σοφία and κύριος τῆς δόξης here? If here a distinction were to be made between wisdom as a heavenly blessing of salvation in the sense of apocalyptic theology and the crucified Christ the argument in 2:8 would be simply incomprehensible both in the context and especially religio-historically. The sentence takes on meaning only under the presupposition that θεοῦ σοφία and κύριος τῆς δόξης mean the same thing, but that is to say, if from 2:6 on θεοῦ σοφία is to be understood as a designation of Christ. θεοῦ σοφία *is here a christological predicate and denotes nothing other than the person of the* κύριος τῆς δόξης *himself*" (p. 71).

This argument—so far as I have understood it correctly—in no way proves what is desired. First, the interpretation would not be possible at all if the σοφία in 2:6 ff. actually is the "heavenly blessing of salvation." For this blessing of salvation is, as the passage cited by Wilckens ([1], p. 66, n. 5) shows (cf. also TWNT VII: 488-89; 504), precisely the perfect wisdom itself, in which the perfected righteous ones some day will participate, but never the Messiah.[32]

Nevertheless in 2:6 ff. we have to do with a *presently* revealed and bestowed wisdom. Thus in any case σοφία denotes a part or parts of the divine plan of salvation, as exegetes heretofore have with great unanimity explained on the basis of the late Jewish parallels, and 2:8 shows that this divine plan of salvation culminates in the cross of Christ. If the archons had known the plan of God's hidden wisdom which is completed in the event of the crucifixion, Paul thinks, they naturally would not have crucified the Lord of glory. This logic is unmistakable and neither "in the context" nor "religio-historically" is it "simply incomprehensible." To the extent that we are recipients of a gift through the fulfillment of God's plan of salvation (2:12), the σοφία which is actualized in such a gift is of course also a blessing of salvation, but naturally not the heavenly blessing of salvation of wisdom in the sense of Jewish apocalyptic.

Moreover the equation σοφία = celestial Christ in 2:6 ff. is already ruled out because the wisdom of which Paul speaks in 2:6 ff. is proclaimed by him only to the perfect.[33] But the Corinthians are still νήπιοι; he has not yet been able to speak to them the σοφία of 2:6 ff. He cannot even do it now (3:2). But it cannot be that Paul means to say that he has not yet been able to

[31] How so?

[32] It is utterly unlikely that the abstract entity of the eschatological salvific blessing "perfect wisdom" has anything at all to do with the equation Christ = Sophia (thus U. Wilckens, [1], p. 73). Much more likely is the connection of this equation with the hypostatized wisdom of late Judaism which is sent to men; thus also, correctly, U. Wilckens, [1], pp. 205 ff.

[33] Not "the perfect proclaim wisdom," as U. Wilckens, [1], p. 71, quotes it.

proclaim *Christ* to the Corinthians! Thus in 2:8 σοφία cannot be = Christ,[34] as is the case in the fine saying in Ign. Eph. 17.2: "λαβόντες θεοῦ γνῶσιν, ὅ ἐστιν 'Ιησοῦς Χριστός." Finally, it is also inconceivable that in I, 1:17–3:3 Paul alternates between σοφία in a general sense and σοφία as a proper name for Christ without any indication of the intended sense at a given point, as Wilckens' argument assumes. In I, 1:30 Paul had just explicitly described the relation of Christ and wisdom: "Christ Jesus, who has become to us wisdom from God and righteousness and sanctification and redemption." This description excludes any thought of a Christ-Wisdom myth. It is not possible that Paul then in 2:6 can be using σοφία as a title of Christ when he writes, "But we speak wisdom among the perfect . . . ."

A somewhat different arrangement is found in the argument with which Wilckens attempts to establish his thesis in [2], pp. 93-94. Here he starts out from the fact that Paul develops the *descensus* conception in 2:8-9 in direct reference to the Gnostic theology in Corinth. To be sure, while that would not prove the equation σοφία = Χριστός, it would prove the existence of a Christ-redeemer myth in Corinth. Nevertheless the apostle is quite familiar with the *descensus* conception, as is shown for example in II, 8:9 and Phil. 2:5 ff., and there is nothing to require the assumption that in I, 2:8-9 Paul is appropriating an argument of the Corinthian Gnostics. Indeed this assumption is moreover unlikely because with it Paul would be conceding to the Corinthians that they fully possessed the *true* wisdom of the cross of Christ in contrast to the archons. But precisely this is what he decisively contested with them, and even in the argument of 2:6-16 there is contained the charge against the Corinthian false teachers that their purported wisdom is nothing other than that worldly wisdom with which the archons of this world have crucified Christ because they did *not* comprehend *God's* σοφία. Wilckens offers a brief argument in behalf of his thesis a third time in TWNT VII: 520. In 2:6 Paul is purported to say that he spoke in pneumatic discourse *of* a wisdom of God, namely the eschatological blessing of salvation, which is reserved in heaven by God for our glorification. This wisdom, Wilckens now says somewhat more cautiously, is "apparently" identical with the "Lord of Glory." But apart from the fact that the "Lord of Glory" is not reserved in heaven as our blessing of salvation but is proclaimed as the crucified one—the *cross* is the mystery which has been determined beforehand for our glory, and which remained hidden from the archons—in 1:6-7 Paul does not say that he is speaking *of* a wisdom, as Wilckens amends the text in order to make possible the equation Wisdom = Christ, but he says in good Gnostic terminology that he (too) is speaking *wisdom,* i.e., is a "Gnostic."

138

While Wilckens attempts from I, 2:6 ff. to show the Corinthian Gnostics as representatives of a Sophia-Christ-redeemer myth, E. Brandenburger (pp. 68 ff.) seeks to prove from I Cor. 15 that the heretics in Corinth knew Christ as redeemer in the form of the second Adam-Anthropos. According to Brandenburger, in I, 15 Paul is not concerned with the resurrection as such, but only with the *futurity* of the resurrection, which is denied in Corinth.

[34] U. Wilckens, [1], unfortunately, breaks off his interpretation with 2:16!

Under this presupposition "one can assume" (p. 72) that with the corresponding idea of Adam-Christ in 15:21-22 Paul is appealing to the views of his opponents and is turning their own ideas against them: through the second Adam, Christ, we *shall be* raised.

Now those in Corinth who denied the resurrection in fact did not venture to deny any hope of the future but only the futurity of the resurrection. Nevertheless Paul's argument in I, 15 as a whole and individual verses such as 12, 19, and 32 leave no doubt at all that *Paul* sees in his opponents people who deny *any* expectation of the future (see below, p. 155). Then, however, Brandenburger's argument on 15:21-22, which indeed even apart from this strikes me as quite arbitrary, collapses; for I would not know what occasion the text gives for the assertion that in this passage Paul is adopting conceptions which were employed in Corinth.

Brandenburger further bases his thesis on 15:45 ff. The conclusiveness of the procedure of proof in this verse, that is, that there is a second, pneumatic Adam because there was the first, the psychical Adam, is supposed to depend on the knowledge in Corinth of the contrast between ψυχή and πνεῦμα, and this is also said to be shown by the undoubtedly polemical vs. 46. Of course! But even so, nothing is said thereby about a doctrine held in Corinth of the pneumatic Anthropos-redeemer Christ! The neuter τό πνευματικόν cannot possibly be completed with ἄνθρωπος, and if one wishes to do it anyway, Christ as *redeemer* cannot be meant by the πρῶτος πνευματικός ἄνθρωπος; for the position of the Gnostics in Corinth refuted in vs. 46 places the pneumatic *ahead* of the psychical. The eschatological redeemer, however, cannot appear *before* the psychical person whom he redeems. Rather the outlook which is criticized in vs. 46 says that the pneumatic substance of man is earlier than his physical body, that is, that man is in essence Pneuma; *over against this* Paul puts the pneumatic element in the figure of Christ in the second place, in order to make it clear that man, who is in essence σάρξ, first finds the way to life by means of redemption. In Gnosticism the *first* man is always the *upper* man as distinguished from the *second* man as the *earthly* man or as the earthly husk of the "first" man. The first man corresponds to the ἔσω ἄνθρωπος, the second to the ἔξω ἄνθρωπος. In Gnosticism there never occurs a redeemer myth in which the *redeemer* is presented as the first man. This is shown precisely by the evidence adduced by Brandenburger (pp. 77 ff.), and his statements on pp. 155 ff. are not able to overshadow this set of facts. The attempt, made as a kind of hint, to understand the πρῶτος-ἔσχατος "apparently also" qualitatively (p. 75) is a poor effort to deal with an embarrassing problem. Gnosticism understands the pair of concepts "first man"—"second man" *anthropologically*. Thus it is not possible to deduce from I, 15 an Anthropos-redeemer myth represented in Corinth and referring to Christ.

III. The Corinthian Gnosis as Gospel

Paul's polemic at the beginning of I Cor. tells us positively nothing about the content of the wisdom being proclaimed in Corinth. In fact, at first glance one could even doubt whether with this wisdom Paul is thinking at all of a specific knowledge or a definite kerygma. οὐκ ἐν σοφίᾳ λόγου (I, 1:17) probably does mean "not in wise discourse." Similarly, in 2:4 it becomes clear that Paul fears that the Corinthians will let themselves be won by the oratorical cleverness of the new teachers. which Paul can—and will—oppose only with preaching in fear and trembling, so that faith may rest, not upon human wisdom, but upon the power of God. Thus Paul sets himself against the rhetorically elaborated eloquence which the Hellenist treasured in the highest measure and regarded as a necessary precondition for any genuine education. Perhaps some in Corinth had denied, not altogether incorrectly, that the apostle had this education. Of course the charge which Paul takes up with his admission that he is an ἰδιώτης τῷ λόγῳ (II, 11:6) hardly refers to a lack of schooling in oratory, but concerns the fact reproved by his opponents, that he represented a "theology of the Word" instead of defending his apostolic activity essentially with pneumatic-ecstatic displays (see p. 177). And the Corinthian judgment on the Pauline epistles, that they are weighty and impressive (II, 10:10), makes us doubt even more that people in Corinth were critically occupied with Paul's language style and formal rhetoric (see pp. 176-77). Thus it must be acknowledged as likely that in I, 1:17 ff. Paul is conducting a polemic against discourse ἐν σοφίᾳ λόγου on his own part and at his own initiative. Cf. G. Friedrich in O. Michel, p. 182.

However. it becomes clear in the entire section that when Paul rejects this wisdom, he means not only the form of the matter but its content as well. In 2:1 the two stand side by side: λόγος and σοφία, and the σοφός, the γραμματεύς and συζητητής of 1:20 are not first of all brilliant orators but representatives of a quite definite wisdom, for Paul a wisdom of this world, to which he counters not with a foolish oratory but with the foolishness of the cross. They must have given expression in elaborate discourse to their own theology with the same determination with which the teachers of wisdom set themselves against certain theological teachings of Paul. Thus the apostle is engaged in a polemic against the wisdom in form *and* content of the conflicting proclamation. It is possible that some in Corinth were employing a polished form of speech. The question, however, is whether the Corinthian opponents would agree that their preaching was a σοφία καθ' ὑπεροχήν, or whether this expression is not rather to be explained in terms of Paul's polemic, which then of course would cause the necessary objectivity to vanish.

Now I, 3:18, εἴ τις δοκεῖ σοφὸς εἶναι, lets us see that in Corinth some actually held themselves to be wise, and the entire section 2:6-3:3 is explained only if Paul here is defending himself against the charge that in Corinth he had neglected the necessary preaching of σοφία (cf. also II, 10:4-5) . Thus the content of the Corinthian preaching was in some way a doctrine of knowledge, so that on the basis of wisdom in form *and* content some actually felt superior to the preaching of Paul. Paul sets himself against this *content* when in his polemic he affirms that he wished in Corinth to know nothing but Jesus Christ and him crucified. Apparently people in Corinth were stressing a knowledge the content of which was not the cross.

140

Of course in Corinth not only σοφία but above all γνῶσις was used as a *terminus technicus* for this preaching. This is seen in I, 8:1, where in the formulations Paul surely refers to the expressions in the congregation's letter. In view of the fact that in the preceding letter (I, 10:14-22) Paul had forbidden participation in pagan cultic meals, the question now is whether then the eating of meat sacrificed to idols, which is sold in the markets everywhere, is objectionable, a judgment that was disputed by the new teachers with the statement that "πάντες γνῶσιν ἔχομεν." Striking and instructive in this statement is the fact that γνῶσις appears without the article. "It is not simply definite knowledge with respect to the εἴδωλα that is meant, but something general; they feel themselves to be people for whom 'knowledge' is characteristic" (J. Weiss, p. 214) . That expresses the attitude which stands behind this "Gnosis" appropriately, even though undoubtedly in the present case the concept must be especially referred to the knowledge of the reasons which allow the eating of meat sacrificed to idols. But I, 13:8 ff. also shows that essentially more is meant thereby. As in I, 1 Paul sets in opposition to the λόγος τοῦ σταυροῦ the λόγος τῆς σοφίας, so here he confronts faith, hope, and love with Gnosis. Actually the two contrasts are essentially the same. Thus Gnosis is the content of the new preaching in Corinth; for it cannot very well be disputed that the section I, 13:8 ff. is polemical. It is just as polemical as the whole of chaps. 12–14, which take a position against too high an estimation of certain spiritual gifts. Paul points to the imperfect and incomplete character of these gifts in time and to their ending with the end of time. He does this in order to contrast them with faith, hope, and love, i.e., the acceptance of the word of the cross, as the perfect, permanent, and certain, and thus to show the Corinthians a ὁδὸς καθ' ὑπερβολήν. The distinctive thing therein is just this, that Paul labels all the individual features of the Corinthian theology with the overarching concept of "Gnosis." It is not accidental that he concludes the discussion of the spiritual gifts with the reference to it (cf. p. 95, n. 23) . As also later in II, 11:6 (see below) he is aware that "Gnosis" is the essence of the Corinthian proclamation or the central spiritual gift.[35] Thus in Corinth we actually have to do with "Gnostics."

When in I, 1, in the fundamental discussion Paul says σοφία instead of γνῶσις, this is probably to be accounted for above all by the fact that here he intends to deal with content *and* form of the heretical preaching in the broadest scope, and for this purpose the word γνῶσις is not suited, because as a *terminus technicus* it has a distinct meaning. Paul himself presupposes such a technical sense for this expression in I, 12:8, 14:6, and even 13:8, even though one can with justification doubt that he personally made exact distinctions between the λόγος σοφίας, the λόγος γνώσεως, and the λόγος διδαχῆς. Paul also still appears not at all to have recognized the special peculiarity of the Corinthian Gnosis precisely as "Gnosticism." In I, 1 he is polemicizing against it as against a special instance of the Greek preaching of wisdom in general, and in that case σοφία is naturally much more appropriate than γνῶσις as a label for that teaching.[36]

141

Reitzenstein[37] has in passing concretized the thesis that in I, 13:8-13 Paul takes up polemically the term γνῶσις which is used in Corinth; he says that in Corinth some were using a fixed formula, "πίστις, γνῶσις, ἀγάπη, ἐλπίς." The apostle has become acquainted with this formula. He has eliminated "γνῶσις" and in vss. 8 ff. has justified the elimination, and on the other hand has adopted the shortened formula, "πίστις, ἀγάπη, ἐλπίς," as that which truly abides. This interpretation has the advantage that thus the thoroughly non-Pauline conception[38] that πίστις and ἐλπίς are eternal (cf. Rom. 8:21 ff.; II, 5:7) can be accounted for, in terms of the external compulsion to adopt in the polemic a formula already at hand. Lietzmann[39] and others therefore have also followed Reitzenstein's explanation.

Arguing against this thesis is the fact that Paul uses the same fixed formula already in I Thess. 1:3 and 5:8 (cf. Col. 1:4-5); thus it was already familiar to him in the abbreviated form when he had not yet collided with Gnosticism and when he still had no occasion for the elimination of γνῶσις (cf. I, 1:5; 12:8; 14:6, *et passim*).[40] Besides,

[35] Cf. Reitzenstein, [1] (3rd ed.), pp. 384-85.

[36] Cf. Col. 2:8, where φιλοσοφία clearly stands for γνῶσις. See G. Bornkamm in *Das Ende des Gesetzes* (1952), p. 143.

[37] [1], p. 383. Cf. H. Jonas, [2], pp. 45 ff.

[38] One could perhaps attempt to prove that according to Pauline views the openness of Christian existence which is expressed in "faith" and "hope" remains even in the consummation. But this would not affect the statement that the concepts πίστις and ἐλπίς in Paul particularly and only denote the openness of the *earthly* existence of man.

[39] *An die Korinther*, pp. 67-68; the bibliography there also; cf. R. Bultmann, TDNT I: 710, n. 78.

[40] Of course this argument would be greatly weakened if I Thess. was not written until during the so-called third missionary journey (and then close to Epistle B

among the many diverse formulas which doubtless existed already
early in Hellenism, Reitzenstein has not certainly proved the stereotyped combination "πίστις, γνῶσις, ἀγάπη, ἐλπίς" which is assumed   142
especially in Corinth. His sources moreover are quite late, though
undoubtedly not directly dependent upon Paul. Finally, nowhere else
in the Corinthian correspondence do πίστις and ἀγάπη appear in the
mouths of the Corinthians.[41] Anyone who thinks with me therefore
that μένει does not have to be translated, as a strict *temporal* antithesis to the quite far removed (cf. TDNT IV: 575) πίπτει, καταργη-
θήσονται, and παύσονται, by the words "remains forever,"[42] but wants
to interpret it (as a solemn conclusion to all the statements περὶ τῶν
πνευματικῶν, cf. p. 95, n. 23) in close conjunction with the preceding
verses; in *material* contrast to all that is partial, imperfect, and transient, which does not and cannot deserve our trust, there remain to us,
as the reliable ὁδὸς καθ' ὑπερβολήν for here and now, faith, hope, and
love, which cannot cease because, oriented to what is imperishable,
they bestow on us imperishability (cf. Rom. 1:17*b*; 5:5)[43]—one who
agrees with this will not agree with Reitzenstein's ingenious combination. I leave the question open, since the concept "γνῶσις" in the
mouth of the Corinthians in one way or another is assured.

Finally, II, 11:4-6 should be considered. The sequence of thought
may be summarized as follows: "You are pleased when people proclaim to you another Jesus, another Spirit, and another gospel than
I have preached to you. But you must then listen to me also, for with
respect to Gnosis I am not inferior to these apostles." It is evident that
the γνῶσις in vs. 6 is the governing concept of the kerygma of the
other Jesus, the other Spirit, and the other gospel. With the polemical
arrangement of the entire passage, however, it cannot be doubted that
with "Gnosis" Paul also takes up the expression which was used in
this connection in Corinth. That proves once more that Gnosis is for
the Corinthian schismatics the central expression for their proclamation.

It is uncertain whether we may support this statement with a reference to I, 15:34. Nevertheless it is not ruled out that here, in view

---

in point of time), which appears more and more likely to me. Cf. now Vol. 2, pp.
132 ff.

[41] *Pure* Gnosticism also excludes the concepts πίστις and ἐλπίς, since it puts
knowledge in the place of faith, and ἐξουσία or ἐλευθερία in place of hope. And it
is still questionable whether ἀγάπη is possible on the lips of libertine Gnostics.

[42] We must not overlook that in 13:13 Paul expressly maintains the special position of ἀγάπη, which οὐδέποτε πίπτει, over against πίστις and ἐλπίς, perhaps because he sees the greatness of ἀγάπη precisely in the οὐδέποτε πίπτει, which does
not hold true in such temporal definiteness for πίστις and ἐλπίς.

[43] Paul would thus be thinking only of the existential significance of faith and
hope, which in contrast to ἀγάπη in their very structure naturally are not eternal.

of those who glory in their γνῶσις θεοῦ, Paul deliberately affirms:
143   ἀγνωσίαν γὰρ θεοῦ τινες ἔχουσιν. The same could also hold true for
II, 10:5, where Paul is polemicizing against πᾶν ὕψωμα ἐπαιρόμενον
κατὰ τῆς γνώσεως τοῦ θεοῦ.[44]

What kind of Gnosis was being preached in Corinth?

"Gnosis" as *terminus technicus* is found not only in Hellenism, but
also in the Old Testament. The decisive difference[45] in the meaning
of Gnosis in these two comprehensive religious spheres becomes clear
when one compares Poimandres I, 3, "μαθεῖν θέλω τὰ ὄντα καὶ νοῆσαι
τὴν τούτων φύσιν καὶ γνῶναι τὸν θεόν," with Hos. 6:6, "ולא חפצתי חסד
וזבח ודעת אלהים מעלות." For the Hellenists the γνῶσις θεοῦ is the understanding of the being of God, for the Jews the knowledge of the will
of God. Correspondingly, there the γνῶσις ἀνθρώπου is the understanding of human existence (Corp. Herm. 11:21: οἶδα τίς ἤμην . . . οἶδα τίς
ἔσομαι), here the understanding of human obligation. There is no
need to question that in Corinth people spoke of Gnosis in the Hellenistic sense. Precisely from the perspective of the λόγος τοῦ σταυροῦ,
which as God's eschatological word in judgment and grace is the
highest expression of the divine will, Paul polemicizes against the
wisdom of the Corinthians, which is perfect in itself. And just so he
places faith, hope, and love as the obedient response of man to God's
word in Jesus Christ over against Gnosis, which is not understood as
promise and demand but as assured *telos*. Finally, in I, 8:1 ff. there is
a polemic *expressis verbis* against the unbiblical γνῶσις, which is lacking in ἀγάπη, since it does not seek to awaken and order the will of
man, but through knowledge excuses man from all responsible willing.

Now there existed in the Hellenistic area a whole series of religious
phenomena in which the concept "Gnosis" was an essential *terminus* of
religious language. Unfortunately we do not yet have a somewhat exhaustive investigation of the origin and distribution of this concept.
The existing studies (the literature in TDNT I: 689) are in part
highly one-sided and therefore to be used in their conclusions with
caution. Thus it appears to me to have been most unfortunate and
confusing when Reitzenstein[46] makes precisely the Corpus Hermeticum
the basis for his investigation of the expression "Gnosis." In this late
collection of Hellenistic writings there is a blend of so many influences
of various kinds that from this very source one is constantly compelled

---

[44] We must also ask whether the ἐπιγινώσκειν in I, 14:37 and the polemical
"εἰ δέ τις ἀγνοεῖ, ἀγνοεῖται" in the following verse were not consciously written in
144   view of the Corinthian *Gnostics*.

[45] On this in details and on the following in general, cf. R. Bultmann in TDNT
I: 689-719, art. "Gnosis."

[46] [1] (1927, 3rd ed.), pp. 284 ff.

to raise the question of the actual origin of the individual terms. Reitzenstein thinks that he has found the home of the technical use of the word "Gnosis" in the mystery cults, in which the supra-sensory vision of God was thus designated. A passage from Corp. Herm. 10.5 may serve as an example: a precondition of the vision is rest, "τότε γὰρ αὐτὸ ὄψει, ὅταν μηδὲν περὶ αὐτοῦ ἔχῃς εἰπεῖν. ἡ γὰρ γνῶσις αὐτοῦ καὶ θεία σιωπή ἐστι καὶ καταργία πασῶν τῶν αἰσθήσεων." But that this ecstatic vision, which indeed originally had nothing in common with a theoretical knowledge but was a metaphysical experience of the most powerful reality, a mystery which actually created ἀνακαίνωσις, real μεταβολή, and παλινγεννησία, could originally have been called "Gnosis" is ruled out.

Instead, one is much nearer to the source of this conception when one considers the passages of the Corpus Hermeticum in which according to Reitzenstein the "mystical language is more or less strongly transferred into the philosophical realm" (Die hellenistischen Mysterienreligionen, p. 288). A section from Corp. Herm. 11.21 may serve as an example: "ἐὰν δὲ ... εἴπῃς ..., 'οὐκ οἶδα τίς ἤμην, οὐκ οἶδα τίς ἔσομαι,' τί σοι καὶ τῷ θεῷ; οὐδὲν γὰρ δύνασαι τῶν καλῶν καὶ ἀγαθῶν, φιλοσώματος καὶ κακὸς ὤν, νοῆσαι. ἡ γὰρ τελεία κακία τὸ ἀγνοεῖν τὸ θεῖον, τὸ δὲ δύνασθαι γνῶναι καὶ θελῆσαι καὶ ἐλπίσαι ὁδός ἐστιν εὐθεῖα ἰδία τοῦ ἀγαθοῦ φέρουσα καὶ ῥᾳδία." The language of this section— further examples are found in Reitzenstein—is certainly not mystical. Also, "the conception of the mysteries" does not "everywhere shine through" as Reitzenstein (p. 294) thinks. But the entire section stands in the closest connection with myth, and indeed with genuinely Gnostic myth, the intent of which is to explain what God is, who we are, whither we are going. To possess Gnosis means nothing other than to know just this myth in its existential import. For this use of the term we have also the earliest witnesses by far, for example in the Test. XII (a selection of passages in TDNT I: 702, n. 59) and now above all in the recently discovered Dead Sea Scrolls (cf. pp. 76-77). In the essential elements it may be traced back without difficulty to the Greek usage, as it has been splendidly characterized by R. Bultmann.[47] He writes, among other things, "On the other hand, the one who sees really 'has' this reality, and is thus assured that he can control as well as know it . . . . Hence the knowledge of what really is can be the supreme possibility of existence, for in it the one who knows encounters the eternal and participates in it" (p. 692). But this means that the existential significance of γνῶσις in the Greek world and of "Gnosis" is so much the same that the concept could without difficulty 145

[47] TDNT I: 689-92.

pass from that sphere to this, even though the object of knowledge
146   was somewhat changed.

On the other hand, the use of the concept γνῶσις in the mystery
religions, in which it occasionally denotes the process through which
supernatural powers are imparted in substance to man, can be explained neither from these religions themselves nor from the Greek
147   usage. Rather in the early association between mystery cults and actual
Gnosticism, the concept γνῶσις passed over, along with Gnostic conceptions, into the vocabulary of the mystery religions. So far as I can
see—and precisely the passages cited by Reitzenstein can impart this
vision to us—it is of course found there only when the primitive-
mysterious conception of a more or less substantial event is already
extensively spiritualized. And that is a characteristic sign that the expression γνῶσις was originally alien to the mystery cults and was never
connected with the actual conception of the mysteries. Moreover—and
in the present connection this is important—it was never the central
concept in the mystery texts. It is an *additional* designation of the central event.

In genuine Gnosticism the story is different. Some examples from
the abundance of those that could be cited may document this assertion. Iren. I, 6:1: "Perfection will be when all that is pneumatic is
shaped and perfected by γνῶσις, that is to say, the pneumatic men who
have τελεία γνῶσις, about God and Achamoth." Iren. I, 21.4 (cf. I,
13.6) on the Marcosians: "The perfect redemption is the knowledge
of the ineffable greatness itself. That is to say, while defect and harm
have come about through ignorance, through γνῶσις the entire state
of things evoked by ignorance would be taken away, ὥστε εἶναι τὴν
γνῶσιν ἀπολύτρωσιν τοῦ ἔνδον ἀνθρώπου." Hipp. Phil. V, 6.6: "ἀρχὴ
τελειώσεως γνῶσις ἀνθρώπου, θεοῦ δὲ γνῶσις ἀπηρτισμένη τελείωσις."
Hipp. VII, 27: "According to them (the Basilideans) the good news
is the γνῶσις of the upper world, . . . which the great Archon did not
148   know." In conclusion we may cite a portion of the famous Naassene
hymn, following the translation by Harnack:

> "Then Jesus said, "Look, O Father,
> Upon this afflicted being
>
>   .   .   .
>
> For his salvation, Father, send
> Me, that I may descend,
>
>   .   .   .
>
> and the secret of the holy way,
> *Gnosis* I call it, to him proclaim." (Hipp. V, 10.)

In all these passages it becomes clear that deliverance, perfection, and redemption consist solely in Gnosis, but the Gnosis also actually suffices for the securing of salvation. At the same time the examples already show what is the actual content of this saving knowledge. The classic formulation of it probably is to be found in Clem. Alex., in Exc. ex Theod. 78.2, where the author speaks of the knowledge, "who we were and what we have become, whence we come and whither we go, whither we hasten and from what we are redeemed, what concerns our birth, what our rebirth" (cf. Hipp. Phil. VI, 26 = 204.8 ff.) .

This Gnosis—and of course Reitzenstein quite rightly recognized this—is not simply theoretical knowledge. Indeed, the speculative Gnosis which has not entered into association with mystery piety is lacking any conception according to which man first becomes Pneuma by means of Gnosis or through the θέα θεοῦ or any other technical action, that is, through any development in substance. For the real Gnostic nothing more in this sense takes place. He only *becomes aware* of what has already happened, i.e., what he himself is and for what he therefore is destined.[48] Thus Gnosis does not *bestow* divine nature upon the Gnostic—this occurs in the mystery cults through some sort of magical act, for which the designation Gnosis cannot possibly have been the original—but it causes him to *recognize* his divine nature and the way to his, and that means to its, redemption.[49] Therewith he, like the initiate in the mystery cult—and here is the point of contact for the transition of the set of ideas into the language of the mysteries—receives the assurance of immortality. For this reason such a becoming aware of himself is an event of no less significance than the transforming vision of the initiate. For only such knowledge about himself liberates the Pneumatic from the fetters with which the demons had bound him. Only with such knowledge is the Pneuma in a position

149

150

---

[48] Cf. Epiph. 26.13 (see p. 56) ; Iren. I, 21.5 (see p. 53) ; Reitzenstein, [2], p. 20; *Pistis Sophia* and Books of Jeu, *passim;* Act. Thom. 15; Exc. ex Theod. 78; Schlier, [2], p. 142.

[49] Interesting in this connection is a saying of Jesus from Pap. Oxyr. 654, which is now found in Coptic as the second (third) saying in the Gospel of Thomas from Nag Hammadi. "Jesus said: If those who lead you say unto you: Behold, the Kingdom is in heaven, then the birds of the heaven will be before you. If they say unto you: It is in the sea, then the fish will be before you. But the Kingdom is within you, and it is outside of you. When you know yourselves, then shall you be known, and you shall know that you are the sons of the living Father. But if you do not know yourselves, then you are in poverty, and you are poverty." (Quoted from the trans. by R. McL. Wilson, in Hennecke-Schneemelcher-Wilson, I: 511.) Here we apparently have a Gnostic interpretation of the ambiguous and, in Gnosticism, favorite (cf. e.g., Hipp. V, 7.20 = 83.12; Gospel according to Mary = Hennecke-Schneemelcher-Wilson, I: 341; Coptic Gospel of Thomas 24; 113; cf. p. 69) saying of Jesus from Luke 17:21, according to which the kingdom of God "ἐντὸς ὑμῶν ἐστιν." The salvation ("kingdom of God") of the Gnostic rests in the Pneuma which is to be found in man. Therefore self-knowledge is the way to salvation.

to find the way to the heavenly home. One may compare with this the clear passage in Hipp. V, 16.1, where the Peratae say, "We alone have recognized the compulsion of becoming and are exactly instructed about the ways in which man has come into the world, and we alone can make our way through the destruction and come out safely." [50]

The concept of Gnosis is at home in this realm of conceptions. Man is by virtue of his *genesis* divine. He has always been divine, and has not just become so through a mysterious act. The disastrous thing is that he is not informed as to his origin and therefore as to his nature. He is asleep or intoxicated.[51] The demons have given him the narcotic potion of forgetfulness. He is redeemed out of this condition of ignorance through knowledge, namely through knowledge of himself, through a self-knowledge of course which necessarily includes knowing about God[52] and the demons by which the being of man is positively and negatively determined. This Gnosis however now guarantees immortality, which the man who is φύσει πνευματικός[53] always possessed in his substance and now in the possession of Gnosis can also realize. Therefore the soul of the Gnostic, according to Iren. I, 21.5, can say to the powers on its ascent: "I know myself, *et scio, unde sim, et invoco incorruptibilem Sophiam, quae est in Patre, mater autem est matris vestrae, quae non habet patrem, neque conjugem masculum. Femina autem a femina nata efficit vos, ignorans et matrem suam, et putans seipsam esse solam: ego autem invoco eius matrem.* As soon as the comrades of the Demiurge hear this, they are greatly frightened and recognize their root and the race of their mother. Those however enter into their possession and throw off their fetters" (cf. Iren. I, 6.4; II, 4.3). Thus Gnosis is not theory but power, salvation, deliverance, freedom; it is simply blessedness. Gnosis is gospel. Gnosis is to the Gnostic what πίστις is for Paul, indeed it is more, in that ἐλπίς is superseded, and ἀγάπη has become unimportant.[54] Anyone who possesses Gnosis is free (cf. Iren. I, 24.4).

Thus the concept "Gnosis" as the central term is native and original in that religious movement which has always borne, and certainly with historical justification in the narrower sense bears, the name "Gnos-

---

[50] Cf. Prov. 8:14, where Gnosis speaks: "ἐμὴ βουλὴ καὶ ἀσφάλεια, ἐμὴ φρόνησις, ἐμὴ δὲ ἰσχύς."

[51] Papyrus Oxyrh. 1 (following Hennecke-Schneemelcher-Wilson, I: 106-7): "Jesus says: I stood (up) in the midst of the world, and in the flesh I appeared to them and found all drunken, and . . . they are blind in their heart." Cf. the biblical passages listed in R. Bultmann, [2], I: 174-75; further, e.g., Corp. Herm. 1.27; 7.1, 2; Od. Sol. 38.12 ff.

[52] "And anyone who has come to know himself has arrived at the good in itself which is above all being" (Cor. Herm. 1:19).

[53] Exc. ex Theod. 56; Clem. Alex. Strom. IV, 13.89; Iren. I, 6.1.

[54] Cf. R. Liechtenhahn, *Die Offenbarung im Gnostizismus,* pp. 99 ff.

ticism." Here and *only* here it is simply the theological expression. If therefore "Gnosis" was the central concept among the Corinthian Pneumatics—and after what has been said above there can hardly be any doubt about this—we probably may now affirm that the Corinthian heresy involved a well-defined Christian Gnosticism. We have recognized not only its Christology as genuinely Gnostic, but now also the "Gnosis" itself. And the latter is true not only because this can be shown to be the concept standing at the center of the Corinthian theology, but most of all because the distinctive feature of the Gnosis in Corinth is that it takes the place of faith, hope, and love (I, 13:3), is "another gospel" (II, 14:4), and thus bears in itself not mere knowledge but salvation and redemption. This is shown above all in the section I, 1:17–3:3, which constantly contrasts the kerygma of the cross and the preaching of wisdom. Thus the latter occupies a position in the Corinthian preaching which the cross as saving fact occupies in Pauline theology.[55] Paul quite correctly sensed that people in Corinth were proclaiming another *gospel* than the one he had proclaimed. It is very characteristic that he does not add, as he does in Gal. 1:7, "ὃ οὐκ ἔστιν ἄλλο." In Corinth it is actually a matter of good news of redemption, not of enslavement to a pseudo-evangelical law.[56] And precisely this holds true in general of the γνῶσις of the religion that is Gnostic in the narrower sense, as we have seen above.

The following consideration also points in this direction. The interpretation of the section I, 2:6–3:1 ff. has always been sensed as a difficulty. Here there suddenly appears in Paul a doctrine of wisdom which —formally, at any rate—is genuinely Gnostic and *against* which in the preceding section Paul emphatically set himself to the same extent; for when he says that true wisdom is the crucified Christ, this is an expression that is not only materially but also "formally" anti-Gnostic: the wisdom of the *cross* of Christ demands the obedience of faith (I, 1:30-31) and is valid for *all* men.

In 2:6 ff., however, Paul speaks of a σοφία which concerns only the τέλειοι or πνευματικοί and apparently consists in the communication of hidden truths (2:7). This is the genuinely Gnostic concept of knowledge. What is found in 2:6–3:1 could be the precise exposition of a Gnostic. This has been correctly seen by U. Wilckens ([1], pp. 52 ff.,   152

---

[55] We may not expect that Paul would specifically have waged a polemic more frequently against the *expression* "Gnosis" if this judgment should be correct; for this concept is common to his own religious language. Hence Paul can sensibly object only to the *content* of the Corinthian Gnosis, and this is done, as the further course of our work will show, at every step.

[56] It seems to me uncertain whether it follows from II, 11:4 that Paul's opponents in Corinth also called their message a "gospel," as Windisch (p. 327) assumes.

especially p. 60; cf. G. Bornkamm in TDNT IV: 819-20). How do these statements come about?

There is no question that we may understand them only in terms of the dispute with the teachers of wisdom in Corinth. But does it suffice to speak of an "approximation" of Paul to the Corinthian doctrine of the Pneuma, which is necessary for the sake of "a common language" and because above all "important elements of the Corinthian Pneuma doctrine are also for Paul himself incapable of surrender" (Wilckens, [1], p. 92)? Certainly not! For the problem indeed lies precisely in the fact that Paul had long since surrendered or had never held the distinction between νήπιοι and τέλειοι or σαρκικοί and πνευματικοί, as it occurs in 2:6 ff. as a Gnostic distinction; for to Paul *all* Christians are through faith πνευματικοί, even if the gifts of the Spirit are variously imparted.

In 2:6 ff. Paul confesses that he has actually withheld from the Corinthians the σοφία which consists in hidden wisdoms. We do not learn of what kind are these teachings of wisdom which are not imparted. Naturally it is not a matter of the message of the "wisdom" of the cross of Christ, which Paul indeed has not withheld from the Corinthians, but of "mysteries," such as Paul sets forth in Rom. 11:25 ff. and I, 15:51.[57] Thus there is no question that the *content* of the σοφία for the τέλειοι in Paul's case was not gnostically determined. Even in 2:6 ff. Paul omits any instructing with such "wisdoms," which he in no way holds to be necessary for salvation;[58] indeed he even *must* omit this instruction, since the disunited and puffed-up Corinthians are first and foremost νήπιοι ἐν Χριστῷ (3:1). This is a typically Pauline expression. While the Gnostic leads the νήπιοι by means of Gnosis to τελείω-σις—for the νήπιος is indeed just an ἰδιώτης τῇ γνώσει—Paul regards the νήπιοι as those who in their ζῆλος and their ἔρις reveal a defect *of faith*. They are not yet worthy or mature enough to have "hidden mysteries" imparted to them. Thus the whole series of statements ends appropriately in a charge against the Corinthians and the state of affairs among them.

To what purpose then all the statements in 2:6 ff.? The only explanation is that Paul must defend himself against the charge that he has withheld from the Corinthians the communication of σοφία,

[57] Thus for Paul in this wisdom it is primarily a matter of knowledge of particulars in God's plan of salvation. Cf. U. Wilckens, [1], pp. 70 ff., who of course thinks that in 2:6-8 σοφία is the perfect wisdom as an eschatological blessing of salvation which is prepared in heaven for the righteous. But this is impossible, since in 2:6 ff. Paul is speaking of a σοφία which he possesses *now* and also is communicating *now*.

[58] Otherwise he could not have kept it a secret in his preaching in Corinth! But at that time he was determined to know only of the crucified Jesus Christ (I, 2:2).

namely of "hidden mysteries" which God "reveals" through his Spirit to the Pneumatics. Thus he himself is no Pneumatic at all, they said, but a Sarkic, and therefore all the more of course not an apostle.

This charge causes Paul no little embarrassment. He too is an ecstatic, he too is a master of glossolalia, he too proclaims "mysteries" from the depths of Deity (I, 15:51; Rom. 11:25 ff., 33 ff.). It is true that in principle he has gone beyond this form of piety. The crucified Christ is his wisdom, for whose sake he regards all else as refuse. He would rather speak five words with rational meaning than ten thousand with tongues (I, 14:19; see pp. 173 ff.). He does not wish to be judged according to his ecstatic experiences, because they are experiences outside the body of Christ (II, 5:11 ff.; 12:6; see pp. 187 ff.). But the factual surpassing of this ecstatic piety still does not mean a fundamental rejection of it. Therein lies the difficulty into which Paul falls in his encounter with Gnosticism, and which he causes us.

His reaction is skillful. After he has expounded, up to 2:5, the nature of *true* wisdom, he now shows next that he is quite able also to teach a σοφία in the sense of the Corinthians. He possesses throughout a practical and theoretical mastery of τὴν σοφίαν ἐν μυστηρίῳ, τὴν ἀπο-κεκρυμμένην, ἐν διδακτοῖς πνεύματος λόγοις. In 2:6-16 this proof is well accomplished—in spite of occasional polemics against those who contradict him (2:13), *too well* for our liking. Consequently the charge against Paul is unjustified.

Now comes the more difficult task. Paul must explain why he has not proclaimed this σοφία. If the epistle were not a polemical writing but a theological treatise, he would now indeed have to show again how little *this* σοφία counts for in comparison with the described σοφία τοῦ Χριστοῦ τοῦ ἐσταυρωμένου (cf. II, 5:11 ff.; 12:1 ff.; I, 14:1 ff.). This would be of great use to *us*, but less so for the sharp debate with the false teachers in Corinth; for in Corinth people wanted indeed to hear of precisely *this* σοφία, in order to recognize Paul as a Pneumatic and an apostle; it is only for that reason that he comes to speak of it at all. Now he could not very well make good the previous failure to communicate the σοφία which was missing in Corinth, especially since that would have made it clear that its Gnostic character was to be recognized only in its form and not in its content, though it was the latter which mattered to the Corinthian heretics. Furthermore, he certainly did not *wish* to do it, since thereby he would have unduly increased the importance of the σοφία ἐν τοῖς τελείοις which, in spite of everything, he treasured very little. Thus Paul passes abruptly to the attack and explains that even now he still must withhold the desired σοφία from the Corinthians, since they are still νήπιοι and σάρκινοι. But the σοφία is intended for πνευματικοί—on this there is unanimous agreement. The Corinthians, however, are νήπιοι and σάρκινοι because ζῆλος and ἔρις are still dominant among them. Thereby the contrast of πνευματικοί and σαρκικοί is bent back again into its historic meaning and in this way retroactively de-gnosticized even in 2:6-16; the critical distance from the σοφία ἐν τοῖς τελείοις which indeed is in no wise communicated is maintained, the charge against him is averted, and Paul returns to his theme of I, 1:12, which now is given further treatment.

If this interpretation is correct, then in 2:6-16, the understanding of the σοφία held by the false teachers in Corinth is actually reproduced.[59] But that wisdom which is known to the Pneumatics by virtue of their divine Pneuma, which is spoken to the τέλειοι, of which the Psychics know nothing and which also remained hidden from the archons of this world, is the *Gnostic* wisdom.

But if the Gnosis is correctly characterized in the sentence, "τίνες ἦμεν, τί γεγόναμεν, ποῦ ἦμεν, ποῦ ἐνεβλήθημεν, ποῦ σπεύδομεν, πόθεν λυτρούμεθα, τί γέννησις, τί ἀναγέννησις" (Clem. Alex., Exc. ex Theod. 78), then the further task for us is to determine what the Corinthian heretics held themselves to be, how according to their opinion this being of theirs was related to the world and to what extent the knowledge thereof signified salvation and blessedness. In this task a look at Gnosticism in general may show us the way along which we have to proceed.

It is the peculiarity of the Gnostic doctrine of the Christ that it represents a special case of the general doctrine of man, insofar as "Christ" is not in general identical with the self of man, as is the case in the system of a pre-Christian Christ Gnosticism described in Introduction A. While we have already proven the christological conception which is expressed in the *mythological* understanding of the "Χριστὸν κατὰ σάρκα οὐκέτι γινώσκομεν"[60] among the false teachers in Corinth who thereby were shown to be genuine Gnostics, now, when we inquire of the Corinthian epistles as to what view of man was represented in the Gnostic circles in Corinth, we have to give attention to just *this* point, that the rejection of the Χριστὸς κατὰ σάρκα in Gnosticism generally matches the rejection of the ἄνθρωπος κατὰ σάρκα. Again, the affirmation of a man κατὰ πνεῦμα necessarily corresponds to the rejection of the "man of flesh," and indeed the former must form the actual self of man, if one does not want to assume that man has rejected himself.

---

[59] In this I am in agreement with U. Wilckens ([1], pp. 60 ff.). However, I am unable to see that in 2:6 ff. Paul is repeating details from the preaching of the Corinthian Gnostics. The concepts and conceptions of 2:6-16 have always been familiar to Paul.

[60] II, 5:16; on this, cf. below, p. 302.

Thus we are confronted with the task of investigating whether the Corinthian epistles permit us to recognize that people in Corinth (1) rejected man in his entire earthly existence and (2) sought and found the exclusive worth of man in a supra-terrestrial pneumatic substance which was affirmed of him.

IV. The Corinthian Anthropology

1. The Attitude Toward σάρξ

a) I, 15   154

On the first problem we first of all consider I, 15. We noted earlier that this chapter belongs to Epistle A. Lietzmann, who acknowledges that here we have the treatment of a new theme "without internal or external connection with the preceding" (*Kommentar*, p. 76), conjectures that the congregation's letter was the occasion also of the discussion of the problem of the bodily resurrection. But then Paul would have begun here also "περὶ τῆς ἀναστάσεως," or something of the sort. The fact that between 15:58 and 16:13 a bit of response to the congregation's letter is inserted is full indication that chap. 15 as well as 16:13 ff. belonged to Epistle A. It is not unimportant to know this, because at the time of this first epistle Paul had only very limited acquaintance with the situation within the Corinthian community and we must therefore be cautious about drawing from these parts of the epistle too-hasty conclusions about the state of things in Corinth. By way of specific indications in this respect the following may be inferred from our chapter:

1. Paul had proclaimed the gospel of the resurrection to the entire congregation, and it had believingly accepted this message (15:1, 11).

2. Now, however, some among the Corinthians are saying that there   155
is no resurrection of the dead (15:12).

3. At the same time, though, there are in Corinth Christians who are having themselves baptized for the dead (vs. 29): ἐπεὶ τί ποιήσου- σιν οἱ βαπτιζόμενοι ὑπὲρ τῶν νεκρῶν. The way in which Paul speaks of the custom of proxy-baptism clearly shows that this baptism did not belong to his kerygma. On the contrary, it must be concluded from vs. 29b, εἰ ὅλως νεκροὶ οὐκ ἐγείρονται, τί καὶ βαπτίζονται ὑπὲρ αὐτῶν, that it is those who deny the resurrection themselves who practice this vicarious baptism and whose contradictory conduct Paul cites as an argument against them (cf. pp. 257 ff.; thus also J. Weiss, *in loc.*).

4. Verse 46, whose polemical thrust is obvious, presupposes that people in Corinth held the pneumatic to be prior to the psychic.

5. On the other hand, it is seriously to be doubted that people in

Corinth had posed the questions in vs. 35. ἀλλὰ ἐρεῖ τις is a formula of the diatribe (cf. J. Weiss *in loc.*) which is also found in James 2:18 and there takes up a *surmised* objection of the opponents. The same is to be assumed here. Indeed already at that time all the scorn of the enlightened pagans for orthodox Judaism was based upon the question of vs. 35. Verses 35-36 thus say nothing about circumstances in Corinth but only reflect Paul's view about those circumstances (cf. also R. Bultmann, [4], pp. 10 ff., 66-67).

156

Now the apostle's statements in I, 15 leave no room for doubt that Paul is of the opinion that the Corinthians were denying any hope of the hereafter.[61] Such beliefs were not strange to his time. Epicurus represented it in exemplary fashion with a reference to the fact that the soul, closely connected with the body, can no longer exist after the dissolution of the body. Such teaching destroys all hope. With some justification it invites one to follow the principle, "Let us eat and drink, for tomorrow we die" (vss. 19, 32). Did the τινές (vs. 12) in Corinth take their stand on this radical Epicurean position, as Paul apparently thinks? Undoubtedly not. Indeed one may not establish this with a reference to vs. 11, as does J. Weiss, because the heretics would have conceded at least the resurrection of Christ. For vs. 11 speaks of the community which had once come to faith and in which *now* some say "ἀνάστασις νεκρῶν οὐκ ἔστιν" (vs. 12). But it is simply inconceivable that people attached themselves to an Epicurean or similar party in the Christian community without changing their outlook. Besides, outside this passage in Epistle A there is no other hint that Paul has before him radical skeptics. The opposite is the case (cf. only I, 4:8). And finally: Anyone who has himself baptized for the dead has still some hope for the dead. Thus Paul was in error

157

when he assumed that some in Corinth were asserting that death ends it all. Albert Schweitzer's thesis[62] that those in Corinth who denied the resurrection represented the ultraconservative line, according to whose teaching only those who were alive at the return of the Messiah had any hope, similarly runs aground on the presence of proxy-baptism.

Since on the other hand the fact cannot be dismissed that in Corinth the resurrection was disputed, Paul's adversaries must have held a spiritualistic expectation of the hereafter. This was widespread in philosophical and mythological form in numerous nuances, yet there probably is no question that it was not direct influences of Greek

---

[61] J. Schniewind (*Nachgelassene Reden,* pp. 110-39) does not observe this in his exposition of I, 15, which for this reason is quite strange.

[62] *Die Mystik des Apostels Paulus,* p. 94; similarly A. Schlatter, *Die korinthische Theologie,* pp. 62 ff.

philosophy, of which clearer traces are nowhere to be discovered in the Corinthian epistles, but the Gnostic myth imported into Corinth that was the basis of the denial of resurrection. Again it is the τινές, thus a small number of persons, who assert that "ἀνάστασις νεκρῶν οὐκ ἔστιν." They are the same ones who hold themselves to be wise (I, 3:18), think that they possess Gnosis (I, 8:2), come with letters of recommendation (II, 3:1), proclaim another Jesus (II, 11:4), and must take it from Paul that in truth they ἀγνωσίαν θεοῦ ἔχουσιν (I, 15:34). The Gnostic custom of proxy-baptism also fits well with them (see pp. 257 ff.). The denial of the resurrection of the body is for Gnosticism a foundational dogma, the proclamation of which within the heretical Corinthian theology we would have had to postulate if Paul did not make certain with his statements in I, 15 that people in Corinth were seriously concerned with this controversial question. Of course it is not to be assumed that the form in which the Gnostics clothed their rejection of the resurrection belief was the same one which appears in II Tim. 2:18 and is expressed there in the formula ἀνάστασιν ἤδη γεγονέναι[63] but is also attested of Gnostics elsewhere. One may compare Iren. I, 23:5: "Through his [Menander's] baptism, that is to say, his pupils receive the resurrection, thenceforth cannot die, are imperishable, eternally young and immortal." Of course in substance what is expressed in this spiritualized terminology of the resurrection is nothing other[64] than the general doctrine of the immortality of the soul as it is represented, according to Justin, Dial. 80, by so-called Christians (namely Gnostics), οἳ λέγουσιν μὴ εἶναι νεκρῶν ἀνάστασιν, ἀλλ᾽ ἅμα τῷ ἀποθνήσκειν τὰς ψυχὰς αὐτῶν ἀναλαμβάνεσθαι εἰς τὸν οὐρανόν. But precisely in his ignorance of the actual situation Paul would not have been able to cite the Gnostic doctrine

[63] Thus Kümmel in Lietzmann's Commentary on p. 79, 1. 13; von Soden, *Sakrament und Ethik bei Paulus*, p. 23, n. 1.

[64] I cannot see what the distinction is supposed to be which Kümmel is asserting in Lietzmann's *Commentary* on p. 79, 1. 13 (cf. also Schniewind, *Nachgelassene Reden*, pp. 110 ff.). If the Gnostics are speaking of the already accomplished resurrection, this is only an attempt to express their own teaching in the traditional terminology. Irenaeus explicitly states this when, in discussing the Simonians, he says: "*Tantum autem absunt ab eo, ut mortuum excitent (quemadmodum Dominus excitavit, et Apostoli per orationem, et in fraternitate saepissime propter aliquid necessarium, ea, quae est in quoquo loco, Ecclesia universa postulante per jejunium et supplicationem multam, reversus est spiritus mortui, et donatus est homo orationibus sanctorum), ut ne quidem credant hoc in totum posse fieri: Esse autem resurrectionem a mortuis agnitionem eius, quae ab eis dicitur, veritatis*" (Iren. II, 31.2). Similarly Tert., de resurr. 19: "*Vae, qui non, dum in hac carne est, cognoverit arcana haeretica: hoc est enim apud illos resurrectio.*" Here one should also compare Johannine passages such as John 5:24; 11:25, etc. Cf. further Schniewind, *Nachgelassene Reden*, p. 116, n. 2.

with "ἀνάστασις οὐκ ἔστιν" if people in Corinth were asserting ἀνάσ-
160 τασιν ἤδη γεγονέναι."

The motivation for the Gnostics' denial of the resurrection is the
Gnostic dualism whose mythological background is too well known
for it to require a detailed presentation here.[65] Man, so far as he is
σάρξ, is for the Gnostic not only perishable but also despicable. The
flesh, which is buried, is the largely anti-godly, but at best—in the
Jewish sphere—worthless, dwelling of the human self. The idea that
this lifeless prison must first be awakened to life before the man himself attains genuine life appears to the Gnostic self-consciousness as
blasphemy. "Redemption extends only to the soul, the body cannot
but by its nature disintegrate" (Iren. I, 24.5).[66] One last remnant of
the Persian–late-Jewish conception of the resurrection body, completely separated from its original meaning, is the view which is widespread in Gnosticism but is basically alien to it, that the redeemed
soul upon its ascent or thereafter receives a heavenly garment. But this
garment is of divine origin and no more a prison of the soul but its
adornment.

Thus the sentence "ἀνάστασις οὐκ ἔστιν" is not for the Gnostic as
it is for Paul an assertion which plunges into the most profound
hopelessness, but the triumphant message of one who can renounce
all hope because he already possesses by nature his salvation. The
Gnostics are φύσει σωζόμενοι. Hence Valentinus can explain (in Clem.
Alex. Strom. IV, 13.18) his preaching to the hearers: "'Απ' ἀρχῆς
ἀθάνατοί ἐστε καὶ τέκνα ζωῆς ἐστε αἰωνίας, καὶ τὸν θάνατον ἠθέλετε
μερίσασθαι εἰς ἑαυτούς, ἵνα δαπανήσητε αὐτὸν καὶ ἀναλώσητε, καὶ ἀπο-
θάνῃ ὁ θάνατος ἐν ὑμῖν καὶ δι' ὑμῶν. ὅταν γὰρ τὸν μὲν κόσμον λύητε,
ὑμεῖς δὲ μὴ καταλύησθε, κυριεύετε τῆς κτίσεως καὶ τῆς φθορᾶς ἁπάσης."
To such triumphant consciousness the church can only oppose the
greater seriousness of her message: "And let no one of you say that this
163 *flesh* is not judged or raised" (II Clem. 9.1).

As the sarx of the deceased no longer interests the Gnostic, so also
he knows no more of the living κατὰ σάρκα. It is one and the same
thing to say ἀνάστασις οὐκ ἔστιν and to assert οὐδένα οἴδαμεν κατὰ
σάρκα. For the person who is under the sway of Jewish thought and is
not familiar with Hellenistic anthropology, the latter expression, if it is
made in isolation from the myth, must be meaningless, and the former

[65] Tert., de resurr. carn. 5, of Menander: "This our transient and frail body,
which they do not hesitate to describe as the evil in general, is likewise a creation
165 of the angels."

[66] Irenaeus' protest against this runs thus: "*Qui quidem resurgent in carne, licet
nolint, uti agnoscant virtutem suscitantis eos a mortuis: cum justis autem non
annumerabuntur . . .*" (I, 22.1). Cf. further, Justin, Dial. 80.4; Iren. V, 31.2.

nihilistic. Thus it is only natural when Paul, who in spite of his numerous Gnostic terms yet here no more than elsewhere shows a direct acquaintance with the Gnostic myth, holds the invitation, "φάγωμεν καὶ πίωμεν, αὔριον γὰρ ἀποθνήσκομεν" (I, 15:32) to be the only appropriate inference from the Corinthian schismatics' denial of the resurrection.   164

If I Clement in the last analysis was called forth by Gnostic arguments in Corinth (cf. W. Bauer, *Rechtgläubigkeit und Ketzerei im ältesten Christentum*, pp. 99-108, and below, p. 298), in I Clem. 23-27 we may have before us a wholly corresponding misunderstanding. It is highly improbable that in these chapters, only I, 15 is taken up again without any specific reason. Of the same kind also is the erroneous inference from Menander's assertion that his pupils could not die, could not grow old, and were immortal (Iren. I, 23.5), that Menander promised his followers bodily immortality. Justin (Apol. 26.4) apparently interpreted things thus and hence was understandably amazed that "even now" some agree to this, while Menander was undoubtedly thinking of the immortality of the Pneuma-self. In Ps.-Cl. Rec. I, 54 Dositheus and Simon Magus, who as Samaritan *Gnostics* denied the resurrection of the dead, are counted with the Sadducees, surely in the conviction that like the latter they denied any life after death. The same opinion may stand behind the remark of Hegesippus: "αἱ δὲ αἱρέσεις αἱ προειρημέναι οὐκ ἐπίστευον οὔτε ἀνάστασιν οὔτε ἐρχόμενον ἀποδοῦναι ἑκάστῳ κατὰ τὰ ἔργα αὐτοῦ" (Eus. CH II, 23.9). Similar misunderstandings are also to be seen elsewhere in the early church (cf. Hilgenfeld, *Ketzergeschichte* . . . , p. 156). It is hard to   166 tell what Polycarp conceives (Polyc. VII, 1) under the denial of the resurrection: "Anyone who does not confess the testimony of the cross is of the devil. And anyone who explains the words of the Lord according to his own wishes and asserts that there is neither resurrection nor judgment is the firstborn of Satan." In any case the Gnostic juxtaposition of denial of the resurrection and rejection of the cross, seen in this passage and occurring also in Corinth, is interesting.

Even though Paul had evidently heard only quite generally that according to the opinion of certain circles in Corinth ἀνάστασις νεκρῶν οὐκ ἔστιν, and in I, 15:3 ff. did not adduce the proof of tradition for the resurrection of Christ because he knew that some were denying precisely this also, still it is obvious that the Corinthian Gnostics denied that the buried Jesus of Nazareth had arisen on the third day.   167 This heretical opinion was not particularly conspicuous because the living Christ—to be sure not resurrected but ascended—stood at the center of the whole Gnostic theology, and for Paul and his communities resurrection and ascension were still one *single* act.   168

b) II, 4:7 ff.

II, 4:7 ff. also is to be understood in terms of the polemic against those circles in Corinth which interpreted the weak body as transitory and perishable, scorned it, and denied its resurrection. The polemical aim of the preceding verses is evident, even though Paul is cautious in his formulations and does not address anyone directly. Some in Corinth had accused the apostle by saying that his gospel was "hidden." In response to this Paul affirms that the unconcealed gospel of his opponents consists in their proclaiming themselves, while his gospel remains hidden only to those who do not recognize the glory of Christ Jesus as the Lord of the gospel that is proclaimed.[67]

This treasure, that is, this message which is to be preached, as Paul now continues in the section which interests us, is held by the apostles in earthen vessels, so that, as Lietzmann correctly translates it, men can *recognize* that the superlative power of this preaching does not stem from man himself—he in his weakness would not be capable of this —but from God. Paul surely would not have stumbled upon the curious idea of regarding the weak body as the dwelling or the vessel of the γνῶσις τῆς δόξης τοῦ θεοῦ ἐν προσώπῳ Χριστοῦ, which he still understands quite abstractly, if polemics had not suggested the image to him.[68] The Gnostics in Corinth, who preach *themselves* as gospel, proclaim their Pneuma-self, the possession of which already is redemption (cf. pp. 183-84). In the myth however the Pneuma is quite really the treasure which dwells in the vessel (to the Gnostics contemptible) of the body.[69] The weakness and perishability of the body was to the Gnostic the best proof of its unworthiness. Paul, to whom the Hellenistic-Gnostic dualism is foreign and for whom *soma* and man are simply identical (cf. R. Bultmann, [2], § 17), must explain or interpret bodily weakness otherwise. In the view of the apostle he does this in our passage clearly with an indication that human weakness (because for Paul *bodily* weakness is *human* weakness) guards us against understanding the vital strength which is in us, by means of the light of the knowledge of Christ as ἐξ ἡμῶν, instead of as a gift of the χάρις τοῦ θεοῦ, as do the opponents whose strength is precisely *themselves* in their being as Pneuma. At this point Paul in a veiled polemic formally takes up the argument of the Gnostics. For him also

[67] Cf. the parallel statements in II, 3:4-6 and pp. 183-84.

[68] Windisch (p. 141) thinks: "Apologetic and polemical motifs do not appear here," for "it is utterly incredible that judaizing disciples of Jesus would have inferred from Paul's sufferings the inauthenticity of his apostolate." But this judgment, in itself correct, shows only how a dogmatically fixed opinion as to the identity of Paul's opponents in Corinth bars the way to an objective interpretation.

[69] Cf. Barn. 7.3 (cf. 11.9): τὸ σκεῦος τοῦ πνεύματος. Cf. II, 5:1 ff.

the body is now the earthen vessel of that which he believes and preaches. But—and this is the anti-Gnostic tenor of the expressions from vs. 7 on—the weakness of this body may not mislead us to the conclusion that it is reprehensible, but it is to be esteemed as a *factum* which is meaningful for the salvation of man. The knowledge of the weakness which belongs to *us ourselves* shows us that our δύναμις by the same token is not from us but from God; it therefore preserves us from falling back into the unbelieving existence of one who seeks his salvation (as does the Jew) in his good intentions or (as does the Gnostic) in his good being. *Our whole being* is a being in weakness; our strength belongs to God.

Our passage, which thus presupposes for the Corinthian heresy the dualism of σάρξ and πνεῦμα which scorns the body and which Paul rejects, shows that we have correctly interpreted the ἀνάστασις οὐκ ἔστιν of I, 15:12 in terms of the derogatory estimate of the body in Gnosticism. It is obvious that the apostle, as distinguished from the case in 1, 15, is no longer of the opinion that the Corinthians intend with the rejection of the *soma* to abandon themselves to nothingness. One may with good reason doubt that in the meantime he had so grasped the Gnostic anthropology that it is no longer inexplicable to him how the one does not necessarily include the other. But Paul has become cautious in his polemic and limits himself to setting forth quite objectively a positive evaluation of the bodily sufferings of the apostle. He thereby of course fends off attacks against the significance of suffering corporeality as such and so against the depreciation of the corporeal in general which was for him impossible.

In vss. 8-9 Paul portrays in the style of the Cynic-Stoic diatribe[70] the apostolic suffering in detail, then to summarize it in vs. 10: "πάν-τοτε τὴν νέκρωσιν τοῦ 'Ιησοῦ ἐν τῷ σώματι περιφέροντες, ἵνα καὶ ἡ ζωὴ τοῦ 'Ιησοῦ ἐν τῷ σώματι ἡμῶν φανερωθῇ." The question is what is to be understood by ζωὴ τοῦ 'Ιησοῦ, here and in vs. 11, which repeats vs. 10 in explanation. In no case is Paul thinking here of the future resurrection, as Lietzmann (*in loc.*) thinks, for the life is now already in effect along with νέκρωσις. We are compelled by the formal structure of vss. 8-11 to understand the two ἵνα clauses in parallel with the four participles in vs. 8 introduced with ἀλλ' οὐκ. Of course not in such a way that the ζωὴ τοῦ 'Ιησοῦ would be shown simply in the preservation, existing in spite of whatever distress, from an utter physical end. Paul intends rather to say that in such preservation the power of the gospel in the believers is preserved. It is the φωτισμὸς τῆς γνώσεως τῆς δόξης τοῦ θεοῦ ἐν προσώπῳ Χριστοῦ, the "exuberance,"

70 Cf. R. Bultmann, [4], pp. 27, 80.

powerful in the believers, of the life of the proclaimed Lord, who does not allow the θλιβόμενοι to become crushed, the ἀπορούμενοι to become discouraged, preserves the διωκόμενοι from all sense of forsakenness, and keeps destruction away from the καταβαλλόμενοι. The Christian, but preëminently the persecuted apostle, thus constantly bears about with himself the sufferings of Jesus, in order that the power, not human but divine, of the gospel, precisely the ζωὴ τοῦ ᾿Ιησοῦ, be revealed in his mortal body. Because against the dark background of the apostolic suffering the δύναμις of the gospel in the apostle becomes especially visible, the paradoxical sentence, "ὥστε ὁ θάνατος ἐν ἡμῖν ἐνεργεῖται, ἡ δὲ ζωὴ ἐν ὑμῖν" (vs. 12) holds true.

170

The following sentence is obviously a failure syntactically. It appears to me as though Paul had in mind saying,[71] "ἔχοντες δὲ τὸ αὐτὸ πνεῦμα τῆς πίστεως, οἴδαμεν ὅτι ὁ ἐγείρας τὸν κύριον ᾿Ιησοῦν καὶ ἡμᾶς σὺν ᾿Ιησοῦ ἐγερεῖ καὶ παραστήσει σὺν ὑμῖν. By means of this sentence a safeguard is provided against a possible misunderstanding of the quite riskily formulated vs. 12. Paul intends to say, "If death is at work in us, and life in you, that still does not mean that we do not ourselves receive life." Rather, "Since we (you Corinthians and we apostles) have the same spirit of faith (by means of the addition 'τῆς πίστεως' the expression is—perhaps intentionally—de-gnosticized even in its formulation, for ἔχοντες τὸ πνεῦμα would be purely Gnostic), we know that the one who raised the Lord Jesus will also raise us (the apostles) and present us together with you (the Corinthians)." Paul lets himself be misled by the inserted quotation into anticipating the main clause with an interim idea ("καὶ ἡμεῖς πιστεύομεν, διὸ καὶ λαλοῦμεν"), so that the main expression can be attached only participially which naturally does not aid in the understanding of the sentence.

The assertion that the polemic against the Gnostics in Corinth, who held the mortal body in contempt, prompted Paul to give an expressly affirmative evaluation in our passage to the weakness of the body is supported by the observation that in vss. 5-14 there are whole passages, not yet discussed, in which Paul employs the simple name Jesus. The frequent appearance in these verses of the proper name Jesus, unusual for Paul, has already caught the attention of many a commentator. Thus Heinrici writes in the eighth edition of Meyer's Kommentar, in loc., p. 159: "Note further how in vss. 10-11 Paul uses only the name ᾿Ιησοῦς, and how he uses it repeatedly. . . . Striking also is the repeated article, which elsewhere ordinarily stands only before the appellative

---

[71] One could almost think that Paul could not have continued better than with I Thess. 3:8: "ὅτι . . . ζῶμεν, ἐὰν ὑμεῖς στήκετε ἐν κυρίῳ."

Χριστός. The concrete human manifestation of Jesus . . . is to be made vividly real." Heinrici does not ask *why* precisely the Christ κατὰ σάρκα is to be made thus vividly real. This is done by Bengel in an interpretation which is of course impossible for Paul: "*Saepius in hoc toto loco Paulus hoc nomen solus ponit, quam alias solet; itaque hic singulariter sensit dulcedinem eius*" (on II, 4:10).

Now it is theoretically possible that Paul speaks thus here because in the present context he is thinking on his own accord exclusively of the Christ κατὰ σάρκα. But then it would be strange that already in 4:5 he says Ἰησοῦς and in 10*b*, 11*b*, and 14, where he is thinking of the resurrected one, he does not choose Χριστός as he normally would have done. If one recalls also that of the total of nine passages in which Paul in the original language writes the simple Ἰησοῦς, six appear in our section, one will hardly be able to doubt that Paul used this formulation for polemical reasons. It is only natural, when he sets the fate of the human σάρξ in decided connection with the Χριστὸς κατὰ σάρκα, with the suffering and risen Jesus, to whom the ἀνάθεμα of the Gnostics applies, when thus, contrary to his custom elsewhere (cf., e.g., Rom. 6:4, 8; see p. 132, n. 23), he adopts the Gnostic separa- 171 tion of Jesus and Christ in terminology, in order to fight for the insepa- rability of the two in substance, that is, for the recognition of the *Christos ensarkos*. For in fact he cannot provide a better motivation for the affirmation of the ἄνθρωπος σωματικός than with a reference to the Christ who *came in the flesh*. Of course it is certain that the Gnostics were not to be convinced by this. But with his deficient knowl- edge of the Corinthian heresy Paul could not go this far in his infer- ences, even though his stressing of the Ἰησοῦς in II, 4:7 ff. may have been motivated in part by the knowledge of an ἄλλον Ἰησοῦν of the opponents.   172

c) II, 11:29-30; 12:5, 9-10, etc.

Closely connected with II, 4:7 ff. are the passages II, 11:29-30; 12:5, 9-10, and to some extent 13:4. There can be no doubt that in all these passages Paul stresses bodily weakness for polemical reasons, and that thus some in Corinth in some way had made a negative judgment on physical weakness. It is hardly necessary to offer proof of this gen- 173 erally recognized fact. Now it is usually assumed that some in Corinth were especially offended by the physical weakness *of Paul* and for this reason declared him to be unfit to be an apostle. That would of course be a most strangely motivated judgment about him, but one could perhaps understand it, if the text required this interpretation. But this by no means is the case. As in II, 4:7 ff., it is nowhere evident that anyone made Paul's *weakness* a charge against him in particular.

And conversely, it is nowhere evident that the Corinthians on their part had boasted of their physical strength, as would then be expected. Nowhere does Paul therefore set himself against a boasting on the basis of physical advantages, although it is to be presumed that he not only defends his weakness but also attacks the strength on the opposite side. Thus in that usual explanation it is only a matter of an explanation produced in a dilemma, which moreover should be impossible in view of the Gnostics, because it has as a presupposition a very positive evaluation of corporeality as such.

But since the negative judgment of the false teachers in Corinth about physical weakness is indisputable, in the background of the passages cited above there can stand only the well-known assertion that the bodily weakness proves the nothingness of the body, a principle against which Paul must contend, since for him, thinking non-dualistically, the nothingness of man is simply asserted. Thus it is understandable that Paul seeks for a *theological* explanation of bodily sufferings, for his opponents also are arguing theologically: the corruptible and miserable body cannot be divine. Thus it is understandable why Paul is not concerned about *his* weakness but about corporeal ἀσθένεια in general. (It should be clear that in II, 12:5 ff. Paul wants to be understood only as a type of a true Christian existence.) But thus also does the negation of his opponents become understandable for the first time at all, a negation which would remain an enigma if people had been denying Paul certain "religious qualities" because of his σκόλοψ τῇ σαρκί. Finally now, one also no longer misses the necessary attitude of the apostle toward the *position* of the Corinthian schismatics upon which their negation of the body rests, that is to say, his attitude toward the appeal to a Pneuma-self which guarantees life in Dynamis, into which of course we can enter in more detail only later.

d) II, 10:2 ff.

II, 10:2 ff. may also be considered briefly. In the circles in Corinth antagonistic to Paul some had accused the apostle of walking according to the flesh. Whether the κατὰ σάρκα reproduces the Gnostic accusation verbatim, as I should assume, or whether Paul only cites it in this way cannot be determined with certainty. Paul refutes the charge: "ἐν σαρκὶ περιπατοῦντες οὐ κατὰ σάρκα στρατευόμεθα." The question is how the κατὰ σάρκα of vs. 2 or the corresponding expression on the lips of the opponents is to be understood. In any case the terminology is of Gnostic origin. The Pneumatic lives here on earth 174   ἐν σαρκί: his Pneuma-self is bound in and to the flesh, even if in moments of highest ecstatic experience it can temporarily be loosed from the flesh. On the other hand, the Pneumatic in no case lives κατὰ σάρκα, that is, as if he *were* flesh, so far as he has and realizes Gnosis. He *is* indeed Pneuma and in his knowledge already possesses the ἐλευθερία from all fleshly power. Both expressions, whose anthropological-mythological original sense is at once evident, are used in Paul metaphorically without distinction, and in fact in a sense which embraces the field of ethics. The "old man" acts, thinks, and lives κατὰ σάρκα (Rom. 8:4, 5, 12, 13; II, 1:17; 11:18) or ἐν σαρκί (Rom. 7:5; 8:8-9) in his unchristian, sinful conduct. How is κατὰ σάρκα in our passage in the mouth of the Corinthians to be understood? If one chooses, as is generally done, the figurative meaning, then fancy has free range to determine the substance and content of the accusation. That this understanding is false cannot be proven unconditionally. But everything argues in favor of interpreting κατὰ σάρκα here in the purely mythical sense.[72]

1. The very people who make the charge live without hesitation κατὰ σάρκα in the Pauline sense, i.e., sinfully. The investigation of Gnostic ethics will show this. Thus in their mouth the statement that Paul is living κατὰ σάρκα would be no accusation at all if the κατὰ σάρκα were to be understood historically. But this is how it actually is to be taken. Besides, it appears hardly conceivable that one could at all make the charge against Paul of sinful conduct in such generalities as would be the case here. The reference to II, 12:16 and 4:2[73] is hardly adequate to support such an assertion. Nowhere else is a similarly sharp judgment pronounced on the apostle.

2. Paul's answer, "ἐν σαρκὶ γὰρ περιπατοῦντες οὐ κατὰ σάρκα στρατευόμεθα," presupposes that Paul was at least basically informed about the mythical background of the accusation. For the positive statement, "ἐν σαρκὶ γὰρ περιπατοῦντες," is utterly unjustified as a refutation of the mere charges of sinful conduct. In the κατὰ σάρκα Paul mistakenly hears, thanks to the terminology used, a criticism of his moral conduct. But he also correctly understands it to be a reproof of his "desire to be in the flesh," [74] or at least he regards this content of the κατὰ σάρκα as possible. This combination of quite divergent judgment is as im-

[72] There is hardly any passage in Gnostic literature in which the dualistic mythology which originally lay behind the κατὰ σάρκα can be so easily recognized as in the statements of the anti-Gnostic Paul in I, 2:12-3:4, esp. in 3:1-4. To see this, one need only consider this passage separated from the Pauline theology, which perhaps is almost easier than the opposite would be. Cf. pp. 151 ff.

[73] II, 1:17 of course comes later.

[74] Paul already knew that the "to desire to be in the flesh" was for his Corinthian opponents a culpable fact, and already in Epistle C (II, 5:6 ff.; see pp. 268 ff.; II, 4:7 ff.; pp. 160 ff.) he had taken a stand against the depreciation of somatic existence. Hence it is only natural that he is conscious also now of this position of his opponents.

possible and incomprehensible for him as it is for the Gnostics. He
now counters it with the sentence which both justifies his position and
dismisses the charge: "If we do walk in the flesh, we still are not
contending according to the flesh." Only thus does the phrase "ἐν
σαρκὶ γὰρ περιπατοῦντες" make sense. In it, the σάρξ in the expression ἐν σαρκί means the natural, worldly existent substance, and on
the other hand, in the designation κατὰ σάρκα, it means the sphere
of that which is hostile toward God, sinful.

In addition, there is the fact that, as Rom. 7:5 and 8:8-9 show, Paul
elsewhere is not acquainted with the contrast ἐν σαρκί and κατὰ σάρκα.
The latter therefore is to be interpreted in our passage in terms of
the concrete specific situation and accordingly condemned by the opponents, who understood κατὰ σάρκα mythically and thereby compelled Paul in his refutation now on his own part to fill the expression ἐν σαρκί with its substantial meaning, which of course is already
present in it in somewhat diluted form (cf. II, 5:6 ff.; see pp. 268 ff.) .

3. In the broader context of the sorrowful epistle it becomes clear
that some were just as energetically denying Paul's possession of the
Pneuma—in the eyes of the Gnostics the actual human self—as some
were here declaring him to be a man of flesh. It is the most obvious
thing to assume that the two assertions complement each other. Then,
however, σάρξ is to be understood here, as is πνεῦμα elsewhere, in the
direct, substantial sense and not to be grasped as ethical and figurative.
On this point one may also compare the statements below, on pp. 197 ff.

If one admits this argument to be valid, then it would be proved
anew that Paul's adversaries regard the substance of flesh as something
contemptible and vain, hold existence ἐν σαρκί as an existence unto
death, and consequently represent an extremely dualistic anthropology[75]—which is to say that here we are dealing with Gnostics κατ'
ἐξοχήν.

2. The Gnostic Self-consciousness

If what has been said in the foregoing section IV, 1 is in essence
correct, then it is certain that the anthropological dualism of Gnosticism, which leads to a radical devaluation of the fleshliness of man,
was represented in Corinth. Now then the question as to the nature
of the real "Self" of man must be posed in a thoroughgoing fashion.
If the Gnostics declare the σῶμα, which for Paul is indissolubly bound
with the human self, to be empty and vain, but without thereby

---

[75] On the basis of II, 5:6 ff. as well as of II, 12:1-10, this thesis can be convincingly demonstrated. Yet the presuppositions for the exegesis of these passages
are still lacking; this will be remedied on pp. 268 ff. and 209 ff. respectively.

abandoning themselves to nothingness, who is the essential man, man in his essence, who allows the Gnostic to look with contempt upon his body?

The concepts, names, and figures of speech for the real human Self are numerous in Gnosticism and vary with the respective environment: light, spark of light, seed of light; inner man, immortal man, hidden man; Philo, like the Hermetic writings, prefers the concept νοῦς; elsewhere in Hellenistic Gnosticism the concept πνεῦμα predominates; the Orient can speak of the "I," the Self, the living or vital Self, the spiritual "I." On this, cf. H. Jonas, [1], pp. 210 ff. Both the Gnosticism whose language Paul speaks and the Gnostic movement with which he collides in Corinth prefer the expression πνεῦμα for the essential "I" of man.

Therefore, if we inquire now about the self-understanding of the Gnostics in Corinth, we must first follow the traces of the Pneuma conception of the Corinthian heretics. Consequently we shall inquire about the existential import of such self-consciousness, and finally we must attempt more precisely to determine the mythological background of the Corinthian doctrine of the Pneuma.

a) The doctrine of the Pneuma
II, 11:4

In the passage II, 11:4, which we have already treated once, Paul explains that in Corinth some received a πνεῦμα ἕτερον ὃ οὐκ ἐλάβετε. "πνεῦμα λαμβάνειν" is a fixed expression of primitive Christian language (John 7:39; 14:17; 20:22; Acts 2:38; 8:15 ff.; 10:47; 19:2; Rom. 8:15; I, 2:12; Gal. 3:2) which is foreign to the Old Testament and may have been native to the mystery cults.

The Pneuma which some in Corinth receive is different from that which some others have received, thus different from that which Paul had taught in Corinth. Now in terminology at least the Pauline doctrine of the Pneuma is strongly influenced by Gnosticism. One need only read the passage Rom. 8:4-10, in which the Gnostic dualism of σάρξ-πνεῦμα is expressed undisguisedly, with a sharp rejection of the σάρξ and a substantial conception of the Pneuma. But just as vs. 3 and vs. 11 show that the lowliness of the σάρξ does not consist in its having been created but in its condition caused by sinful man, so passages like Gal. 5:17, 25; Rom. 8:27 and 12:11 allow us to see that for the apostle the Pneuma is not a life-guaranteeing inalienable possession but a gift of divine grace which is ever anew to be confirmed [76]

---

[76] At this point we cannot go into detail on these distinctions, but it is at once clear that the Gnostic anthropology, for which the Pneuma is the human self,

(cf. R. Bultmann, [2], § 38, 3). In the last analysis Gnostic terminology of the Pauline doctrine of the Pneuma is nothing but the often more corrupt than correct form into which the Christian Paul's essentially Jewish thought has flowed. Hence one may say with confidence that the Pauline conception of the Pneuma stands in fundamental opposition to the corresponding Gnostic conception with which we have become acquainted in the Introduction A in a special form, and that Paul therefore must necessarily have regarded the Gnostic Pneuma doctrine as the proclamation of a ἕτερον πνεῦμα set in opposition to his own.

Of course we cannot conclusively prove *from this passage* that the "other Pneuma" in Corinth actually is the Gnostic one, but it may be difficult for the person who doubts the appearance of avowed Gnostics in Corinth more precisely to characterize the heretical view of the Pneuma in Corinth. If one notes that with the mention of the ἄλλος Ἰησοῦς and the ἕτερον εὐαγγέλιον Paul refers to two central and at the same time concrete doctrinal elements of the false teaching which he is opposing, then the preaching of the ἕτερον πνεῦμα, mentioned at the same time, cannot have been much less significant and specific. It is therefore ruled out that the apostle here distinguishes the "other Spirit" of the Gnostics from the one familiar to him as generally and indefinitely as in Rom. 8:15 he places the πνεῦμα δουλείας in contrast to the πνεῦμα υἱοθεσίας or in I, 2:12 contrasts the πνεῦμα ἐκ τοῦ θεοῦ with the πνεῦμα τοῦ κόσμου (*contra* Windisch, *in loc.;* Heinrici, *in loc.,* and others).[77] If, as Lütgert thinks,[78] it had been a matter only of some hyper-Pauline fanatics in Corinth, who, in an exaggerated estimation of the Spirit once proclaimed to them by Paul, place *this* Spirit too strongly in the forefront of the church's doctrine and praxis, Paul would not have been able to speak of *another* Pneuma which was being preached *in opposition* to his own. It may be remarked only in passing that those who, with Baur, see the Corinthian schismatics as Judaizers stand helpless before our passage. If one searches for a phenomenon within or on the border of the Christian communities in the time of Paul in which a Pneuma doctrine opposed to the Pauline doctrine occupied a significant place, one will in fact be able to think only of Gnosticism. Even without our adducing the results of the entire foregoing investigation for the interpretation of our passage, we

---

while the *soma* is that which comes to man from without, forms the exact opposite to the Pauline image of man, which sees in the *soma* the man himself and in the Pneuma the added element (cf. I, 15:46).

[77] Cf. Lütgert, *Freiheitspredigt und Schwarmgeister in Korinth*, pp. 62 ff.

[78] "Here Paul has to do with opponents who . . . wish to prove that they have brought the Spirit in a greater measure than he in his weakness was able to do" (p. 70).

may say with some certainty that it presupposes a Christian-Gnostic heresy in Corinth.[79]

I, 15:46

This conclusion is confirmed by I, 15:46: "ἀλλ' οὐ πρῶτον τὸ πνευματικὸν ἀλλὰ τὸ ψυχικόν, ἔπειτα τὸ πνευματικόν." To complete this, only ἐστίν is needed, but not σῶμα (thus e.g. Bachmann-Stauffer, *in loc.*), which would not have been allowed to drop out. The verse again takes up emphatically and in fundamental form the fact, already expressed clearly in vs. 45, that the first man is psychical and the second is pneumatic. The polemical thrust of the verse is therewith unmistakable, although, or just because, a counterthesis is nowhere represented in the context. The front against which vs. 46 is aimed must have been clear at once to the reader. There is no question that again we must think of the intruders in Corinth who are being fought all along the way, especially since the assertion that the Pneumatic is earlier than the Psychical is the most significant expression of the whole Gnostic understanding of being. The Psychical, within which according to widespread Gnostic terminology one must reckon the Sarx also and therewith the entire κόσμος οὗτος, is the prison formed by the demonic powers for the incarceration of the heavenly Pneuma, and the entire confidence of the Gnostic rests upon his knowledge of this fact and his consequent joy over the vanity of the world, whose dissolution is brought about by the return, guaranteed to him by his pneumatic nature, into the Pleroma of the "First," into the fullness of the Pneumatic.[80] The church's protest against this self-understanding, which in our verse is expressed in admittedly thoroughly mythological form, is only self-evident. The priority of the Pneumatic over the Psychical indeed signals the end of the preaching of repentance and grace, while

178

179

[79] With apparent correctness Windisch remarks that the λαμβάνετε in the second part of vs. 4 is superfluous; even the πνεῦμα still would have had to be *proclaimed!* Now it is true that the λαμβάνετε anticipates the ἀνέχεσθε. Therefore, following the lead of Baljon, Schmiedel, and others, he wishes to strike out the λαμβάνετε as an interpolation. The λαμβάνετε is in fact conspicuous and awkward. When Paul nevertheless inserted it, he must have been conscious of the fact that people were not *proclaiming* the πνεῦμα in Corinth (thus differing from Paul) —a conception perhaps still possible for Paul, even if πνεῦμα κηρύσσειν is not found—but that they are bringing the other πνεῦμα in such a way that one is not instructed about it, but can only *receive* it. But precisely this is the characteristic feature of the Gnostic πνεῦμα, namely, that it is not brought near in proclamation or manifested in faith, but only becomes manifest when it is produced in ecstasy and thereby evokes such ecstasy in other Pneumatics. Precisely this must have happened in Corinth, as is shown by Paul's formulation in II, 11:4.

[80] In his exposition of the story of creation Philo also identifies the first man as the one who is a partaker of the Pneuma (leg. all. I, 31-32; cf. Reitzenstein, [1], pp. 343 ff.; [3], pp. 107 ff.). Cf. also Philo, de opif. mundi 134 ff.

conversely the placing of the Pneumatic later is supported by the awareness that the life imparted in the gift of the Spirit is the free gift of God who stoops to lost and sinful flesh. If one considers this, there can be no doubt of the anti-Gnostic thrust of our verse, which thus points back to a purely mythological Pneuma doctrine that is disseminated in Corinth. That however at the same time assures our exposition of II, 11:4 and secures a firm basis from which the remaining sections of the Corinthian letters, which exhibit a special importance of the Pneuma doctrine within the heresy opposed by Paul, must be explained. For even if in individual passages the assumption of a hyper-Pauline fanaticism *perhaps* would suffice for the explanation, still in I, 15:46 the Gnostic-mythological background of the Corinthian Pneuma conception emerges clearly. But since it would be completely unjustified to assume two wholly different heresies in Corinth, both of which regarded the Pneuma as central, one must also understand against the background of the Gnostic myth those sections of the Corinthian epistles polemicizing against a false Pneuma conception, even though they do not directly refer to the myth.[81]

I, 7:40b

I, 7:40b is to be placed in the same context. With κἀγώ Paul again takes up the subject already contained in δοκῶ. It is foolish to dispute the fact that therewith Paul sets himself off polemically from those who with an appeal to the πνεῦμα θεοῦ propound a view opposed to

[81] In connection with this verse it is further worthy of note that it clearly breaks the continuity of the passage. Verse 47 not only is a direct continuation in substance of vs. 45, but it also appears to be still grammatically dependent on the ἐγένετο in vs. 45. A rearrangement placing vs. 46 before vs. 45 (J. Weiss, *in loc.*) is not possible, because vss. 45-47 would be proving the idea set forth in vs. 46, that the pneumatic is prior to the psychic, while according to the larger context, they are obviously meant to document on the basis of the Scripture the presence of the pneumatic *in general*. To place vs. 45 in parentheses and to add "σῶμα" to vs. 46 (cf. Lietzmann's Commentary, *in loc.*) also fails to eliminate the difficulty.

Therefore one should seriously consider whether vs. 46 is not to be excised as a gloss. This is all the more likely, the less likely it appears that at the time when in I, 15 Paul betrays a most superficial acquaintance with the heretical eschatology, he had such a precise knowledge of the conceptions of the Pneuma held by the Corinthians that in vs. 46 he can systematically and pertinently combat them. Verse 46 then would be a marginal comment written by one of Paul's anti-Gnostic adherents in Corinth in view of the opposing Gnostic thesis which Paul substantially, though unintentionally, refutes in vss. 45 and 47, and as a confirmation of this Pauline statement. This comment must have been intended for the Gnostics to whom the letter was also available. Verse 56 of the same chapter, which is undoubtedly a gloss, could come from the same hand. This judgment in no way changes the interpretation of vs. 46. A decision—whether gloss or not—can therefore be left open here, even though the former of the two alternatives appears to me by far to be the more likely.

Paul's opinion (Heinrici, *in loc.*) .[82] How the possession of the Pneuma was for the heretics reason and cause for issuing binding instructions on the problem of marriage will be explored later. Here we are content with the renewed confirmation of the thesis that the Pneuma played a crucial role in the theology in Corinth opposed by Paul, and that the individual placed value upon πνεῦμα θεοῦ ἔχειν. Thus what was at issue was not an abstract speculation about the Spirit, as it was common in the later church, but the personal possession of the Pneuma substance. This feature of the Corinthian Pneuma doctrine did not emerge explicitly in the previously considered passages, even though the Gnostic pneumatology necessarily implied it. Paul's claim that he possesses the Pneuma *exactly* as the Gnostics do must not delude us, with all the similarity in terminology, about the fact that the structure of the Pneuma as well as the state of ἔχειν is to be defined in terms of the respective and different understanding of self and the world. The Gnostic "has" the Pneuma as his own Self and hence in fact is in himself ἱκανός for the ministry of the new covenant (II, 3:5-6), which *inter alia* is performed also in the instructions on the problem of marriage, and that indeed in a way which, as we shall see, once again is genuinely Gnostic. Paul "has" the Pneuma as a gift of God, and therewith also his ἱκανότης for spiritual office, dependent upon the Pneuma, is a gift of the Kyrios bestowed upon the unworthy (Gal. 1:15-16).

I, 12–14

In conclusion, I, 12–14 also should be considered here briefly. περὶ δὲ τῶν πνευματικῶν (I, 12:1) can be read as a neuter or as a masculine. The majority of exegetes who venture a decision here at all translate it in an analogy to 14:37 as "concerning the pneumatic persons," and indeed correctly. This of course cannot be proved beyond question. It would be certain if it could be proved that the community had inquired only about the specific case treated in 12:3 which concerned the Pneumatics. In this case a general inquiry "concerning spiritual gifts" would have been out of place. Now 12:4–14:40 in no way creates the impression that Paul is answering definite questions of the community's letter. He rather appears to be attacking excesses and undesirable distortions in the use of the gifts of the Spirit among the ζηλωταὶ πνευμάτων (14:12), of whom he had an *oral* report. Also arguing in favor of the personal translation of τῶν πνευματικῶν is the fact that not only vs. 3 but also the whole of the three chapters dealt   182

---

[82] Cf. I, 2:1, 3; II, 10:7; 11:21, *et passim*.

with persons as bearers of spiritual gifts, but not with the content of this giftedness.

But if we read 12:1 as "concerning the Pneumatics," it becomes clear at once that there was in Corinth a group of Christians who claimed for themselves the title of πνευματικός as a characteristic which distinguished them from the other members of the community. Such a self-understanding is un-Pauline. According to Paul every believing Christian has the Pneuma. The conception of the special caste of the Pneumatics who look down upon the mere believers is, on the other hand, genuinely Gnostic. Thus we must also under-
183   stand the instruction carried through in I, 12–14 in terms of the great dispute with the heretics in Corinth who proclaim the ἕτερον πνεῦμα. In fact this connection is indicated as early as 12:3: Jesus is cursed by just those people who are set apart from the rest of their community by their special possession of the Pneuma. Since the curse was spoken from the point of view of the Gnostic myth, the Pneuma doctrine against which Paul sets himself must also be that of the mythological Gnosis.

A consideration of 12:4-11 leads to the same conclusion. The aim of this section is not the assertion of the distinctiveness of gifts of grace but the affirmation that all *charismata* are wrought by ἓν καὶ τὸ αὐτὸ πνεῦμα. Therefore they are all alike to be esteemed as pneumatic (vss. 12-13), none is to be despised, none to be made absolute (vss. 14-27), and everyone therefore is to be satisfied with the gifts which are imparted to him (vss. 28-30). Thus some in Corinth not only highly treasured certain spiritual gifts, but held them to be πνευματικὰ κατ᾽ ἐξοχήν. The whole section cannot be directed simply against the special evaluation of some, because Paul himself urges, "ζηλοῦτε τὰ χαρίσματα τὰ μείζονα" (12:31). Thus he too makes distinctions in the significance of the *charismata* for the community. But he speaks for their *basic* equality, for πάντα ἐνεργεῖ τὸ ἓν καὶ τὸ αὐτὸ πνεῦμα.[83] This very point must have been contested. Those holding the views which Paul means to touch with his statements regarded the πνεῦμα as the originator only of quite special "spiritual gifts" (in the Pauline sense) and therefore also claimed only a quite special group of persons as spiritual men. According to them the φανέρωσις τοῦ πνεύματος (12:7) is not given ἑκάστῳ πρὸς τὸ συμφέρον, as Paul asserts it em-
184   phatically as *his* understanding of the Spirit.

When Paul in vs. 9 counts πίστις among the spiritual gifts, he

---

[83] Cf. H. Greeven in ZNW 44: 3, n. 6: "The enumerations (12:8-10, 28, 29-30) have the task of showing that glossolalia is only *one* among many spiritual gifts." Cf. E. Käsemann, [2], pp. 169-70; H. Jonas, [2], pp. 44 ff.

again clearly tries to include *all* members of the community among
the Pneumatics. Hence there is no reason not to understand πίστις
here in its usual Pauline sense. The apostle means to say that to one
the gift of preaching (λόγος σοφίας, λόγος γνώσεως) is given, to another ("only") the faith which is wrought thereby. Naturally that
does not rule out the preachers' also possessing *pistis* themselves, but
the striking evaluation of faith as a spiritual gift guarantees the assertion that all Christians are Pneumatics in the same way.

Thus once again Paul's polemic proves itself to be directed against
a genuinely Gnostic doctrine of the Pneuma and therewith against
the Gnostic Pneumatics of 12:1. That in them we have to do with
ultra-Pauline fanatics is impossible because of 12:3, and because of
the necessity of seeing the Pneumatics here attacked in connection
with II, 11:4; I, 15:46, etc. It is also excluded because a mere extension
of the Pauline doctrine of the Pneuma could lead at the most to an
excessive esteem for definite utterances of the Pneuma and therefore
a special striving for these, but not to the formation of an exclusive
clique of Pneumatics who reserved to themselves the possession of the
Pneuma. The latter phenomenon is typically Gnostic and, in spite of
I, 3:1 ff., is absolutely un-Pauline.   185

In view of this situation it is to be expected that Paul does not use
the term "πνευματικά" in the sense of "χαρίσματα," because the expression then would be subject to misunderstanding in the Gnostic
meaning. Since 14:1*a b* certainly is a redactional addition (see p. 95,
n. 23), the masculine rendering of τῶν πνευματικῶν (12:1) may for
this reason also be assured, especially since nowhere else in Paul do we
find the equation "πνευματικά" = "χαρίσματα."

The question as to which charisma was held by the Corinthians to
be simply *the* gift of the Spirit is plainly answered by chap. 14.[84] It is
the speaking in tongues upon which the highest value is placed in
Corinth. This speaking in tongues is portrayed by Paul as an ecstatic   186
condition: "ἐὰν γὰρ προσεύχωμαι γλώσσῃ, τὸ πνεῦμά μου προσεύχεται,
ὁ δὲ νοῦς μου ἄκαρπός ἐστιν" (14:14). In the speaking in tongues only
the Pneuma which dwells in the body is active. The natural mental
functions of man, on the other hand, are not involved. It is easy to

---

[84] Of course chap. 12 also has already answered the question, as H. Greeven has
fittingly observed (*Propheten, Lehrer, Vorsteher bei Paulus*, p. 3, n. 6): "The fact
that, from chap. 12 on, Paul has glossolalia in mind is betrayed in the enumerations
in 12:8-10, 28, 29-30. Each time glossolalia (with its accompanying *hermeneia*)
stands at the end—and indeed with emphasis! For when in vss. 29-30 the enumeration of vs. 28 is repeated with the question μὴ πάντες . . . , the series breaks off
with χαρίσματα ἰαμάτων, then of the remainder to take up only glossolalia (and to
add *hermeneia*)—for in this context it is the main concern." Cf. H. Greeven, "Die
Geistesgaben bei Paulus," in *Wort und Dienst* (1959), p. 119.

recognize that here Paul is thinking wholly hellenistically. Those who were speaking in tongues did not conceive the process differently. That fundamentally distinguishes speaking in tongues from the other spiritual gifts, which do not occur ἐν ἐκστάσει. The conclusion which Paul draws from this is of course only that he assigns glossolalia a low rank since it does not serve to edify the congregation. The special kind of utterance of the Pneuma in the speaking in tongues does not, on the other hand, lead him to the conclusion that this Pneuma is not effective in the charismata which occur ἐν νοΐ. His interpretation of the Pneuma as the gift of God indwelling all *believers* does not permit that. As is so often the case in Paul, here Hellenistic conception and Jewish thought come into sharp collision.

Different is the attitude of the *Pneumatics* toward ecstatic gifts. For them everything depends on giving themselves and others a proof of the Pneuma dwelling within them. Because the presence of the Pneuma as the real Self is a guarantee of life, such a proof is *for them* clear but also exhaustive demonstration of their religiosity, while for Paul talk of the Pneuma is only a form—of course inadequate—of expression for his message of God's grace which demands faith. For this reason to *him* the technical proof that the Pneuma is materially present does not mean any reassurance. He must strive for the confirmation and verification of the spiritual gifts (Gal. 5:25), just as he must hold *all* expressions of the Christian life including πίστις and ἀγάπη to be effects of the Spirit (I, 13; I, 12:9).

These opposing interpretations lead to the apostle's polemic in chap. 14. The opponents of Paul naturally have the terminological tradition on their side, and it is no wonder when it is obvious to the Corinthians that the sign of the indwelling Spirit is not a λόγος τῆς διδαχῆς found ἐν νοΐ, as Paul had asserted and taught, but only the Spirit's ecstatic utterances. This explains the fact that the Corinthians became ζηλωταὶ πνευμάτων (14:12), for only the possession of the Spirit—and Paul himself would not have been able to dispute this—guarantees salvation.

Of course chap. 14 does not yield compelling proof that those whom Paul is attacking are Gnostics in the technical sense of this word, but it is assured by the context. Ecstatic practices are widespread elsewhere throughout Hellenism, though outside Gnosticism and related phenomena predominantly in the internalized form of a personal vision of God, if one disregards the primitive religions. In the Hellenistic sphere during New Testament times cultic ecstasy belongs peculiarly to Gnosticism (in the comprehensive sense, including the mystery cults), and the speaking in tongues as a special form of ecstasy may have

187

been perfectly at home in mythological Gnosticism, if we may trust 188
the extant reports.[85] This latter fact is accounted for by the great
interest in glossolalia in the Gnostic myth. The Pneuma-Self of man
is a personal being or a part of such a being and therefore speaks a
language of its own, the heavenly "language of tongues." [86] In the
ecstasy which closes out the νοῦς, the Pneuma itself speaks in this its
own ἑτέρα γλῶσσα (Acts 2:4) ἐν ἀγγελλικῇ φωνῇ.[87] The term, "to speak
in another language" or in "the language of angels" may have been the
original label for this way of speaking which later, under the influence
of the other meaning of γλῶσσα (= "incomprehensible words") developed into the *terminus technicus* γλώσσαις λαλεῖν[88] (cf. Behm in
TDNT I: 722 ff.). Speaking in tongues in general and the *language*
of tongues in particular appeared to prove the assertion and the consciousness that a heavenly being dwells in man as his actual self. This
fact thus makes it understandable that the glossolalia which is also
elsewhere connected with ecstatic practices enjoyed in Gnostic circles
an esteem and an extended observance not to be discerned anywhere
else.[89] Speaking in tongues as *the* form of manifestation of ecstatic
religiousness and also as the central expression of the piety of Paul's
Corinthian opponents in general also allows at least the inference
therefore, if one considers chap. 14 in itself, that Paul's adversaries
in Corinth were mythological Gnostics in the *inclusive* sense of this
designation.[90]

[85] Cf. the excursuses in Lietzmann and J. Weiss and the bibliographies given
there.

[86] H. Greeven in ZNW 44, n. 39: "In glossolalia primitive Christianity did not
hear the helpless stammering of the person in ecstasy for whom, under the vision of
heavenly revelation, language failed and, so to speak, shattered. It is not the ruins
of human speech, but superhuman language that is perceivable on the lips of those
who speak in tongues."

[87] Test. Job 48.3; cf. Reitzenstein, [2], p. 57, where still further evidence for 189
this view is collected; cf. I, 13:1.

[88] That the expression γλώσσαις λαλεῖν could develop as a *terminus technicus*
is adequately shown by the wide distribution of speaking in tongues among those
who were interested in it.

[89] The length at which Paul speaks of glossolalia must not lead us astray to the
opinion that in the primitive Christian communities outside Gnosticism it was of
general and customary usage. What would we know about glossolalia in primitive
Christianity if Paul had not been compelled for polemical reasons to make the
statements in I, 14? The redactor who inserted Acts 2:5-11 apparently no longer
knows what to do with the λαλεῖν ἑτέραις γλώσσαις, and Paul, faithful to his principle that he would rather speak five words with reason than a thousand in ecstasy,
must have conducted his missionary work *without* speaking in tongues.

[90] Even Goethe, by the way, concerned himself in a not uninteresting fashion with
the question, "What does speaking in tongues mean?" (*Sämtliche Werke*, Cotta,
XXXI: 269, "Zwo wichtige, bisher unerörterte Biblische Fragen").

II, 10:1, 10

In conclusion, at this point we must consider the two quotations which Paul cites, more or less word-for-word, in II, 10:1 and II, 10:10 as the accusations made by his adversaries. What are they supposed to express on the lips of the *Gnostics?* Thus what did some in Corinth claim emphatically for themselves while they denied it to Paul? In these passages the commentators usually think in general of the apostle's physical weakness and his lack of oratorical skill and then compare with "ὁ λόγος ἐξουθενημένος" the passages I, 2:1-4 and II, 11:6—"the ἐξουθ. thus means first of all the inartistic form of Pauline speech" (Windisch, p. 306) —with κατὰ πρόσωπον ταπεινός and ἡ παρουσία τοῦ σώματος ἀσθενής the fact deduced from II, 4:10, 12:7 ff.; Gal. 4:14 and 6:17 that Paul was chronically ill—"more important than a weak voice and unimpressive gestures (J. Weiss) will have been a certain lack of assurance, of skillfulness and presence of mind, which probably was grounded in disturbances of the nervous system (slight neurasthenia?)" (Windisch, p. 293). These parallels seem to me to be overestimated.

Now if one notes the section 10:1-12, it is at once clear that the charges of the Gnostics have reference to the deficient *exousia* in the apostle's proclamation. *This* is missing because his appearance is ταπεινός, i.e., humiliatingly poor, when compared with the weighty tones of the epistles; because it is ἀσθενής, "not impressive" (Lietzmann) ; indeed, because his preaching (ὁ λόγος, vs. 10) is simply contemptible, altogether other than his weighty and forceful (vs. 10) letters would lead one to expect. But it is equally clear that neither the charges themselves nor Paul's reply suggests that this *exousia* was lacking in the apostle's appearance because he was sick or not rhetorically trained. Both are rather excluded, the latter because it is inconceivable that the style of the Pauline letters was in very serious contrast with that of his speech. But since the letters are just as vigorously praised for a certain matter as his speech is held in contempt for the same matter, Paul's style of language cannot possibly have been the basis for such divergent judgments, regardless of how one evaluates it or how it was evaluated in Corinth. As for the physical weakness, it is hardly conceivable that anyone could make it an accusation against Paul at all, if one was criticizing his apostolic authority. That *the Gnostics* did this is utterly excluded. That would indeed in any case have been another sign of conduct κατὰ σάρκα. As a Gnostic one cannot reproach someone for his conduct κατὰ σάρκα (II, 10:3) and hold him to be foolish when he glories in his bodily weakness (II, 10:12; cf. pp. 185-86) and at the same time reprove this his weakness as such.

But it is not to be doubted that Paul here is disputing Gnostic accusations. 192

Precisely because and while we must understand the words against the apostle as utterances of the *Gnostics,* their background now becomes clear also: the Pauline preaching is so contemptible because it is accomplished ἐν νοΐ, not in the (gnostically understood) ἀπόδειξις πνεύματος καὶ δυνάμεως (I, 2:5). This repeated charge against Paul, that he is not a Pneumatic, is also expressed in the quotations in II, 10:1, 10; this is assured not only because here we must be faced with the genuinely Gnostic charge, but also because, bracketed by vs. 1 and vs. 10, in vss. 3-4 there appears the assertion of the opponents that Paul is still behaving as a Sarkic—thus not as a Pneumatic—and in vs. 7 the apostle objects to the fact that some have denied him the Χριστοῦ εἶναι, which means, as we shall show later (see pp. 197 ff.), the πνευματικὸς εἶναι. All four charges (vss. 1, 3, 7, 10), as also the one refuted in vs. 12 (under the assumption of the longer text; see pp. 185-86), thus have in the same way the aim of denying Paul's possession of the Pneuma.

However, thus, and only thus, are the Gnostic assertions *themselves* fully comprehensible. The letters must have appeared to the Gnostic actually as weighty in meaning (βαρύς, vs. 10). We may for example take up Epistle B and attempt to read it in terms of the conceptual world of the Gnostics. It can then be understood in long sections wholly as an expression of a decided Gnostic self-consciousness (θαρρεῖν, II, 10:1). If we consider e.g. the section 2:6–3:3, or chaps. 12 and 14 with the sentence, "I thank God that I speak with tongues more than you all" (14:18), or passages like 2:4; 7:40; 8:1; 9:1, etc., we see at once why the Gnostics had to regard the letters as ἰσχυρός, that is, as a sign that Paul at least claimed the pneumatic *exousia* for himself, even though they considered it foolish (II, 10:12) that in writing and also in fact when present he renounced the ecstatic demonstration of this *dynamis.* Since the Gnostics are unable to understand this renunciation, they rightly make Paul's "unpneumatic" appearance during his interim visit an accusation against him. He appeared to them ταπεινός, that is, as a Pneumatic weak and beggarly. Therefore also his proclamation which is found solely ἐν νοΐ could only be contemptible (ἐξουθενημένος).[91] His presence was simply wretched (ἀσθενής) when compared with his letters. In practice, the *exousia,* asserted in writing and grounded in the possession of the Spirit, was completely lacking. 193

[91] Käsemann (ZNW 41 [1942]: 35) wants to refer the ἰδιώτης τῷ λόγῳ (II, 11:6) also to the incapacity for pneumatic discourse. This is possible! 194

That does not mean that Paul himself recognized this background
of the criticism against him. He apparently understands the reproaches
of the Gnostics only as a disputing of his apostolic authority, without
seeing through the mythological basis of this disputing or even missing
such a basis. Just as his adversaries did with his, he fills *their* concepts
with *his* conceptions, in order to conclude that they are disputing his
very belonging to Christ (vs. 7), thus see him still behaving as a sinner
(vs. 3), therefore naturally also dispute his ἐξουσία εἰς οἰκοδομήν (vss.
8 ff.; cf. II, 13:10) announced in his letters, especially since they could
not determine during his brief stay in Corinth that he was able or
willing to take action successfully and with authority against disobedience (vs. 5; vs. 10; cf. 13:3). Paul thinks therefore that some are
charging that he intended only to frighten them with his letters (vs.
9). To all this Paul then can counter with nothing other than τὰ
κατὰ πρόσωπον (vs. 7), which of course on all his presuppositions
would be fully sufficient.

Paul does not see that precisely τὰ κατὰ πρόσωπον,[92] that is to say,
the ecstatic productivity which is claimed in writing but is lacking
in fact, evoked the Gnostic charges. Since we have investigated this
background of the Gnostic criticism, the Gnostic self-consciousness
has nevertheless once more become evident in the utterances of the
Gnostics themselves.

II, 13:9a is to be considered and evaluated under the same perspec-
tives as II, 10:1, 10. The ἀσθένεια here charged against Paul personally
is the weakness of the παρουσία τοῦ σώματος which, in contrast to the
Gnostics, who are δυνατοί, is lacking any *pneumatic* δύναμις. Thus II,
13:9a *is* not to be separated from II, 10:10. The same holds true for
II, 11:21a.[93]

That may conclude the consideration of those passages in which Paul
conducts a polemic directly against the doctrine of the Pneuma held
in Corinth. In spite of all the criticism which perhaps would be possible on isolated statements, it may stand as a conclusion of the investigation that the apostle is fighting specifically Gnostic views. Some
in Corinth held the Pneuma to be the real Self of man, which existed
before the creation of the human body. The possession of it is, as

[92] I consider II, 10:7a not to be an interrogative sentence (thus, e.g., R. Bultmann).

[93] κατὰ ἀτιμίαν λέγω, like the entire context, must be understood in an ironic
sense, and so cannot mean, "to *your* shame I must say," but "to *my* shame I must
confess." Therefore with ὡς ὅτι the well-known charge that Paul is only a weak
Sarkic is introduced explicitly as a *quotation* (cf. II, 5:19; II Thess. 2:2, and H.
Windisch, p. 348): "How weak we were!"—that is, when we were with you and
failed to display any pneumatic *dynamis*.

such, life, and the demonstration of this possession in the state of ecstasy is therefore the most important function of religious existence.

b) Self-praise 196

Before we inquire whether it is possible more precisely to determine the mythological background of this Pneuma teaching, we consider briefly the Gnostic's assurance of salvation which is based upon it. The church fathers already sensed the arrogance of the Gnostics as blasphemy and rejected it. A splendid example of this self-esteem is offered by Iren. I, 13.6. This passage may stand here for many. The 197 pupils of Marcus call themselves the Perfect: *"quasi nemo possit exaequari magnitudini agnitionis ipsorum, nec si Paulum aut Petrum dicas, vel alterum quendam apostolorum: sed plus omnibus se cognovisse et magnitudinem agnitionem illius, quae est inenarrabilis virtutis, solos ebibisse. Esse autem se in altitudine super omnem virtutem: quapropter et libere omnia agere, nullum in nullo timorem habentes. Propter enim redemtionem et incomprehensibiles et invisibiles fieri iudici."* To Christian understanding of being, the Gnostic self-esteem must appear as presumptuous. The Gnostic is by nature redeemed. His ultimate salvation cannot even be open to doubt, for he cannot lose his pneumatic substance. Redemption, so far as he acknowledges any such 198 as coming from God at all, is as much in God's interest as in his own.[94] He is indeed a lost fragment of divine substance. With this, the Gnostic has a certainty of salvation which is not at all to be compared with genuine Christian assurance of salvation. The future demands nothing 199 more of him; he hardly expects anything from it. He is able already to anticipate it in ecstasy, in those moments in which the self leaves the body and temporarily attains the heavenly goal. Abiding ἔκστασις, i.e., ultimate being outside the fetters of the body, indeed signifies for him perfection. Out of this assurance of salvation there necessarily grows a self-esteem which must appear as scandalous arrogance to the apostle, who μετὰ φόβου καὶ τρόμου (Phil. 2:12) is working out his salvation and does not claim ἤδη ἔλαβον, ἤδη τετελείωμαι (Phil. 3:12).

I, 4:7 ff.

I, 4:7 ff. certainly is to be classified in this connection. The transition 200 from vs. 6 to vs. 7 is somewhat abrupt. It becomes understandable when one observes that in vs. 6b two ideas overlap. The verse is first directed against a person's taking special glory in being a teacher. This

---

[94] Cf. Act. Joh. 85 (see M. R. James, *The Apocryphal New Testament*, p. 250): "We thank thee that thou art in need of a redeemed human nature" (? The Greek text appears corrupted). Od. Sol. 4.9 perhaps is a polemic against such a conception.

is absurd because, as the example Paul-Apollos has shown (vs. 6a),
both are servants of the Lord in the same way (3:5). But at the same
time Paul also condemns boastfulness in general. Even Paul and
Apollos do not engage in a boasting exchange, but work together and
with modesty (3:6-7). The κατὰ τοῦ ἑτέρου at the end of vs. 6 can
refer either to a teacher or to a member of the community. However
one decides this point, it is certain that in vs. 7 Paul refers back only
to the φυσιοῦσθε of vs. 6b and now takes up a clear theme: the rejection of the arrogant self-consciousness of the Gnostics. That should
not mean that Paul was more precisely informed about the anthropological presuppositions of this attitude. However, Chloe's people must
have pictured the opponents for him quite accurately, for the polemic
in vs. 7 fits the Gnostic self-consciousness precisely: "τίς σε διακρίνει"
= "who distinguishes you?" This is to be completed with the answer:
no one. According to the precise meaning of the word διακρίνειν, the
Corinthian Christians addressed here regarded themselves as distinct
from others. The consciousness of being separate from all non-
Pneumatic persons, however, is the most fundamental expression of
the self-consciousness of the Gnostic.

"τί δὲ ἔχεις ὃ οὐκ ἔλαβες; εἰ δὲ καὶ ἔλαβες, τί καυχᾶσαι ὡς μὴ λαβών;"
That the Christian has received all in which he could glory—and for
just this reason cannot boast—is for Paul irrefutably true. There is
nothing about man himself that is worth boasting about (Rom. 3:23).
With the Gnostic it is just the reverse. For him only that which he *is* is
worthy of boasting. He has *received* from the demonic powers the contemptible body. Thus Paul's line of argument does not touch him,
since he cannot agree with its presuppositions. Nevertheless he is exactly characterized with the "τί καυχᾶσαι ὡς μὴ λαβών;" A comparison
with Irenaeus (I, 6.4), who says of the Gnostics in general: "They
desire to have in their possession as their own property the grace that
is from above," may help us understand Paul when he continues, "ἤδη
κεκορεσμένοι ἐστέ; ἤδη ἐπλουτήσατε; χωρὶς ἡμῶν ἐβασιλεύσατε." In connection with these words one thinks automatically of the already-
mentioned passage in Phil. 3:12: "οὐχ ὅτι ἤδη ἔλαβον ἢ ἤδη τετελείωμαι," which, probably written in Ephesus, stems from the same situation.[95] Passow (cf. J. Weiss, p. 106) fittingly characterizes the consciousness which is expressed with ἤδη: "It is a determinative particle

[95] It is logical to assume that the Gnostics who are conducting a mission in
Corinth have come by way of Philippi (cf. II, 3:1; p. 224). Since in them we have
to do with Gnostic Jews, Phil. 3 would be splendidly explained, with its polemic
against the Jews ('Εβραῖος in vs. 5; cf. II, 11:22!) and the τέλειοι (vs. 12), which
certainly has reference to only *one* group, if one assumes that here Paul has in
mind those very "Corinthian" Gnostics. Phil. 3 then might well fall about the
time of Epistle D. Cf. now Vol. 2, pp. 182 ff.

which according to its construction from ἦ and δή signifies *confidence* (ἦ) which is based upon evident observation (δή) ." However, at the same time is portrayed the Gnostic self-consciousness which gives Paul occasion for the bitter questions: "Are you really already satisfied? Are you actually already rich? Have you attained dominion without us?" One may place beside this a note of Irenaeus (I, 23.5) about Menander: "He added that the magical arts taught by himself bestowed power over the angels who made the world. That is to say, through his baptism his pupils receive the resurrection, henceforth cannot die, are eternally young and immortal." The basic feeling of the Gnostic, who boasts of his salvation as a sure possession and basically expects nothing more of the future, is expressed with equal clarity in both cases. The Pneumatic in essence is no longer at all regarded as man and, according to the Gnostic myth, he is not (cf. I, 3:4; Reitzenstein, *Hellenistische Mysterienreligionen*, p. 341) .[96] One may also compare Clem. Alex. Strom. IV, 23.149: "τούτῳ δυνατὸν τῷ τρόπῳ τὸν γνωστικὸν ἤδη γενέσθαι θεόν" (cf. IV, 6.40) . In contrast to this, there is expressed in the apostle's cry, "ὄφελον γε ἐβασιλεύσατε, ἵνα καὶ ἡμεῖς ὑμῖν συμβασιλεύσωμεν," the fundamentally different attitude of the one to whom his life not only still is always before him, but who also promises this life to all the believers, not to a favored, exclusive group of Pneumatics. The conception here which originally underlies the βασιλεύειν is typically Gnostic,[97] without our having to assume that Paul is consciously taking up an expression used in Corinth.[98] The Pneumatic, when he is in possession of Gnosis, rules over the demonic angel powers which seek to restrain him in the fetters of matter. On this point, cf., in addition to the passage from Iren. I, 23.5, cited above, also I, 25.3, where it is said of the Carpocratians: "They perform magical arts . . . and assert that they have the ἐξουσία πρὸς τὸ κυριεύειν ἤδη over the archons and creators of this world." Paul of

201

[96] Very significant is Corp. Herm. 10:9: "ὁ γὰρ γνοὺς καὶ . . . ἤδη θεῖος."

[97] The expression here cannot stem from a Stoic or Jewish conception (thus J. Weiss and others) . All the less so since in this passage Paul obviously is thinking of the future consummation at the end of time, while the Stoic on the other hand speaks of the conquest of drives, passions, and the world *in* the world. However, the Jewish view which must be underlying here, namely that lordship over the world comes to the Jewish people in the end-time, is unknown to that late Jewish tradition in which Paul was trained. In it there rather dominates the conception that the redeemed stand under the βασιλεία τοῦ θεοῦ, even though the *Gnostic* idea that they together with God rule over the *cosmos* may already have been known in certain circles.

[98] But cf. lines 5-9 of the saying from Oxyrh. Pap. 654 (following Hennecke-Schneemelcher-Wilson, I: 100) : "Let not him cease who is seeking (until he) has found, and when he has found (he will be amazed, and when he) has been amazed, he will reign an (d he who has come to royal rule will) find (?) rest" (= Clem. Alex. Strom. V, 14.96, cf. II, 9:45) .

course uses βασιλεύειν in a figurative sense, but therewith he intentionally or unintentionally strikes the mythological foundation of the
consciousness of perfection of the Corinthian schismatics, which in I,
6:1 ff. also becomes clear in non-Gnostic terminology (cf. II Tim.
2:12).

I, 4:10

As in I, 4:7-8, in 4:10 and 5:2 Paul turns against the arrogance of his
adversaries, who obviously look down in scorn upon Paul from the
assurance of their religious possession. No additional information is
202   gained by 5:2. The idea of 4:7-8 is repeated in briefest form. More
important is 4:10: "ἡμεῖς μωροὶ διὰ Χριστόν, ὑμεῖς δὲ φρόνιμοι ἐν
Χριστῷ· ἡμεῖς ἀσθενεῖς, ὑμεῖς δὲ ἰσχυροί· ὑμεῖς ἔνδοξοι, ἡμεῖς δὲ ἄτιμοι."
The individual expressions may have been chosen by Paul himself,
even if the passage II, 10:10 presupposes ἰσχυρός and ἀσθενής, and
II, 11:19 φρόνιμος, in the mouth of the opponents. But in any case
they again splendidly fit the situation as well of the opponents as also
—in contrast therewith—of Paul. As compared with their cleverness
the apostle intended to be, and had to be, a fool. In view of their
strength, which was based upon the quality of their being in substance,
Paul could not but appear as weak, since his strength existed only in
the decision, to be made anew again and again, to yield himself to
God precisely in the affirmation of this weakness: ὅταν γὰρ ἀσθενῶ,
τότε δυνατός εἰμι (II, 12:10). Thus while Paul is all that he is in
weakness, and also wishes to be judged only accordingly (II, 12:6),
the genuine being of the Gnostics consists in the divine power of their
spark of the Pneuma, whereas they regard that which one "sees and
hears" (II, 12:6) in them, i.e., all corporeality with its weaknesses,
as not at all belonging to them themselves—to their Self (cf. pp. 211 ff.).

Now already in I, 4:10 the theme is introduced which wholly pervades Epistle C and the sorrowful epistle but also is continually promi-
204   nent in Epistle B:[99] the struggle about the apostolic authority of Paul
or of the apostle in general. The later the epistles are, the more is the
character of the whole discussion altered as a result of the personal
attack against Paul. This of course does not mean that its content is
changed. Paul opens the battle with an attack upon the basic religious
attitude of his opponents: their arrogant self-estimate, based upon
Gnosis, with all its religious-ethical consequences. This is the situation
as it is found in Epistle A and predominantly also in Epistle B. The

---

[99] Chap. 2 is already directed against the charge that Paul is lacking in the
necessary preaching of wisdom. 4:3; 7:40, and 9:1 ff., e.g., clearly presuppose attacks
against him.

answer of the Gnostics consists in their denying Paul the right to speak at all as an apostle, that is as an authorized preacher of the Christian kerygma.[100] This is a skillful and, from the Gnostic standpoint, also an appropriate defense. For when Paul, rejecting Gnosis, boasts of his weakness, he therewith confesses himself to be a non-Gnostic or non-Pneumatic and therefore in the eyes of his opponents, for whom only the Pneumatic actually *is* anything, he shows up as nothing. As II, 12:11 shows, this accusation had been made very clear to him, even though Paul may hardly have perceived its concrete mythical background. Paul is counted among the worthless class of the Sarkics (II, 10:3; cf. II, 12:11). His apostolic πεποίθησις is without foundation. It is clear that the attack against Paul is being launched from the very position against which he fought quite generally at the beginning of the dispute. When he now defends himself against personal attacks, he has not shifted the battlefront and with it the basic issue of the battle.

One can also formulate it thus: the dispute about Paul's apostolic rights is simply a dispute about anthropology—anyone who is not Pneuma is all the more not an apostle—and therefore Paul, when he rejects the enemy's charges against his office, is fighting the same battle which he himself began with the attack against the Pneumatics. Thus we have indeed already adduced, in the consideration of the negative side of Gnostic anthropology, two passages, in II, 4:7 ff. and II, 10:2-3, which stem from the discussion about the apostolate, and now, in the investigation of the positive side, we proceed accordingly.

II, 4:2-5

First we shall consider II, 4:5. Here becomes visible the more precise argument for the view that every apostle must be a Pneumatic in the Gnostic sense. For the apostle's assertion that his opponents proclaimed themselves is altogether correct and will not have been disputed by them. They preach that which they are, and therefore naturally must expect of the other apostles that they are the same. Hardly anywhere does the Gnostic self-consciousness appear so vividly as here. The Gnostic lives because he *is*. He has not received true life as a gift, has not himself seized it. Rather, it is given with his actual being. He is

---

[100] From this perspective we can easily account for the polemical expression ὑπερλίαν ἀπόστολοι (II, 11:5; 12:11) which has so frequently stimulated the imagination of the exegetes, for it is precisely as *apostles* that Paul's opponents put themselves above him. Similarly, Paul's sharp polemic against the ψευδαπόστολοι in II, 11:13 ff. is only natural if he, who knew himself to be an ἀπόστολος Ἰησοῦ Χριστοῦ, was being denied and accorded this position. Paul must turn this contrast around, and then, in view of his genuine apostolate, that of the opponents necessarily appears as pretended, false, devilish.

blessed in any case through his pneumatic nature (Iren. I, 6.2). For this reason, as an apostle he also cannot *pass on* this life. He cannot proclaim it to the hearers as something which comes to them from without and is to be grasped. The apostolic message is for him the knowledge of man himself, and indeed of that which man always already *is*.[101] To preach himself or to realize himself in ecstasy and therewith also to help another toward the knowledge of his Self is the task of the Gnostic apostle. Knowledge of oneself is redemption. Hence the Gnostic proclaims *Gnosis,* but he himself is its content.[102] One hardly needs to put Paul, for whom man himself is dead and can live only by the Word which comes forth from God, alongside this view in order fully to grasp the Gnostic self-understanding in all its limitlessness.

209

But from this angle now a clear light also falls on vss. 2-4. The charge that Paul's gospel is hidden is connected, on the lips of the Corinthians, altogether concretely with Paul's rejection of ecstatic practices and their theoretical exposition as Gnosis, and thus with the neglect of self-proclamation. Paul cannot become manifest in this manner because a gospel thus understood is indeed a εὐαγγέλιον ἕτερον which he has not received and passed on (II, 11:4). He commends himself through the φανέρωσις τῆς ἀληθείας (4:2). Obviously with φανέρωσις just as with καλύπτειν he is employing expressions of his opponents (see pp. 190-91). If II, 5:11 ff. (see pp. 187 ff.) is compared with this, the ring is closed: the φανέρωσις which is there demanded of Paul is, as a comparison of vs. 11a with vs. 13a shows, the ἔκστασις through the absence of which Paul's gospel appears in the eyes of the Gnostics to be hidden.

II, 3:4 ff.; 10:12 ff., and other passages

In 3:4 ff. the same basic idea is found as in II, 4:5-6. Already in 2:16 Paul, having in view the apostolic ministry, had posed the question: "καὶ πρὸς ταῦτα τίς ἱκανός;" of course without explicitly answering it or giving the argument for the obvious answer, "we." In the defense of his office he first allows himself to be attracted to an interim idea, only to return in 3:4 to the theme of 2:16b. The answer to the question, "who is sufficient for the apostolic office?" is given with a hardly

---

[101] On this, cf. pp. 149-50. It is amazing how fittingly Paul has grasped his opponents' consciousness of existence, even where he still is not at all acquainted with their myth.

[102] May we adduce as a *substantive* parallel to this the following passage from Ign. Philad., which is a polemic against a Jewish Gnosticism? "ἐὰν δὲ περὶ 'Ιησοῦ Χριστοῦ μὴ λαλῶσιν, οὗτοι ἐμοὶ στῆλαί εἰσιν καὶ τάφοι νεκρῶν, ἐφ' οἷς γέγραπται μόνον ὀνόματα ἀνθρώπων" (6:1).

mistakable side-glance at those who regard themselves, by virtue of their own being, as ἱκανοί. For in view of the substantive parallel in 4:5 and the polemic in 2:17–3:3 it cannot be doubted that 3:5 is polemical in this way. The significance and the mythological background of this self-satisfaction for our problem has just been adequately evaluated.

II,10:12-13 is to be cited here also, especially if the longer text is correct: "οὐ γὰρ τολμῶμεν ἐγκρῖναι ἢ συγκρῖναι ἑαυτούς τισιν τῶν ἑαυτοὺς συνιστανόντων. ἀλλὰ αὐτοὶ ἐν ἑαυτοῖς ἑαυτοὺς μετροῦντες καὶ συγκρίνοντες ἑαυτοὺς ἑαυτοῖς οὐ συνιᾶσιν. ἡμεῖς δὲ οὐκ εἰς τὰ ἄμετρα καυχησόμεθα, ἀλλὰ . . . ." The undeniable difficulty in this text lies in the αὐτοί at the beginning of the second sentence. If it refers to the opponents, without question οὗτοι would be expected. The shorter text, which omits οὐ συνιᾶσιν. ἡμεῖς δὲ, removes this difficulty in an illuminating fashion. Of course the longer text is tenable under *one* presupposition. If one assumes that the Gnostics had accused Paul by saying that *he* was not sensible, and Paul skillfully returned this charge with the same words, "They are not *themselves* being sensible," the αὐτοί makes sense and is quite in place. II, 10:12-13, then, freely translated, would read: "We are not so arrogant that we are among those who recommend themselves. Rather they *themselves* are not reasonable who measure themselves by themselves and compare themselves with themselves. *We*, however, do not boast on the basis of an invalid standard . . . ." [103] Arguing against this understanding of the passage is only the fact that such a charge remains a mere conjecture, albeit in my judgment an attractive one. For all the preceding verses bear witness to similar charges: Paul was ταπεινός in his presence in Corinth (vs. 1), he walks according to the flesh (vs. 2), he is not Χριστοῦ (vs. 7), he is personally weak and contemptible (vss. 10-11). These accusations, which taken together in substance deny the apostle any claim to be a Pneumatic in the Gnostic sense,[104] are well followed by the defense against the further reproach that Paul is not being sensible when he glories in his weakness, the cross of Christ, the resurrection of the dead, or even in himself as in I, 9, thus in any case in the flesh.

210

211

[103] Käsemann ([1], pp. 56 ff.) reads from the shorter text that people were charging against Paul that he lacked the "μέτρον τοῦ κανόνος." Even if this were the case, it would still be far from meaning that the heretics in Corinth are judging Paul according to a standard issued by the *Jerusalem* authorities, as Käsemann infers. Nevertheless it is not to be overlooked that the expression "μέτρον τοῦ κανόνος" is introduced by Paul in vs. 13 because he can boast of an authentic standard, namely "ἐφικέσθαι ἄχρι καὶ ὑμῶν," while he denies precisely this to his opponents (cf. also R. Bultmann, [1], pp. 21-22).

[104] On vs. 1, cf. pp. 176 ff.; on vs. 2, cf. pp. 164 ff.; on vs. 7, cf. pp. 197 ff.; on vss. 10-11, cf. pp. 176 ff.

This is, on the lips of the Gnostics, a solemn and, from their stand-point, justified reproach which in no way "turns out much too dim and hazy" (Windisch, p. 309) in its utility.

212   Arguing against the shorter text is first of all the fact that it has very little attestation, and then the fact that the Western witnesses which alone come into consideration are *very* poor witnesses. Further, it should be remembered that the shorter reading is the easier one, whose skillful construction[105] by a redactor who took offense at the difficult αὐτοί is more easily conceivable than the insertion, which is difficult to account for, of the οὐ συνιᾶσιν. ἡμεῖς δὲ. The expression is good Pauline language in both forms of the text, though in view of the situation in Corinth it does not appear to me very clever of Paul if with the shorter text he claims for himself in this one passage what he has repeatedly reproached his opponents for claiming: that they commend themselves, preach themselves, are perfect in themselves (cf. I, 4:7 ff. ;II, 3:5-6; 4:5; 10:12a, 18),[106] even though of course he does this only in form.

Windisch (see p. 309) can only assert that "measuring and compar-ing oneself with oneself" when applied to the opponents yields no immediately enlightening meaning because he does not observe the character of the opponents and the direct parallels in I, 4:7 ff.; II, 3:5-6, and 4:5. The "staying with oneself" is in every way the charac-teristic feature precisely of the Gnostic.[107] Even the shorter text pre-supposes this, since Paul in fact claims for himself (in correct fashion) the self-measurement and self-comparison *practiced* (in a wrong fashion) by his opponents. For this reason it should rather be said that the literal sense is lacking in the *shorter* text since here "to measure oneself by oneself" is identical with the measuring κατὰ τὸ μέτρον τοῦ κανόνος οὗ ἐμέρισεν ἡμῖν ὁ θεὸς μέτρου (vs. 13), that is with the "being commended of *God*" (vs. 18).

The decision as to which text is to be preferred may be left to the reader. In any case this passage also may be placed in the context being discussed here. The longer text, which I consider correct, would of course speak a plainer language.

Since for the Gnostic everything depends on his Pneuma-Self, self-

[105] Cf. the similar, utterly ingenious editorial method in Gal. 2:5.

[106] If the shorter text is to be preferred, it could only be the offense at this strongly felt clumsiness which prompted the redactor by means of the insertion of the "οὐ συνιᾶσιν. ἡμεῖς δέ" to connect the offensive characterization in 12b to the opponents in Corinth.

[107] Not, of course, of the Judaizer! He measures himself or his achievements in terms of the demands of the law. Therefore Schmiedel, e.g., along with most other exegetes, must prefer the shorter text, for II, 10:12b "does not fit (in the longer form) the Judaizers at all" (*Kommentar, in loc.*).

commendation and self-comparison is the most pertinent, necessary, and by no means unethical expression of his religiousness. In vs. 18 213 Paul once more sets his own piety over against that in a summary way, and indeed with the same polemical thrust: "οὐ γὰρ ὁ ἑαυτὸν συνιστάνων, ἐκεῖνός ἐστιν δόκιμος, ἀλλὰ ὃν ὁ κύριος συνίστησιν."

We may be content with only mentioning other passages which belong here. They provide no significantly new viewpoints but underscore what has already been said.

The spiritual weapons of the apostle are powerful λογισμοὺς καθαιροῦντες καὶ πᾶν ὕψωμα ἐπαιρόμενον κατὰ τῆς γνώσεως τοῦ θεοῦ (II, 10: 4-5). The Gnostics, against whom this sentence is directed, of course will have contradicted Paul, that precisely the true γνῶσις τοῦ θεοῦ demands their spiritual pride, which may be meant here by ὕψωμα. 214

We have already referred earlier to II, 12:11: "οὐδὲν γὰρ ὑστέρησα τῶν ὑπερλίαν ἀποστόλων, εἰ καὶ οὐδέν εἰμι." That Paul is "nothing" is meant on the lips of the Gnostics, in the special sense of their myth. It is denied that he possesses the Pneuma, and therefore as a sarkical person he actually is a "nothing," a fragment of dead substance, for the *sarx* is nothing.

We may briefly refer to II, 13:9, the polemical formulation of which of course is not provable: "χαίρομεν γὰρ ὅταν ἡμεῖς ἀσθενῶμεν, ὑμεῖς δὲ δυνατοὶ ἦτε," and in conclusion I, 7:40b may be considered once more: "δοκῶ δὲ κἀγὼ πνεῦμα θεοῦ ἔχειν." This passage allows us conclusively to decide that some in Corinth preached and naturally also practiced certain views with regard to marriage, with explicit reference to the possession of the Pneuma. The self-consciousness of the Corinthian Pneumatics, who as such are not only perfect but *eo ipso* also authorized apostles, therewith clearly comes to light.

II, 5:11-15 215

In this connection also belongs the section II, 5:11-15. I shall treat it in a somewhat more thorough way since hardly anywhere does the helplessness of the exegetes who see Paul fighting against the Judaizers become clearer than in this passage, where they have brought forward an immense number of more or less obscure expositions. To go into the many interpretations of this section in detail, though, seems unnecessary.

In vs. 11 Paul is following the substance of vs. 10: the φόβος τοῦ κυρίου is the fear of the βῆμα τοῦ Χριστοῦ. In the following, however, a new theme is then set forth. Reitzenstein's attempt to interpret vs. 13 as a full parallel to vs. 9 (ἐκστῆναι = ἐκδημῆσαι) (*Hellenistische Mysterienreligionen*, p. 372) has rightly met with general rejection.

It is because the apostle is aware that he must appear before the judgment seat of Christ that "he persuades men," while he is "manifest to
God." Exactly what this means is at first difficult to say. The broader
context will of course make it clear. Verse 11*b* can at first be left out
of consideration. Paul asserts, in a parenthetical remark, that he hopes
also to be "manifest" to the Corinthians, and then continues with the
apologetic assurance that he is not commending himself again. Thus
he considers it possible that the expression in vs. 11 might be charged
against him as self-commendation. But that was not his intention. He
intended rather with it to give the Corinthians an ἀφορμή so that they
could counter those who glory ἐν προσώπῳ. This ἀφορμή, joined with
γάρ, is once more repeated in vs. 13: "εἴτε γὰρ ἐξέστημεν, θεῷ, εἴτε
σωφρονοῦμεν, ὑμῖν." The ἀνθρώπους πείθομεν must be paralleled in the
present context by the εἴτε σωφρονοῦμεν, ὑμῖν, and the θεῷ δὲ πεφανερώμεθα must be matched by εἴτε ἐξέστημεν, θεῷ. Then follows the
argument in support of this conduct: the love of Christ thus constrains
us. Just as Christ was present for all in his death, so are we also to be
present for all, that is, for others. That brings the course of thought
back again to the beginning of vs. 11, only that in the place of the fear
of the βῆμα Χριστοῦ there appears obedience in view of the σταυρὸς
Χριστοῦ. But this is not a contradiction for Paul, for the judging Christ
is the crucified Christ, so that the arguments given at the beginning
and the end of the sequence of thought for the apostle's conduct
described in vs. 11*a* and vs. 13 are identical.

What now is the characteristic feature of the conduct claimed by the
apostle, and how can this conduct be held before those in Corinth who
boast in the presence of Paul as proof that this boasting is a glorying
ἐν προσώπῳ?

Of what are the adversaries in Corinth boasting? The polemical
thrust of the entire section is obvious. It is clear also that Paul finds
himself in a defensive position. The attacks apparently were directed
against his apostolate. In any case it is true of the entire Epistle C
elsewhere that it is refuting such attacks, indeed not as vigorously as
the sorrowful epistle, but more comprehensively than the occasional
remarks in the preceding epistle (I, 9:1 ff.). The same polemical situation is already to be presupposed for our section, because the verses
5:18-21 which conclude it very clearly have in mind *only* the apostle.

Now people in Corinth were claiming for themselves the rights of
apostles by pointing to pneumatic-ecstatic experiences of all kinds, the
absence of which in Paul appeared to prove that he was not an apostle.
In fact Paul defends himself also in our present passage against the
charge that he is not a Pneumatic and *therefore* not an apostle. This
is done with the same argument as is found in I, 14—there without

special reference to the office of apostle. There, exactly as later in II, 12:1-10, Paul indeed does not reject the pneumatic experiences, but he depreciates them, since they are an expression of individual religion only and yet profit the community none at all: "ὁ λαλῶν γλώσσῃ ἑαυτὸν οἰκοδομεῖ. ὁ δὲ προφητεύων ἐκκλησίαν οἰκοδομεῖ" (14:4). For this reason he would rather speak five words τῷ νοΐ than a thousand ἐν γλώσσῃ (14:19). For ὁ λαλῶν γλώσσῃ οὐκ ἀνθρώποις λαλεῖ ἀλλὰ θεῷ (14:2). This verse is reminiscent even in wording of II, 5:11, where now of course there is specific thought of the apostle: "ἀνθρώπους πείθομεν, θεῷ δὲ πεφανερώμεθα." Behind the πείθειν, as is widely recognized by the exegetes, is concealed the hateful charge of the Corinthian heretics that Paul knows how to "persuade" only.[108] In vs. 13 Paul uses, instead of this, his own more pertinent expression "σωφρονεῖν." Therewith he emphatically declares that he *intends* nothing other than to proclaim the gospel to the community in sober preaching, to "persuade" them with the word. For those who have the Pauline conception of the apostolate, there can in fact be no better ἀφορμή against those who do not acknowledge Paul as an *apostle* than an explicit reference to the *preaching* of the apostle. The concept ἀπόστολος in Paul is not yet hardened into the narrow designation of office of a certain circle of disciples, but is still alive in the original sense of "emissary" (cf. I, 12:28; II, 8:23; 11:13; Phil. 2:25). The apostle of Jesus Christ is the one commissioned for the proclamation of the gospel before others (II, 5:18 ff.), and Paul devotes all his energy to going as far as possible in this mission (II, 10:13). It is his boast to have aroused as much faith as possible in the power of Christ (II, 3:1 ff.). Thus it is the decisive, and indeed basically the only, mark of the apostle to be present in the community for others. While the individual may also have the right to live out his individual religion, it is the right and the duty of the apostle to refrain from doing this, in the service of the community. *For this reason* he prefers to speak five words with his intellect than a thousand in ecstasy, *for this reason* he speaks only unwillingly of his visions.

This *aphormē* of course will hardly have convinced the *Gnostics*. Not that they did not place a certain value upon preaching, so far as it was the communication of Gnosis. But they conceded a right to such preaching to no one who was not a Pneumatic and who could not be identified as such by the ecstasy over the possession of the Pneuma. Paul defends himself against such a demand: εἴτε γὰρ ἐξέστημεν, θεῷ

216

217

---

[108] In an independent formulation, Paul would have used κηρύσσειν, παρακαλεῖν, or something of the sort (cf. R. Bultmann, [1], p. 13). The same charge word for word apparently is present in Gal. 1:10, a point on which cf. Vol. 2, pp. 39 ff.

or θεῷ πεφανερώμεθα.[109] He deliberately refrains from producing for the community his own religious possession (for thus in fact he regarded the pneumatic endowment). It suffices for him if in this respect he is manifest to God. Toward men he fulfills his apostolic ministry of πείθειν.

The equation ἐξιστάναι = φανεροῦσθαι appears to me to be certain, because of parallelism of vs. 11a and vs. 13 which is compellingly demanded by the context of our passage. Thus one may not give the φανεροῦσθαι in vs. 11 the sense of the same expression in II, 3:3 (cf.

218   II, 4:2). This cannot be done because in vs. 11a as in vs. 13 undoubtedly there is a genuine conflict which in vs. 11a cannot be dissolved by reading "we are manifest to God (as true apostles) by virtue of the fact that we persuade men." Paul is rather affirming that he refuses to give the demanded φανέρωσις because it is only God's concern, while on the other hand he holds the reproved πείθειν as a concrete exercise of the apostolic office to be the proper proof of just this office. With φανεροῦσθαι as well as with πείθειν Paul adopts the term employed in Corinth, which he then in vs. 13 replaces with his own term. Thus φανεροῦσθαι means a making manifest of the Pneuma in

219   ecstasy.

I, 12:7 shows that this is Gnostic language: "ἑκάστῳ δὲ δίδοται ἡ φανέρωσις τοῦ πνεύματος πρὸς τὸ συμφέρον." "φανέρωσις τοῦ πνεύματος"

220   is—this much may be evident—a fixed expression. Even though I am not acquainted with a parallel, I should nevertheless confidently assert that it, along with the abundance of concepts encountered in vss. 8 ff., is of Gnostic origin, especially since φανέρωσις is foreign to the LXX [110] and even in profane Greek is at least unusual. Paul uses φανέρωσις τοῦ πνεύματος in vs. 7, corresponding to his conception of the Pneuma, of course in an indirect (passive) sense: the Pneuma is revealed by means of the gifts of the Spirit. The original meaning of this formula, as it must be determined from II, 5:11 to have appeared in Corinth,

222   meant on the other hand a direct revelation of the Pneuma in ecstasy.

I would assert moreover that the Gnostics are being quoted not only in II, 5:11, but that in II, 4:2 and 11:6 also Paul is referring to the

223   Gnostic demand for φανέρωσις τοῦ πνεύματος. The passage 4:2-3 is a response to the opponents almost word by word. Already in ἀπειπάμεθα τὰ κρυπτὰ τῆς αἰσχύνης most interpreters assume a thrust against these or even a parrying of special charges which they had made against Paul. We need only compare II, 12:16 with μὴ περιπατοῦντες ἐν παν-

221   [109] On this, cf. the parallel in I, 14:28, where Paul says of the Pneumatics who speak in tongues: "ἑαυτῷ λαλείτω καὶ τῷ θεῷ"—thus not of the community.
     [110] "φανεροῦν" only in Jer. 40:6; "φανερός" eight times, yet never in connection with "πνεῦμα."

ουργία μηδὲ δολοῦντες τὸν λόγον τοῦ θεοῦ. Verse 3 certainly is quoting the Gnostics. And finally, vs. 2b is reminiscent of II, 10:12 (cf. 3:1; 4:5), where Paul makes the charge of *self-commendation* against his adversaries because they glory in their possession of the Pneuma instead of in the ministry. That Paul in this context names the φανέρωσις τῆς ἀληθείας in deliberate opposition to the φανέρωσις τοῦ πνεύματος as the standard of *his* recommendation appears to me very probable, especially since except for I, 14:7, where indeed the usage is not original, φανέρωσις does not appear elsewhere in Paul (or in the rest of the New Testament). Still more likely seems this state of things in II, 11:6, where the issue is, just as concretely as in II, 5:11 ff., the parrying of the super-apostles who had made the charge against Paul that he was an ἰδιώτης τῷ λόγῳ (vs. 6a), did not possess γνῶσις (vs. 6b), and was deficient as to φανέρωσις (vs. 6c). Unfortunately the text is corrupt. Hence we cannot say with certainty *what* Paul actually intends to reveal. Certainly not τὸ πνεῦμα, as the Gnostics would like, or ἑαυτούς, as some manuscripts read, which then could be understood also in the sense of Gnosis. It is most likely that it should be completed by adding an αὐτήν (*scil.* τὴν γνῶσιν) to the undoubtedly correct φανερώσαντες. Still we cannot go beyond conjectures. It is enough to say that here Paul probably is acceding to the Gnostic demand for φανέρωσις in a non-Gnostic fashion. 224

With all this, one may feel assured that πεφανερώμεθα in II, 5:11a looks back to the Gnostic demand for φανέρωσις τοῦ πνεύματος, even if one cannot agree with all that has been said. In vs. 11b, Paul very finely converts the expression into the meaning which is close to his heart: Precisely in that I as an apostle preach to the community, but keep the "manifestations of the Spirit" between myself and God I hope also to be "manifest" to you, manifest precisely as the one who is commended through the φανέρωσις τῆς ἀληθείας πρὸς πᾶσαν συνείδησιν ἀνθρώπων ἐνώπιον τοῦ θεοῦ (II, 4:2). That clarifies the meaning of the entire passage II, 5:11-13. Verses 14-15 in conclusion offer the reason for the apostle's conduct. The apostle has to exist not only for himself or for his own individual relationship to God but for all men, because Christ has died for all men, too. Indeed, still more. Christ is not simply our example, whom we emulate in this task, but as Christians we have died with him, in order also to live with him and for him; for the apostle this means ἐν σωφροσύνῃ ἀνθρώπους πείθειν.

It is truly puzzling to me when Windisch, along with many other exegetes, finds the ἀφορμή, which Paul declares he is giving in vs. 12, in all the following statements, particularly in 6:1-10. There Paul obviously declares only that he is concerned with fulfilling his apostolic office in every situation without giving anyone an occasion for complaints. What is the use of such an ἀφορμή if people are basically disputing Paul's right at all to call himself an apostle? Besides, it is literarily absurd for Paul in 5:12 to announce an ἀφορμή but to say everything else, and then in 6:3 ff. to bring it in without any further reference to it. According to the wording of the passage the ἀφορμή must be concretely contained in the immediate context.

Of course Windisch also thinks (p. 179) that vs. 13 is not comprehensible as an ἀφορμή καυχήματος. Such a judgment is pardonable. But when he then says: "Some must occasionally . . . have accused him (*scil*. Paul) of using his experiences for his self-commendation, of boasting of them as over against those who are not blessed with such circumstances, of seeking with them to establish special apostolic prerogatives . . . ," such a total distortion of the facts goes somewhat too far.[111] On that point Heinrici already had better knowledge. On vs. 13 he writes: "According to the context one expects the ἀφορμὴ καυχήματος to be introduced with γάρ," and this is then basically correctly defined thus: "Thus the ἀφορμὴ καυχήματος lies in the verifiable accomplishments for the οἰκοδομή of the community."

In fact, seen from Paul's standpoint there is no better ἀφορμή against the attacks of the super-apostles in Corinth than the reference to the fact that as an apostle he actually is performing his ministry in persuading (πείθομεν, 5:11)[112] the community in sobriety (σωφρονοῦμεν, 5:13), while *they* with all their self-glorying are to be disgraced because with their individual ecstatic religiosity (5:11) they are indeed "manifest" to God, but do not possess the only decisive mark of the apostle, the missionary preaching.

With this I shall conclude the consideration of section II, 5:11-15. The passage is understandable only if here also Paul is defending himself against the Gnostics who appear everywhere else; thus the attitude of these Gnostics is once again brought out: They expect of Paul an ecstatic φανέρωσις τοῦ πνεύματος, so that thereby he might be proved to be a Pneumatic in the sense of mythological Gnosticism. Only such a Pneumatic is anything at all (II, 12:11); only he therefore can also make the claim that he is an apostle.

---

[111] Similarly still A. Oepke, TDNT II: 460, who thinks that people were making the *accusation* against Paul that he was "out of his mind."

[112] Paul argues thus briefly already in I, 9:1 ff., where, as he explicitly emphasizes, he is defending himself against his accusers. He is an apostle *because* he, who was called by an ὄρασις of the Lord (cf. p. 356), has founded the community in Corinth by his preaching. It is only this successful activity that seals his call and, therewith, his apostolic *office*.

c) The mythological background
II, 13:3

We have earlier shown the Pneumatics in Corinth to be typically Gnostic. Now we must ask whether the mythological background of the Corinthian doctrine of the Pneuma can be more precisely determined, that is, whether a special form of the myth which is, in any case, Gnostic can be deduced. We shall start out from II, 13:3: "ἐὰν ἔλθω εἰς τὸ πάλιν οὐ φείσομαι, ἐπεὶ δοκιμὴν ζητεῖτε τοῦ ἐν ἐμοὶ λαλοῦντος Χριστοῦ, ὃς εἰς ὑμᾶς οὐκ ἀσθενεῖ ἀλλὰ δυνατεῖ ἐν ὑμῖν." This passage presupposes that people in Corinth doubted that Christ was actually speaking in Paul, and looked to him for proof to the contrary. The apostle meets this disparaging demand with the threat that upon his forthcoming visit in Corinth he will not spare them, but will come in the power of Christ. The meaning of vs. 3b is difficult to discern: "ὃς εἰς κτλ." Either the relative clause still belongs to the quotation, and then Paul is adopting it in irony: "a proof of Christ who, as you say, is not weak toward you but strong in you," or it depends in substance on the οὐ φείσομαι: "you expect a proof of Christ which, as you will then see upon my appearing, is not weak toward you but strong in you." The third possibility, that Paul is quite generally conceding to the Corinthians that among them Christ is strong and not weak, is excluded. For that is indeed their own self-conscious assertion which he elsewhere constantly reproves and, as 13:5 shows, also doubts. Of the other two explanations, the latter is to be preferred, since only thus does vs. 4 follow intelligibly.

Some had made the charge against Paul that Christ is weak in him, or is not to be found in him at all, and this charge, which the apostle—to be sure, incorrectly—apparently connects with his physical weakness, he refutes with the christologically grounded reference (vs. 4a) to the paradoxical situation in which the apostle, with Christ at once strong and weak (vs. 4b; cf. 4:7-11; see pp. 160 ff.), stands; precisely *as such* he will be δυνατός among the Corinthians.[113]

The fact that the Corinthians were of the conviction that Christ was strong in them or they were strong in him is not called into question by the choice of this explanation.

What is interesting to us above all now is the demand of the Corinthians for a proof of the Christ who speaks in Paul. What does it mean? The terminology in which this demand is expressed is purely Gnostic and presupposes the Gnostic Christ myth as we have already become acquainted with it in Introduction A. The Pneuma dwelling in individual men is identical with Christ—ὁ κύριος τὸ πνεῦμά ἐστιν,

225

[113] Cf. II, 10:4, 8, 11; 13:10; I, 2:4; 5:4.

II, 3:17—thus a proof of the Christ who speaks in a man is the evidence of the Pneuma dwelling in him. In its original mythological meaning such a request consequently expresses the demand for ecstatic speech, i.e., above all, speaking in tongues. If this demand is met, then it is proved that one is dealing with a Pneumatic, in whom a part of the Pneuma-Christ resides.

In my opinion the Corinthians propounded their demand in this unblurred mythological sense. In itself, it is of course not impossible "τοῦ ἐν ἐμοὶ λαλοῦντος Χριστοῦ" was used metaphorically. Paul shows to what extent the terminology of the Gnostic myth could be made useful for genuinely historical thinking also. It could be accidental that the expression appearing here is not found in Paul. But it still is more than questionable whether the mythological Gnostics themselves could employ their own terminology in a figurative, demythologized sense. Besides, the Corinthians with their seeking for the proof of the Christ who is speaking in Paul make a quite concrete demand which had to be fulfilled just as concretely, and only then are they ready to recognize him as an apostle, that is, to hear what he has to say; for the apostolic rights are indeed the exclusive theme of the entire sorrowful epistle. Thus the δοκιμή which is to be produced cannot consist in Paul's somehow preaching more christologically or proving in his bearing toward the wicked members of the community that Christ *actually* is speaking in him. People will in fact recognize what *Paul* says as Christian statements only when it first is shown that *Christ* actually is speaking in him. Thus a preliminary σημεῖον is demanded (thus also Windisch, *in loc.*). But after all we have seen already, this can mean only that Paul shows that he too is a Pneumatic, and thus that he plainly possesses the gift of the Spirit, that is to say, ecstatic endowment. The language of our verse, however, expresses this demand only if we understand it in the original sense, not as metaphor.[114] Thus ἐν τινὶ λαλῶν Χριστός is to be equated with τὸ ἐν τινὶ ὂν πνεῦμα, so that in this way we obtain a vivid confirmation that the Corinthians identified the Pneuma with Christ.

It is also worthy of note that "δοκιμὴ τοῦ ἐν τινὶ λαλοῦντος Χριστοῦ" still probably cannot mean *"some kind of evidence* that the man is

---

[114] The question of what the *Corinthians* sought with their demand for a proof of the Christ who was speaking in Paul strangely has seldom been posed by the exegetes (and never correctly answered). But this is necessary, because the Corinthians cannot possibly have used the expression in the sense in which Paul takes it: to impose on them himself an unsparing punishment in the power of Christ. Of course Windisch thinks this (p. 417), since he incomprehensibly overlooks the fact that precisely the προημαρτηκότες καὶ οἱ λοιποὶ πάντες are demanding the proof of the Christ who is speaking in Paul. But if one poses the question, any answer other than the one given above is hardly possible.

speaking in Christ's mind" but *"direct proof, immediate guarantee of the speaking Christ himself."* But if, as is not to be doubted, this   227
proof coincides with the revelation of the Pneuma, then Christ and the Pneuma are actually identical; thus the Corinthian Gnostics are representatives of the myth described in Introduction A. W. Lütgert, who basically follows this same argument, thinks only of a proof of the heavenly Christ, because he also sees the Pneuma of the Corinthians still too much in the Pauline, demythologized sense as a heavenly gift, but not as the *other* Pneuma of II, 11:4, i.e., as the real self of the Gnostic.

If, after all this, the expression in 13:3 that interests us must be understood directly in its mythological content, this in no way means that Paul understood it thus. It is, on the contrary, only obvious that he, to whom this terminology was quite as familiar in its figurative sense as it is to us, while he did not at all know the real meaning, adopted the concrete demand of the Corinthians with the only understanding of it possible to him.[115] That this actually was the case is shown by the naïvely positive estimate of the Corinthians' demand in essence. We shall be able to observe the same phenomenon in the corresponding passages yet to be treated. It quite naturally does not occur to Paul to satisfy the demand of the Corinthians with a reference to his own speaking in tongues, even though, as I, 14:18 shows, this would have been no trouble to him and although, as is evident from II, 12:1 ff., he did not feel hindered in making such a reference within the context of his "foolish" boasting.[116]   228

Let us pause a moment at the actual outcome of this last investigation: the Corinthian Gnostics identified Christ and the Pneuma. Their Pneuma-Self is a part of the cosmic Christ who in primitive times took up residence in the bodies of all Pneumatics and intends to liberate his members imprisoned on earth. Thus they are representatives of the anthropological Christ myth. Here the specific conclusions of our Introduction A acquire their special significance for our theme.

---

[115] He was probably completely unaware of the strangeness of the Gnostic terminology for his utterances. The case is different, apparently, with the author of the Epistle of Barnabas: "ἐν τῷ κατοικητηρίῳ ἡμῶν ἀληθῶς ὁ θεὸς κατοικεῖ ἐν ἡμῖν. πῶς; ὁ λόγος αὐτοῦ τῆς πίστεως, ἡ κλῆσις αὐτοῦ τῆς ἐπαγγελίας, ἡ σοφία τῶν δικαιωμάτων, αἱ ἐντολαὶ τῆς διδαχῆς, αὐτὸς ἐν ἡμῖν προφητεύων," but then also without any interpretation: "αὐτὸς ἐν ἡμῖν κατοικῶν . . . ὁ γὰρ ποθῶν σωθῆναι βλέπει οὐκ εἰς τὸν ἄνθρωπον ἀλλὰ εἰς τὸν ἐν αὐτῷ κατοικοῦντα καὶ λαλοῦντα" (16:8 ff.).

[116] If one considers that this is the case although Paul has already for some time been debating with the same opponents, this fact becomes most instructive as to how much he is captive to his own thoughts and how little he has approximated actual Gnosticism or even understood it, in spite of his amazingly far-reaching appropriation of Hellenistic-Gnostic conceptions and concepts. Only for this reason can he be as naïve in his use of Gnostic terminology as he actually is (cf. pp. 132-33).

We had stated that this myth was resident in the Jewish area: the people who are proclaiming it in Corinth are Jews. In the earliest period, and long before Paul's missionary journeys, it was widespread in the Syrian-Phoenician region: they are Hellenistic Jews who are proclaiming to the Corinthians the Pneuma-Christ who dwells within man. It is naturally inclined to create in them a special apostolic consciousness of mission: that the Corinthian Gnostics and super-apostles were driven by such a missionary self-consciousness is unmistakable. Hence we need not marvel at the appearance of the anthropological Christ myth. According to all that we know of the earliest Christian Gnosticism—and the earliest source is the terminology widely distributed in the Pauline letters and kindred writings, a terminology which presupposes the figure of the inner Christ—it rather is almost to be expected that the Gnostics of Jewish origin, who are conducting a "Christian" mission at the same time as Paul, will hold this myth. They evidently travel on the tracks of Paul through Asia Minor and Greece, sent with letters of recommendation from community to community, and since the area whence they started out is not far from that point where Paul began preaching the crucified Christ, it is possible that they had already been active for a long time in Pauline congregations even of the early period before it came to a debate with Paul in Galatia and Greece which also is the first hostile encounter between Christianity and Gnosticism at all that is known to us for sure.

II, 13:5

Now we follow the further traces which the Corinthian epistles have preserved for us of the myth which was being represented in Corinth.

The idea of 13:2*b*-3 is continued in vs. 5, after the nonessential theological comment of vs. 4 (see pp. 193-94). When some demanded of Paul that he prove that Christ is in him, the apostle turns the point of the weapon the other way: "ἑαυτοὺς πειράζετε εἰ ἐστὲ ἐν τῇ πίστει, ἑαυτοὺς δοκιμάζετε· ἢ οὐκ ἐπιγινώσκετε ἑαυτοὺς ὅτι ᾽Ιησοῦς Χριστὸς ἐν ὑμῖν;" Since the Corinthians are firmly of the opinion that Christ is in them, and Paul also knows this, the clause "ἢ οὐκ ἐπιγινώσκετε ἑαυτοὺς ὅτι ᾽Ιησοῦς Χριστὸς ἐν ὑμῖν;" can only have the same skeptical meaning as the preceding demand for self-examination, thus with the sense of, "Or do you *not* recognize among yourselves that Christ is in you?" "εἰ μήτι ἀδόκιμοί ἐστε": "Then you would indeed be unproved!" When Paul here equates the ἐν τινὶ λαλῶν Χριστός with the Χριστὸς ἐν τινί in general, this certainly corresponds to the real intention of the Corinthians. They wish to hear or to see that Christ is *speaking* in Paul in order to recognize therein that he actually *is* in him, thus that Paul himself is a Pneumatic. Unfortunately it cannot be said whether in his use of "Ἰησοῦς Χριστὸς ἐν ὑμῖν" Paul consciously is following an expression of the Corinthians which originally expressed a challenge to him, or whether he himself generalizes the expression from 13:3. It is beyond question that the Corinthians spoke of the "Christ who is in man" just as they did of the "Christ who speaks in him" (cf. pp. 206-7).

II, 10:7

But now it is from this starting point also that the much discussed and disputed passage II, 10:7 is to be explained: "εἴ τις πέποιθεν ἑαυτῷ Χριστοῦ εἶναι, τοῦτο λογιζέσθω πάλιν ἐφ᾽ ἑαυτοῦ, ὅτι καθὼς αὐτὸς Χριστοῦ, οὕτως καὶ ἡμεῖς." Paul understands the Χριστοῦ εἶναι—there can be no serious dispute over this—in the most general sense, namely, = to belong to Christ, to be a Christian (cf. I, 3:23; 15:23; Gal. 3:29, *et passim*). However, it is just as certain that the formula was used in Corinth as a slogan by Christians against Christians and hence must have a quite specific meaning.[117] A reference to I, 1:12 puts this beyond all doubt. Windisch, Kümmel, and others think in this connection that with the appeal to Christ the special status of the apostle's ministry is to be grounded. In the first place, this is surely correct, for the whole discussion in the sorrowful epistle turns upon this theme. More important, however, is the question of what then is the *substance* of what is said with the Χριστοῦ εἶναι. How *can* ἡμεῖς Χριστοῦ ἐσμεν in the mouth of the Corinthians mean, "We have the position which you, Paul, claim unjustifiably for yourself, since you are not Χριστοῦ"? Are Paul's adversaries appealing to a personal acquaintance with Jesus Christ? Or are they saying that one can receive instructions only from the words of the Lord handed down? There is not the slightest reason for such an assumption. It is rather ruled out by the negative attitude of the Corinthian Gnostics toward the historical Jesus, quite apart from the fact that such an outlook could hardly have been expressed with Χριστοῦ εἶναι. If, with Lütgert and others, one thinks of revelations of the exalted Christ, one comes somewhat nearer to answering our question. But manifestations of the heavenly Christ are never directly mentioned in the Corinthian epistles. Instead, Paul's opponents always appeal to their possession of the Pneuma as such in their opposition to him. Therefore even here also ἐγώ εἰμι Χριστοῦ in the mouth of the Corinthian Gnostics as evidence of apostleship can mean nothing other than "ἐγώ εἰμι πνευματικός," and indeed in retrospect to all

230

231

---

[117] J. Weiss writes in his commentary, p. xxxvii: "Here Χριστοῦ εἶναι must be understood in a special, narrower, emphatic sense."

spiritual gifts *kat' exochen*. Anyone who is a Pneumatic, and *only* one who is a Pneumatic, is anything at all; naturally only he can qualify as an apostle. That is indeed the basic Gnostic thesis, as it has repeatedly appeared up till now. But if the Χριστοῦ εἶναι in the mouth of the Corinthians has the exact technical sense of πνευματικὸς εἶναι, and if some were denying Paul's being a Pneumatic with the expression that "he is not Christ's," then in view of the fact that Paul had before him decided Gnostics, the only thing possible is to interpret the Χριστοῦ εἶναι (= ἐν Χριστῷ εἶναι) [118] in the original, mythological sense. Only thus in fact is it comprehensible as a distinguishing and clearly identifying slogan in communities in which the expression was quite familiar, ever since Paul's preaching, as a general designation for the Christian position. The emphasizing of the fact that one is Christ's thus corresponds exactly to the assertion that one has the Spirit (I, 7:40). Because Christ himself is the Pneuma, or each individual Pneuma is a part of the Christ, the manner of expressing it can be changed at will, as in fact the prophets of Celsus can say in the same context: "ἐγὼ ὁ θεός εἰμι ἢ θεοῦ παῖς ἢ πνεῦμα θεῖον" (the passage is quoted on pp. 276-77).

Arguing in favor of such a mythological understanding of the slogan "Χριστοῦ ἐσμεν" is also the fact that the Χριστοῦ εἶναι obviously is inserted as a complement to the "ἐν σαρκὶ εἶναι" of vss. 3 ff. Some had accused Paul of walking κατὰ σάρκα. He refutes this charge with a reference to τὰ κατὰ πρόσωπον, namely: "If anyone thinks that *he* is Christ's, let him consider that just as he is Christ's, so are we." Naturally this line of argument is possible only if the Gnostics opposed the ἡμεῖς Χριστοῦ ἐσμεν to the derogatory ἐν σαρκί in such a way that in these formulas the two modes of existence conceivable to the Gnostic were expressed. However, since the being ἐν σαρκί in vss. 3 ff. was mythologically understood by Paul's opponents and referred to the man who still lived in the flesh, i.e., in merely fleshly substantial selfhood (cf. pp. 164 ff.), the Χριστοῦ εἶναι in the mouth of the Gnostics likewise cannot be said historically, and cannot express the consciousness of being able as this undeniably sarkical self to live only out of Christ's power. It must rather affirm the substantially different self which as light is fundamentally distinguished from the darkness of the *sarx*, that is, the Pneuma-self. Thus Χριστοῦ εἶναι is directly equivalent to πνευμα (τικὸς) εἶναι. Here the genitive Χριστοῦ is, to be more specific, a *genitivus partitivus:* every individual is a part of the cosmic Christ. Besides the frequent Χριστοῦ εἶναι in Paul's writings the οἱ τοῦ Χριστοῦ 232 of I, 15:23 and Gal. 5:24 may also go back to this Gnostic usage. Judg-

---

[118] This equation in Paul, e.g., in Gal. 3:28-29.

ing from the formula-like character of the οἱ τοῦ Χριστοῦ, it was hardly
formed *ad hoc* by Paul. But if the Χριστοῦ εἶναι is to be taken in this
mythological sense, we can further affirm that the meaning of this
expression cannot be limited to the discussion about the apostolate,
in which it appears in 10:7, but is relevant for anthropology in general.
Thus those who speak of a Christ *party* are correct, rather than those
who think only of Christ *apostles*.   233

I, 1:12

Inseparably connected with our passage is the ἐγὼ δὲ Χριστοῦ (in the
mouth of the Corinthians: ἐγώ εἰμι Χριστοῦ) of I, 1:12. The opinion
held by Bachmann, Windisch, and others, that the Christ party of
I Cor. has not the slightest to do with that of II Cor., is untenable.
One can propound such a thesis only if one has preconceived opinions
about the circumstances in Corinth, for the texts themselves do not
in the least demand such an interpretation. Even if not only some four
to five months lie between Epistle B and the sorrowful epistle, it requires quite a bit of imagination to suppose that a second outspoken
"Christ party" suddenly emerged in Corinth, a party which has in common with the first only the wording of the slogan. In view of the close
connection among the whole body of Corinthian epistles which has
repeatedly emerged in the preceding study, the substantial connection
between I, 1:12 and II, 10:7 also is beyond any doubt. But then the
same holds true for I, 1:12 as was noted in connection with II, 10:7.
The ἐγώ εἰμι Χριστοῦ is the watchword of those who hold their own
Self, the spark of the Pneuma lying in the prison of the body, to be a
part of the cosmic σῶμα Χριστοῦ. Thus they would have been able also
to assert in a sharpened fashion, "ἐγώ εἰμι ὁ Χριστός," as the Gnostics
in Epiph. XXVI.9 (see p. 54) do. Of course it is unlikely that they did
speak thus. The *genitivus partitivus* Χριστοῦ of the typically Gnostic
EGO EIMI formula expresses the consciousness which best conforms
to the myth that man is only a part of the Christ.[119] It would be going
too far afield to show the connection of this formula with the EGO
EIMI formulas which were widespread in other Gnosticism in manifold variations.[120] The common elements of this formula language

[119] The fact that Paul understood the "ἐγώ εἰμι Χριστοῦ" simply as the motto
of his opponents confirms again that the appeal to the possession of the Pneuma or
of the Pneuma-Christ stood at the center of the Corinthian heresy which is thereby
identified as Gnostic.

[120] To be compared with the literature on this problem cited by E. Stauffer in
TDNT II: 343 ff. is R. Bultmann's excursus in his commentary on John, p. 167, n. 2,
and esp. E. Schweizer, *EGO EIMI* (1939) .

                                                        234

with the ἐγώ εἰμι Χριστοῦ of the Corinthian Gnostics are of course evident.[121]

235   All this already indicates that I reject the thesis, greatly favored in recent exegesis and strongly assailed above all by J. Weiss, that the ἐγὼ δὲ Χριστοῦ is a gloss.[122] Some assert reservations about the genuineness of this clause because immediately thereafter Paul, with the μεμέρισται ὁ Χριστός, poses a question which, after the ἐγὼ δὲ Χριστοῦ of those who apparently claim the whole Christ, appears utterly uncalled for, and besides, in I, 3:23 he makes the Christ slogan his own without embarrassment.

But both are thoroughly pertinent if Paul understood the Christ slogan for what it was and as it was familiar to the Corinthians: the slogan of a group which precisely with its appeal to Christ was disturbing the unity of the congregation, a group which thus was misusing the only correct watchword, by using it to divide the body of Christ. Then the "μεμέρισται ὁ Χριστός" is in place, for the clause then is asking: "Is the σῶμα Χριστοῦ, the ἐκκλησία, divided?" But then there also is no occasion for Paul to have the use of this expression in I, 3:23 forbidden; no one can take it in his mouth as the Corinthian party motto; thus now as well as then no one will consequently accuse Paul 236   of recommending to the Corinthians that they join the "Christ people."

It seems to me, though, that something still more precise can be said about I, 1:12-13. The exegetes have noted repeatedly and often adduced against the authenticity of the "ἐγὼ δὲ Χριστοῦ" that with "μὴ Παῦλος ἐσταυρώθη κτλ." Paul intentionally overlooks this last slogan and refers only to the first three slogans. Exactly! But then it suggests itself also to think of the "μεμέρισται ὁ Χριστός" as directed only against the

---

[121] To be sure, the ἐγώ εἰμι formulas preserved for us everywhere already contain a nominative (as subject or predicate nominative) instead of the *genitivus part.*, and thus are self-expressions of the redeemer κατ' ἐξοχήν. That demonstrates the understandable fact, already mentioned in various connections, that in the struggle with the church, Gnosticism already quite early had to refrain from the extreme self-expression of every Gnostic which is formulated in the ἐγώ εἰμι Χριστοῦ, since it intolerably exposed the redeemer figure of Christ to every idiosyncrasy. But the widespread use of the genitive formula is shown, e.g., by the frequent Χριστοῦ εἶναι in Paul and the formula οἱ τοῦ Χριστοῦ in I, 15:23 and Gal. 5:24 (see p. 65), two ways of speaking which can best be explained in terms of the language of the Gnostic myth. Thus it would be a mistake to make a fundamental distinction between the ἐγώ εἰμι formula with the genitive (as a predicate nominative) and those with a nominative. We must only free ourselves from the traditional notion that the genitive in I, 1:12 can only be the genitive of *party* allegiance. Even if Paul must understand it thus (see below), this does not rule out the possibility that the Gnostics understood it in the sense of their belonging in *substance* to the Christ-primal man.

[122] J. Weiss (pp. 15-16) has rightly rejected other attempts at explanation (Räbiger: the fourth part is to be connected with each of the three preceding ones. 238   Von Dobschütz: the fourth part is to be understood as Paul's personal confession).

"ἐγώ εἰμι Χριστοῦ." Lütgert already had stated that the "μεμέρισται ὁ Χριστός" was directed *only* "against the Christ party" (*Freiheitspredigt und Schwarmgeister in Korinth*, p. 91). *In the first place,* there thus results a perfect rhetorical pattern, one that is abundant in vivid language: 237

ἐγὼ μέν εἰμι Παύλου, ἐγὼ δὲ Ἀπολλῶ, ἐγὼ δὲ Κηφᾶ,
ἐγὼ δὲ Χριστοῦ. μεμέρισται ὁ Χριστός;
μὴ Παῦλος ἐσταυρώθη ὑπὲρ ὑμῶν, ἢ εἰς τὸ ὄνομα Παύλου ἐβαπτίσθητε;

In the second place, then already in I, 1:12-13 the line of battle in Corinth comes clearly into view: the apostle's people against Gnostics, tradition against Spirit (see below). And *third,* "ἐγὼ δὲ Χριστοῦ. μεμέρισται ὁ Χριστός" can be understood as a wordplay which is as skillful as it is weighty, which will, however, mislead anyone who does not comprehend the situation.[123]   239

One also misses in the following discussion any reference to the Christ watchword. But apart from the fact that such a reference perhaps is found in 4:10, one could expect a more detailed discussion of wording of the slogan only if Paul had correctly perceived its meaning.   240
But that is not the case even at the time of the sorrowful epistle. And in Epistle B Paul conducts a steady polemic against the *position* which is expressed in the ἐγώ εἰμι Χριστοῦ. If one were to strike out the last of the four little clauses in vs. 12, then the Gnostic party which is responsible for all the disorder would not even be mentioned; for that it is concealed behind Paul, Apollos, or Cephas is completely ruled out. But Paul could not possibly have left unnoticed precisely the Gnostic slogan. And if one nevertheless foolishly seeks for it in the ἐγὼ δὲ Ἀπολλῶ or the ἐγὼ δὲ Κηφᾶ, then one cannot help having to see definite partisan theology also behind the remaining slogan. But

[123] The following interpretation of the passage also should be considered: If one assumes that Paul has grasped, at least in principle, the conception which stands behind the ἐγώ εἰμι Χριστοῦ, the μεμέρισται ὁ Χριστός could either ask whether the Christ is divided up into individual men, as the anthropological Christ myth asserts, or (as is more likely in view of Paul's knowledge of the situation) whether Jesus Christ is divided into the Christ κατὰ σάρκα and the Christ κατὰ πνεῦμα, so   241
that one could acknowledge the latter only with disregard for the former.
Lütgert, who apparently does not have in mind the equation Χριστός = ἐκκλησία, remarks, in continuation of the passage cited above on μεμέρισται ὁ Χριστός: "Such an objection would be a proper answer if they (the Christ party) are claiming for themselves a part of Christ in a special sense. We would have to know more of this party if we expected rightly to understand the objection." As an objection to the anthropological Christ myth or to the dualistic Christology, the "μεμέρισται ὁ Χριστός" is an undoubtedly proper and fitting answer. But in the light of all that we have been able to determine, I consider it unlikely that Paul had comprehended the position of his opponents to the extent presupposed by all these explanations, quite apart from the fact that it apparently is Paul's intention in I, 1:13a to charge the "Christ party" with the rending of the *community.*

at the very moment in which one assumes two distinct battlefronts against which Paul is aligned in Corinth, the problem of the Corinthian heresy becomes insoluble.

Since moreover in II, 10:7 the ἐγώ εἰμι Χριστοῦ is presupposed as a watchword in Corinth, it is in any case a curious solution born of a predicament when one excises the same formula in I, 1:12 as a gloss that can be explained as such only with a fanciful imagination.

If ἐγώ εἰμι Χριστοῦ is the watchword of those against whom in all his letters Paul takes a position as against a single front, then the other three slogans are directed against the fourth, and on their part form —at least in this discussion—a united party which is not fighting within itself but whose strength lies precisely in the fact that over against the Gnostics it can appeal [124] to Paul as well as to Apollos and Peter.[125] Such an appeal may have been strengthened by Gnostic attacks on the authority of the church's apostles in general. As for example the passage from Iren. I, 13.6, quoted on p. 277, shows, such attacks are common in later Gnosticism. Basically, however, the appeal rests on the fact that some in opposition to the new teachers referred to the old ones.

Thus in Corinth apostolic tradition stands against free pneumatic status! The appeal to the Christ without against the appeal to the Christ within! The invocation of witnesses against the self-testimony! The message mediated through men against the ἐν τινὶ λαλῶν Χριστός! Precisely in I, 1:12-13, where Paul treats and rejects the "Christ" slogan and "apostle" slogans separately, the fundamental unity of the "apostle people" against the "Christ people" becomes clear.

242

[124] One must not forget that the community in Corinth consisted of a not inconsiderable number of *house* churches. The oldest ones had been established by Paul, and they appealed above all to Paul in their opposition to the Gnostics. Others, which on the basis of the agreement of Gal. 2:9 must be found in *Jewish* homes, are a result of the missionary work of Peter. They undoubtedly were not anti-Pauline—Paul assumes that they read and heed his epistle just as do the "Paulinists"—but in their opposition to the Gnostics they understandably appealed primarily to Peter. The majority of the communities can be traced back to Apollos. Hence they appealed to Apollos and to the gospel as *he* proclaimed it to them, and hoped also to see him again among them (I, 16:12), without thereby coming into any tension with Paul. The *various* slogans with apostles' names within the *unified* anti-Gnostic front therefore are nothing unusual, but a phenomenon whose absence would have to be a puzzle to us.

[125] It cannot be determined *with certainty* whether Peter was personally in Corinth, whether disciples of his did missionary work there in his name, or whether individual Corinthians had come into contact with him elsewhere. I regard the first of these alternatives as by far the most likely. Of course it cannot be proved, but still less is it possible to prove the opposite, as M. Goguel has attempted in *Rev. d'hist. et de philos. relig.*, 1934, pp. 461 ff. The mistake of Lietzmann, who has argued emphatically at various places *in favor* of Peter's stay in Corinth, was that he understood the activity of Peter as directed against Paul. Criticism could properly begin

243   here.

It is possible that there were also certain tensions in the "apostolic" group. However, this is not likely, and Paul at all events does not presuppose such tensions. According to I, 4:6 the expressions about Paul and Apollos are meant by him only figuratively. Thus he does not at all assume that people in Corinth are appealing to him and Apollos as to opposing party leaders (see p. 202, n. 124), and thus also did not intend to convince the Corinthians that they are in error when they do this. Instead, he has chosen himself and Apollos, who, as the Corinthians also know, have no conflicts of any kind, as an example for genuine division into parties. The actual opposing party, however, is that of the Gnostics, as 4:7-8 shows. It is actually what he has in mind. This gives a good internal motivation for the abrupt external transition from 4:6 to 4:7. If Paul did not speak directly, it was simply because the circumstances which he had in mind were not sufficiently well known to him. | 244

It is also worthy of note that at every point in I, 1–4 where Paul is reproving specific things, a connection with the three slogans about the apostles is not evident. And naturally just as little is one of these "parties" even once mentioned in any other passage in the epistles. | 245
And when in 3:3–11:21 ff. Paul comes back to the watchwords, this evidently is not done basically in order to combat known partisan activities against him among the individual followers of apostles, but out of the specific occasion of being obliged to prove that the Corinthians are still sarkics. Of course he appeals decisively not to the partisan disputes as evidence, but to the wrongness of the "καυχᾶσθαι κατὰ σάρκα," that is, of appealing to man instead of Christ.[126] And the slogans offer an occasion at least externally for such a complaint. In any case Paul nowhere knows anything of the occasionally conflicting views of the Paul group and the Apollos group, and all the less of the followers of Cephas.

Finally, I, 1:12-13 also shows, under the interpretation given above, that Paul is not assuming conflicts among the apostles' people. For the "μεμέρισται ὁ Χριστός" is indeed addressed to the "Christ people," i.e. to the Gnostics, and indeed *only* to them. *They* are destroying the unity of the community that is built "on the foundation of the

[126] ζῆλος and ἔρις are indeed mentioned in I, 3:3*b*, but there is nothing to argue for understanding these disputes here as quarrels between the old members of the community, while everywhere else where Paul mentions them, they appear between the intruding Gnostics and the "apostolic people." The γάρ in vs. 4, which contains the slogans, indeed does not refer to the ζῆλος καὶ ἔρις, but to the σαρκικὸς εἶναι at the end of vs. 3. Thus the slogans cited are not meant to prove the presence of controversies, but by means of a new argument to prove the assertion that the Corinthians are still σαρκικοί because they are making their appeal to men.

apostles." The complaint against the apostles' groups, on the other hand, runs: How could you appeal to men instead of Christ? That is what the σαρκικοί do (I, 3:3-4). Or was Paul crucified for you? There is only one slogan for Christians: "ἐγώ εἰμι Χριστοῦ" (I, 3:23)! The fault of the apostles' people is this, that in the effort to preserve the unity of the church against the Gnostics (thus!), they are appealing to men instead of Christ.

The often-proposed opinion that the teachers of wisdom in 1:17–2:5 are Apollos' followers is impossible. Apollos would have had to reject the cross and yet remain Paul's friend! And how then would the sharp polemic in 1:17–2:5 against the preaching of "Apollos" agree with the stressing in 3:4 ff. of the concord between Paul and Apollos (cf. 16:12)? Even J. Weiss (p. xxxiv) must concede that in view of the abrupt change in attitude in 3:10 ff. as compared with 3:3-9, Apollos and his followers cannot possibly be meant in 3:10 ff. But, since the polemic against the σοφοί in 3:18 ff. is indissolubly connected with 3:10-17, neither can the target of Paul's attack in 3:10-17 be the mysterious Cephas group. The problem of this passage is soluble only if Paul here is conducting a polemic against the Gnostics, who *actually* are meant by the μετασχηματισμός in 3:3-9 (cf. Lütgert, pp. 99-100).[127]

Similarly, however, the entire polemic of both canonical Corinthian epistles is aimed in substance at the immigrant "Christ people," that is, the Gnostic representatives of the anthropological Christ myth, together with their Corinthian partisans, and in this alignment of battle lines, there stand on Paul's side all those who rely upon the apostolic tradition.[128] It is surprising how precisely this situation corre-

---

[127] In fact, in the last analysis one cannot isolate the polemic against the "preaching of wisdom" which is found in I, 1–3 from the corresponding polemic in the rest of the epistle. Thus one would have to make Apollos, the friend of Paul, into the champion of the anti-Pauline mythological Gnosticism in Corinth, who with letters of recommendation has sneaked into the community (II, 3:1) and now, while his followers rave against Paul in Corinth, in Ephesus basks in the sunlight of the friendship of his great opponent and acts as if he knows nothing of what is going on. Impossible! Here one can no longer build the *pons asinorum* that the followers of Apollos had drawn "false consequences" from Apollos' preaching. Gnosticism is no misunderstanding of the Pauline *kerygma* and in no wise can be so, by its very nature, especially since Paul moreover already presupposes Gnosticism.

[128] De Wette has already seen all this, in principle quite correctly, though of course from his contemporaries and successors he hardly received much more for his labors than an uncomprehending wagging of the head, in spite of this perceptive insight which was far in advance of his time. Cf. e.g., "While the parties of Paul, Apollos, and Cephas acknowledged apostolic authority, the Christ party scorned the authority of all apostles." "They named themselves after Christ . . . because their leaders claimed to have a secret, direct fellowship with Christ by means of visions and revelations (inspiration)." ". . . could these Pneumatics or

sponds to the situation during the later great battle against Gnosticism, in which the appeal to apostolic doctrine and tradition was the chief weapon of the church's heresy fighters against the free pneumatic.

Thus in Epistle B Paul has already formed a *fundamentally* correct estimate of the situation in Corinth. Here, as later, he is acquainted with only the *one* antithesis of the "Christ people" against those who cherish the apostolic tradition, but of course, here, as later, has not recognized the "Christ people" as Gnostics or understood them as such in their concerns. How little Paul comprehended the situation in Corinth *in detail* is shown precisely in I, 1:12 by his placing in parallel, without embarrassment, the Christ slogan and the apostle slogans. This is possible because Paul erroneously understands the ἐγώ εἰμι Χριστοῦ in the demythologized sense which was familiar to him; I belong to Christ, am a Christian (thus still in the sorrowful epistle, II, 10:7!). He may himself have coined the other forms in their precise form *ad hoc* after the pattern of this catchword-like slogan of the Christ group. Thus one may by no means reject the interpretation in the sense of the myth, as given here, of the Corinthian formula ἐγώ εἰμι Χριστοῦ, with the correct assertion that in I, 1:12 Paul cannot possibly have thought of an identity of substance of the "apostle people" with their apostles.

In summary it may be said that not only the total context of the epistles but even the correct interpretation of I, 1:12-13 and of the statements in I, 1–4 following therefrom convincingly demand that we think of only *one* enemy front. Since these four chapters forbid the view that followers of one of the apostles were agitating against Paul, and since later in the Corinthian letters Paul does not indicate with a single word that he connects one of the false teachings which he is opposing with Peter or Apollos, it naturally follows that only the Christ people come into consideration as the opposing party. Indeed they also appear at least in the sorrowful epistle as Paul's adversaries with the same watchword as in I, 1:12, and it could be shown how precisely this slogan of theirs fits into the unified picture of the heretical theology in Corinth which we have been able to form on the basis of the preceding study. Paul cannot be expected to have taken a position frequently or in a thoroughgoing manner especially against

Gnostics, whose Gnosticism likely was of a Jewish kind, place value upon Jewish lineage." "It was quite natural that those Corinthians who were converted by Paul held to the authority of this apostle. But now others had been converted by Apollos, and these held to him." ". . . it appears quite natural that the Jewish Christians in Corinth chose Peter as their head. But he was not thereby for them a hostile opponent to Paul . . . ; for even Peter did not find himself in this opposition." (*Das NT griechisch mit kurzem Kommentar*, nach W. M. L. de Wette [Halle, 1885], pp. 109-10).

the appeal to Christ; for in fact he was not familiar with its actual background, and he could not at all properly object to the *wording* of the Christ slogan, because he had borrowed it from the Gnostics to describe his own stance of faith (cf. I, 3:23). And in fact Paul conducts the *material* polemic against the Χριστοῦ εἶναι by taking a stand against the Corinthians' doctrine of the Pneuma and the Gnostics' καύχησις based upon it.

I, 4:10

We have not yet considered all the passages in which Paul's polemic could refer to the anthropological Christ myth. I, 4:10 also comes into consideration: "ἡμεῖς μωροὶ διὰ Χριστόν, ὑμεῖς δὲ φρόνιμοι ἐν Χριστῷ." What is striking in this passage is the alternation of διὰ Χριστόν and ἐν Χριστῷ. Since a material distinction between the two formulations is not at once apparent, most exegetes explain it as an "attractive" (J. Weiss) rhetorical variation. This explanation naturally is possible and also adequate in itself, especially since Paul likes to vary his prepositions. Of course if one observes that our verse is unquestionably polemical, and in fact is aimed at the puffed-up Gnostics who boast of the "Χριστὸς ἐν ἡμῖν," then one should nevertheless ask whether the change in expression is not prompted by a polemical interest. If one does this, then one also notes that the Pauline expression which adopts the language of the Gnostics, "φρόνιμοι ἐν Χριστῷ" (cf. II, 11:19), corresponds exactly to their myth. ἐν Χριστῷ εἶναι, another formula for "Χριστοῦ εἶναι," is indeed for the myth as for Paul fully equivalent to "Χριστὸν ἐν ἑαυτῷ ἔχειν." The conception of the cosmic σῶμα Χριστοῦ, whose parts the individual Pneuma-selves are, allows the view that the individual man is in Christ, as well as the view that Christ lives in the individual man.

Heinrici says on our passage: "Note how Paul does not repeat διὰ Χριστόν; the Christian sham-wisdom had different interests." I consider it in fact most highly probable that Paul deliberately intended by means of the διὰ Χριστόν to set himself apart from the ἐν Χριστῷ of his opponents. Without being clear about its exact meaning, he did comprehend that the ἐν Χριστῷ of the Gnostics had nothing more to do with the meaning which he assigned to this expression. The διὰ Χριστόν, however, in contrast to the quite general ἐν Χριστῷ, which in figurative usage was capable of any interpretation, required a quite definite conception of the relationship of the individual to Christ. The διά may be translated, similarly to that in II, 4:5 and 4:11, as "for Christ's sake," or, better, "through Christ's instigation." It then expresses, perhaps deliberately, the fundamental personal distinction

between Christ and the individual man. Whatever may be the case
as to the details, it appears to me not unlikely that with the φρόνιμοι
ἐν Χριστῷ precisely as with the ἐγὼ δὲ Χριστοῦ Paul consciously is
referring to a usage of language employed by the Corinthians and
thereby unconsciously to the anthropological Christ myth.

II, 11:23

II, 11:23 also belongs in this context: "διάκονοι Χριστοῦ εἰσιν;
παραφρονῶν λαλῶ, ὑπὲρ ἐγώ." The basic context of this passage, with
all those previously considered which expressed that the Corinthians
appeal to Christ in a quite special way, is beyond any doubt. Of course
at first glance one can be puzzled since the designation διάκονοι
Χριστοῦ neither conforms to the inflated self-consciousness of the
Gnostics nor exactly corresponds to their Christ myth. Indeed it is not
impossible that the Gnostics occasionally were able to describe themselves as servants of Christ. The individual, as a part of the whole
σῶμα Χριστοῦ, particularly in view of the "Christ" who had entered
into Jesus, perhaps could have been called διάκονος Χριστοῦ and, as   248
an apostle, in a certain way even felt himself to be such. But this is
not very likely.

It is rather to be assumed that the non-Gnostic formulation is to
be attributed to Paul. Within the discussion about the apostolate,
from his presuppositions he could not understand the Χριστοῦ εἶναι
of his opponents in any way other than that they thereby claimed a
special servant relationship to Christ. To be sure, he denied that there
was actually such a servant relationship on their part, but this does not
change the fact that he can first, without taking a position, cite their
claim which he thus interprets, that they are servants of Christ, since
he is concerned only with claiming for himself this title rightfully
and emphatically.

In view of the intention of the Gnostics it would of course have
been more correct and less subject to misunderstanding if Paul had
written, as in vs. 7, only: "Χριστοῦ εἰσιν; παραφρονῶν λαλῶ, ὑπὲρ ἐγώ."
But Paul obviously intends now to speak specifically of the apostolic
office. Hence he interprets the Χριστοῦ εἶναι as διάκονος Χριστοῦ εἶναι,
and from his point of view this interpretation is altogether pertinent;
for people were disputing his apostolic *servant* relationship to Christ
because he was not "Christ's," without its being clear to Paul that his
opponents were basically concerned simply with anthropology. Hence
the Pauline interpretation of the bare Χριστοῦ εἶναι is in itself of course
incorrect. But *thus* considered it is no less incorrect when in what
follows Paul alludes to his *peristaseis*. For any Gnostic will laugh at

him if he intends to prove therewith that he is "Christ's." The mistaken understanding on Paul's part of the anthropological myth of the Gnostics is thus the ultimate cause of the erroneously interpretative formulation, "διάκονοι Χριστοῦ εἰσιν," which with this exposition argues for, not against, the fact that some in Corinth under the slogan "ἐγώ εἰμι Χριστοῦ" identified themselves entirely substantially with the heavenly Pneuma-Christ.

That Paul places the comparison between his perception of the apostolic ministry and the missionary concern of the Gnostics under the rubric διάκονος/διακονία could be connected *in general* with the widespread distribution which the term διάκονος has found in Hellenism for the designation of religious emissaries. *In particular* Paul again takes up the concept διάκονος from II, 11:15, where it apparently had been introduced by Paul himself.

Of course now anyone who asserts that 11:23, like 11:22, offers a word-for-word expression of the Gnostic Corinthians cannot demand that one *prove* to him the contrary. But the interpretation given here is in any case unobjectionable and therewith the only one given in the context of our study as a whole. I should doubt, moreover, that with the almost identical formulations in vs. 22 Paul intends to reproduce nothing but verbatim labels of the Corinthians. In these words Paul takes up, in what are probably his *own* formulations, the fact that the false teachers in Corinth are boasting of their Jewish origin. *His* interpretation of the Χριστοῦ εἶναι of his opponents with the διάκονοι Χριστοῦ εἰσιν is no different.

That Jewish-Christian Gnostics, in spite of their depreciation of the flesh, could and did glory in their connection with the Old Testament people of God in a certain frame of reference is explained from the fact that the Old Testament even to many Gnostics—especially to those of Jewish origin—was a book of revelation, and the salvation-history, including the "Son of Man," insofar as it could be understood prophetically, had in no way lost its significance. In this connection one may note a comment about the Valentinians in Iren. I, 3.6: *"Et non solum autem ex Evangelicis et Apostolicis tentant ostensiones facere . . . , sed etiam ex Lege at Prophetis, cum multae parabolae et allegoriae sint dictae, et in multa trahi possint ambiguum per expositionem . . ."* or the Old Testament quotation of the Naassene Preaching in Hippolytus. The Jewish Gnostics with whom Ignatius, according to Ign. Philad. 8.2, debated, also held very deliberately to the authority of the Old Testament.[129]

---

[129] Also in Phil. 3:2 ff., a passage which may well have been directed against the same Gnostics (cf. Vol. 2, pp. 47 ff.) , it is presupposed that Paul's opponents boasted

II, 12:1-10

A further reference to the anthropological Christ myth represented in Corinth is perhaps to be inferred from the section II, 12:1-10. Of course this part of the apostle's "talking like a fool," which actually forms the center of the entire sorrowful epistle, is also informative about other previously discussed conceptions of the Corinthian schismatics. This justifies a somewhat more thorough examination of this passage.

Windisch writes (p. 368) : "It is nowhere *here* indicated that the opponents also can boast of such visions," and from this he concludes that Paul here is boasting of unique advantages which played no role at all in Corinth. While in 11:22-23 we read, "they—I too," or "they—I all the more," here it is, "I alone." One can express such a judgment only if one basically misunderstands the nature of Paul's boasting in the sorrowful epistle.[130] Paul is prompted to his unseemly boasting only by the fact that his opponents are appealing, for the grounding of their position, to certain advantages which Paul does not recognize as such. But since some are disputing Paul's apostolic rights because he does not possess these Corinthian distinctions, he must prove that he too has them at his disposal. In that very act he falls into the awkward position of boasting of such things as, according to his opinion, one may not at all boast of possessing.

Now it is from this perspective that 12:1 is to be understood. Following the only possible text, one offered by P[46] H G L *et al.,* it may

254

---

of their Jewish ancestry. Indeed, they even placed value upon circumcision and perhaps even practiced it in their communities. This is not, in itself, surprising. The practice of circumcision is also attested for us elsewhere among Jewish Gnostics (the Ebionites, cf. Epiph. XIX.5; XXX.2, 26 ff.; Elchasaites, cf. Hipp. IX, 14.1; Cerinthus, cf. Epiph. XXVIII.5; Dositheus, cf. article in *Realencyclopädie*). It will everywhere have had the sense of symbolizing the annihilation of the *sarx*, a significance which may well lie in the mythical background of the "circumcision of Christ" in Col. 2:11. Of course it is strange then that Paul never wages a polemic against circumcision in Corinth. However, one can imagine without difficulty that the Gnostics did not propagate this custom, which was not very significant for them, and which must have encountered the very sharpest opposition in the strictly Pauline and moreover almost purely Gentile-Christian community in Corinth— a kind of behavior that would have been inconceivable for Judaizers (cf. also Vol. 2, pp. 27 ff.). For *Gnostics* this does not mean that they were hypocrites who concealed their own Jewish views.

On the significance of the Jewish tradition for most branches of Gnosticism, cf. among others W. Bousset, [1], pp. 324 ff.; G. Strecker, *Das Judenchristentum in den Pseudoclementinen*, pp. 162 ff.; L. Goppelt, *Christentum und Judentum im ersten und zweiten Jahrhundert*, pp. 130 ff. Unfortunately, today the inference is often drawn from the ever more clearly recognized wide distribution of Jewish Gnosticism in pre-Christian times that Gnosticism is also of Jewish *origin* (see pp. 77-78).

253

[130] Thus most recently H. J. Schoeps, [3], pp. 75-76, 81.

be translated freely as follows: "I am compelled to boast; although it is utterly absurd, I come now . . . ." Later, in 12:5 ff., Paul expressly, emphatically, and redundantly declares that he, the apostle—and the entire sorrowful epistle is in fact concerned only with this subject— could in no way boast of the pictured experiences. He boasts of his weakness. Thus he has spoken unwillingly and under compulsion of the ὀπτασίαι and ἀποκαλύψεις; but what would have compelled him to do this but the boasting of his adversaries in the same area? Thus if one wishes to deny that Paul here *also* is boasting of the visions, one must then stand the course of thought of the entire sorrowful epistle on its head and moreover make the legitimate charge against Paul that he does glory in *himself*, not in Christ, his own weakness, his ministry. For one who agrees in essence with the foregoing statements of this study it is also evident, even apart from our present passage, that the Corinthian Gnostics knew and practiced ecstatic raptures. Also the detailed exegesis, especially of vss. 2-3, will show that the text is fully understandable only if Paul here is yielding to the demand of the Corinthians that he demonstrate on his own part their advantages.

255

Besides all this, there is the fact that if he here would boast of his quite personal advantages which supported his apostolic office, in the first place Paul would have to name the vision of Christ at Damascus, upon which in fact his claim to that office actually is based elsewhere (Gal. 1:12; I, 9:1; 15:8). The fact that here he does not mention this vision in the face of the Corinthians, although his office is nowhere attacked as vigorously as in the dispute with them, shows that Paul is standing in a decidedly defensive position in which the opponents dictate his choice of weapons; and the Damascus experience has for Paul a fundamentally different character from that portrayed in 12:1 ff. Even there, where he is not even boasting, he selects a "polemical" boast. Thus in II, 10:12-18, because the adversaries invade alien territory; in II, 11:23-33, because they are boasting of their strength. Finally, strictly speaking Paul would contradict his negative estimate, expressed in Epistle B (I, 12–14; cf. pp. 171 ff.) and in Epistle C (II, 5:11-15, cf. pp. 187 ff.), of the pneumatic experiences, so far as they do not remain limited to the realm of personal religion, if he now all at once and voluntarily boasts *to others* of that which concerns no one but God and himself (I, 14:2; II, 5:13). Our entire passage is rather permeated with bitterness over the fact that the apostle is compelled by the ἐν προσώπῳ καυχώμενοι (II, 5:12) to engage in the same utterly unbecoming boasting.

The meaning and form of the Gnostic experiences to which Paul alludes are at once evident. While they last the Pneuma-self of man anticipates the conditions of the future perfection. Thus the "soul" of the Gnostic leaves the body and temporarily is submerged in the cosmic σῶμα Χριστοῦ. This practice presupposes a sharp dualism of body and soul and is not only found in Gnosticism of all kinds but is also well known in Hellenism. For its occurrence, examples, and lists of the literature I refer to the excursus in Lietzmann, *in loc.*, to the statements in Windisch, pp. 374 ff., and to Reitzenstein's *Hellenistische Mysterienreligionen*, pp. 403-17. That which Paul calls ὀπτασίαι and ἀποκαλύψεις—it cannot be said with certainty whether the Gnostics used the same terms—is thus the highest form of ecstasy. While during the speaking in tongues the Pneuma did not leave the body, but performed only as in principle detached from it, during the ecstasy it leaves behind it the prison cell of the body and actually beholds the heavenly world, its true homeland.

256

257

We must raise the question whether during his portrayal in 12:2 ff. Paul was thinking of a celestial journey in this hellenistically Gnostic sense. The question is to be answered in the negative. Two reasons may suffice here to demonstrate this.

In the first place, the Gnostic dualism is foreign to Paul. We have previously been able repeatedly to ascertain that he simply did not understand it with the Gnostics. For proof of the contrary one cannot point to II, 5:1-10. This section will be investigated more fully later on, but it may be said now that in it Paul is waging a polemic with all emphasis precisely *against* a bodiless existence of man, and indeed apparently because he cannot imagine such an existence.

In the second place, the twice-stressed affirmation that he did not know whether he had been ἐν σώματι or ἐκτὸς τοῦ σώματος during the rapture shows that Paul at least considers it *possible* that he did *not* leave the body. Therewith, however, the central concern pursued by the Gnostic dualist with the practice of his celestial journey, namely the liberation from the body, is directly and apparently deliberately denied (on this, see below).

Nor may we infer, of course, that Paul was thinking of a bodily ascension to heaven in the Jewish sense. The parenthetical comments in 12:2-3 rather show that the question as to the form of the rapture did not interest him at all (see below). What mattered to him was only the fact that he had been in Paradise, that is, that in a moment of his earthly life he had once already reached the heavenly goal, that for a moment faith became sight (cf. II, 12:1: ὀπτασίαι, and II, 5:7). Therewith however the *scope* of his statements coincides exactly with the actual concern of the Gnostics, for whom everything hinged on their asserting their salvation already in the present as an assured possession, and their proving this fact by means of a public demonstration of ecstasy. Precisely as in the polemic in I, 4:7 ff. against his satisfied opponents who have "become kings" and the corresponding passages already treated, Paul also shows here that he has recognized the existential basic attitude, the self-consciousness of the Gnostics, so precisely that he can methodically examine it even though the mythical background of such an attitude has not become clear to him.

Now it is again typical how Paul existentially evaluates his own experience of rapture which anticipated vision, and which the Gnostics compelled him to mention. He speaks of the perfected "I" as though he himself was not at all the one who experienced this. It is customary to explain this by saying that the apostle is speaking in modest style. But this affirmation does not suffice; for as little as Paul wishes to boast, he still intends from the very first to leave no doubt about it; on the contrary, the very thing that is important to him is that *he* is the one who has had these revelations. If in Paul's way of speaking a certain modesty is given expression, it is certainly not such *false* modesty and naturally much less a formal, rhetorical one, which also is foreign to Paul elsewhere and is completely out of place in the sorrowful epistle.

The use of the third person becomes understandable only when one sees it against the background of the Gnostic "immodesty." We have determined that Paul repeatedly takes a position sharply against the assertion of his opponents that they already here and now had achieved the ultimate existence. His "basic religious feeling" is, in spite of all his certainty of salvation, that of the "not yet." He affirms the "already now" only in faith. While ecstatic experiences of all kinds are for the Gnostics a normal, fitting, and appropriate expression of their present, perfected existence, Paul in his rapture experiences what he one day will be, not what he already is now. While the Gnostic thus sees *himself* in Paradise, it is by no means the Paul who is a man and apostle walking in faith who has heard the ἄρρητα ῥήματα. Paul could not at all have made this point and therewith the contrast to the Gnostics any more vividly and impressively than by making a fundamental distinction between his present Self and this his future Self. He is the ἄνθρωπος ἐν Χριστῷ who he will one day become and already has been temporarily, fourteen years earlier, in a moment of most marvelous and exalted experience. Thus the modesty of the apostle is the attitude of the believer who knows about his future without having it in his possession. And when this is emphasized by him here in such a striking fashion, it is done in view of the fact that under compulsion he boasts even of a perfection experience vis-à-vis those

258

who only naturally renounce modesty on the basis of similar but differently interpreted experiences.[131]

The following verses also may be shown to be prompted exclusively by the anti-Gnostic tendency, that a judgment of a man in terms of the ὑπερβολὴ τῶν ἀποκαλύψεων—and the Gnostic self-consciousness indeed is based upon this—is utterly wrong, since the only objective expression of our present form of existence is the weakness in which the believer experiences and receives the power of Christ. Paul's distinction applies to the Gnostics who boast ὑπὲρ ἑαυτῶν when they refer to their ecstasies: "For *this* (other) I will glory; for myself however I glory only in my weaknesses." Verse 6 follows this somewhat strangely with γάρ: "That is to say, if I wanted to boast (of this experience for myself instead of for this one), I would not be committing a folly; for I spoke the truth. But I (prefer to) refrain, so that . . . ." Thus Paul probably knows that *he* has experienced the same thing which had happened to that other man in so marvelous a fashion, but he also knows that he cannot simply identify himself *hic et nunc* with that man, "so that no one may form a judgment about me beyond what he sees in me or hears from me, in terms of the marvelous exceptional phenomena of the revelations," that is, so judge him on the basis of his 259 ecstatic experience as though he himself were already no longer the Paul κατὰ σάρκα who still stands before them, visible and audible, but the other one, who is already perfected.

It appears certain to me that this is the sense of vss. 6b and 7a. Whether the text as transmitted to us is in order is, of course, more than questionable. One expects something like the following Greek wording: "μή τις εἰς ἐμὲ λογίσηται ὑπὲρ ὃ βλέπει με ἢ ἀκούει ἐξ ἐμοῦ κατὰ τὴν ὑπερβολὴν τῶν ἀποκαλύψεων." Then "κατὰ [132] τὴν ὑπερβολὴν τῶν ἀποκαλύψεων" would be an adverbial phrase modifying λογίσηται. If anyone wishes to conjecture thus, his conjecture would in any case be as justified as the diverse attempts at producing an intelligible text which the commentaries exhibit. Since the sense of the verse cannot

---

[131] It is entirely possible that Paul has adopted this way of speaking of the other "I" somehow from the language of the mysteries, in which the self of man as the actual "I" attained to the vision, while the ordinary "I," the natural, sarkic man, remained on earth. But this is still a long way from meaning that Paul connected the Gnostic-dualistic conception with it, as Reitzenstein ([1], pp. 415 ff.) immediately deduces from the terminology. It is true that elsewhere also Paul constantly makes use of dualistic language for his own conceptions, and it certainly can be shown that here Paul is not thinking as a dualist (see above).

[132] λογίζομαι κατά is customary; cf. Rom. 4:4. If with λογίζεσθαι instead of κατά the mere dative could stand, the present (Egyptian) text perhaps could be maintained.

be in doubt, a more detailed examination of the question, still not
certainly soluble, of the original text need not be pursued.

Although Paul thus would have had the same rights as the Gnostics
to boast of his perfected self, he abstains from this so that no one will
get the idea that he is boasting of *himself* and then pass the judgment
on him that his actuality *hic et nunc* does not at all agree. In contrast
to the Gnostics, Paul knows that he ἐνδημῶν ἐν τῷ σώματι ἐκδημεῖ ἀπὸ
τοῦ κυρίου (II, 5:6),[133] and for this reason he is glad in the last analysis
that he has a thorn in the flesh which makes clear to him at all times
that the earth is the reality of Christians, too. Paul is not deceived
about his existence: "ὅταν ἀσθενῶ, τότε δυνατός εἰμι." [134] By the
"modest" way in which Paul relates the experience demanded of him,
as also by his personal confession in 12:6 ff., he makes it impossible
for anyone to interpret his experience, about which he would have
preferred to be completely silent, in a Gnostic sense, and at the same
time he indirectly aims a sharp attack at the arrogant feeling of per-
260   fection of his opponents.

Thus in essence the peculiar background of the statements in II,
12:1-10 is exhibited, and with it anew the Gnostic self-consciousness of
the Corinthians clearly emerges. Now we must go on to point to two
details of our text which are not without significance for us. First,
it is striking that in 12:2, where he speaks of his other self, he refers
to this as an "ἄνθρωπος ἐν Χριστῷ." He claims the "ἐν Χριστῷ εἶναι" in
the figurative sense in general for the ordinary Christian, that is, also
and precisely for the one who glories in his weakness. When he limits
261   it here to the perfected man he makes use of the pure Gnostic conception. For to the Gnosticism of the "inner Christ" everyone who is "in
Christ," i.e., every Pneumatic, is perfect, while to the person who
lives only in the tangibility of the earthly sarkical existence, this
predicate cannot possibly apply. But when Paul, in contrast to his
usage elsewhere, employs the "ἐν Χριστῷ" in 12:2 in a genuinely Gnostic way, in that he applies it only to the ecstatic Pneumatic, not to believers in general, the question is, what prompted him to do this? Either
the expression "ἄνθρωπος ἐν Χριστῷ" as a technical designation for the
person in ecstasy is known and familiar to him so that he does not sense
the tension in which it stands to his manner of speaking elsewhere,
or he adopts the expression from the terminology of the Corinthian

---

[133] This basically un-Pauline formulation to express his consciousness of his
transitory character of course is occasioned by the polemic also (see pp. 269-70).

[134] The opposing attitude becomes splendidly clear in the speech of a Gnostic
in Clem. Alex. Strom. III, 1.2: εἰσελήλυθα ἐγὼ εἰς τὰ ἅγια, οὐδὲν δύναμαι παθεῖν.
This contrast will let us sense how firmly the apostle's statements in II, 12:7 ff. are
rooted in the concrete situation.

Gnostics reported to him. Unfortunately a decision between these two possibilities cannot be reached. Perhaps the two are related. If one holds the latter in some form to be correct, one acquires new evidence of the anthropological Christ myth held in Corinth.

More important than this problem is the question which is posed by the repeated parentheses εἴτε ... εἴτε ... in vss. 2-3. What does Paul mean to say by these? We have already noted that he declares thereby that he has no interest in establishing the particular form of the ecstatic experience. This of course remains to be proved and must be more specifically explained. According to Lietzmann, *in loc.*, the specific meaning of the double parenthesis consists in the fact that thereby "the mysterious character of the experience is painted in unsurpassed fashion." But nowhere in Paul do I have the impression that he shows any interest in mysterious portrayals. They certainly do not correspond to the tone of the sorrowful epistle, and even the presentation of the rapture, which was occasioned only by polemical necessity, follows in brief, succinct matter-of-factness. If Paul had intended to paint the mysterious character of his experience, he surely would have found better words for that purpose than the very sober-sounding parentheses.

Windisch (p. 374) affirms that here Paul shows himself to be familiar with two different forms of the heavenly journey, and appears to be of the opinion that the apostle is also informing his readers twice that he does not know whether he had gone to heaven in the Greek-Gnostic manner in genuine ecstasy, or whether he experienced the rapture bodily in the Jewish manner. This is at once more relevant than Lietz-   263
mann's statement, but it still is not an explanation of the passage, for the question is just what prompted the apostle to insert the two parenthetical remarks. Besides, in the foregoing investigation we have been able constantly to determine that any acquaintance on Paul's part with the Hellenistic-Gnostic anthropology is as good as ruled out.

The polemical thrust of the entire section, II, 12:1-10, demands that the parentheses also, for which a motivation can be attributed from the context only artificially, be investigated with a view to whether they do not have their motivation in the debate with the Gnostics. If this is done, their meaning immediately becomes clear. The Gnostics emphasized that during their rapture they were ἐκτὸς τοῦ σώματος. Being perfected means for them in fact nothing other than having left the prison-house of the body. The word ἔκστασις within the Gnostic usage is definitely to be explained from this point of view,[135] and for

[135] See G. Schrenk, *Studien zu Paulus* (1954), p. 107; H. Noetzel, *Christus und Dionysos*, p. 12.

the experience of the heavenly journey it holds true that "οὐδὲν ἐν σώματι ἀληθές, ἐν ἀσωμάτῳ τὸ πᾶν ἀψευδές" (Stob., Ecl. I, 41.1 [Wachsmuth 275.18; cf. 276.5 ff.]) .[136] That these views were also familiar to the Gnostics in Corinth has been adequately demonstrated, and that Paul had already learned of them at the time of the sorrowful epistle is surely evident from II, 5:1-10, where, as will be shown further below, he vigorously protests against this conception.

The same protest, however, is expressed in the statement that Paul does not know whether the ἄνθρωπος ἐν Χριστῷ experienced his rapture ἐν σώματι or χωρὶς τοῦ σώματος. This is aimed directly at the Gnostics who placed the highest value upon the ἐκτὸς τοῦ σώματος εἶναι. For Paul this question is at least without significance. In fact he does not know its background. For him the experience as such alone is important, while for the Gnostic everything depends on the actual ἔκστασις. We do not know *how* Paul conceived of the experience in detail. *Whether* he did so at all can seriously be doubted. In keeping with his total outlook he must have been of the opinion that during the rapture he had experienced the ἀλλαγή of the σῶμα τῆς σαρκός and existed as σῶμα πνευματικόν.[137] But such a conception probably will have gone too far for him. At any rate starting from his presuppositions he could not at all understand what the Gnostics meant by the stressing of the "ἐκτὸς τοῦ σώματος." For Paul a non-somatic human existence is not conceivable. He knows of no substantial, personal "I" which could subsist within itself. The man who is no longer *soma* is no longer at all.[138] Hence it already goes too far when one tries to read from the "εἴτε ἐν σώματι εἴτε χωρὶς τοῦ σώματος" that Paul nevertheless reckons with the *possibility* that he had been in rapture ἐκτὸς τοῦ σώματος. In our passage he is guided only by the negative interest of denying any significance for the ἐκτὸς τοῦ σώματος so emphatically held by the Corinthians. Paul does not intend to make any sort of *positive* affirmation with the parentheses, and for this reason one may not cite them for the presentation of the *Pauline* conception of the *soma*. The statement, "I know not whether out of the body," means in the context of Pauline anthropology, "I do not know how this is of interest to you. In fact, I do not even know how you visualize it at all." Naturally he does not say this, and rightly so, since nothing would be gained by such a fundamental discussion for his primary theme, the parrying of the haughty self-esteem of his opponents. In the parentheses he be-

---

[136] Cf. also Asc. Jes. 7.1 ff.: "In this condition in which I prophesied . . . I saw a sublime angel . . . . And he said to me: . . . you will not learn my name, for you must return into this your body."

[137] I Cor. 15:44 ff.

[138] Cf. R. Bultmann, [2], § 17.

comes a Gnostic to the Gnostics, when he apparently concedes the possibility of an existence ἐκτὸς τοῦ σώματος, but only in order thereby to be heard in his ultimate concern: However we conceive of our existence, the opinion that we are perfect and no longer are in need of the grace which is powerful in the weak is in any case mistaken. But precisely for this reason the repeated parenthetical remark is most instructive for the *Gnostic* conception of the *soma* which is passed on by it alone. In it we find it once again confirmed that for Paul's adversaries the actual Self of men abiding in the body is their Pneuma-spark, that everything hinges on releasing this Self from the fetters of the body and experiencing already here, as far as possible, the ultimate perfection, and that therewith finally the *soma* is scorned and repudiated as that which is alien and inimical to men.

So much for the meaning of the section II, 12:1-10. I hope that I have shown that it becomes understandable only in the setting of Paul's dispute with his Gnostic opponents, but that under this presupposition it is at the same time valuable in providing knowledge of the views held in Corinth. If in this respect the passage offered us nothing new, still the earlier conclusions of our investigation could find extensive confirmation. The relative correctness of the opinion that in our passage Paul is speaking without direct reference to the corresponding experiences of his opponents lies in the fact that he refrains here from directly contesting the opponents' views, as was done, for example—erroneously—in I, 15. The reason for the indirect polemic which is found in II, 12:1-10, as to a large extent in the later epistles, is to be sought in the fact that the apostle is aware that he is much too little informed about the actual form of the Gnostic proclamation to be able to mount a fundamental attack with any prospect of success. The experiences which he had had with his first epistle, particularly in the debate about the resurrection, will have prompted him to be cautious. Thus he concerns himself with setting forth his own views in a constant antithesis to the views of his opponents as he understands them, yet without actually mentioning the latter in the polemic. Thereby in case of errors on his part he renders impossible all complaints that he is falsely representing the position of the Gnostics and yet, where he has correctly understood them, he also is understood by the Corinthians. And we have been able repeatedly to observe how clearly he perceived the presumptuousness of the Gnostic self-consciousness, in spite of his ignorance of the theoretical-speculative foundations.

On p. 63 we have already referred to the Gnostic concepts in II, 3:17, which in its original mythical sense says exactly what the Corinthians as representatives of the anthropological Christ myth were proclaiming in Corinth: "ὁ κύριος τὸ πνεῦμά ἐστιν," [139] i.e., the Kyrios Christ and the Pneuma-spark which lives in every Pneumatic as his real self are one and the same, though divided, person.[140] I hope that I have succeeded in presenting proof that the Gnostic Christ myth, which we examined in our Introduction A as to structure and distribution, according to all appearance was represented by the Gnostics in Corinth in pristine purity.

Now II, 3:17 can also point us to our new subject, the Gnostic ἐλευθερία, which according to II, 3:17 is necessarily given with the Pneuma of the Kyrios: οὗ δὲ τὸ πνεῦμα κυρίου, ἐλευθερία. It cannot be proved with certainty that the *expression* "ἐλευθερία" was used in the heretical circles in Corinth; I, 9:1, 19, and 10:29 are not sufficient to serve as proof. It is not difficult, however, to prove that the *matter* always connected with the myth is present.

V. The ἐλευθερία of the Gnostics as an Attitude Toward the World

266   *1. General Remarks*

On the lips of the Gnostics, ἐλευθερία is a strictly eschatological concept. To the Gnostic myth the world appears as a mixture of divine and demonic substance. The empirical phenomenon of man himself owes its existence to such a mixing. The separation of the opposing elements and the return of the celestial light-elements to the Pleroma are the *telos* of all cosmic occurrences. For man this means that he has reached the goal of his history when he has released his true self, the divine Pneuma, from the bonds uniting it to the lower, sarkical substance, when he has been *set free* from the world.[141] ἐλευθερία thus is the *telos*, the ἐλεύθερος is the perfected person. Even if this *telos* actually comes only after death, still the Gnostic knows himself already *in fact* to be a liberated person. He has in fact the Gnosis which

---

[139] Cf. pp. 58-59.

[140] I venture to raise the question whether II, 3:17, 18*b* is not a marginal comment of the Corinthian Gnostics which slipped into the text early:

   ὁ δὲ κύριος τὸ πνεῦμά ἐστιν.
   οὗ δὲ τὸ πνεῦμα κυρίου
   ἐλευθερία
   καθάπερ ἀπὸ κυρίου πνεύματος.

This would solve all the difficulties of the passage. I surmise the same for II, 5:16. Both verses come from Epistle C. On this, cf. now pp. 315 ff. below.

[141] On this, cf., e.g., Hipp. VII, 32.2: Carpocrates speaks of the soul, "ἣν καὶ διὰ πάντων χωρήσασαν ἐν πᾶσί τε ἐλευθερωθεῖσαν ἀνεληλυθέναι πρὸς αὐτόν (scil., τὸν ἀγένητον θεόν);" cf. VII, 32.7 and VII, 32.8: "ἐλευθερωθήσονται τοῦ μηκέτι γενέσθαι ἐν σώματι." Unfortunately, Schlier, in his article "ἐλευθερία" TDNT II: 487 ff., fails
to consider the Gnostic usage, which precisely for Paul is indispensable.

guarantees him, φύσει πνευματικός, the ultimate deliverance. Where 268
the knowledge of the fact that I am Pneuma or *pars Christi* is present,
freedom is a *present* reality (Iren. I, 13.6; I, 23.3; I, 24.4; Hipp. VI,
19.7). Therewith however the contempt for the *sarx* and the denial of
the resurrection is the most central expression of the Gnostic consciousness of freedom.

In his ecstasies the Gnostic experiences ever anew the fact that in
principle he has already gained his freedom. The ecstatic praxis is
thus a further expression of the ἐλευθερία gained through Gnosis.

Since the Pneumatic in possession of Gnosis is already here sure of
his freedom, the religious καύχημα which Paul found so arrogant in
the Corinthians is a normal and legitimate outcome of their self-understanding; the self-glorying therefore is the third expression we have
observed of the gnostically understood freedom.

Since the man existing as Pneuma sees through the nothingness of
the *sarx* and has already achieved the detachment from it, his attitude
toward the world will always be a negative one. As such it can be
expressed in either of two ways: The Gnostic in strict asceticism avoids
any contamination of his pneumatic substance by the sarkical sphere,
or, in the consciousness of the invulnerability of the pneumatic quality,
he demonstrates his freedom in unrestrained libertinism,[142] as is the
case according to Hippolytus' report (VI, 19.7), for example, among
the Simonians. "Down to the present day they have no scruples about
doing, as *free people,* whatever they will." Thus also the Marcosians,
who according to Iren. I, 13.6 say of themselves: *"esse autem se in altitudine super omnem virtutem: quapropter et libere* (ἐλευθέρως) *omnia
agere, nullum in nullo timorem habentes"* (cf. I, 23.3), for οὐ γάρ
ἐστι φύσει κακὸν ἀλλὰ θέσει (Hipp. VI, 19.8),[143] and such a *"θέσις τῶν
ἀγγέλων τοῦ κόσμου"* does not affect the Pneumatic.[144] Asceticism and
libertinism thus are a further expression of the Gnostic ἐλευθερία of
the same kind, regardless of all outward difference between them. We
are concerned now with this latter aspect of ἐλευθερία, since we have
already discussed the former.

It would be incorrect simply to identify the theme thus posed as that
of the Gnostic ethic. The libertinism of Gnostic observance is related
to only a part of the moral principles. The general moral code naturally is just as valid for the conduct of the Gnostics among themselves
as for other men. It is in no way to be justified in terms of the myth

---

[142] Clem. Alex. Strom. VI, 111: "πᾶσα πρᾶξις γνωστικοῦ κατόρθωμα." 269
[143] Cf. Hipp. VI, 19.5: "νομιζομένῳ κακῷ." Iren. I, 25.4. Clem. Alex. Strom. III,
2.6-9.
[144] Cf. Ign. Eph. 8.2: "πράσσειν οὐ δύνανται . . . οἱ πνευματικοὶ τά σαρκικά" (cf.
Gal. 5:16). Iren. III, 15.2.

that one part of the Pneuma should lie to or deceive another, and so on. Another principle holds true for the relation of the Pneumatic to the Hylic, but this need not concern us here. The conduct characterized as libertine or ascetic moves in a realm which for the understanding of the genuine Gnostic is excluded from the whole religiously relevant sphere. If ethics is a religious concept, then Gnostic asceticism, as well as Gnostic libertinism, is no ethical problem at all. The church's heresy fighters indeed do not recognize this, but if one determines what they have to bring forward as charges against their opponents, one finds that they are basically only two: unchastity and the eating of meat sacrificed to idols, or the ascetic antipodes of these[145] (cf. Rev. 2:14, 20; Iren. I, 6.3). Both forms of conduct are closely related to the commerce with the *sarx,* that substance which is "nothing," hostile to God, and "inhuman," and is detached from the ethical sphere.[146] Thus Iren. I, 28.2 tells of certain Gnostics, who also practiced community of women, that they asserted that God *does not trouble himself* about participation in sacrificial meals of the heathen.

Every freedom for conduct with respect to the *sarx* is grounded in the freedom from the *sarx.* Iren. I, 6.2: "*Quaemadmodum enim choikum impossibile est salutem percipere, sic iterum quod spiritale impossibile esse corruptelam percipere, licet in quibuscunque fuerint factis.*" Against just this Gnostic libertinism, which must have been practiced in his native Rome in his time (cf. Shepherd of Hermas, Sim. IX, 22), Hermas conducts a polemic when he has his Shepherd speak: "Preserve this flesh pure and unspotted, ἵνα τὸ πνεῦμα τὸ κατοικοῦν ἐν αὐτῇ may give it a good testimony . . . . For both (σάρξ and πνεῦμα) belong together and they cannot be stained in isolation" (Sim. V, 7; cf. Sim. VIII, 6.5). The anthropological schema of Gnosticism (see pp. 30-31) is altogether clear here in spite of the breaking of its consistent dualism with its ethical consequences. On the

---

[145] The following passage from the Gospel of the Egyptians preserved by Clement of Alexandria, e.g., offers a typically Gnostic argument for sexual continence. To Salome's question, "How long will death have power?" the Lord answers, "So long as ye women bear children," for just so long is the Pneuma, ever again in need of redemption, poured forth into the world. The same tendency is shown by the following passage from the Gospel of Philip, in a fragment preserved in Epiph. XXVI, 13. The soul says, "'I . . . have not sown children to the Archon'. . . . But if it should prove that the soul has borne a son, it is kept beneath until it is in a position to recover its children and bring them back to itself" (Hennecke-Schneemelcher-Wilson, I: 166, 273).

[146] The Gnostics' charge that Paul treats the community as σαρκικοί (1st ed., cf. pp. 80 ff.) therefore in its concrete situation could have been an answer to the ethical instructions given by Paul in Epistle A. The Gnostics could not more aptly and concisely refute Paul's reproof and his ethical demands than with the remark that they applied only to sarkic persons and therefore were, at least for the Gnostic conventicles and their partisans, an intolerable demand.

common responsibility of body and soul one may compare further the interesting parable, in the extant form certainly antilibertine, of the blind man and the lame man in the Apocryphon of Ezekiel in Epiph. Haer. LXIV, 70.5 ff. (corresponds in essence to Synhedrin 91a b; IX: 33-34, Goldschmidt); further, II Clem. 9.1 ff.   275

Of course the freedom of the Gnostic can be limited for religious, not truly ethical, reasons. This occurs not only in asceticism but in a certain way also in libertinism, when unchastity and idol worship are understood as parts of the battle against the powers of darkness.[147] Thus it is said of the Valentinians in Iren. I, 6.4 that they asserted literally: "Whoever is *in* this world (i.e., the Gnostic as contrasted with the Psychic, who is *of* this world and for whom the reverse holds true) and does not love a woman so that he subdues her is not of the truth and does not attain the truth" (cf. Iren. I, 25.4; 26.4; 31.2). Here the freedom which in any religious libertinism is in some way religiously grounded becomes compulsion.[148]

In the eating of εἰδωλόθυτον, along with the indifference with respect to the *sarx*, still another formulation of the Gnostic self-consciousness plays a role. Above all, when it is a matter of participation in the heathen cult itself, the ultimate reason for this freedom is the consciousness that the Pneumatic has dominion over the demons, that for him their dominion has ended, that for him they already are, practically speaking, a nonentity. Therefore he can participate in the heathen cultic ceremonies without having to fear that the demons would endanger his salvation. Gnosis in fact is not subject to being stolen. Naturally the right to unchastity can also be similarly grounded. One may compare for example Jude 8, where in the polemic against the Gnostics it is said: "οὗτοι ἐνυπνιαζόμενοι σάρκα μὲν μιαίνουσιν, κυριότητα δὲ ἀθετοῦσιν, δόξας δὲ βλασφημοῦσιν." Thus according to Hipp. VI, 41 the Gnostic Marcus tempts to shame with the rationale that it is "according to his doctrine without danger, for they belonged to the perfect Power and had a part in the ineffable Might."   275

So much for fundamentals. If we look now at the situation in Corinth, it at once becomes evident that libertine tendencies were at work there in sexual matters as well as with regard to the "meat

---

[147] Cf. H. Schlier in *Neutestamentliche Studien für Rudolf Bultmann* (1954), pp. 79-80.

[148] Similarly Hipp. VI, 19.5 (Wendland, 146.11 ff.), according to whom the recognized "redemption" among the Simonians apparently was supposed to be documented by moral dissoluteness: "All earth is earth, and it does not matter where one sows, only that one does sow; but they even call themselves blessed because of the alien mixing, since they assert that it is perfect *agapē* .... In other words, nothing supposedly evil can gain power over them, for they are redeemed" (cf. Epiph. Haer. XXI, 4.1-2).   277

sacrificed to idols." One could perhaps infer a tendency to asceticism from I, 7, but this would hardly be correct (see below). That *the same* party preached and practiced libertinism *and* asceticism together, as Lütgert *et al.* think, is utterly impossible for reasons of logic.

The libertinism in Corinth must now be examined more closely, above all with respect to its connection with the Gnostics. Arguing against any such connection appears to be the fact that in Epistle C and in the sorrowful epistle Paul engages in practically no polemics at all against moral grievances, although precisely these epistles contain the sharpest polemics and also make most clearly evident the Gnostic attitude of the Corinthian Pneumatics, while on the other side the two earlier epistles, written at a time when Paul had understood his opponents even much less than later, contain extended sections in which Paul takes a stand against libertine conduct. But anyone who proposes with this certainly correct observation to be able to dispute the identity of the morally lax Corinthians who are opposed at first with the later emerging "super-apostles" and their following[149] mistakes the character of the entire debate. We have already indicated in various points that partially already in Epistle B, predominantly in Epistle C, and almost exclusively in the sorrowful epistle it is Paul's apostolate that is under discussion. Just after the apostle's first intervention in the affairs of the Corinthian community, some from the Gnostic side had denied that Paul, as a non-Pneumatic, had the right at all to give instructions of a religious or ethical kind. Paul was compelled thereby first of all to take care to insure that his apostolic authority was recognized in Corinth before he could with any prospect of success begin to reestablish the full Christian order in the sense of his first epistle. That the latter is his real intention in the sorrowful epistle is fully evident in this epistle itself. The whole epistle consists of two major parts of wholly different content. The break comes before II, 12:19. With "πάλαι δοκεῖτε ὅτι ὑμῖν ἀπολογούμεθα" Paul is looking back on all that has been said previously in which in fact he had defended himself. The aim of these statements was of course intended in the last analysis to be the edification of the community: "τὰ δὲ πάντα, ἀγαπητοί, ὑπὲρ τῆς ὑμῶν οἰκοδομῆς." Such οἰκοδομή appears to him

278

---

[149] Thus also Käsemann, [1], pp. 33 ff.. who would grant to chaps. 10–13 their own problematic, because "the relative independence of this part is immediately evident." This is certainly true, but the task which this concession poses still is that of explaining the peculiar problematic, which lies in the relative independence of the sorrowful epistle, in terms of the context of the entire debate. Käsemann on the other hand considers this section in isolation, does not note the constantly recurring connections with the preceding correspondence, and then on the basis of the passages which are distinctive for chaps. 10 ff. construes a picture of the situation which now in turn rules out any connection with the preceding discussion.

urgently needed, for he fears that at his arrival in Corinth he will not find the community as he would wish (12:20), that moral grievances of all kinds are widespread in it, and that therefore he will be compelled to take unsparing action (13:2) against those who have sinned and have not yet repented as Christians (12:21). Paul gives solemn assurance: "Now I am coming to you the third time. On the testimony of two or three witnesses every matter is to be established. I have already said during my second visit and now repeat, being absent, to those who had sinned beforehand and to all the rest, that when I come again, I will not spare" (13:1-2). Of course he cherishes the hope that this threat will suffice; for "διὰ τοῦτο ταῦτα ἀπὼν γράφω, ἵνα παρὼν μὴ ἀποτόμως χρήσωμαι κατὰ τὴν ἐξουσίαν ἣν ὁ κύριος ἔδωκέν μοι εἰς οἰκοδομὴν καὶ οὐκ εἰς καθαίρεσιν" (13:10).

With all this Paul explicitly confirms that it is the ultimate aim of his comprehensive apology to create the preconditions for the reestablishment of proper moral conditions in Corinth. The main topic of the first two epistles has not been dropped but has only been necessarily given a subordinate position for the moment. Thus there exists a close connection between the statements in II, 12:19–13:10 and the paraenetic sections in Epistles A and B.

Moreover, the remark that Paul had taken steps with reference to the matters having to do with morality during his second (interim) visit (13:2), as well as the πρό in προημαρτηκότες (12:21; 13:2), which can refer only to sins which occurred before the interim visit, points back into the past and therewith to the conditions pictured in the earlier epistles. If we observe also what Paul censures in the sorrowful epistle by way of specific grievances in Corinth, we see that, besides the dissensions which in the brief catalog of vices in II, 12:20 are cited with eight different expressions, they are the typically Gnostic sins of ἀκαθαρσία, πορνεία, and ἀσέλγεια (ἀκαθαρσία here, like πορνεία, defilement with sexual impurity; ἀσέλγεια on the other hand probably gluttony in the heathen feasts of meats sacrificed to idols; cf. Tert. Apol. 39; Iren. I, 25.3). And we meet just these sins also in the first two epistles to the Corinthians, both in the detailed treatment and at the head of the list of vices in I, 6;9. Thus Paul has in no way undertaken a shift in fronts in his later epistles.

That the *libertines* in Corinth are *identical* with the Gnostics in the same place, and thus that Paul is not always fighting against two different fronts, not only is certain because the libertine conduct is typically Gnostic, but is also confirmed by the fact that the address to which II, 12:19–13:10 goes is the same one to which Paul directs II, 10:1-12, 18. This becomes completely clear in 13:3 ff. Some had demanded of Paul a proof of the Christ who was speaking in him. Paul

279

proposes to provide this δοκιμή by calling those who demand this to account for their *sins;* for they would have had occasion first of all to ask themselves whether Christ was "in them." Likewise for example in I, 8:1 ff. the connection of Gnostic terminology and theology with the libertine tendencies becomes clear.

280   Worthy of note in this connection is Phil. 3:18-19, a passage which, as we have already stated (p. 208, n. 129 and Vol. 2, pp. 47 ff.) , may have been in opposition to the same group of Gnostics which was active in Corinth. Here Paul is fighting τοὺς ἐχθροὺς τοῦ σταυροῦ τοῦ Χριστοῦ, ὧν ὁ θεὸς ἡ κοιλία καὶ ἡ δόξα ἐν τῇ αἰσχύνῃ αὐτῶν. Gnostic theology as it is expressed in the rejection of the cross and libertinism belong together. Especially instructive is the formulation "ἡ δόξα ἐν τῇ αἰσχύνῃ αὐτῶν." It is in fact a sign of Gnostic honor, i.e. of pneumatic self-consciousness, to demonstrate the shamefulness of the flesh through immoral conduct.

The foregoing statements may be supplemented by a reference to II, 5:10, a passage which we shall examine later in more detail in the context of the entire first part of the fifth chapter. For our subject of the moment the only thing of interest is the fact that Paul concludes a section which obviously is a polemic against the Gnostic views of last things with a paraenetic allusion which undoubtedly applies to the same opponents: "For this reason we strive . . . to be well-pleasing to him. For we must all appear before the judgment seat of Christ, that each one may receive his reward for what he has done with his *soma,* whether it is good or evil" (II, 5:9-10) .

Thus if we can already say that the Gnostics are responsible for the libertine tendencies in Corinth and that down to the time of the sorrowful epistle they were exerting their disruptive influence in this respect, we must now confirm these judgments on the basis of the passages of the earlier epistles in which Paul proceeds directly against specific Gnostic "sins." For this we take as a working basis the literary-critical division already given and consider first Epistle A, then Epistle B.

281   ## 2. The Problem of the Meats Sacrificed to Idols

The "μὴ γίνεσθε ἑτεροζυγοῦντες ἀπίστοις" at the beginning of the part of Epistle A preserved for us identifies the theme of this entire epistle. After the general exhortations in II, 6:14–7:1 Paul demands that sanctification be perfected in the fear of God (II, 7:1) , since, as he makes clear in I, 9:24-27 in a figure, not all who are in the community will also automatically receive the "incorruptible victory crown." This is typologically established in 10:1-13 with an Old Testament example.

From that point then there follow, down to the concluding salutations, four concrete problems with which Paul warns against a relapse into paganism: participation in pagan sacrificial rites (10:14-22); unchastity (6:12-20); lack of discipline during the Lord's Supper and the congregational gatherings in general (11:2-34); and skepticism about the resurrection (15:1-57). The thrust of the entire Epistle A is therewith so clear that it cannot be doubted that Paul was of the opinion that some in Corinth had again turned to paganism more strongly than is permissible for Christians. He does not yet see other problems, and he shows that he is not informed as to the reasons for that stance in Corinth. Significant of course is the fact that he does not reckon with an already accomplished direct return to paganism. The libertinism is a Christian phenomenon. Paul has the impression that some in Corinth in certain circles disregarded the separation from paganism. Even if this opinion is only very conditionally correct, still there can be no doubt that the concrete questions which Paul touches in his criticism were being debated in Corinth. For chaps. 11 and 15 this is indeed immediately clear, and for the other two sections it can be inferred with certainty from Paul's manner of argumentation. Paul addresses his words to those who know how to combine unchastity and participation in the pagan cultic meals with the Christian position and explains to them with a reference to their own ability to judge (6:15-16, 19; 10:15, 18) that this obviously is not possible. Of course he appears not yet to have material for making specific charges.

We consider first of all 10:14-22. Paul sets himself against the participation in meals of the meats sacrificed to idols, thus in cultic ceremonies in the service of pagan gods. On such cultic meals one may consult the excursus in Lietzmann, *An die Korinther,* on 10:21 and the literature cited there. Sacral meals preceded by a sacrifice were widespread in various forms in the New Testament times. Insofar as they belong to the broader area of the mystery cults, their origin is oriental-mythological, and their original meaning is that the individual enters into substantial connection with the cult's god. The conception of the κοινωνία τοῦ θεοῦ mediated through such table fellowship was of course later often spiritualized, yet without giving up the animistic terminology. Even Paul adopted the latter, as precisely our passage shows, without being obliged therewith to think of a substantial connection with the respective cult god. It is clear, however, that in principle he regarded the Lord's Supper precisely as he regarded the pagan idols' meals. The eucharistic rite of the community, just like the meals of the pagan cults, has the aim of uniting the participants with the god who is invoked therein. Hence it is impossible to hold that a participation in both ceremonies is permissible if one places any value on the fellowship with the σῶμα Χριστοῦ. Not as though in the sacrificial meals of the idols a supernatural quality were actually imparted. In this respect the meat that has been sacrificed to idols means nothing (10:19a). The vain demon can do nothing to man. But *on the other hand* the sacrifice is objectionable: a *man shows* by it that he is turning to the demons (10:20), and this means that God is being tried (10:22). Anyone who in the Supper celebrates the fellowship with Christ cannot at the same time be a κοινωνὸς τῶν δαιμονίων, even if only outwardly, because he is persuaded that the idols are nothing. "μὴ θέλε, ἃ μὴ θέλει ὁ κύριος" is the gloss appropriately made by Severian (according to Lietzmann, *in loc.*), and von Soden (*Sakrament und Ethik*, p. 24) interprets very properly: οὐ δύνασθε, i.e.: "It is *historically* prohibited to sit at Christ's table and at the table of demons." Thus Jesus' saying that no man can serve two masters is applicable here.

Paul does not doubt that the Corinthians who were addressed consciously intend to be Christians. With them he is of the opinion that the idols are nothing. But to take part in the ceremonies of sacrifices to idols means simply to tempt God. Without giving more specific proof of this, he appeals to their Christian capacity of judgment. Thus we obviously are not dealing with lax members of the community who do not themselves take seriously their being Christians or are "not yet properly awakened from the drunken condition of pagan immorality" (J. Weiss, p. xxix). With people of this kind Paul would have had to argue differently. He is addressing the Corinthians not about indifference or ignorance but about a clearly defined but incorrect view of the Christian condition that tends to paganism.

It is, however, typically Gnostic to participate in pagan cultic meals from a deliberately "Christian" stance. The demons have indeed been conquered. This needs to be demonstrated. The Gnostic is ἰσχυρός— only that Paul warns against feeling oneself stronger than God (10:22). Most highly instructive is a comment of Irenaeus about the Valentinians (I, 6.3): "They eat heathen sacrifices without hesitation and do not believe that they are defiled by it, and at every festival of the heathen and every banquet in honor of the idols they are the first to appear." The Gnostics not only exhibit a certain indifference with regard to the sacrifices to idols, but they deliberately partake of fleshly pleasures—in addition to unchastity Irenaeus also mentions attendance at battles among wild beasts and between gladiators—in order thus to demonstrate their victory over the powers of the *sarx:* "They, who immoderately serve the lusts of the flesh, however also assert that one must offer what is sarkical to the sarkical and what is pneumatic to the pneumatic" (Iren. I, 6.3). They are Gnostics also who according to Rev. 2:14, 20 in Pergamon and Thyatira are teaching the churches φαγεῖν εἰδωλόθυτα καὶ πορνεῦσαι, for they also assert of themselves that they had learned τὰ βαθέα τοῦ σατανᾶ (Rev. 2:24).[150] Just because they have learned the deep things of Satan, they can or even must take part in the heathen cult. Probably on the basis of this passage from the Apocalypse Irenaeus also asserts concerning the Nicolaitans: "They teach that it is of no significance when one practices adultery or eats meat sacrificed to idols" (I, 26.3), and he cites as an utterance of Basilides the statement that one "can scorn the sacrifices to idols and regard them as nothing, and may take part in them without hesitation" (I, 24.5). We may also compare a passage from Justin's Dial. 35.1-6 (following Goodspeed). Trypho objects: "καὶ μὴν πολλοὺς τῶν τὸν Ἰησοῦν λεγόντων ὁμολογεῖν καὶ λεγομένων Χριστιανῶν πυνθάνομαι ἐσθίειν τὰ εἰδωλόθυτα καὶ μηδὲν ἐκ τούτου βλάπτεσθαι λέγειν" (vs. 1). In these people, as Justin explicitly states in his answer, we have to do with Gnostics, that is to say, with Marcians, Valentinians, Basilidians, Satornilians, and others, who ἀντὶ τοῦ τὸν Ἰησοῦν σέβειν ὀνόματι μόνον ὁμολογεῖν (vss. 5-6).   282

Thus in Epistle A Paul takes a stand against such Gnostic tendencies in the Corinthian church, of course without having precisely understood the attitude of his opponents. From Epistle B we learn the reaction of the Corinthians to these admonitions. περὶ τῶν εἰδωλοθύτων is the subject of the connected section 8:1–9:23 + 10:23–11:1.   283

In Epistle A Paul warned against εἰδωλολατρία (10:14); now he speaks only of εἰδωλόθυτον.[151] Already in this is shown a significant shifting of the theme. The community, so far as it acknowledges Paul's authority, has taken a stand, apparently without reservation, on the anti-Gnostic position represented by Paul in 10:14 ff., that participation in the worship of idols is forbidden for Christians. But thereupon there arises a new problem, the question whether then one may eat the meat that has been sacrificed to idols, which is available everywhere.   284 Someone asks Paul for information on this point and from the outset points out that people in Corinth had "Gnosis" and knew that the idols and the pagan gods no longer have any meaning. Therewith of course the community adopts the Gnostic argumentation (see pp. 141 ff.), the form of which we cannot reconstruct in detail since we do not know to what extent Paul is referring to the congregation's letter in 8:1 ff.   285

Paul's position on this question is such that he (a) in principle

---

[150] This is a genuinely Gnostic assertion; see the article "βαθός" in TDNT I: 517-18.

[151] Even in 8:10, where of course Paul chooses an extreme example, he is concerned only with the eating of εἰδωλόθυτον, not with the participation in the cult as such.

affirms the Gnosis but (b) wants to see it directed by love (8:1-3). This general proposition then is applied to the concrete problem of eating meat sacrificed to idols. *We* indeed have the knowledge of the nothingness of the gods to whom the meat was offered (a) (8:4-6), but since not everyone possesses this knowledge, we must forgo our *exousia,* if the occasion arises, out of love for the weaker brethren (b) (8:6-13). In chap. 9 Paul cites himself as an example of such authentic demonstration of Christian existence in freedom.[152] There is no reason for excising chap. 9 from this context,[153] especially since the argument follows the same pattern of thesis and antithesis as in chap. 8. In (a) 9:1-12a (14) Paul asserts his right to support by the churches; in (b) 9:12b (15)-23 he explains and justifies his renunciation of this *exousia.* The first section in vss. 1 ff. is interrupted by a little apology,[154] while the second opens out into a more comprehensive presentation of the apostolic renunciation of the *exousia* than would have been required by the theme of the right to support in itself (vss. 19-23). After 10:23-24 have once more led back to the actual theme in the "a-b" pattern, the whole set of statements περὶ τῶν εἰδωλοθύτων is closed with quite specific instructions for conduct in public with regard to meat

287

---

[152] It is utterly unjustified to assume that on the Gnostic side Paul was denied his apostolic right because of this restraint (thus still Käsemann, [1], p. 36). Even II, 11:7-12 and 12:13 do not assume this. The reference to Paul's autarchy is in any case incomprehensible as an *accusation,* because such restraint is unquestionably commendable. At the most, people would have been able to say, "See, he is refraining from using his apostolic rights. Thus he himself does not claim to be an apostle." But this contradicts the whole tendency of the opponents' attacks, which everywhere else are directed specifically against Paul's apostolic *claims.* In addition, there is the fact that in I, 9 Paul first explicitly establishes his right to support by the community, in order then to be able to boast of his renunciation of it. But one never defends himself thus against charges which arise directly out of the fact that the apostle *has* this right. We must not be led astray by the polemical vss. I, 9:1 ff. into assuming for all of chap. 9 the same direct polemic orientation. Verses 1-3 are a parenthetical remark which is sharply set off by vs. 3 from what follows (Nestle makes an incorrect separation). At most we may ask whether Paul had been accused of being deficient in love for the Corinthians in comparison with his love for the Macedonians (II, 11:11). But even this is unlikely.

286

On the other hand, II, 3:1 and 5:12a probably refer back to the "self-glorying" in I, 9 (cf. I, 4:14 ff.). But Paul does not allow himself to be impressed by the charge of self-praise. Later he emphasizes again that he has a right to boast of his renunciation of his apostolic rights (11:7 ff.; 12:13). Of course from the Gnostic side this attitude is answered with the spiteful charge that Paul uses deceit to exploit the community for these purposes by means of the collection (II, 12:16; see pp. 108-9). This charge was all the more weighty since the heretics who had come to Corinth also apparently renounced support by the communities; cf. II, 11:7-12 and *The Office of Apostle,* pp. 219 ff.

[153] Not only does 10:23-24, esp. vs. 24, follow directly on 9:19-23, but above all 10:23 ff. presupposes the whole course of thought of 8:1–9:23.

[154] Verse 3b unquestionably belongs to the preceding as a concise conclusion to the parenthetical remark. It is impossible to assume that people were *accusing* Paul because of his renunciation of the right of support (cf. n. 152, above).

sacrificed to idols (10:25-30) and a summary of what has been set forth in terms of principle (10:31–11:1).

The detailed exposition of this part of Epistle B is of no more interest to us here than the understanding of Christian existence that underlies the Pauline argument. On this latter point one may secure information above all from R. Bultmann, *Theology*, § 39. However we note once more the connections which exist on this problem between Epistle A and Epistle B. In Epistle A Paul is arguing with a genuinely Gnostic manner of conduct. This cannot be said unconditionally of Epistle B. If the church in principle affirms the Pauline statements, then it may eat all meats without hesitation, since the Corinthians indeed πάντες γνῶσιν ἔχουσιν. In any case one is not justified in doubting this latter assertion out of hand. That Paul had learned of "weaker ones" in Corinth or had even received some communication directly from them, that "strong" and "weak" anti-Gnostics stood over against each other there, is unlikely, especially when one considers that the Pauline limitation, "ἀλλ' οὐκ ἐν πᾶσιν ἡ γνῶσις," directly contradicts the thesis of his followers in Corinth—"πάντες γνῶσιν ἔχομεν." Perhaps the writers of the church's letter after Paul's answer reflected upon the fact that there were also "weak ones" in the community. But at the time of the composition of their letter they considered themselves all to be strong, i.e. in possession of true Gnosis. If this Gnosis was ready to have regard for a brother, it showed itself thereby to be undergirded by the awareness of the historicality of man and determined to be subordinated to the "being known by God." One probably may at once assume that the majority of the congregation accepted this Pauline standpoint or continued to hold it. But this does not alter the fact that the Corinthians' appeal to Gnosis, as it may be inferred from 8:1 ff., is typically Gnostic in form and content. One could of course argue thus without remaining bound to the mythical thinking to which any curtailment of ἐξουσία is absurd or even perverse. But in any case it is clear that in the wider background of the church's letter also there stands that group which out of a pure Gnostic understanding of existence stands up for an unrestrained exercise of ἐξουσία and which Paul addressed in Epistle A; indeed even now he sees the church still under that group's influence. And conversely, in the fact that the inquiry περὶ τῶν εἰδωλοθύτων ultimately is to be traced back to people who possess γνῶσις (in the technical sense of the word) and boast that "πάντα μοι ἔξεστιν" (10:23), one may see a confirmation of the fact that the inclination to εἰδωλολατρία which Paul had fought a little earlier also goes back to pronounced Gnostics.

3. The Problem of Unchastity

In Epistle A the section I, 6:12-20 concerns itself with the second major problem of the gnostically understood *eleutheria*, namely with πορνεία. Paul begins with the Gnostic slogan which he also mentions again in Epistle B (10:23) : "πάντα μοι ἔξεστιν." This slogan has always caused great difficulties for the study of concepts. It is well known that ἐξουσία has three basic meanings (cf. with caution Foerster in TDNT II: 562-63). *First,* it designates, approximately equaling δύναμις, the possibility or capacity, the outward force or inward power, to do something or to have it done, in the widest sense. *Second,* not always strictly distinguished from the first meaning and in any case presupposing it, it stands as the equivalent of authorization, permission, to do something, regardless of whether it involves a legitimately given or an arbitrarily taken freedom to act. And *third,* the word figuratively signifies the powers themselves which have the power.

Now in Gnosticism precisely as in the Stoa ἐξουσία is employed as a *terminus technicus.* Which influence is present in I, 6:12 ff.? Certainly not Stoic influence, as for example J. Weiss, *in loc.,* ventures to suggest and Dupont, *Gnosis,* V § 2, recently asserts. Neither in I, 6:12 nor in 10:23 does it have to do with the ability of the individual to be *in a position* because of complete self-determination to do, allow, and endure any sort of action, but with the freedom in the possession of Gnosis to be able to do anything without the Self being influenced thereby in any way. Thus while the Stoa uses ἐξουσία in the first meaning of this word, the Gnostics apparently apply it to the second. But even in Gnosticism ἐξουσία in this second meaning is not found as a *terminus technicus.* Gnosticism is familiar with the first and third usages. In one case ἐξουσία is a designation for the supra-terrestrial powers, mostly of a demonic kind (e.g. I, 15:24) and in the other case it designates, in the first meaning, the power which the Pneumatic possesses by reason of his pneumatic quality and with which he lords it over the demonic ἐξουσίαι as well as the human non-Pneumatics[155] and remains in magical nourishing connection with his heavenly Self. Reitzenstein ([1], pp. 363 ff.) is certainly correct in explaining the use of ἐξουσία in II, 10:8 and 13:10 in these terms, even though he again neglects to distinguish terminology from Gnostic conception in Paul. But it remains useless for one to seek in Gnosticism for a technical use of ἐξουσία in the sense of authority or permission for any moral or immoral action, that is for the use of ἐξουσία in the second sense cited above. This is because the ἐξουσία of the Gnostic for the conduct

---

[155] Cf. Corp. Herm. I 28; 32; Iren. I, 23.5; 25.3; Od. Sol. 22.4; R. Bultmann, commentary on John, p. 36, n. 1.

described in I, 6:12 ff. and 10:23 ff. is not based upon a special permission of some higher court, but is a direct concretizing of that ἐξουσία with which he lords it over the demons and their creation, the σάρξ. Gnostic libertinism is, as we have seen, not an ethical problem. *Gnosis* bestows upon the Pneumatic the ἐξουσία or ἐλευθερία—the two concepts are interchangeable—for every *desired* contempt for fleshliness. Thus πάντα μοι ἔξεστιν does not mean for the Gnostic, "Someone has given me permission," but, "For me (as a Pneumatic) it is a matter of free choice to act thus; for me no peril is involved therein." Thus according to Hipp. VI, 4 the Gnostic Marcus recommends ἁμαρτάνειν "διὰ τὸ εἶναι τῆς τελείας δυνάμεως καὶ μετέχειν τῆς ἀνεννοήτου ἐξουσίας." Anyone who has the power to scorn the κυριότητα also has the freedom to "defile" the σάρξ (Jude 8). The saying of the Gnostic Marcus makes it clear then that the freedom of the Gnostic to do precisely what is unbecoming is based upon his pneumatic *being*. He does not have authorization or permission to act in a libertine fashion but the *essential* capacity and ability to act thus. He has power over the creators and lords of the σάρξ and thus power over the flesh itself.

Thus in substance the "πάντα μοι ἔξεστιν" corresponds exactly to the "πάντες γνῶσιν ἔχομεν" of 8:1 (cf. 8:9). With both slogans the Corinthian Gnostics justify their freedom to take part in pagan cultic meals or, if they wish, to be able to eat sacrificial meats. In both cases Paul apparently affirms the slogan as such; but in both cases he also wants to see it limited by love. Therewith the equation πάντα μοι ἔξεστιν = πάντες γνῶσιν ἔχομεν confirms our judgment that the ἐξουσία of the Gnostics for fleshly behavior is based upon the awareness of the nothingness of the σάρξ, thus in the *being* of the Gnostic; because for the Gnostic "Gnosis" is not knowledge of obligation but of existence. Hence the formula "πάντα μοι ἔξεστιν" employs ἐξουσία in the first meaning given.

In Corinth "πάντα μοι ἔξεστιν" means, "Everything is permissible for me, who in possession of Gnosis have *exousia* over the demons," a principle which the Gnostic uttered and practiced with respect to the "deeds of the flesh." Of course it would be theoretically possible that there is some Cynic influence present here (see the passage in Lietzmann on I, 6:12), even if one will hardly be able to explain how in a Christian community Cynic principles could be proposed emphatically as a part of the kerygma, but in the context of the Corinthian epistles only Gnostic tendencies naturally come into consideration.[156] Paul

289

---

[156] On this, cf. Iren. II. 32.2, where it is said of the Gnostics, "*qui quidem Epicuri philosophiam, et Cynicorum indifferentiam aemulantes, Iesum magistrum gloriantur, qui non solum a malis operibus avertit suos discipulos, sed etiam a*

must have heard from Stephanas and his people that some in Corinth
were conducting propaganda with this slogan. That the community
members adhering to Paul accepted it forthwith I regard as excluded,
and in the church's letter it certainly had not been mentioned, especially since Paul had in fact already criticized it.

In I, 10:23 the apostle takes up the formula in itself to pursue the
line of thought further. It is not necessary to excise vs. 23 (J. Weiss).
What should have prompted the redactor to repeat, in somewhat varied
form, vs. 6:12? That would in no way comport with his careful kind
of revising.

Now the apostle's argument in 6:12 ff. is most curious. The theme
of the entire section is πορνεία. How can Paul, as regards *porneia*,
affirm in principle the "πάντα μοι ἔξεστιν," as he nevertheless undoubtedly does in vs. 12? And what is the meaning in this context of
vs. 13*a*: "τὰ βρώματα τῇ κοιλίᾳ καὶ ἡ κοιλία τοῖς βρώμασιν. ὁ δὲ θεὸς
καὶ ταύτην καὶ ταῦτα καταργήσει"? The train of thought in vss. 12-13
is satisfactorily explained only if one assumes that Stephanas has told
Paul that some in Corinth, by appealing to the slogan "πάντα μοι
ἔξεστιν," are explaining that one can eat anything without discrimina-
tion and can engage in sexual intercourse in every way without reservations, and are supporting this view by pointing out that the σῶμα
together with the κοιλία is perishable.[157] It is beyond any doubt *that*
some in Corinth were teaching this. The reference to the *exousia* to
be allowed to eat anything naturally holds true in a special way for
the eating of meat sacrificed to idols (10:23). Of course Paul has not
yet become aware of this. The theme is urgent for him for the first
time in Epistle B. Therefore he unhesitatingly affirms the thesis of
the Corinthians insofar as it pertains to food (in contrast with I, 8:1 ff.
= Epistle B; cf. pp. 227-28). He denies it with reference to πορνεία:
"τὸ δὲ σῶμα οὐ τῇ πορνείᾳ ἀλλὰ τῷ κυρίῳ, καὶ ὁ κύριος τῷ σώματι" (vs.
13*b*).

290   If Paul agrees with the freedom to eat because the κοιλία is perishable, such a train of thought still is basically un-Pauline. Corresponding to Pauline belief and thought would be an argument from Christian *eleutheria* such as is found in I, 10:29-30. The present argument,
however, is typically Gnostic-ahistorical, an indication that here Paul
is actually repeating the reasons of the Gnostics which have been
reported to him. The same holds true also for the second question.
The real *Pauline* motivation for the rejection of *porneia* is not given

---

sermonibus et cogitationibus, quemadmodum ostendimus." To Irenaeus such a
juxtaposition is obviously and rightly inexplicable.

293   [157] Similarly also J. Weiss, *in loc.;* cf. also Phil. 3:19 (see Vol. 2, pp. 79-80): ". . .
ὧν ὁ θεὸς ἡ κοιλία."

in vs. 14 with a reference to the fact that the *soma* is raised, but in vs. 15 with the declaration that τὰ σώματα are members of Christ. The assertion that the σῶμα would be raised and thus is imperishable again is best explained if therewith Paul is taking up the Gnostic thesis that has been reported to him, that the body is mortal, perishable, and therefore exempt from "ethical" principles, now of course in a negative sense.   291

With such an explanation of our passage we acquire not only once again an indication of the two central problems of Gnostic libertinism, but above all also a confirmation of the fact that this libertinism was justified in a specifically Gnostic way, i.e., with a reference to the perishability of the fleshly substance. Of course then the question still remains open as to why Paul at first affirms the "πάντα μοι ἔξεστιν" although it in no case holds true for πορνεία. One must acknowledge a certain lack of correctness in Paul's train of thought. It would be   292
fully explainable if the slogan, like so many other Gnostic terms, was already familiar to Paul in a Christianized meaning, perhaps with an anti-Judaistic thrust. Then the πάντα would hold true from the outset *cum grano salis* and in Paul's understanding would be limited to the adiaphora. Even for the Gnostics it does not have an absolute validity, but only with respect to the *sarx*. Moreover, it should be asked to what extent *Paul* fills the "πάντα μοι ἔξεστιν" with the meaning "I can do all things," which indeed is to be affirmed more unconditionally than the "I may do all things." Of course this whole question is ultimately without significance for our topic.

The detailed exegesis of the entire section, which except for the first verses does not especially note the anti-Gnostic battlefront, is likewise of little interest for our problem. With its parrying of the Gnostic depreciation of bodily existence, vs. 14 already points toward chap. 15, which indeed likewise belongs to Epistle A. It is noteworthy how little here as elsewhere in the two early epistles Paul recognized his adversaries as "Gnostics." When he writes "ἢ οὐκ οἴδατε, ὅτι τὸ σῶμα ὑμῶν ναὸς τοῦ ἐν ὑμῖν ἁγίου πνεύματός ἐστιν, οὗ ἔχετε ἀπὸ θεοῦ"(vs. 19), such a question is grist for the mill of the Gnostics, who from such a fact draw the inference which uniquely corresponds to the mythological sense of this conception, that the dwelling place of the Pneuma as the prison of the Self deserves nothing but contempt. Hence it is only logical when on the basis of this and other passages (e.g., I, 2:6–3:3) they demand of Paul that he prove now that he actually is a Pneumatic as he has claimed. And further, it is quite understandable when in the later epistles, particularly in Epistle C, Paul is in every way more cautious and reserved in his statements.

In Epistle B chaps. 5 and 7 are to be compared on the question of sexual relations. We consider first chap. 7, which is in response to questions in the church's letter. In the first place, it is not always clear what is actually under discussion here, particularly in the section on the "virgins." Still less is it immediately clear from which standpoint the church's letter was composed. On the other hand, we are in the fortunate situation—and this is by far the most significant thing for our investigation—of proving on the basis of 7:40 that it was the Gnostics who were in the background of the entire set of questions about marriage. Paul concludes the thorough discussion of the problems related to marriage with the declaration as concise as it is emphatic: "δοκῶ δὲ κἀγὼ πνεῦμα θεοῦ ἔχειν." Though this polemical remark first is joined to vss. 30-40, it nevertheless acquires the weight it deserves only when one regards it as a closing comment to the whole chapter. Perhaps vs. 25 and vs. 35 are prompted by a similar polemical intention. Of course the connection of the concluding remark with what immediately precedes it is important, for from it may be inferred that some on the side of the Pneumatics were of the opinion that it is *not* better for the widows to remain unmarried. Naturally such a γνώμη still is not unconditionally libertinistic, yet it shows the Gnostics' strenuous effort not to allow any restriction of sexual freedom. The protest against the widows' remaining single is thus in our case a part of a libertinistic program.

But what now was the view of the *community?* In the discussion of the problem of meat sacrificed to idols we saw that the community which wrote the letter to Paul was decidedly submissive to the apostle. The same may hold true correspondingly for the question about marriage. If with respect to the idol sacrifices they wrote, "If we cannot participate in εἰδωλολατρία, does that mean that we also may not eat the εἰδωλόθυτον even though we all have 'Gnosis'?" then the inquiry about marriage may have run accordingly, "If intercourse with prostitutes is forbidden us, does this mean that even in marriage we are to refrain as far as possible from sexual intercourse or must even dissolve our marriages or remain unmarried?" As an answer to such an inquiry 7:1-24 at once becomes understandable. In principle Paul affirms the unmarried state and continence (vss. 1, 8), but in practice, since not all have this *charisma* (vs. 7), he does not will that people refrain from sexual relations in marriage (vss. 2-6) or remain unmarried if it is not in their power (vs. 9). Divorce among Christians is directly forbidden by Christ (vss. 10-11); divorce from a mixed marriage is to be avoided if at all possible (vss. 12-16). Direct inferences as to the views of the Gnostics in detail cannot be drawn from this passage, even though in view of vs. 40 it is to be inferred that it was the Gnostics who in principle argued against continence and for divorce when it was desired.

We are in no way justified in speaking on the basis of vss. 1-24 of explicit ascetic tendencies in Corinth.[158] The community quite simply demands of its apostle a clear statement of position on the question of Christian marriage, after he has emphatically pointed out the impossibility of πορνεία for Christians. Of course there may have existed in certain circles of the "Paulinists" the effort to go further than Paul in welcoming or even demanding continence, which then also resulted in the community's letter.

The section περὶ τῶν παρθένων (vss. 25-38) has always caused special difficulties. It is certain that it is unitary in theme, and that vss. 25-28 do not treat another problem than is treated in vss. 36-38 (contra Lietzmann). It cannot be a question simply of the attitude of unmarried maidens, for this problem has already been discussed in vss. 8-9, apparently in response to the letter of the Corinthians. In modern times the only correct view has increasingly prevailed, that our section refers to the custom of the syneisaxis. This practice is not originally Gnostic-ascetic, even though according to Iren. I, 6.3 it seems to have appeared among the Valentinians, but catholic, as the history of these spiritual marriages shows (see the catalog of literature and passages in Lietzmann, p. 36). Precisely from Paul's attitude as it is expressed in 7:7, 26, 40, et passim is it understandable when a bridal pair, who were baptized, refrained from carrying their betrothal forward into marriage, since they knew that ὁ καιρὸς συνεσταλμένος ἐστίν (vs. 29) and παράγει τὸ σχῆμα τοῦ κόσμου τούτου (vs. 31), without their necessarily dissolving their connection.[159] Out of this then there later developed the ascetic practice of syneisaxis. It can properly be doubted whether there existed already at the time of our epistle a permanent vow and in general a fixed form of such nonsexual marriages.[160]

---

[158] Even Paul is not thinking ascetically in principle, although of course he does not show any high estimate of marriage. But the combating of desire is indeed characteristic of asceticism, and this Paul does *not* demand. Anyone who does not have from God the *charisma* to remain unmarried should marry without hesitation. It is not because of the inferior worth of the corporeal, but because of the θλίψις to be expected in the approaching end-time that it is better not to touch a woman (vs. 28).

[159] W. G. Kümmel (*Neutestamentliche Studien für Rudolf Bultmann*, BZNW 21 [1954]: 275-95) treats this problem very instructively, thoroughly, in principle correctly, and I believe conclusively. It only remains to be desired that the explanation of Paul's attitude had been extended beyond I, 7:32-35 to include vss. 29-31: ὁ καιρὸς συνεσταλμένος ἐστίν.

[160] Kümmel (in Lietzmann's Commentary on p. 37, l. 4) is correct insofar as he doubts the possibility of the development of "so extreme an ascetic custom in a Christian community which is only a few years old." But syneisaxis in fact was not introduced as an ascetic practice in the narrower sense, into which it was developed only after the appearance of ascetic tendencies in Christianity, but as an "eschatological" practice, and thus is no more to be regarded as ascetic than is Paul's attitude

297

299

Now the Gnostics understandably pressed for dissolution of such relationships, with which people were placed under an unnecessary yoke (vs. 35). On the other side, old members of the congregation of the Pauline persuasion or even already with ascetic tendencies of a moralizing, certainly not of a mythological, kind will have argued for the maintenance of the spiritual vows. Therefore the community inquires of Paul περὶ τῶν παρθένων, and the apostle again gives the advice to leave standing the existing relationships, without having scruples *in principle* if the betrothed people marry (vss. 36-38) or one of the betrothed persons marries a third person, as apparently is presupposed in vs. 28 (J. Weiss). Thus again in the inquiry of the community which is thoroughly loyal to the apostle Paul, Gnostic tendencies do not become directly evident, even though the entire discussion as such was first provoked by the Gnostics, as vs. 40 shows with certainty.

Finally, there appears to have been in the church's letter an inquiry concerning the remarriage of widows. On this Paul takes a position precisely like that on the other problems: In principle they are permitted to marry, but it is better if they can refrain from doing so 298 (vss. 39-40). This question too, as is immediately evident from vs. 40, was ultimately prompted by the Gnostics, who argued for sexual relations without limitation and for whom a prohibition of remarriage naturally was absurd.

In summary, it may be said of chap. 7 that the entire discussion evidently was occasioned by the Gnostics, who wanted to concede no restriction of any sort on sexual license. Paul's statements of course allows us to recognize *directly* only his own views and those of the community loyal to him, since except for vs. 40 he is not conducting a polemic. It is likely that certain circles in the church had doctored Paul's "have as if not having" with its practical consequences for the relationship of the sexes to one another into the law of "not being allowed to have." Of course even here one can hardly speak of real asceticism, and it is completely wrong to assume a special ascetic party which stands in opposition to Paul, or even to attribute to the *one* Gnostic party the libertine as well as the allegedly ascetic features, as 301 Lütgert for example does.

In chap. 5 Paul takes up an especially gross case of πορνεία which had occurred in Corinth and of which he had heard by an oral report from Chloe's people. Naturally Paul did not think that this was the only instance of unchastity in Corinth. Already at the time of Epistle

---

toward marriage in general. The rise of such an eschatological custom however is 300 possible precisely and only in earliest Christianity.

A he knows of πορνεία in the community, and even now he gives instructions which go beyond the specific individual case (vss. 9-13). Thus Paul hears that unchastity is being practiced in the community and discusses, by way of example, the case which is probably the grossest that has come to his attention, that a man is having sexual relations with his stepmother. Obviously it cannot be proved that this happened under the appeal to Gnostic *eleutheria,* but in view of the total situation in Corinth this is certainly the most likely assumption. The contrary would have to be asserted with good reasons if one were to hold it to be correct. The fifth chapter itself does not offer such reasons. On the contrary, the fact that a community to which Pauline church discipline was not unknown allowed such a case of unchastity to occur without disciplinary intervention indeed probably shows that the evildoer belonged to that Gnostic *ecclesiola in ecclesia* from which the writers of the church's letter knew themselves to be dissociated from the first. Moreover, Paul apparently seeks the πεφυσιωμένοι (vs. 2) —and these are the Gnostics with their haughty self-consciousness—in just the circles to which the offender belonged. Unfortunately it cannot be said with certainty whether the arrogance mentioned in vs. 2 refers specifically to the extremely libertine conduct of the unchaste person. In any case one should seriously take into consideration the *possibility* that unchastity and arrogance are related as cause and effect, a relation whose motive Paul indeed does not recognize or understand; for this reason also he cannot go into the connection in more detail, but its structure as such still is sketched even in Paul's thought in the transition from 5:1 to 5:2.

If the father of the offender had already been dead, the description, "πορνεία ἥτις οὐδὲ ἐν τοῖς ἔθνεσιν," and especially the punishment demanded would be too harsh, even though such a union was forbidden by Jewish and Roman law. Precisely to the believing, non- 302 legalistic thinking of Paul the visit to a prostitute may have appeared significantly more immoral than a marriage with the perhaps very youthful widow of the father. The offender must have had sexual relations with the wife of his father who was still alive. That similar things took place among the Gnostics is shown for example by Iren. I, 6.3: "Again, others *openly* and without shame take the women who please them away from their husbands and make them their own wives." With these words Irenaeus describes precisely the occurrence which was the occasion for Paul's statements in I, 5.   303

4. The Problem of Wearing the Veil

The passage under discussion is I, 11:2-16. In this section of Epistle   304
A, Paul is arguing that the women should keep their heads covered

during worship. Since the covering of the head in religious ceremonies
305   was a rigid rule indeed in the Orient and among the Jews but not in
Greece, Kümmel (Lietzmann, on p. 53, l. 17) thinks that here Paul is
fighting "for the introduction of an oriental-Jewish custom into the
Corinthian congregation, against which the resistance of the local
custom is directed." This is not wholly correct, for vs. 16 clearly says
that this non-Greek practice was evident and encountered no resistance
in all Paul's Greek communities, and therefore certainly ever since he
306   had founded them. Corinth cannot have been an exception. Instead,
recently an attempt had been made by contentious persons (vs. 16) in
Corinth to abolish the previously customary observance, and Paul is
fighting for its *preservation*. It is likely from the outset that the
recently appeared Gnostics are responsible for these efforts also, but
it can also be demonstrated in detail.

It must be Paul's effort pertinently to defend the old custom in the
face of the newer ones. Then of course one marvels first at the exposition of the distinctions between God, Christ, man, and woman. It
is true, the statement that man is set over woman seems to prove that
what holds true for man does not at all have to apply to woman in
the same way, but it includes no justification at all for the view that
the woman is to wear the veil. Besides, in vss. 11-12 Paul in effect takes
back all that he has previously asserted with reference to the inequality
of the sexes.[161] And the stressing of the equality of man and woman
doubtless corresponds to Paul's actual judgment (see below). But this
means that in vss. 3-9 the apostle is not arguing with full freedom, but
is pressured in a certain direction by the views of the adversaries.
This view can only have been that with a reference to the equal status
of the two sexes some were declaring the custom regarding covering the
head during worship, which was different for men and for women, to
be irrelevant. Over against this, Paul takes his stand on the inequality
of the sexes.

The train of thought in vss. 3-9 now becomes so obscure because
at the same time Paul makes the impossible effort to prove the *necessity*
of woman's wearing the veil with the same argument, although this
argument only makes sure the *possibility* that the woman in contrast
to the man must wear a headcovering, since she is not equal to the
man in every way. Therefore it is useless to search for an actual advance

---

[161] Lietzmann very freely concedes, without being corrected by Kümmel on this
point in the new edition of the Commentary: "Here is it incomprehensible to
us why Paul did not omit vs. 3 together with the forced play on words (namely
vs. 4)." Characteristic also is Godet, *Der erste Brief an die Korinther*. J. Weiss ([1],
p. 271) remarks on I, 11:3-4: "I do not make any claim to understanding the text
as it has been handed down."

in thought in these verses. Paul struggles desperately with the material, yet without being able rightly to achieve his intention. Verse 3 sets forth the assertion that man and woman are not on the same level. In vss. 4-5a, there follows the other assertion, that the man must not cover his head, but the woman must cover hers. The second thesis is not derived from the first, but does presuppose it. The combination of the two assertions underlies the following vss. 5b-6: If the woman thinks that she, like the man, can leave off the headcovering, then she is also to let herself be shorn like a man—whereby she would be placed on a level with the prostitute. But if this appears disgraceful to her, then would she please also cover her head? Man and woman just do not stand on the same level, and therefore the same thing does not apply to both. In vs. 7 there follows an abortive argument that the man in contrast to the woman may wear his hair unbound. In essence vs. 7 says only that the man in general stands above the woman—the old thesis which in vss. 8-9 in addition receives its biblical justification. That puts an end to this theme. Paul sensed that he would not reach his goal in this way. Nevertheless, the very fact, which becomes evident, that the *opponents forced* him to stress the inequality of the sexes, and this clearly against his real intention, can help us to recognize the views of these opponents. They argue for the "emancipation" of woman, that is, for her complete equality. But this is genuinely Gnostic. If the Pneuma is the real self of the person, then the person ("man") is neither male nor female, but a part of the cosmic σῶμα Χριστοῦ which in every respect is equal with others. Differences of sex belong only to the sphere of the *sarx* and therefore cannot serve to judge the person.

Paul unintentionally confirms this when in vss. 3-9 he argues from the basis of sexual differences rooted in creation, only then in vss. 11-12 to affirm that ἐν κυρίῳ all differences are taken away. Of course Paul has transformed the mythical side-by-side arrangement of the kinds of existence into a historical sequential one. The mythical origin of the schema that is employed, however, is unmistakable. This becomes even clearer in Gal. 3:28, where Paul writes: "οὐκ ἔνι Ἰουδαῖος οὐδὲ Ἕλλην, οὐκ ἔνι δοῦλος οὐδὲ ἐλεύθερος, οὐκ ἔνι ἄρσεν καὶ θῆλυ· πάντες γὰρ ὑμεῖς εἷς ἐστε ἐν Χριστῷ Ἰησοῦ." This is, at least in terminology, pure Gnosticism.[162] Cf. also the fragment from the gnosticizing

[162] I regard Gal. 3:26-28 as a liturgical piece of Gnostic origin which, already employed in pre-Pauline Hellenistic communities, was taken over by Paul and by him was demythologized by means of the catchword "διὰ τῆς πίστεως" (similarly Rom. 3:25; πίστις ἐν Χριστῷ is never found elsewhere in Paul; cf. Schlier, commentary on Galatians, p. 127; this points to the insertion of the "διὰ τῆς πίστεως"). Without this phrase the passage offers purest Gnosticism. Paul let himself be led by the beginning of the piece to quote it in its entirety in the present context.

308   Gospel of the Egyptians preserved in Clement of Alexandria and in
       II Clem. 12.2: The Lord says that the kingdom will come "when you
       tread underfoot the garment of shame, and when the two are one (see
       pp. 79 ff.), and the exterior is like the interior (i.e. when only the
       soul is present), and the male with the female, so that there is neither
309   male nor female" (see Hennecke-Schneemelcher-Wilson, I: 168-69).[163]
       The preference of Gnostic systems for male-female primal beings is
       related to such anthropology.[164] This idea of the unity of the sexes
       in Christ must have been familiar in the Gnostic circles from which
       Paul's redeemed-redeemer terminology stems and with which in fact
       the Corinthian Gnostics also are closely connected. But then it was
       also a concern to the Gnostics to demonstrate this unity of man and
       woman ἐν Χριστῷ, as it apparently was being done most recently in
       Corinth.[165]

       The further train of thought is as follows: In vs. 10 at last apparently
       a concrete reason is given for the necessity of wearing the veil. This
       verse is presently to occupy our attention somewhat more closely. In
       vss. 11-12 there follows then the already mentioned statement which

---

Verse 26 fits quite well into the train of thought, in which of course the change of
person shows that from vs. 26 on, Paul is no longer formulating freely. Verses 27-28
on the other hand break the train of thought; for it is not exactly the same whether
one is buried by baptism ἐν Χριστῷ or, as Paul wishes to prove, is made righteous
in God's sight by faith. Furthermore, it is not clear what the stressing of the
equality of all Christians before Christ is supposed to mean in the total context.
Paul then of course does not reflect further on this, and vs. 29 is connected with
vs. 28 only terminologically, while on the other hand it is substantively connected
with vs. 26.

The Gnostics must have spoken the formula, whose attractive force in that time
one can well imagine, after baptism in a liturgical act to the newly baptized. (Does
Gal. 4:6—cf. Rom. 8:15—somehow continue the formula?) In addition to I, 12:13,
the same tradition is utilized in Col. 3:10-11 (cf. Rom. 10:12), and indeed in Col.
quite independently of the passage in Gal. 3:26 ff.; for the "πάντα καὶ ἐν πᾶσιν
Χριστός" shows a mythological thinking that is independent in comparison with
Gal. 3:28 and which is not to be attributed to the author of Col. In place of the
"synthetic" manner of speaking in Gal. 3:28, "You are all one in Christ," in Col.
3:11 the same mythological conception is formulated "analytically": "There are no
310   longer any distinctions of the σάρξ, for Christ, who is in all, is all."

[163] Among the Valentinians this conception later occurs in narrative form: the
clothing of the first men with animal skins signified clothing in the flesh and hence
the beginning of sexual differences (Gen. 3:21). God had created man as a sexless
being (Clem. Alex., Exc. ex Theod. 55; cf. J. P. Steffes, Das Wesen des Gnostizismus
[Paderborn, 1922], p. 186).

[164] Cf., e.g., Hipp. V, 7; Iren. I, 14.1; I, 30.3; V, 14; II Clem. 14.1 ff.; H. Schlier,
311   Ignatius, pp. 91 ff.

[165] That Paul's argument for the inequality of the sexes in I, 11:3 ff. is anti-
Gnostic is also shown by the corresponding statements in I Tim. 2:13-14, which,
like the entire epistle, are written with an anti-Gnostic orientation. In both passages there is clearly disclosed a common motif of the polemic against the Gnostic
"unity movement" which was offered by the Old Testament-Jewish tradition (cf.
Dibelius on the Pastoral Epistles, in loc.).

corresponds to Pauline thinking, that ἐν κυρίῳ all distinctions are taken away. Since the problem being debated functions exclusively within the community, and indeed for Paul that means "ἐν κυρίῳ," the apostle therewith in effect nullifies the entire preceding argument. He certainly sensed this, for in what follows he appeals solely to his readers' capacity for sound judgment: "Judge for yourselves; is it becoming for the woman to call on God in prayer with her head uncovered?" But even nature itself for him teaches nothing more than that cutting the hair is disgraceful for a woman; the covering for the head is no longer discussed: "And does not nature itself teach you that it is a disgrace for a man to wear long hair, but for a woman an honorable thing, since it is given to her as a covering?" Then because even thus Paul does not achieve his aim, he concludes the fruitless presentation abruptly: "εἰ δέ τις δοκεῖ φιλόνεικος εἶναι, ἡμεῖς τοιαύτην συνήθειαν οὐκ ἔχομεν, οὐδὲ αἱ ἐκκλησίαι τοῦ θεοῦ" (vs. 16).

With this apodictic conclusion the apostle in substance concedes that he too is unable to justify the wearing of the veil. Nevertheless he attempts such a justification and does not break through to the freedom of the believers which he himself represents in Rom. 14 and I, 8 and which he is willing to have restricted only out of regard for his brother; thus in fact he appears to contradict himself. This shows that he knows that he is dealing with opponents who do not, like himself, represent the *eleutheria* of the ὡς μή which is bestowed on the person who is obedient in the faith, but teach a freedom which as a proving of Gnosis itself redeems and therefore is loveless and unhistorical and the practicing of which is necessary.

Not that Paul had already grasped the background of the Corinthians' attitude. He had hardly heard more than that some were *demanding* the abolition of the veil and thus were interpreting it as an obligatory religious act. This must however show him that it is no longer *his* gospel, which in principle had to allow freedom in this question, that stands behind that demand, but some "other gospel" (II, 11:4). In the face of this situation he can secure obedience to his kerygma only by elevating the maintenance of the tradition to a commandment, for only in the presence of such a concrete demand will the division of minds be made in this case. With respect to the problem of covering the head as such this attitude naturally means an unevangelical legalism. But for Paul it is in fact simply a matter of the Christian stance of faith, which is lost where the veil *may not* be worn. If one sees Paul's statements in I, 11:2-16 against this background, one will have to agree with them fully in their ultimate intention and only deplore the fact that in consequence of his defective knowledge of the opponent's heresy the apostle was unable to make his attack

312

fundamental and therewith clearer, but *in the last analysis* one cannot say that in 11:3-10 Paul "did not achieve the Christian clarity of Gal. 3:28" (Kümmel in Lietzmann, p. 55, 1. 15) .[166]

313   Now we must examine vs. 10. What reason is given here for the wearing of a headcovering and why is it inadequate? "διὰ τοῦτο ὀφείλει ἡ γυνὴ ἐξουσίαν ἔχειν ἐπὶ τῆς κεφαλῆς διὰ τοὺς ἀγγέλους." That is, literally, therefore (because woman is beneath man) the woman must wear an authority on her head because of the angels. The only possible explanation of this verse, which is accepted everywhere even by the modern exegetes, was given already by Tertullian: " 'Propter angelos' scilicet quos legimus a Deo et caelo excidisse ob concupiscentiam feminarum" (Virg. Vel. 7, following Lietzmann, p. 55). The headcovering then had an apotropaic effect, and thus possessed the ἐξουσία to fend off the demonic angel powers.[167] It is of course wrong to have in mind here above all the erotic lustfulness of the ἄγγελοι, as is the case in Tertullian and in Lietzmann, *in loc.*, for Paul certainly is clearly not thinking of this. As a reason that the *man* does *not* need to wear the veil, he is able to say only that man stands above woman. διὰ τοῦτο something else holds true for the woman, not because she is especially threatened by the demons on account of her sex. When Paul immediately thereafter asserts the equality of the sexes ἐν κυρίῳ, the whole motivation of vs. 10 of course becomes untenable of itself. Besides, there is the fact that the person who is ἐν κυρίῳ, according to Paul's opinion, also no longer needs to fear the demonic powers. Whoever stands under the protection of the κύριος no longer needs magical instruments for defense against the evil angels. This Gnosis, which Paul plainly represents during the discussion about meat sacrificed to idols, he denies here in the interest of an argument which of course is fruitless.

What interests us now above all is the fact that the real meaning of the veil as a protection against the demons was familiar to the Gnostics also. But then we learn a further and perhaps the most important reason which prompted the Gnostics to take a stand against the custom of the covered head for women during prayer: Anyone who is a Pneumatic, who possesses Gnosis, has no more reason to fear the persecutions of the powers of darkness. He is in fact already freed from

---

[166] The judgment is justified with respect to the lack of clarity with which Paul represents his concern, but not with respect to the clarity of his theological perception.

[167] On this, cf. now Kümmel in Lietzmann, [1], on p. 54, 1. 15. Also to be compared is E. Rohde, who remarks in *Psyche* (Kröner's Taschenausgabe, Vol. 61, n. 150) : "When the mother provides the child that is to be exposed with a crown made of olive branches (Eur. Ion. 1433 ff.) , this is just as much an apotropaic instrument
314   as is the Gorgon's head on the wrap which she also sends along with the child."

them; he has become a ruler. He "stands in the heights above all power and needs to fear no one" (Iren. I, 13.6). To such self-awareness the custom of wearing a veil as ἐξουσία διὰ τοὺς ἀγγέλους must be an expression of a wholly un-"Christian" anxiety. Paul must have been in full agreement with the Gnostics here. He is put in the wrong even by his own standards when he goes on record for the maintaining of the veil, and therefore he also fails to justify this observance. But because the Gnostics are pressing for the practicing of Gnosis since their salvation rests therein, Paul must here demand full renunciation of the ἐξουσία, since only in the fulfillment of such a demand is the false way of salvation closed. Because Paul therewith in our situation only apparently establishes a nonevangelical law, but in truth takes a stand for a historical understanding of life over against the mythological one of the Gnostics, his demand should be approved in principle, and indeed in such a way that this affirmation includes the declaration that the person who today would demand the headcovering for women on the basis of I, 11:2-16 would thereby be working directly against the sense of this passage.

It probably may be assumed that with the apostle's statements the problem was decided in passing for the community which adhered to him, that the women also thereafter wore their headcoverings in worship. In the further correspondence this question is not taken up again. In fact, when Paul begins the section with a word of praise, this probably presupposes that he knows that the community in its totality rejects the demands of the Gnostics, so that with his statements he intends above all to stiffen their backs against the φιλόνεικοι.

5. The Problem of the Silence of Women in the Church

I, 14:33b-36 stands in a unique conflicting connection with I, 11:2 ff. While in the latter Paul at once presupposes that the women pray and prophesy in the gatherings of the church, here he forbids them any such utterance. This contradiction is easy to recognize and is not to be disputed with the unfounded assertion that in 11:2 ff. Paul is talking about house worship or something similar, or that in 14:33b ff. a special kind of utterance of the women, not more precisely described, is meant, and that their public praying and prophesying is not forbidden (Heinrici, Kümmel, et al.). Some have resolved the difficulty by excising vss. 34-35 as a gloss patterned after I Tim. 2:11-12. They appeal to the W-Text, which has vss. 34-35 only after vs. 40. But the Western reading is the obvious emendation of a redactor who felt, not altogether incorrectly, that the note about the appearance in public of women breaks the connection of the instructions about prophecy and speaking in tongues. Nevertheless it is not to be denied that vs. 33b belongs to vs. 34, that vs. 36 therewith looks back on the entire section vss. 33b-35, and that thus the position of the disputed section in today's text is unassailable. One would have to rule out vss. 33b-36, but then of course *cannot* any longer appeal to the Western tradition.[168]

The whole difficulty, however, is easy to solve if one notes that the two contradictory parts belong to different writings. In Epistle A Paul is objecting to the appearance of women unveiled in the Corinthian worship. That he concedes their speaking in public as such, although it was not the custom in Pauline congregations, will be due to the fact that Stephanas or at any rate he himself had mistakenly failed to connect this custom with the new libertine tendencies in Corinth, which *inter alia* demanded that the veil be laid aside. Otherwise Paul would have had to protest even here. The public cultic activity of women was familiar to Hellenism, and Paul shows himself extremely free to

318 change position on these externalities in themselves. Passages such as 11:2 ff. and 14:33b ff. are explained in terms of the concrete situation which compelled Paul to oppose the innovations of his opponents with the demand, concretized in detail, for the preservation of the traditional practice. Since he obviously did not sense that the active participation of women in the cultus was demanded by the Gnostics, it is characteristic of his freedom that he tolerates this practice without

319 contradiction. At the time of Epistle B he is better informed; hence he now demands that the Gnostic custom, which allows women to engage in public prayer and certainly also in speaking in tongues, be

320 once again discontinued. On this point it is interesting that he *now* refers briefly to the tradition and sets forth the practice in other communities as normative,[169] without attempting again a fruitless theo-

321 logical motivation for this originally Jewish observance. In judging Paul one must keep in mind the special cause which compelled him, in the last analysis against his intention, to limit Christian freedom in this way, and one then will readily accept, without qualms and naturally also without legalism, passages like 14:33b ff. as Pauline. One will then also, at the deepest level, feel no contradiction between 11: 2 ff. and 14:33b ff. It is the same correctly understood Christian freedom

322   [168] Cf. H. Greeven, "Propheten, Lehrer, Vorsteher bei Paulus," p. 7, esp. n. 19.

   [169] One should note that references, almost the same in wording and at any rate the same in motivation, to the custom in the Pauline communities in 4:17 and 7:17 are, like that in 14:33, from Epistle B. This not only argues for the correctness of our literary-critical analysis and against the theory of J. Weiss, that these passages are interpolated (cf. p. 89, n. 13); it also shows that Paul was well aware of the peculiar course of his argument in I, 11:2-16, now in the new epistle draws the teaching from there, and employs the reference to the συνήθεια in the ἐκκλησίαι θεοῦ as an essential argument in the debate.

which lets Paul allow the activity of women in the cult there and
forbid it here.

In this case the Gnostics naturally justified their ἐλευθερία, just as
in the issue about the veil, with a reference to the pneumatic equality
of man and woman. The Pneumatic indeed is no longer a man and
hence obviously not a sexual being. Man and woman are one in Christ.
One may imagine oneself for a little in the thought-world of mythological Gnosticism and will at once sense that for the Gnostic it must
have been sheer nonsense when the Pneuma dwelling in a female *sarx*
was supposed to be silent while the fragment of the primal man imprisoned in a man was permitted to speak. However in Corinth in the
whole affair it may have been primarily a matter of speaking in
ecstasy. Examples of active participation of women in the cult can be
cited from later Gnosticism in large numbers. I mention only Priscilla
and Maximilla from Montanism and the prophetesses of Marcus in   323
Iren. I, 13.3, and from earlier times the fact, later mythologized, that
Simon had a constant companion (Helena) who possessed the gift of
prophecy. Post-canonical Judaism—not so much the Old Testament—   324
in contrast excluded any cultic service of women. It is worthy of note   325
that in his communities Paul in principle continued the Jewish tradition.   326

To be sure, it cannot be *proved* that the new abuse, introduced only
in Corinth (vs. 36), of having women to speak in the assemblies, is of
Gnostic origin, for the close connection of this problem with that of
speaking in tongues in the statements of Paul could not be of the
proving kind. Yet such a proof could be demanded only by the person
who rejects[170] the conclusions of the present work in the broadest scope.

VI. The Sacraments

1. General Observations

The answering of the question as to the attitude of the Corinthian
schismatics toward the sacraments enables us again to point to the
basic Gnostic attitude of these heretics and at the same time contributes
to the better understanding of some passages in the Corinthian epistles.
First we must clarify the position of the Gnostic on the sacrament in
principle.

[170] Anyone who does this, however, should note that the parallel statements in
I Tim. 2:11-12 also can rightly be understood only against the background of the
anti-Gnostic orientation of the entire epistle; indeed, the peculiar evaluation and
high regard for childbearing among women in I Tim. 2:15 (cf. 5:14) also begins
to make sense only as an antithesis to the mythologically grounded Gnostic asceticism
(I Tim. 4:3). Dibelius has already correctly recognized this in his commentary
(*Pastoralbriefe,* 2nd ed., pp. 30-31).

327

328

Fundamental is the fact that to the genuine Gnostic any sacramental piety is alien. This is very clearly established in Irenaeus' account concerning the Gnostics' teachings about redemption in I, 21.4: "But others . . . say that it is not necessary to complete the mystery of the ineffable and invisible power by means of visible and perishable creations, the incomprehensible and incorporeal by means of the corporeal and that which can be experienced. The knowledge of the unutterable Greatness itself is rather the perfect redemption. After defect and suffering had arisen through ignorance, the entire state of things that had been produced by ignorance is taken away διὰ γνώσεως. Hence Gnosis is the redemption of the inner man . . . . For through knowledge the inner man is redeemed, and the knowledge of all things satisfies them. And this is the *true* redemption." This passage leaves nothing to be desired in clarity. When nevertheless in numerous Gnostic sects sacramental usages were practiced, this is occasioned by the fact that even pure Gnosticism could not escape the syncretistic tendencies of the age, and especially with the mystery cults, which were kindred in essence,[171] it practiced a lively exchange. But it is typical that the eucharist as a sacrament is almost wholly lacking.[172] This is due above all to the fact that the conception, in some way still connected with cultic meals of all kinds, and originally stemming from the mysteries, that the food eaten is connected with the flesh or blood of the cult's god, made the adoption of such forms of cultic worship impossible for Gnosticism. One could not hold in contempt the sacral meals of the heathen and at the same time say that his own rituals with a corresponding connection with sarkical substance were religiously appropriate.[173] Flesh and blood are simply deserving of con-

---

[171] Later Gnosticism which is particularly well known to us, of course, moreover is significantly influenced by the early catholic church and its view of the sacraments which has a strong touch of the mysteries about it.

[172] By no means is the custom, widespread in certain Gnostic circles, of the cultic eating of bread and salt to be compared with this (esp. in the Clementines; cf. Bousset, *Hauptprobleme*, pp. 303 ff.). It has nothing to do with the Supper.

[173] Very clear is Ign. Smyrn. 7.1, where it is told of the Gnostics: "εὐχαριστίας . . . ἀπέχονται διὰ τὸ μὴ ὁμολογεῖν τὴν εὐχαριστίαν σάρκα εἶναι τοῦ σωτῆρος ἡμῶν Ἰησοῦ Χριστοῦ. . . ."

329

If a cultic observance of the supper was known, under the influence of the Great Church, also in Gnostic circles, people were compelled, with the disregard for the flesh of Jesus, somehow to interpret the action symbolically. This did happen. Hence I am certain that the peculiar exposition of the act of the Lord's Supper in I, 10:16-17 goes back to Gnostic tradition. It is certain that "σῶμα τοῦ Χριστοῦ" in this context cannot mean, on the lips of Paul, the church (thus, correctly, K. Stürmer in EvTheol, 1947, p. 51, in spite of Kümmel in Lietzmann, *in loc.*); the parallel to "αἷμα" in vs. 16 will not allow this. Otherwise the parallel between Supper and mystery meal, on which Paul's entire argument in I, 10:14-22 is built, would in fact be lost. But it should be just as much beyond doubt that in vss. 16b and 17 Paul is taking over a fixed formula which he attaches to his saying about the cup and after which—making use of traditional Jewish formulas (J. Jeremias, *Eucharistic Words of Jesus* [1955], pp. 21 ff.) —he constructs this saying. Verse 17 seems to me to show the Aramaic background of this piece especially clearly. Verse 17 also offers an explanation of the "σῶμα τοῦ Χριστοῦ" which leaves no doubt that *originally* the church was meant to be understood thereby, an interpretation which indeed does not fit at all into the present context. What is the source of this formula? Not the "breaking of bread" of the primitive community (Acts 2:42), but a Gnostic construction of this observance, in which the divided bread was interpreted to mean the division of the σῶμα Χριστοῦ, and the unity of the bread to mean the unity of the individual members of the Pneuma. As to terminology and conception of the piece itself, the best proof of this is offered by the words of the eucharistic prayer in Did. 9 (cf. J. Jeremias, p. 35, n. 5), which certainly stem from gnosticizing tradition and in which what is formulated analytically in the saying about the bread in I, 10:16-17 is said synthetically: "ὥσπερ ἦν τοῦτο τὸ κλάσμα διεσκορπισμένον ἐπάνω τῶν ὀρέων καὶ συναχθὲν ἐγένετο ἕν, οὕτω συναχθήτω σου ἡ ἐκκλησία ἀπὸ τῶν περάτων τῆς γῆς εἰς τὴν σὴν βασιλείαν (Did. 9.4; on the subject, cf. Epiph. Haer. XXVI, 13, and XXVI, 3; see p. 56). We have become sufficiently acquainted with such variation in the language of the myth of the redeemed redeemer (cf. pp. 62 ff.; p. 239, n. 162), so that no more proof is required that for the *myth*, I, 10:16b says the same thing as Did. 9.4 (cf. 10.5). That neither Paul nor the author of the Didache knew of the mythological original sense of these passages appears to me, to be sure, self-evident. But by the determination of the "Sitz im Leben" of these pieces we can recognize that even in genuine Gnostic circles the practice of the Supper or of the breaking of bread could be maintained as a cultic observance, but only with definite, purely symbolic meaning, without any reference to the σάρξ of Christ. (J. Jeremias, p. 85, with others, misses the words of institution in the prayers of the Didache. But this is precisely their characteristic mark, that these are replaced by the Gnostic interpretation of the act. It is impossible to explain this absence in terms of arcane discipline.)

E. Käsemann, (EvTheol, 1947/48, pp. 264 ff.; cf. J. Jeremias, p. 131), who does sense the tension between I, 10:16a and 16b-17, curiously holds vs. 16 to be community tradition, and vs. 17 to be Pauline interpretation. But it is utterly incredible that with the "traditional" piece, which moreover is genuinely Pauline, Paul exactly fits the context in 10:14-22 which he has conceived, but of all things, loses the connection with his "own" idea (which nevertheless is clearly anchored in the tradition—Did. 9.4). The saying about the bread in 10:16b-17 also is identified in the context as tradition in contrast to the saying about the cup, because it is established that in certain circles of earliest Christianity, indeed in the early Jerusalem community among other places (cf. Bousset, *Hauptprobleme*, p. 307), only the eating of bread ("breaking of bread") possessed cultic significance (disputed by Jeremias, pp. 82 ff., in a dubious interpretation), while nowhere was the Supper celebrated only with wine, as we should expect if in our passage Paul is using his own saying about the bread to fill out a saying about the cup that has been handed down to him.

Of course the Supper in dual form did not always remain unknown to all the Gnostic circles. This is shown by the aforementioned eucharistic prayers of the Didache, which interestingly stem from J e w i s h-Christian–Gnostic tradition; for it may be regarded as certain that in them we have to do with revised Jewish table prayers (cf. R. Bultmann, [2], pp. 40-41; M. Dibelius in ZNW 37 [1938]: 32-41; article "Abendmahl," in RGG). Not only does their saying about the bread contain a Gnostic meaning, but in the saying about the cup also the cultic action is bound up with the genuine Gnostic myth. Underlying the saying περὶ τοῦ ποτηρίου, "We thank thee, our Father, for the holy vine of thy servant David, whom thou hast allowed us to recognize through thy servant Jesus," is not some Old Testament tradition but the widespread conception of the cosmic tree of life, which frequently appears as a vine (cf. among the Mandaeans, then also in one of the sources of John [John 15:1 ff.]; cf. Sir. 24.22 ff.; cf. E. Schweizer, *EGO EIMI*, pp. 39 ff.) and

demnation, and because the anathema applies to the Christ *kata sarka,* any cultic action which depends upon this *sarx* is an impossibility.[174]

It is a different matter with baptism and with anointing. Both practices of the catholic church were not unknown in later Gnosticism (Iren. I, 21). Of course in pure Gnosticism their meaning could only be that the redemption that had already occurred in Gnosis was symbolized in such ceremonies; it could not consist in their effecting the redemption. Where the person first receives the Pneuma through initiation we find ourselves in the sphere of influence of the mystery cults which in origin were sharply distinguished from Gnosticism. When the genuine Gnostics in the section from Irenaeus quoted above reject baptism and anointing, of which Irenaeus had spoken earlier, because the secret of the invisible power cannot be perfected by anything that is visible, this shows that in the sphere of *pure* Gnosticism sacraments can only be symbols of an event which occurs independently of them. Thus the anointing is done with balsam oil "because this ointment is a *type* of the fragrance that is above all" (Iren. I, 21.3). The symbolic meaning of baptism lay in the fact that with the baptismal act the liberation of man from the prison cell of the body was symbolized by the drowning of the "(old) Adam." Since in certain Gnostic circles Christ's death on the cross was understood also as the liberation of the heavenly Pneuma from the fleshly substance which was slain on the cross,[175] this provides the explanation of the line of argument in Rom. 6:3-4: "Or do you not know that all we who are baptized into Jesus Christ are baptized into his death? Now we have been buried with him by baptism into death, so that, just as Christ was raised from the dead by the glory of the Father, we also should walk in newness of life."

---

in Gnosticism is a figure for the cosmic primal man-redeemer (E. Käsemann, [2], pp. 69 ff.; Schlier, [2], pp. 48 ff.; on this, cf. Ps. 80:9-20, which was allegorically interpreted in this sense [because of the vine of *David!*]; see H. Lietzmann, *Mass and Lord's Supper,* p. 190). Since the wine was connected with the vine thus understood, one could employ the cup as well as the bread in the Gnostic cult (cf. Schlier, [2], p. 55, n.). As to meaning, of course this Gnostic cultic meal had as little in common with the Hellenistic meal as with the primitive community's meal custom, even though the fact of a Gnostic supper with the broadly drawn interpretation of the cup quite generally points to the decisive influence of the Hellenistic community.

[174] The abominable supper of the Borborians portrayed by Epiphanius (Haer. XXVI) can confirm this, since here instead of bread the male semen is used, and instead of wine, menstrual blood, and this because these secretions are regarded as the locus of the Pneuma, which in this way is to be preserved from being diffused in the world. For the same reason these Gnostics, who regard the begetting of children as a grievous sin, eat the embryo which they have taken from the mother's womb (Haer. XXVI, 5). One may compare here also the well-known magical ceremonies of the Gnostic Marcus in Iren. I, 13.2, who apparently practiced hocus-pocus with the Supper.

[175] Cf. Col. 2:11-12; 2:20–3:4; Hipp. VII, 33.2; X, 21.3 = Iren. I, 26.1.

Of course Paul transposes the whole conception visibly into the historical realm, but unblurred remains the originally Gnostic idea that baptism is a symbol for the fact that the individual will experience the same happy destiny which Christ has experienced as the ἀπαρχὴ τῶν μελλόντων: the ascent of the πνεῦμα ἐν τῇ ἀπεκδύσει τοῦ σώματος τῆς σαρκός (Col. 2:11; note the context in which this passage appears   330 in Colossians). With such a purely symbolic interpretation certain sacral actions *could* find admission even into the pure Gnostic cult.   331 They were not able to acquire special significance here. They always remained manifestations on the periphery of the religious life of the genuine Gnostic.[176] In particulars the attitude toward such sacraments was varied; only the rejection of cultic meals is general and, as we said, highly characteristic of the Gnostic understanding of existence.[177] Interesting in this connection is the absence of the sacraments in John. Of course he is acquainted with baptism (3:22; I John 2:20, 27; 5:6-7), without ascribing to it any meaning. The Supper is never mentioned and is first inserted by the editor in 6:51b-58 and 19:34b (on this, see now R. Bultmann, *Theology*, II: 54, 58-59). Without prejudice to the   333 fact that John is no Gnostic κατ' ἐξοχήν, there is revealed, in this more than indifferent[178] attitude of the writer of the Fourth Gospel toward

---

[176] Exceptions confirm the rule (cf. Bousset, *Hauptprobleme*, chap. VII). Thus   332 the high regard for baptism in the Mandaean texts is to a large extent historically and geographically conditioned. The baptist movement in the Orient is age-old, and baptist sects at the Jordan are certainly older than Mandaeism and Gnosticism in general. That Gnosticism readily found admittance in eschatologically motivated or at least seriously religious baptismal fellowships is just as evident as the fact that it had to maintain so far as possible the central practice of this baptismal fellowship (cf. O. Cullmann in *Neutestamentliche Studien für R. Bultmann* [1954], pp. 44-45). Hence one may no longer expect to find a coherent system in such syncretistic phenomena. The chaos of the Mandaean texts offers a perfect example of such syncretism of Gnostic observance.

Those initiations which are supposed to enable the soul during its ascent to deceive the demons and to overcome the numerous fortifications of the demonic world do not belong here. In a later time they are widespread (*Pistis Sophia*). Just so, as time goes on, magical-mysterious piety is syncretistically superimposed upon pure Gnosticism, a procedure which is inseparably bound up with the deterioration of the genuinely Gnostic self-consciousness. Sin was again sensed, the already conquered demons threatened more powerfully than ever, and in place of the grand liberty of the one who knows there appeared the anxious concern about salvation and with it often a flood of the most varied mysteries designed to give aid.

[177] If one compares with this the praxis of the mystery cults in which meals κατὰ σάρκα to a large extent stood at the center of the cultic observances, it becomes clear that mystery religions and Gnosticism at the outset were fundamentally separate. Only the later development gives us a certain right to describe the mystery religions also as Gnostic.

[178] Cf. John 17:19; perhaps in the "ὑπὲρ αὐτῶν ἐγὼ ἁγιάζω ἐμαυτόν" there is a reference to the words of institution of the Supper, revealing the intention which led the author of the Fourth Gospel in a special way in his appropriating the high-priestly prayer: to create a substitute for the establishing of the Lord's Supper (cf. R. Bultmann, commentary on John, *in loc.*).

the sacraments, the Gnosticism which stands in the background of his terminology and theology.[179]

2. The Supper

Here we must discuss the section I, 11:17-34. Here also Paul touches on problems which had been made known to him from the oral accounts of Stephanas and his companions. Again, as in 11:2-16, it involves happenings in the congregational gatherings. It is typical that Stephanas, in contrast to his other reports, in this respect was relatively well informed. For if he had become acquainted with the unedifying situation in Corinth only on his journey through, he could of course have informed himself best about the external conditions in the gatherings, in other words, through his own observation (cf. p. 101). There are two things which Paul now censures in detail. First (πρῶτον) the σχίσματα in the community which become evident in the meetings (vss. 18-19). Paul apparently had not been able to learn more precisely from Stephanas what was involved in these conflicts. It will have been a matter of more or less vehement disputes between the Christ people who had come in, i.e., the Gnostics, and the apostle people, who defended the ecclesiastical tradition.

The πρῶτον (vs. 18) is not formally taken up again by a δεύτερον and also is not replaced by the οὖν in vs. 20, which rather points back to the συνερχομένων ὑμῶν of vs. 18 (J. Weiss). In substance of course the δεύτερον πρόβλημα to which the πρῶτον points is broached in vss. 20 ff. with the discussion of the disorder in the celebration of the eucharist, which could never have been called σχίσματα or αἱρέσεις (cf. I, 1:10).[180] We have to ask: (1) What was the ordinary course of the observance of the Supper as it was introduced by Paul and now is again demanded, and (2) of what kind are the abuses which have recently spread in Corinth during the observance?

On (1): people met—probably on Sunday and certainly separate 334 from the "preaching service" [181]—in order to partake of the common

---

In this connection the observation is interesting that there is a close affinity between John 17 and the eucharistic prayers of the Didache discussed above, pp. 246 ff. (cf. E. Lohmeyer, ThRs, 1937, p. 304).

[179] J. Jeremias (p. 125) rejects the assertion that the Gospel of John "rejected the Eucharist or regarded it as superfluous," with the argument: "Where in the history of the apostolic age do we find the slightest support for so weighty a thesis?" The answer is: "in all Christian Gnosticism!"

[180] Otherwise Rom. 3:2, where the "πρῶτον" does not have any point of reference, even in substance.

[181] Oscar Cullmann's thesis (Early Christian Worship) that in the primitive church there was no community worship without the observance of the Supper is

κυριακὸν δεῖπνον. They began only when the entire congregation was assembled (vs. 33). After a prayer of thanksgiving the bread was broken and divided (vs. 24). When that had been eaten (vs. 25a), in the same way, i.e., after a corresponding prayer, the cup with the wine was passed around (vs. 25). With this meal and probably also during this meal the death of the Lord was to be proclaimed (vs. 26).

It is not to be assumed that Paul should have observed the κυριακὸν δεῖπνον otherwise than as he "received from the Lord." Of course that is the opinion of most exegetes, who see the Supper of the Pauline communities more or less as an "Agapē." But there is nothing here to indicate that a meal to satisfy hunger belonged to the observance. On the contrary! Paul expressly orders: "If anyone is hungry, then let him eat at home, so that you may not come into judgment" (vs. 34a).[182] Thus he tolerates no profanation of the sacred act which would blur the fact that what is involved is the enjoyment of the bread and wine of the Lord. People are to eat and drink at home. "Do you not have houses for eating and drinking?" (vs. 22). Thus it is utterly unjustified to draw close connections between the Pauline observance of the Supper and the later *agapae,* the origin of which is obscure (J. Weiss, Lietzmann, Bachmann, Heinrici, and many others). But the Hellenistic cultic meal of Paul is also fundamentally separated from the primitive community's breaking of bread. Only bread and wine were taken, and that in liturgical form and under the presupposition that the participants had already satisfied their hunger at home. Of course this does not mean that one only received a bread crumb of the weight of our communion wafer, but already with Paul the κυριακὸν δεῖπνον no more served as an ordinary meal than does our observance of the Supper today.[183]

335

untenable. Try as one will, one cannot even claim that Cullmann attempts a serious exegetical grounding for his theory. I, 11 and I, 14 and their relationship to each other are not even discussed; the epistle of Pliny is thrust aside. Correctly seen is the fact that according to the evidence of our sources, there was never an observance of the Supper without the proclamation of the Word. Still one may not simply turn this rule around, as Cullmann does.

[182] "Not to refrain from coming at all, but to come without a ravenous appetite," is Bachmann's (*in loc.*) gloss on the verse. But this is strained.

[183] Against this assertion one cannot adduce the "μετὰ τὸ δειπνῆσαι" (vs. 25; cf. Luke 22:20) as a presupposition for the *Pauline praxis* of a general meal for satisfying hunger in which more than the bread that was broken at the beginning was eaten, between the two cultic meals. Paul always speaks only of the partaking of bread and wine, and nowhere does he have in mind a meal for general enjoyment, which he expressly relegates to the homes, or for a favor. Further, according to vs. 26, only the partaking of bread and wine has cultic significance. But there can be no doubt that in vs. 26 Paul is looking back on the *entire* action just portrayed, in which therefore no act of eating apart from the cult can have taken place. Once this is recognized, we do not need to concern ourselves with the problem of what the "μετὰ τὸ δειπνῆσαι" is supposed to be saying in the bit of tradition. As a

On (2) : recently however the observance of the eucharist appeared to Paul to be developing into such profane meals. Some Corinthians were coming into the place of meeting and beginning, even before the cultic δεῖπνον was opened (vs. 33), to partake of a meal that they had brought, and were continuing to do this even during the common φαγεῖν (vs. 21a). That it was always customary to take along food and then to eat it in common cannot be inferred from Paul's words.[184] Quite the contrary. Paul is not censuring them because the individual eats by himself, but because a profane meal is taken at all in place of the κυριακὸν δεῖπνον: "συνερχομένων οὖν ὑμῶν ἐπὶ τὸ αὐτό, οὐκ ἔστιν κυριακὸν δεῖπνον φαγεῖν· ἕκαστος γὰρ τὸ ἴδιον δεῖπνον προλαμβάνει ἐν τῷ φαγεῖν" (vss. 20-21). The disorderly church members apparently came with the intention from the outset of eating an ordinary δεῖπνον out of provisions which they themselves had brought instead of observing the common cultic Supper. The expression "ἴδιον δεῖπνον" thus stands in contrast to "κυριακὸν δεῖπνον" (vs. 20) as the significant cultic meal, not in contrast to some *common* meal" which, without altering its nature, was divided into nothing but individual meals.[185] Wholly without support is the assertion, frequently found in explanation of 11:20-34, that because of some bad experiences Paul *now* is demanding the separation of cultic meal and the meal for satisfying hunger, which evidently had previously been combined. *It is inconceivable that Paul is peremptorily altering a practice which he himself had introduced and which was customary in all his communities, by making it appear that the alteration is the return to the* παράδοσις *of the Lord which had been given to him.* If a meal for satisfying hunger out of common stores had previously been customary, Paul would have had to press for the restoration of the common meal for satisfying hunger in place of the individual meals if he wanted to reestablish the old arrangement. Yet this is his intention when he points to the already well-known and practiced tradition. Instead of this he sends the meals for the satisfying of hunger back to the homes, and his aim in doing this certainly was not for convenience to give a mask to the

comparison with Matt. and Mark shows, it is a later indication of the situation (cf. Lietzmann, *in loc.*), and could perhaps refer to the passover situation (cf. J. Jeremias, p. 87). If Paul was conscious of this, it signified no difficulty for the praxis of his observance, since in fact he intended not to imitate a passover feast but to observe a cultic meal which was limited to bread and wine. Of course, if he debated with this passage of his tradition fragment at all, he must rather have thought of the eating of the broken bread, which in outward form and amount of the bread eaten will at least have had more of the character of a genuine meal than in our observances of the Supper.

[184] We do not know who arranged for the communal bread and wine.

[185] Of course the cultic meal was a communal meal, but what Paul is reproving is the disruption of the cultic, not of the communal.

lack of spirituality which lies in the lovelessness of gluttony, nor was
it because he had received a new and different *paradosis* from the
Lord, but because that was where those meals had always belonged.
What a strange apostolic instruction it would have been if Paul newly
allowed the rich, who previously shared with the poor from their
abundance, first to eat and satisfy their hunger at home alone, only
thereafter to observe with the hungry the common cultic meal, which
now leaves these still hungry!

The consequence of the ἴδιον δεῖπνον is that ὃς μὲν πεινᾷ, ὃς δὲ μεθύει
(vs. 21b). The two expressions probably are not to be understood
literally. It is no more to be assumed that during the gathering some
actually became drunk than that in the Christian community of that
time which was certainly marked by sacrifice and love there were
people who could not even get enough to eat. Paul only wishes drasti-
cally to indicate the consequences of such conduct and means that
the one eats none at all while another is gluttonous. Then he con-   337
tinues: "μὴ γὰρ οἰκίας οὐκ ἔχετε εἰς τὸ ἐσθίειν καὶ πίνειν"; that is, must
you eat your meals in the meeting place because you have no houses?
Naturally the answer is "no." But then (vs. 22b) for Paul the only
alternative explanation of the strange conduct is that brethren who did
not bring anything are to be shamed by the ἄτακτοι, who thereby
despise the ἐκκλησία τοῦ θεοῦ. The τοὺς μὴ ἔχοντας may also be translated "those who possess nothing." Then Paul would have surmised
specifically that the rich by this action intended to shame the poor, by
enjoying a feudal banquet in the presence of the poorer community
which resigns itself to bread and wine. But this is a long way from
meaning that previously the rich had shared with the poor or that
Paul at all countenanced the ordinary meals. He rather is himself seeking for an explanation of the disquieting conditions in Corinth and
is asking whether, since it certainly is not for a lack of space at home
that some were eating in the meeting place in the evening, the disorderly ones intended to despise and to shame the community and the
brethren for their poverty. But even this, if it should prove true, is   338
not what is reprehensible, but the ordinary eating of a meal in itself.
Anyone who nevertheless under such presuppositions partakes of the
cultic meal eats it unworthily, since he does not appreciate the special
character of this meal and puts it on a level with profane meals (: μὴ
διακρίνων τὸ σῶμα [vss. 27-30]). Thus for this reason one ought to
satisfy his hunger at home, and then begin and carry through the
celebration of the eucharist in company in the traditional liturgical
form (vss. 33-34).

It appears to me that this state of things is clear. Paul is not objecting to the fact that individual Corinthians are giving up the previous

custom of "eating out of a single bowl" and instead of this are eating the meal they have brought for themselves alone. His objection is rather that certain people deliberately intend to reduce the formerly
339 purely sacral meal into a profane repast. The former explanation not only has no support in the text, as we have seen, but also is impossible because such self-centered people would have filled themselves at home and would rather have brought less for the fellowship. Anyone who thinks in such self-seeking terms would not display his attitude *ad oculos*. In addition, it seems to me not very credible that in the young churches, which reckoned daily on Christ's *parousia*, a loveless attitude of this kind could have attained such a widespread acceptance. Thus vs. 22*b* certainly no more than vs. 22*a* gives an explanation of the conduct of the ἄτακτοι, which for Paul at the time of Epistle A was
340 just as inexplicable as it would be for us if we possessed only Epistle A.

However, the whole situation now at once becomes fully comprehensible when we recognize that the conduct which was so abhorrent to Paul was a deliberate demonstration of the Gnostics who are well known from the later epistles and who thereby were opposing the sacrament of the body and blood of Christ. This is already indicated by the general observation that the beginning of this abuse must coincide in time approximately with the advent of the Gnostics and by the fact that the other two reprehensible practices within the congregational gatherings, the women's praying unveiled and the disputes in I, 1:18 ff., both were caused by Gnostics. And the actual behavior of the unworthy ones is just what we would have to expect from the *Pneumatics*. For them a cultic meal at the center of which stands the crucified, sarkical Jesus is inconceivable.[186] If they nevertheless participate in the Supper, this is done from the outset not in order to observe the κυριακὸν δεῖπνον but to eat a profane meal. It cannot be said with certainty whether this was meant to be only a negative demonstration, or whether from the Gnostic side people connected a positive meaning with it. The former, however, is by far the more likely, especially since the conduct of the Gnostics showed no sort of tendency toward the *agapē*, the love-feast.[187] Then the unholy behavior of the Pneumatics

---

[186] Schniewind (see p. 130, n. 21) points to this context.

Cf. also U. Wilckens in EvTheol 18 (1958): 365. In principle correctly, even though very generally, W. Lütgert (*Freiheitspredigt und Schwarmgeister in Korinth,* pp. 131 ff.) points, for explanation of the abuses at the Supper in Corinth, to the "contempt for the sacrament that appears with any spiritualism"; the Corinthian heretics do not believe "that the Supper establishes real communion with Christ."

[187] It may be considered whether the Gnostics of Jewish origin with their practice referred directly to the sacral meals of the Jewish house congregations. If this were the case, of course it still would not mean that a religious meaning was also ascribed to this tradition.

Even the Gnostics whom Ignatius is combating because they reject the church's

would reveal their exaggerated self-consciousness, and with his charge
that they despised the ἐκκλησία τοῦ θεοῦ and the brother who did not
live in the same *eleutheria,* Paul may have put his finger exactly on
what the Gnostics intended.[188] Their attitude toward the Lord's Supper
then was not different in principle from that toward the sacrifices to
the idols.[189] For them neither meal had any cultic meaning, since the
"accursed" Jesus was just as much a "Nothing" as were the gods of the
heathen. However, they welcomed these meals as an opportunity to
fill the κοιλία with βρώματα as a demonstration—ὁ θεὸς καὶ ταύτην καὶ
ταῦτα καταργήσει. Upon the community and the individual brother
who did not yet possess the Gnosis which led to such doings they
looked down in scorn.

Thus the unedifying happenings at the Supper are best explained
from an action of those who were striving, out of their knowledge of
the absurdity of the Lord's Supper, to sabotage the cultic observance
and to transform it into an assembly with a profane feast.

A noteworthy parallel to such conduct is afforded in Jude 12: "οὗτοί
εἰσιν οἱ ἐν ταῖς ἀγάπαις ὑμῶν σπιλάδες συνευωχούμενοι ἀφόβως." The
situation corresponds fully to that of Corinth: the Gnostics—that such
are being combated in Jude indeed requires no proof—are taking part
in the *agapae* of the community. Unfortunately it cannot be said

---

Supper on account of its connection with the σάρξ of Christ (see pp. 246 ff.) likewise have their own communal meal, for in Smyrn. 8-9, Ignatius takes a stand
against those who celebrate the eucharist or *agapē* without the bishop as the guaran-
tor of correct doctrine, though of course we do not hear anything of the character
of this celebration.

Finally, it should be remembered here that even in the gnosticizing Jewish sects
with which we have become acquainted through the recent discoveries from the
Dead Sea, non-sacramental fellowship meals are common. On this, one may compare K. G. Kuhn in EvTheol, 1950/51, pp. 508-27, who attempts, with basic justification, to show connections between all these customs of meals and banquets.
Of course *dependence* certainly cannot be proved; cf. J. Jeremias, pp. 31 ff.

[188] G. Bornkamm's remark that "not a syllable is said about Gnostics and their
alleged attempts at sabotage" ([2], p. 348) is indeed correct, but this still is no objection to my interpretation. For unfortunately Paul does not give us any indication *at all* of the reasons for the disorders in the Supper at Corinth. *Every* interpretation is thrust back in the same way on conclusions *a posteriori*. But still the
connection of 11:18-19 with 11:20 ff. leaves no doubt at all that it was the divisions
in the community which in the last analysis caused the unedifying conduct of some
at the observance of the Supper. Even Bornkamm himself, a little before the
passage cited (p. 345, *et passim*), traces the disorder at the Corinthian observances
back to the "Gnostic experience of the Pneuma" of the Corinthians!

[189] B. Reicke's explanation (*Diakonie, Festfreude und Zelos,* pp. 252-93) mentioned earlier already pointed in this direction, since he correctly recognized the
Corinthian heretics as Gnostics. Of course Reicke's explanation is inconsistent, since
he illogically describes these Gnostics as both libertines and judaizing fanatics for
purity: as libertines they revel *generally,* and as Judaizers they revel *among themselves.* Reicke also proceeds from the unfounded identification of the Corinthian
meal as an *agapē.*

whether these *agapae* were cultic meals, love-feasts, or both. Still the cultic element may at least have played a role in them, since the mere eating together at the *agapae* in fact was not an accusation which belonged at the head of the catalog of vices in vss. 12-13, and the ἀφόβως may mean a lack of reverence in the presence of God to whom the meal is dedicated, and hence may stand in parallel to the longer statements of Paul in I, 11:27 ff.

It may be assumed that after the arrival of Epistle A the community no longer tolerated such tendencies. At any rate the problem is not taken up again in the later correspondence.

3. Baptism

Two sections of the Corinthian letters can be connected with this problem, namely I, 1:13-17 and 15:29. The former however is certainly to be eliminated. The passage can be explained most simply if Paul here is not referring to certain views of baptism held by the Corinthians but is arguing hypothetically, in order to demonstrate to the Corinthians the absurdity of appealing to men. The mystery conception that the baptized person enters into a close and perhaps even substantial connection with the God in whose name he was baptized, so that he then could say "ἐγώ εἰμι τοῦ θεοῦ" (then the God's name) was widespread in Paul's time (cf. Reitzenstein, [2], pp. 219-20). Baptism in the name of "Christ" in fact has the same meaning in its mythical significance. On the basis of this presupposition Paul proves that it is an absurdity to appeal to a man as is done in the first three watchwords in vs. 12: Were you baptized in Paul's name, so that you could now call yourselves by his name as your cult's god? (vs. 13c). Thank God, Paul says, that I did not baptize many. So then at least no one can get the idea of asserting falsely that he was baptized in my name, that is, that I myself have baptized him in my own name (thus Paul presupposes that others certainly had not baptized in his name and at the most he could have done this out of arrogance). The argument naturally is ironic; Paul knows precisely that no one in Corinth is claiming to have been baptized in his name. But for exactly this reason the absurdity of the slogans, "ἐγώ εἰμι Παύλου," and so on, which make sense only if some actually had been baptized in the names of men, must become very clear to the Corinthians.

It is impossible that people in Corinth placed special value upon baptism being administered by the personal teacher (J. Weiss, *in loc.;* cf. Reitzenstein, [1], pp. 40-41) and felt themselves to be bound in a special way to the baptizer, to whom they therefore also appeal with ἐγώ εἰμι . . . . For there were of course practically *no* people there who had been baptized by Paul, nor surely by Peter, personally. They would have had to call themselves after Paul's helpers and the members of their own church who had baptized, and this apparently did not happen. Paul's statements are rather on the contrary based on the knowledge that people in Corinth could not possibly think of any close fellowship between baptizer and baptized mediated through baptism, and that therefore they would be bound to see on their own the absurdity of the apostle slogans.   341

I, 15:29 however is of significance for us: "But what shall they do who are baptized for the dead?" Thus there were Corinthians who had themselves baptized for those who had died. It is absurd to dispute this, as Bachmann and Schlatter, for instance, have attempted to do in a more than dubious fashion.[190] The passage does not say how and why this baptism was performed. We must also doubt whether Paul was familiar with the form and meaning of this custom.

We have said earlier (p. 155) that in all probability the same people practiced the custom of proxy baptism who denied the ἀνάστα-σις νεκρῶν.[191] Verse 29b suggests this: "εἰ ὅλως νεκροὶ οὐκ ἐγείρονται, τί καὶ βαπτίζονται ὑπὲρ αὐτῶν"; Since only some (τινές, 15:12) asserted that there is no resurrection of the dead, and there are also only certain people (οἱ βαπτιζόμενοι, vs. 29) who have themselves baptized as proxies, Paul's line of argument in vs. 29 has meaning only if the two groups were identical. Thus there were Gnostics among whom vicarious baptism was in vogue. This is confirmed by the fact that the custom is proven in Gnostic circles and *only* in them, while the church objected to it. Lietzmann (*Kommentar, in loc.*) quotes an account of John Chrysostom concerning the Marcionites: "For if one of the catechumens among them dies, they conceal a living person beneath the bier of the departed one, approach the corpse, talk with the dead person, and ask him whether he intended to receive baptism. Thereupon the person who is concealed, speaking from beneath for the other who does not answer, says that he did indeed intend to be baptized, and then they baptize him for the departed one." This corre-   342
sponds to a report by Epiphanius about the Cerinthians (Haer. XVIII, 6.4) : "καί τι παραδόσεως πρᾶγμα ἦλθεν εἰς ἡμᾶς, ὡς τινῶν μὲν παρ' αὐτοῖς προφθανόντων τελευτῆσαι ἄνευ βαπτίσματος, ἄλλους δὲ ἀντ' αὐτῶν εἰς ὄνομα ἐκείνων βαπτίζεσθαι, ὑπὲρ τοῦ μὴ ἐν τῇ ἀναστάσει ἀναστάντας αὐτοὺς δίκην δοῦναι τιμωρίας βάπτισμα μὴ εἰληφότας, γίνεσθαι δὲ ὑποχειρίους τῆς τοῦ κοσμοποιοῦ ἐξουσίας. καὶ τούτου ἕνεκα ἡ παράδοσις ἡ ἐλθοῦσα εἰς ἡμᾶς φησι τὸν αὐτὸν ἅγιον ἀπόστολον εἰρηκέναι 'εἰ ὅλως

---

[190] A splendid assembling of the various expositions is already found in Godet's   343
commentary.
[191] See Stürmer, [2], pp. 173 ff.

νεκροὶ οὐκ ἐγείρονται, τί καὶ βαπτίζονται ὑπὲρ αὐτῶν.' " To be compared also is Philastrius, Haer. 49, who gives a corresponding report of the Montanists. Finally, we cite a passage from the sixth canon of the third Council of Carthage (379) : "*Item placuit, ut corporibus defunctorum eucharistia non detur . . . deinde cavendum est, ne mortuos etiam baptizari posse fratrum infirmitas credat*" (following Lietzmann). That on the church's side people were not in agreement with such a practice is also shown by Tertullian, Marcion V, 10, and de resurr. 48.[192]

The passages cited unconditionally assure the meaning of the passage I, 15:29. That they all are derived from this verse, which was misunderstood in the sense of a baptism for the dead, is an assertion of which we can take note only in disbelief (thus Bachmann-Stauffer, p. 452, n. 1).

The practice of baptism by proxy cannot have arisen in Gnosticism itself, but was probably taken over along with baptism in general from the mystery cults (see documentation and literature in Lietzmann, *in loc.*). However, it is hardly accidental that precisely the baptism by proxy for deceased persons was common among Gnostics. We have already said that genuinely Gnostic baptism cannot have a realistic meaning, since Gnosis as such is redemption. But precisely for this reason the Gnostic's concern for the relatives who departed without Gnosis must be greater than among the Christians, who ultimately could wait patiently for the grace of God even for the deceased who were unbaptized. From this perspective it is understandable that some were anxious to substitute the magical act of baptism for the dead for the Gnosis which the dead were lacking. For Gnosticism, then, baptism for the dead in principle takes on a greater significance than the baptism of living Gnostics, which in fact could have only a symbolic meaning. It accords well with this that no account of the Gnostic baptismal praxis has been handed down to us in the Corinthian epistles other than the report of proxy baptism. That may of course be accidental, but at any rate it is characteristic.

We do not know how the Gnostics conceived of the effects of the βαπτισμὸς ὑπὲρ νεκρῶν in detail. In any case they must have thought of a magical effect through which the deceased, in spite of a lack of Gnosis, still experienced the liberation from the power of the demonic forces and was led homeward to the Pleroma. It may rightly be doubted that this conception had among the Gnostics the concrete content of meaning of the mystery theology down to the last detail. The Jewish *oblationes pro defunctis* however cannot even be adduced as a parallel

[192] Cf. A. Hilgenfeld, *Ketzergeschichte*, pp. 381, 417.

of the *baptismum pro defunctis* (*contra* Stauffer, *Theology*, p. 299, n. 544), much less as its source.

The effect of the baptism for the dead was magical in nature. Therefore we may also cite as a direct parallel the custom, attested by *Pistis Sophia*, that the living perform the mysteries for the dead, which protect the latter from the persecutions of the demons.[193] Only here it is no longer simply a matter of baptism, but of a whole series of various mystery rites as they were common in later Coptic Gnosticism, and which of course were also of the highest significance for those still living for whom the power of pure Gnosis no longer sufficed.

However, if in the baptism by proxy we are dealing with a specifically Gnostic usage which was observed in Corinth only in very recent times, we cannot assume that Paul knew any more about it than he tells us in I, 15:29. In I, 11:30, a section of the same Epistle A, we hear of an uncommon number of deaths in the community. Precisely the relatives of these departed ones will have had a willing ear for the Gnostic teachings, since it was in fact taught them "ἅμα τῷ ἀποθνήσκειν τὰς ψυχὰς τῶν νεκρῶν ἀναλαμβάνεσθαι εἰς τὸν οὐρανόν" (Justin, Dial. 80; cf. Iren. V, 31.2), and therefore several baptisms for the dead may have occurred. Stephanas hears of this and tells Paul, to whom this notice is valuable, since he thinks that therewith he can lead those who deny the resurrection from their own presuppositions *ad absurdum*. Thus Paul himself has in general no position with reference to baptism by proxy, which he here encounters for the first time, so the   348
exegete does not need to rack his brain, while its significance for the Gnostics who practiced it is clear at least in principle.

With this we can conclude the treatment of the Corinthian schismatics' view of the sacraments. It has confirmed precisely what the basic observation led us to expect for a still relatively pure Gnosticism: The position on the Supper is outspokenly negative, while there appears not to be a characteristic general teaching on baptism. An exception to this is provided by the special form of baptism by proxy, which however is historically demonstrable as specifically Gnostic practice as well as explainable from intrinsic, internal reasons.

VII. Eschatology

Under this subject, we must explore above all the section II, 5:1-10; for the rest, we shall only refer to what we have said from time to time previously on the subject of "Gnostic eschatology."

First we shall consider vss. 1-5. From time immemorial they have been among the passages of Epistle C which have occupied the exegetes

---

[193] *Pistis Sophia*, ed. Schmidt, pp. 153-54, 211-12.

260 Gnosticism in Corinth

in a special way. People have attempted to read out of these verses everything imaginable, above all for the Pauline expectation of the future. Paul is here no longer counting on the Parousia; he regarded the death of the believer to be the normal thing; he is thinking only of the Parousia. Again: Paul had the conception that the departed one received the heavenly body immediately after dying; he must first endure a state of nakedness; he is clothed at the Parousia. Further: the old garment will first be taken off before the new is put on; the new will be put on over the old and will swallow it up; after putting off the old robe man still has a pneumatic garment over which the new will be placed—and so on. Of course with all this abundance of conflicting views, which could easily be expanded, there is general agreement on one thing:[194] in II, 5 the picture of the future has been altered from that of I Thess. and I Cor.,[195] and we even know the reason for it: the experiences in Asia (II, 1:8 ff.) have evoked the alteration (Windisch)! But Rom. 13:12! Very slight difficulties are caused for the exegetes in general by the fact that on this view Paul must also have changed his whole anthropology and now all at once knows of a Pneuma-soul which can exist as the real man even without the *soma*. These difficulties are removed then by a reference to the passage II, 12:2, which however may not at all be invoked for the presentation of the *Pauline* anthropology (see pp. 214 ff.), and to Phil. 1:23, which, employing a widely used formula of pagan *origin* (see A. Deissmann, *Light from the Ancient East,* p. 303, n. 1), nevertheless cannot possibly carry the burden of proof which is allotted to it. In any case one entertains no doubt that Paul has just begun to think in Hellenistic fashion.

Now of course we have to admit frankly that our section confronts us with utterly insurmountable difficulties if we wish to use it immediately as a source for determining the Pauline anthropology and eschatology. In that case almost anything can actually be read from it, as the various exegeses prove. But these exegeses all proceed from false presuppositions, since they do not take note of the polemical aim of our passage. This aim is so conspicuous that it is simply incomprehensible how in the commentaries of Lietzmann and Windisch, to say nothing at all of the earlier ones, it could fail to be mentioned even as a possibility. According to Windisch, *in loc.,* what is involved here is a "meditation about passing over into the beyond." It was Rudolf Bultmann, so far as I can see, who first in recent times in principle proposed the correct way to the exposition of II, 5:1-10 (*Exegetische Probleme . . .*).

[194] In this, cf. the commentaries. P. Hoffmann, *Die Toten in Christus,* pp. 4 ff.

[195] More recently, e.g., Althaus in TLZ, 1950, p. 254.

Paul's manner of argument in these verses can in fact be understood at all only if he is not setting forth *ad hoc* to the community the most elementary foundations of his preaching, which could never have been unknown to the community, but is defending it against contrary views which have recently been brought into play. The subject about which Paul is concerned at first, namely the assertion of a celestial corporeality in the consummation, is treated with an unmistakable reference to a divergent opinion. In addition, there is the fact that Epistle C as a whole is polemically oriented. The only striking thing is that to a large extent and especially clearly in our section this polemic is conducted with a certain moderation in expression. The reasons for this reservedness, which naturally makes the understanding of our passage more difficult, have already been set forth (see pp. 98-99).

Under this presupposition, however, it is only with the greatest caution that the exegete can infer from the existing text expressions which go behind what is directly set forth. The nature of the Pauline argument is necessarily determined to a large extent by the opponents against whose attack Paul must defend himself. And beyond that, it is only natural when in terminology and conception Paul follows his opposition so far as this is possible, in order better to be heard in his real concern. In so doing he is only following an obvious law of such discussions. If this is observed, there is not the slightest reason for the assumption that in this passage Paul was setting forth an altered expectation of the future on the basis of a Hellenistic-Gnostic anthropology. On the contrary, even here he does not even exhibit a correct understanding of Greek dualism and of the eschatological problems connected with it. The following exegesis is to make this clear.   353

Paul begins with "οἴδαμεν γάρ." The γάρ connects the forthcoming statements with the end of chap. 4. This connection is justified in terms of material. The passage 4:16-18 had opened up the view on τὰ αἰώνια. This watchword is taken up again in 5:1 with οἰκίαν αἰώνιον. With this the theme of 5:1 ff. is plainly indicated. Paul is now concerned with τὰ αἰώνια, with eternal matters.

His situation with respect to this theme is by no means an enviable one. In Epistle A this problem had already been thoroughly discussed and, as it appeared, unequivocally answered. Since the false teachers in Corinth denied the resurrection, for them, according to the apostle's opinion, everything ended with death, while he only needed to remind the church of what they had already received from him (I, 15:1). Significantly now there emerges in the treatment of τὰ αἰώνια in II, 5: 1 ff. neither the question about the resurrection in general nor even the charge that the opponents denied every human hope for the future. Paul must in the meantime have comprehended that his adversaries

354   denied the resurrection *and* affirmed an "eternal life." He cannot conceive of this, since for him the annihilation of the human body is the annihilation of the man, and thus human existence after death is possible only through the resurrection of the dead, i.e., through the re-creation of the man as σῶμα πνευματικόν. This self-evident equation, aliveness = corporeality, however, Paul cannot prove, since he cannot even imagine a disembodied life. For him the equation is a tautology. But just as little is he able substantively to refute his opponents, since against them indeed he would have been able only to repeat the obviously defective argument of I, 15.

One can easily understand then that with οἴδαμεν at first he simply is offering, as a fact which in his opinion is beyond doubt for any Christian, the assertion ὅτι ἐὰν ἡ ἐπίγειος ἡμῶν οἰκία τοῦ σκήνους καταλυθῇ, οἰκοδομὴν ἐκ θεοῦ ἔχομεν, οἰκίαν ἀχειροποίητον αἰώνιον ἐν τοῖς οὐρανοῖς.

Our verse says nothing about *when* Paul is expecting the dissolution of the earthly "tent dwelling." This question does not interest the apostle at all, even in what follows, where he obviously has the Parousia constantly in mind, as a comparison of vs. 4 with I, 15:52

355   suggests.

The figure of the tent as the dwelling place of the "I" is widespread especially since Plato, and is typically dualistic. When Paul adopts it, this of course does not mean that he too regards the tent, i.e. the earthly body, as the outer covering of the real Self. The figure is far less adequate for his conception than for the original dualistic one, but he can adopt it at once, since as a Jew he also can abstract the "I" from the *"Dasein"* as such. But this "I" is then actually a bare abstraction and can no more be equated with the dualistic "Self" than can the shadow-souls of men in Sheol. The terminology of "house" or "tent," which does not appear elsewhere in Paul, may, as in II, 4:7, have been taken over directly from the opponents, but in any case it corresponds to their intention. They assert that we have *no* οἰκοδομὴ ἐκ θεοῦ when the earthly covering is laid aside. This is the view of the Gnostic dualism which is held in Corinth, and the figurative language which Paul uses is thoroughly suited to it.[196]

In vs. 2 Paul justifies the assertion that an οἰκοδομὴ αἰώνιος awaits us: for in this (tent) we indeed sigh, since we longingly anticipate being clothed with our heavenly abode.[197] A strange justification! In

---

[196] Cf. e.g., Hipp. VI, 34: "According to them this material man is like an inn or a place of residence . . . ." Cf. also H. Jonas, [1], p. 102; Corpus Hermeticum 13.12; 13.15. Of course in view of its pessimism toward the world, Gnosticism prefers the

357   figure of the "dungeon" or "prison."

[197] On οἰκητήριον as dwelling place of the Self, cf., e.g., Hipp. VI, 9.4-5. (136.18-19) ; VII, 29.22 (214.13) .

vs. 1 Paul cannot have intended to say that in eternity we would live not *without* but *with* a resurrection body; for vs. 2 offers no justification for such a point of view within an intra-dualistic (!) dispute. But vs. 2 also does not prove that we shall receive a new bodily form, i.e., continue to live, *at all*. Paul has learned in the interim that even in the opinion of his opponents death is not the end of everything, so that for this reason alone a basic controversy on that point, as in I, 15, would be out of place. Apparently the argument has to do only with the special *quality* of the new body. The habitation that is prepared for us is no longer ἐπίγειος, no more an easily shattered σκῆνος, but ἀχειροποίητος, αἰώνιος, and ἐν τοῖς οὐρανοῖς; for in our earthly body indeed we sigh and *longingly wish* for the heavenly habitation. It thus must be worth our yearning. "Since man is not created for a habitation which so confines him, there must be another one for him which is adequate to his nature—that is the logic of the argument," writes Windisch (pp. 160-61) and therewith in essence captures Paul's train of thought.

356

358

359

Thus already in vs. 1 the stress is not so much on the assertion *that* οἰκοδομὴ ἐκ θεοῦ ἔχομεν, but on the *features* of this habitation, as indeed is already shown by the emphatically postpositive "οἰκίαν ἀχειροποίητον αἰώνιον ἐν τοῖς οὐρανοῖς," on which the weight of the sentence rests, and by its contrast to ἐπίγειος and σκῆνος. This observation is instructive. In his argument Paul apparently is aware that his opponents (although they inexplicably nevertheless believe in a life after death), with a reference to the weakness and perishability of the corporeal, reject the celestial corporeality[198] and hence wish to remain "naked"—an altogether accurate awareness on his part. Paul meets this Gnostic justification of a disembodied state worth striving for by pointing to the higher, unearthly and divine quality of the heavenly habitation for which we rightly yearn.

Verse 3 follows upon this in a very unusual way: "εἴ γε καὶ ἐνδυσάμενοι οὐ γυμνοὶ εὑρεθησόμεθα" (at least if we,[199] after we have been clothed, are not found naked). The clause contains an almost intolerable tautology. Hence the emendation of the Western collateral tradition which serves to relieve this problem (ἐκδυσάμενοι instead of ἐνδυσάμενοι) is easily understandable. It is inconceivable that the W-text of all the texts should have preserved the original reading here.[200] To prefer it (J. Weiss, [2], II: 535; R. Bultmann, *Exegetische*

---

[198] This reference, which Paul has understood also elsewhere, appears on the lips of the Corinthians at every turn (see pp. 160-61; 176).

[199] To translate εἴ γε καί with "da ja" (= "since indeed"; thus Lietzmann, *et al.*) is linguistically impermissible (cf. Kümmel in Lietzmann, on p. 120, l. 25).

[200] Surprisingly many emendational W-readings are found in II, 5:1-10.

Probleme) therefore means in effect to conjecture with the W-redactor. In addition, indeed the ἐνδυσάμενοι of vs. 3 obviously takes up again the ἐπενδύσασθαι of vs. 2. Finally, this smoothing of the text in vs. 3 immediately presents a new difficulty, "for how can a person who has been *unclothed* yet be preserved from nakedness?" (Windisch, p. 162). Thus it must be read as ἐνδυσάμενοι. The attempt to avoid the tautology by understanding ἐνδυσάμενοι as in apposition to οὐ γυμνοί: "at least if we are (at all) clothed, are not found naked," is grammatically hardly to be held, and moreover it does not give any real satisfaction (see Windisch, p. 162).

On the other hand the verse becomes completely comprehensible in terms of the polemical situation. Since the Corinthian adversaries do not deny an existence beyond death, Paul *must* assume that they yearn to be clothed with a new corporeality just as he does.[201] Hence the (ἐπ) ενδύσασθαι, which as such he therefore in fact does not even seek to prove, had to hold true for them also. But at the same time he must also have heard that the same people in Corinth described the condition of the perfected as bodilessness, as γυμνότης. For Paul such a double assertion is inconsistent. The "naked" person is the *dead* person.[202] Paul can sense only as paradoxical the assertion that as a person living in eternity (ἐνδυσάμενος) one is naked. How can the living person be dead, and the existing person be nothing!

Paul expresses just this lack of understanding in vs. 3: We long for the heavenly existence (vs. 2) —at least if we as clothed are not found naked, i.e. as living are not found dead; for then our yearning does have meaning, for as one who has been clothed one obviously is not found naked! Thus, Paul thinks, people in Corinth surely must see that one cannot at the same time hold to an eternal life *and* a bodiless state in that life. The inner contradiction of the Corinthian assertions alone should show that Paul is right!

Paul is obviously arguing more cautiously than in I, 15. But he is arguing from the same misunderstanding or lack of understanding of his opponents' position. There, in view of the denial of the resurrection, he appeals to the baptism for the dead which is irreconcilable with that denial; here, in view of the affirmation of a life after death, he appeals to the nakedness which rules out this life—in both cases in order to carry his opponents' assertion *ad absurdum*. In both cases he displays an utter lack of understanding for the dualism of his op-

---

[201] For Paul this need not be a radical contradiction of the denial of the resurrection which he knows, in the moment when he has in mind only the Parousia, as is certainly the case in II, 5:1 ff.

[202] "By nakedness is . . . to be understood neither a disembodied state nor an existence without a spirit, but the absence of being . . ." (Stürmer, *Auferstehung und Erwählung*, p. 180).

ponents, whose "I" is not bound to a body and therewith to the resurrection in order to be able to exist. Therefore his argument cannot have been convincing in either case.

Paul only apparently abandons this digression, which was probably meant as much to be irony as argument, when in vs. 4 he repeats the argument of vs. 2: καὶ γὰρ οἱ ὄντες ἐν τῷ σκήνει στενάζομεν βαρούμενοι, ἐφ' ᾧ οὐ θέλομεν ἐκδύσασθαι ἀλλ' ἐπενδύσασθαι, ἵνα καταποθῇ τὸ θνητὸν ὑπὸ τῆς ζωῆς; i.e. once again. The longing under the burden of this perishable tabernacle shows that a house of life awaits us (vs. 2). But Paul adds: for indeed we are not sighing because we wish to be unclothed,[203] i.e. killed, but because we await the clothing with the body of eternal life. Thus in vs. 4 in fact Paul takes up both vs. 2 *and* vs. 3. ἐκδύσασθαι takes the place of γυμνός: our yearning sighing shows the inconsistency of holding that the *nakedness* is a goal of our hope worth striving for, for we are not yearning for death! And as living ones, which we mean to be, we are not dead, as clothed ones we are not naked (vs. 3)! Thus vs. 4 is not merely externally but also in thought a repetition of vss. 2-3.

Interesting and instructive after all is the figurative expression ἐπενδύσασθαι in vs. 2 and vs. 4, which in the present context says subtiantially the same thing as the ἀλάσσειν in I, 15:51-52: there is not a moment of nakedness, i.e. of nonexistence, between the earthly and the heavenly life. The new garment is put on over the old one, which is destroyed thereby. Death is *swallowed up* by life. The image, which was chosen in the interest of harmony with the figurative language of the entire section, is strange to us, but precisely for this reason most highly instructive for the added interest which Paul has in the assertion which is inescapable for him, that there is no such thing as a mere ἐκδύσασθαι. Mere "unclothing" would in fact mean the end of human existence.

At the same time, however, the ἐπενδύσασθαι also points to the Gnostic *thesis,* over against which Paul sets this expression as *antithesis:* the goal of the Gnostic is the ἐκδύειν of *any* and *every* body and therewith the γυμνότης of the Pneuma-Self, which precisely and only in such freedom from any corporeal existence has attained the *eschaton.*

Whom now is Paul actually hitting with his argument in II, 5:1-4?

---

[203] Here also of course we have to do with Gnostic conceptuality which may likewise have been used in Corinth. Cf., e.g., the passage from Oxyrh. Pap. 655 which is misunderstood by J. Jeremias (*Unknown Sayings of Jesus,* pp. 16-17) : ". . . He himself will give you your garment. His disciples say unto him, When wilt thou be manifest to us, when shall we see thee? He saith, When ye shall be stripped and not be ashamed . . . ."

The Gnostics? No, because for them the putting off of the body by
no means signifies death. He is hitting only the "Paulinists," i.e., those
who think as he does and who therefore naturally do not even need
such instruction. Paul is in a somewhat helpless situation. He must
prove that there is no existence at all without a *soma*, and that therefore there *must* be a heavenly habitation for those who believe in a
life after death. But that there can be no such thing as a *soma-less*
existence is for him a fact the opposite of which he cannot imagine,
which he thus also is not even able to prove and which, if he does
not wish at the outset to invite the charge of defective Gnosis, he may
not even express directly because he knows that his opponents—incomprehensibly—are disputing precisely this. The fact that in spite of
this almost desperate situation Paul adopts a position on this question
at all shows that in Corinth the problem was a focal point of discussion, probably not least on the basis of I Cor. 15.

Verse 5 concludes the train of thought: "ὁ δὲ κατεργασάμενος ἡμᾶς
εἰς αὐτὸ τοῦτο θεός, ὁ δοὺς ἡμῖν τὸν ἀρραβῶνα τοῦ πνεύματος." The verse
is hardly polemically formulated. Paul rather intends by it to escape
from the fruitless polemic and at last to point to the grace of God
which alone is important. In spite of this the verse allows us clearly
to recognize the fundamental contrast which separates Paul from the
Gnostics. For them the Pneuma itself is life, for which reason they
also long for liberation from any *soma* which restrains the Pneuma.
For Paul the Pneuma is God's initial gift to the person who has laid
hold in faith upon the life promised to him, a pledge that God will
actually give him eternal life if he "walks in the Spirit" (Gal. 5:25).
Thus the Pneuma is not the ζωή itself, nor is the ζωή already the possession of man. The life is rather a free gift of God which still awaits
man, even though he already possesses it in faith, and which will be
manifested in his existence as σῶμα πνευματικόν.

I have deliberately examined this section in somewhat more detail
since in it we can clearly see how much the understanding of the
Corinthian epistles in details depends on the possession of a proper
picture of Paul's opponents and of the dispute as a whole. For the rest,
however, we are here again in the first place concerned with completing
this picture.

It is at once clear that Paul adopts a position against such people
who not only like himself yearn for liberation from the σῶμα τοῦ
θανάτου τούτου, but wish to remain naked after the laying aside of the
σῶμα χοϊκόν. This view presupposes the Gnostic dualism which we
have ascertained among the Corinthian schismatics: the real Self has
an existence independent of corporeality. Now it is noteworthy that
within Gnosticism itself the opinions diverge as to whether the soul

having ascended to heaven would again receive a garment. Even a superficial survey of the appearance of the various views shows that the later the time, the more common is the thesis of the celestial garment in Gnosticism, and it is widespread above all in the vicinity of Judaism and the mystery cults. I mention only the gnosticizing late-Jewish eschatology,[204] Mandaeans[205] and Manichaeans, and even the 362
mysteries,[206] where the originally Persian and the Jewish conception of the resurrection in a new corporeality of man who without a body is nonexistent has its influence everywhere (cf. Bousset, [1], p. 303). 363
The conception of a heavenly garment is foreign to pure mythological Gnosticism. The soul, or the Pneuma-spark, is a part of the great σῶμα of the primal man and on the return into the Pleroma takes again its original place in this cosmic organism. The more this simple mythological basis disappears, so much the more can the view of the gar- 364
ment awaiting one in heaven find acceptance. If Gnosticism in Corinth, in spite of its undeniable closeness to Judaism, explicitly held to the idea that the Self goes to heaven naked and there finds no new cloth- 365
ing, this indicates that in that Gnosticism the myth was still in force in relatively pure and unbroken form—a fact that is fully confirmed by what has been developed in the course of the present work. To such Gnostics *any* habitation appeared as fetters which hinder the return into the Pneuma-unity of the primal man. The new body, as it obviously was being taught in the Pauline communities, must have meant to them, if they built this view into their anthropological scheme, a new prison of the soul. Yet the whole interest of the Corinthian schismatics reached its peak in that their Pneuma-sparks ἅμα τῷ ἀποθνήσκειν hastened unclothed into the Pleroma, without being recast into a new prison by the demons along the way.

We cannot say how this heavenly pilgrimage is thought to have been accomplished for them in detail. Anz (*Ursprung des Gnostizismus*), in a fruitful one-sidedness, holds the ascent of the soul through seven heavens to be the central doctrine of Gnosticism. But the Babylonian number seven of the planetary spheres is not the only form, and, as Bousset has already shown (*Die Himmelsreise . . .*, pp. 43 ff.), is not even the oldest form of the Gnostic cosmological speculation. Paul

[204] Greek Enoch 22.8-9; Eth. Enoch 51.1; 62.15-16; Asc. Jes. 9.9; Apoc. Abr. 13.15.

[205] Lidzbarski, *Johannesbuch,* p. 121 (cf. p. 194.1, *et passim*); Sauriel speaks: "'Go forth, thou soul. Why dost thou still watch over the body?' Then it said to him, 'You wish to take me out of the body, Sauriel; first show me my garment (and clothe me with it), then take me forth and lead me thither.'" As a sign of the disparate materials which were handed down by the Mandaean texts, one may compare Lidzbarski, *Ginza,* p. 517, l. 22: "Naked I was brought into the world, and empty I was taken out of it."

[206] Cf. Reitzenstein, *Hellenistische Mysterienreligionen,* 1st ed., pp. 32 ff.

himself is familiar with the older (three or four) number, as II, 12:1 ff. shows (cf. Windisch, pp. 371 ff.). To the Judaism of his time, in addition to the number seven, the number ten also was well known. Later Gnosticism knows up to 360 heavenly spheres. But we may not assume an extensive interest in mere aeon speculation among the much more existentially interested Gnostics in Corinth, especially since they lived in the lively awareness that the power of the demons of all spheres is already broken. Nevertheless whatever of this might have come to Paul's ears he would not have felt to be heretical. His demonology is Gnostic in its basic features (cf. I, 2:7 ff.), even though it stands on the periphery of his theology. In view of the triumphant consciousness of the apostle's Corinthian adversaries who in their ecstatic experiences have already accomplished the journey ἐκτὸς τοῦ σώματος to the heavenly home without difficulty, one may by no means assume that the description of the ascent and the imparting of the secret words, means, and ways, which served to outwit and overcome the watchmen at the gates of the individual spheres, possessed any essential significance for them. Such theories are widespread in the speculative Gnosticism of the later times, often to the point of absurdity, for example in the *Pistis Sophia,* but are alien to the early period. For this early period the knowledge about the origin of the Self, the mythological fact of the Χριστὸς ἐν ἡμῖν, is simply the mystery whose knowledge already guarantees the consummation and liberates one from all fear of the lower powers of which he who sees before him unending perils of the ascent never rids himself. And whatever may nevertheless have been taught in Corinth by way of special mysteries of the ascent will have been in the secret discipline. Hence it is in no case to be demanded that Paul must have taken a position against a specifically Gnostic doctrine of the heavenly journey of the soul, if an explicitly mythological kind of Gnosticism was being held in Corinth.[207]

If in 5:1-15 Paul set himself against the views of his opponents which in the narrower sense are eschatological, vss. 6-8 aim at combating their arrogant self-consciousness, while vss. 9-10 have in mind the Gnostic libertinism.

In vss. 6-8 the sentence structure is not in order. Verse 6 is an anaco-

---

[207] This is to be maintained, e.g., against K. Stürmer (*Auferstehung und Erwählung,* pp. 45-46), who does not wish to identify Paul's opponents in Corinth and instead of this, like Lütgert speaks of "exuberant displays of a pneumatic enthusiasm which is reminiscent of the cult of Dionysos." For "what constitutes the essence of Gnostic Gnosis is not that it bears a pneumatic-charismatic stamp, but that it . . . imparts magical knowledge and powers for the conquest of the spirits and the mastery of the demons." One must not make the later Colossian Gnosticism—which is difficult to characterize anyway—into a yardstick for Christian Gnosticism in general!

luthon. Through the parenthesis in vs. 7 which explains vs. 6, in dictating Paul lost the overall view of the entire construction, and in vs. 8 he adds an independent clause. Already for this reason the train of thought is obscured. In addition, there is the fact that in vs. 6 the confidence expressed in θαρροῦντες οὖν πάντοτε is apparently weakened by the distressing statement that we today still dwell far from the Lord. Windisch, in loc., thinks that Paul must have written concessively: we are of good courage although we know . . . . Finally, even the use of σῶμα in vss. 6 and 8 not only strictly contradicts the view expressed in I, 15:44 ff., according to which the σῶμα ψυχικόν is swallowed up by a σῶμα πνευματικόν, but also the immediately preceding assertion that man will never be without an οἰκητήριον. For there need be no question that the οἰκοδομὴ ἐκ θεοῦ in 5:1 fully corresponds to the σῶμα πνευμα-τικόν in I, 15:44. But in vss. 6 ff. Paul is not speaking of the move into another οἰκία, a new σῶμα, but in genuinely Gnostic fashion of the leaving of the σῶμα, in order to be with the Lord.

We shall master these manifold difficulties only if we once again strictly observe the polemical aim of the entire section. We have recognized that the Gnostics held themselves to be already perfected, had in fact already been loosed from the σῶμα, as the ecstatic experiences proved, thus dwelt in the vision, lived ἐν κυρίῳ, and did not confidently "search after" but "had already obtained." Paul now addresses himself to this self-satisfied state. θαρροῦντες οὖν πάντοτε looks back on the fact that the Pneuma is given to us as a pledge that we shall after all live hereafter and hence also may expect an οἰκητήριον ἐξ οὐρανοῦ. Thus on the one hand we live in such confidence. It is possible that the θαρρεῖν, which here means a hopeful certainty (cf. II, 7:16), is already chosen in conscious antithesis to the βασιλεύειν (I, 4:8) of the Gnostics. But on the other hand we know "ὅτι ἐνδημοῦντες ἐν τῷ σώματι ἐκδημοῦμεν ἀπὸ τοῦ κυρίου." As in 5:1, by an εἰδότες Paul introduces a fact which is disputed by the Gnostics. They live only apparently in the body and in fact already in the Lord,[208] i.e. in the cosmic σῶμα Χριστοῦ. They already walk by sight, against which Paul expressly affirms: "διὰ πίστεως περιπατοῦμεν, οὐ διὰ εἴδους." Even the fact that Paul here uses πίστις in the sense, otherwise alien to him, of provisionality as over against perfect vision shows that he is engaged in a polemic, and for that reason he cannot freely select his terminology. It is possible that he

[208] The terms "ἐνδημεῖν" and "ἐκδημεῖν," which appear in the New Testament only in this passage, may have been taken over by Paul from the language of the Corinthian Gnostics. They are dualistic, at any rate, and in conjunction with "κύριος" they also presuppose the Gnostic myth. Of course this is somewhat blurred in Paul, when instead of the Gnostic "ἐκ τοῦ κυρίου" he writes "ἀπὸ τοῦ κυρίου" vs. 6), and instead of "ἐν τῷ κυρίῳ," "πρὸς τὸν κύριον" (vs. 8).

had heard of Gnostic attacks in Corinth against πίστις on behalf of γνῶσις and εἶδος. Further, in the assertion, unheard of for Paul's historical way of thinking, that as Christians we live, not ἐν Χριστῷ but far from the Lord, it becomes evident that he is combating a myth which takes the ἐν Χριστῷ literally and compels Paul now also to think in mythical terms.

369

"Since we now on the one hand have the confidence that even after death a future awaits us, and because on the other hand we know that so long as we are in the *soma* we live far from the Lord—for we walk by faith and not by sight—our striving is directed toward our leaving the body and walking with the Lord,"—Paul must originally have had the sentence in mind in something like this form if he did not, as is quite possible, have in mind the idea of vs. 9 as the main clause: Because we live in such confidence and such consciousness, "we concern ourselves with being well-pleasing to God even now." It is true that the construction is broken by vs. 7. Hence in vs. 8 Paul once more picks up vs. 6. Thus the polemical stress in vs. 8 lies on the "θαρροῦμεν δὲ καὶ εὐδοκοῦμεν μᾶλλον," not on the statement as to the content of the wish. *That we live only in confidence and still wish but do not already possess, in other words, the still-believing in contrast to the already-seeing is the declaration intended by Paul in vss. 6-8.* His clothing it in such a positive form is typical of the entire indirect polemic of Epistle C. Because for Paul the firm *hope* in the future is expressed in the θαρρεῖν, he naturally cannot concessively subordinate the expression connected with εἰδότες to the θαρροῦντες, as Windisch insists. The two participial constructions in vs. 6 are in Paul's intention unitary, not only in form but also in content, and they attest, over against the exclusive "already now" of the Gnostics, the hopeful "not yet" of the believer.

There still remains the task of explaining the un-Pauline use of σῶμα. Other than here, it occurs in Paul's writings also in II, 12:2-3. In both passages Paul not only comes "very close" (R. Bultmann, [2], I: 201) to Hellenistic-Gnostic dualism, but he speaks in purely Gnostic fashion; the question is only whether Paul here shows himself to be influenced in his thinking by the dualistic depreciation of the body in comparison with an actual Self. I believe this question should be answered in the negative from the very first. In my opinion it is unthinkable that Paul had two contrary anthropologies and could change

370

them at will. Still in vss. 1-5 he in fact took the position that without a σῶμα a man no longer exists, and therefore he vigorously defended the belief in the fact of a new bodily existence in the consummation. When immediately thereafter in vss. 6-8 he speaks of the σῶμα as something simply to be given up and abandoned, he must mean the σῶμα ψυχικόν or τῆς σαρκός, τοῦτο τὸ σῶμα. But why, just as in II, 12:2-3, does he not say this, as he does in I, 15; II, 5:1-5, and often elsewhere? The reason must be the same as in this other passage, which displays the purely Gnostic usage: to the Gnostics Paul becomes a Gnostic, in order to win the Gnostics. He knows that they are interested in being freed from the body, that their striving is "ἐκδημῆσαι ἐκ τοῦ σώματος καὶ ἐνδημῆσαι πρὸς τὸν κύριον." It is against this thesis, the realization of which would for him mean the end of a man, that he addresses himself in vss. 1-5. Now, in vss. 6-8, he is concerned only with refuting the assertion of his opponents that they are already walking ἐν Χριστῷ. This arrogance and the libertinism arising out of it, in other words the basic existential attitude, appears to have been for him after all the most offensive element in the Corinthian theology. Again and again he addresses himself to it, whether in a direct polemic, or under the watchword "ἀσθένεια," or, as in this passage, with a reference to the "not yet." And in order to be heard correctly on this decisive issue, he first of all grants in vss. 6-8 that our striving is simply aimed at release from the body. For that which he wants to say now, the problem of vss. 1-5 is in fact irrelevant. By taking the standpoint of the Gnostics he avoids having the opponents reject him at the very outset because his presuppositions are false. So long as we live in the body we are absent from the Lord, we are not yet perfected; we must, as vss. 9-10, concluding the train of thought, declare, remain conscious of the judgment bar of God which is yet to come. So long as we live in τοῦτο τὸ σῶμα, Paul naturally *thinks* and would actually have to say, but he deliberately omits it, since he would then in fact presuppose a σῶμα πνευματικόν which his opponents deny and which would hinder them from hearing his crucial concern. Regardless of whether a new *soma* awaits us or not, Paul wants to say, we are *not yet* made perfect, and to the Gnostics, whom he constantly has in view, this is as it must be said: "So long as we are still in the body we are absent from the Lord, we still yearn for him or for being in him." One must with good reason doubt that even this so "Gnostic" argument could have been successful. For the heretics already were disputing *the fact* that the "tarrying still in the body" was a matter of any kind of significance. They were not only in the Pauline sense ἐν Χριστῷ, but also in the real-mythical sense and had already as good as left the *soma*. It was for just this reason that they placed such great value upon their ecstatic experiences. Their arrogant self-consciousness was for them nothing less than justified and a suitable, fitting expression of their present perfected and bodiless existence. This assertion must have come to Paul's ears later, as the parentheses in II, 12:2-3 show. Whether it was already known to him at the time of Epistle C is unlikely because of vss. 6-8, especially since in the entire epistle only the scorning (4:7 ff.), not the overcoming of bodily existence by his opponents, concerns him.[209]

Whatever may be the case on that question, in our verses we acquire a confirmation of the unbelieving consciousness of perfection of the Gnostics in Corinth and moreover an indication that they acknowledge only *one soma*, from which they desired to be set free, in order then in the nakedness of their pneumatic existence ultimately to occupy in the Pleroma of Christ the place promised to them. For determining the Pauline anthropology, in particular for the Pauline conception of the *soma*, the wording of our passage may in no case be adduced. To the Gnostic Paul becomes a Gnostic. Their—and indeed only their—anthropology is therefore to be seen directly in vss. 6-8, which like the parenthetical remarks in II, 12:2-3 are in their outlook neither genuinely Pauline nor ungenuinely Pauline, but genuinely un-Pauline.

Verses 9-10 conclude the train of thought which in three sections offers a polemic that is masterfully conducted. The grammatical difficulties in vs. 10 need not concern us, since the meaning of the verse is clear. Windisch (p. 168) thinks: "Here Paul suddenly checks the train of thought by inserting in the midst of it the watchword εὐάρεστοι αὐτῷ εἶναι, a surprising but genuinely Pauline expression." But a look at the polemical orientation of the whole section shows that the new theme logically grows out of the preceding argument. Out of the Gnostics' consciousness of perfection and their awareness of being already ἐν κυρίῳ, and thus out of the Gnostic *eleutheria* there arose, as we have seen, the indifference toward the actions of the *sarx*. It is only logical when Paul, after he has parried the Gnostics' exaggerated self-esteem, also takes a position against their libertinism. This occurs again in the indirect way which is characteristic of our passage.

In vs. 9 the "εἴτε ἐνδημοῦντες εἴτε ἐκδημοῦντες" causes some difficulty. Is σῶμα or κύριος to be supplied here? The certainty with which the majority of exegetes decide for σῶμα is hardly justified. The series of participles (Kümmel in Lietzmann, on p. 121, l. 50) surely cannot settle anything here. In essence one can only plead that it would be beside the point to argue thus: Because we want to *come* to the Lord, we strive to be well-pleasing to him, whether we *are* with him or not. But if we add to the participles σῶμα as a definition of place, we are confronted with the necessity of assuming that even after the metamorphosis man must still strive to be well-pleasing to the Lord in order

---

[209] Possibly the Gnostics' rejoinder to 5:6 ff. shines through in 10:3 and 12:2-3.

to be able to *come* to him, and that is an idea for which there simply is no place in Pauline apocalyptic. It will not do simply to translate the participles "in this way or in that" (Windisch, *in loc.*), since their special, clearly defined meaning was at once clear to the readers from the preceding verses. Finally, it must also be stated that for Paul himself an "εἴτε—εἴτε" was not at all under debate. In fact, he had just declared unequivocally (vss. 6-8) that we are still *in* the body and *absent* from the Lord.

Once again, not merely the theme selected by Paul as such but also the formulation in detail becomes comprehensible only when we observe the cautious polemic which is expressed therein. The transition from vs. 8 to vs. 9 formally corresponds entirely to that from vs. 5 to vs. 6: The thesis set forth in the preceding is ignored, so that the thought propounded in the following can be heard directly. We are still in the body and absent from the Lord, Paul asserts in vs. 8, and he continues: Regardless of whether we find ourselves in the body—in the Lord—or out of the body—of the Lord—we must in any case concern ourselves with being well-pleasing to him. For Paul the truth 371 of this new thesis stands firm, quite apart from whether one agrees with what was asserted in vss. 6 ff., for in any case the βῆμα τοῦ Χριστοῦ still awaits us. Once again Paul becomes a Gnostic to the Gnostics, in order to win the Gnostics. He will hardly have been successful with it, for the Gnostics, who really were already ἐν Χριστῷ, naturally were no longer interested in the judgment at all (cf. Iren. I, 13.6). But Paul was so far from understanding the situation because he did not recognize the basic attitude of his opponents in its structure at all.

But what is to be supplied to the participles to complete their meaning? For purposes of our investigation the question is, in the last analysis, irrelevant. In any case the un-Pauline concession expressed in the εἴτε—εἴτε makes it evident that Paul's opponents were conscious of the already attained perfection of their existence. If σῶμα should be added, the passage would mean: Because we wish to come to the Lord we strive to be well-pleasing to him, regardless of whether we walk here on earth in the body, as we assert, or without the body, as you Gnostics apparently think. Therewith the parenthesis in vs. 9 would offer an exact parallel in substance to the two parentheses in II, 12:2-3. But it has already been determined that it is unlikely that already in II, 5 Paul was aware of the ἐκτὸς τοῦ σώματος (II, 10:2 ff.; 12:2-3) of the Corinthian opponents. In vs. 6 Paul presupposes as undisputed that we are still ἐν σώματι, and from this he draws the apparently disputed conclusion that we are still absent from the Lord.

He must then also, from a rational point of view, concede in the parenthesis in vs. 9 this ἐν τῷ κυρίῳ—ἀπὸ τοῦ κυρίου which is under discussion, but not the presupposition, in his judgment universally valid, of the ἐν σώματι εἶναι. Moreover, the διὰ τοῦ σώματος in vs. 10 is hardly possible if Paul had earlier admitted that one might possibly already live ἐκτὸς τοῦ σώματος. The absolute use of σῶμα in vs. 10 shows that here Paul is thinking especially of the Gnostics. They are responsible for what they do διὰ τοῦ σώματος, since according to Paul's opinion they indeed obviously still live in it, regardless of whether they fancy themselves already to be ἐν κυρίῳ or not.

The above-mentioned difficulty, that with the supplying of κύριος to the participles in vs. 9 the διό would be out of place since the argument then is lacking in strict logical force, is naturally to be acknowledged. But the same illogic is shown in a certain manner in the entire section 5:1-10, in which Paul several times concedes what has previously been denied at the moment in which he expresses a new concern. And in vs. 9 Paul clearly is passing over to a new theme. In the process in this case the pedagogical illogic contains a probably intentional fine irony: Since we indubitably are only on the way to the Lord (vs. 8), we strive to be well-pleasing to him, whether it is true that we are with the Lord (as you Gnostics indeed curiously assert) or that we are still absent from him. The brevity and lack of clarity of the "εἴτε ἐνδημοῦντες εἴτε ἐκδημοῦντες" may hence have been chosen by Paul deliberately or unintentionally, in order to conceal the lack of strict logic in the train of thought which was difficult for him at best.

372 　 Of interest now is the fact that Paul closes his polemic against the Corinthian theology, which indeed begins in 4:7 with the rejection of the scorn for the weak body, with a paraenetic appeal. The sorrowful epistle in fact also ends in this way. Therewith, however, even in this case Paul is not simply following a familiar method. Rather this phenomenon is grounded in the concrete situation on which he is expressing himself. Paul takes offense of the deepest sort at the libertinism of the Gnostics as the obverse side of their perfectionism, just as he does at the perfectionism itself. The ultimate aim which he set for himself was that of leading the community back to the sobriety of its believing existence and to the related ethical awareness of responsibility. That he does not argue more decisively here for that aim probably is not so much because the preconditions for it are lacking—in contrast to the sorrowful epistle, in Epistle C he sees the community as a whole still on his side—as rather because even in the handling of this question he places some restraints upon himself in order to avoid the difficulties which could result from his vague knowledge

of the exact situation in Corinth and which he would escape in the forthcoming personal visit.[210]

VIII. The Functions of the Community[211]

1. General Remarks [212]

The Gnostic communities in principle possessed only one function: to awaken the Pneuma-selves slumbering in men and to gather them to the unity of the primal man.

The most important representative of this function was in the early period of Gnosticism the missionary, the apostle, who carried Gnosis into all the world and everywhere sounded the call to the sleeping Pneuma thus: "ἔγειρε, ὁ καθεύδων, καὶ ἀνάστα ἐκ τῶν νεκρῶν" (Eph. 5:14). At the time of the birth of Christ and thereafter no religious movement besides the Christian movement organized and executed such an extended and deliberate missionary work as the Gnostic enterprise. Simon travels in the western part of the empire, while Mani travels in the east and sends missionaries into all the world, so that in a short time his teaching is widely disseminated. Irenaeus meets the apostles of the Marcosians in Asia Minor as well as in the Rhone valley (Iren. I, 13.5,7), and the prophets of Celsus can be found everywhere in Phoenicia and Palestine (Origen, Cels. 7.8-9). Many of those who have rank and name among the heads of Gnostic schools appear in Rome, where Marcion also organizes his successful world mission. Gnosticism is not disseminated by means of occasional missions as are for example Judaism and the mystery cults, but through apostles who are sent forth. Far removed from all magical cults these messengers are zealous for their message which brings to light that which was hidden. No wonder! The *individual* Gnostic is redeemed only when *all* are redeemed. The individual man has not yet reached the goal of perfection so long as the *one* man is not perfect, the primal man whose parts the individual selves of men are. Every Pneuma must say to the other: ". . . so long as you are not called my own, I am not what I was" (Acta Joh. 100).

Hence the missionary "office" is the real function of the Gnostic

---

[210] A comparison of 5:9-10 with 12:19–13:10 moreover clearly shows the basic difference in the situations out of which Epistle C and the sorrowful epistle arose.

[211] This section replaces pp. 243-47 of the first edition. In the meantime I have published separately in *Das kirchliche Apostelamt* (ET, *The Office of Apostle in the Early Church* [1969]) the investigation of the ecclesiastical and the Gnostic office of apostle which I had in mind at the time of that first edition. The following section presupposes this investigation.

[212] I was not able to examine the Heidelberg dissertation of Heinz Kraft, *Gnostisches Gemeinschaftsleben* (1950), since neither the university library nor the theological faculty in Heidelberg has a copy of it.

community. So far as this function is attended to by emissaries who are sent forth into the world, it is a matter of an explicitly apostolic function, and ἀπόστολος was also the title of the Gnostic missionaries who in Paul's time were hurrying into the world in order to disseminate Gnosis. I have discussed this in the aforementioned study of *The Office of Apostle.* Hence I content myself here with a reference to pp. 159-92 of that study.

The more Gnosticism was spread abroad, and the more dense the network of its communities in city and countryside became, the more did the apostolic function become subordinate to the local tasks. Now it was necessary in any given place to separate the Pneumatics from the Sarkics, to gather together the former, to make them certain of their redemption, and to guard the Pneuma against further dispersion in the world. This task was achieved above all in the ecstatic representation of the Pneuma-self and the ecstatic liberation, prompted in other men also thereby, of the Pneuma-spark from the fetters of the body. The *terminus technicus* for this procedure is προφητεύειν, and the bearer of this function is the προφήτης.

One may compare, for example, how Iren. I, 13.3 pictures the stirring of a woman to be a "prophetess" by the Gnostic Marcus: " 'ἄνοιξον τὸ στόμα σου καὶ προφήτευσον'. τῆς δὲ ἀποκρινομένης 'οὐ προεφήτευσα πώποτε καὶ οὐκ οἶδα προφητεύειν,' ἐπικλήσεις τινὰς ποιούμενος ἐκ δευτέρου εἰς κατάπληξιν τῆς ἀπατωμένης φησὶν αὐτῇ. 'ἄνοιξον τὸ στόμα σου (καὶ) λάλησον ὅ τι δήποτε, καὶ προφητεύσεις.' ἡ δὲ χαυνωθεῖσα καὶ κεπφωθεῖσα ὑπὸ τῶν προειρημένων, διαθερμαθεῖσα τὴν ψυχὴν ὑπὸ τῆς προσδοκίας τοῦ μέλλειν αὐτὴν προφητεύειν τῆς καρδίας πλέον τοῦ δέοντος παλλούσης, ἀποτολμᾷ λαλεῖν ληρώδη καὶ τὰ τυχόντα, πάντα κενῶς καὶ τολμηρῶς, ἅτε ὑπὸ κενοῦ τεθερμαμμένη πνεύματος . . . καὶ ἀπὸ τούτου λοιπὸν προφήτιδα ἑαυτὴν ὑπολαμβάνει καὶ εὐχαριστεῖ Μάρκῳ τῷ ἐπιδιδόντι τῆς ἰδίας χάριτος αὐτῇ" (text following W. Völker, *Quellen zur Geschichte der christlichen Gnosis* [1932], p. 137). "Thus we can see what προφητεύειν and prophet actually signify: it stands for ἐν πνεύματι λαλεῖν and is expressed in fanatical, ecstatic phenomena" (G. P. Wetter, *Der Sohn Gottes,* p. 74. Naturally the apostle did not perform his function differently from the prophet; the apostle is only a wandering or sent prophet).

The closest parallel to the portrayal by Irenaeus of Marcosian prophecy is presented by the Gnostic prophets whom Celsus had seen in Phoenicia and Palestine. Origen (Cels. 7.3-15, esp. 7.8-9) debates with the presentation and interpretation of this prophetism given by Celsus. Thus we learn that these missionaries not only are called prophets but also appear as "redeemers" and represent themselves to be "θεὸς ἢ θεοῦ παῖς ἢ πνεῦμα θεῖον." Their discourse ends with "ἄγνωστα καὶ πάροιστρα καὶ πάντη ἄδηλα," whose meaning "no one who is in his right mind" can comprehend, while "foolish persons and conjurors" can interpret this discourse as they like. That ecstatic glossolalia is being portrayed here is unmistakable.

On the *title* of prophet in Gnosticism one may compare further Rev. 2:20, the prophetess Jezebel; Lidzbarski, *Ginza* 43.28–45.2; 25.26-30, where there is a polemic against the *many* apostles and prophets who appear as redeemers and in favor of the *one* emissary;[213] Eus. CH IV, 7.7, the prophets Barkabbas, Barkoph, *et al.* among the Basilideans; IV, 22.6, the Gnostics brought forward "ψευδόχριστοι, ψευδοπροφῆται, ψευδαπόστολοι" (cf. Justin, Dial. 82.2; Ps.-Clem. Hom. XI, 35) ; V, 13.2; Tert., Haer. 30, Philumene, the prophetess of Apelles; Hermas, Mand. XI; Clem. Alex., Strom. VI, 6.33.2; Epiph., Haer. XL, 7, etc. Even Mani is called a prophet; cf. G. P. Wetter, pp. 16, 21. Cf. also Heracleon in Origen, Comm. in Joh. 2:14 = Preuschen, p. 70.3 ff. More in D. Lührmann, *Das Offenbarungsverständnis . . .* , pp. 36-37.

The significance of ecstatic prophetism in Gnosticism led the church early to a critical attitude toward its own prophetic office. Already Paul distinguishes between the actually ecstatic speaking in tongues and the προφητεύειν in understandable discourse (see below) . Soon attempts were made to find more suitable standards in order to be able to separate false prophecy from true: Did. 11 ff.; Justin, Dial. 82; Hermas, Mand. XI, *et passim*. With the introduction of the anti-Gnostic apostolic norms the ecclesiastical prophetism wholly disappears in the second century;[214] the Pseudo-Clementines set in opposition to the many prophets the one prophet Christ; the new prophecy of Montanism is most sharply opposed, and so on. Thus the prophetic "office" was surrendered to the Gnostics.

In the time of Irenaeus a Pneumatic like Marcus still showed the undiminished strength of such Gnostic prophetism. In the assemblies of the Marcosians it is determined by lot whose task it is on a given occasion to προφητεύειν (Iren. I, 13.4) . Thus *everyone* was eligible for the task. But the prophet stood above all ordinary men, "whether Paul or Peter or some other of the apostles. They (*scil.* the Marcosians) knew more than anyone else and had alone imbibed of the greatness of the Gnosis of the unutterable Dynamis and stood in the heights above all Dynamis" (Iren. I, 13.6) .

Of course even in Gnosticism, as time went on, the function of the prophet was complemented or replaced by the office of the *teacher*. Over the long run a high ecstatic-pneumatic pitch cannot be maintained or evoked at will. Hence it soon became necessary to keep the

---

[213] *The Office of Apostle*, pp. 185 ff.
[214] E. Fascher, *Prophetes* (1927) , pp. 216 ff.

words of the prophets in the memory and to repeat them. The teacher was required especially where people confessed a heavenly redeemer who *once* in the primordial age or—like Christ—in the more recent past had brought Gnosis, so that it might be preserved for all time.

While the church relied on the apostolic tradition especially in the anti-Gnostic, i.e. the anti-fanatical, deployment, Gnosticism was compelled by the slackening of pneumatic enthusiasm to accept the idea of tradition.[215] The difference from the church was marked by the fact that insofar as it could not base its teachings on a living prophetic office and so far as the apostolic literature could not be reinterpreted, Gnosticism had to appeal to secret traditions.[216] Such traditions formed the foundation of the later Gnostic doctrinal structures and often abstruse systems. The whole of the literary remains of Gnosticism stems from Gnostic circles with a diminished enthusiasm; the authors were διδάσκαλοι. The Gnostic apostles and prophets were hardly productive literarily, a fact which is for the most part overlooked in the evaluation of Gnosticism (see p. 79). This acknowledgment will guard against placing too heavy an emphasis on the functions of the teacher in the early period of Gnosticism and in the strongly enthusiastic Gnostic circles in general. The teacher first came into action where the prophet failed.

Thus the functions of the Gnostic community were looked after by apostles and prophets, followed after some interval by the teacher. This triad of apostles-prophets-teachers, with or without the third member, is familiar to us from the Gnostic literature and from the church's literature which borders on Gnosticism: Clem. Alex., Ecl. ex proph. 23; Lidzbarski, *Ginza*, pp. 25.26-30; 43.28–44.2, 21-25; Ps.-Clem. Rec. IV, 35; Hom. 11.35; Mart. Pol. 16.2; Herm. Sim. IX, 15.4; 16.5; 25.2; Vis. III, 5.1;[217] Eus. CH IV, 15.39; 22.6; Did. 11.3; 13.1-2; 15.1, *et passim;* Rev. 2:2, 20; 18:20; Eph. 2:20; 3:5; 4:11; I Cor. 12:28-29; Origen, Comm. in Joh. 2:14. After what has been said, it appears to me to be certain that this group of offices was native to Gnosticism.[218] Such an origin explains also the often-noted "charismatic" character of the apostles and prophets in the circle of the other officers of the primitive church such as presbyters and bishops, deacons and evangelists.

Now if we turn our attention from these general remarks to the situation in Corinth, in view of the decidedly pneumatic-ecstatic appearance of the false teachers there, we must reckon with the possi-

[215] Cf. R. Bultmann in TDNT I: 695.

[216] H. v. Campenhausen, *Ecclesiastical Office and Spiritual Authority*, pp. 157 ff.; *The Office of Apostle*, p. 284.

[217] Cf. I Tim. 2:7; II Tim. 1:11, and on this, *The Office of Apostle*, pp. 51 ff.

[218] *The Office of Apostle*, pp. 226-27.

bility that in them we encounter apostles and prophets, but not teachers. This expectation is confirmed. Paul is not combating Gnostic teachers, much less a Gnostic doctrinal system. He is arguing with Gnostic Pneumatics who do not teach but intend to persuade by their appearing. The scorning of the body, the libertinism, the disorder at the Lord's Supper, the conduct of the women in worship, the ecstatic evidence of the Pneuma-self, the "arrogance," and so on: all this is not so much taught as demonstrated. Even the rejection of the Jesus in the body and of his cross occurs during ecstasy: I, 12:3.

The Corinthian ecstatics, however, pass themselves off as apostles and prophets who know themselves *as such* to be far superior to the church's teachers.[219]

2. The Apostles

The false teachers in Corinth dispute Paul's apostolate. It is true that nothing of this is yet detectable at the time of Epistle A. This is understandable, for it is only with this epistle after all that Paul makes use of his authority as founder and teacher of the community over against the Corinthian false teachers. Thus in I, 15:9 Paul can still quite naturally call himself the least of all the apostles, who is not worthy to be called an apostle.

But already in Epistle B it becomes clear how the Gnostics in Corinth react to the Pauline claim to be able to exert apostolic authority in the community. Paul decisively resists the contesting of his apostolic dignity: "Am I not an apostle? Have I not seen Jesus, our Lord? Are you not my work in the Lord? If I am not an apostle to others, still I am one to you; for you are the seal of my apostleship in the Lord. This is my defense against those who accuse me" (I, 9:1-3; see below, p. 383) .

The remnant of Epistle C consists almost entirely of a defense of the Pauline apostolic rights, even though the term "apostle" does not occur in the part of the epistle that is preserved. On the change, detectable here, in the form of the argument between Paul and his opponents from an objective to a personal discussion, see pp. 182-83 and 290.

That it is the *apostle* who is speaking in Epistle C is discernible at once in the first verse extant: through the apostles God sheds abroad the fragrance of the knowledge of himself (II, 2:14-16) . In vs. 16*b* Paul asks who possesses the ἱκανότης for such an office, and in what follows down to 3:18 he answers: he himself, to whom the ministry of the new covenant was delivered by God. For this reason, the apostle continues in 4:1-6, he *rightly* takes up such a ministry undeterred by

---

[219] On the suppression of the ecclesiastical teachers by the Gnostic pneumatics, cf. Gal. 6:6 = Vol. 2, pp. 21-22; I Thess. 5:12-13 = Vol. 2, pp. 121-22.

the hateful accusations of his opponents, and, even though he bears the treasure of the apostolic ministry in earthen vessels (4:7-15), he does not grow weary in his ministry (4:16-18). The prospect of conquering the hardships of his ministry in eternal glory then gives occasion in 5:1-10 for handling anew the question of eschatology which since Epistle A was already important in the argument with the Corinthian adversaries (see pp. 259 ff.). But from 5:11 on, Paul again is already concerned with the defense of his office, and this theme is not left again in 5:11–6:10; then finally in 6:11-13 + 7:2-4 it turns into the heartfelt and fervent plea that the Corinthians in the future recognize him as their apostle.

In Epistle D, the sorrowful epistle, the same theme is continued in sharpened form. In II, 10:1-18, apologetic and polemic evoked by it alternate. Always the issue is the apostolic authority of Paul, which is being contested. This is shown by key words like ταπεινός (10:1), κατὰ σάρκα (10:2), Χριστοῦ εἶναι (10:7), ἡ παρουσία ἀσθενής (10:10), ὁ λόγος ἐξουθενημένος (10:10), self-commendation (10:12 ff.), and so on. To all this Paul counters: "I think that I am not behind the super-apostles in any respect" (11:5). With this he begins the forced comparison between himself and the super-apostles. He too has preached without pay (11:7-15); he has labored and suffered more than they (11:16-33); like them he has ὀπτασίαι and ἀποκαλύψεις to exhibit (12: 1-10). Thus he does not fall behind the super-apostles; he has not withheld from the Corinthians the signs of the apostle (12:11-12). Once more he must defend himself, this time against the charge of being a sorcerer instead of an apostle, one who makes a business of God's word (12:13-19). Only then can he, in a continuing polemic and apologetic, announce his, the *apostle's,* third visit to Corinth (12: 20 to the end of the epistle). Cf. supplementary note 208.

It is clear that in Corinth people do not contest the point that the proper ecclesiastical authority is that of the apostle. On the contrary! They expressly assert this in order at the same time to deny that Paul is an apostle. Only against this background do Paul's statements become understandable.

But where in Corinth is this *proper* apostolic authority shown? In the false teachers themselves! For these do not appeal to some human authorities who are the proper apostles. They are rather *themselves* apostles. Paul angrily and mockingly calls them ὑπερλίαν ἀπόστολοι (11:5; 12:11), and sharply describes them as ψευδαπόστολοι, ἐργάται δόλιοι, μετασχηματιζόμενοι εἰς ἀποστόλους Χριστοῦ (11:13), but therewith he adopts precisely the self-designation of the Corinthian false teachers.[220] He must therefore compare himself with them when he on his own part exhibits the σημεῖα τοῦ ἀποστόλου (12:12).[221]

Whose apostles are the Corinthian adversaries? In II, 11:13 Paul calls them apostles of Christ. If he had been able in any way to make the charge against them that they were apostles of *men*, he, himself an apostle of Christ, surely would not have refrained from doing so. So little do they come on a human authority, however, that as Gal. 1–2 shows, they rather on the contrary accuse *Paul* of being an apostle of men.[222]

That these Christ apostles are *Gnostic* apostles is shown by their demand for the σημεῖα τοῦ ἀποστόλου. In response to this demand Paul points to his σημεῖα, τέρατα, and δυνάμεις, an obvious formula, as is shown for example by Rom. 15:19; I Thess. 1:5; II Thess. 2:9; Heb. 2:4 (cf. I Cor. 2:4 and even Deut. 7:19; Jer. 39:21 LXX): ἐν δυνάμει 373 σημείων καὶ τεράτων, ἐν δυνάμει πνεύματος. δύναμις πνεύματος: *that* is apparently the sign of the apostle as it is disclosed in ecstasies, speaking in tongues, and the variety (ποικίλαις, Heb. 2:4) of similar miraculous phenomena in the apostle himself—this is the original meaning of the *entire* formula.

Since for Paul the *success of preaching* is the sign of the apostle (II, 10:13, *et passim;* cf. *supra*, pp. 187 ff., and *The Office of Apostle*, pp. 33 ff.), even in Rom. 15:17 ff. and in I Thess. 1:5 (cf. Vol. 2, pp. 101-2), and precisely there, where he uses the same formula, he could hardly have connected a concrete conception with its origin. We never hear from Paul himself that he has performed miracles after the fashion of the account of the apostles in Acts (e.g. Acts 3:1 ff.; 5:1 ff.; 9:32 ff.; 13:6 ff.; 14:8 ff.; 20:9 ff.; cf. Matt. 10:8), and even in II, 12:12 he certainly is thinking of the miraculous effect of the *word*.[223] But what his opponents demanded were ecstatic proofs of the Pneuma-Christ who lived in Paul.[224] Although Paul probably does not connect 374 this demand with the formula σημεῖα τοῦ ἀποστόλου—perhaps by design—nevertheless in his "foolish boasting" he complies with it. II, 12:1 ff. with the reference to the ὀπτασίαι and ἀποκαλύψεις experi-

[220] Thus also D. Georgi, [1], pp. 39-40.

[221] This E. Käsemann ([1]) disputes in an otherwise instructive essay. According to him, the Corinthian heretics are an official delegation of the Jerusalem community, and the original Jerusalem apostles are meant by the ὑπερλίαν ἀπόστολοι or the ψευδαπόστολοι. That this understanding of II, 10–13 is untenable has been so splendidly demonstrated by R. Bultmann ([1], pp. 20 ff.) that here I only refer to this refutation; cf. further above, p. 120; pp. 209 ff.; and *The Office of Apostle*, pp. 177-78. To be added to Bultmann's arguments is the fact that there were never *original apostles* in Jerusalem who were legal authorities; cf. *The Office of Apostle*, pp. 82 ff.

[222] See Vol. 2, pp. 13 ff.

[223] See Vol. 2, pp. 101 ff.; *The Office of Apostle*, pp. 36-37, 213-14; cf. also Rev. 2:2.

[224] Paul presupposes this meaning of σημεῖα in I, 14:22.

enced by Paul is, gnostically understood, the proof of the δύναμις πνεύματος which lived within Paul and hence is a decisive sign of the
apostle, as also the ecstatic form of discourse rejected by Paul in I, 14
(see pp. 171 ff.) and in II, 5:11 ff. (see pp. 187 ff.) is for the Gnostics
a proof of the Christ who is speaking in Paul (II, 13:3; see pp. 193 ff.) ,
so that in this way Paul would have been able to acknowledge the
Gnostics as Christ apostles.

I have discussed the form and nature of this Gnostic apostolate in
detail in *The Office of Apostle* (see esp. pp. 159 ff., 204 ff.; 211 ff.) and
here can content myself with the remarks above. They will suffice for
the assertion that *Gnostic* apostles were appearing in Corinth.[225]

3. The Prophets

Apostles and prophets have the same function in Gnosticism. The
difference between them, which therefore is not always conceptually
maintained, is only that the prophets who were sent out on the mission
could bear the title ἀπόστολος. Thus in the Gnostic congregational
assemblies the apostles also appear as prophets and, when after a successful mission they pass on to another place, they leave behind in the
community their prophets. It is, however, understandable that in the
discussion of ecstatic experiences in the community gatherings at

---

[225] I need not here take up in detail D. Georgi's ([1], pp. 40 ff.) discussion with
my derivation of the apostolate from Gnosticism. In our present context it is of
interest only that there were Gnostic apostles. This cannot be denied and is not
disputed by Georgi.

His discussion mentioned above is based in large measure upon misunderstandings. For example, he accuses me of having failed to note W. Bauer's thesis that
orthodoxy and heresy are clearly to be defined only in later times. Now this thesis
forms one of the presuppositions of my derivation of the apostolate from Gnosticism! Of course if Georgi means that in Paul's time ecclesiastical and Gnostic
Christianity are not yet to be separated, he cannot appeal to Bauer in support of
this assertion. For though Bauer states that orthodoxy and heresy *as such* were
not separated from the very first, still he never put forth the foolish assertion that
Gnostic, Hellenistic, and Jewish Christianity as well as Jewish and Christian Gnosticism in their recognizable distinctions did not exist side by side.

A misunderstanding also underlies the objection which Georgi takes over from
G. Klein (*Die Zwölf Apostel*, p. 63, n. 277) , to the effect that a special apostolic
claim is inconceivable in Gnosticism if apostolic and pneumatic self-consciousness
coincide. But I have never asserted that "apostle" in Gnosticism is more than a
description of function or that the self-consciousness of the apostle is different from
that of the Pneumatic. The attack against Paul's apostolic claim which is launched
from Corinth intends therefore clearly to unmask Paul as a non-Pneumatic.

I regard as decidedly inapt the assertion of Georgi that the understanding of the
apostle in Paul is still unexplained. This assertion, which is comprehensible only as
a confession of perplexity, is already refuted by a reference to the triad—apostles,
prophets, and teachers—which already was taken over by Paul, or by the fact that
for Paul the apostolic circle is capable of precise delineation (even to the assertion
that after himself no one has been called to be an apostle) .

Corinth it is not the apostolate but prophetism that is under consideration. It is true that even for I, 12–14 the superscription does not read
περὶ τῶν προφήτων but περὶ τῶν πνευματικῶν. However, προφήτης and
πνευματικός are interchangeable concepts, as I, 14:37 shows. The προφητεύειν is a function of the Pneumatics, for which in principle every
Pneumatic must be qualified. Thus, as we have already seen, in the
community gatherings of the Marcosians, lots are cast among all the
Pneumatics to determine who is to attend to the task of προφητεύειν
at a given time.

In I, 12–14 especially we learn of Paul's attitude toward the spiritual
gifts of the πνευματικοί. Paul is convinced that all spiritual gifts are
wrought by the same Spirit and therefore are equally worthwhile
(chap. 12). In the gifts of the Spirit in the narrower sense he distinguishes between γλώσσαις λαλεῖν as incomprehensible discourse and
προφητεύειν as understandable discourse ἐν πνεύματι. Since the edification of the community is the standard of measurement for the practicing of the gifts of the Spirit in the community's gathering, he wants
to have the speaking in tongues banned from the meetings unless an
interpreter is present (chap. 14). Love surpasses all these spiritual
gifts, as chap. 13 conclusively (see p. 95, n. 23) says.

We shall not repeat here what we gathered on pp. 171 ff. from chaps.
12–14 about the situation in Corinth. Here, however, some things
should be added.

Chapter 14 does not offer the portrayal of a *normal* service of worship in the Pauline communities. Paul is speaking only of the actually
ecstatic forms of the life of worship. Even προφητεύειν is in fact such
a form of ecstatic piety. The Spirit comes upon the prophet *suddenly*
(14:30), so that the danger exists that several will engage in προφητεύειν at once (14:31). New "revelations" are imparted to the prophets,
as 14:29-30 shows. The προφητεύειν is distinguished from the γλώσσαις
λαλεῖν only by the fact that the latter is incomprehensible to the ordinary hearer. Paul does not discuss the whole question because it was
of interest for the communities he had founded in general but because
it had recently become of interest to the Corinthians: "ἐπεὶ ζηλωταί
ἐστε πνευμάτων" (14:12). Paul himself in his epistles hardly ever
appeals to a prophetic inspiration, and even in the meetings of the
community something else stands in first place: "ὅταν συνέρχησθε,
ἕκαστος ψαλμὸν ἔχει, διδαχὴν ἔχει, ἀποκάλυψιν[226] ἔχει, γλῶσσαν ἔχει,
ἑρμηνείαν ἔχει" (I, 14:26). Two or at the most three ecstatics are to
come forward in the meetings with speaking in tongues or prophesying

[226] Here as in I, 14:30 ἀποκάλυψις stands for προφητεία; for the "prophet" receives "revelations."

(14:27 ff.). Paul is quenching the Spirit! In fact, all the instruction in I, 12–14 shows that the Corinthians previously had not learned from Paul at all about the phenomenon of the πνευματικὰ κατ' ἐξοχήν. They only now learn that he too can speak ἐν ἀποκαλύψει and γλώσσῃ (I, 14:18-19; II, 12:2 ff.). Paul had *taught* πανταχοῦ ἐν πάσῃ ἐκκλησίᾳ (I, 4:17; cf. 7:17; Rom. 16:17; Gal. 6:6). The communities were indeed still full of νήπιοι and σάρκινοι, as Paul states in I, 2:6–3:2. Certainly he would have preferred that instead of their becoming ζηλωταὶ πνευμάτων (I, 14:12) they had remained νήπιοι and had been satisfied with the teaching which they had received.

It is clear that the whole problem of "prophecy" had been first of all brought to Corinth by the Gnostic Pneumatics. Paul is still too much bound to the ecstatic praxis to be able to renounce it generally, as the church later did. [227] So he does the best he can: he declares all gifts of the Spirit to be equally important, in order thus to neutralize the preference for the ecstatic phenomena; he places love higher on the scale than speaking in tongues and prophesying and in chap. 14 deliberately distinguishes between private and edifying utterances of ecstatic piety. Only the latter have their place in worship.

375   This distinction is in its present form typically Pauline. Gnosticism has no acquaintance with it thus. The portrayals of the Marcosians' worship by Irenaeus and of that of the prophets of Celsus by Origen (see pp. 276-77) show that among these prophets there is no distinction made between understandable and incomprehensible ecstatic speech; here even the speaking in tongues is called προφητεύειν.[228] Paul, who deliberately distinguishes between γλώσσαις λαλεῖν and προφητεύειν, therefore also has no separate word for the person who speaks in tongues. Beside the προφήτης stands the γλώσσῃ τις λαλεῖ (14:27). Hence the problem of the πνευματικὰ κατ' ἐξοχήν is likewise only provisionally solved by the Pauline distinction; for the prophet who said the "ἀνάθεμα Ἰησοῦς" (I, 13:3) indeed had also spoken understandably!

Moreover, in Corinth, following what has been said, among the Pneumatics the *whole* complex of the ecstatic πνευματικά for which the ζηλωταὶ πνευμάτων strive and which Paul sorts into γλώσσαις λαλεῖν and ἑρμηνεία and προφητεύειν could bear the designation of προφητεύειν. The Pneumatics were simply *prophets*. This is shown conclusively by I, 14:37-38: "εἴ τις δοκεῖ προφήτης εἶναι ἢ πνευματικός, ἐπιγινωσκέτω

---

[227] Cf. I Thess. 5:19 ff. = Vol. 2, pp. 124 ff.

[228] "This was obviously the idea that most Christians had of prophecy. Paul gave the word a radically new significance and contrasted it with glossolalia" (G. Bornkamm in NTS 4 [1958]: 98). Of course it is not certain whether Paul was the first to make this distinction.

ἃ γράφω ὑμῖν ὅτι κυρίου ἐστὶν ἐντολή. εἰ δέ τις ἀγνοεῖ, ἀγνοεῖται." The reference to the Gnosis of the purported Pneumatics and prophets in Corinth is unmistakable in these verses. But this also means that the   376 Pneumatics in Corinth represented themselves to be prophets when they went into action in the community's gatherings for purposes of worship.   377

CONCLUSION

I. A Review

First of all we may state that the conclusions of our Introduction B in the investigation of the heretical theology in Corinth have been confirmed throughout.

The literary-critical analysis has been repeatedly confirmed in the exposition. The insight into the special character of Epistle A, which with its predominantly paraenetic contents leaves out any insight of Paul into the backgrounds of the unsatisfactory conditions in Corinth and hence is very significantly different from Epistle B, which presupposes Epistle A and the community's answer to it, renders good service not only in the exegesis of I, 15 but above all in the investigation of the Gnostic *eleutheria*. The awareness that in II, 2:14–6:13 + 7:2-4 we probably have to do with the torso of one of Paul's writings coming before the sorrowful epistle has been constantly strengthened. And the special situation of the joyful epistle and of II, 9 which is closely connected with it has been conclusively proved by the fact that the corresponding sections could never be adduced for the presentation of the heretical Corinthian theology. The joyful epistle is thus instructive as to the connections between Paul and the community which is obedient to him: the Gnostic heresy is no more thought of with a single word. Perhaps the "οὐκ ἐν σοφίᾳ σαρκικῇ" (II, 1:12) is a reminiscence of previous debates, and the "ὡς πάντα ἐν ἀληθείᾳ ἐλαλήσαμεν ὑμῖν" (II, 7:14) may have been written out of the consciousness of Paul's rehabilitation, which has become obvious, against his opponents' charges, if it does not look back to II, 1:13, which is more likely. II, 8:18 ff. is presumably a reaction to the charges against Paul in the matter of the collection, as vss. 20-21 above all indicate. But the fact is inescapable that Paul intentionally avoids carrying the previous theological discussion any further.

If we disregard the joyful epistle and the letter of recommendation (E) which is connected with it, then with *one* exception we not only have been able but have also been obliged to explain all the larger sections of the Corinthian epistles in terms of the situation which developed because of the penetration of the Gnostics into the Corinthian community. Therewith has been confirmed the other thesis stated at the outset, which said that it stands to reason that *all* the individual questions handled in the epistles must be investigated with a view to whether they had not developed out of *the* problematic which certainly lies at the basis of a great number of themes. The one exception is provided by I, 6:1-11, the disputes before heathen courts. N rally here too Gnostics or Gnostic motifs could have played a part. But nothing can any longer be discerned as to the background of this point of controversy.[1] If, as is not ruled out, the σοφός in vs. 5 is meant in a polemical-ironic sense, it could, just like the genuinely Gnostic sins of πορνεία and εἰδωλολατρία which in vs. 9*b* are placed at the head of the catalog of vices, indicate that even here Paul has not lost sight at least of his real opposition.[2]

The *midrash* in II, 3:7-18 forms a special problem. It stands within the statements with which Paul is defending his apostolic rights in Epistle C. Out of the apologetic assertion that Paul has received the empowering for the ministry of the new covenant from God (3:4-6) there develops the presentation of the glory of this ministry in 3:7-18. On the interpretation of this section, which is not polemical in details,[3] see pp. 315 ff.

S. Schulz, "Die Decke des Moses" (ZNW 49 [1958]: 1-30), has attempted to produce proof that in this section Paul adopts and polemically revises a *midrash* of his Jewish Christian opponents in Corinth. In this model Moses' unique vision of God is supposed to have been expounded as a type of the vision of God of all Christians. Schulz's argument has not convinced me. Of course it is beyond question that the *technique* of the *midrash* in II, 3:7-18 is traditional. It is uncertain whether *this midrash* had Jewish or Christian models.[4] In my judgment Paul's text does not allow us to recognize such models and so far as I know there are no parallels. Thus II, 3:7-18 could represent an original Pauline *midrash*. Even less can I recognize that Paul has made only a gloss on a model that lay before him, so that this model can still be reconstructed. And that this model should have been played into his hands from the hands of his Jewish Christian opponents is a thesis which simply is unfounded.

D. Georgi ([1], pp. 246 ff.) also thinks that the solution cannot suffice which understands the whole text as a *midrash-like* insertion. Therewith it is not explained "how Paul could at all come to speak of the tables of the law and

---

[1] On the theological exposition of this passage one may consult E. Dinkler, "Zum Problem der Ethik bei Paulus," ZThK 49 (1952) : 167 ff.

[2] Cf. *ibid.*, p. 180, where Dinkler reckons with the possibility that the employment of the heathen judicial system is a deliberate demonstration by people in Corinth for whom civil law had nothing to do with their religion. It is in fact possible to understand in such a way the situation which stands back of I, 6:1-11 in terms of the demand of Gnostic libertinism to connect the fleshly with the fleshly and the spiritual with the spiritual.

[3] Otherwise, e.g., J. Jervell, *Imago Dei*, p. 177.

[4] "We encounter no passage in the old rabbinical literature in which there would be a reference to the 'veil of Moses' in Exod. 34:33 ff." (Billerbeck, III: 516).

of the figure of Moses" (p. 247). The reason for it, according to Georgi, can only be that the opponents were occupying themselves with the figure of Moses. But that is a mere assertion! The question as to why Paul concerns himself here with the figure of Moses is however to be answered simply: because it afforded him the appropriate material for his *midrash*. To be sure it is obvious that 3:1-6 and 4:1 ff. are polemical in particulars,[5] but for just that reason the nonpolemical character *in particulars* of 3:7-18 is set in bold relief. The presentation of the significance of the motif of tradition and of allegory in Hellenistic and late Jewish propaganda, which Georgi discusses explicitly and instructively (pp. 83 ff.), still does not take the place of proof that II, 3:7-18 is "exceedingly polemical" since Paul is commenting in this section on a scriptural proof of his opponents. That such a "disconnected argument" (pp. 248-49) as that in II, 3:7-18 can be explained only with such a thesis does not tally in itself and besides, in the statement about the disconnectedness, proceeds from modern presuppositions which in the investigation of an allegorical *midrash* should as much as possible be left aside, since this *midrash* wants to be understood in terms of the logic which is peculiar to its exegetical form and also can be understood thus without strain (see below, pp. 315 ff.).[6] I cannot even regard Georgi's exposition of the *midrash* as a hypothesis, which is how he wishes to have it regarded.

378   Cf. now also G. Friedrich in O. Michel, *Abraham unser Vater*, pp. 184-85.

Above all the third result of our introductory investigation has been strikingly confirmed, namely the thesis that there was only *one* battle-front in Corinth and that Paul also takes a stand only against this *one* heresy, an assertion which almost compellingly resulted already from

---

[5] See in D. Georgi, [1], pp. 246 ff., 285 ff. To be sure, Paul's text appears to me to be overinterpreted with the detailed reconstruction of the opponents' theologoumena undertaken by Georgi, and thus often obscured rather than illumined. Since the peculiar nature of the opposition can be deduced only from Paul's polemic, one is always in danger of employing the hermeneutical circle, unavoidable here, in such a way as to construe problems in the text which are not present to begin with, in order then to solve these with the help of his own thesis. This is everywhere said in self-criticism, yet it appears to me that Georgi himself has fallen victim frequently to this danger, particularly in the interpretation of II, 3-4.

[6] Of course the *midrash* in II, 3:7-18 has already in the past been explained as polemical in details. A history of the exegesis of this passage would show that at any given time, the opponents inferred from the other parts of the epistle were also found in 3:7-18. Those of the Tübingen school, e.g., saw Judaizers being opposed here, A. Schlatter ([1], pp. 30 ff.) saw his Palestinian enthusiasts, and so on. This shows the *fundamentally* debatable character of a detailed polemical explanation of this passage, which then is rightly rejected by most of the commentaries. One may compare with this such a sober and correct judgment as that of H. Windisch (p. 112): "Certainly there is a connection between 3:1-6 and 7-18 (cf. vs. 3 and vs. 6). But what is fixed there only in axiomatic brevity and indeed in specific application to the Corinthian community and its apostolic founders is here discussed in broad terms in the form of a *midrash*, free from all specific application .... The passage looks like a literary insertion; the material is conceived independent of the epistolary situation, and since the apology is taken up again in 4:1 ff., the pericope could easily be removed without any harm being suffered by the context of the epistle."

the preliminary investigation. One may attack the conclusions of the present investigation on details, doubt the tenability of the exegetical basis on occasion, and find the picture of the schmismatics in Corinth mistakenly drawn as to detailed features: the fact that without any necessity of doing violence to the text it was possible to draw a unified picture of the Corinthian heresy,[7] into which every passage which can at all be adduced for this topic fits without difficulty, undoubtedly speaks for the clarity of this picture as well as for its fundamental correctness.

While heretofore for the most part the Corinthian epistles have been explained under the presupposition of a double battlefront in such a way that the polemic in all the epistles is fairly equally aimed against the various fronts, D. Georgi [1] has recently taken the position that the opponents in II, i.e. in II, 2:14–7:4 + 10–13 (Epistles C and D) are different from those in I, and G. Bornkamm [1] recommends this solution of his pupil as "the most illuminating explanation of the question" (p. 15).[8] Bornkamm adds the critical remark: "With rare passion W. Schmithals argues for the identity of battlefront in all the letters of Paul" (p. 16). Now in any case it is no more strange for the battlefront to be the same than for it always to be changing. Here—and on this I am in agreement with Bornkamm—it must be settled on "exegetical grounds" (p. 17). I think that I have done this. Passion would be out of place here. $\qquad$ 379

What I say with passion is that this question is correctly approached methodologically only when one investigates the *whole* body of epistolary literature coming into question or in the investigation of parts keeps in view the whole (see pp. 345 ff.; Vol. 2, pp. 175 ff.). Otherwise there is the danger of construing different fronts where only one is present. Precisely the dissertation of D. Georgi offers the best proof of this.

G. Bornkamm summarizes Georgi's characterization of the false teachers in II as follows: "Here the *new* invasion of Paul's opponents into Corinth is taken seriously and with a challenge to one of the previously customary labels their picture is drawn entirely according to the pattern of the heathen miracle workers who were widespread in late antiquity, the most famous examples of which are Apollonius of Tyana (Philostratus), Alexander of Abonuteichos, and Peregrinus Proteus (Lucian). The type represented by them is confessedly a highly characteristic phenomenon in the field of competition of the most widely varied religions in the age of syncretism. They are wandering prophets, sorcerers, healers, give themselves out to be emissaries of a deity, who ballyhoo their δύναμις and by means of revelations and miracles make a show of it. Important for us is the fact that the primitive

---

[7] Cf. also F. Büchsel, *Der Geist im Neuen Testament*, p. 390; L. Goppelt, *Christentum und Judentum*, . . . pp. 129-30; G. Eichholz in *Basileia: Walter Freytag zum 60. Geburtstag* (1959), pp. 56 ff.; E. Dinkler in RGG (1960, 3rd ed.), IV, col. 18; W. Marxsen, pp. 75-76. $\qquad$ 380

[8] Cf. also Feine-Behm-Kümmel, *Introduction to the New Testament*, pp. 210-11.

Christian mission in the Hellenistic area apparently made every effort to resist these rivals; even Paul, as I Thess. 2:1-12 shows, had to demarcate himself energetically from them. But it is no less important that this type also prevailed and was copied in popular Christianity in considerable measure. Everything argues for the view that Paul's opponents in II Cor. with their understanding of Christ, their behavior, their preaching, and in the style of their propaganda are to be reckoned as belonging to this type" (pp. 15-16).

In essence, I am able to agree with this throughout, including the reference to I Thess. 2:1-12 (see Vol. 2, pp. 98 ff.). In fact everything does argue for the view that the false apostles in Corinth are to be reckoned as belonging to this type of traveling Pneumatics. I hope that the present investigation as well as my book on *The Office of Apostle* will have led to this conclusion. Only I do not understand how therewith another front than in I Cor. is indicated, and how a person can think that he is able with *such* a presentation to refute the unitary description of the Corinthian heresy presented here.

θεῖος ἀνήρ is a collective concept. The Gnostic apostles as we have described them are splendidly characterized by G. Bornkamm with this concept and its exposition. That in I Cor. primarily the teaching of Paul and his opponents, and in II Cor. the personal authority of the two are discussed is easily understandable and well argued (see pp. 182-83, 279-80). To separate the fronts because of this shift within the advancing discussion means to make the impossible attempt to pull apart the message and the messenger.[9] This is all the less permissible since the dispute about the apostolic office including the question of the right to support already begins vigorously in I, 9:1 ff.—in Epistle A of course it still had no place; see pp. 279 ff.—and the description of the "wandering prophets . . . who ballyhoo their δύναμις and by means of revelations and miracles make a show of it" rests no less on I, 12–14 than on II, 10–13. Conversely, almost all the "doctrinal questions" from I Cor. recur in II Cor., as our investigation has shown. In addition, not only is the *title of apostle* for extra-ecclesiastical Hellenistic θεῖοι ἄνδρες attested only among *Gnostic* apostles, but there are no primitive Christian missionaries other than the Gnostic ones who are proven to have appeared as θεῖοι ἄνδρες.[10] Because D. Georgi does not note this, the heretical missionary move-

---

[9] The fact that only in II Cor. do we learn anything more definite about the *person* of the opponents cannot be adduced as proof of newly arrived opponents in II Cor., because the Gnostics whom Georgi recognizes for the debate of I Cor. must ultimately also have invaded the community from without, even though Paul does not explicitly mention this fact in I Cor. For Georgi will hardly want to assert that the Corinthian Gnosticism developed out of Paul's preaching within the community in Corinth itself, although this sometimes seems his intention (cf. [1], pp. 13-14, 220, 303).

And where were the adversaries of I Cor. during the correspondence of II Cor.? That in II Cor., because of the new opponents, Paul makes overtures to the old adversaries and feels compelled "to show how close to him are the Corinthian Gnostics" (Georgi, [2], p. 95), who nevertheless reject the crucified Jesus and deny the resurrection, certainly is not an idea that is to be taken seriously (cf. [1], pp. 14, 220, 304).

[10] D. Georgi ([1], pp. 210 ff.) indeed points to the way in which Luke in his book of Acts and in Luke 10:17 ff. portrays the missionary activity of the apostles;

ment in Corinth which he has reconstructed, in spite of—or precisely because of—his excellent religio-historical excursus, hangs entirely in midair and the labor applied to this excursus remains in the last analysis wasted [11] (cf. also p. 282). An organized Christian missionary movement, stemming from Palestine, of Hellenistic Pneumatics and θεῖοι ἄνδρες, whose fundamental distinguishing mark was their ecstatic mode of appearance, who conduct an antinomian Gentile mission and yet are not Gnostics, who bear the technical designation of "apostles," who regard Jesus not as exalted *Kyrios* but as θεῖος ἀνήρ—Georgi has not been able to prove the existence of such a movement for earlier or for later.

If he had taken into account the *entirety* at least of the Corinthian epistles, indeed if he had at least subsequently drawn the radius which he proposed ([1], p. 29; cf. below, p. 346), his description of the false apostles in Corinth, which is correct on essential points, would not have been able to lead him to the postulation of a second front there, especially since he himself does not emerge without the thesis that in many respects the opponents in I Cor. and II Cor. meet and that in both cases we have to do with missionaries with a decided ecstatic-pneumatic self-consciousness[12] (cf. [1], pp. 229 ff., 243 ff., 292 ff.).

For what Georgi otherwise adduces by way of actual or alleged differences between I Cor. and II Cor., he himself apparently regards as not very important. Hence it also says nothing for the separation of the opposition into two fronts:

II, 11:4 is said to contradict I, 12:3 ([1], p. 285; [2], p. 95); on this, see p. 352.

Only in II Cor. do we learn that the opponents are Jews ([1], p. 220; [2], p. 95); of course, for it is only in II Cor. that the dispute shifts *at all* into

---

but still this portrayal only shows how at the beginning of the second century, in the Hellenistic environment of the Lucan Christian community—presumably in Asia Minor—some conceived of the activity of the apostles. The Pauline writings and the other Christian literature of the first century, on the other hand, do not allow the thesis that in primitive Christianity outside the Gnostic movement there were missionaries who appeared as θεῖοι ἄνδρες. Therefore it is not accidental that the only "Christian" θεῖοι ἄνδρες who appear in the interesting description of the Hellenistic missionaries given by Georgi ([1], pp. 83-205) are of *Gnostic* observance ([1], pp. 117 ff.).

[11] The long section in Georgi's work on "Mission in neutestamentlicher Zeit" (Mission in New Testament Times; [1], pp. 83-218) very diligently assembles a comprehensive body of material which embraces Jewish apologetic, Josephus and Philo, Hellenism and Gnosticism, the Stoic diatribe and primitive Christianity, beggars before the synagogues, Jewish interpreters of dreams and merchants, Simon Magus and Elchasai, and much else besides. Nevertheless one stands rather helpless in the presence of this material which is assembled to form almost half of the work and unfortunately is entirely unsatisfactorily differentiated. For it has long been undisputed that, like Paul himself, his opponents also are to be placed somewhere in the sphere of these missionary efforts.

[12] Of course to infer such a self-consciousness also from the question of the right to support (D. Georgi, [1], pp. 234 ff.) appears to me to be mistaken. Rather, the Corinthian opponents in I and II Cor. themselves so little demanded support by the community that they could even make the gathering of a collection for Jerusalem into a charge against Paul; cf. *The Office of Apostle*, pp. 219 ff.

the personal sphere, for which reason it also says nothing that only in II Cor. are the letters of recommendation mentioned,[13] only in II Cor. does Paul attack the alien apostles *personally,* and only in II Cor. is there a discussion of the pneumatic mighty acts as *proof of missionary authority (ibid.)* .

It is alleged that in II Cor. there is lacking any debate with libertinism ([1], p. 220) ; on this, see pp. 223, 383.

The opponents' Christology in II Cor. is not Gnostic ([1], pp. 14, 282 ff.) , since it in fact proclaims the exalted one, but also brings forward in the Corinthian community the historical Jesus not as the crucified one but as θεῖος ἀνήρ.[14] I do not see how one can reach this conclusion from II, 5:16 (on this, see pp. 302 ff.) ; II, 13:3 ff.; II, 11:4 (on this, see pp. 132 ff.) , and II, 4:5 ff. (ζωὴ 'Ιησοῦ is supposed to have been a heretical catchword in Corinth!) . Hence on pp. 282 ff. Georgi works with concepts like "apparently," "evidently," "probably," "it is to be presumed," and so forth. II, 5:16 would most readily lend itself to use for his thesis, yet even this passage at best says only that *some* positive understanding of the historical Jesus among the Corinthian opponents is to be assumed; but see pp. 302 ff. Georgi's hypothesis already hangs in midair because a θεῖος-ἀνήρ Christology still is not proven, not only in II Cor. but in the Pauline era at all.[15]

In view of all this it is not surprising, even though strange, that at the close of his original dissertation Georgi stated: "Hence these wandering preachers (*scil.* in II Cor.) must not unconditionally themselves have been Gnostics." This sentence is no longer found in this form in the printed edition. Yet Georgi now speaks matter-of-factly in the same way of the "commonalities" of the old and the new adversaries, who *combine forces* against Paul ([1], pp. 303-4) ! That appears to me to be a fatal result for an investigation which intended to prove for II Cor. precisely other adversaries

381

383

384

---

[13] The section on the letters of recommendation ([1], pp. 241 ff.) makes little sense in the study as it now stands. In the original dissertation it was a different matter. There Georgi regarded it as inexplicable "why Gnostic Pneumatics should have placed value upon letters of recommendation." For him this serves as an important argument against the Gnostic character of the opponents in II Cor. He has properly omitted this line of argument. Now he holds ([1], p. 244) these letters of recommendation even to be "something like chronicles of the pneumatic feats of the opposing preachers."

382

I would not allow myself such a judgment about the contents of the letters of recommendation, about which in fact we know nothing. Nevertheless I am fully in agreement with Georgi in this respect: "Self-commendation and commendation through letters of recommendation must not be mutually exclusive; they rather lie in the same line" ([1], p. 90) . See further p. 115 above.

[14] Conversely, W. Bieder ("Paulus und seine Gegner in Korinth," pp. 324-25) recently asserts that for Paul's opponents in Corinth Jesus is "simply the crucified one, not the Lord."

[15] If there was an early Christian movement in which Jesus was esteemed "as an outstanding Pneumatic" (D. Georgi, [1], p. 286) , it was Gnosticism, in which Jesus was occasionally represented as an exemplary Gnostic (see p. 48, n. 109) . It is not permissible to refer to the Synoptic tradition in this connection. It is true that here features of the Hellenistic θεῖος ἀνήρ conception are transferred to Jesus in large measure, but it is the *exalted Kyrios* of Hellenistic circles who is supposed to be represented herewith.

than for I Cor., though of course under this presupposition an unavoidable conclusion; for the question as to the whereabouts of the opponents from I Cor. naturally cannot be left unanswered if they no longer appear in II Cor. (cf. p. 290, n. 9). Actually they "no longer" appear because a change of fronts did not take place at all.

G. Friedrich (in O. Michel, *Abraham unser Vater*, pp. 181 ff.) describes the opponents in II Cor. in extensive agreement with D. Georgi. To be sure, he holds them to be the people of Stephen who according to Acts 6–8 were 385 expelled from Jerusalem.

II. Summary

Has it been successfully proven that the heretical theology in Corinth was a genuine Gnosticism? We have said in the Introduction A, I, what is after all to be called Gnosticism in the proper sense. Under A, II, we became acquainted with a genuinely Gnostic system. It involved a system of Jewish Christ Gnosticism. Our special attention was called to the equation occurring in this system of primal man = Christ and to the purely anthropological significance of the Christ figure which was based on that equation. But at the same time we noted—even though only incidentally—other features of this Christ Gnosticism: the significance of Gnosis itself; the anthropological dualism, with which were connected on the one hand libertinism and on the other hand the doctrine of the ascent of the soul; the absence of a redeemer myth; the emphatic self-consciousness of the Christ Gnostics; their conspicuous consciousness of mission, and so on. The Jewish character of this Gnosticism was expressed not only by the terminology and by the use of the Old Testament, but above all by the decided weakening of the cosmic dualism.

We encounter all these features again in the heretical theology in Corinth, so that the assertion appears justified that in it we have to do with representatives of a Jewish Gnosticism, as it lies before us in various shadings, for example in the "Great Proclamation" and in traditions of the Naassene Preaching and as it was represented by people such as Simon, Menander, Dositheus, Cerinthus, and others. In this manner the fact that between Paul and his opponents in Corinth a cosmic dualism was not discussed finds its illuminating explanation. Even the Simonian system of the "Great Proclamation," for example, has no specifically dualistic cosmology, although man is further seen dualistically. This is in a certain way inconsistent, but precisely such inconsistency shows that Gnostic systems without a pronounced cosmic dualism nevertheless are to be classed as genuinely

Gnostic, insofar as the Gnostic anthropology continues to be maintained in them.[16]

On the Jewish character of the Corinthian Gnosticism some concluding remarks must be made in view of the present state of research. That the false teachers in Corinth were Jews was already to be inferred from many passages in the Corinthian epistles. They not only were of Jewish nationality but also placed special value upon their ancestry (cf. p. 208). Therefore the Old Testament obviously stood in high regard with them (see pp. 77-78). It is possible that they could practice the custom of circumcision, perhaps with a symbolic significance (p. 209). Even if one does not venture to adduce Phil. 3 (see Vol. 2, pp. 60 ff.) or even the Galatian epistle (see Vol. 2, pp. 9 ff.) as substantial parallels, there can be no doubt that the Corinthian false teachers consciously appeared as Jews. Thus from the teaching as well as from the teachers the Jewish character of the Corinthian Gnosticism becomes evident (incidentally one more reason for holding to the unity of the battlefront in the epistles). Naturally this does not mean that here a connection is found into which Judaism has entered with Gnosticism, as the majority of researchers assert who do not venture to decide between F. C. Baur and D. Schenkel (cf. H. Windisch, p. 26). A "judaizing Gnosticism" or a "Gnostic *Judaismus*" is an absurdity and never existed.[17] F. Godet somehow imagines that the "super-apostles" were members of the "Jewish priestly caste and of Pharisaism" who wanted to force the Mosaic law on Gentile Christians also. But then "no doubt they added, once they were on Greek soil, elements of a theosophical kind to the gospel of the apostle, in order thereby to make their doctrine more acceptable to the speculative taste of the educated (! I 1:26 ff.) Christians of Greece." In the end Godet finds it possible to agree with the words of Kniewel, "who has described the Christ party as 'the Gnostics before Gnosticism'" (*Der erste Brief an die Korinther*, p. 39). But only one of the two is possible: Judaism or Gnosticism. Pure Gnosticism rules out the way of the law as a way of salvation in any form. When Godet conceives of Cerinthus as the type of the Corinthian heretics, this does an injustice

---

[16] See the first edition of the present work, pp. 241-42.

[17] To this extent—but no further—H. J. Schoeps and others are correct in their protest against speaking of a "Jewish Gnosticism"; cf., e.g., Schoeps in TLZ 81 (1956), cols. 420-21.

Of course there could just as well be a Jewish or Jewish-Christian Gnosticism, and thus a *Gnosticism* in the setting of Judaism or of Jewish Christianity with certain influences from the setting which did not alter the Gnostic substance, as well as a gnosticizing Judaism or Jewish Christianity, in other words, a *Judaism* or *Jewish Christianity* with certain external borrowings from Gnosticism—there could have been these, I say, just as well as there could be a Christian Gnosticism and a gnosticizing Christianity.

to his conception of Cerinthus' false doctrines, for the latter certainly was no Judaizer. To be sure he is correct in substance in this reference, for Cerinthus lets us clearly recognize the association of genuine Gnosticism and a certain observance of the Old Testament tradition as we encounter that association in Corinth, since he (according to the representation of Epiphanius above all) was indeed a Jewish but nonetheless a genuine Gnostic (cf. Vol. 2, pp. 25-26). Very sensitive, even though historically hardly justified, is the observation which stands behind the assertion of Epiphanius, Haer. XXVIII, 4, that I Cor. was written against Cerinthus. The agreements of the Corinthian Gnosticism with Cerinthus go astoundingly far. Even the territory which they covered apparently coincides, so that here relatively close connections will have existed, an observation which is repeated with respect to the Galatian epistle (see Vol. 2, pp. 25-26).

Thus, as much as the existence of a Gnostic Judaism is to be disputed, just as much can the existence of a Jewish Gnosticism be asserted.[18] In our work we have followed *one* branch of this Jewish Gnosticism and in the Introduction A have already called attention to how strongly late Judaism was influenced from the side of the Gnostic terminology and conceptual world. On the other hand in fact the role which the Old Testament plays in Gnosticism in general is an indication of the significant influence of the specifically Jewish Gnosticism. To be identified more or less—but especially more—as Jewish-Gnostic are groups like the Elchasaites, Hemerobaptists, Masbothaeans;[19] sects such as the Sethians, Cainites, and the Baruch Gnosticism; men like Simon, Elchasai, Cerinthus, Dositheus, and others. Not infrequently Jewish Gnostics are meant by the *Minim* in the oldest parts of the Talmud.[20]

The emergence of Jewish Gnosticism is by no means utterly mysterious. It is evident from the Introduction A, I, that I regard Mesopotamia as the homeland of genuine Gnosticism, which developed there as a movement with pronounced peculiarities of the understanding of the world and the self, in the early period of the Diadochi with the meeting of the Greek and the oriental spirit under a heavy use of the

[18] Cf. R. Reitzenstein, [1], pp. 104 ff.: P. Steffes, pp. 35 ff., 57 ff.; K. Schubert, pp. 94 ff.; M. Friedländer, [1]; [3], *passim;* H. Graetz, *Gnostizismus und Judentum* (1846); U. Wilckens, [1], p. 67; E. Lohse, *Märtyrer und Gottesknecht* (1955), pp. 165-66; G. Quispel, [2], pp. 475 ff.; J. Jervell, pp. 123-24; Feine-Behm-Kümmel, pp. 154 ff.; E. S. Drower, pp. XV, 101; M. Simon, *Die jüdischen Sekten zur Zeit Christi* (1964), esp. pp. 92 ff.

[19] See K. Rudolph, [1], pp. 222 ff.; Hegesippus, e.g., knows of a whole series of sects, for a part of which of course only the name is known to us (in Eus. CH IV, 22).

[20] M. Friedländer, [1], pp. 169 ff.; H. J. Schoeps, [2], p. 50; G. Quispel, [2], pp. 475 ff.; K. J. Kuhn, in *Judentum, Urchristentum, Kirche,* BZNW 26: 39 ff.

various myths of the Orient.[21] But Mesopotamia is also, since the Exile, the second home of Judaism. There, by assimilation to Jewish traditions, Gnosticism gained entrance even within the Jewish population and, as Jewish Gnosticism, migrated to the Mediterranean along the indicated paths of the Jewish influence which was lively everywhere in the Orient.[22] In Palestine, the stronghold of Jewish orthodoxy, it could not be held in its original form and had to be assimilated to the conservative theology. If all the sources were preserved for us, certainly a wide scale could be exhibited, ranging from pure Gnosticism of Jewish observance as it was developed in Mesopotamia, by way of the manifold varieties of Jewish Gnosticism and of gnosticizing Judaism, to late Jewish orthodoxy, which cannot deny certain influences of this Gnosticism in anthropology and eschatology.[23] Unfortunately these sources are in large measure lacking. Still preserved for us is that which later Judaism held to be tolerable. The actually heretical items which would be most interesting to us have, insofar as there was any literary production at all (see above, p. 79), disappeared along with the heretics themselves. But Jewish Gnosticism fell victim to the combined efforts of Jewish and Christian heresy fighters. If only a little is preserved for us of the texts of pure Jewish Gnosticism, this is due also to the fact that Jewish Gnosticism early was absorbed into Christian and other forms of Gnosticism. Jewish traces still confront us everywhere in the later Gnostic sources.[24]

Jewish Gnosticism existed *alongside* the proper, "orthodox" Judaism which at the time of the beginnings of Christianity of course was not yet narrowed into rabbinism but embraced Pharisees and Sadducees, apocalypticists[25] and Essenes and other groups, and *alongside* Jewish

---

[21] Cf. H. Jonas, [3], p. 3.

[22] On the distribution of Jews in Babylonia, see K. Rudolph, [1], p. 52 (Literature); K. G. Kuhn, "Die Sektenschrift und die iranische Religion," ZThK 49 (1952): 310; R. McL. Wilson, [2], pp. 1 ff.; P. Dalbert, pp. 12 ff.; T. Hopfner, *Die Judenfrage bei Griechen und Römern*, Abhandlungen der deutschen Akademie der Wissenschaften in Prag, 8 (1943): 6.

A certain preparation of Judaism for Gnosticism is to be found in what W. Kamlah (*Christentum und Selbstbehauptung* [Frankfurt, 1940]) calls the "overcoming of the Israelite-Jewish historicality," i.e., the abandonment of the national-sociological self-assertion and its religious foundations (cf. *ibid.*, pp. 21-51, 124 ff.). Nevertheless the strong gnosticizing of Judaism was possible only in the communities of the Diaspora, part of which had been in existence since the exile, from which then certain Gnostic elements penetrated to the very center of orthodox Judaism (see pp. 71 ff.).

[23] Cf. W. Bousset, [3], pp. 14 ff., 57; H. J. Schoeps, [3], p. 76, n. 1.

[24] On the Mandaeans one may compare, e.g., K. Rudolph, [1], pp. 80 ff.; [2], pp. 382 ff. There is hardly a single branch of Gnostic tradition that does not have Jewish elements. Cf. p. 78, n. 200.

[25] On the independence of the late Jewish apocalyptic theology, see D. Rössler, *Gesetz und Geschichte*, WMANT 3 (1960).

Hellenism which to be sure has become better known to us only in Philo, its outstanding representative. Its distribution and special character however are beyond any doubt.[26]

Thus late Judaism was a phenomenon which in no respect was second to early Christianity in complexity. On both sides are found three different religious forms circulating under the same name, naturally with different shadings and influences, but in the distinctive components still clearly different: orthodoxy, which was represented in Christianity at first by the Palestinian Jewish Christians; Gnosticism; and Hellenism, which found its most famous expression in early Christianity in Paul. One may ask whether there was in Judaism a phenomenon after all which combined all the disparate elements. It was not nationality; not circumcision, which for example was discontinued[27] by Hellenistic Jews;[28] not even the Old Testament canon as a whole; perhaps the Pentateuch, but even this only possibly. And in Christianity it was only the name of Christ which still could hold together the extremes, not even his person, since certain Gnostics could, in favor of the Pneuma-Christ, curse the man Jesus, who *alone* possessed significance for the extremely Jewish Christian circles.

This fact lets us better understand the beginnings of Christianity. The various expressions of Christianity cannot possibly have sprouted from a *single* root. Certainly, the confession of Christ—not of Jesus!—held together all the forms in which early Christianity was manifested.[29] But the diversity in the outward forms does not lie grounded in this confession—in which it rather was still pronounced—but in the fact that Judaism, from whose presuppositions alone early Christianity may be explained, exhibited the same diversity of forms.

The transition from the manifold forms of Jewish orthodoxy and of Jewish Hellenism to the variety of ecclesiastical Christianity can be shown with sufficient clarity in the extant sources.

But for the development of Christian Gnosticism the same thing[30] holds true in principle which is to be said about the origin and the beginnings of the Christianity which later became orthodox.[31] In that

---

[26] Cf. R. Reitzenstein, [1], pp. 417 ff.; P. Dalbert, *Die Theologie* . . . , *passim*, e.g., pp. 25-26.

[27] Cf. I, 7:18 and H. Lietzmann, *in loc.;* I Macc. 1:15; Josephus, Ant. XII, 5.1; J. Leipoldt, *Die urchristliche Taufe im Lichte der Religionsgeschichte* (1928), pp. 4-5; E. Lerle, *Proselytenwerbung und Urchristentum* (1960), pp. 48 ff.; T. Hopfner, *Die Judenfrage bei Griechen und Römern* (1943), p. 54.

[28] Cf. W. Foerster, *Neutestamentliche Zeitgeschichte*, II (1956) : 233.

[29] Of course there were also communities which confessed Jesus without confessing him as the Christ (see Vol. 3, p. 34, n. 71; p. 116). But in such a case do we have to do with Christian communities?

[30] Cf. E. Käsemann, *New Testament Questions of Today*, pp. 19-20.

[31] The earliest church fathers were correct in deriving Christian Gnosticism

connection it is interesting that Christian orthodoxy is essentially of
Hellenistic observance, utterly in contrast with Judaism, in which the
Palestinian-conservative tendency prevailed as orthodox. The reasons
for this need not be investigated here, but it should be emphasized
that orthodoxy did not stand at the beginning of the development and
assert itself victoriously against the assaults of Judaists and Gnostics,
but was the end-point of a history whose active figures could be clearly
classified as heretical and orthodox only after the battle was won. It is
the merit of W. Bauer's fine book, *Rechtgläubigkeit und Ketzerei im
ältesten Christentum,* to have shown that still at the close of the second
century large areas, especially in the eastern part of the Roman empire,
were entirely or almost entirely free of orthodoxy even though they did
not lack Christian communities. In fact I have no doubt that in Edessa
as well as in Egypt from the beginning onward a more or less Gnostic
Christianity was common, in the face of which the church was able
only slowly to prevail. And it appears to me that Bauer has also convincingly demonstrated that around the turn of the century in Paul's
missionary territory in Asia Minor the Gnostics stood alongside the
"Orthodox" at least equally as strong (*ibid.,* pp. 65-98). This observation is of interest for us because it shows that the debate between
ecclesiastical and Gnostic missions, first recognizable in the Corinthian
epistles, was not at all terminated by Paul. If, as one may concede to
W. Bauer at least as a justifiable possibility, I Clement was occasioned
by a renewed penetration of Gnostics into the Corinthian community
(pp. 99 ff.),[32] some forty years after the debate which we have investigated a very similar situation will have developed, this time of
course caused by Christian Gnostics.

It is regrettable that "orthodoxy" silenced the "heretics" where it
could not overcome them and has preserved for us only the documents
of its own history. Therefore, for the problem of early Christian Gnosticism exactly as with the characterization of Jewish Gnosticism, we
are dependent to a large extent upon inferences drawn from polemical
literature of the church and upon literarily relatively late Gnostic

---

directly from pre-Christian Jewish heresies; their voices are much too little heeded.
One may compare, e.g., Hegesippus in Eus. CH IV, 22.5, 7, who not unjustly counts
Simon with the Jewish heresies out of which Christian Gnosticism grew directly.
Epiphanius also begins his history of the heretics, not without reason, with Jewish
sects (cf. A. Hilgenfeld, p. 81). Cf. further Ep. Ap. 1; 7.

[32] Unfortunately one hardly learns from I Clem. any details about the circumstances in Corinth, but still the main themes of the epistle coincide precisely with
those of the Corinthian epistles. I Clem. is directed against controversies in the community, against haughty arrogance toward God and the brethren, against the
denial of the resurrection, against the turning away from *agapē,* and against the
surrender of the traditional form of worship. What else but Gnosticism could come
into consideration as the adversary here?!

sources, which for the most part have been made known to us accidentally through discoveries in the dry lands of the Orient, or through Gnostic sects which like the Mandaeans have remained active down to the present. Anyone who does not *wish* to be convinced here cannot be convinced. But then it may be expected that the other persuasions will be set forth with tenable reasons. The accounting for Gnosticism out of Christianity is no longer acceptable. The more the study of the New Testament encounters traces of Christian Gnosticism, the more puzzling becomes the question as to its origin, if one does not refer directly to heretical Judaism and does not judge the origin of Christian Gnosticism in principle other than that of later orthodoxy and that of the Judaistic heresy.

388

Only thus is explained also the abundance of diverse kinds of Gnosticism which is already presupposed in the New Testament and, precisely like the variegated Hellenistic Christianity, continues individual pre-Christian traditions. I call attention to the Corinthian Gnosticism, whose terminology Paul knew and which with its myth of the "Christ ἐν ἡμῖν" probably was common in the Syrian-Samaritan region. Alongside this is the Gnosticism known from the Johannine writings, to which the substantial connection between man and redeemer obviously is foreign and which precisely for this reason, and not accidentally, exhibits close contacts with the gnosticizing Judaism that stands close to orthodoxy. This can be deduced from the Testament XII, the Damascus document, and other texts and is well known from the Mandaean tradition and the recently discovered Dead Sea manuscripts. The pre-Pauline hymn to Christ in Phil. 2, like the theology which stands in the background of Colossians and Ephesians, shows that in certain Gnostic circles one could even fit the crucified One into the theological system. Besides, in addition to libertinism, Gnostic-ascetic tendencies also are opposed (Col. 2:16-23; Titus 1:14-15). This brief survey shows how diverse early Christian Gnosticism was, just as Jewish Gnosticism and gnosticizing Judaism were, and it certainly is not too much to say that, seen as a whole, even the individual expressions of early Christian Gnosticism have their precursors in Judaism. Thus there can be no serious doubt that Christian-Gnostic sects like the Sethians, Cainites, the Baruch Gnosticism of Justin,[33] and others were originally purely Jewish and venerated a hero of Jewish history as a redeeming bringer of Gnosis. The figure of Christ can mostly be

---

[33] Cf. R. Reitzenstein, [1], p. 60.

On the Baruch Gnosticism of the Gnostic Justin, cf. E. Haenchen, "Das Buch Baruch," ZThK 50 (1953) : 123 ff. This quite instructive study splendidly shows the dissolving of the original simple redeemer conception into a more elaborately told myth.

readily dissociated out of these systems.[34] Through the fact that its
second home was also the home of Gnosticism the Jewish nation was
clearly predestined to become an important mediator of the new religion to the West after the alien way of thinking had once found
entry into Judaism. Therefore also it is no accident but historically
conditioned that not only in the Corinthian epistles but also probably
in Colossians (cf. 2:16) and certainly in the Pastorals Jews are fought
as originators of the Gnostic heresy (Tit. 1:10, 14; I Tim. 1:7),[35] and
if the battle line of Ignatius in his epistles is a single one,[36] "Ἰου-
δαισμός" (Magn. 8:1; Philad. 6.1) denotes simply a Gnosticism.[37]

So much for the origin of Christian Gnosticism. It was my intention
only to draw the major line in which the Corinthian heresy which
we have investigated forms one point. That this latter was, according
to all appearances, common in the Syrian region or in the fringes of
that region has been stated and argued in various ways.

Syria is well attested as a hotbed of heresy, and indeed Antioch itself
in the post-apostolic era is anything but an undisputed stronghold of
orthodoxy (W. Bauer, pp. 65-72). If it is only in Asia Minor and
Greece that the apparently first collision between Paul and pure Gnosticism occurs, this shows, first, that the activity of the apostle in Arabia
(Gal. 1:17) and in the Syrian-Cilician region must have been locally
limited, and, second, that probably as an inheritance from the Jewish
era, the exchange between Hellenistic and Gnostic communities was
not very active and that both groups were hardly very numerous. The
struggle in Corinth itself which we have followed sounds like the pre-
lude to the great debate between church and Gnosticism which reached
its climax in the middle of the second century.

It is to be regretted that the combative fathers of the later church
in their struggle against Gnosticism no longer possessed the same

---

[34] This can be seen very clearly, e.g., in the Gnostic sect of the Melchizedekians,
for whom Christ is "only the shadow of Melchizedek" (O. Michel, *Der Brief an
die Hebräer*, Meyer *Kommentar*, XIII [8th ed.]: 160). Originally Melchizedek was
revered in Jewish or Samaritan Gnostic circles as the redeeming bearer of Gnosis.
Numerous traces of this have been preserved in various streams of tradition, among
others even in rabbinical polemics (see O. Michel, pp. 159 ff. and the literature
listed there). The ascendancy of Christianity then compelled the Melchizedekians
also to fit the Christian redeemer figure in their system, in which of course it was
and remained superfluous (Hipp. VII, 36; X, 24; Epiph. Haer. LV, 1; Ps.-Tert.
Haer. 88). Cf. *The Office of Apostle*, p. 138, n. 181.

[35] "The more ancient Gnosticism is, the more Jewish it is," writes T. Zahn (according to W. Lütgert, p. 47).

[36] This is disputed—incorrectly, of course—e.g., by H. Schlier, [2], p. 109.

[37] Ign. Magn. 8.1: "μὴ πλανᾶσθε ταῖς ἑτεροδοξίαις μηδὲ μυθεύμασιν τοῖς παλαιοῖς,
ἀνωφελέσιν οὖσιν. εἰ γὰρ μέχρι νῦν κατὰ νόμον Ἰουδαϊσμὸν ζῶμεν, ὁμολογοῦμεν χάριν
μὴ εἰληφέναι." According to Magn. 8.2, the assertion that there is not only *one* God
also belongs to these mythical heretics of "Jewish" origin.

thoughtful insight into the basic differences in Christian and Gnostic understandings of the world and of self which Paul at once gained from his genuine Christian attitude in spite of, or perhaps even because of, his defective knowledge of the mythologial background of the Gnostic self-consciousness. For this reason the ultimate victory over Gnosticism was bought by the church at a high price.

APPENDIX: TWO GNOSTIC GLOSSES IN II CORINTHIANS[1]

It is always awkward when in the interpretation of a text one must work with glosses. To excise a gloss always means an interference with the existing text, and however well founded may be the assertion that precisely thereby the *original* text is restored, still such an assertion is always at the mercy of every kind of contradiction.

On the other hand, it is utterly unscientific to interpret a text with the intention of proving the passages suspected of being glosses to be in the original text in any case. Anyone who knows even a little about the manuscript transmission of ancient texts must reckon in his interpretation with the possibility that his text contains intended or unintended additions. Only the unbiased testing of each individual case can elevate the suspicion to the level of probability or a greater or lesser degree of certainty, or prove the unlikelihood or the unjustifiability of such a suspicion.

In the ideal case it would follow that a passage should be interpreted as a gloss if

a) the section in the text that is in question is not unanimously attested,
b) it interrupts the context,
c) it is not even understandable in the context,
d) for reasons of language or of contents it must have been composed by a strange hand, and
e) it is in itself understandable and explainable as a gloss.

I. On II, 5:16[2]

We are concerned first with II, 5:16, probably the hardest *crux interpretum* of II Corinthians, which is not poor in such *cruces*. The verse is given as a conclusion from the preceding text. Hence we first must discern the meaning of the vss. 5:11-15. It is the merit of R. Bultmann[3] to have opened the way to the correct understanding of this section: On

---

[1] This first appeared in EvTheol 18 (1958) : 552-73; the version presented here has been revised, corrected, and expanded.

[2] Of the more recent literature I mention J. Cambier, "Connaissance charnelle et spirituelle du Christ dans 2. Cor. 5,16" (*Littérature et théologie pauliniennes, Rech. Bibl.* V [Brussels, 1960]: 72-92) ; J. B. Souček, "Wir kennen Christus nicht mehr nach dem Fleisch," EvTheol 19 (1959) : 300-314.

[3] [1], pp. 12 ff.

302

the one hand he points out that here as generally in large parts of II Cor. Paul defends his apostolic office, and on the other hand he shows that in vss. 11-15 Paul is debating with Gnostic Pneumatics and how he does it. I myself have adopted this interpretation in the foregoing investigation (pp. 187 ff.) and have expanded it. With reference to these two works I can briefly summarize the contents of the vss. II, 5:11-15 here:

The specific accusation of the Gnostic apostles was that Paul could only "persuade" men,[4] as some put it scornfully, i.e., that, as Paul himself formulates it, he could only soberly proclaim the word (σωφρονοῦμεν), instead of his demonstrating that φανέρωσις τοῦ πνεύματος (vs. 11) in ecstasy (vs. 13) which proves him to be a Pneumatic. Paul counters by saying that the ecstasy that is demanded concerns only his personal relationship to God (vss. 11, 13). But precisely as an apostle he has to live for others (vs. 13); one who has died with Christ can no longer live to himself (vss. 14-15). Hence the love of Christ compels him to preach the gospel to others (vs. 14). To boast of such a ministry is a glorying "ἐν καρδίᾳ," while on the other hand to boast of ecstasies is a glorying "ἐν προσώπῳ" (vs. 12). Paul does not intend with these statements to commend himself; rather the Corinthians are to hold up before those who dispute Paul's apostolic rights just this, that precisely where in refraining from ecstatic demonstrations he speaks the word soberly, Paul is performing the true apostolic ministry, which indeed is to be a ministry to others (vs. 12).

Thus vss. 5:11-15 offer a train of thought which is complete in itself. Both vss. 16 and 17 follow with ὥστε. Here lies a first difficulty. Is vs. 17 a conclusion from vs. 16, or does vs. 17 refer back past vs. 16 to vss. 14-15, so that a *double* conclusion is attached to the section 5:11-15? The answer cannot be difficult: vs. 17 is an immediate conclusion from vss. 14-15. "With vs. 17, beyond the special case handled in vs. 16, the general conclusion from . . . vss. 14, 15 is . . . given." [5] Verse 17 indeed describes in other and general concepts precisely that which vss. 14-15 said with a particular aim. The person who had "died with Christ" is "in Christ." "The old" has "passed away" through such a death. The "new" which has come into being is the "living no longer to self" of vs. 15.[6] This connection is so clear that one should not attempt to understand vs. 17 as a conclusion from vs. 16, as for example H. Windisch[7] does, although he sees that vs. 17 would "follow better

---

[4] The same charge from the same mouth appears in Gal. 1:10; see Vol. 2, pp. 39 ff.

[5] H. Lietzmann, p. 126; cf. R. Bultmann, [1], p. 17: "Verse 17 unfolds the idea of the ἄρα οἱ πάντες ἀπέθανον of verse 14."

[6] Cf. the exact parallel in Gal. 6:14-15.

[7] *Der zweite Korintherbrief*, p. 189.

on vs. 15." [8] The double conclusion from vss. 14-15 is of course syntactically unusual, but one will have to agree with P. Schmiedel [9] that Paul could "without too much negligence attach both ὥστε's to 15." I see fewer difficulties for the understanding of vss. 14-17 thus than if one tries to make vs. 17 comprehensible as a conclusion from vs. 16 because, as G. Heinrici [10] puts it, there would be set forth in the special case of vs. 16 the general situation which is expressed in vs. 17. (But can one infer the general from the particular in this way?)

But however one decides here, it is clear that vs. 16 not only would not be missed in the context, but that without vs. 16 the difficulties would be removed which are present in the hardly discernible logical connection of vs. 14 to vs. 17 or in the doubled ὥστε. Of course this fact lacks a great deal of being sufficient reason for excising vs. 16 as a gloss, as has been attempted occasionally.[11]

But vs. 16 offers still further difficulties. It is indeed given as an inference from vss. 14-15. Therefore a logical connection must be shown between vss. 14-15 and vs. 16. R. Bultmann ([1]) has attempted with great ingenuity to cite this proof. I reproduce this attempt in brief:

Those who glory ἐν προσώπῳ (vs. 12) are boasting of "outwardly visible advantages," and Paul's boasting on the contrary is—ἐν καρδίᾳ—a glorying "in the invisible." In vss. 14-15 then Paul sets forth how and why he has turned from the "world of the visible" to the "invisible." "In vss. 14-15 there is a double affirmation: (1) negatively, that Paul in his worldly appearance is not significant, and therefore there cannot be a καυχώμενος ἐν προσώπῳ; and (2) that he is what he is in the service of others." "The apostle (the Christian) is dead with respect to the sensible bodily existence, so that all καυχᾶσθαι ἐν προσώπῳ (vs. 12) is at an end." Verse 16 now draws from that the necessary inference: "Since with us all it is all over with respect to the sarkical existence, the world of the senses, our judgment concerning men may not and cannot be any longer oriented to the world of the senses." Therefore, so the Corinthians are to conclude, "you must not adhere to those who ἐν προσώπῳ καυχῶνται . . . . Instead, you as καινὴ κτίσις must also understand me as καινὴ κτίσις. This inference Paul leaves to the readers."

Hence in this interpretation vs. 16 necessarily belongs to the train of thought of Paul from vs. 11 onward, for this train of thought indeed

[8] *Ibid.,* n. 2.

[9] *Die Briefe an die Corinther,* p. 245.

[10] *Der zweite Brief des Paulus an die Korinther,* p. 210.

[11] D. Völter, *Paulus und seine Briefe,* pp. 88 ff.; also, in *Theol. Tijdschrift,* 1889, p. 301. Cf. J. Weiss, *Paulus und Jesus* (1909) , p. 27.

ends only with the unexpressed inference which is to be supplied after vs. 16.

It is, however, in my judgment inconceivable that Paul would leave unspoken the very conclusion to which his entire argument is supposed to be aiming. Already on this point Bultmann's attempt to connect vs. 16 closely with the preceding verses appears to me to fail.

Moreover, the subject in vss. 12-15 is not at all the end of "worldly appearance." When Paul says that he has died with Christ, this can only mean, as always with him, that he has died to *sin*, here concretely the sin of "living for self." Thus in vss. 14-15 Paul is not affirming that he is not significant in his "worldly appearance" but that the old man is dead to sin. He is not portraying his turning from the world of the visible to the world of the invisible, but from the service of sin to the service of righteousness. Thus also the glorying ἐν προσώπῳ is not a boasting of outwardly visible advantages but the false, unfounded glorying of the "old man," while the glorying ἐν καρδίᾳ is the justified glorying of the new man. Thus also the apostle is not dead "with respect to the sensible bodily existence"—how is one to conceive of that at all—but with respect to sinful existence, his *ungodly* glorying! 389

But then vs. 16 no longer fits, if one tries to understand it as a necessary continuation of the argument of vss. 12 ff.! For now indeed —if we maintain Bultmann's outline of the line of thought[12]—by analogy it must follow: Therefore man must be judged according to whether he is old man or new man.[13] But in *no* case does vs. 16 say that. For whatever is to be understood by "Χριστὸς κατὰ σάρκα," Paul could indeed conceive of Christ as an outwardly visible man, but not as the "old man." Hence Bultmann's argument characteristically displaces the meaning of vss. 12-15 in order to be able to fit vs. 16 into the line of thought.[14]

[12] Of course its weakness is in the fact that vss. 14-15 specifically justify Paul's conduct that is under attack, namely his sober preaching, while the thought that is required for vs. 16, that the apostle or even the Corinthians are rendered capable of a new *judgment about others,* is quite remote from these verses.

[13] Verse 17 then as a consequence drawn from vss. 14-15 also speaks of the old and the new man, a sign that our understanding of vss. 12-15 is correct.

[14] D. Georgi ([1], p. 255, n. 3) objects: "The alternative offered by Schmithals, . . . either 'boasting of outwardly visible advantages' or 'the false, unfounded boasting of the old man,' actually is not an alternative, but it is a matter of two sides of one and the same thing, wherein the second is Paul's theological characterization of the first . . . . Bound up therewith is a misunderstanding, already revealed in the work on Gnosticism, of the dialectical character of the Pauline argument as Bultmann has persuasively worked it out." Here the actual state of affairs has been turned upside down. Of course I do not contradict the first sentence. But Georgi should not direct this objection against *my* interpretation but against that of Bultmann! Georgi has not understood that I am criticizing Bultmann for the very reason that he (Bultmann) establishes this alternative in order to make vs. 16 comprehensible in the context; for precisely because in II, 5:11 ff. Paul formulates

It will not be worthwhile to refute other, less satisfactory attempts
to fit vs. 16 into the course of thought from vs. 11 onward. For it is
390 evident anyway that vss. 11-15 set forth a self-contained argument:
Paul wishes to give the community an indication as to how they can
defend his authoritative apostolic office as over against the rivals who
charge him with a deficiency as regards ecstatic experiences (vs. 12).
This "ἀφορμή" stands in vs. 11 and is repeated in vs. 13: ecstasies as
an expression of personal religion do not belong to the ministry of the
apostle. The sober communication of the message of salvation to others
on the other hand is the best proof that Paul is an apostle. Verse 11a
at the beginning of the argument, like vss. 14-15 at its end, offers the
justification for such right conduct: the fear of the Lord or the love
of Christ—rightly understood the two are one for Paul—demands
obedient service to others. Any further statement is not necessary in
this well-rounded argument.

Of course this still does not prove that vs. 16 could not logically and
analogously be connected with vss. 14-15. It remains the most often
selected possibility to understand vs. 16 indeed not as conclusion and
climax of the train of thought but in fact as one of the "characteristic
Pauline parentheses." [15] Verse 16 then introduces a new idea, which
is logically joined to vss. 14-15 thus: Because we have died with Christ,
i.e., have become new creatures, thus because we no longer live to ourselves, we no longer know anyone according to the flesh, and so forth.
The discomfort which seizes the exegetes in such logic is understandable. For what the apostolic "living for others," of which vs. 15 speaks,
has to do with the *estimations* concerning others, of which vs. 16 speaks,
is in fact utterly without explanation. One would have to do as
H. Lietzmann does and connect vs. 16 with the πάντες ἀπέθανον of vs.
14, which now undergoes a new interpretation that no longer takes
vs. 15 into account. But with such a leap in thought Paul expects too
much of the reader.

Of course the interpretation which considers vs. 16 a parenthesis
becomes still more problematical if one inquires as to the material
content of the parenthetical idea expressed in vs. 16. Here fantasy has
abundant room to play, and the expositors indeed have not been
sparing with venturesome interpretations.

It is most plausible to think of the parenthetical idea as having

his argument "dialectically," vs. 16b is incomprehensible and Bultmann's attempt to
eliminate that dialectic is understandable. I do not presume to deny that my interpretation means "a clear retreat from Bultmann's analysis" (D. Georgi, [1], p. 255).
But in view of the fact that Georgi has fundamentally misunderstood the discussion
with Bultmann, this sentence is nevertheless distressing.

[15] H. Lietzmann, p. 125. J. Weiss, *Paulus und Jesus* (1909), p. 27.

arisen out of the concrete polemical situation in which Paul found himself. That would at least somewhat account for it. H. Lietzmann[16] thinks accordingly that in vs. 16b Paul is defending himself against the charge of his judaizing opponents that he has no personal acquaintance with Jesus to show. In such an interpretation then emerges the well-known problem of whether vs. 16b gives information about a direct acquaintance of Paul with Jesus. In vs. 16a also, H. Lietzmann sees a refutation of boasting on the basis of earthly advantages which certain people claim, without being able to say anything more specific about this. This most plausible interpretation already runs aground— apart from all the rest—on the fact that in Corinth Paul is indeed debating with Jews but by no means with Judaizers. His opponents are indeed themselves the ones who reject the cross (I, 1:17 ff.) and can even utter an "ἀνάθεμα ᾽Ιησοῦς" (I, 12:3). How are these people supposed to have been self-assertive with respect to Paul with their personal knowledge of the fleshly Christ! [17]

Bo Reicke[18] has correctly sensed this. Therefore he interprets vs. 16 in passing to mean that Paul *concedes* to the docetic Gnostics: Even though earlier I knew Christ in an earthly manner, yet now I know him only pneumatically, as you do. This is the best explanation I have found of vs. 16 if it is understood as a parenthetical thought, even though, as we shall see presently, it is not tenable.

391

The other expositions, out of whose "confusingly large number" H. Windisch[19] has compiled the most important, are not able even to give a concrete motivation for the parenthesis. But still one may not forgo an explanation, not even if one holds vs. 16 to have been added later by Paul.[20] We can spare ourselves the work here of developing and refuting these numerous attempts at interpretation in detail, because every commentary contains such refutations and is generally convincing. But above all such labor is unnecessary because it can be shown that vs. 16 cannot have been written by Paul at all, whatever it may intend to say as to contents.

The following investigation may prove this. It is to be assumed that vs. 16a and vs. 16b may only be seen in perfect parallelism. Further, the twofold possibility of connecting the "κατὰ σάρκα" to the verbs or to the substantives is to be considered separately. One cannot, as for example H. Windisch does, determine in advance that both forms

---

[16] HNT 9, *in loc.*

[17] Our verse after all should not be drawn into the discussion of the question of the so-called historical Jesus, which is remote from the verse, from the Corinthian epistles generally, and indeed even from the whole of primitive Christianity.

[18] *Diakonie, Festfreude und Zelos*, p. 277.

[19] *Der zweite Korintherbrief*, pp. 186 ff.

[20] See in P. Schmiedel, *Die Briefe an die Corinther*, p. 245.

proceed from the same motivation. That could be, but it can be asserted only after the exegesis has been done. The author of the verse must have used the doubled κατὰ σάρκα in the same way in both places. Finally, a comment about Paul's use of κατὰ σάρκα must be mentioned in advance. Wherever Paul places κατὰ σάρκα with substantives (Rom. 1:3; 4:1; 9:3, 5; 8:5; I Cor. 1:26;[21] 10:18) the person in his physico-psychical character is meant; thus κατὰ σάρκα denotes man insofar as he is *naturally born*, and in contrast to all additional "spiritual" connections and objectivities; in this use κατὰ σάρκα means the same as φύσει or ἐκ φύσεως.[22] With verbs, on the other hand, with the exception of Gal. 4:23, 29, κατὰ σάρκα is used ethically. And in the truest sense of the saying this exception proves the rule, for the verb γεννᾶν, which in itself already expresses the natural-born state, here possesses its own rules. For it could in fact even be omitted in both passages or be replaced by εἶναι. No judgment is being expressed about birth or procreation. Rather the *one born* is characterized as ἄνθρωπος κατὰ σάρκα, i.e., as a man of mere "createdness" with "pneumatic" significance. Thus Gal. 4:23, 29 in fact belongs to those passages in which κατὰ σάρκα applies to substantives and in form stands closest to Rom. 8:5a.

The uniqueness of this dual usage is not accidental. In it Paul is adopting Gnostic concepts. Gnosticism divides man into the two contrasting parts σάρξ and πνεῦμα. This dualism allows a distinction between man κατὰ σάρκα, that is, man insofar as he is σάρξ, and the same man κατὰ πνεῦμα, that is, insofar as he is Pneuma.[23] But in Gnosticism man is κατὰ σάρκα in the entirety of his createdness. From this perspective one can understand Paul's usage which can call man σάρξ—to this extent wholly in agreement with the Old Testament— and can distinguish him as such from himself κατὰ πνεῦμα—in this respect really foreign to the Old Testament.

For Gnosticism the createdness of man, i.e. man κατὰ σάρκα, is an expression of the evil. The real man is the ἄνθρωπος κατὰ πνεῦμα.

[21] This passage is no exception. I do not know precisely what is the intention of R. Bultmann's remark: "But when the 'wise' are called 'wise after the flesh,' the addition does not mean 'so far as they are empirical phenomena within the world,' but ' (wise) so far as a wisdom according to the norms of "flesh" is concerned'; 'the wise' is equivalent to a verb in the above discussion" ([2], I: 238) . In any case Paul intends to say: You are not *born* wise, you are not φύσει σοφοί, but have your wisdom ἐν Χριστῷ (I, 1:30) .

[22] R. Bultmann, [2], I: 237.

[23] Cf. the First Book of Jeu 3 = Schmidt-Till, pp. 259.30 ff.; *Die Geschichte von Joseph dem Zimmermann* (TU 56 [1951]) , 2.6; 4.2; 17.14; Sah. 23.8; 30.8; 31.7.

In the background of Rom. 8:5, οἱ κατὰ σάρκα ὄντες . . . there is, correspondingly, the Gnostic division of *humanity* into the group of the mere Sarkics, who possess no spark of Pneuma, and that of the Pneumatics, for whom the σάρξ is the dwelling of the real Self.

Hence any action which occurs κατὰ σάρκα, i.e., in such a way as if the essential man were σάρξ, is reprehensible. Such activity occurs in the sphere of enmity against God, of the demonic, of the vain, empty, and perishable. From this perspective is explained the usage, unthinkable for the Old Testament, that all action κατὰ σάρκα is a sinful action.

Thus with the double and characteristically distinguished usage Paul stands firmly in the Gnostic tradition, though he naturally does not also adopt the dualism with its condemnation of the ἄνθρωπος κατὰ σάρκα, but makes the alien terminology serviceable to his Old Testament-historical way of thinking.

Now let us attempt to understand vs. 16 under the presupposition that the κατὰ σάρκα is related to the verbs. Until recently this possibility was rejected by a majority of those exegetes who make a distinction here at all.[24] In reading one is inclined purely intuitively in vs. 16a to connect κατὰ σάρκα with οὐδένα. And since vs. 16b only takes up again the wording of vs. 16a with an emphatic relocation of Χριστόν, vs. 16b cannot negate this interpretation which to be sure is only emotional.

But how impossible it is to make the reference apply to the verbs is shown by the following consideration: In this case κατὰ σάρκα can indeed only have the ethical sense, and Paul would be arguing: "From the moment when I died with Christ I know or judge no one any longer in a sinful way. Yea, even though I once knew Christ as a sinful man, yet no longer do I now." The absurdity of such an argument is obvious if one once puts himself in the situation of the writer. For if one no longer regards anyone in a fleshly manner, then it is obvious that Christ—the very Christ with whom one has died to such judgment —is the first one who is regarded κατὰ πνεῦμα, so that a person could not possibly get the idea of inferring: Because we no longer regard even Christ κατὰ σάρκα, we naturally also no longer regard any other man in a fleshly manner.[25] That would be the same as if—to offer an extreme example—a murderer should say, "From now on I will not kill a fly; indeed, even if I earlier have killed men, I now will do so no more."

[24] It has recently been represented by O. Michel in EvTheol 14 (1954) : 22 ff., esp. p. 23; also by E. Schweizer in TWNT VII: 130-31; J. B. Souček (see above, p. 302, n. 2) , p. 304. Also in the Revised Standard Version of 1946, "even though we have known Christ after the flesh" is replaced by "even though we once regarded Christ from a human point of view." This is followed by the revised Luther text of 1956.

[25] Nevertheless this still E. Schweizer's understanding of it in TWNT VII: 130.27-28: "He himself intends no longer to judge anyone thus (scil., according to human standards) . Verse 16b shows how absurd that would be." But this is precisely what vs. 16b does not show.

The argument of vs. 16 then would have meaning, if any, if κατὰ σάρκα were to be referred to the objects, as will presently be suggested; for it is understandable when one attributes to the Χριστὸς κατὰ σάρκα a greater significance than to the ordinary man κατὰ σάρκα. But to conclude that, since one does not even regard Christ any longer κατὰ σάρκα, one has no sinful opinion any longer about men in general, is absurd.

This objection would not be answerable even if one wanted to understand vs. 16*b* not as heightening but only following the preceding, wherein Christ would be mentioned then for illustration or as an example of the declaration of vs. 16*a*. For since εἰ καὶ cannot reasonably be understood in any way but as a heightening, this would not only be an awkward dilemma, but Christ would then remain the most inappropriate special case conceivable for the opinion that Paul intends to know *no one* any longer in a fleshly sinful way.

Hence there remains only the possibility of connecting κατὰ σάρκα with the substantives. Then according to Paul's usage, κατὰ σάρκα must have the psychical-physical sense which we have described. But how are we to imagine that Paul intends to know no one anymore in his morally neutral, psychical-physical appearance? [26] How should one avoid this? What would be reprehensible about it? Surely Paul is not a Gnostic!

Further, and above all, this interpretation is not possible because the Χριστὸς κατὰ σάρκα of vs. 16*b* is of decisive significance in the salvation-history for Paul, and indeed precisely in view of the dispute with the Corinthians who declare Ἰησοῦς, that is the Χριστὸς κατὰ σάρκα, to be without significance and even curse him. The polemic against the ἄλλον Ἰησοῦς[27] and the emphasizing of the cross[28] signify just as decisive a clinging to this Χριστὸς κατὰ σάρκα as do the passages Gal. 4:4; Rom. 1:3; 9:5, and many others. Thus it would be foolish to seek to assert that Paul wants to know nothing of the naturally born, crucified, and resurrected Jesus of Nazareth. In what way he holds him to be significant is an entirely different question which does not belong here.

Even if one refers the κατὰ σάρκα to the substantives, therefore, vs. 16 is not comprehensible on the lips of Paul.

Now the majority of the exegetes thread their way between the Scylla and Charybdis of these two closed possibilities by wrongly attributing to the Χριστὸς κατὰ σάρκα a sense which it never had with

[26] Cf. J. B. Souček, "Wir kennen Christus nicht mehr nach dem Fleisch," p. 307.
[27] II, 11:4; cf. pp. 132 ff.
[28] I, 1:17 ff.; cf. pp. 135 ff.

Paul elsewhere, and cannot have. F. C. Baur[29] explains that the Christ κατὰ σάρκα is the Messiah of Judaism. H. Windisch thinks (p. 188) that the Χριστὸς κατὰ σάρκα is "Jesus before the Passion," the "savior in Palestine," the "teacher and prophet," whom Paul wants to know no longer. H. Lietzmann (p. 125) interprets it thus: There is "for me no one any longer whose earthly circumstances trouble me in any way, . . . not even the circumstances of the earthly life of Christ." Thus the Χριστὸς κατὰ σάρκα is the Christ in the "circumstances of his earthly life." G. Heinrici (p. 206) formulates somewhat more precisely: To know someone according to the flesh means "to know someone according to merely human appearance, to know him in such a way that one has formed a judgment about him according to what he is by virtue of his natural and earthly form of existence." For Jesus, then, according to Heinrici, Paul no longer knows the Jewish ancestry,[30] the Davidic origin,[31] or the circumcision.[32] Similarly Bengel, *in loc.*: "*Secundum carnem, secundum statem veterem, ex nobilitate, divitiis, opibus, sapientia.*" R. Bultmann ([1], p. 17) thinks: ". . . since with all of us it is all over with respect to the sarkical existence, the world of the senses . . ."; cf. in *Faith and Understanding*, I: 217: Christ "is a Jew according to the flesh (Rom. 9:5) ." According to D. Georgi ([1], pp. 282 ff.) the Χριστὸς κατὰ σάρκα is the θεῖος ἀνήρ, endowed with a "sensational life-force" and as an "outstanding Pneumatic" paralleled with Moses, of Paul's Corinthian opponents.   392

These examples may suffice. They could be enlarged at will. Common to them all is the fact that the significance of the κατὰ σάρκα was so softened that at least vs. 16*b*, and in part even vs. 16*a*, can be understood in the context of Pauline theology. These interpretations also allow one in part to leave open the question of the syntactical connection of the κατὰ σάρκα. A Christ who is known only from worldly appearance is in fact also to be recognized only in his worldly appearance. That these interpretations also do not rightly regard the total context need not be noted further here, for they are all disposed of with the observation that understanding of the κατὰ σάρκα presupposed in them appears nowhere in Paul and is even ruled out for him.

When Paul uses κατὰ σάρκα in a neutral sense—and an ethical indifferentism of this designation is assumed by all these interpreta-

[29] "Die Christuspartei in der korinthischen Gemeinde," *Tübinger Zeitschrift*, 1831.

[30] But look at Rom. 9:5!

[31] But look at Rom. 1:3!

[32] But look at Gal. 4:4!

tions—he does indeed always refer to the worldly appearance, but always understands this in such a way that it embraces the whole man in his natural, begotten state. To this also belongs his activity, for example as teacher, and also his appearance, his cleverness, and so on. But never does κατὰ σάρκα designate a man purely spiritualized in view of individual ones of his mundanely perceivable qualities or activities with the explicit exception of his psychical or physical createdness. Yet that must be the case with the above-mentioned interpretations, since in fact it ultimately is none other than the mundanely perceivable Christ who was born of the seed of David, came under the law, and was hung on the cross. Paul certainly knows *this* Christ. And Paul likewise certainly can never leave out of account this mundanely perceivable Christ when, as in Rom. 1:3 and 9:5, he speaks of the Χριστὸς κατὰ σάρκα. He certainly could have said that he no longer wished to know (or acknowledge) the circumcision, the ancestry, etc., of men and of Christ. But he could not express that with "no longer to know Χριστὸς κατὰ σάρκα." Χριστὸς κατὰ σάρκα is the circumcised descendant of David, Jesus of Nazareth, and as the crucified One he stands at the center of the Pauline theology. It is contrary to all rules of exegesis when in the presence of such a clear and excellent attestation of what Χριστὸς κατὰ σάρκα means in Paul's writings, one attributes, in such a difficult verse as the present one, to the κατὰ σάρκα a sense which not only is undocumented but which we also can understand as derived from the actual meaning only with our modern abstract way of thinking.[33]

This is all the more true since Paul indeed is not even the creator of this terminology. Perhaps he then would have been able to stand over against it with some freedom. But he in fact unconsciously uses the already given Gnostic language and therefore can understand by τὶς κατὰ σάρκα nothing at all but man in all his creatureliness; more-

[33] According to D. Georgi ([1], pp. 291-92), "Schmithals fails to see that according to Paul's opinion the form of manifestation and the empirical character of the object of knowledge as such do not define Christian existence. The resurrection of Christ and the fact of the new creation are rather the noetic presupposition even for the understanding of pre-Christian and non-Christian existence . . . ." Of course I agree with this. But where have I failed to see this? In our passage this problematic is not even under discussion if, as Georgi rightly and very decidedly does, one denies the connection of the κατὰ σάρκα to the verbs of knowing (p. 291). For then it is a question of what κατὰ σάρκα in Paul's writings means, if this concept more precisely defines man as the *object* of knowing. And here the answer is unequivocal: it means man simply in his character of an "empirical phenomenon within the world." This is no awareness of the "new creation," but of philology! We may readily concede to Georgi (p. 292) that nowhere in Paul is this man "immediately and in himself accessible to knowledge." But this does not alter the fact that this man κατὰ σάρκα who is inaccessible to immediate knowledge is simply the earthly empirical man (Jesus) who as such—under whatever aspect of mediated Christian knowledge—is the Alpha and Omega of Pauline faith.

over, he *may* not understand by this anything else if he wants still to be understandable to his hearers; for even for these the Χριστὸς κατὰ σάρκα is indeed not the "historical Jesus" of the nineteenth century but the crucified Jesus of Nazareth.

Thus vs. 16 not only breaks the connection of vss. 14-15 with vs. 17, but in my opinion it cannot at all be made comprehensible as Pauline. It is to be excised as a non-Pauline gloss. Thereby the train of thought of II, 5:11-17 ff. is relieved of any extraordinary exegetical difficulty. Verse 17 follows the preceding insofar as it no longer asserts only the "living for others" but the whole new creation of man as a result of dying with Christ—the terminology of the mysteries is evident—and leads to the following verses, in which the office of the new-creating proclamation is praised, which indeed is the proper office of the apostle: the main apologetic theme is not abandoned!

The meaning of the gloss likewise can now be seen at once if one no longer has to bring it into harmony with Pauline theology. The glossator says that he intends to know no one anymore in his natural existence, not even Christ. For Christ this means that the earthly figure of the man, the man Jesus as the dwelling of the celestial light-being, is rejected. Thereby the source of the gloss also is already cleared up. It stems from the hand of one of the dualistic Gnostics to whom the apostle's polemic in 5:11 ff. applies. One may assume that some such person, whether a converted member of the community or one of the immigrant heretics themselves, read the epistle and thereupon wrote in the margin at vs. 17 the comment which slipped into the text in an early copy as vs. 16. It must be conceded to the glossator that his inference is thoroughly logical if he understands vs. 17 in the Gnostic sense. And since with "εἴ τις ἐν Χριστῷ" Paul is speaking in Gnostic terminology which was still being employed in Corinth in its original mythological sense,[34] the Gnostic inference is but self-evident.[35] For the Corinthian form of early "Christian" Gnosticism, "Christ" is indeed the sum of all the Pneuma-sparks, and thus in this sense every Pneumatic is "τοῦ Χριστοῦ,"[36] i.e., a part of the heavenly Pneuma-Christ. But whoever is "of Christ" or "ἐν Χριστῷ," and thus in the final analysis is himself "Christ," looks with contempt upon the σάρξ. Indeed he has seen through it as the vain creation of the demons, and he knows that the body is only the prison-house of the inner Pneuma-

[34] Cf. pp. 193 ff.

[35] Cf., e.g., the Gnostic parallel from Od. Sol. 17.4: "He broke off my fetters/I received the face and form of a new person/and I walked in it and was redeemed."

[36] I, 1:12; II, 10:7.

Christ. No longer to know anyone according to the flesh, no longer to know even the crucified Christ, is the triumphant victory cry of the Gnostics who in Paul's words think of themselves as already rich, as already having attained lordship (I, 4:8). Thus the sense of vs. 16 is:

ὥστε (i.e., because for the person who is ἐν Χριστῷ, everything old, even the old man of flesh, has passed away);

ἡμεῖς (i.e., emphatically: we Gnostics; we who set for ourselves the Χριστοῦ ἐσμεν in opposition to a Παύλου κτλ. ἐσμέν);[37]

ἀπὸ τοῦ νῦν (i.e. from the time when we know ourselves to be ἐν Χριστῷ, ever since we possess the Gnosis about ourselves, since our ecstatic experiences reveal to us the inner Pneuma-Christ. One might assume that the glossator was a recently "converted" former member of the Pauline community in Corinth);

οὐδένα (no man);

οἴδαμεν (this is not to be weakened but is to be taken in the fullest sense: he does not even exist for us; we will have nothing to do with him: Matt. 25:12);

κατὰ σάρκα (insofar as he is naturally born; so far as he is visible and tangible, so far as he is body, creation of the demons);

εἰ καὶ ἐγνώκαμεν (γινώσκω instead of οἶδα, because there is no form of οἶδα with a perfect tense significance. Naturally the glossator is not thinking of a personal acquaintanceship with Jesus but means: Even if to us members of the young Gnostic community acquaintance with the crucified Jesus and his significance has earlier been imparted by the preaching, for example, of Paul, this now concerns us no longer. Certainly not all the members of the Gnostic community in Corinth came out of the church's community there. Thus not all had to deny their "knowledge" of the fleshly Christ. Hence the real conditional clause which usually causes so much perplexity to the theologians and philologists; see R. Reitzenstein, [1], pp. 374 ff.);

κατὰ σάρκα Χριστόν (this is the "Jesus" of II, 11:4, to whom the anathema of I, 12:3 pertains, thus the earthly dwelling of the heavenly Pneuma-Christ);

ἀλλὰ νῦν (i.e., from now on, however, since we know ourselves to be "in Christ");

οὐκέτι γινώσκομεν (he concerns us no longer).

Therewith vs. 16b now rightly follows vs. 16a in an intensification; for it is still more venturesome to reject the figure of Jesus of Nazareth, who outside the extremely dualistic area had the highest significance

[37] Cf. I, 1:12.

as Messiah, as θεῖος ἀνήρ, as ἐσταυρομένος and ἐγηγερμένος, than the earthly appearance of the ordinary man, whose transformation indeed even Paul awaits with longing. This holds true especially if the glossator was up until recently a member of the Pauline church community. It is only natural that later Gnostic exegesis made use of this verse in order to prove that Christ did not have a body of flesh.[38]

Thus of the five conditions stated above for the ideal determination of a gloss, four are met. Lacking only is the disunited literary attestation. Now this lack is also frequently found elsewhere in genuine glosses. If, as our interpretation suggests, the original letter of Paul apparently already had the gloss added in Corinth, then we may not even expect that the later tradition would exhibit vs. 16 in any way other than unanimously.

It is evident that the interpretation given here satisfactorily solves all the problems of II, 5:16 and splendidly reestablishes an interrupted connection. A "better" exposition might hardly be possible, if one does not regard it as "bad" in general to reckon with glosses in the biblical literature.

From Paul's polemic, we can deduce with utter clarity *that* the false teachers in Corinth were Gnostic dualists and that they sharply rejected especially the crucified Jesus, i.e., the Christ κατὰ σάρκα, proclaimed by Paul, just as they rejected the body of man in general.[39] II, 5:16 now fits splendidly into this picture as a Gnostic gloss and thus succeeds in confirming points of information already gained.   393

II. On II, 3:17-18[40]

It has always been difficult for the exegetes to fit vs. 17 into the context intelligibly. It cannot be disputed that the verse interrupts the connection in a way which is not at once understandable and unnecessarily obstructs the flow of thought.[41] Verse 18 best follows directly after vs. 16.

In addition, there is the fact that the identification of Christ and

---

[38] E.g., Faustus Manich. in Calovius, *Bibl. ill.*, pp. 463-64.

[39] See pp. 124-41.

[40] On the following, see the sensitive study by J. Hermann, *Kyrios und Pneuma* (1961).

[41] "But since vs. 18 refers to the taking away of the veil, it is evident that vs. 17 is an auxiliary sentence . . ." (G. Heinrici, p. 134). P. Bachmann (p. 172) speaks of the "uncertainty in general which has often appeared in the exposition with reference to fitting vss. 17-18 into the context." H. Windisch (p. 124) calls vs. 17 a "parenthetical remark," "which at first glance interrupts the course of thought in a manner difficult for us to comprehend." "In such a cohesive train of thought (i.e., of vss. 16 and 18), what is the sudden insertion of the Spirit and of freedom supposed to mean?" (M. Dibelius, *Botschaft und Geschichte*, II: 128).

Pneuma, as it appears explicitly to be achieved by Paul here, is thoroughly un-Pauline. This is, of course, disputed by many exegetes, especially since from F. C. Baur to W. Bousset,[42] thus from the idealistic perspective as well as from the religio-historical perspective, some had thought that in the equation κύριος = πνεῦμα they had found a foundation of the entire Pauline Christology. But Bousset let himself be led astray by Paul's terminology. It is correct that in their original meaning, Paul's concepts which originated in Gnosticism had equated Christ with the Pneuma.[43] This is still clearly expressed where Paul speaks this language.[44] Nevertheless there can be no doubt that Paul makes a strict distinction in his *mind* between Christ and the Spirit.[45] Christ bestows the Spirit; the Spirit is a medium of the Christ at work.[46] The functions which Christ and the Spirit perform are indeed in essence the same, but this must not obscure the fact that as to person Christ is in principle separate from the Pneuma. Paul adopts the substantial conception of the Pneuma which often appears in his theology as an alien element indirectly by way of the pre-Pauline Christian communities from Gnosticism, and with the help of his Jewish tradition he transforms the Spirit which was originally identical with Christ into an instrument through which Christ becomes effectual with respect to man. The difficulty which the fitting of the Pneuma into his theological thinking caused him is already shown in the fact that he appears constantly to alternate between the Greek conception of a Pneumasubstance which occupies space and the abstract Jewish conception, according to which only the divine δύναμις belongs to the Pneuma of God. And from the same cause springs the very inability to distinguish between the effects of the κύριος and the πνεῦμα and therewith the capacity for confusing the two concepts to a considerable extent after the Gnostic example,[47] which then misleads the exegetes into the really untenable judgment that vs. 17a is the key to the Pauline Christology.[48]

[42] *Kyrios Christos* (1st ed.) , pp. 126, 142 ff. See in E. Güttgemanns, *Der leidende Apostel und sein Herr,* pp. 342 ff.

[43] Cf., e.g., Epiph. Haer. XXX, 3: "εἰς αὐτὸν ἦλθε τὸ πνεῦμα, ὅπερ ἐστὶν ὁ Χριστός, καὶ ἐνεδύσατο αὐτὸν τὸν Ἰησοῦν καλούμενον." Hipp. X, 21: "πεπονθέναι τὸν Ἰησοῦν, τὸν δὲ Χριστὸν ἀπαθῆ μεμενηκέναι, πνεῦμα κυρίου ὑπάρχοντα." According to Hipp. VI, 49.5, the Gnostic Marcus calculated the numerical values for "dove (= Holy Spirit) and Alpha and Omega (= Christ) both at 801. Thus Christ = Pneuma (cf. H. Leisegang, *Die Gnosis* [4th ed.], p. 41) . See also pp. 58-59; 63, n. 152. Cf. also Iren. I, 13.5; Hipp. VI, 36; Ign. Magn. 15; II Clem. 14.4.

[44] E.g., Rom. 8:9-11; see above, p. 63; I, 15:45.

[45] E.g., II, 13:3; cf. G. Friedrich in *Wort und Dienst,* 1952, p. 64.

[46] Gal. 4:6-7.

[47] Cf. 4:4-7; Rom. 8:9-11.

[48] On the basic question one may compare R. Bultmann, [2], § 38, who also provides the necessary evidence, and on the details, W. G. Kümmel in H. Lietzmann, on p. 113, ll. 23-32; H. Windisch, *Der zweite Korintherbrief,* p. 125; E. Fuchs, *Christus und der Geist bei Paulus* (1932) , pp. 5-6.

Hence vs. 17a cannot be meant in the sense of an identification of κύριος and πνεῦμα. Besides, this interpretation makes the verse a "superfluous parenthetical christological remark," [49] and M. Dibelius rightly affirms that then one can all the less comprehend "why this basic principle is expressed just here, between an Old Testament quotation and its application." [50]

394

395

In recent times vs. 17 has been understood by most as an exegetical gloss by Paul to clarify vs. 16.[51] The verse is then to be set in parentheses, so that vs. 18 follows directly after vs. 16, which in fact alone is correct, and serves to simplify for the reader the interpretation of vs. 16. Whether this explanation is correct can be said only after the train of thought of the entire context is clarified.

Paul finds himself in dispute with those who contest his apostolic rights. Over against them he describes to the community his ministry of the new—not the old—covenant, as a ministry of the Spirit—not of the letter (3:4-6).

Even the ministry of the old covenant was performed in glory, as Paul infers from Exod. 34:29 ff., although it was a transient ministry. How much more, Paul argues by inference, will the ministry of the new, abiding covenant be a glorious one (3:7-11)!

In such hope the ministry of the New Testament apostle is performed in great boldness and not in the fashion of Moses. The remark from Exod. 34:33 ff. to the effect that in connection with the proclamation of the law Moses veiled his face for a time is interpreted by Paul to mean that the Jews should not see the perishable nature of the Mosaic law (3:12-13). Moses is here the type of the apostle; in comparison with his lowly ministry the glory of the New Testament apostle should appear especially brilliant. The consequences of this veiling were that the Jews did not recognize the provisional character of their law. Indeed, their minds were so blinded that even yet today in the reading of the books of the old covenant this concealing veil hides from them the correct understanding of those books. It has not disappeared, because it can be taken away only by Christ, that is, because only from the perspective of Christ can the true significance of the law and therewith the provisional character of the old covenant be recognized (3:14).

In vs. 15 and vs. 16 the two expressions of vs. 14 are repeated in

[49] W. G. Kümmel in H. Lietzmann, on p. 113, ll. 23-32.
[50] M. Dibelius, *Botschaft und Geschichte.*
[51] See W. G. Kümmel in H. Lietzmann, on p. 113, ll. 23-32, and the literature listed there; also, *Kirchenbegriff . . . ,* p. 46, n. 19a. M. Dibelius, *Botschaft und Geschichte.*

essence and in the same order. "But to this day a veil lies over their hearts when 'Moses' is read" (vs. 15). "But when one turns to the Lord, the veil is taken away" (vs. 16). Verse 18 then logically follows this: "But we all (i.e., first 'we apostles,' and then Christians generally also) reflect with unveiled face the glory of the Lord," i.e., we put no veil over our faces but preach with great boldness (vss. 12-13), without fear, since we proclaim not the transitory law but the glory of the Lord.

If we understand vs. 18 thus, then in this concluding verse as in the entire midrash the subject is the contrast "Moses-Paul," i.e., the ministry of the old and that of the new covenant. That the emissaries of Christ, in contrast to Moses with his veiled countenance, reflect the glory of the Lord—precisely this is the παρρησία which according to vs. 12 distinguishes them from the ministers of the old covenant.

To be sure, vss. 15 and 16 brought with them a distinctive shift in thought as compared with vss. 13-14, which they repeat. While according to vss. 13-14 the covering lay over the face of Moses, according to vss. 15-16 it lay upon the hearts of the Israelites. It is easy to assume that Paul writes down vss. 15 and 16, which otherwise have nothing new as over against vss. 13-14, in order to give expression to this shift. But then in vs. 18 also it is no longer the apostles but the community that is the subject, and we should have to read: "We (Christians) all however behold with unveiled face (i.e., without having a veil upon our hearts) the glory of the Lord." [52]

Since κατοπτρίζω in the middle voice actually means "to look at one-self in a mirror"—a meaning which is equally unfavorable to either of the proposed translations—a decision cannot be made on linguistic grounds, even though the well-known parallel in Philo, Leg. all. III, 101 suggests the translation "behold": "μηδὲ κατοπτρισαίμην ἐν ἄλλῳ τινὶ τὴν σὴν ἰδέαν" means, in the context of the passage, "Moreover I should not like to behold as in a mirror your form in any other." Then the entire vs. 18 would remain within the mystery conception—which of course Paul is using only as a figure—: by means of the vision of God the beholder himself is transformed into the God. On this, cf. especially Apul. Met. 11:23-24; Od. Sol. 13.

An eschatological view effectively concludes the midrash: "In the same figure we are changed from glory into glory." The comment "καθάπερ ἀπὸ κυρίου πνεύματος" follows somewhat awkwardly. The conclusion of the midrash would be better without it.

[52] Similarly, in II, 5:1-10 the apologia of the Pauline apostolate is expanded by an excursus dealing with the entire community.

Thus the sense of our passage is completely clear even without the exegetical gloss. No reader would miss vs. 17 or in its absence be unable to understand the preceding or the following verses. On the contrary, precisely as our commentaries show, vs. 17 renders the interpretation of the entire passage uncommonly difficult, and that not only because it is superfluous and also as a gloss has a restrictive effect,[53] but also because it offers no precise explanation of vs. 16 at all.

First of all we must observe the following: vs. 16: "ἡνίκα δὲ ἐὰν ἐπιστρέψῃ πρὸς κύριον, περιαιρεῖται τὸ κάλυμμα" repeats analogously, only with transposed signs, vs. 14b: ". . . μὴ ἀνακαλυπτόμενον ὅτι ἐν Χριστῷ καταργεῖται." Every reader will therefore at once identify the κύριος of vs. 16 with Christ, who is meant as in vs. 14, and Paul himself was able in vs. 16 to quote Exod. 34:34 only because he intended just this. The connection of vs. 14 to vs. 16 is so clear here that a special reference to this fact was superfluous. But if Paul should still have held a corresponding exegetical gloss to be necessary, this could only have read: "ὁ δὲ κύριος ὁ Χριστός ἐστιν," i.e., by the κύριος of the Old Testament quotation Christ is meant, but never "ὁ δὲ κύριος τὸ πνεῦμά ἐστιν." If this sentence is Pauline, in any case the thought would thereby be carried forward; for κύριος and πνεῦμα are *not* identical for Paul. Thus it is excluded that vs. 17a is an exegetical comment on vs. 16.

This already makes it clear that neither in itself nor in the context can vs. 17 be made comprehensible as Pauline. The following reflections can support this awareness.

Even vs. 17b does not explain vs. 16. Verse 16 affirms that for the person who turns to the Lord the veil is taken away, that is, the understanding of the law is disclosed. It is simply incomprehensible how this fact can be explained by the word "ἐλευθερία." The concept "ἐλευθερία" indeed embraces very much more than what is expressed in vs. 16; and one does not determine the meaning of a passage that is already clear in itself when one joins to it an abstract broader concept. Thus vs. 17 does not compel the awareness that now vs. 16 is rightly explained, but the question as to what Paul then really means to say with vs. 16 when he expressly appends to it the reference to ἐλευθερία. No answer is given to this question, for vs. 18 likewise refers back to vs. 16 without giving the slightest indication that Paul intended to have the correct knowledge of the law understood as freedom in any

[53] Such a gloss would, moreover, be unique in Paul. Gal. 3:16, where a new thought is introduced, and Gal. 4:24 as well as Rom. 10:6 ff., where an allegory is offered, are not parallels (*contra* W. G. Kümmel in H. Lietzmann, on p. 113, ll. 23-32) ; I Cor. 15:56, however, is a non-Pauline gloss'

sense. Naturally it would not be impossible to connect the insight into the real meaning of the Mosaic law with Christian ἐλευθερία as Paul understands it, perhaps in such a way that understanding of the aim of the νόμος means freedom from the law of death. But therewith Paul not only would be introducing a new thought which is alien to the context—not bondage but the transient glory of the law was the subject—he would have also had to explain this thought if people were to understand what he meant. So, as the text now reads, the concept ἐλευθερία in vs. 17 hangs wholly in midair, since it neither serves as an exact clarification of vs. 16, the meaning of which it rather obscures, nor provides any parenthetical thought that is obvious or self-evident or that advances the line of thought.[54]

In conclusion, one final consideration which affects all expositions of the passage: If Paul wishes to move from the κύριος to the concept of ἐλευθερία, why does he require for this the detour by way of the πνεῦμα, by explaining (as for example H. Lietzmann, *in loc.*, thinks) : "The κύριος mentioned in the quotation (as person) however is (as substance) the Pneuma, and only where the πνεῦμα is is there free-dom . . . ." Why does he not make freedom dependent directly upon Christ here also, as is constantly done elsewhere (cf. I, 7:22-23, 39; 9:1; Gal. 2:4; 5:1), and write something like: "But when one turns to the Lord (= Christ), the veil is taken away; for where the Lord is, there is liberty (from the law of death, or something similar)"? If that were here, then perhaps one could overcome the reservations against the isolated and unexpected emergence of ἐλευθερία. But it is not here, and thus the extremely peculiar fact that Paul unnecessarily, indeed confusingly, and contrary to his custom involves the Spirit in his statements in vs. 17 remains enigmatic and unexplainable, quite

397

[54] The exegetes give varied definitions of it even in terms of contents. H. Lietzmann, *in loc.*: freedom is asserted here "in apostolic self-consciousness." W. G. Kümmel in H. Lietzmann, *in loc.*: ". . . he becomes free from the enslaving powers of this world, and thus also from the slavery of the law." P. Bachmann, [2], p. 175: the freedom is "the freedom which is first of all inward, but then is also shown in conduct, relationships, and works. It has its life from the Lord and his Spirit, and thus it draws from the most high and most powerful and bestows upon men who are formed by it free and sure movement in the clarity and immediacy of the fellowship with God and of self-expression." H. Windisch, p. 126: "Here freedom means being free from all the veils that hinder the knowledge of God and his salvation and the communion with God and the understanding of God . . . , furthermore the release from all the burdensome prescriptions of the law (Acts 15:10), from the entire apparatus of the Mosaic cult." G. Heinrici, p. 137: "To have a veil upon the heart and to be spiritually free are opposites." P. Schmiedel, p. 229: "Ἐλευθερία in this context is freedom from the law and its κατάκρισις." M. Dibelius (*Botschaft und Geschichte*, II: 130): ". . . Freedom (of immediate access to God)."

apart from the fact that the form of this involvement—Christ = Pneuma—is absolutely un-Pauline.

Thus it will not do to try to fit vs. 17 into the context of the whole midrash in a sensible way. Now the following observations also are interesting:

The midrash II, 3:7-18 is typically Jewish or rabbinical, not only in its manner of argument and its style but also in its language. Even vs. 8—ή διακονία τοῦ πνεύματος—is good Jewish material (Ezek. 36: 25), and the mystery terminology used in vs. 18a certainly is in this form Paul's *Jewish* inheritance.[55] On the other hand vs. 17 and vs. 18b offer pure Gnosticism in conceptuality *and* conception. This difference is so striking that it would have to attract special note even if the exposition of vs. 17 caused no difficulties.

Further: vs. 18b—καθάπερ ἀπὸ κυρίου πνεύματος—is a most infelicitous comment in this passage. Not because it could not possibly fit into the context. It is indeed rather unusual to consider the κύριος from two wholly different sides in *one* sentence: we are changed into the same image (of the *Lord*) as by the *Lord* of the Spirit—but this is not the most peculiar thing. More important is the fact that the midrash has a good liturgical ending that is so effective that one cannot avoid the suspicion that the following piece was added only later. And moreover there is the fact that vs. 18b, precisely like vs. 17, calls attention to itself by its Gnostic language as a foreign element in the midrash.

If one takes all this together, the consideration may be justified as to whether vs. 17 together with vs. 18b should be excised as non-Pauline glosses. It is immediately evident that thereby all the exegetical difficulties in vss. 12-18 caused by vs. 17 would be eliminated and the conclusion of the midrash would afford an eminently clear continuity. Moreover, the certainly necessary terminological unity of the midrash would thus be restored. But we would also obtain a gloss which by virtue of its form is so striking that there can hardly be any doubt as to its original unity:

> ὁ δὲ κύριος τὸ πνεῦμά ἐστιν.
> οὗ δὲ τὸ πνεῦμα κυρίου,
> ἐλευθερία
> καθάπερ ἀπὸ κυρίου πνεύματος.

The important thing is only to recognize the meaning of this gloss. Its language points to a Gnostic origin. And in fact it can splendidly

---

[55] Cf. the evidence in H. Lietzmann, HNT 9, *in loc.*

be understood on the lips of one of the Corinthian Gnostics against
whom Paul is writing. The apostle's letters undoubtedly played a role
in the discussion within the Corinthian community; they had been
read also by the Gnostics, who of course still belonged within the
community. We have already seen that one of them provided the
epistle with marginal comments. From the same hand comes the comment which originally stood in the margin beside the last sentences
of the midrash and which, broken into two parts, in a recopying
slipped into the text itself.

The glossator obviously was concerned about the concept of ἐλευθερία—a typically Gnostic concept, which was of significance in Corinth.[56] For the Gnostic, ἐλευθερία signified primarily the freedom from
the world in a wholly real sense, that is to say, the liberation of the
πνεῦμα from the σάρξ and its sphere, and therefore secondarily the
freedom from all the ethical directions which had reference to the
σάρξ. That this subject was of current interest in Corinth is shown,
for example, by the discussion about eating meat sacrificed to idols
in I Cor. (cf. 8:1; 9:1; 10:29), where Paul clearly takes a stand against
an unrestrained practice of ἐλευθερία.[57] In direct opposition to the
view of Paul, our glossator argues for the unrestricted validity of the
gnostically understood freedom.

Moreover his remark is evidently an exposition of the quotation
which Paul gives in vs. 16, only naturally in a Gnostic sense! Paul intends by vs. 16 to be saying: anyone who turns to the Lord recognizes
the law in its provisionality. The Gnostic radicalizes this. For him
the Christ-Kyrios and the Pneuma which dwells in man are identical.[58]
Thus to him the passage from Exodus is saying: "Anyone who turns
to the *Pneuma* recognizes the transitory character of the law." But
where the Pneuma is, there freedom reigns for the Gnostic.[59] The
Pneumatic is liberated from the sphere of the terrestrial including
the laws connected therewith.[60] This conception is necessarily given
with the myth.[61] "To take away the veil from the law" or "to recognize
the law" therefore has, in Gnostic exposition, the meaning: to recognize

[56] See pp. 218 ff.
[57] On this, see pp. 224 ff.
[58] Cf., e.g., the passages cited above, p. 316, n. 43.
[59] Cf. the Coptic Gospel of Philip 73 = Leipoldt-Schenke, p. 52: "The bridal
chamber is not provided for the beasts, nor for the slaves or defiled women, but
it is provided for *free* men and women through the *Holy Spirit*."
[60] Cf., e.g., Iren. I, 6.4: "We, the Psychics, who are of this world, need continence and good works, in order thereby to attain to the place of the center; but
they, the πνευματικοί and τέλειοι, by no means have such need."
[61] πνεῦμα stands in radical opposition to σάρξ, and the law is a work of the
creator of the world, the evil deity.

that the law is a creation of the demons[62] and therefore is not valid for the Pneumatics. Thus with his comment the Gnostic intends to say: "Since Christ and the Pneuma are identical, but with the Pneuma of the Pneumatic is given at the same time ἐλευθερία, the sense of Exod. 34:34 is: the Christian—as Pneumatic—is free from the law."

As far as wording is concerned, Paul naturally also could have drawn this latter inference.[63] But he could not argue as the Gnostic did. For one thing, he cannot equate κύριος and πνεῦμα. For with him the detour by way of the Pneuma would be incomprehensible, though for the Gnostic it is necessary since the name for the individual self of man which lives in ἐλευθερία is not κύριος but πνεῦμα. And finally, Paul in fact also would at least have had to clarify the concept ἐλευθερία, if one does not already exclude the possibility that he introduces it into the context at all, while the Gnostic refers with it to one of his catchwords.

On the gloss itself it remains to be said that on the lips of the Gnostics the two genitives were meant as expressions of identity and therewith take up the thesis of vs. 17a. "Κύριος πνεύματος" means "the Lord, who is the Spirit"; correspondingly, "πνεῦμα κυρίου" means "the Spirit, who is the Lord." [64]

Thus it is true once more that the text without the presumable gloss affords a good connection in contrast to the presently existing text; that the supposed gloss is explainable neither in the context nor even in itself as Pauline; finally that it does however in itself acquire an excellent interpretation as a marginal comment from the hand of one of the Gnostics in Corinth. Since the gloss presumably was written on the margin of the original epistle, it is not surprising that it has a unanimous literary attestation.

The gloss stands in the same epistolary fragment[65] in which is found also the inserted verse II, 5:16. In view of the fact that corresponding

[62] Cf., e.g., Epiph. Haer. XXVIII, 1: Cerinthus asserts, "τὸν νόμον καὶ τοὺς προφήτας ὑπὸ ἀγγέλου δεδόσθαι," and according to Haer. XXVIII, 2 this angel is regarded as "οὐκ ἀγαθός." Cf. H. Schlier, Der Brief an die Galater, Meyer Kommentar VII (1949, 10th ed.) : 111 ff.

[63] For the Gnostics freedom from the law means libertinism; for Paul it means the possibility of a new obedience.

[64] If the major premise is accepted, then we have an explicit confirmation that the Gnostics in Corinth identified Christ with the Spirit (which dwelt in themselves). For one who accepts the explanation of II, 3:17 proposed here, the fundamental correctness of the studies on pp. 193-218 would be confirmed at first hand. Quite incidentally the interesting observation is to be made that the Gnostics in Corinth in principle recognize the authority of the Old Testament, a fact which of course is only obvious among Jewish Gnostics and is also elsewhere assured for the Corinthian heretics (cf. pp. 294-95).

[65] Epistle C; cf. pp. 96 ff.

marginal comments are not to be found in the other epistles, this may give support to the correctness of our interpretation.

Both glosses are to be attributed to the aim of deriving a decisive pro-Gnostic thesis from the *text of Paul himself*.[66] But what is striking about both of them is above all their elaborate stylistic construction. In the last passage considered, it produces an outright affected effect. Instead of writing "οὗ δὲ τὸ πνεῦμα, ἐλευθερία," the glossator expresses his thought in a form which is indeed permissible but still verbose: "οὗ δὲ τὸ πνεῦμα κυρίου—ἐλευθερία—καθάπερ ἀπὸ κυρίου πνεύματος." No less elaborate in form is the construction of II, 5:16: "ὥστε ἡμεῖς ἀπὸ τοῦ νῦν οὐδένα οἴδαμεν κατὰ σάρκα. εἰ καὶ ἐγνώκαμεν κατὰ σάρκα Χριστόν, ἀλλὰ νῦν οὐκέτι γινώσκομεν."

And here also the expression is overdone. Instead of the conditional sentence, a simple "not even Christ" would have sufficed.

It is not at all Paul's way to speak thus. Even if perhaps rhythmic prose had not remained without effect on him,[67] still any merely rhetorical interest is foreign to him. On the other hand, Paul charges against his Corinthian opponents that they loved to talk in vain σοφία λόγου (I, 1:17) and to win men ἐν πειθοῖς σοφίας λόγοις, as is evident from I, 2:4. One cannot ask for better examples of such an artistic but empty manner of speaking than the two glosses which we have established. Paul's criticism of the ὑπεροχὴ λόγου (I, 2:1) of the Corinthians who speak in διδακτοῖς λόγοις of human wisdom (I, 2:13) exactly fits the affected form of the two Gnostic marginal comments. Thus even in this not uninteresting way we secure a confirmation of the close connections between the two passages regarded as un-Pauline and the Corinthian Gnostics.[68]

W. G. Kümmel (Feine-Behm-Kümmel, p. 211) regards it as "extremely improbable" "that glosses of Paul's opponents could have succeeded in getting unnoticed into the text of the archetype lying at the basis of our manuscripts." I see no difficulty here. Why should a Gnostic not have been able to make marginal comments on the original writing? And no one who holds the passages involved to be Pauline can insist that a later copyist would have had to recognize these comments as un-Pauline and excise them.

---

[66] The method of Paul's Gnostic opponents of finding support for their theses in passages of the Pauline epistles or in the conduct of Paul himself is also demonstrable elsewhere: II Thess. 2:2 (cf. Vol. 2, p. 149); Gal. 5:11 (cf. Vol. 2, p. 28). Of course they do not therewith mean to appeal to Paul as a Gnostic comrade-in-arms. All the passages cited rather show the same not unskilled line of argument, of presenting Gnostic opinions as the logically consistent interpretation of Pauline principles: even Paul must concede this or that, they argue.

[67] Blass-Debrunner (7th ed.), pp. 224 ff.

[68] See I, 1:12; cf. pp. 199 ff.

The explanation of II, 5:16 and 3:17-18 given here naturally does not depend on the asserted suspicion that they were Paul's Gnostic opponents in Corinth who made these marginal comments. That Gnostic glosses are involved in both verses appears to me to be the only possible interpretation of these verses. That these glosses come from the hand of the adversaries whom Paul personally combated seems to me to have in its favor a well-founded likelihood.

SUPPLEMENTARY NOTES

1   On the following, cf. R. Haardt in U. Bianchi, *Le Origine dello Gnosticismo*, pp. 161 ff.

2   This holds true all the more for the definition which G. van Groningen (*First Century Gnosticism, Its Origin and Motives* [Leiden, 1967]) gives to Gnosticism. He holds it to be at the core a nonreligious movement which sought with the aid of science to conquer the world and to control the cosmos. Magic and astrology, nature philosophy and Pythagorean as well as Aristotelian influences shaped the original Gnostic, Simon Magus. Van Groningen regarded the religious form of the later syncretistic Gnosticism as an only loosely fitting garment. This obviously strongly modernizing interpretation of Gnosticism is hardly correct, but this fact interests us less than van Groningen's observation: "This ancient spirit of scientism, seeking to express itself in religious terms and contexts, is by no means dead. It will not die as long as sinful man lives" (p. 186). Christian Science and theosophy, Toynbee and Tillich, A. Schweitzer and Bishop Robinson, the modern trust in science and materialist philosophy serve as examples for van Groningen of the present locus of this "Gnosticism."

3   Correctly S. Arai in U. Bianchi, pp. 181 ff.; K. Rudolph in *Kairos*, 1967, p. 109.

4   Cf. now also S. Arai in U. Bianchi, pp. 179 ff.; K. Rudolph in *Kairos*, 1967, p. 108; E. Haenchen, *Gott und Mensch* (1965), pp. 16-17.

5   Cf. H. Koester in *Gnomon* 33 (1961): 595. On the subject, cf. also P. Pokorný, *Der Epheserbrief und die Gnosis*, pp. 40 ff.

6   P. Hoffmann, *Die Toten in Christus*, pp. 31 ff.; C. Colpe in U. Bianchi, pp. 429 ff.; L. Troje in *Museum Helveticum* V (1948): 98 ff.; H. Langerbeck, *Aufsätze zur Gnosis* (1967), pp. 113-14; A. A. T. Ehrhardt in StTh IV (1952): 154-55; P. Pokorný, pp. 43-44; A. Dieterich, *Eine Mithrasliturgie*, pp. 199 ff.; W. Bousset, [2], pp. 518-19.

Cf. K. Holl, *Gesammelte Aufsätze*, II: 6.   7

Cf. H. M. Schenke, "Hauptprobleme der Gnosis," *Kairos* 7 (1965) :   8
117-18.

Colpe also follows the method criticized here in his article ὁ υἱὸς   9
τοῦ ἀνθρώπου (TWNT VIII: 403 ff.) ; he does this by inquiring after
"counterparts" among religious parallels in question and affirming (p.
414.29) "unfailingly serious differences." Then in the search for the
historical roots of the Jewish Son-of-Man figure, he consistently arrives
at the conclusion "that the history of the Son-of-Man conception within
history is to be inferred from Jewish apocalyptic itself" (p. 422.26 ff.) .
The religio-historically fundamental fact that the concept and the
figure of the celestial "man" represent an entity which overlaps with
Jewish apocalyptic is regarded by Colpe as unimportant and is ignored
(p. 422.8 ff.) .
For criticism of Colpe's method of working in general, cf. the discussion by G. Widengren in OLZ 58 (1963) : 533-48.
R. Haardt (*Die Gnosis* [1967], pp. 22-23) is mistaken when he gives
it as my opinion that the Gnostic system described in the following
is *the* fundamental Gnostic system or basic model which underlies all
other expressions of the Gnostic myth. I do regard the structure of
this system as relatively old, e.g., in comparison with systems which
have a redeemer myth. But it is of interest to us only as a *particular*
system, namely as the one appearing, in my opinion, in Corinth.

Hence it is not correct that I regard the Apophasis "as a genuine   10
work of Simon himself"—thus W. Foerster in U. Bianchi, p. 191.

Cf. H. v. Campenhausen, *Die Entstehung der christlichen Bibel*,   11
BhTh 39 (1968) : 161-62.

The investigation of the Apophasis by J. H. Frickel (in U. Bianchi,   12
p. 197) also leads to this view. His study comes to the conclusion that
Hippolytus did not quote the Apophasis itself but rather a para-
phrasing commentary on it. Cf. *ibid.* in *Studi di Storia Religiosa della
tarda antichita* (Messina, 1968) , p. 49: "The 'Apophasis Megalē' may
. . . with great probability be regarded as the original system which
underlies . . . the other systems."

Cf. the fine study by H. Schlier, "Der Mensch im Gnostizismus" in   13

Besinnung auf das NT (1964), pp. 97 ff. Further, W. Foerster, "Die Naassener" in *Studi di Storia Religiosa della tarda antichita,* pp. 21 ff.

14   W. Foerster (see preceding note), e.g., neglects this necessary differentiation.

15   Correctly seen also by C. Colpe in U. Bianchi, pp. 442-43. Cf. also W. Foerster (see note 13), pp. 26 ff. *Contra,* incorrectly, B. A. Pearson, in JBL 86 (1967) : 305.

16   Cf. N. A. Dahl, *Das Volk Gottes* (1963, 2nd ed.), p. 115.

17   The three secret words which, according to Saying 13 of the Gospel of Thomas, Jesus communicates to Thomas, whose "master" he does *not* wish to be, may have been: σὺ εἶ ἐγώ.

18   According to Saying 24, the disciples find the place where Jesus dwells within themselves: thus Jesus is their real self. Hipp. VIII, 15 quotes Monoimos: εὑρήσεις αὐτὸν ἐν σεαυτῷ.

19   Otherwise Epiphanius must have exchanged "Jesus" and "Christ" and be speaking of Cerinthus' Jesus, who, as "vessel" of the Christ, experiences the ordinary human fate. But Cerinthus would hardly have been able to speak of an apocalyptically conceived general resurrection of the dead.

20   Cf. II Clem. 15.3-4.

21   Cf. also S. Arai in U. Bianchi, pp. 182-83, who moreover attempts to prove a similar development also for the Gospel of Truth: S. Arai, *Die Christologie des Evangelium Veritatis* (Leiden, 1964), pp. 120-21.

22   Cf. further M. Bouttier, *En Christ. Étude d'exégèse et de la théologie pauliniennes* (Paris, 1962) ; P. Pokorný, pp. 55-56.

23   The historically meant Johannine μένειν ἐν αὐτῷ or ἐν ἐμοί (*scil.* Χριστῷ) may intentionally replace a substantially meant, Gnostic εἶναι ἐν . . . ; cf., e.g., John 6:56; 15:4. Pertinent passages from the Corpus Hermeticum in Pokorný, p. 56.

24   E. Güttgemanns, *Der leidende Apostel und sein Herr,* pp. 252 ff.; Pokorný, pp. 34 ff., 50 ff.

Cf. also P. Pokorný, pp. 56-57.   25

Contrary to E. Güttgemanns' objection (p. 108, n. 80), the idea of   26
substitution does occur everywhere in the myth; *on behalf of* his
"body," the redeemer takes upon himself the trouble of the descent, the
burden of suffering in the darkness, and the battle at the ascent, to
bring Gnosis to that "body" and to blaze the trail into the celestial
world. As the πρόδρομος he is followed by his emissaries who, in the
world, suffering under the menacing grip of the demonic powers, act
ὑπὲρ Χριστοῦ by gathering together the σῶμα Χριστοῦ. Cf. further
W. Bousset, *Kyrios Christos* (ET, 1970), p. 169.

E. Lohse (in Meyer *Kommentar* IX, 2 [1968, 14th ed.]: 121-22 and   27
in NTS 11 [1965]: 213) may be correct when in his exposition of Col.
he connects the Χριστὸς ἐν ὑμῖν with the Christ who is preached among
the nations. But since we are asking not about the meaning of the
author of Col. but about the original meaning of the obviously already
existing material which he employed, Lohse's exposition, contrary to
his view, in no way affects our religio-historical evalution of Col. 1:26-
27.

Cf. Hipp. VIII, 12-15; X, 17; Iren. I, 12.3; 30.1.6; further material in   28
H. M. Schenke, [2], pp. 6 ff.

Cf. further G. Iber, *Überlieferungsgeschichtliche Untersuchungen*   29
zum Begriff des Menschensohns im NT, Diss. Heidelberg, 1953, pp.
37 ff.; C. Colpe in TWNT VIII: 403 ff.; H. Balz, *Methodische Pro-*
bleme der neutestamentlichen Christologie, WMANT 25 (1967) : 61 ff.

H. F. Weiss, *Untersuchungen zur Kosmologie des hellenistischen und*   30
palästinischen Judentums, TU 97 (1966) : 305 ff.

C. Colpe, TWNT VIII: 413, n. 67.   31

Cf. further C. Colpe, TWNT VIII: 413; K. Rudolph, *Theogonie,*   32
Kosmogonie und Anthropogonie in den mandäischen Schriften,
FRLANT 88 (1965) : 297-98; *Apokalypse des Adam,* ed. A. Böhlig and
P. Labib, *Koptisch-gnostische Apokalypsen aus Codex V von Nag*
Hammadi, p. 96.

H. F. Weiss, art. "Menschensohn" in RGG [3rd ed.], IV, cols. 874 ff.   33

34   Cf. the methodological reflections of Reitzenstein in R. Reitzenstein
        and H. H. Schaeder, *Studien zum antiken Synkretismus,* p. 129.

35   K. Rudolph in WZUJ, 1963, Sonderheft, p. 93 (Literature); R.
        Bultmann, [5], p. 12.

36   Here also possibly belongs the fact that the two-aeons schema in
        apocalyptic not seldom is transposed out of the temporal into the
        spatial category; see the literature in E. Grässer, *Der Glaube im He-
        bräerbrief* (1965), p. 176, n. 159.

37   H. Conzelmann, "Die Mutter der Weisheit," in E. Dinkler, ed.,
        Zeit und Geschichte (1964), pp. 225 ff.; K. Rudolph in *Kairos,* 1967,
        p. 118; C. Colpe in TWNT VIII: 412 (Literature); H. F. Weiss,
        Untersuchungen zur Kosmologie . . . , TU 97 (1966): 181 ff.

38   H. Ringgren, "Qumran and Gnosticism," in U. Bianchi, pp. 379 ff.;
        K. Rudolph, "Stand und Aufgaben der Erforschung des Gnostizis-
        mus," WZUJ, 1963, Sonderheft, esp. pp. 92-93; also, [1], pp. 226-27;
        H. Braun in ThRs 29 (1963): 194; also, *Qumran und das NT,* II
        (1966): 136 ff.; E. Käsemann, *Exegetische Versuche und Besinnungen,*
        II: 28-29.

39   Cf. further G. Quispel, "Gnosticism and the NT," in J. P. Hyatt, ed.,
        The Bible in Modern Scholarship (1965), pp. 252 = VC 19 (1965):
        65 ff.; D. Georgi in E. Dinkler, ed., *Zeit und Geschichte,* pp. 269-70,
        according to whom Gnosticism is oriented "to the intention of the Old
        Testament"; E. Schweizer in ZNW 57 (1966): 199; G. Kretschmar in
        EvTheol 8 (1953): 354 ff.

40   P. Pokorný (pp. 40 ff.) employs H. M. Schenke's analysis in his at-
        tempt to account for the origin of Gnosticism, in similarly uncon-
        vincing fashion. According to his opinion, before the emergence of
        Gnosticism man was conscious of being related in essence to deity and
        was also of the opinion "that the objective cosmos does not harmonize
        with a higher spiritual substance . . . . People longed for a liberation
        from this oppressive environment. Even before the rise of actual Gnos-
        ticism, the view had been formulated that redemption consists in
        knowledge of self and in the ascent of the soul" (p. 45). The "con-
        scious Gnostic revolt" began with a "stratagem": "The invisible most

high God was equated with a celestial being and the creator-God was made a subordinate servant. This was done on the basis of the perennially troublesome and debated passage Gen. 1:26-27: man, or the spiritual power dwelling within him, is, according to this, a likeness of the highest deity" (p. 46).

For criticism of Schenke's construction, see K. Rudolph in OLZ 59 (1964), cols. 574 ff.

Cf. further A. Adam in U. Bianchi, pp. 296, 300; A. Böhlig, in U.   41
Bianchi, pp. 109 ff.; H. Jonas in J. P. Hyatt, pp. 279 ff., 288 ff.; K. Rudolph in *Kairos,* 1967, pp. 112-13; E. Käsemann, *Exegetische Versuche und Besinnungen,* II: 28-29; J. Maier, *Vom Kultus zur Gnosis* (1964), pp. 23 ff.; K. Schubert, "Jüdischer Hellenismus und jüdische Gnosis," in *Wort und Wahrheit,* 18 (1963) : 455 ff.; A. D. Nock, "Gnosticism," HTR 57 (1964) : 255 ff.

The Gnostic "Apocalypse of Adam" from Codex V from Nag Ham-   42
madi also shows a purely Jewish influence; cf. A. Böhlig and P. Labib, pp. 96 ff.

Cf. further Böhlig, "Der jüdische und judenchristliche Hintergrund in gnostischen Texten von Nag Hammadi," in U. Bianchi, pp. 109 ff.; K. Rudolph in TLZ 90 (1965), cols. 321-22; also in WZUJ, Sonderheft, 1963, pp. 92 ff.; J. M. Robinson in ZThK, 1965, pp. 333-34.

With respect to the deficiencies in the literature, the same situation   43
prevails for the mystery cults as for early Gnosticism, even though the motives for the lack of literature were quite diverse in both places; cf. A. Dieterich, pp. 52-53.

J. Barr, *The Semantics of Biblical Language* (1961), pp. 237-38, ob-   44
jects—hardly justifiably—to H. Schlier's exposition.

On this metaphor, greatly cherished in almost all religious move-   45
ments, cf. further A. Dieterich, pp. 128-29; H. Windisch, pp. 320 ff.; E. Preuschen, *Zwei gnostische Hymnen* (1904), pp. 30-31, 40-41; II Cor. 11:2; Herm. Vis. I, 3.4; III, 9 ff.; IV, 2.1-2.

As man and Son of Man—Hipp. VIII, 12-15; X, 17. As spirit and   46
body—II Clem. 14.2-4.

Cf. K. Rudolph, *Theogonie, Kosmogonie und Anthropogonie . . . ,*   47
FRLANT 88 (1965): 271-75, 336, 345.

48　　This judgment presupposes the literary-critical analysis of the Thessalonian epistles as it is proposed in Vol. 2, pp. 91 ff., 139 ff.

49　　Hypotheses about the division of the Corinthian epistles were also variously proposed after the aforementioned work of C. Clemen, which gives a full account of the earlier literature. One may compare, e.g.: C. Clemen, *Paulus*, I, II (1904); R. Drescher, "Der zweite Korintherbrief und die Vorgänge in Korinth seit Abfassung des ersten Korintherbriefes," *ThStKr*, 1897, pp. 43-111; A. Halmel, *Der zweite Korintherbrief des Apostels Paulus* (1904); H. Lisco, *Die Entstehung des zweiten Korintherbriefes* (1896); D. Völter, *Paulus und seine Briefe* (1905); the literature down to 1922 is discussed by E. Golla, *Zwischenreise und Zwischenbrief* (1922); further, cf. J. Héring, [1], pp. xii ff.; [2], pp. xi ff.; A. Schweitzer, pp. 49-50; J. Weiss, [1], pp. xl-xliii; H. Windisch, pp. 11 ff. (Literature); E. Dinkler in RGG (3rd ed.), IV, col. 18; C. H. Dodd, NTS, 1953, pp. 80 ff., 83 ff.; R. Bultmann, [1], p. 14, n. 16; G. Bornkamm, [1], pp. 1 ff.; B. Rigaux, *Saint Paul et ses lettres* (1962), pp. 153 ff.; W. Marxsen, pp. 77 ff.; F. Hahn, p. 81, n. 8; D. Georgi, [1], pp. 16 ff.; P. Cleary, CBQ 12, 1950, pp. 10 ff.; A. M. G. Stephenson, "Partition Theories on II Corinthians," *Studia Evangelica*, II, Part I (1964): 639-46; C. Bjerkelund, *Parakalo*, n. d., pp. 141 ff.; W. H. Bates, "The Integrity of II Corinthians," NTS 12 (1965): 56-69; J. Harrison, "St. Paul's Letters to the Corinthians," *Exp. Times* 77 (1965/66): 285-86; A. Q. Morton, "Dislocation in 1. and 2. Corinthians," *Exp. Times* 78 (1966/67): 119.

H. Conzelmann (pp. 13 ff., *et passim*) holds that a literary-critical analysis of I Cor. is not absolutely necessary. One could understand the epistle as a unity. His opinion on chap. 9 is characteristic: "With reference to the literary questions one will have to acquiesce in a *non liquet* and concede the advantage to the conservative view" (p. 179, n. 5). Why this latter? Since Conzelmann acknowledges the composite literary character of other epistles, in the exposition of I Cor. he should not be allowed to ask whether its integrity can be maintained if necessary, but only whether it can *better* be explained with the assumption of its integrity than with the opposite assumption.

50　　P. Gaechter (*Petrus und seine Zeit* [1958], pp. 311-37) treats I, 1:2 in detail. He gives the conclusion of his study in the following paraphrase: "Paul sends his blessing to the church of God as it has taken form in Corinth, and this means to all those together who through their sanctification have been brought together into unity in Christ Jesus, but also to all individually who have been called to be holy, in their association with those who as official leaders of worship call on the name of our Lord Jesus Christ, in whatever place they are, whether those who are in Corinth, the location of the addressees being summoned to holiness, or those who at present are with us in Ephesus"!

Cf. further Vol. 2, pp. 185 ff.

By having the writings of Paul addressed to the executors of the apostle's legacy and thus to all his congregations or to their leaders, the author of the Pastoral Epistles skillfully avoids the difficulty of making epistles to individual congregations binding upon the whole church. In I, 1:2b he solves this problem as well as possible, but still in essence quite crudely.

W. Michaelis ([2], p. 26) doubts that *the same* controversies are 51 meant in I, 11:18 and I, 1-4. But this doubt certainly cannot be justified exegetically, as would be required, but can only be ruled out (see below). J. Munck, *Paul and the Salvation of Mankind*, pp. 136-37, wants to understand the passage in I, 11:18-19 eschatologically: "In the last days, which are not far off, many in the Church will fall away, and thereby endanger the Church's continued existence." But it is impossible to regard the αἱρέσεις of I, 11:18-19 as a "part of the future misfortunes, of the Messianic sufferings." Paul rather hears that divisions are now present.

Of course, cf. I, 5:1. 52

Cf. E. Güttgemanns, p. 88, who of course objects: "But this over- 53 looks that, according to Paul, along with the kerygma of God's raising of Jesus the credibility of the preacher also was involved" (cf. vs. 15). However, the circle of the preachers of the resurrection of Jesus, whose credibility of course is not called in question in 15:9, by no means coincides with that of the apostles. Decisive for our question, however, is simply that in 15:9 Paul still senses no necessity of defending the legitimacy of his *apostolate*.

Even in I, 8:10 Paul chooses only an extreme example practiced 54 in Corinth of the use which the possessor of Gnosis makes of his freedom to hold the idols in contempt and to eat the meat sacrificed to idols; this example is not at all directed against the *worship* of idols. Paul therefore does not by any means forbid participation in the idols' meals, but only wishes to see them avoided for the sake of love.

Conversely, 10:1-22 treats only of cultic meals, of the worship of idols, not of the eating of meat sacrificed to idols. In this section Paul simply is forbidding participation in the idols' meals.

55   Of course H. v. Soden (*Sakrament und Ethik bei Paulus,* pp. 21-22) attempts to maintain the unity of the section 8:1–11:1, without answering the objections that argue against such unity.

Further, G. Bornkamm ([2], esp. pp. 346 ff.) has not succeeded in convincing me that both sections can be understood in a proper interpretation of the Pauline intention as a unitary sketch. As we have seen, I, 8:10 does *not* amount to a bridge connecting the two sections. The remarkable statement that "some compiler sought precisely here a shockingly poor place for the introduction (insertion?) of B (= 9:24–10:22)," that nevertheless "the interruption by Paul himself is quite suggestive" and "the connection of 9:24-27 to 9:23" is "too close," is still an admission that Bornkamm's exegesis could not really clear away the doubts about the unity of the section; for I do not understand how the same train of thought in a compiler is shockingly poor and yet in Paul himself is quite sensible. I regard the insertion by the compiler under the circumstances to be extraordinarily skillful.

Strange also is the argument, "If I Cor. 10:1-22 had actually stood in the warning epistle of I Cor. 5:9, then the Corinthians would in fact not have misunderstood the apostle but understood him correctly, and Paul would now be beating a retreat . . ." ([2], p. 315); for if the *substantive* relationship of I, 5:9 to I, 10:1-22 is seen correctly here, then both passages in *the same* epistle would be all the more impossible. But actually I, 5:9 has no immediate connection with I, 10:1-22; for *here* Paul is forbidding participation in the heathen cult, and *there* he is interpreting an assertion which people would have been able to misunderstand as a prohibition of commerce with pagans altogether. I, 10:1-22 provides no occasion for such misunderstanding, though II, 6:14 ff. probably does (see above, pp. 94-95).

56   G. Bornkamm ([2], p. 347) also admits that a sharp break is to be made before I, 9:24 (and not first at I, 10:1). Above all H. W. Bartsch (*Entmythologisierende Auslegung* [1962], pp. 172 ff.) has not only noted the caesura before I, 9:24 but also splendidly described it. This observation and description is especially valuable because Bartsch pays no attention at all to the literary-critical problems but bases his judgment solely on the course of the Pauline argument. Cf., e.g.: "In the simile of the race it is no more a matter of the exercise of a liberty which exists by right, which only now and then must be given up for the neighbor's sake, but a matter of the necessity of ἐγκράτεια beyond all liberty whether rightly or unjustly existing" (p. 172).

57   Otherwise G. Bornkamm, [1], pp. 34-35, n. 131.

The handling of the same theme in the two passages is moreover 58
very different: there peremptory, here didactic; cf. E. Dinkler in ZThK
49 (1952) : 168.

This assignment proves useful in the interpretation and is supported 59
by it; see pp. 230 ff. Otherwise C. Maurer, "Ehe und Unzucht nach
I Cor. 6, 12–7,7" in *Wort und Dienst*, 1959, pp. 159 ff. His argument
that the "no" to unchastity in 6:12-20 and "the full 'yes' to marriage"
(p. 169) in 7:1-40 form a substantial unity speaks, in view of the au-
tonomy and mutual independence of the two sections, rather for the
skill of the editor than for the hand of Paul. Moreover, to find in chap.
7 a *full* "yes" to marriage appears to me very optimistic.

H. Conzelmann, p. 353, writes: "If vs. 13 were to follow directly 60
after 15:58, it would likely be detached from it by Schmithals as a
doublet. The same holds true for vs. 15, which according to Schmithals'
rule must *introduce* a paraenesis, and hence is to be separated from
vss. 13-14."

Not at all! I Thess. 5:14-22, e.g., shows how extensive concluding
admonitions after all can be; alongside this, I, 15:58 + 16:13-14 looks
modest in scope. Who could suspect a doublet here?

And the immediate juxtaposition of general concluding exhortations
(I, 15:58 + 16:13-14) and the particular admonition to give heed to
certain functionaries (16:15-18) is found, e.g., also in I Thess. 5:12-13
+ 5:14 ff.; Phil. 4:1-3 + 4:8-9; Col. 4:2-6 + 4:7-9.

Thus if one attempts to verify Conzelmann's objections, the original
connection of I, 15:58 with 16:13 ff. is confirmed.

W. Michaelis ([2], p. 25) disputes this equation with the argument 61
that in II, 6:14–7:1 Paul is warning against mixing with paganism,
"while the sentence from the earlier letter meant in I Cor. 5:9 must
have referred, as Paul makes explicit in 5:10 ff., precisely to living
together with sinners within the community." I do not see this alternative. Quite the contrary! In I, 5:9 ff. Paul shows that there is paganism
still within the community; one should separate oneself from purported
brethren who live in a pagan manner. This is also *meant* in II, 6:17
and, since the quotation employed in II, 6:17 actually could be misunderstood as a demand to "leave the world," it is interpreted and
made more specific in I, 5:10 ff.

On II, 6:14–7:1 cf. also N. A. Dahl, "Der Epheserbrief und der ver-
lorene erste Brief des Paulus an die Korinther," in O. Michel, pp. 65 ff.

H. Braun in ThRs 29 (1963) : 221 ff. (Literature) ; J. A. Fitzmyer,

"Qumran and the Interpolated Paragraph in 2. Cor. 6,14–7,1," CBQ 23 (1961) : 271-80.

62   J. Müller-Bardorff ("Zur Frage der literarischen Einheit des Philipperbriefes," p. 603, n. 28) agrees with the suggested analysis in essence, but holds II, 6:14–7:1 to be non-Pauline and makes the following arrangement: 11:2-34; 10:1-22; 6:12-20; 15:1-58; 16:13-24. His remark that I, 6:24 ff. [sic] is "with a certain likelihood secondary" remains incomprehensible; does he mean 9:24 ff.?

63   Many students surmise that I, 4:14-21 belongs to the conclusion of an epistle. In that case Epistle B would have to be divided into two writings, with I, 1–4 in one of them, and the remainder in the other. This conjecture is possible but not necessary. Besides, a comparison of I, 4:17 with I, 16:10-11 shows that if we assume two separate writings, these two epistles can have been written with only a brief interval between them.

64   G. Iber's attempt to maintain the original unity of I, 12–14 is stimulating but not convincing: "Zum Verständnis von I Kor. 12,31," ZNW 54 (1963) : 43 ff. H. Conzelmann (NTS 12 [1966]: 241) thinks that the basic component of chap. 13 had been composed by Paul independent of the contemporary context, but then expanded by Paul and subsequently inserted between chaps. 12 and 14 as a strengthening of his argument about the charismata. But then it would remain incomprehensible why Paul has given chap. 13 such an awkward place instead of putting it after chap. 14. And is it true that chap. 13 *strengthens* the argument in chaps. 12 and 14? Chapter 13, which certainly refers back to already formulated material, still goes beyond chaps. 12 and 14. Cf. now also H. Conzelmann, pp. 255 ff., 275, where he argues with more restraint.

65   It is possible that, as J. Müller-Bardorff (p. 604, n. 49) assumes, the conclusion of the epistle in 13:11-13 stems from the "joyful epistle" (see below), but it is unlikely. For 13:11 fits in well as the closing paraenesis to the sorrowful epistle and better than to the joyful epistle. Moreover, one finds the "quotation" from the sorrowful epistle, to which Paul refers in the joyful epistle in II, 2:3, in II, 13:10, since in 1:23, and 2:3, 1, Paul takes up ("quotes") the thought of II, 13:10, as A. Plummer, *II Corinthians*, pp. 49-50, has already seen. Cf. also II, 2:9 with II, 10:6.

Thus also J. Héring ([2], p. 13); on this W. Michaelis in TLZ 83   66
(1958), col. 509. Otherwise W. Marxsen, p. 82, who in regard to II,
9:5 incorrectly speaks of brethren *sent in advance.*

Cf. also J. Weiss, [2], I: 349.   67
R. C. Tannehill (*Dying and Rising with Christ,* p. 94) very vigorously sets forth the substantive connections between 7:2-4 and 7:5 ff.
which betray a literary break at this point. But these connections,
which are actually present though to be sure exaggerated by Tannehill,
do affect only those expressions which characterize the Corinthian
situation in all stages, and in addition attest the skill of the redactor.

The utter contrast between the friendly part of the letter a) and the 68
angry chaps. II, 10–13, in which Paul fears that the community has
already slipped away from him, cannot be eliminated by a reference
to II, 11:1*b* (thus W. Michelis, [1], p. 181), rgeardless of how one
understands the ἀλλὰ καὶ ἀνέχεσθέ μου.

Cf. now also G. Bornkamm, [1], pp. 16 ff., who once again effectively 69
argues the description of II, 10–13 as the sorrowful epistle; D. Georgi,
[1], pp. 16 ff.
Cf. W. Marxsen, pp. 80-81.   70

G. Bornkamm ([1], pp. 31-32), following the lead of others, has   71
chap. 9 written and sent *after* chap. 8. Titus then is the bearer of the
joyful epistle. This, however, is nowhere indicated. The difference in
the commendation of the messengers argues for the view that chap. 9
was delivered by Titus. W. Marxsen (p. 82) also puts chap. 9 later
than the joyful epistle (with chap. 8). His argument that in chap. 9
Paul is boasting to the Macedonians of the collection in Achaia, exactly the reverse of chap. 8, suggests, however, that at the time of chap.
9 the success of the Macedonian collection was not yet as visible as at
the time of chap. 8, particularly since Paul in fact boasts to the Macedonians only of the *intention* (9:2) of the Christians of Achaia, not
of the results of their collection.
D. Georgi ([3], pp. 56 ff.) thinks that neither chap. 8 nor chap. 9
can be connected with the joyful epistle (F), and regards both chapters as two independent letters written in close succession as recom-
mendations of the collection. Georgi's reasons for detaching chap. 8
from the joyful epistle, however, are not convincing. Georgi begins
from the incorrect presuppositions that II, 7:5 reflects an unfriendly
reception of Paul among the Christians of Macedonia and that Titus

is the bearer of the joyful epistle. Moreover, it is also quite unlikely, from general considerations, that in the joyful epistle Paul should not have said anything about the collection.

72   J. S. Semler (*Paraphrasis II epistulae ad Corinth.*, Praefatio b and pp. 238-39) already had considered the question whether chap. 9 was not addressed to the Achaian communities other than Corinth.

73   D. Georgi ([1], pp. 16 ff.) and G. Bornkamm ([1], pp. 21 ff.) also are of the conviction that II, 2:14–7:4 is an *independent* fragment of a letter. Cf. already A. Halmel, *Der zweite Korintherbrief des Apostles Paulus* (1904), pp. 79 ff., 106.

Cf. also Halmel, *Der Vierkapitelbrief im 2. Kor. des Apostels Paulus* (Essen, 1894). Cf. also H. Windisch, pp. 19, 225, who indeed takes the passage in question as a self-contained unit, but would relocate it before II, 1:12 or after II, 7:16. Cf. further W. Marxsen, pp. 79-80.

74   G. Bornkamm thinks with respect to II, 1:13 ff. that it "would be quite conceivably their appeal to the announcement of the visit in I, 16:5 ff. Here the anticipated route of travel indeed is different (Ephesus-Macedonia-Corinth) from that in II, 1:15-16 (Corinth-Macedonia-Corinth). Still the mere question of the route hardly was a stone of offence for the Corinthians, but the fact that Paul still owes them the promised longer visit, which alone can justify the expression δευτέρα χάρις (II, 1:15)—corresponding to his first working in Corinth when he founded the church there." However, (1) this understanding of δευτέρα χάρις appears to me to be inadequately grounded and incapable of such a grounding; (2) 1:15 (first to you, then to the Macedonians) and 2:1 ff. show that in fact the itinerary was under discussion; the complaint against Paul was not the delayed visit but the unreliability of his word: II, 1:17 ff.; and (3) the plan of I, 16:5 ff. could yield no basis at all for a complaint, since Paul in fact is carrying through with this very plan!

The view that I connect the δευτέρα χάρις in II, 1:15 with the interim visit which took place, as Bornkamm says in his further argument, must be a misunderstanding. Or does Bornkamm mean to say that the πρώτη χάρις which is presupposed by the "δευτέρα χάρις" is the interim visit? This is of course my opinion.

75   According to G. Bornkamm ([1], pp. 24 ff.) the composition of II Cor. was concluded with Epistle D, because according to a law of form for early Christian literature the warning against false teachers and false prophets belongs at the end of an epistolary piece or anything of

the sort. This is a good and attractive hypothesis, but of course nothing more. Cf. Vol. 2, pp. 198 ff.

J. Héring ([1]; [2]) shows himself to be very much interested in 76 this question; nevertheless his reflections are not free from contradictions; cf. the detailed discussions by W. Michaelis in TLZ 75 (1950), cols. 343 ff.; 83 (1958), cols. 508 ff.

Also not very satisfactory is R. Batey, "Paul's Interaction with the Corinthians," JBL 84 (1965): 139-46. Many of the relevant details given by D. Georgi ([3], *passim*) are more created than exegetical; on this, see my discussion in TLZ 92 (1967), cols. 668 ff. J. C. Hurd, *The Origin of I Corinthians* (1965), seeks in an extensively speculative fashion to illumine the events preceding I Cor., i.e., actually Epistle B. The author is well-read, particularly in the literature of the nineteenth century. However, this qualification and some individual correct observations cannot gloss over the fact that he fails in his historical attempt to shed light on the pre-history of I Cor. W. G. Kümmel has said (in TLZ 91 [1966], cols. 505 ff.) what is necessary by way of criticism.

Of course this assumption is not necessary; cf. W. Michaelis, [1], 77 p. 175.

For the sake of comparison I offer the following earlier analyses, 78 which in significant measure diverge from one another: J. Weiss, [2], pp. 271 ff.:

A: I, 10:1-23; 6:12-20; 11:2-34; 16:7 (?), 8-9, 20-21 (?); II, 6:14–7:1
B^1: I, 7-9; 10:24–11:1; 12:1–16:6, 7 (?), 15-19 (?)
Letter about the collection II, 8
B^2: I, 1:1–6:11; 16:10-14, 22-24 (?)
C: II, 2:14–6:13; 7:2-4; 10–13
D: II, 1:1–2:13; 7:5-16; 9
M. Goguel, *Introduction au Nouveau Testament*, IV, 2 (1926): 72-86:
A: II, 6:14–7:1; I, 6:12-20; 10:1-22
B: I, 5:1–6:11; 7:1–8:13; 10:23–14:40; 15:1-58; 16:1-9, 12
C: I, 1:10–4:21; 9:1-27; 16:10-11
D: II, 10:1–13:10
E: II, 1:1–6:13; 7:2–8:24
F: II, 9:1-15
The place of the rest cannot be determined.
J. Héring, [1], pp. xiii ff.; [2], pp. xii-xiii.
A: I, 1–8; 10:23–11:1; 16:1-4, 10-14
B: I, 9:1–10:22; 11:2–15:58; 16:5-9, 15-24

C: II, 10–13
D: II, 9
E: II, 1–8

The considerable differences in the various analyses must not lead to the conclusion that thereby the ones responsible for the analyses themselves refute the possibility or necessity of a literary-critical analysis of the epistles—C. K. Barrett, *A Commentary on the First Epistle to the Corinthians* (1968), p. 14, argues in this direction; instead, they must be the occasion of our seeking the best analysis possible.

79   Cf. also the cautious "I hear" in I, 11:18 = Epistle A.

80   Of course the name of Chloe is missing in the greeting list addressed to Ephesus in Rom. 16; this makes her origin in Ephesus appear to me very doubtful. Perhaps Chloe's people came neither from Ephesus nor from Corinth.

81   Thus G. Bornkamm again most recently speaks ([1], p. 19) of "the so surprisingly successful interim epistle of the apostle." Similarly W. Marxsen, pp. 79-80, likewise without justification.

82   Cf. now Vol. 2, pp. 132 ff.
      It could then, e.g., be that some appointment with Timotheus prevented Paul from a longer stay in Corinth.

83   Thus recently again G. Bornkamm ([1], p. 9): ". . . immediately thereafter."

84   Cf. II, 12:18.

85   Did Paul not mention in the sorrowful epistle the revived change in travel plans? II, 12:14 and 13:1 leave open the question of which route Paul will take. Thus at the time of Epistle D (or only later? thus W. Marxsen, pp. 88-89) Paul could have abandoned *without announcement* the plan presumably (see p. 99) announced in C (II, 1:13) to travel *directly* from Ephesus to Corinth (II, 1:15-16), only telling Titus personally of the change. This led to the accusation reflected in II, 1:13, which Paul cannot easily parry in II, 1:13 ff., 23, since the apostle apparently only now, i.e., in Epistle F, communicates in writing the change in travel plans which in the meantime has been put into effect. Cf. H. Windisch, p. 75, on II, 1:23: "The justification must be new to the Corinthians; apparently Paul had thought that

without any further explanation he could substitute the epistle for a visit."

Most recently to my knowledge E. Golla (*Zwischenreise und Zwi-*   86
schenbrief [1922]) has attempted to deny the existence of an interim epistle (and of the interim visit) at all. His attempt does violence to the text.

Over against the sequence, "interim visit—Epistle C—intervening event—sorrowful epistle," G. Bornkamm ([1], pp. 23-24), followed by W. Marxsen (pp. 80-81), would like to maintain the traditional sequence of "Epistle C—interim visit—intervening event—sorrowful epistle." Compared with the course of events as a whole, of course, this is hardly "a significantly divergent account" (p. 23, n. 89). Against the first-mentioned sequence Bornkamm objects: "I cannot see how one can tear apart the three things mentioned in the closest conjunction (interim visit, episode, and sorrowful epistle). Besides, in 2:14–7:4 there is not found the slightest reference to the visit that allegedly had just taken place" (p. 24). The second objection says nothing, because—for whatever reason—the letter fragment C contains *no* indications *at all* (anymore?) of the situation. The first argument is incomprehensible to me, since I do not at all pull apart the interim visit, episode, and sorrowful epistle. That the incident took place during the interim visit, as Bornkamm thinks, is nowhere indicated. On the contrary, it is excluded, since it was the incident that caused the change in travel plans (II, 2:1 ff.). Thus it must have intervened *after* Paul's departure from his interim visit and naturally before the sorrowful epistle. For when should the earlier travel plans described in I, 1:15, the abandonment of which was charged by the Corinthians against Paul, have been in effect in Corinth if not at and after Paul's departure from Corinth?

D. Georgi ([1], p. 27, n. 1) also holds firm to the traditional sequence, since the intervening event must have occurred during the interim visit: "for the λύπη of which Paul speaks in 2:1 ff. must indeed have been connected with the interim visit." But why? To conclude from the "personal vehemence" of the sorrowful epistles that here Paul makes "reference not to what is reported to him but to a very recent personal experience" is not only illogical but even fatal. For this reflection presupposes that Paul withdrew from immediate confrontation by flight, in order to make good from a safe distance by vehemence what he lacked in courage. But then it would remain incomprehensible how in the sorrowful epistle the discussion is conducted without reference to the interim visit and the interim event which allegedly happened in that connection.

Cf. also D. Georgi, [3], pp. 44 ff.

H. Ulonska (in EvTheol 26 [1966]: 379) argues in favor of the order "Epistle C—interim visit—Epistle D": "That is to say, with this arrangement Paul's completely different basis of argument against his opponents in the sorrowful epistle can be explained: He has recently become acquainted with them, he understands their language, he perceives their gnostically oriented polemic." This suggestion proceeds from the incorrect assumption that Epistle D shows a completely different basis of argument from Epistle C. Actually, however, the *basis* of the Pauline argument in C almost totally coincides with that in D; the amount of information possessed and the points of contention show no essential difference. The measure of the Corinthians' estrangement from the authority of his gospel assumed by Paul is different. But now Epistle F shows that at the time of Epistle D Paul had had too gloomy a view. Hence the difference between Epistles C and D can hardly go back to the apostle's own outlook. In other words, there was no visit by Paul to Corinth between Epistles C and D, but indirect and evidently sketchy reports about the situation there.

87   Thus again D. Georgi, [3], pp. 44, 51.

88   Naturally Paul also had to inform the Macedonian churches of the sudden change in his travel plans. The embassy of Timotheus and Erastus to Macedonia mentioned in Acts 19:22 may have served that purpose. In the letters to Corinth this visit of course is not mentioned; yet we learn from II, 1:1 (= Epistle F) that when he was in Macedonia, Paul had Timotheus (again) with him.

89   The charge that Paul is preaching for money apparently already stands back of Paul's apology in I, 9:4-23, although there Paul hardly connected this charge with the collection. Nevertheless in the same epistle (B) he already takes precautions against slanders connected therewith: I, 16:3. Again in Epistle C he refutes corresponding accusations: II, 7:2.

The reaction to the charges against Paul is shown then in the commendation concerning the collection in the joyful epistle, II, 8:18-21: Paul sends with Titus two brethren chosen by the churches "so that no one may blame us about this generous gift which we are administering, for we aim at what is honorable not only in the sight of the Lord but also in the sight of men" (cf. II, 9:5).

Incidentally Paul must, at almost the same time, defend himself against similar-sounding charges which, brought forward in similarly massive form, are meant to undermine his apostolic authority in Thessalonica also; on this, see Vol. 2, pp. 103 ff.

Cf. further H. Lietzmann, *in loc.;* G. Delling in TDNT VI: 273;   90
W. Hartke, *Die Sammlung und die ältesten Ausgaben der Paulusbriefe,* p. 14.

The explicit mention of Titus and his companion in II, 12:18 presupposes with some likelihood that both names had been cited in Corinth in connection with the charges against Paul. Both were in Corinth on the occasion of the collection (II, 8:6), and this observation confirms the conjecture that the accusation encountered in II, 12:16 was related to the collection. Cf. H. Windisch, pp. 402, 404.

The use in II, 2:11 (Epistle F) of πλεονεκτεῖν, which has often been   91
felt to be strange and in Paul especially surprising, ". . . to keep Satan from gaining an advantage over us" (RSV), may be making reference with a play on words to II, 12:17-18 (Epistle D; cf. II, 7:2; 9:5). Similarly, in I Thess. 4:6 (cf. with I Thess. 2:5) Paul apparently is playing with the concept πλεονεκτεῖν (see Vol. 2, pp. 113 ff.).

Thus it is not justifiable to assert that "the only thing that we know   92
for certain about the severe letter is that Paul demanded the punishment of one of the church members" (J. Munck, p. 170), a broad assertion with which the argument often is unjustifiably made against the assignment of II, 10–13 to the sorrowful epistle, since in II, 10–13 no sort of punishment of an evildoer is demanded.

Some time after sending the sorrowful epistle Paul leaves Asia and   93
travels to Macedonia. There he meets Titus (II, 7:6; later than expected: II, 2:12-13) and Timotheus (see note 88). It cannot be determined whether the event reported in II, 1:8 ff. occurred before or after the sending of the sorrowful epistle. Cf. further W. Michaelis, [3], pp. 67 ff.

Cf. H. Lietzmann on II, 8:17.   94

Cf. W. Michaelis, [3], pp. 75 ff.   95

D. Georgi ([2], p. 96) writes: "This setting of the boundaries rests   96
in essence on the presupposition that Paul actually carried through with his intention, expressed in I Cor. 16:8, to leave Ephesus before (*sic!*) Pentecost. But there is no compelling proof of this. Quite the

contrary." What is the meaning of "proof" and "quite the contrary"? The *contrary* is what one would have to *prove!* For Paul intends to leave Ephesus *after* (!) Pentecost. This plan is part of the larger itinerary which includes the gathering of the collection, Jerusalem, and Rome. This trip, as for example the organization of the collection shows, was long agreed upon with several communities. Paul could hardly alter it essentially at all or allow any considerable delay in it. Any such considerable delay would have had to leave its traces at least in the later correspondence. This did not happen. "Quite the contrary!" The "course of events" does not show—indeed, it rules out the possibility—that Paul suddenly extended his sojourn in Ephesus for about a year, as Georgi would like, in order to make a place for the agitation of two countermissions emerging in Corinth independent of each other and in succession (see above, pp. 289 ff.) .

In [1], p. 28, Georgi thinks that eight months is too short a period, because Paul stayed in Ephesus about two and one-half years. I have no desire to dispute the latter point, but I do not understand what connection there is between the length of Paul's stay in Asia Minor during his third journey and the duration of the confusion in Corinth.

Cf. also T. Zahn, pp. 318 ff.; W. Michaelis, [3], pp. 73-74. Of course there is nothing to indicate that, as Michaelis thinks, Timotheus' trip mentioned in I, 16:10 was a trip for the collection, and because of the separation between 16:1-4 and 16:1 it is even unlikely.

97   If, as we have surmised, about October Paul travels through Macedonia toward the south and spends the following passover again in Philippi or (on this, cf. E. Haenchen, [2], pp. 515 ff.) Troas, about six months would be available for the trip to and from Achaia. The three months—a round number—"in Hellas" (Acts 20:2-3) fall within this time. This fits together well.

Cf. further E. Haenchen, [2], pp. 514-15. Haenchen's remark which represents a *communis opinio:* ". . . above all, Paul was in Corinth . . . where he wrote the epistle to the Romans (Rom. 15:22-29) " is uncertain in both parts. From Rom. 15:22-29 it emerges with some certainty only that Paul is writing the epistle in Achaia. And the striking statement that Paul has stayed three months in Ἑλλάς (only here in the NT) rather argues *against* a longer stay specifically in Corinth, and after all that had gone before this is easily understandable—in spite of I, 16:7.

It is true that the Gaius of Rom. 16:23, in whose presence Paul is writing to Rome, apparently is a Corinthian (I, 1:14). But ξένος by no means has to mean that he was *host* to Paul and the community when Paul was writing to Rome. He could just as well be a *guest* with them outside Corinth.

According to W. Hartke, Titus 3:12-15 is part of a genuine epistle of Paul which was written to Titus in Macedonia in the time which we are discussing here. I consider this an attractive and well-justified conjecture. Paul then spent the winter in Nicopolis before he visited Corinth in order there to put to sea (Acts 20:3). From there he writes (to Titus in Corinth?) the lines in Titus 3:12-15.

In recent times, cf. further H. J. Schoeps, [3], pp. 69 ff.   98

In the two epistles Paul does not suggest with a single word that he   99
is fighting against two different groups of opponents in Corinth. This fact must not be ignored.

D. Georgi ([2], p. 96) thinks that the differentiation is a *methodo-*   100
logical exigency. Certainly! But this does not mean that an investigation must presuppose differences in *its object.* On Georgi's study, see esp. pp. 289 ff.

The brief span of time covered by the correspondence also does not   101
allow us to investigate individual letters or parts of letters without relating them to the rest of the correspondence in order thus to be able clearly to determine the background of the polemic at least for parts of Paul's writings. The results achieved by such a method justify skepticism from the outset. Thus E. Käsemann ([1]) treats II, 10–13 without any attention to the rest of the correspondence (see above, p. 120; p. 185, n. 103). J. Munck, pp. 135 ff., examines I, 1–4 and II, 10–13 in isolation. H. Koester in RGG (3rd ed.), III (*s.v.* "Häretiker im Urchristentum") isolates I Cor. and II Cor. from each other and affirms a different line of battle for each. Similarly D. Georgi ([1]), who in the correctly reconstructed epistles C and D sees the battle waged against opponents other than those in I Cor., and G. Friedrich in O. Michel, pp. 181 ff.

U. Wilckens ([1]) examines only I, 1–2, but nevertheless rightly judges: "But from the results of our analysis, everything else which Paul indicates *in the two Corinthian epistles* about the theology of the Corinthian adversaries can be understood without further ado in the very same context" (p. 212).

Thus for the answering of the question about Paul's adversaries in Corinth, it is methodologically indispensable to take as a basis all the correspondence with Corinth. This method does not mean any prejudging of the question as to Paul's adversaries, but is rather the presupposition of any decision.

In essence this is the opinion of D. Georgi also ([1], p. 29). Although he writes: "Thus it is advisable . . . to choose a relatively narrow text basis as point of departure for the actual investigation," he regards it as necessary "then to ask how far outward from there the radius may be drawn." One will surely understand Georgi correctly when he wishes to give expression to the opinion that the conclusion reached on the narrow textual basis must also be open to corrections which prove to be necessary when one draws the radius. That he entirely omits in his investigation to draw this radius is another matter.

D. W. Oostendorp also neglects the comparison with I Cor. which seems necessary (*Another Jesus*, pp. 5, 81-82). R. Baumann, *Mitte und Norm des Christlichen*, exegetes only I, 1:1–3:4, but in spite of this narrow foundation makes a judgment about the Corinthian situation in general. It is no accident that this judgment is not very satisfactory.

To this I may append one further remark on method. From the course of events set forth above it emerges with certainty that Paul was at first only poorly, later better, but hardly ever fully informed about conditions in Corinth and their background. In view of the distance between Ephesus and Corinth, the only occasional connection between them and the largely indirect information, this is only natural. It is methodologically demanded that in any individual exegesis this fact be taken into account. One must reckon with deficient information and therefore also with misunderstandings on the part of the apostle. It is altogether possible that the interpreter, who reads the first pieces of the correspondence in the light of the last and can understand the limited emergence of the false teachers in Corinth from a far more comprehensive knowledge of their religious movement, is able better and more correctly than the apostle himself to interpret individual statements of Paul about conditions in Corinth. This holds true in particular if in Corinth Paul is encountering a doctrine which he had not encountered elsewhere, and which therefore was unknown to him from the ground up. The exegete, however, must reckon with this.

Knowledge of this state of affairs and of the method of investigation appropriate to it undoubtedly does not render the interpretation easy, but it does make it possible for the first time. W. Marxsen, pp. 55-56 also sees this very properly (cf. "Exegese und Verkündigung," *Theologische Existenz heute* 59: 46, n. 5), especially in view of the significance of the method sketched for exegesis that is theological in the narrower sense. The necessity of such a method is in any case hardly to be disputed. At any rate it is pointless to caricature it, as one reviewer of the first edition does, instead of refuting it. One can argue in seriousness only about its use in any given case. Unfortunately G. Friedrich (in O. Michel, p. 194) also fails to do this. Cf. further Vol. 2, p. 68, n. 123.

Utter misunderstanding of the heuristic distinction between the views of the opponents and the Pauline interpretation of these views is shown also by E. Güttgemanns. To the detriment of his exegesis, he proceeds from a modern version of the dogma of inspiration and has Paul in every case completely informed about the situation in distant Corinth and about the theology of his Gnostic opponents. Güttgemanns irritably rejects the consideration, necessary in view of the mostly indirect information, of whether in every case Paul possessed adequate news: "Thus Paul is notoriously incapable of thinking" (p. 114, n. 111). As though thinking could be a substitute for information! Cf. also note 154.

On the other hand, P. Hoffmann (*Die Toten in Christus,* e.g., pp. 239 ff.) splendidly considers the possible difference between the Pauline understanding of his adversaries' views and these views themselves, as well as the misunderstandings which might possibly arise therefrom. Cf. also W. Marxsen, pp. 83-84; E. Haenchen, in RGG (3rd ed.), II, col. 1653; E. Dinkler, in RGG (3rd ed.), IV, cols. 18-19.

There is a related distinction, moreover, when, following the lead of others H. Conzelmann (*The Theology of St. Luke,* pp. 73 ff.) explains individual passages of the Lucan literature under the assumption that the evangelist was not familiar in detail with the geography of Palestine. Vico had already observed and in principle thought through the problem in method which lies at this point: cf. R. G. Collingwood, *The Idea of History,* pp. 68-69.

Letters of recommendation were very common in antiquity and, in view of the many charlatans, indispensable. For the intercourse between Christian congregations Paul himself gives several examples of these; cf. H. Windisch, pp. 103-4; H. Lietzmann, p. 110.   102

Cf. *The Office of Apostle,* pp. 219 ff.   103

Cf. further W. Bauer, p. 56.   104

"Die Christuspartei in der korinthischen Gemeinde," *Tübinger   105 Zeitschrift,* 1831; "Einige weitere Bemerkungen über die Christuspartei in Korinth," *ibid.,* 1836; "Beiträge zur Erklärung der Korintherbriefe I," *Theologisches Jahrbuch,* 1850; "Beiträge zur Erklärung der Korintherbriefe II," *ibid.,* 1852.

106   *Ecclesia Corinthia* . . . . Schenkel's work was discussed by F. C. Baur in the *Jahrbücher für wissenschaftliche Kritik*, 1839.

107   W. M. L. de Wette, *Kurze Erklärung der Briefe an die Korinther* (1855, 3rd ed.), pp. 2 ff. In his *Lehrbuch der historisch-kritischen Einleitung in die kanonischen Bücher des NT* (1848, 5th ed.), pp. 262 ff., de Wette gives instructive information on the discussion between F. C. Baur and D. Schenkel and their disciples as well as on the views of the earlier exegetes.

108   Its theses are rather fully adopted by F. Büchsel, *Der Geist im Neuen Testament*, pp. 367 ff., nevertheless with the noteworthy assertion: "An ethnicized Judaism which had close connections with the origins of Gnosticism would thus have been the soil in which the Corinthian fanaticism was rooted" (p. 395).

109   Yet E. Haenchen in recent times talks about how the "Corinthian Gnosticism" has "developed through an incorrect exposition of the Pauline preaching" (*Die Botschaft des Thomas-Evangeliums* [1961], p. 71). Of course such a judgment is rare nowadays. But cf. also J. M. Robinson, "Kerygma und Geschichte im NT," ZThK 62 (1965): 302.
       It is true that the opinion of U. Wilckens (in *Theol. Viat.* VIII [1961/62]: 292) now is not greatly different: "In Corinth what happened was nothing but that non-Jews who had become Christians through Paul's ministry have grasped the gospel proclaimed by Paul from the outset in a non-Jewish frame of reference, which in the course of the years had an increasingly strong effect in a troubled internal history of the community: an obvious and therefore understandable process." Now such a process certainly is not in itself impossible. But it still cannot transpose the Pauline preaching into an utterly anti-Pauline, highly mythological Gnosticism such as Wilckens himself correctly sees Paul fighting against in Corinth ([1], *passim*). Moreover, the arrival of apostles who invade the Corinthian community from without is not to be doubted (II, 3:1), as then in fact the emergence of the false teaching in the Pauline community in Corinth was an event to be set within rather narrow limits of time.

110   Cf. F. Büchsel, pp. 371-72.

111   *Novum Testamentum Graece* (Groningae, 1898).

112   Cf. further W. Bauer, p. 104; L. Goppelt, pp. 126 ff.; B. Reicke, pp. 273 ff.; U. Wilckens, [1], *passim*.

[1], p. 60; [2], p. 335.   113

On this, cf., e.g., Justin, Dial. 16:4; 47.5; 95.4; 96.1; 108.3. H. Strack,   114
pp. 66-67.

Cf. also G. Eichholz in *Theologische Existenz heute* 77: 11 ff.   115
Not every ecstatic and pneumatic utterance is glossolalia, as O. Cullmann ([1], p. 225) seems to assume. Because curse and confession are
spoken as understandable words, he detaches I, 12:3 from its connection with chap. 12 and interprets it as follows: Christians in Corinth
were being forced into the cult of the emperor; therein they had to
curse Christ. When they did this, they excused themselves in the community afterward with a reference to Matt. 10:17 ff.: the Spirit had
inspired them with the curse. This speculative explanation is not to be
justified in any of its parts. I, 12:3 belongs in its setting and therefore is connected with occurrences in the worship services (W. G.
Kümmel in Lietzmann, p. 61, 1. 12). That the problem of the sacrifice
to the emperor was already a current one for the Christians in Paul's
time is undocumented and unlikely. Matt. 10:17 was, even if it were no
vaticinium ex eventu, certainly unknown to the Pauline communities.
K. Maly ("I Kor. 12,1-3, eine Regel zur Unterscheidung der
Geister?" BiblZ, NF 10 [1966]: 82 ff.) also unjustly takes offense at the
fact that a pneumatic-ecstatic utterance in understandable language
resulted. He regards the "anathema Jesus" as a Pauline counter-
formulation to the "Kyrios Jesus," which has the function only of
"marking off the boundaries of the liberty which the Spirit brings"
(p. 89). Of course these would then be quite broad limits! Such a
criterion would at the most say nothing. Fitting criticism of Maly is
offered by N. Brox, BiblZ, NF 12 (1968): 103 ff.
Unsatisfactory are the reflections on our passage offered by D. Lührmann, *Das Offenbarungsverständnis* . . . , pp. 28-29.

This deals a fatal blow to the curious explanation which our pas-   116
sage has received most recently from O. Huth (in *Symbolon, Jahrbuch
für Symbolforschung,* Band 3, ed. by J. Schwabe, n. d. [1962?], pp. 28-
29): "In view of this text one must ask who uttered this anathema,
and the answer can only be 'John the Baptist.' For it can be spoken
only by the authoritative man of the religious band to which Jesus
once belonged."

Cf. John 20:31. The Latin fathers, like Clement and Origen, read   117
in I John 4:3, πᾶν πνεῦμα ὃ λύει τὸν Ἰησοῦν, and A. v. Harnack
(*Studien* I: 132 ff.) regards this reading, which in any case gives the

Gnostic meaning precisely, as the original one. On the other hand, Sinaiticus, which reads 'Ιησοῦν κύριον and the Koinē with the reading 'Ιησοῦν Χριστόν obliterate the reference to the dualism of the Gnostic Christology which lies in the bare 'Ιησοῦν. Moreover, from the repeated mention of the "Pneuma" in 4:1-3 it may be inferred that, as was the case in Corinth, the denunciation of "Jesus" came about through the pseudo-prophets mentioned in vs. 1 , in pneumatic-ecstatic discourse.

118   Cf. W. Wilkens in EvTheol 18 (1958) : 365; H. Braun in ZThK 48 (1951) : 289.

119   It remains a mystery to me how E. Güttgemanns (p. 64, n. 59) can give it as my opinion, allegedly expressed in the foregoing section: "Hence Paul does have a *theologia crucis,* but he does not notice that this was involved *with* the ἀνάθεμα 'Ιησοῦς." It is true that I am unable to see that in I, 12:3 Paul emphatically has the *earthly* Jesus in mind when he quotes the current primitive Christian confessional formula κύριος 'Ιησοῦς. In my judgment, the existing wording is overtaxed with such refinement of exegesis as is undertaken by Güttgemanns (pp. 65 ff.) .

120   On the following, cf. now the fine essay by N. Brox, "Anathema Jesous" (I Cor. 12:3) in BiblZ, NF 12 (1968) : 103 ff., who still points out that already Origen himself in his exegesis of I, 12:3 uses the Ophites' curse in explanation. Therewith he also explicitly contradicts the view of B. A. Pearson ("Did the Gnostics Curse Jesus?" JBL 86 [1967]: 301 ff.) that the Ophites had not cursed Jesus, but Origen had waged a polemic against them and explained that with their connection with the snake they themselves fell under the curse pronounced against the snake—an obvious distortion of what Origen says twice.

H. Conzelmann (p. 242) follows Pearson without noting the criticism by Brox. He calls the exposition given above "fantastic" and sees it as "refuted by the fact that the Corinthians without a problem acknowledged the Credo of Jesus' death and resurrection (15:1 ff.) ." But this alleged fact is an incorrect construction by Conzelmann (see note 168 on page 360) . And it is not evident to me that my explanation leaves out of consideration 12:4 ff. because there Paul assumes that the Corinthian Pneumatics had actually received the Spirit and hence could not curse Jesus: Where in I, 12–14 does Paul say that those enthusiasts who deny cross and resurrection, preach sexual libertinism, and divide the community actually have received the Spirit? I, 12–14 does have in mind that community which listens to Paul and has written to him!

Conzelmann himself holds the "Jesus is accursed" to be a counter-formulation *ad hoc* to "Jesus is Lord' (p. 241). It is true that therewith he imputes to the apostle a maximum of banality, indeed of stupidity; for would Paul not have sensed that he is emptying the confession "Jesus is Lord" of any specific content if he lets it first be limited by a "Jesus is accursed"? Since on the basis of the Corinthians' inquiry (vs. 1) Paul gives a formal explanation (vs. 3)—vs. 2 is actually a parenthesis; the γνωρίζω ὑμῖν (vs. 3) takes up again the οὐ θέλω ὑμᾶς ἀγνοεῖν—in vs. 3 only the catchwords from the Corinthian inquiry which reflect the events in Corinth can have been taken up; cf. Brox, p. 105.

J. Munck ("The New Testament and Gnosticism," StTh 15 [1961]: 121 187) considers it an "unhistorical conception of time" when, as is widely customary today, one attempts to describe and to understand the Gnosticism of the first century with the help of Gnostic documents and anti-Gnostic accounts of the second century. According to his opinion "such a correspondence of doctrine, in spite of the intervention of at least a century . . ." is "a miracle which no one who takes miracles seriously would believe in." Indeed, he regards such a method as "a striking proof of the decline of exegetic research since the thirties." This is beyond my comprehension. Is there then also no "correspondence of doctrine" between the *ecclesiastical* Christianity in the first century and in the second century?

Cf. Hennecke-Schneemelcher-Wilson, I: 313; W. Eltester, "Freund, 122 wozu bist du gekommen?" in *Neotestamentica et Patristica* (Leiden, 1962), pp. 75 ff.

Cf. also G. Eichholz in *Theologische Existenz heute* 77: 11 ff.; 123 B. Reicke, pp. 275 ff. E. Güttgemanns, pp. 62 ff.

Cf. now W. Auer, "Jesus oder Christus," in *Bibel und Kirche* 14 124 (1959) : 3-12; D. Georgi, [1], pp. 282 ff.

Even πίστις ᾽Ιησοῦ (Rom. 3:26) may possibly be a traditional way 125 of speaking.

Since F. Neugebauer (*In Christus*, p. 45) counts fourteen Pauline 126 passages with the simple "Jesus," while I on the other hand count thirteen—the difference is explained by the fact that I have counted the double occurrence in I Thess. 4:14 as only a single one—his remark (p. 49, n. 23) is incomprehensible: ". . . Schmithals appears not to have included all the passages, for I count 8.5 more passages than does he."

Neugebauer thinks moreover (without justification) that " 'Jesus' in Paul never means the merely earthly Christ." Instead "Jesus" is "for Paul the proclaimed one as the one who through his death on the cross has wrought salvation" (pp. 48-49). It is far from my intention to dispute the latter point, but that can "never at all" be the specifically characteristic feature of the use of the simple name "Jesus." Cf. only the threefold designation "Jesus" for the resurrected One in II, 4:10-14. Cf. now also D. Georgi, [1], pp. 282 ff.

W. Kramer (*Christos, Kyrios, Gottessohn*, AThANT 44 [1963]: 199 ff.), using a point of view which is not perceivable to me, counts, instead of the entire 28, only 17 passages with the simple Ἰησοῦς or ὁ Ἰησοῦς. He denies that Paul uses the simple (ὁ) Ἰησοῦς in any special way. Therewith he incorrectly attributes to me the opinion that the simple Ἰησοῦς does not denote Jesus as the bearer of the salvation event. This already shows that he does not at all perceive the real problematic of the simple Ἰησοῦς in Paul. This also shows his wholly inadequate form- and tradition-critical analysis of the passages which he considers, which does not allow Paul's usage to be elicited with sufficient differentiation.

127   I do not understand why Güttgemanns (p. 113, n. 109) makes the objection *against* my statements: "What concerns Paul is . . . precisely the identity of the heavenly Kyrios with the earthly Jesus," for this is exactly what I intend with the concept *Christos ensarkos*. Of course therein I have not asserted that Paul employs the *concept ensarkos* (*contra* Güttgemanns, p. 275, n. 28).

128   Cf. further G. Klein, p. 58, n. 248 (Literature).

129   To be sure, D. Georgi ([2], p. 95) thinks that "II Cor. 11:4 *contradicts* I Cor. 12:2" (apparently he means 12:3), for in II, 11:4 "the name Jesus takes on a *positive* significance for the opposing theology"; for "if for the opponents it were not a matter of the earthly Jesus, Paul would never have been able to say that they were speaking of another Jesus but, as in I Cor. 12:3, would have had to say that they were denying (or cursing) Jesus" ([1], p. 285, n. 6). But here the exegete is obviously making an unjust demand of Paul. Is not the Jesus cursed by the Gnostics "another Jesus" than Paul's? That in 11:4 it cannot be Gnostics who are apostrophized because the understanding of the earthly Jesus is "a rather unimportant question for Gnosticism" ([1], p. 285) is an astounding assertion.

Further, one may not appeal to the κηρύσσει in II, 11:4. It is chosen on account of the ἐκηρύξαμεν and says nothing about what significance the "other Jesus" possessed for the Corinthian theology.

J. M. Robinson, appealing to D. Georgi, writes in ZThK 62 (1965) : 328: ". . . all signs indicate that this other Jesus—somewhat as in the signs-source—is a miracle-worker endowed with power and δόξα . . . ." I am unable, however, to discover any of these signs anywhere.

"Thus the heightened emphasis upon the cross in I Cor. 1:18 ff. and 130 2:2, 8 is Paul's christological antithesis to the Corinthian rejection of the crucified One" (Güttgemanns, p. 64) —a proper comment, in which the only thing I do not understand is why Güttgemanns poses it *against* my interpretation.

The connection is made by means of the antithesis βαπτίζειν— 131 εὐαγγελίζεσθαι.

Cf. now also the (first) Apocalypse of James 31 (25). 15 ff. = A. 132 Böhlig/P. Labib, p. 41.

Cf. U. Wilckens, [2], p. 84; E. Peterson, pp. 43 ff. 133

Thus the false teachers in Corinth are "enemies of the cross of 134 Christ" (Phil. 3:18) , as are the false teachers in Philippi (see Vol. 2, pp. 77-78) .

U. Wilckens ([1], pp. 5 ff.) has thoroughly exegeted the first chapter 135 of I Cor. He not only inquires about Paul's opponents, but wishes also to understand the Pauline polemic "in its structure and its special intention" (p. 4) . This leads to a comprehensive investigation with a breadth which to be sure is often wearisome as well. With respect to our subject I can gratefully affirm the gratifying agreement of the two investigations: "Paul stands over against a teaching for which . . . the *cross* of Christ had no saving significance" (p. 20) .

Cf. also H. Conzelmann, "Paulus und die Weisheit," NTS 12 (1966) : 236 ff. R. Baumann (*Mitte und Norm des Christlichen*) also correctly works out the "theologia crucis" as "center and norm of what is Christian" on the basis of an exposition of I, 1:1–3:4. His exposition suffers, however, from the fact that he assumes as background of the Pauline statements only personal rivalries in Corinth which were caused by an overestimation of the charisma of pneumatically and rhetorically persuasive wisdom discourses. Thereby the Pauline antithesis loses some of its sharpness and suggestiveness.

136   E. Güttgemanns (pp. 148 ff.) seeks also to support this thesis with
II, 13:4. He traces the unusual ἐξ ἀσθενείας back to a Gnostic theologoumenon quoted by Paul in this passage: "The crucifixion of Jesus is
an act of a demonic power whose essence is ἀσθένεια. Only for this
reason can it appear as abrogated in the Corinthian Gnosis: Because
with the crucifixion the earthly *Jesus* has fallen victim to the demonic
ἀσθένεια of the *sarx,* the Gnostic in his apostolic existence no longer
has to do with him, but only with the pneumatic-dynamic *Christ."*
Even though this exposition fits well into our picture of the Corinthian
heresy, still it appears to me to put an excessive amount of strain on
the ἐξ, which obviously was simply prompted by the following ἐκ and
expresses the well-known Pauline idea that Jesus Christ was crucified
in or on the basis of his weakness (= his humiliation to our weakness).

137   Cf. H. Koester in E. Dinkler, ed., *Zeit und Geschichte,* p. 75, n. 20.

138   A detailed debate with U. Wilckens from the pen of K. Prümm is
found in the *Zeitschrift für katholische Theologie* 87 (1965) : 399-442;
88 (1966) : 1-50; unfortunately it is completely in error as to method.
Very pertinent, on the other hand, is the thorough critical discussion
by H. Koester in *Gnomon* 33 (1962) : 590 ff. Cf. also K. Niederwimmer,
"Erkennen und Lieben," *Kerygma und Dogma* 11 (1965) : 79-80.

139   Cf. the evident response to the σοφοί in Corinth in I, 6:5 and also
Rom. 16:19 (see Vol. 2, pp. 170-71).

140   It is true that in I, 1:25, 30 Paul speaks positively of σοφία, but it
is clear that precisely therewith he adopts the Corinthian concept in
order polemically to fill it with new content. The wisdom known by
the *called ones* is Christ, who likewise has been described as the *crucified One.* Here I note the gratifying agreement with the investigation
of U. Wilckens ([1]).

141   This is all the more true since the concept σοφία was familiar to
him from the Jewish tradition. According to E. Peterson (pp. 44 ff.),
in I, 1:18 ff. Paul is referring back directly to the praise of σοφία in
Bar. 3.9–4.4.

142   But now cf. Saying 115 from the Coptic Gospel of Philip (= Leipoldt-Schenke, p. 50): "The husbandry of the world exists by means
of four forms: people gather things into the barn because of water,
earth, wind, and light. And God's husbandry likewise exists by means

of four forms: πίστις, ἐλπίς, ἀγάπη, and γνῶσις. Our earth is faith, because in it we take root. But the water is hope, because we are nourished by it (?). The wind is love, because through it we grow. But the light is knowledge, because through it we ripen." The triad of πίστις-γνῶσις-ἐλπίς is found in Lidzbarski, *Johannesbuch* (57.17 ff.).

Thus E. Lövestam in *Studia Theologica* 12 (1958) : 83-84; B. Reicke,   143
p. 280.

This verse in fact speaks explicitly and apparently ironically to   144
those in Corinth who hold themselves to be "prophets" and "pneu-matics." But certainly we are to refer to I, 1:5 and perhaps also to II, 2:14.

The identity of this *significance*, to which Bultmann refers in TDNT   145
I: 692-93, is not made questionable by the fact that the Greek gains his knowledge in the main rationally and the Gnostic gets his by means of revelation, illumination, and vision. D. Georgi ([2], p. 94) neglects to distinguish between the existential significance of Gnosis and the way to its achievement. Therefore he mistakenly disputes a paralleling of the Greek and the Gnostic concept of knowledge, particularly with an unjustified appeal to Bultmann's article cited above. In spite of that he should not have been able to write that "in principle . . . the clarity of Greek knowing" escapes the "Gnostic" Gnosis. The irrationalism of Gnostic knowledge in no way means for the Gnostic that his Gnosis is lacking in clarity.

The Greek does not speak of γνῶσις θεοῦ (E. Norden, pp. 87 ff.).   146
This is in harmony with the fact that for him γνῶσις is essentially bound up with "seeing" (R. Bultmann in TDNT I: 691-92). The transferral of the Greek concept of knowledge to the knowledge of God occurred in the Orient and probably is originally joined with the emergence of the "Gnosis" (E. Norden, pp. 95 ff.). Cf. further S. Arai in U. Bianchi, p. 180.

Cf. further p. 33, n. 20.   147

Od. Sol. 26.12 is also characteristic: "For it suffices to have Gnosis   148
and (therein) to find rest."

Cf. further the passages in E. Norden, pp. 102-3; Iren. I, 21.5; Corp.   149
Herm. I, 19; 21; Pirqe Aboth 3.1; Acta Andr. 6; Acta Thom. 15; Tert., de praescr. haer. 7.5; G. Widengren, "Der iranische Hintergrund der

Gnosis," ZRGG 4 (1952) : 103-4; Evang. Ver. (from the Jung Codex) 22.13 ff.

150   We acknowledge that the heavenly vision, the sight and ecstasy and the μεταβολή wrought thereby in the mysteries cannot originally have been called "Gnosis"; but of course this does not mean that the *way* upon which the Gnostic gains his knowledge was not vision and ecstasy, *visio* and ἀποκάλυψις. D. Georgi ([2], pp. 94-95) does not distinguish the two. That he moreover asserts that I deny an ecstatic and visionary form of the Gnostic process of knowing is incomprehensible to me; cf. e.g., pp. 171 ff. and 279 ff. above.

151   That this Gnostic conception stems from pre-Gnostic oriental myths is shown by Widengren in *Sakrales Königtum im Alten Testament und im Judentum* (1955), pp. 66 ff.; cf. Ps. 78:65; 7:7; 35:23; 59:5-6; 44:24; Isa. 51:9. Cf. further H. Jonas, [1], pp. 113-18.

152   Cf. now also D. Lührmann, *Das Offenbarungsverständnis* . . . , pp. 113 ff. H. Langerbeck (*Aufsätze zur Gnosis* [1967], pp. 103 ff.) accordingly develops from this passage his original thesis that later Gnosticism is a systematic unfolding of Pauline theology which on its own part should and must have been understood by every Greek as the fulfillment of Platonism. These proposals, however, are not tenable. Unsatisfactory also is the view of H. Conzelmann, "Paulus und die Weisheit," NTS 12 (1966), who thinks that we still are not obliged to assume for I, 2:6 ff. a developed Gnosticism. Similarly R. Scroggs, "Paul, ΣΟΦΟΣ and ΠΝΕΥΜΑΤΙΚΟΣ," NTS 14 (1967) : 33 ff., who distinguishes in Paul between "kerygma" and "theology" and counts the wisdom doctrine offered in I, 2:6-16 as theology which is concerned with apocalyptic speculations of a wisdom type. But one ought to study this passage precisely in the light of the fact that elsewhere Paul knows *no* separation of kerygma and theology; instead, he develops the kerygma theologically, and his theology as the expression of the kerygma. R. Baumann, pp. 171 ff., also deliberately plays down the religio-historical problematic of our passage.

153   R. Baumann (p. 267, *et passim*) asserts that Paul does not envision a difference in *content* between the solid food for the mature and the milk for the infants. The only difference involved method and form. But that too hastily eliminates the essential problematic of our passage which lies in the fact that Paul undoubtedly claims to have a special wisdom for the mature, although he does hold as important only the

"word of the cross" which applies to all men, and elsewhere knows no esoteric proclamation.

Cf. H. Rusche, "Die Leugner der Auferstehung von den Toten in der korinthischen Gemeinde," *Münchener Theol. Zeitschrift* 10 (1959): 149-51.   154

J. H. Wilson (ZNW 59 [1968]: 90 ff.) explains that in his preaching in Corinth Paul had indeed spoken of the resurrection of Jesus but not of the resurrection of Christians. Now he must make up for his omission. But apart from the fact that I, 15 is not really made understandable from the perspective of this thesis, it is impossible to assume that nothing should have been said about the resurrection of the dead by Paul at all and in Corinth after about twenty years of missionary practice—and the death of half a Christian generation!   155

Contrary to E. Güttgemanns' view (pp. 79-80) the reflections in paragraph 5 here neither presuppose that Paul had "bad information" nor intend to *accuse* the apostle of not being fully informed. Of course Güttgemanns has not recognized the heuristic function of such reflections. This is shown by the strange assumption that I turn possibly existing misinformation into an *accusation* against the apostle. Wholly different, e.g., is P. Hoffmann's (p. 239) treatment of I, 15, which begins with the statement as sober as it is appropriate: "For the exegesis of the passage it is important above all to distinguish the Pauline understanding of the opposing views. The question of the actual views of the opponents has a lesser significance for the exegesis."   156

Thus already R. Bultmann, [2], I: 169.   157

Thus also R. Bultmann, [1], p. 4; H. Weinel, p. 383; E. Käsemann in ZThK 54 (1957): 18: S. M. Pavlinek in *Comm. Viat.* 1 (1958): 64, n. 28; U. Wilckens, [1], p. 212; W. Bauer, p. 104. This exegesis is confirmed by I Thess. 4:13-18; see Vol. 2, pp. 116 ff.   158

Cf. Tert., de praescr. haer. 33.7.   159

E. Güttgemanns (p. 67) objects: "Therewith Schmithals overlooks the fact that the opponents' thesis is nowhere given as ἀνάστασις οὐκ ἔστιν, but ἀνάστασις νεκρῶν οὐκ ἔστιν (vs. 12). Now the Corinthians rejected only this latter, but not the ἀνάστασις in general." Now I cannot conceive of an ἀνάστασις that would not be ἀνάστασις νεκρῶν.   160

Even the formula ἀνάστασιν ἤδη γεγονέναι means the resurrection of the
dead! That I *presuppose* that the Corinthian Gnostics would not have
been *able* to say ἀνάστασιν ἤδη γεγονέναι is, in view of the Gnostic
parallels which I have cited on p. 157, one of the assertions of Güttgemanns (pp. 67-68) which are incomprehensible to me. The question is
only whether they *did* so or whether Paul *understood* them thus. But
the latter is ruled out by the clear formulations ἀνάστασις νεκρῶν οὐκ
ἔστιν and εἰ ὅλως νεκροὶ οὐκ ἐγείρονται (vs. 29). When Güttgemanns
(p. 75) quotes vs. 12 in this form, "But if the deceased Jesus *alone* is
proclaimed as already risen, how then can some of you say, 'There is
no *more* future resurrection of the dead, *because all resurrection has
already universally occurred, and that indeed to the living,*'" the *inter-
pretamenta* of Güttgemanns (italics mine) are smoothly inserted into
the text of Paul. The same is true of the rendering of vs. 29: "If the
ἀνάστασις in general (ὅλως) refers not to the νεκροί but only to the
living . . . ." Of course with such veiled conjectures anything can be
proved.

Now it is true that Güttgemanns thinks that "it is only from the
Gnostic thesis that the resurrecion has already occurred universally
that the temporal spacing-out of the resurrection becomes understandable," as Paul proposes in vss. 23-28 (pp. 70-71). But for Paul this spacing-out goes without saying, since Christ has indeed already risen, but
the Christians have not. I am unable to see that vss. 23-28 represent
an "incomprehensible divergence from the subject" and "possibly"
must "even be excised by literary-critical procedures" (p. 74) if they
are not directed against the Gnostic thesis of the already generally
experienced resurrection. With them Paul is working precisely in the
theme of chap. 15, and the homologous manner of discourse in vss.
23-28 does not allow the idea of pointed polemic even to arise for an
unbiased reader.

Of course Güttgemanns' interpretation is not aimed at a basically
different estimation of the Corinthian situation from the one we have
given. He is only attempting to avoid the assumption that Paul has
misunderstood the Corinthian adversaries as denying the hope of the
future. But the very exegetical dislocations required for such avoidance
show the necessity of such an assumption.

P. Hoffmann, pp. 240 ff., judges correctly. Cf. further J. M. Robinson
in ZThK 62 (1965): 304-5.

161   At most one could point out that with Gnostic talk about the already
generally experienced resurrection the eschatological reserve is *ex-*

pressly abandoned; cf. H. A. Wilke, *Das Problem eines messianischen Zwischenreichs bei Paulus,* AThANT 51 (1967) : 60.

Plotinus, Enn. III, 6.6.71-72 (ed. E. Bréhier) : ". . . the true resurrec- 162
tion is a resurrection from the body." Papyr. Oxyrh. 654, 1. 31 = Hennecke-Schneemelcher-Wilson, I: 102; Eph. 5:14; Hipp. V, 8: "ἡ ἀνάστασις ἡ διὰ τῆς πύλης γινομένη τῶν οὐρανῶν." Acta Joh. 98; Pistis Sophia
100 = Schmidt-Till, 180.34; Acta Pauli 14; Coptic Gospel of Philip 23;
63; Lidzbarski, *Ginza,* 437.19 ff.; the Epistle to Rheginos from the Nag
Hammadi find: "We shall ascend to heaven like rays of the sun. . . .
This is the spiritual resurrection, which swallows up the psychical and
fleshly resurrection" (de resurrectione, ed. Malinine-Till-Quispel-
Puech [Zürich, 1963], pp. 45-46). Cf. further passages in E. Güttgemanns, pp. 68 ff.; H. W. Bartsch in ZNW 55 (1964) : 266; H. N.
Schenke in ZNW 59 (1968) : 123 ff.; J. M. Robinson in ZThK 62
(1965) : 310.

Cf. Ep. Ap. 21 ff.; 26; Iren. I, 22.1; apocryphal epistle to the Corin- 163
thians 24-25 = *Kleine Texte* 12:17.

P. Hoffmann (pp. 245-46) thinks that Paul did recognize "that the 164
Corinthian Gnostics had a hope of the hereafter, but from the perspective of his conception of the hereafter, which is indissolubly bound
up with the hope of the resurrection, he did not acknowledge this
anticipated condition of incorporeality as a blessing." This is not impossible.

Cf. Tert., de praescr. haer. 7; Justin, Dial. 62.3; Lidzbarski, *Ginza,* 165
39.4-5; 40.12 ff.; Iren. V, 31.1.

Such misunderstandings or deliberate misinterpretations apparently 166
are found also in the Talmud, insofar as the Minim, who deny the
resurrection, are to be understood to denote Gnostics; cf., e.g., TSanh.
13.4; RH 16*b*, 34.

That at the beginning of his discussion of the question of the resur- 167
rection in I, 15 Paul makes a detailed reference to the resurrection of
Jesus would be inexplicable if he could proceed on the assumption that
the fact of Jesus' resurrection was undisputed in Corinth. The assertion, occasionally encountered, that the false teachers in Corinth did
not deny the resurrection of Jesus is therefore untenable, especially
since it is also without any basis elsewhere in the text. It is curious that

even U. Wilckens agrees with this erroneous thesis (in *Dogma und
Denkstrukturen,* ed. by W. Joest and W. Pannenberg [1963], p. 61,
n. 11); for he correctly regards Paul's opponents in Corinth as Gnostics. But Gnostics deny the (bodily) resurrection altogether and as
such, without being able to distinguish between the body of Christ and
that of the Christians. Cf. "οἱ δὲ λέγοντες ἀνάστασιν οὐκ εἶναι τῆς
σαρκὸς . . . οὐ πιστεύουσιν, ὅτι ὁ νεκρὸς (*scil.,* κύριος) οὕτως ἀνέστη
(apocryphal epistle to the Corinthians 24-25). In Ign. Smyrn. 1.2 a
Gnostic tradition is reworked which reinterprets the Easter confession
to say that Jesus arises into the body of the church (see p. 59, n. 140).

For the assumption that the Corinthians had not denied the resurrection of Jesus, people usually claim support from vss. 13 and 16, where
Paul makes it clear to the readers that the confession of Jesus' resurrection also collapses with the denial of the resurrection in general.
But does Paul mean to say to the Corinthians, "If you correctly deny
the resurrection of the dead, then to be consistent you would *have* to
deny the resurrection of Jesus also—which you acknowledge"? This
latter is precisely what Paul does not express, and after vss. 1-11 he
cannot even *mean* this. In vss. 13-16 Paul is not arguing from the
allegedly acknowledged resurrection of Jesus, the contesting of which
he rather clearly presupposes in vss. 1-11, but on the basis of the resurrection of the dead which is contested in principle, and he makes clear
the consequences which result from this contesting, without reflecting
on the question to what extent people in Corinth had already drawn
such consequences. Cf. also E. Güttgemanns, p. 58.

168   H. Conzelmann, EvTheol 25 (1965), writes (pp. 10-11) of the Corinthians: "They do not doubt that 'Christ' [*sic*] has died. But they
are oriented exclusively to the resurrection. They are not Gnostics,
but Spirit enthusiasts . . . , they separate Christ's resurrection from his
death. They spiritually leave death behind them." Conzelmann justifies
this differentiation between Gnostics and Spirit enthusiasts with the
statement that "Paul presupposes that the confession of faith is
acknowledged in Corinth"—a principle which undoubtedly holds true
for Paul's community, but not for the heretics who precisely in I, 15
are plainly distinguished from the community, and whose assertion
that there is no resurrection of the dead betrays anything but an agreement with the church's confession of Christ, however this assertion
may have been understood. Besides, I do not comprehend how a
Spirit enthusiasm which *spiritually* leaves death behind can appeal to
the primitive Christian confession of the bodily resurrection of Jesus.
Anyone who as an enthusiast denies that there is a resurrection of the

dead can appeal on behalf of his denial only to the Spirit-Christ, not to the resurrected One.

In his commentary in I Cor. also Conzelmann thoroughly defines the opposition in I Cor. in terms of the repeated stereotyped axiom that Paul's opponents in Corinth had not contested the confession of Jesus as the crucified and resurrected Christ (pp. 29, 48, 52, 55, 242, *et passim*). It is largely with this axiom that differing analyses are refuted.

To be consistent, then, Conzelmann must detach Paul's statements in I, 1:18 ff., which place the "cross" in opposition to "wisdom," from 1:12 ff., the polemic against partisan divisions, although the argument in chap. 3 again ends in the question of parties and even Conzelmann does not wish to deny that Paul's opponents boasted of their wisdom (3:18)!

And it is equally consistent when he understands I, 15:1-11 as a communication of the confession of faith *acknowledged without doubting* even by Paul's opponents. Indeed he himself sees that in view of the verses mentioned this understanding is hardly possible; it does appear that Paul is producing "an impressive series of witnesses and therewith a proof of the resurrection of Jesus" (p. 304). But since Conzelmann's maxim, *presupposed* even here—where it still has to be proved—that "in Corinth the resurrection of *Jesus* is not at all doubted," this appearance *must* be deceptive. The import of the enumeration of witnesses is rather "to establish the resurrection of Jesus as a *past* event" (p. 306); in vs. 6 the stress is placed upon the fact that some have already died—an interpretation in my judgment almost grotesque and not to be documented from anything in I, 15:1-11, which would be untenable even if the Corinthian adversaries had not actually doubted the resurrection of Jesus.

For this cardinal element in his entire exposition, Conzelmann now appeals to 15:11 and to 15:13. But in 15:11, it is demonstrable that alongside κηρύσσομεν there stands the ingressive aorist ἐπιστεύσατε, which deliberately avoids the πιστεύετε to be expected in Conzelmann's interpretation, and with the help of which Paul obviously seeks anew to enjoin the now *threatened* confession of the *beginning;* cf. 15:2.

In 15:13 Paul adds to the affirmation implied in 15:12, "if Christ has risen, then there is also a general resurrection of the dead," its converse, "if there is no resurrection of the dead, then Christ also has not risen." Conzelmann (p. 313) thinks that Paul intends (as in vs. 29) to refute his opponents from their own presuppositions: "Since you acknowledge the resurrection of Jesus, to be consistent you must also affirm the resurrection of the dead." Otherwise the sentence would be "formal logical inference drawing." Yet this alternative is constructed with a view to what is to be proved; for in vs. 13 Paul in no way indicates that he intends to refute the Corinthians from their own presuppositions. Actually the function of the change from vs. 12 to vs. 13, repeated from vs. 15b to vs. 16, lies beyond that alternative in establishing the unity and indissoluble connection between the resurrection of the dead and Jesus' resurrection, as vs. 20 then in fact explicitly draws the conclusion from vss. 12-19: Jesus has risen *as the first of all who sleep;* Christ's resurrection is not a solitary case.

Hence the train of thought altogether runs as follows:

1. Christ has actually risen; *this can be proved:* vss. 1-11.
2. But Christ's resurrection must be understood as the dawn of the general resurrection of the dead: vss. 12-19.
3. Hence it follows from Christ's resurrection that the dead in general will rise: vss. 20 ff.

The point of departure for the argument here is by no means the acknowledged, but the provable (and, in view of the Corinthian situation, first and foremost to be proved: vss. 1-11) resurrection of Jesus.

If therefore one follows Conzelmann's advice to determine the Corinthian position on the basis of "what is to be drawn from the text" (p. 29), one cannot base this position on the view that the Corinthians who denied the resurrection nevertheless acknowledged the resurrection of Jesus. This assertion rather is revealed to be a premise which is not only religio-historically untenable but also unsuited to the texts.

169   Unfortunately R. C. Tannehill (*Dying and Rising with Christ,* pp. 84 ff.) in his exposition of our passage does not consider the specific reference of the Pauline statements. The exposition of D. W. Oostendorp (*Another Jesus,* pp. 59 ff.) remains entirely unsatisfactory; see my review in TLZ 93 (1968), cols. 503-4.

170   Cf. *The Office of Apostle,* pp. 48 ff., 222 ff.

171   Cf. note 127.

172   I am bewildered by E. Güttgemanns' charge (p. 97, n. 25; p. 98, n. 30; p. 125, *et passim*) that with my exposition of II, 4:7 ff. the "theologia crucis" is in principle eliminated. I am even more perplexed to read that therewith I give up on understanding the Pauline train of thought. In passing Güttgemanns interprets the passage to mean that in his sufferings Paul, as apostle, makes the crucified One immediately manifest. The sufferings of Jesus are, so to speak, repeated in the suffering of his apostle. Hence Güttgemanns can speak of a "demon-

stration of identity" (p. 119) or can say that Paul is defending his Christology at one and the same time (!) with his apostolic rights (p. 117, n. 135). The sufferings of the apostle are to be described as a "christological epiphany" (p. 195), the bodily existence of the apostle acquires "christological relevance" (p. 134). Thereby the apostle moves out of the community and becomes, with Christ, something over against it (pp. 195, 324 ff.).

Now here *I* would speak of a—threatened, at least—elimination of the "theologia crucis." In other words, if one does not, with Güttgemanns, make it into a mere formal principle, this "theologia crucis" is constituted by the unrepeatable "once-for-all" of Jesus' sufferings, which as so unique an event can be present only in the proclamation at all times, but never in fulfillment of existence of some outstanding Christian officeholders. The variation of the "Christus prolongatus" offered by Güttgemanns in conscious association with the mystic-Gnostic idea of identity (p. 139) makes it appear, on the other hand, in principle a matter of private preference whether the glory of God is beheld in the suffering of Jesus or in the suffering of his apostle, and the purportedly radical contrast of this concept of apostle to Gnosticism (p. 139) is in fact only a very relative one.

However, in II, 4:7 ff. Paul defends himself precisely against the unreasonable demand of his Gnostic opponents that he overestimate the apostolate christologically; this he does by affirming that the *true* proclaimers of the gospel (in II, 4 Paul is by no means speaking exclusively of the *apostles*, as Güttgemanns assumes) bear this treasure in earthen vessels, so that it must be clear to everyone that the superlative power of this gospel comes solely from God and not at all out of the existence of the messenger (4:7) —*this* is *theologia crucis*, which brings man, and above all the apostle, to naught, not the epiphany-bearer of Deity. Therewith neither a connection between weakness and gospel nor a positive function of weakness for the gospel is disputed, as Güttgemanns incomprehensibly attributes to me (p. 97). Instead, the connection of the two is rather affirmed, to be sure in a way required by the text itself and the context of the Pauline theology. Güttgemanns—I turn his charge (p. 97, n. 25) back on him—turns both into the opposite.

The same appears to be the case in Galatia: Gal. 4:12 ff.; see Vol. 2, pp. 34-35. 173

Cf. Gal. 2:20. 174

175   Paul's statement in I, 3:1 ff. that he has been able to deal with the Corinthians only in the sphere of "sarkic" speech afforded his opponents a good opportunity to discredit Paul as a "sarkic" in their sense and to call on Paul himself as a witness to the fact. As we have seen, they did not let this opportunity slip.

176   Cf. W. Lütgert, p. 115.

177   D. W. Oostendorp's exposition (pp. 17 ff.) seems to me to be entirely misleading. He says that Paul's (judaizing) opponents made the charge against him that he lacked the necessary "spiritual power" to deal with the moral lapses of the Corinthians who are still entangled in paganism.

178   All the less is Ἀδάμ to be added, as E. Brandenburger, *Adam und Christus,* thinks, without noting the neuter in vs. 46.

179   "It is clear that this sentence is meaningful only if Paul thinks of a doctrine which asserts just what he denies here" (O. Cullmann, [1], p. 168). Thus also many other interpreters.

180   Cf. W. Bousset, *Kyrios Christos* (ET, 1970), p. 178.

181   If vs. 46 belongs to the original text, it is formally to be regarded as a parenthesis; cf. E. Brandenburger, p. 74, n. 4.
        Unfortunately E. Güttgemanns (p. 57, n. 21) abhors my arguments on vs. 46 as a distortion which withholds from the reader some important information.
        On the problematic of the temporal relation of "spiritual" and "fleshly," cf. Ps.-Clem. Hom. 16 ff.

182   Thus in I, 14:37-38, e.g., Paul addresses, just as bitterly and ironically as he speaks in 14:36, those in Corinth who represent themselves as prophets and Pneumatics. Cf. most recently G. Eichholz in *Theologische Existenz heute* 77: 8-9.

183   Cf. also Gal. 3:2; 5:25; 6:1; see Vol. 2, pp. 32 ff.

184   Naturally this does not mean—as all the commentators say—"for the *common* profit"; for that is not found here. Paul rather means that there are no unprofitable gifts of the Spirit (as the "Pneumatics" think with regard to the non-ecstatic gifts of grace within the Pauline

communities); *all* gifts of the Holy Spirit are profitable gifts. Cf. D. Lührmann, pp. 27-28.

Cf. R. Bultmann, [2], I: 158; on I, 3:1 ff., see pp. 151 ff. above. 185

On this, cf. W. Bauer, *Der Wortgottesdienst der ältesten Christen* 186 (1930), pp. 33 ff.; J. Behm in TDNT I: 722 ff.; S. D. Currie, "Speaking in Tongues," *Interpretation* 19 (1965): 274 ff.; J. P. M. Sweet, "A Sign for Unbelievers," NTS 13 (1967): 240 ff.

The προφητεύειν also denotes an immediate utterance of the Spirit 187 and according to evidence from I, 14 it is highly esteemed in Corinth. Although the προφητεύειν—like the speaking in tongues—presumably was first introduced in Corinth by the Gnostics, since it is done in rational discourse, Paul does not wish to reject it so long as it remains in the framework of good order (I, 14:29 ff.). On the phenomenon of προφητεύειν, cf. further pp. 275 ff.

This judgment does not mean that glossolalia is not also found else- 188 where. Even in rabbinic Judaism ecstatic phenomena occur. Primitive Palestinian Christianity undoubtedly also was acquainted with enthusiastic movements. Whether speaking in tongues belonged to these is of course questionable. Cf. also H. Grass, *Ostergeschehen und Osterberichte*, pp. 312-13.

Cf. *Die Geschichte von Joseph dem Zimmermann*, 23.1 (Sahidic) = 189 S. Morenz in TU 56: 19; W. Bauer, *Der Wortgottesdienst der ältesten Christen* (1930), p. 34.

"When you see miserable, persecuted, and perfect ones whom a 190 bodily ailment and infirmity befalls, do not ridicule them in your hearts. For only the bodies formed of flesh and blood become contemptible through suffering and infirmity; the soul does not become contemptible through suffering and infirmity" (Lidzbarski, *Ginza*, p. 42.13-18).

I do not understand why E. Güttgemanns, in his justified under- 191 taking to interpret the Corinthian epistles consistently in terms of an anti-Gnostic front, repeatedly (e.g., p. 125; p. 138, n. 17; p. 139; p. 156, n. 16; pp. 164-65) states that the Corinthian Gnostics had accused Paul of the *weakness* of his somatic existence and from this inferred his "dependence on the *sarx* which is put off in the heavenly-pneumatic existence" (p. 139). For the Gnostics the demand for *stronger* somatic existence would have been only the irrational demand for strengthening the demonic power, while the *weakness* of the *sarx* demonstrates precisely the weakness of its demonic masters. Actually Paul nowhere gives occasion for the conjecture that the Corinthian adversaries had taken offense at his bodily weakness; they rather accused him of positive *evaluation* of the (suffering) body.

192   When E. Güttgemanns (p. 138) infers from the statements on p. 176 that I completely deny "that Paul was sick or oratorically uneducated," he misunderstands my argument. There I am denying only that the charges encountered in II, 10:1, 10, refer to the apostle's lack of education in rhetoric or his illness.

193   Or ἐν λόγῳ μόνον, as the equivalent Gnostic charge runs, according to I Thess. 1:5; cf. Vol. 2, pp. 98 ff. I Thess. 1:5 confirms in detail the exposition given here.

194   Of course since in vs. 6 Paul is proceeding according to the principle of vs. 5 and is crossing swords with his opponents in his "foolish talk," one must give a sharper focus to E. Käsemann's interpretation. It is indeed his opponents who scorn the non-pneumatic Logos and use Gnosis as well as the ecstatic revelations of the Pneuma itself as their identification. In this very respect, Paul says in II, 11:6, he is not inferior to them. Of course he takes care, in doing his foolish boasting, clearly to fill λόγος, γνῶσις, and φανέρωσις with *his* content, since otherwise the foolish equation would evaporate. Indeed in vs. 6a, Paul can only *mean* that perhaps he is in fact lacking in the necessary schooling in rhetoric, but not in the γνῶσις of the gospel of the crucified Christ (cf. II, 4:4 ff.) and not in the φανέρωσις of the truth (cf. II, 4:2). *His* content for the concepts prescribed by the opponents, therefore, is directly anti-Gnostic.

195   D. W. Oostendorp (pp. 20 ff.) concludes, from the fact that in 10:1-11 Paul promises strong measures in Corinth, that the opponents had demanded sharp intervention against the moral abuses and Paul concedes to them the right to make such a demand. But one cannot overlook the fact that here as elsewhere Paul directs his threat against his opponents themselves.

196   On the following, cf. F. Büchsel, pp. 369 ff.; K. Deissner, *Paulus und die Mystik seiner Zeit* (1918), pp. 54 ff. *passim*.

See further corresponding passages on the following pages. Cf. 197
further Iren. I, 6.4; 23.5; 25.3; II, 26.1; III, 15.2; Tert., de praescr.
haer. 41.4; Ep. Ap. 38; 50; Rev. 3:17; I Tim. 6:3-4; Herm. Sim. IX, 22
and the parallels cited by M. Dibelius in HNT, in loc.; I Clem. 13.1;
14.1; 16.2; 17.5; 21.5; 30.1, 8; 57.2; Ign. Smyrn. 6.1; Trall. 4.1; 7.1;
Corp. Herm. IV, 5.

Most obvious are the parallels in the anti-Gnostic passages of the
other Pauline epistles; on Philippians cf. Vol. 2, pp. 69 ff.; on I Thess.
cf. Vol. 2, pp. 98 ff.; on II Thess. cf. Vol. 2, pp. 142 ff.; on Gal. cf. Vol.
2, pp. 33 ff.; on Rom. cf. Vol. 2, pp. 167 ff.

"Those to whom that Spirit (πνεῦμα) comes will live under all cir- 198
cumstances (πάντη πάντως)" (Pap. Berol. 8502 = Apocryphon of
John 67.1 = Till, p. 175).

". . . the Pneumatics gave to themselves the unmediated reality 199
which was achieved by means of vision" (H. Jonas, [2], p. 44).

Cf. W. Lütgert, pp. 117 ff.; cf. I Thess. 5:1-11 = Vol. 2, pp. 119 ff. 200

With the typically Gnostic ἤδη, cf. further the so-called Gospel of 201
Truth from Nag Hammadi: "Be not worm-eaten, for you have *already*
cast it out. Be not to yourselves a place for the devil, for you have
already brought him to nought" (*The Gospel of Truth,* Kendrick
Grobel, trans., p. 144; Codex Jung 33:17 ff. = H. M. Schenke in TLZ,
1958, col. 498) ; Iren. III, 15.2; I, 25.3; John 3:18.

Further, de resurrectione, ed. Malinine-Till-Quispel-Puech (1963),
p. 49.15-16: "You already (ἤδη) have the resurrection." Corp. Herm.
X, 9; ὁ γὰρ γνοὺς καὶ ἀγαθὸς καὶ εὐσεβὴς καὶ ἤδη θεῖος. Philo, de vita
cont. 13.

Cf. Corp. Herm. I, 26; Acta Joh. 92: "Jesus, those whom you chose
yet do not believe you. And my Lord answered him: you are right; they
are (still) men."

Καὶ ὑμεῖς πεφυσιωμένοι ἐστέ; The concept φυσιοῦν which appears 202
here as also in I, 4:6 is found in the New Testament, other than in the
similarly anti-Gnostic passage in Col. 2:18, only in Paul, and indeed
in his work only in Epistle B to Corinth (cf. II, 12:20). Thereby the
polemical use of this term even in the passages not yet mentioned is
proved: I, 4:18-19 (the πεφυσιωμένοι assert that Paul will no longer let
himself be seen in Corinth) ; I, 8:1, similarly I, 13:4 (ἡ γνῶσις φυσιοῖ,
ἡ δὲ ἀγάπη οἰκοδομεῖ).

On the later anti-Gnostic use of the term, cf., e.g., Ign. Smyrn. 6.1; Trall. 4.1; 7.1.

Cf. the Coptic Gospel of Thomas 2; Pistis Sophia 96 = Schmidt-Till, p. 148.10; Hipp. V, 8.2, 30; Acta Thom. 136 = Lipsius-Bonnet II, 2, p. 243.10; the Coptic Gnostic "Untitled Work" from Nag Hammadi's Codex II, 173.1-14.

203 κυριεύειν is found alongside βασιλεύειν; cf., e.g., Iren. I, 25.3; Clem. Alex. Strom. IV, 13.89. Cf. also the (second) Apocalypse of James 56 (50).2 ff., ed. A. Böhlig/P. Labib, p. 78.

With ἤδη κεκορεσμένοι ἐστέ E. Haenchen (*Die Botschaft des Thomas-Evangeliums* [1961], p. 71) properly compares Saying 60 of the Gospel of Thomas: "Blessed are the hungry, for the body of him who desires will be filled," and on this offers the commentary: "He who in the abundance of the world remains unsatisfied and in spite of all that the world offers him feels his unappeased hunger is satisfied by the knowledge that he is a son of the living Father."

204 Cf. R. Bultmann, [1], p. 3.

205 That is to say, from the presumptuous position of the Gnostic pneumatic state; cf. F. Büchsel, pp. 381 ff.

206 Otherwise D. Georgi, [2], p. 95. From the judgment: ". . . first in II Cor. (more precisely in 2:14–7:4 and 10–13) Paul proceeds against false apostles and discusses pneumatic feats as proof of missionary authority," he concludes that the opponents of II Cor. are different from those of I Cor. But the dispute about apostleship begins already in I, 9:1 ff., and the fact that the discussion of pneumatic feats, as it is found in I, 12–14, recurs in Epistles C and D within the dispute about apostleship reflects only the progressive course of the debate with the same opponents, and not the appearance of other false teachers; cf. further p. 290.

207 U. Wilckens ([1], p. 94) infers from I. 4:3 ff. that the Corinthians had "summoned Paul before a sort of pneumatic court." This is possible, but it seems more likely to me that in I, 4:3 ff. Paul is reacting to his disqualification as pneumatic person and apostle, pronounced long ago—possibly even in ecstatic discourse—by the heretical Corinthians.

208 In this connection we must once more examine the thesis of E. Güttgemanns that the apostle in his existence as a suffering one makes the

crucified Christ directly manifest. In consequence of this concept of the apostle, the apostolic existence is fundamentally distinguished from other Christian existence, which does not possess this character of an epiphany (p. 195) ; the apostle stands with Christ *over against* the community. Güttgemanns must therefore emphasize that in the passages which he exegetes to support his thesis, it is specifically and only *apostolic* existence that is in question; cf., e.g., pp. 95-96; p. 114, n. 111; p. 125; p. 145, n. 21; p. 155, n. 14; p. 174, n. 19, *et passim*. However, not only do the individual texts contradict the theory of the christological epiphany character especially of the apostolic existence in Paul (cf., e.g., note 172), but also the view that Paul makes so basic a distinction at all between apostolic existence and Christian existence fails because of the wording of Epistles C and D, which Güttgemanns uses. One need not even refer to I, 12, where the apostolate is represented as one charisma of the Christian *community* alongside many others. It suffices to point to the fact that precisely in Epistles C and D the apostolic *title* remains without any significance for Paul's argument; in Epistle C it does not occur at all, and in Epistle D it appears only as a self-designation or on the lips of the Corinthian Gnostics.

Now of course there is an ancient dispute over the question of how the "we" which predominates in Epistles C and D is to be understood: as a literary plural, by which Paul means only himself; as a specifically apostolic "we"; as a "we" which includes Paul and all his missionary co-workers; as a general Christian "we"; as a "we" that includes Paul and Timotheus, who purportedly joins him in sending the letter?

It is certain that there is no indication that we are exclusively to count in the "we" a collaborator who is named, if at all, in the lost protocols of Epistles C and D, and that there is also no occasion for limiting the "we" to the circle of the actual apostles who are never named. An exposition of both epistles in context shows rather that the "we" has primary reference to the members of the community in general who are active in mission, hence the *"apostles"* in the general and broadest sense, that Paul now and then restricts it to himself (e.g., II, 3:1) , but frequently extends it to include the entire community. Particularly in Epistle C it can be shown how in constant change and with easy transition Paul anchors the missionary existence in Christian existence in general, and brings Christian existence to a point in the missionary charisma (cf. H. Windisch, p. 34) . This apparently is done intentionally, in view of the attacks which are meant to discredit him as an apostle, in order to avoid any opposing of apostle to community and to put them both together over against the Kyrios Christos as also over against the adversaries. The community is to understand the attacks against Paul as directed against herself, since the common faith is at stake.

Unfortunately, Güttgemanns does not take into account these connections but assumes at once that in Epistles C and D Paul has in mind pointedly and exclusively the *apostolic* existence, and this in its contrast to the community; but this is precisely what has to be proved. His position is further weakened by his failure to clarify his *concept* of the apostle employed herein. Thus his repeated polemic against the view chosen in the present study, that no basic distinction is made by Paul in the sense of I, 12 between apostolic existence and Christian existence in general (cf. *The Office of Apostle,* pp. 21-22) remains without evident support.

209   Cf. further Arnobius II, 33: "You wrongly place the salvation of your souls in yourselves." Characteristic is the frequent use of Luke 17:21 in Gnostic texts; alongside the saying quoted on p. 149, n. 49, cf. also the following: "Take care that no one lead you astray with the words, 'Lo, here!' or 'Lo, there!' For the Son of Man is within you. Follow after him! Those who seek him will find him" (Gospel of Mary 8.14 ff. = Till, p. 65). Cf. further p. 68. H. Jonas fittingly describes "the sufficiency for salvation claimed by the Pneumatics, the immediate self-attainability of a perfection which already here was enjoyed to the full as a surety of itself" ([2], p. 44).

210   Incidentally, a precise parallel is offered by I John 4:5. The Gnostics, who accuse the members of the Great Church that they are "of the world," are answered: αὐτοὶ ἐκ τοῦ κόσμου εἰσίν = they are *themselves* of the world.

211   Still vs. 12, with the ironic parrying of a comparison with those who commended themselves, returns a charge of the Corinthians against Paul, as II, 3:1 and 5:12 surely show.

212   Cf. H. Lietzmann, pp. 208-9; H. Conzelmann in TWNT VII: 893-94.

213   To this corresponds the significance of μιμεῖσθαι for the Gnostics, especially for the Gnostic apostles; cf. *The Office of Apostle,* pp. 216 ff.

214   In addition, the comparison which Paul "ventures" in II, 11:21 ff. following the "pattern" of the Corinthians lets something of the claim of the Corinthian false teachers show through.

On the following, cf. R. Bultmann, [1], pp. 12 ff. Bultmann has   215
greatly furthered the understanding of II, 5:11-15, even though the
mistaken reference to vs. 16 (see pp. 302 ff.), which Bultmann wishes
above all to explain, encumbers his exegesis and somewhat obscures
the outcome. As compared with Bultmann's essay, the study of J. B.
Souček, "Wir kennen Christus nicht mehr nach dem Fleisch," EvTheol
19 (1959) : 300 ff., which is concerned essentially with the understanding of II, 5:16, repersents a step backward, since Souček hardly considers the polemical-apologetic situation of the passage. On the other
hand, E. Käsemann ([1], pp. 67 ff.) has shown the proper way to the
understanding of the section. Cf. also H. Schwantes, *Schöpfung der
Endzeit*, pp. 29 ff. and more recently E. Güttgemanns, pp. 282 ff., esp.
pp. 298 ff., who successfully seeks to explain the passage II, 5:11–6:10
theologically on the basis of the "Gnostic hypothesis."

Hence Paul cannot deny his opponents the title of apostle as such,   216
but at the climax of the debate can only address them as "lying
apostles" (II, 11:13; cf. 11:5; 12:11). Connected with this is the fact
that in the defense of his missionary service in Epistle C Paul does not
even mention the apostolic title, since in the matter of the gospel it
is of no consequence.

Cf. *The Office of Apostle,* pp. 32-33. H. Windisch (p. 179) moreover   217
rightly calls attention to the change in tense between ἐξέστημεν and
σωφρονοῦμεν. The aorist obviously stands for what happened occasionally, and the present for what happens regularly, the ordinary behavior.

Of course this sense, attested by II, 3:3, apparently occurs *also* in   218
the clause, "But we are evident to God," which therewith in a certain
sense takes on a double meaning; for vs. 11*b* may be consciously related to this incidental sense (see below).

R. Bultmann ([1], p. 13) thinks that the θεῷ δὲ πεφανερώμεθα κτλ.   219
is directed "obviously against the charge of secrecy"; certainly, but
against the charge that Paul is concealing from the Corinthians that he
is an ecstatic, i.e., that he lets nothing be seen of the (asserted or demanded) ecstatic and pneumatic revelations.

Cf. already J. Weiss ([1], pp. 298-99) : "Very curiously, ἡ φανέρωσις   220
τοῦ πνεύματος appears in place of τὸ χάρισμα, whereat a never-ending
dispute arises as to whether the genitive is subjective or objective. The
thought however probably is (as in II, 4:10-11) that τὸ πνεῦμα φανεροῦται, and this not through the activity of the Christians, so that he

would be the object, but that he *reveals himself* in their doing. But it is curious that this is not verbally expressed, as ἐν δὲ ἑκάστῳ φανεροῦται τὸ πνεῦμα πρὸς τὸ συμφέρον. ἡ φανέρωσις τοῦ πνεύματος must already have been a form of *terminus technicus* like χάρισμα."

Cf. further D. Lührmann, pp. 27-28.

221   F. C. Baur has already established in *Theol. Jb.* IX (1850) : 182 ff., that the ἐκστῆναι can refer only to actual ecstasies—he points to I, 14:18 and II, 12:1.

222   A. Oepke has already noted, in TDNT III: 591, the "Gnostic tinge" of the concept φανεροῦν. Above all, however, in the first edition of this book the methodologically and substantially convincing as well as splendidly written study by H. Schulte, *Der Begriff der Offenbarung im Neuen Testament, Beiträge zur Evangelischen Theologie* 13 (1949) , escaped me. Schulte investigates the concept φανεροῦν in the New Testament. She recognizes the Gnostic–anti-Gnostic character of the term and also asserts, with reason, that in the Corinthian epistles Paul has taken it over from the language of the Corinthians (esp. pp. 20 ff., 67 ff.) . The context in which φανεροῦν occurs in the Gnostic or gnosticizing passages cited by H. Schulte is for the most part the manifestation of the *one* heavenly emissary in the flesh. This corresponds to the traditions of Christian Gnosticism and essentially expresses nothing other than the manifestation of the *pneuma* in the *sarx* of one of the many Gnostic apostles. To the numerous items of documentation which H. Schulte adduces I append the following, especially suggestive in our context: the Gnostic Apelles *"in alteram feminam impegit, illam virginem Philumenen, quam supra edidimus, postea vere immane prostibulum et ipsam, cuius energemate circumventus quae ab ea didicit* Φανερώσεις *scripsit"* (Tert., de praescr. haer. 30.6; cf. de carne Christi 6) .

223   Cf. H. Schulte, pp. 20-21, who, probably with justification, also suspects a polemical-ironical coloring in II, 3:3; 7:12: "you with your φανεροῦν." Cf. also E. Güttgemanns, p. 107, n. 75.

224   Perhaps the text of vs. 6*b* still can be kept in its present form. As in vs. 6*a* (see note 194) , Paul intends, by speaking as a fool, to prove that he is not inferior to the "superlative apostles" (vs. 5) . In view of the Gnostic demand for φανέρωσις, Paul asserts with the φανερώσαντες that such "revelation" has taken place, and in fact ἐν παντί = in every respect. This ἐν παντί is deliberately used in place of a definite object, since such an object would have disrupted Paul's foolish com-

parison with his opponents; for Paul does not intend to provide the ecstatic φανέρωσις τοῦ πνεύματος demanded by the Gnostics, while the φανερωσις τῆς ἀληθείας ἐν προσώπῳ Χριστοῦ (II, 4:2 ff.) which he means is scorned by the Gnostics as empty talk. At the same time, with the ἐν παντί Paul counters the charge that his φανέρωσις is incomplete. And then with ἐν πᾶσιν εἰς ὑμᾶς Paul emphasizes that the φανέρωσις was shared with *everyone* in Corinth, by which assertions to the contrary obviously are refuted. Paul himself had given occasion in I, 3:1 ff. for such assertions, which may have prompted his opponents to make the statement that in contrast to Paul they brought to *everyone* the *full* revelation. In the face of this, Paul declares in his role as fool that he is not inferior to these superlative apostles: "We rather have revealed everything to each of you."

The εἰς ὑμᾶς at the end of vs. 4, which has in view Paul's apostolic 225 effectiveness, unquestionably takes up the εἰς ὑμᾶς and the ἐν ὑμῖν of vs. 3b and thus compels us to understand vs. 3b also as a description of Paul's conduct in Corinth. Of course it is possible that Paul is also referring ironically to the assertion of his Corinthian adversaries that Christ is strong in them. Hence the two possibilities mentioned at first would be combined: Do you fail to find a proof of the Christ who is speaking *in me,* and who is strong *in you?* Now when I come to you and no longer spare you, you will see how right you are: Christ will be displayed among you, not as weak but as strong.

E. Güttgemanns follows this interpretation but formulates it quite 226 awkwardly: "Thus people not only failed to find ecstatic phenomena in Paul, but above all they took offense for christological reasons at the apostle's weakness" (p. 146). The "not only . . . but above all" obscures the meaning which Güttgemanns probably also intends, that the ecstatic phenomena themselves represent the christological display.

On this subject, cf. Barn. 16.8 ff.: ". . . ἀληθῶς ὁ θεὸς κατοικεῖ ἐν ἡμῖν 227 . . . αὐτὸς ἐν ἡμῖν προφητεύων, αὐτὸς ἐν ἡμῖν κατοικῶν . . . ὁ γὰρ ποθῶν σωθῆναι βλέπει οὐκ εἰς τὸν ἄνθρωπον ἀλλὰ εἰς τὸν ἐν αὐτῷ κατοικοῦντα καὶ λαλοῦντα."

On the other hand, it appears to me, for the reasons given, less likely 228 that "Paul deliberately distorts the original mythological sense of the words to his own meaning and expects the opponents to understand this" (thus E. Güttgemanns, pp. 146-47, n. 27). Güttgemanns would have to be able to show *why,* with adequate knowledge of his opponents' mythology, in all the correspondence Paul consistently refrains from a discussion of the myth and only takes up its anthropological or theological implications.

229   Cf. *The Office of Apostle*, pp. 159 ff.

230   Thus already D* G and Ambrosiaster, who instead of Χριστοῦ have Χριστοῦ δοῦλος.

231   J. Roloff (*Apostolat—Verkündigung—Kirche*, p. 77, n. 119) thinks of "the consciousness of a special commissioning by Christ." Still this aspect is quite remote from the thought of the opponents and could at most be taken into account for the Pauline understanding. However, Paul can hardly have understood the Χριστοῦ εἶναι here otherwise than in Gal. 3:29 and I, 3:23; 15:23.

232   Cf. Mark 9:41 and E. Klostermann, *in loc.*; see above, p. 59.

233   The equation "Christ party = Gnostics" is held, among others, by B. Reicke (pp. 275 ff.), who to be sure goes further than earlier advocates of this equation in that he introduces the concept of Docetism into this context and lets the appeal to Christ be directed against the earthly Jesus of the church.

234   Further, E. Norden, pp. 177 ff., 210 ff.; E. Stauffer, *Jesus* (Dalp-Taschenbücher 332), pp. 130 ff. The formula serves in the entire ancient Orient for the proclamation of the gods or of God, then also of the ruler and of distinguished men, and of the Gnostic redeemer. Purely Gnostic is the use of the formula if, as in our present case, any Pneumatic can use it. Cf. A. Dieterich, *Eine Mithrasliturgie*, pp. 6, 8, 16-17.

235   Most recently W. Michaelis, [1], p. 172; U. Wilckens, [1], p. 17, n. 2, who of course—correctly—on p. 211 understands the ἐγώ εἰμι Χριστοῦ as a confession of Christ of the Corinthian Gnostics.

236   It already appears in vs. 13 that Paul regards the ἐγώ εἰμι Χριστοῦ as the only proper slogan, so far as the unity of the church is not disrupted thereby. For when he counters those who appeal to *men* by saying "Was Paul crucified for you? Or were you baptized in the name of Paul?" this means: You can be named only for the one who was crucified for you and in whose name you are baptized: Christ.

The chiasm of this passage has also been seen fundamentally cor- 237
rectly by J. Jeremias ("Chiasmus in Paulusbriefen," ZNW 49 [1958]:
145 ff., esp. p. 151; cf. further below, p. 383), who also points to the
frequency with which chiasm occurs precisely in Paul. Jeremias rightly
explains the fact that in vs. 13 only "Paul" appears, thanks to the
apostle's "tact": ". . . in the polemical queries he wishes to leave
Apollos and Cephas out of the picture."

U. Wilckens' objection, "But the *exclusive* attachment of μεμέρισται
ὁ Χριστός to ἐγὼ δὲ Χριστοῦ is already misconceived in terms of the
rhetorical plan of vs. 12" ([1], p. 11, n. 1), is therefore to be turned
around: The rhetorical form of chiasm shows that the μεμέρισται ὁ
Χριστός may be related only to the ἐγὼ δὲ Χριστοῦ.

In "Die sogenannte Christus Partei in Korinth," *ThStKr* 84 [1911]: 238
193 ff., an interesting conjecture is offered by Perdelwitz, who changes
Χριστοῦ into Κρίσπου. He also changes κόσμος in I, 3:22 into Κρίσπος,
but then necessarily would also be bound correspondingly to change
II, 10:7. This point alone is sufficient to cause the collapse of this
fanciful idea.

E. Käsemann (introduction to F. C. Baur, *Ausgewählte Werke*, I:
X) and R. Baumann (*Mitte und Norm des Christlichen*, p. 54), following the lead of others, regard the Christ motto as a sarcastic exag-
geration of the other formulas and thus a bit of Pauline rhetoric. Apart
from all else, this thesis is possible only if one ignores II, 10:7 and lets
Paul's opponents be left unnamed in the slogans.

In the *fourth* place, the following statement corresponds fully to such 239
a division of I, 1:12-13; 1:18-2:16 against the Christ party; 3:1-23
against the apostles parties.

In the *fifth* place, 3:22-23 now also becomes understandable. Some
have stumbled at the fact that here Paul does not mention the Christ
slogan *alongside* the apostle slogans as he does in 1:12, but sets it in
opposition to them; not least of all for this reason, some have excised
the Christ slogan from 1:12 as a gloss. Now one should rather conclude
from this that already in 1:12 Paul sets the Christ slogan apart from
the apostles slogans—as it indeed actually occurs by means of the
chiasm. In 3:1-23 Paul is setting himself exclusively against the καυχᾶσθαι ἐν ἀνθρώποις (3:21), thus against the apostles parties, whose
slogans he rejects, in order to point them to the only slogan of the entire and undivided community: ὑμεῖς Χριστοῦ. *This* slogan is not rejected by Paul, but in I, 1:12 only criticized with respect to its use as
a *partisan watchword*. Paul rejects the *apostle slogans*.

240   Thus it happens that Paul thoroughly sanctions the wording of the
formula and opposes only the use of the ἐγώ εἰμι Χριστοῦ in partisan
strife.

241   Indeed in any case this latter mythological conception stands behind
the *formulation* μεμέρισται ὁ Χριστός. Like its counterconcept, ἑνόω,
etc., μερίζω is a *terminus technicus* in Gnosticism; cf. H. Schlier, [2],
pp. 86, 97-102.

242   Cf. Iren., I, 25.2, according to which the Gnostics exalt themselves
above the apostles because they are "like Jesus," i.e., are themselves
Χριστοί (see p. 49).

243   Cf., e.g., W. G. Kümmel, ThRs 17 (1948): 34 (Literature); 18
(1950): 29, n. 2. The proof that Peter cannot have worked against
Paul in Corinth however by no means says that he did not work in
Corinth at all. This is often overlooked. Even O. Cullmann ([2], pp.
53-54 [Literature]), in his discussion of the problem, still proceeds too
much from the assumption that Peter would have had to appear in
Corinth in a certain competition with Paul, an affirmation for which
there is in fact not a single witness. Moreover, it is to be maintained
against Cullmann, who still reckons with the possibility of Peter's
presence in Corinth, that the passages I, 3:6 and 4:15, in which Paul
sets himself forth as the sole founder of the community, contribute
nothing to the answer to our question. For here Paul naturally is
thinking only of the founding of the *Gentile* Christian community,
while Peter, in case he founded a community in Corinth, founded the
Jewish Christian community, which existed independently alongside
the Gentile Christian community; on this, cf. Vol. 3, esp. pp. 38-62.
      Cf. further W. Bauer, pp. 116-17 (Literature). What Dionysius of
Corinth writes (Eus. CH II, 25) may have its source in I, 1:12, but in
any case it reveals the natural understanding of this passage.
      F. Hahn, *Das Verständnis der Mission im Neuen Testament*, p. 39,
n. 3, also regards Peter's presence in Corinth as not very probable; for
"Paul would have expressed this more clearly." Why? Would this not
have been known in Corinth? Paul is not writing for us! Why should
Peter be named in I, 1:12 differently from Paul and Apollos if like
them he had been in Corinth?
      According to C. K. Barrett (in O. Michel, pp. 1 ff.), Peter was in
Corinth. Paul's opponents appeal to him, though to be sure with a
misuse of his authority. Hence Paul spares Peter and attacks only his
unsought adherents—an interesting variation of the untenable Judaizer
theories.

Thus also B. Reicke, pp. 275 ff.; W. Marxsen, pp. 72-73.   244

J. Munck, pp. 139 ff., rightly refers to this. Of course he makes this   245
the foundation of the untenable thesis that at the time of I Cor. there
was no division created by the false teachers in the community at
Corinth. After he has excised the ἐγὼ δὲ Χριστοῦ as a gloss, W.
Michaelis ([1], p. 172) infers from the same observation that even II,
10:7 does not prove the existence of a Christ party. But this will not
do!

Thus, correctly and in concert with many others, W. Lütgert, p.   246
99, as before him W. M. L. de Wette and F. Godet, who in this section
think of the "Christ people" as Paul's adversaries.

Thus most recently F. Neugebauer, In Christus, p. 109.   247

The Gnostics are not διάκονοι Χριστοῦ but are themselves Χριστοί.   248
So far as they performed a "ministry," it was the ministry as Christ or
even for Christ, in other words, for the restoration of the body of
Christ, of which they themselves are part; the tenants of such ministry
qualify as God's διάκονοι (cf. Acta Thom. 24; Od. Sol. 6.13). The Corinthian apostles also would like to be understood as διάκονοι in this
sense and perhaps even claimed for themselves the title of διάκονος,
which as a technical designation frequently occurs in the New Testament and in its environment, not least of all for the κῆρυξ θεοῦ (see
below).

Cf. H. W. Beyer in TDNT II: 81-93; E. Schweizer, Church Order in   249
the New Testament, pp. 173 ff. (II, 21c); article "Diakon" in RAC;
H. Lietzmann in Kleine Schriften I (= TU 67 [1958]): 148 ff.; D.
Georgi, [1], pp. 31 ff.; further, in Paul in I, 3:5; II, 3:6 ff.; 4:1; 5:18;
6:3-4; Col. 1:23 ff.; Phil. 1:1, et passim (see concordance).

Also the frequent use of διάκονος, διακονεῖν, and διακονία in Epistle   250
C does not allow the recognition of any sort of apologetic or polemical
reference.

In view of the frequent occurrence of these terms in II Cor., the
suggestion that Paul has taken over these concepts from the language
of his opponents (thus, e.g., G. Friedrich in O. Michel, pp. 181 ff.)
is an admittedly appealing but untenable and exegetically indefensible
theory which leads to a bad distortion of the opponents' position. Cf.
J. Roloff, p. 122, n. 288.

251   Anyone who concludes from II, 11:15, 23, that διάκονος Χριστοῦ
was a *self-designation* of the Corinthian adversaries must, with D.
Georgi ([1], pp. 49 ff.), to be consistent brand the ἐργάται (δόλιοι, II,
11:13) also as a self-designation. Moreover, the ἐργάτης is nowhere
proven as a technical title; on the contrary, it is frequent as a figurative
term in primitive Christianity (Mark 10:10 par.) and Paul (Phil. 3:2;
II Tim. 2:15). Thus the concepts ἐργάτης *and* διάκονος in II, 11:13 ff.
may go back to Paul.

252   It cannot be concluded, from Paul's statement that like his opponents he is a "Hebrew," an "Israelite," "Abraham's seed," that
these opponents are of Palestinian origin, regardless of whether in these
expressions we have to do with self-designations of the opponents or
not. This unjustified conclusion is found in D. Georgi ([1], pp. 11, 53,
58, 60), apparently in the interest of setting the opponents in II Cor.
off from those in I Cor. But the three concepts mentioned after all have
no geographic reference, not even a linguistic one. Every conscious
Jew could call himself a "Hebrew." Georgi's erroneous inference leads
to the absurd conclusion that even the Cilician and Hellenistic Jew
Paul, who in II, 11:22 claims the same designations for himself, must
have come from Palestine.

Even if the note in Acts 22:3 is correct and Paul had actually studied
in Jerusalem—his epistles make this appear very unlikely, while in Acts
22:3 the Lucan tendency clearly emerges—Paul still did not thereby
become a Jerusalemite; *contra* D. W. Oostendorp, pp. 12-13.

The Palestinian origin of the false teachers even in II Cor. incidentally is as good as ruled out by the fact that like Paul they were conducting a *non-law-observing* Gentile mission, a fact to which Georgi
nowhere in his work gives due attention, although he does treat the
Jewish mission in the primitive Christian era in detail and instructively
([1], pp. 83-187). But these broad statements fail to focus on the
phenomenon of the non-law-observing Gentile mission and thus on
the problem which is decisive for the question as to the adversaries
of Paul in Corinth.

If the Gnostics were introduced in Corinth *consciously* as Jews, this
was done for purportedly missionary reasons. Such an introduction did
not, of course, mean a recommendation for everyone, but it probably
did for the circles to which above all the Christian mission was directed, namely the God-fearers; cf. Vol. 3, pp. 60 ff.

253   Cf. further H. v. Campenhausen, *Die Entstehung der christlichen
Bibel*, BhTh 39 (1968): 91.

Thus already, and correctly, W. Lütgert, pp. 71 ff.; K. Deissner,   254
Paulus und die Mystiker seiner Zeit (1918), pp. 75 ff.
Cf. now also E. Güttgemanns, p. 155; D. Lührmann, pp. 55 ff.

When J. Munck, p. 186, rejects this interpretation because it al-   255
legedly presupposes "that Paul began this section intending to boast of
his visions, but that by degrees his intention changed," and he finally
gloried in his weakness, such a line of argument only shows a lack of
understanding of the paradoxical character of Paul's unseemly, forced
boasting in the sorrowful epistle.

It is nevertheless probable. Cf. Phil. 3:15, and on this, Vol. 2, pp.   256
72 ff. The connection of ὀπτασία with ἀποκάλυψις shows that the concept ἀποκάλυψις in II, 12 is used, not in a late Jewish-orthodox way, but
in a Gnostic manner. While in "orthodox" late Judaism the ἀποκάλυψις belongs to the primordial age or to the end-time, the characteristic
mark of the Gnostic ἀποκάλυψις is that it is *presently* imparted to the
ecstatic; cf. D. Rössler, *Gesetz und Geschichte*, WMANT 3 (1960) :
65 ff.; D. Lührmann, pp. 39 ff., and also P. Stuhlmacher, *Das paulinische Evangelium*, I (1968) : 76-77.

On the conception of the third heaven, cf. esp. W. Bousset, [3], pp.   257
43-58. A good example of the ecstatic celestial journey is offered now
by the "Apocalypse of Paul," ed. A. Böhlig and P. Labib, pp. 15 ff.

If in his style of speech Paul should be shown to have been in-   258
fluenced by the conception of the double "I," which is widespread in
ecstatic religion (cf. H. Windisch, pp. 369-70), still he empties this
schema precisely of its original meaning; for in the context of that
conception, essential existence is attributed to the celestial "I," while
Paul in his actual existence is set at a distance from this "I." On this
subject, cf. further D. Lührmann, p. 58.

Cf. Phil. 4:9.   259

For all that, it is to be noted that the section II, 12:1-10 stands in a 260
context in which specifically the apostolic claim of Paul and of his
adversaries is being discussed. A demand was being made of Paul for
a proof of his ὀπτασίαι and ἀποκαλύψεις, because up to this point some
are not willing to recognize him as an *apostle*. In that Paul depreciates
the ecstatic experiences named in II, 12:1, does *not* want to see them
made the basis of a judgment about himself, and instead of this glories
in his weakness, he decisively rejects a defense and justification of his

apostolic rights rooted in fanaticism (see above, pp. 279 ff.) . Cf. K. H. Rengstorf in TDNT I: 440; E. Käsemann, [1], pp. 69 ff.; *The Office of Apostle*, pp. 37-38, 213-14.

To be sure, there is in my opinion no reason (with E. Käsemann, [1], p. 53, and E. Güttgemanns, p. 166) to limit the meaning of χάρις in vs. 8 to the apostolic charisma; cf. W. G. Kümmel in H. Lietzmann, p. 212 on p. 155, 1. 53. But I am still less able even here to share the still more far-reaching exegesis of E. Güttgemanns, according to which in vs. 8 Paul is teaching that "his apostolic infirmity is to be understood as an epiphany of the divine power of the crucified One." Not only do our verses nowhere suggest this basic thesis of Güttgemanns that the apostle *in his person* manifests the crucified One. It is rather specifically contradicted in II, 12:8-10. The apostle's ἀσθένεια does not appear *as* the δύναμις of Christ, but (dialectically) as *presupposition for* the effectiveness of this δύναμις: ἡ γὰρ δύναμις ἐν ἀσθενείᾳ τελεῖται. In *this* sense Paul continues by saying that he will gladly glory in his infirmity, so that the δύναμις of Christ may *abide* with him. The ἵνα does not merely cause "some difficulties" (p. 169) for Güttgemanns' exegesis, but contradicts it; for it cannot be inferred from Paul's words, even by the most generous interpretation, that the apostle clings to his weakness so that the epiphany of the power of the crucified One may *remain unveiled*.

261   Since πρὸ ἐτῶν δεκατεσσάρων and the following parenthesis belong without question to ἄνθρωπον ἐν Χριστῷ, the latter expression cannot simply be equivalent to "a Christian," as F. Neugebauer, pp. 125-26, thinks. For then Paul would be affirming the nonsense that he had been a *Christian* fourteen years earlier and does not know whether he was within or without the body.

262   Thus now P. Stuhlmacher, *Das paulinische Evangelium*, FRLANT 95 (1968) : 77 ff., n. 1, who connects τῇ ὑπερβολῇ as *dativus causae* with λογίσηται and—undoubtedly fitting to the sense intended by Paul—translates: ". . . so that no one reckon to me more than what he perceives in me and hears from me, and indeed (reckon) in consequence of the abundance of revelations."

263   On this, cf., e.g., Test. Abr. 8.3 (Riessler, 1097) : "Then the Lord said to Michael: go and bring Abraham hither in the body and show him all . . . ." Cf. G. Hause, "Entrückung und eschatologische Funktion im Spätjudentum," ZRGG 13 (1961) : 105-13.

264   Although I attempt to make it clear that for the sake of the existen-

tial advantage Paul relativizes the meaning of the *conceptions* on which, for the Gnostics, everything rests, I read in E. Güttgemanns, pp. 157-58: "This view of things has Paul's *theological* battle take place in the realm of *conceptions* and thus makes Paul's theology into the world view which Paul basically already held as a Jew . . . . Here we have a cardinal evidence of how whole realms of theological *thought* are simply set aside when theological exegesis reduces Paul's statement to its conceptual content. Paul's struggle becomes a *religio-historical* debate which possesses only historical value for us." It cannot escape even the hasty reader that with these words the intention of my exegesis is turned upside down. I do not regard it as a bit of "carelessness" on the apostle's part not to be interested in the form of his ecstatic experience, but a considered and deliberate *theological* polemic.

D. Lührmann (pp. 55 ff.), in his essentially correct interpretation   265
of II, 12:1-10, does not consider the two parentheses. It is only thus that he can assert that for the Corinthian heretics there occurs in ecstasy a "transformation into the form of the Pneuma" (p. 59), whereby he is able to place Paul's opponents in II Cor. not so much in the sphere of genuine Gnosticism as in the realm of thought of the mysteries.

On the following, cf. F. Büchsel, pp. 372 ff. Above all one should   266
now note the far-reaching statements of K. Niederwimmer, pp. 54 ff.

Cf. Act. Thom. 19 = Lipsius-Bonnet, II, 2: 129.9; 39 = 156.15-16:   267
"ὃς (*scil.* ἀπόστολος) ἐλεύθερος ὢν γέγονας δοῦλος καὶ πραθεὶς πολλοὺς εἰς ἐλευθερίαν εἰσήγαγες"; 43 = 161.9-10; 167 = 282.2, *et passim;* Coptic Gospel of Philip 13; 73; 110; 114; 123, *et passim;* on II Peter 2:19, cf. E. Käsemann in ZThK 49 (1952) : 274; John 8:32, 36; Od. Sol. 10.3; First Book of Jeu 2 = Schmidt-Till, p. 258.20 ff.; Apul. Met. XI 15.5.

"ἔστιν δὲ οὐ τὸ λουτρὸν μόνον τὸ ἐλευθεροῦν, ἀλλὰ καὶ ἡ γνῶσις" (Exc.   268
ex Theod. 78).

Cf. further Epiph. Haer. XXXI, 5.1; Justin Dial. 1.5; Iren. I, 6.4.   269

"Sin as such does not exist, but you make sin when you do what is   270
of the nature [φύσις] of fornication, which is called sin" (Gospel of Mary 7.13 ff. = W. Till, p. 63; this translation from R. M. Grant, *Gnosticism*, p. 65). Thus fornication belongs only to the realm of the φύσις.

271 Tert., de praescr. haer. 43; Ep. Ap. 27; 39; 1 John 3:6 ff.; 5:2; Eus. CH IV, 7.11 with some justification complains that the libertinism of the Gnostics in the era of persecution simply brought all Christendom under the accusation of immorality, against which the apologists constantly had to defend themselves (cf., e.g., Tert., Apol. 7-8).

272 Cf. further Justin, Apol. I, 26.7; Tert., de praescr. haer. 33.10; Eus. CH III, 28.5; Iren. I, 24.5; 28.2; Tertullian (Apol. I, 7.1) must already defend himself against the charge of the heathen that all Christians ate children who had been sacrificed and that they also practiced incest. Eus. CH IV, 7.11, also refers to this: the Christians have commerce with mothers and sisters and eat impure foods.

273 Cf. also Clem. Alex., Strom. III, 9.63: "I came in order to destroy the work of woman." A polemic against such Gnostic views is also found in I Tim. 2:15; 4:3; 5:14.

274 Cf. further Ep. Ap. 22; 26; 39, end.

275 In the first edition of the present work, pp. 80 ff., I attempted to prove that in I, 3:1 ff. Paul takes over the concept σαρκικός from the lips of his Corinthian opponents. I am no longer certain whether this demonstration can be successfully persuasive. For this reason I have now eliminated the corresponding section.

276 Paul most fittingly described such an attitude: "ὧν . . . ἡ δόξα ἐν τῇ αἰσχύνῃ αὐτῶν" (Phil. 3:19; see Vol. 2, pp. 80-81.).
In the writing "On righteousness," ascribed to the Gnostic Epiphanes, liberty for indiscriminate sexual intercourse is ultimately inferred from the gnostically understood *equality* (see above, pp. 238 ff.) of man and woman and of all flesh: "Hence it is ridiculous when one must hear this saying of the lawgiver: 'Thou shalt not covet'; and still more laughable when it is said: 'that which is your neighbor's.' For he himself, who gave desire, so that it might keep in order the business of procreation, commands that it be restrained, although he withdraws it from no other living being. And the 'thy neighbor's wife,' in order to force commonality into particularity, is an even more laughable utterance" (Clem. Alex., Strom. III, 3.9). "Consequently, God created everything common to man and even joined woman to man in common" (Clem. Alex., Strom. III, 2.8-9).
Even if in the church's polemic against the heretics there is the danger that the accusation of immorality is becoming stereotyped (cf. Dibelius-Conzelmann in HNT 13 [1955, 3rd ed.]: 2), still there can be

no question about the essential justification of this charge, either in details or as a whole.

In view of the situation in Corinth, it is first to be said with some certainty that the *concept* ἐλευθερία played a role there. In I, 9:1 Paul apparently is defending himself against attacks by his adversaries; 9:3 presumably belongs with 9:1-2! There can be some argument as to whether Paul is refuting two or three charges: that he is not free; that he is not an apostle; that he has not had a vision of Christ. But since vs. 1*d* and vs. 2 give the answer to the charge of vs. 1*b* which disputes Paul's apostolic rights, it may be also that in the intervening remark in vs. 1*c* no *special* charge is expressed, but rather the assertion that Paul is no apostle *because* he has not had a manifestation of Christ (see *The Office of Apostle,* p. 26).

Then, however, in 9:1 only the two separate charges are mentioned, that Paul is not free and that he is not an apostle. Paul deals briefly in 9:1-3 with the second charge, which is so important in the later correspondence. Beginning with 9:4, however, he enters into a detailed treatment of the first charge, which is of special interest to him in the context of the question of refraining from eating meat sacrificed to idols. This he does by choosing his personal renunciation of the apostolic right to support as an example to demonstrate the maintenance of Christian liberty. (Thus in chap. 9 we have a chiasm:

a) 9:1*a*
b) 9:1*b*
b) 9:1*c*-3
a) 9:4-23

J. Jeremias has seen this essentially correctly [in ZNW 49 (1958) : 155-56], even though he incorrectly still assigns vss. 4-18 to the defense of the apostolic office instead of to the theme of ἐλευθερία.) In 9:19 as well as in 10:29 Paul again takes up the term ἐλευθερία. The charge that he is not free naturally presupposes that in Corinth personal ἐλευθερία was being stressed. Arguing for this is also the appearance of the same people in Galatia, since in Gal. 5:1, 13, Paul alludes to their assertion that they possessed liberty (see Vol. 2, pp. 35 ff.). I have set forth in the Appendix (pp. 315 ff.) the ways in which II, 3:17 suggests the use of the concept ἐλευθερία among the Corinthian Gnostics.

Cf. further Eus. CH IV, 7.9; Clem. Alex., Strom. II, 117.5; III, 25-26; 277
Const. Ap. 6.10; Epiph., Haer. XXI, 2; XXV, 1.5; 2.5; XXVI, 1 ff.; 9.9;
H. J. Schoeps, [2], pp. 256 ff.

278   Thus also R. Bultmann, [1], pp. 23-24.

279   Arguing that the battlelines in I and II Cor. are *not* the same, D.
Georgi ([1], p. 233, n. 1) disputes the current reference of the sins
named in the second part of the catalog of vices, although he rightly
asserts this specific reference for the controversies named in the first
part.

280   Cf. also Rom. 16:18 = Vol. 2, pp. 167 ff. The Gnostics who are opposed in I John also deny at one and the same time that Jesus has
come in the flesh and that they themselves are sinners; cf., e.g., 1:5 ff.;
4:1 ff.; 5:1 ff.

281   On the following, cf. the fitting statements of K. Niederwimmer,
pp. 204 ff. Further, C. K. Barrett, "Things Sacrificed to Idols," NTS
11 (1965) : 138 ff.

282   Cf. further Eus. CH IV, 7.7: διδάσκειν τε ἀδιαφορεῖν εἰδωλοθύτων
ἀπογευομένους; Hipp. VII, 36.3; Origen, Cont. Cels. VI, 11 (= Koetschau II, 81.22-23) : ἐναδιαφορεῖν αὐτοὺς διδάξας πρὸς τὴν εἰδωλολα-
τρείαν; Iren. I, 28.2.

283   Thus correctly already H. Weinel, pp. 381-82: "It is not a question
of thoughtless eating for the sake of eating, but of eating as a matter of
principle for the sake of liberty."

284   While the Jews were strictly forbidden to eat meat sacrificed to idols
(cf. Billerbeck, III: 377-78; Acts 15:29; Phocylides 31 = Riessler, p.
863; F. Büchsel in TDNT II: 378-79) , the Gnostics took for themselves
the freedom to eat of the εἰδωλόθυτον (Acts 2:14, 20; Iren. I, 26.3;
Justin, Dial. 35.1) as well as the participation in the pagan cult
generally.

285   Further, it cannot be said with certainty whether the "πάντες γνῶσιν
ἔχομεν" was the positive assertion of the Corinthians who were Paul's
followers, who wrote the letter to Paul, or whether in these words we
have a restatement, perhaps even a critical one, of views uttered in
Corinth. The former seems to me the more likely, insofar as Gnosis
was specifically connected with the eating of meat sacrificed to idols;
all claimed to have the Gnosis necessary for this.

286   The assertion, "It is . . . an honor for the community when the
pneumatic person receives his reward" (D. Georgi, [1], p. 298) is

indeed praiseworthy, because it concerns itself with a grounding for the widespread assumption discussed here, but it cannot be confirmed either from the ironic verse II, 12:13 or from religio-historical parallels generally. Always under discussion in antiquity was the *disputed* right of the Pneumatic to support, precisely also in II, 12:14 ff. (*contra* D. Georgi, [1], pp. 234 ff.) .

Cf. note 276.   287

On this, cf. I Thess. 4:3-8; see Vol. 2, pp. 113-14. Worth recommend-   288
ing for our passage now is the exposition by E. Güttgemanns, pp. 226 ff. Seen as a whole, it is fitting, though abundantly lengthy. Cf. further K. Niederwimmer, *Der Begriff der Freiheit im Neuen Testament,* pp. 202 ff.; R. Freudenberger in ThZ 23 (1967) : 106.

For Paul such a principle means that God is blasphemed: Gal. 6:7-8   289
= Vol. 2, pp. 37-38.

Cf. Hermas, Sim. V, 7.2: "Guard yourself against giving room to   290
the idea that this flesh is perishable and hence misusing and staining it." Cf. also Rom. 16:18 = Vol. 2, pp. 167 ff.

Thereby also arises the unique, but for Pauline anthropology note-   291
worthy, statement that the κοιλία is perishable, but that the σῶμα would arise. To the Gnostic such a distinction in principle between κοιλία and σῶμα is incomprehensible. Both are σάρξ and therefore independent of ethical judgment. Paul is thinking from the standpoint of ethics and therefore, when he justifies his ethical judgment with the substance thought of the Gnostics, he comes to that curious distinction between eating, which pertains to the perishable κοιλία, and πορνεία, which pertains to the imperishable σῶμα. Here a comparison of vs. 13*c* with vs. 14 shows that Paul equates σῶμα and "man": man *is* σῶμα and *has* a κοιλία. From vs. 13*c* on, therefore, Paul is *theologically* on his own. Cf. E. Güttgemanns, pp. 226 ff., who correctly points out (p. 229, n. 26) that Paul in non-Gnostic fashion has the perishability of the *sarx* grounded in the eschatological work of God.

Not only II, 10:8 and 13:10, but also I, 8:9 as well as I, 9:4, 5, 6, 12*b*,   292
and 18 show that Paul is using the concept ἐξουσία in a Gnostic manner. Indeed, in chap. 9 he speaks, not of special permission to let himself be supported by the community, but of the freedom and power of such a right to support which is given with the *apostolic office.* The

ἐξουσία is never simply unrestricted liberty, but the power and authority pertaining to a definite *position:* to the Gnostic Pneumatic, to the apostle, and to the Stoic sage. Hence for Paul even the πάντα μοι ἔξεστιν does not mean "everything is permissible for me," in the sense of unrestrained libertinism. Rather, the meaning of the formula is limited for Paul's mind from the very outset by the previously given technical usage in Gnosticism (and the Stoa). *Positively* speaking, this limitation appears, e.g., in passages like I, 2:15; 4:3; 6:2; 7:17 ff.; 8:8-9; 9:19 ff., etc.; negatively in our passages; I, 6:12: οὐ πάντα συμφέρει; and I, 10:23: οὐ πάντα οἰκοδομεῖ.

293　　　"Some justified promiscuity with an appeal to liberty and to the perishability of the body" (F. Büchsel, p. 376).

294　　　Cf. now also C. Maurer, "Ehe und Unzucht nach 1 Kor. 6,12–7,7," in *Wort und Dienst,* 1959, pp. 159 ff., esp. p. 161, who to be sure incorrectly has 7:2-7 also directed against libertinism.

295　　　H. v. Campenhausen (in SAH 2 (1957): 21) also connects vss. 2-6 with the conduct of *married* Christians. That this interpretation had "not previously been set forth" is not surprising to me; cf. further E. Kähler, *Die Frau in den paulinischen Briefen,* pp. 22 ff.

296　　　The reflections in vss. 17-24 are connected with all the previously mentioned cases.

297　　　H. Conzelmann, p. 139, n. 11, declares: ". . . this means to attribute to the community a significant degree of ignorance of language and customs, even to the point of stupidity. In the last analysis, even then πορνεία was a concept." However, I do not understand how a community which was influenced on one side by libertinism and on the other side by an eschatologically motivated striving for continence would be displaying stupidity when it asked its apostle for a comprehensive statement of position on problems of marriage and sex. In this situation the simple prohibition of πορνεία, which cannot have been new to the Corinthians, does not answer all the open questions, and, contrary to Conzelmann's opinion, I have not denied but rather affirmed that in Corinth continence was being advocated by individual members of the community. Only it will not do to label every sort of sexual continence as asceticism in the technical sense. And if the Corinthians' inquiry was simply, "Is sexual intercourse (at all) permitted?" (*ibid.,* p. 139), then not only does Paul's detailed answer in chap. 7 become a puzzle, but it also remains unexplained how an entire Pauline community could come to the point of renouncing sexual intercourse for reasons of asceticism. For Paul as for early Jewish and Christian tradition as a whole, sexual intercourse *in general* was never an ethical problem.

"With the assertion, 'I believe that I also have the Spirit of God,'   298
Paul is not justifying the principle that marriage is permitted, but rather the advice to the widow to refrain from remarriage. From this it results that the Pneumatics attack the Pauline esteem for the unmarried state . . ." (F. Büchsel, p. 376).

Cf. further H. Schlier, [3], p. 272 (Literature); R. H. A. Seboldt,   299
"Spiritual Marriage in the Early Church," *Concordia Theological Monthly* 30 (1959): 103-19; 176-89; E. Kähler, p. 38.

The originally wholly non-ascetic practice of postponing marriage   300
because of the impending messianic woes thus is rooted in apocalyptic thought and presupposes the apocalyptic imminent expectation of the end. Here and there it may well have gained admission from Jewish apocalyptic circles into early Christianity. Paul undoubtedly did not invent it or introduce it. Cf. further RGG (3rd ed.), IV, cols. 560-61.

Thus also W. Schrage, *Die konkreten Einzelgebote in der paulini-*   301
schen Paränese, p. 217, n. 141, according to whom the texts speak "clearly enough for a double front," namely one against Gnostic libertines and one against Gnostic ascetics. Nevertheless: if one wishes to speak of an ascetic "party" in Corinth, this party can have been formed only by the *opponents* of the Gnostic libertines, not on the contrary by these themselves. Thus the people with "ascetic" tendencies are hardly Gnostics, but are seen in protest against Gnosticism. For the fact that libertinism as well as asceticism can be an expression of the same Gnostic self-understanding does not mean that the same Gnostic group could propagate libertinism as well as asceticism. And that *one* Gnostic group was divided on the question of libertinism versus asceticism—thus E. Güttgemanns, pp. 228-29, n. 25—is an extremely improbable assumption, one in no way demanded by the text. D. Georgi's charge ([3], p. 38) that I have "denied the connection between libertinism and asceticism altogether" is not correct, insofar as the point in question is the common anthropological background of the two kinds of conduct. It is true that I deny that the same Pneumatics

at the same time demand asceticism and libertinism, for reasons of logic as well as the lack of religio-historical parallels for such a procedure, and for the Corinthian situation moreover on the basis of the texts, which neither require nor suggest such an interpretation.

302   Cf. Lev. 18:8; 20:11; Deut. 23:1; 27:10; Phocylides 179 = Riessler 869. Of course according to the older rabbinical view which was in force in the time of Paul, marriage with one's stepmother was permitted to the Gentile (Billerbeck, III: 345-46). The proselyte also, even after his conversion to Judaism, might marry his stepmother (Billerbeck, III: 354 ff.). The Roman law which forbade such marriages was binding only on Roman citizens; cf. H. Balternsweiler, "Die Ehebruchsklauseln bei Matthäus," ThZ 15 (1959) : 350-51. Cf. further Philostratus, Apoll. I, 10; VI, 3.

303   Cf. further: "They have their women in common . . . . The man leaves his wife and says, 'Arise and make love to your brother' " (*unde?* Epiphanius, according to W. Schultz, *Dokumente der Gnosis*, p. 162).
         According to Eus. CH IV, 7.11, the Gnostics bring the whole church into disrepute "ὡς δὴ ἀθεμίτοις πρὸς μητέρας καὶ ἀδελφὰς μίξεσιν."

304   On this cf. E. Kähler, pp. 43 ff.; G. Delling, *Paulus Stellung zu Frau und Ehe*, pp. 96 ff.; H. Schwantes, *Schöpfung der Endzeit*, p. 12; M. D. Hooker, "Authority on Her Head," NTS 10 (1964) : 410-16.

305   Cf. Billerbeck, III: 427 ff.

306   When K. Wegenast (*Das Verständnis der Tradition bei Paulus und in den Deuteropaulinen*, WMANT 8 [1962]: 112) gives it as my opinion that in I, 11:2 ff. Paul is attempting again to introduce "a custom created by the Corinthians," he has obviously misunderstood me. The custom of women covering their heads during worship is ancient tradition in the Pauline communities and may go back to Paul, who, as vs. 16 shows, knows a different custom in none of his communities and in this practice must have been following a synagogal custom; cf. J. Jeremias in TLZ 91 (1966), col. 431.

307   Thus already W. Lütgert, pp. 130-31. Cf. E. Haenchen, *Die Botschaft des Thomas-Evangeliums* (1961), p. 72: "The women in the community who are prophesying with uncovered head, against whom Paul sets himself in 11:2 ff., were in all probability Gnostic prophetesses (11:5, προφητεύουσα) ."

Clem. Alex., Strom. III, 13.92. Cf. Coptic Gospel of Thomas 23; 308
Acta Petri 38; Acta Phil. 140; Test. Dom., ed. Rahmani, p. 65; Sophia
Jesu Christi, ed. Till, pp. 228-29.

Hennecke-Schneemelcher-Wilson, I: 298. Cf. further, from the writ- 309
ing "On righteousness" attributed to the Gnostic Epiphanes: "But
these all see (the creation) in common; for there is no distinction
between rich and poor, the people and the princes, the foolish and the
wise, man and woman, servants, freedmen and slaves . . . . The Creator
and Father of all things made no distinction between woman and
man" (Clem. Alex., Strom. III, 6.1-2; 7.1). From this the Gnostic
drew the inference of having the women in common. In the Coptic
Gospel of Thomas it is said in Logion 114 (Leipoldt-Schenke, p. 26;
Hennecke-Schneemelcher-Wilson, I: 522): "Simon Peter said to them:
Let Mary go forth from among us, for women are not worthy of the
life. Jesus said: Behold, I shall lead her, that I may make her male, in
order that she also may become a living spirit like you males. For
every woman who makes herself male shall enter into the kingdom of
heaven"; i.e., that the Pneuma takes away the distinction between
man and woman. Thus in the Book of Baruch of the Gnostic Justin it
is said: "ἡ μὲν γὰρ ψυχή ἐστιν Ἐδέμ, τὸ δὲ πνεῦμα Ἐλωείμ, ἑκάτερα
ὄντα ἐν πᾶσιν ἀνθρώποις καὶ θήλεσι καὶ ἄρρεσι" (Hipp. V, 26.25 =
130.25 ff.). ". . . at the place where there is neither man nor woman,
nor are there figures there, but an indescribable light" (Pistis Sophia
143 = Schmidt-Till, p. 245.32 ff.).

Cf. now also G. Klein, Die Zwölf Apostel, FRLANT NF 59 (1961): 310
195; J. Jervell, pp. 294-95; Coptic Gospel of Philip 49; 102.

Cf. further Hipp. V, 14.3; VI, 18.4; V, 6.5, et passim; Corp. Herm. 311
I, 9, 15 ff.; Papyr. Berol. 8502, p. 28.3 = Till, p. 97, et passim.

Cf. J. C. G. Greig, "Women's Hats—I Corinthians 11:1-16," Exposi- 312
tory Times 69 (1958): 156-57.

On this, cf. now J. A. Fitzmyer, "A Feature of Qumran Angelology 313
and the Angels of I Cor. XI, 10," NTS 4 (1957): 48 ff.

Cf. further J. P. Asmussen, "Bemerkungen zur sakralen Prostitution 314
im Alten Testament," StTh XI (1958): 191-92; M. Dibelius, Die
Geisterwelt im Glauben des Paulus (1909), pp. 18 ff.; Heliodorus,
Aithiopica: "You must therefore without fail show me the phylactery

which according to your account was exposed with the child and which you received along with the other identifying signs. I fear that this phylactery contains some sort of definite magic and is inscribed with magical signs, which make your daughter so abrupt and unapproachable" (*Bibliothek der Alten Welt* [Zürich, 1950], p. 109). From Jewish tradition I cite the following passage, following Billerbeck, III: 439, from Wagenseil, *Sota*, p. 43: "Those who know the tradition write, Where a woman's hair comes out (that is, out of her coiffure, so that it is loose around her head), there the evil spirits come and sit upon it and corrupt everything in the house; and the Gemara lists three things that are a shame for a woman: when she cries aloud, when she shows her body, and when her hair is loose.' " Cf. also Lidzbarski, *Mandäische Liturgien,* pp. 4.13 ff.; Philostratus, Apoll. VII, 22: the prayer frontlets bound on the head also possessed apotropaic significance for the rabbis; cf. Billerbeck, IV: 273.

315   He has "ἐξουσίαν . . . πρὸς τὸ κυριεύειν ἤδη τῶν ἀρχόντων καὶ ποιητῶν τοῦδε τοῦ κόσμου" (Iren. I, 25.3).

316   Most recently E. Kähler, pp. 74 ff.

317   Thus most recently J. Leipoldt, *Die Frau in der antiken Welt und im Urchristentum* (1955, 2nd ed.), pp. 190-91; W. D. Marsch in RGG (3rd ed.), II, col. 1071; E. Schweizer, *Church Order in the New Testament,* n. 783; G. Fitzer, "Das Weib schweige in der Gemeinde," *Theol. Existenz heute* 110: 1963.

318   Cf. A. Oepke in TDNT I: 786-87.

319   Note also Rom. 16:1 (Phoebe); Phil. 4:2 (Euodia); Acts 18:26; Rom. 16:3 (Priscilla).

320   This is shown by the connection of the passage with the entire fourteenth chapter.

321   When G. Blum writes (*Novum Testamentum* 7 [1964/65]: 149-50), "The complete denial of the theological relevance of the reality of the creation on the Gnostic side and the practical consequences resulting from it were for Paul only the immediate impetus for his view and ruling that in Christian worship none but men are called to the various ministries of the proclamation of the Word," the "only" is disturbing. It incorrectly makes the prohibition of women's speaking a "funda-

mental, theological" ruling instead of a confession of the creator and an insight into differences rooted in creation.

Correctly G. Blum, "Das Amt der Frau im NT," *Novum Testa-* 322
mentum 7 (1964/65) : 149-50, who also further follows the explanation offered here.

Therein the Montanists appeal with vigor, and rightly, to Gal. 323
3:26 ff.; Epiph. Haer. XLIX, 2.

Cf. further Rev. 2:20; Thecla in Acta Pauli et Theclae, e.g., in 39; 324
41; 43; Herm., Vis. II, 4.3; Iren. I, 13. 2-3: the Gnostic Marcus leads women into speaking in tongues; Tert., de carn. Chr. 6; de praescr. haer. 6; 30; Eus. CH V, 13: Philumena in the company of Apelles; Epiph., Haer. XLII, 4.5: Marcion lets women baptize; Tert., de praescr. haer. 41.5: "Even the women of the heretics, how impudent they are: they dare to teach, to dispute, to exorcize, to promise heal-ings, perhaps even to baptize" (cf. Syr. Didasc. III, 9) ; women from biblical history who stand in some esteem among the Gnostics are, e.g., Eve, Norea, Salome, Mary, Mary Magdalene, Mariamne, Martha, etc.; extensive material on this in L. Zscharnack, *Der Dienst der Frau . . . ,* pp. 156 ff.; on Mary Magdalene as medium of the revelations of Christ, cf., e.g., the Gospel according to Mary, and therein esp. p. 10.1 = Till, p. 69; cf. further H. Kraft, "Gab es einen Gnostiker Karpokrates," ThZ 8 (1952) : 434-43; G. G. Blum, *Tradition und Sukzession* (1963), pp. 128 ff.

A. Oepke in TDNT I: 786-87; Billerbeck, III: 467 ff.; J. P. Asmussen 325
in StTh XI (1958) : 173 ff.

In the defense against Gnosticism, then, the silence of women be- 326
comes an *emphatic* regulation of the church (cf. already I Tim. 2:11-12; I Clem. 21.7; Syr. Didasc., ed. Achelis-Flemming, TU NF X, 2 [1904]. 76.11 ff.), which did not hold universally for the primitive church, as is seen not only in Paul but also, e.g., in Acts 21:9.

Cf. also I Clem. 21.7. 327

The Gnostic is thereby fundamentally distinguished from the ad- 328
herents to the mystery cults.

Here Ignatius deliberately calls the eucharistic bread not σῶμα, but 329
σὰρξ κυρίου: Philad. 4; Trall. 8; Rom. 7.3. This is the sharpest rebuff

to the Gnostic Docetism against which he is contending (Trall. 10).
Further, the eucharistic discourse in John 6:51c-58, the anti-Docetic
tendency of which is indeed well established (cf. W. Wilkens, "Das
Abendmahlszeugnis im vierten Evangelium," EvTheol 18 (1958) :
354 ff.) , shows how one could argue from the church's side *against*
Gnosticism with the demonstrative emphasizing of σάρξ and αἷμα of
the incarnate Christ as the elements of the Supper. A tendency, of
Gnostic origin, of criticism of the Supper may also be present in the
fragment of the Ebionite gospel which Epiphanius (Haer. XXX, 22.4)
transmits as follows: "They (*scil.,* the false teachers) have the disciples
say, 'Where do you desire that we should prepare for you the Passover
meal?' And they have him answer, 'Do I even desire to eat meat with
you in this Passover?'" Cf. also from the Coptic psalm book (Allberry, *A Manichaean Psalm-Book*) , 87.18: "I have purified you, my
God, from sarx and blood (?) ."

330   Cf. the Coptic Gospel of Philip 43.

331   Cf. further Corp. Herm. IV, 4. If in Gnostic circles a purely symbolic understanding of baptism was not consistently assumed, discrep-
ancies were unavoidable (cf. Mark 16:16) . G. Strecker (pp. 204 ff.)
has demonstrated them for the "Kerygmata Petrou" in the Pseudo-
Clementines. He also refers to Exc. ex Theod. 78.2 (Stählin, III, 131.
16 ff.) : "However, it is not the washing alone that liberates, but also
the Gnosis." According to Hipp. VI, 41.2-4; 42.1, Gnostic baptism is
something preliminary and unimportant in comparison with the "redemption."

332   Cf. further K. Rudolph, [2], pp. 379 ff.; G. P. Wetter, *Der Sohn
Gottes,* pp. 43-44.

333   Cf. also I John 5:6, and on this, W. Wilkens in EvTheol 18 (1958) :
365.

334   G. Bornkamm has written a significant essay, "Herrenmahl und
Kirche bei Paulus" ([2]) , on this section. He rightly proceeds from the
assumption of the one line of battle in I Cor. and for this reason—a
fully correct methodological decision—takes the basis of his interpretation from the pasage I, 10:1-22: "for there the Corinthians appear
. . . as very massive sacramentalists, and in vss. 1 ff. Paul must energetically hold before them the fact that the possession of the sacraments in no wise guarantees eternal salvation" ([2], p. 317) . This char-

acteristic of the Corinthians is not established by Bornkamm himself, but only by a reference to H. von Soden's investigation of "Sakrament und Ethik bei Paulus." In fact on p. 23 we find the following description of the "Corinthian Gnostics," who "are eccentric enthusiasts of the pneuma-belief": "They do not place their confidence decisively in the rational reflection that there are no idol-gods—for even they will not have denied the existence and effectiveness of demons—but in the fact that those who have been consecrated with Christ's sacraments are immune to all powers and therefore have limitless ἐξουσία . . . . For them the Christ-sacrament is the absolute insurance."

(This view is shared also by E. Käsemann in EvTheol 7 [1947/48]: 270 ff. The impossible combination in this description of "eccentric enthusiasts" and "massive sacramentalists" is puzzling. What exegesis supports this description?)

In von Soden, I find (on pp. 7-8) only the following sentences which can be considered as justification: "Even the fathers in the generation in the wilderness, so Paul explains (10:1-12), had received the spiritual consecration, the sacraments; they were baptized in the cloud and in the sea, they had partaken of the spiritual food (the manna) and the spiritual drink (from the miraculous fountain); in the form of the traveling rock Christ was in effect with them and gave them drink. And yet the majority of them were not well-pleasing to God and died in the wilderness without having seen the promised land. This took place as a warning for us Christians. For what had those who were lost in spite of the bestowal of the Spirit done? They had yielded to ἐπιθυμία (the opposite of ἀγάπη), they had practiced idol worship and immorality, they had tempted God and murmured against him. Thus also one who thinks that he has a firm footing—who is initiated and has Gnosis —still can fall. At that time there was nothing more to idols in the world than in the Christian era. What is required, however, is not to fear idols but to fear God; apostasy from God or rebellion against him means the worship of idols! The sacraments are not . . . ."

I have quoted this section at such length because on the basis of it the thesis of the Corinthian sacramentalists is at the point of being hardened into a scientific dogma which requires no more testing. But does this section offer any proof at all for the alleged sacramentalism of the Corinthians? Not at all!

Von Soden has of course correctly recognized the meaning of the section. In 10:1-22 Paul warns the Christians against false security. For not all who run in the race win the prize (9:24-27). Even of the Jews who were led out of Egypt, most of them died on the way, although they all had shared in the spiritual gifts of the present Christ (10:1-13).

The occasion for this warning is the fact that Christians in Corinth, in false security, took part in the cultic sacrificial meals for idols. In order to make clear to them the impossibility of such conduct, Paul draws the parallel, in 10:14-22, between the pagan sacrifices and the Christian Supper. One cannot participate in both rites! Of course this says nothing about where the "secure ones" in Corinth found their security, with which they took part in the idol feasts without peril.

(H. v. Soden would like above all to show in his essay that here Paul is not arguing animistically but historically [pp. 24 ff.]. This is successfully proved. However, it is completely independent of the question of whether the Corinthians are sacramentalists or not.)

The fact that in the interesting midrash 10:1-13 Paul portrays the "Christian" existence of the members of the old covenant typologically as participation in the sacraments now apparently forms the reason for the assertion that the Corinthians were sacramentalists. But this reason does not hold up. Certainly Paul would also have had other possibilities for setting forth the "Christian" status of the generation in the wilderness. But he had to do it somehow. He does it in a presumably traditional but in any case most ingenious typology. This is explanation enough. That he chooses *this* typology may be determined in part by the fact that in 10:14-22 he is arguing with the parallelism of the Supper and the idol feasts. But with all that it is not in the least indicated that the Corinthians were sacramentalists. In the immediate context of the typology Paul does not at all say what it is upon which their security rests; in principle all possibilities are open for it. Thus even v. Soden reckons with two such possibilities: because one "is initiated" and because one "has Gnosis."

But the Corinthians cannot have been sacramentalists, for the reason that they were "eccentric enthusiasts." Naturally the Gnostics in Corinth did not deny the existence of demons. But they were immune against all powers, not by virtue of having received the sacraments but through their *Gnosis,* the possession of which guaranteed the perfection of their pneumatic self. All parts of both epistles unanimously indicate this, and in them hardly anything of a sacramentalism of the Corinthians is to be found (see below). Instead it is explicitly affirmed in I, 8:1 that the πάντα μοι ἔξεστιν as the Gnostics in Corinth practice it in their attitude toward the worship of idols is grounded in the πάντες γνῶσιν ἔχομεν. Finally, when Paul attempts in 10:14-22 to convert those who are participating in the pagan cultic meals by first enlightening them as to the significance of the Supper, which effects a close communion with Christ—and Paul does argue thus!—then he cannot at the same time have been of the opinion that the strong ones in Corinth *on account of* the close association with Christ achieved in the sacraments participate in the idols' sacrificial meals and in 10:1-13 combat the security thus grounded.

In brief, von Soden's thesis is not only unjustified but also untenable. This fact naturally has its consequences for the interpretations of I, 11:17-34 which are based upon it; for this passage obviously does not yield anything for the thesis of *sacramentalists* in Corinth, but rather most pointedly contradicts it.

H. Conzelmann (pp. 228-29) again follows the exposition of H. von Soden. Against my exposition he objects: "It is abstract speculation, that the Gnostics must have thought thus under the compulsion of their purported system" (p. 229, n. 20). This principle can just as easily be used against Conzelmann himself: It is abstract speculation that the Spirit enthusiasts, under the compulsion of their alleged sacramentalism, must disrupt the table fellowship. But of course such flat judgments in fact say nothing at all. The decision lies with the exegesis itself, which of course is performed by Conzelmann only very incompletely. For example, it does not tell us *why* sacramentalist Spirit enthusiasts wish to disturb the community of mealtime celebrations, and why they are even of the opinion that loveless reveling serves them "for spiritual edification" (p. 229). Further, we do not hear why Paul quotes the words of institution, what meaning σῶμα has in vs. 29, and so on. In other words, Conzelmann's explanation does not result from the exegesis of the text. Instead, the presupposition that Paul's opponents are in any case sacramentalists relieves us in this case of the necessity of exact analysis of the apostle's statement.

On this subject cf., e.g., H. Lietzmann in *Kleine Schriften* III (TU 74, 1962): 11, 48 ff.; W. Bauer, *Der Wortgottesdienst der ältesten Christen* (1930), pp. 1 ff. **335**

B. Reicke, pp. 32-33, thinks that Paul "basically" is of the opinion that the Supper is a meal for satisfying hunger.

But even the Supper in Troas, of which a pre-Lucan account is handed down to us in Acts 20:7-12, was a eucharist without the actual character of a meal; cf. E. Haenchen, [2], p. 520.

There is no documentation to show that in primitive Christianity **336** there was ever a meal for the satisfying of hunger between the partaking of the bread and the partaking of the wine. G. Bornkamm ([2], p. 349) places this regular meal for the Pauline praxis *before* the cultic meal, yet he cannot appeal to the μετὰ τὸ δειπνῆσαι as evidence for such a common meal in connection with the cultic meal in Paul; moreover, he himself sees that for Paul the μετὰ τὸ δειπνῆσαι was "only an old liturgical formula" (NTS 2 [1956]: 203) .

337   Thus I do not at all dispute this set of facts, as G. Bornkamm ([2], p. 343) thinks.

338   The questions in vs. 22b are probably meant rhetorically, precisely like the question in 22a, and Paul knows that they will be answered in the negative. Thus they say nothing about the background of events in Corinth beyond what is said in vs. 21.

339   G. Bornkamm ([2], pp. 348-49) objects that in 11:20-21 Paul is not at all protesting against the common meal as such and deduces that therefore he could not do so in 11:22 and 11:34a. I do not understand this logic. In 11:20-21 Paul is not objecting *to anything*, but is *describing* the Corinthian situation: people were not observing the Lord's Supper but were having a common meal. In 11:22 then he is *objecting* to these practices, by simply banishing the common meals to their houses. This cohesive and self-complementing sequence of thought is incapable of misunderstanding and cannot possibly be taken apart.

340   It is understandable that the explanation of the passage just rejected enjoys great popularity; for insofar as the exegetes find the disorders reproved by Paul only in the common meal preceding or joined with the actual sacrament, they render quite manifestly easier the answer to the difficult question about the motives for the disorders which are being reproved. Now one can, of course, account for the unworthy conduct—which was bad enough, as we have seen—with a general lovelessness. (In view of this it does serve as a welcome insight into the difficulties here, though it does not represent any advance in the explanation, when G. Bornkamm, [2], connects the loveless conduct of the ἀνάξιοι with their alleged sacramentalism. For where would there be parallels for a lovelessness grounded in sacramentalism, especially among the sacramentalists themselves?!)

    The real problem of the passage, however, arises now out of the question as to "how far the appeal to the Lord's sayings and the exposition of the significance of the celebration are to serve the purpose of combating Corinthian immorality" (J. Weiss, [2], II: 648-49) , if indeed the abuses do take place only within the regular common meal and the cultic meal had in no way been profaned! G. Bornkamm ([2], pp. 341 ff.; cf. W. G. Kümmel in H. Lietzmann, p. 186, and the literature cited there, p. 59, l. 3. G. Bornkamm's thesis has been taken over by, among others, his pupils U. Wilckens, [1], pp. 212-13; D. Georgi, [2], p. 94) answers—and it is the merit of his essay to have given a sharp definition to the statement of this problem—that the decisive thing is the *interpretation* of the words of institution by Paul. In other words, Paul *interprets* the σῶμα of the words of institution to mean the assembled community, and μὴ διακρίνειν τὸ σῶμα "means to understand that the body of Christ given for us and received in the sacrament unites the recipients into the 'body' of the community and makes them responsible for one another in love" ([2], p. 342). Accordingly Paul does not quote the words of institution because the *cultic* meal was being wrongly celebrated, but because the Corinthians misunderstood the *meaning* of the meal.

But I regard this interpretation as impossible. For since σῶμα in vs. 24 because of the τὸ ὑπὲρ ὑμῶν, and in vs. 27 because of the parallel to αἶμα, undoubtedly must be understood to mean the crucified body, the simple τὸ σῶμα in vs. 29 cannot mean anything else. (Cf. K. Stürmer, "Das Abendmahl bei Paulus," EvTheol 7 [1947/48]: 50 ff.) Apart from that, vss. 27 ff. do not offer an *interpretation* of the words of institution—only vs. 26 does this—but from their simple wording, the meaning of which is presupposed by Paul as obviously well known, they draw the *implication*—ὥστε—for the situation in Corinth. Thus what concerns Paul is the sharpening and focusing of the words of institution themselves, not their *interpretation,* and this means again: the problem in Corinth concerned the *cultic observance.* It is not that the *concept* σῶμα is discussed and interpreted, but that the *contempt* for the σῶμα in the Lord's meal is reproved.

This has been correctly seen by J. Weiss ([1], pp. 283 ff.), H. Lietzmann *(Mass and Lord's Supper,* pp. 207-8), W. Lütgert (pp. 131 ff.), E. Käsemann (ZNW 41 [1942]: 40), and most of the early exegetes. But just then there arises the difficult question: From what cause did such disregard for the sacrament arise? H. Lietzmann has attempted *(Mass and Lord's Supper,* pp. 207-8) explicitly to give an answer to this: The Jewish Christian heretics wish to replace the Hellenistic cultic observance with the Jerusalem custom of a non-sacramental table fellowship. Since it starts out from the situation in Corinth, this answer is methodologically correct, even though in substance it stands or rather falls with the theory about the Judaizers and is hardly tenable because the abuses reproved by Paul can hardly arise from an eschatological table fellowship with the exalted Lord, which moreover even in itself is not proven as a primitive Christian observance.

Cf. also B. Reicke (pp. 252 ff.), against whose thesis, that Jewish Christian fanatics for purity had not wanted to eat with Gentile Chris-

tians, the same reservations arise as against H. Lietzmann's explanation; cf. further G. Bornkamm, [2], p. 315, n. 2.

341   U. Wilckens ([1], pp. 6-17; [2], p. 91) builds his interpretation of I,
1:12 again upon the thesis that the apostle slogans reflected the view,
widely held in Corinth and stemming from the mysteries, that through
baptism the baptized one entered into an especially close relationship
with the baptizer, and that the forming of groups in Corinth rested
on that fact. The ἐγώ εἰμι Χριστοῦ, which does not fit in with such an
interpretation, is excised by Wilckens as a later gloss.

The fact is, first of all, that there is not a single bit of evidence that
in the mystery cults, even when people gathered themselves around
the mystagogue, they called themselves *by his name*. Even the repeatedly cited passages in E. Dieterich, *Eine Mithrasliturgie*, pp. 52-53,
146 ff., say nothing of this sort and are not interpreted by Dieterich in
this sense. The ἐγώ εἰμι τοῦ . . . always denotes the appeal to the *deity*
of the mystery.

But be that as it may, only the conception that the initiate is named
for his *God*—I can only repeat what has been said—forms the foundation of Paul's argument in I, 1:12-ff. Paul says: No one has been baptized *in my name*, especially since I in any case have baptized hardly
anyone; thus the slogan ἐγώ εἰμι Παύλου is absurd. Baptism is performed only in the name of Christ. Hence one cannot be named after
men at all, but only after Christ: ἐγώ εἰμι Χριστοῦ (I, 3:23) .

Since Paul had baptized hardly two families, and Peter, who according to the opinion of most exegetes was never in Corinth, possibly had
baptized no one at all, but in any case not many Christians in Corinth,
the *baptizers* cannot have been the occasion for the forming of the
parallel groups bearing the names of Paul, Apollos, and Peter. People
can have appealed to Paul, Apollos, and Peter only as the normative
teachers. Thus the slogans for the first time make sense as a comprehensive description of the Corinthian community: Paul and Apollos
were, with their respective co-laborers, the two mutually independent
missionaries of the Gentile Christian community in Corinth, and Peter
the missionary or teacher of the Jewish-Christian house churches.

U. Wilckens, who correctly demonstrates from I, 1–3 the penetration
of Gnostic teachers of wisdom into Corinth, would not at all have
been able to say that the division in Corinth goes back to the apostles'
groups: For these teachers of wisdom in any case do not appeal to one
of the "apostles" named, but to their "Christ."

But Wilckens himself sees that then even the ἐγώ εἰμι Χριστοῦ cannot be discarded. On p. 211 he gives this as the *Gnostic* slogan, while
on p. 17 he excises the same formula because it is out of place when

one connects the slogans with the baptizers instead of with the teachers; for Christ certainly does not come into consideration as one who baptized.

One cannot, after all, infer a sacramentalism of the Corinthian *Gnostics* even when one relates the slogans in I, 1:12 to the "apostles" as *baptizers;* for these Gnostics obviously do *not* call themselves by the name of a baptizer. The mistakenly presumed sacramentalism in Corinth would have to be interpreted as an anti-Gnostic reaction.

R. Baumann (pp. 58 ff.) rightly judges this question. Cf. also H. Koester in *Gnomon* 33 (1961) : 591, who correctly shows that the baptizers cannot stand behind the party labels. When J. M. Robinson, agreeing with this, infers that people were appealing to their having been baptized by those who stood in a line of succession from Paul, Peter, or Apollos (ZThK 62 [1965]: 304, n. 11), Paul's argument provides no basis for such a construction.

Recently E. Käsemann reckons in a most massive way with a baptismal sacramentalism of the Corinthian heretics when he affirms that "all the grievances in Corinth" are based upon a sacramental realism "which sees perfect redemption already achieved in that with baptism a heavenly spiritual body was bestowed and the earthly body was degraded into an unreal, perishable cloak" (ZThK 59 [1962]: 273). Unfortunately Käsemann does not indicate from what passages of the Corinthian epistles he infers this connection of baptismal realism and genuine Gnosticism. Cf. also W. G. Kümmel (in Feine-Behm-Kümmel, p. 201), who connects the apostle slogans or "parties" with the baptizers and is thereby compelled to conclude that we can "in no wise determine" what is meant by the "particularistic claim to belong to Christ."

Migne, PSG LXI, col. 347.   342

On this, as the most recent attempt at an apologetic exposition: 343
M. Raeder, "Vikariatstaufe in 1 Kor 15,29?" (ZNW 46 [1955]: 258 ff.) ; cf. J. Jeremias, *Infant Baptism in the First Four Centuries,* pp. 36-37. A detailed survey of the study of the matter was recently given by M. Rissi, *Die Taufe für die Toten* (1962) .

Cf. further most recently K. C. Thompson, "Baptism for the Dead," *Studia Evangelica,* Part 1 (1964), pp. 647-59. He punctuates the text as follows: Ἐπεὶ τί ποιήσουσιν οἱ βαπτιζόμενοι; ὑπὲρ τῶν νεκρῶν; εἰ ὅλως νεκροὶ οὐκ ἐγείρονται τί καὶ βαπτίζονται ὑπὲρ αὐτῶν; i.e., freely translated, "What do these who are having themselves baptized expect to achieve in their baptism? Do they submit to baptism because death does after all have the last word? If this is really so, then why do they let themselves be baptized at all?" In this way baptism for the dead is eliminated, but at the price of an act of exegetical violence. J. K. Howard, "Baptism for the Dead: A Study of 1 Corinthians 15:29," *Evangelical Quarterly* 37 (1965) : 137 ff., has a view like that of M. Raeder: Pagan relatives of deceased Christians have themselves baptized and become Christians in the expectation of being reunited with the departed ones at the resurrection. But this cannot be expressed with ὑπὲρ τῶν νεκρῶν. Cf. further J. D. Joyce, "Baptism on Behalf of the Dead," *Encounter* 26 (1965) : 269-77.

344   Cf. further Clem. Alex., Exc. ex Theod. 22.1-3.

345   Cf. Jeremias, *Infant Baptism in the First Four Centuries*, pp. 36-37.

346   As much as pure *Gnostic* thought excluded magical sacramentalism, just so much did the *substance-oriented* thought of Gnosticism possess an affinity for sacramental praxis, to which the later Gnostic systems therefore not infrequently succumbed. But this in no case is justification for inferring from the baptism for the dead a general sacramentalism of those who had this custom. On the contrary, baptism for the dead does not at all signify the later administering of baptism because of the importance of this act, but a substitute for Gnosis. Thus neither Marcionites nor Cerinthians nor Montanists, among whom baptism for the dead is attested, show detectible sacramentalist features.

A substantive parallel to the baptism for the dead of the Corinthian Gnostics is offered by the Mandaean ceremony of the feast of the dead, which bears the name "Lofāni." "It involves a . . . meal which the family can give at any time on behalf of a deceased person. . . . The meaning of this ceremony is evident: The food is supposed (according to 'magical analogy') to empower the ascending soul and happily to advance it through the Matarātā (interim hell) to its goal; it is 'travel provisions' for the 'soul's journey to heaven.' Thus the meal establishes 'connection' with the departed soul and is supposed at the same time to establish 'fellowship' for it with the world of light" (K. Rudolph, [2], p. 153) . Cf. E. S. Drower, *The Secret Adam*, pp. 68 ff.

See now also E. Güttgemanns, pp. 77-78.

347   Cf. further Esnik von Kolb, *Wider die Sekten*, ed. J. M. Schmidt (Wien, 1900) , pp. 204 ff.; H. Schauerte, "Die Totentaufe," in *Theologie und Glaube* 50 (1960) : 210-14.

Thus it is out of the question to say that Paul approves of this cus-   **348**
tom as such. He states it only because it is useful for his argument,
without passing judgment on it. M. Rissi *(Die Taufe für die Toten*
[1962]), who rightly does not attribute to Paul a magical view of baptism, but incorrectly has him sanctioning vicarious baptism, thinks
therefore that baptism by proxy must be understood as an "act of proclamation and of confession." "The one baptizing, the one baptized
as proxy, and the community intended with this baptism to confess by
means of a sign: We believe in the resurrection of this deceased one,
for whom this baptism is performed" (p. 89). Since according to
Rissi those who practiced proxy baptism were people who denied the
resurrection, this explanation, which is in itself curious and cannot be
inferred from the words of Paul, and which completely ignores the
religio-historical parallels, is all the more untenable.

On the other hand, E. Dinkler (RGG [3rd ed.], VI, col. 958, art.
"Totentaufe") has rightly pointed out that I, 15:29 yields nothing for
Paul's view of baptism, and that what is involved in the proxy bap-
tism for the dead is a Gnostic practice. Of course his reference to Iren.
I, 21.4 in addition to the passages cited above for this latter assertion is
a mistake; Irenaeus relates nothing of a baptism by proxy.

"This is generally recognized," writes J. Jeremias in TLZ, 1955, col.   **349**
745. Cf. also W. Grundmann, "Eschatologisches Denken des Apostels
Paulus," NTS 8 (1961/62) : 17 ff.

P. Hoffmann (pp. 286 ff.) has convincingly shown that in Phil. 1:23   **350**
Paul takes his point of departure from the Jewish conception of an
intermediate state between death and resurrection which was already
understood in late Jewish circles as a state of blessedness. Even though
this late Jewish theologoumenon could be hellenistically influenced,
it still remains in the sphere of non-dualistic Jewish anthropology, and
there is no reason to remove this motif from the Jewish context in its
application by Paul.

Pp. 1 ff.; the most important recent studies on II, 5:1 ff. are taken   **351**
up there also. Cf. further A. Feuillet, "La demeure céleste et la des-
tinée des chrétiens (2 Cor. 5,1-10)," *Rech. de Scienc. Relig.* 44 (1956) :
161 ff., 360 ff. E. E. Ellis , "2 Cor. 5:1-10 in Pauline Eschatology," NTS
6 (1960) : 211-24. Cf. also P. Hoffmann, p. 265, n. 68, who points to
earlier attempts to explain II, 5:1-10 in terms of the polemical situation.

352   Cf. also C. H. Dodd, *New Testament Studies* (1953), pp. 83 ff.;
J. Jeremias in TLZ, 1955, col. 745; J. Dupont, ΣΥΝ ΧΡΙΣΤΩΙ (1952),
pp. 165 ff.; R. Berry, "Death and Life in Christ," SJT 14 (1961) : 60 ff.
Earlier literature in K. Deissner, *Auferstehungshoffnung und Pneumagedanke bei Paulus.*

353   On the following, I point with emphasis to P. Hoffmann's (*Die
Toten in Christus,* pp. 267 ff.) exposition of these verses. It is a
thoroughly successful attempt, in method as well as in substance.
Cf. R. Bultmann, [1], p. 10; [2], I: 169, n. 1.

354   Thus also R. Bultmann, [1], p. 4.

355   Cf. R. Bultmann, [1], p. 10.

356   Thus also R. Bultmann ([1], pp. 9 ff.) apparently understands the
verse.

357   Cf. further P. Vielhauer, *Oikodome,* Diss. Heidelberg, 1939, esp. pp.
34 ff.; R. Bultmann, [1], p. 6; S. Laeuchli, "Monism and Dualism in the
Pauline Anthropology," *Biblical Research* 3 (1958) : 15 ff.

358   "And I was clothed with the garment of thy Spirit and put off from
me the garments of skin" (Od. Sol. 25.8). "Having divested himself of
these perishing rags, he clothed himself with the imperishability"
(Evang. Veritatis 20.30 ff. [*The Gospel of Truth,* trans. Kendrick
Grobel, pp. 66, 68]).

359   Cf. already W. M. L. de Wette, *Kurze Erklärung der Briefe an die
Corinther* (1855, 3rd ed.), p. 213; further, H. Lietzmann, *in loc.* Paul
uses a similar argument in Rom. 8:18 ff.

360   "That is precisely the Gnostic hope as it is broadly portrayed in
Corp. Herm. I, 24-26; γυμνωθεὶς ἀπὸ τῶν τῆς ἁρμονίας ἐνεργημάτων the
redeemed one ascends to the Ogdoad. In XIII, 6 the ἀληθές, which
forms the opposite to the θνητόν, among other predicates which designate the incorporeal nature, is characterized as τὸ γυμνόν. According to
Philo, de virt. 76, Moses senses, at the end, that the component parts of
which he is composed are being dissolved: τοῦ μὲν σώματος . . . περιαι-
ρουμένου, τῆς δὲ ψυχῆς ἀπογυμνουμένης καὶ τὴν κατὰ φύσιν ἐνθένδε πο-
θούσης μετανάστασιν" (R. Bultmann, [1], p. 5). In the same place
Bultmann also refers to Hierocl., in aur. Pyth. carmen, p. 179.18 ff.
(Mullach); Porphyr. Abst. I, 31: γυμνοί τε καὶ ἀχίτωνες . . . ἀναβαίνωμεν;

Corp. Herm. VII, 2. Cf. further Saying 37 from the Coptic Gospel of Thomas: "His disciples said: On what day wilt thou be revealed to us, and on what day shall we see thee? Jesus said: When you unclothe yourselves and are not ashamed, and take your garments and lay them beneath your feet like little children, and tread upon them, then . . . ye shall not fear" (Leipoldt-Schenke, p. 16 = Hennecke-Schneemelcher-Wilson, I: 515); Saying 21: "Mary said to Jesus: Whom are thy disciples like? He said: They are like little children dwelling in a field which is not theirs. When the owners of the field come, they will say: Yield up to us our field. They (the children) are naked before them, to yield it up to them and to give them back their field" (Leipoldt-Schenke, p. 14 = Hennecke-Schneemelcher-Wilson, I: p. 513); Pap. Oxyrh. 655, I b, see in Hennecke-Schneemelcher-Wilson, I: 111; Clem. Alex., Strom. III, 13.92; Saying 36 from the Coptic Gospel of Thomas is also to be interpreted from this perspective: "Jesus said: Be not anxious from morning to evening and from evening to morning about what you shall put on" (Leipoldt-Schenke, p. 16 = Hennecke-Schneemelcher-Wilson, I: 515); the Coptic Gospel of Philip 23: "Some are afraid lest they rise naked. Because of this day they wish to rise in the flesh, and they do not know that those who bear the flesh [it is they who are] naked; those who . . . . themselves to unclothe themselves [it is they who are] not naked" (H. M. Schenke, TLZ 90 [1965], cols. 326-27; this translation from R. McL. Wilson, *The Gospel of Philip*, p. 87); Gr. Physiologus, chap 9; Lidzbarski, *Ginza*, 432.25 ff.: "The envoy who had come to Adam responded and said, 'What is it about the stinking body in which you sojourn, Adam, that pains you and affects you? Is there a body in the house of life? A body does not ascend to the house of life.' " Lidzbarski, *Ginza*, 517.22: "Naked I was brought into the world, and empty I was taken out of it." Philo, de gigant. 53, speaks of that kind of men who "πάντα ἀπαμφιασάμενον τὰ ἐν γενέσει καὶ τὸ ἐσωτάτω καταπέτασμα καὶ προκάλυμμα τῆς δόξης ἀνειμένη καὶ γυμνῇ τῇ διανοίᾳ πρὸς θεὸν ἀφίξεται"; cf. further the passages from Philo in J. N. Sevenster, "Some Remarks on the ΓΥΜΝΟΣ in 2 Cor. 5,3" (*Studia Paulina*, 1953, pp. 204-14), pp. 208-9; leg. all. II, 53-70.

Cf. further Hipp. V, 8.44; the (second) Apocalypse of James, ed. A. Böhlig/P. Labib, pp. 68, 78, 80; H. Windisch, pp. 164-65; H. Lietzmann, p. 120.

It is true that the ancient and particularly Jewish conception that the soul in the heavenly spheres wears a garment is also widespread in Gnosticism (see pp. 266-67). But this is not the *original* Gnostic conviction. For the conception of the celestial garments of the individual soul presupposes the expectation of personal immortality of the individual soul, while according to pure Gnostic views every soul is only a splinter of the *one* person of the celestial primal man, who is reassembled to unity and eternity out of the sum total of the souls. The assertion of the nakedness of the soul is in harmony with this basic mythological outlook. This is found most clearly expressed in the 14th Anathema of the synod at Constantinople (543), at which the teaching of Origen was condemned: "All spiritual natures will become a unity, and the hypostases and the numbers alike will be taken away with the bodies. And the knowledge of spiritual things is followed by annihilation of the worlds and the laying aside of bodies and the taking away of names, there will be oneness of knowledge as of hypostases, and in the full restoration they will be only naked spirit" (cf. in Koetschau, *Origenes,* V: 286; H. Jonas, [2], p. 203).

When in Gnosticism the return of the individual pneuma-spark to the fullness of the pneuma treasury is described in such a way that the individual pneuma *puts on* the "perfect man," the "new man," the "Christ," and so on, this figurative language still does not contradict the assertion of the nakedness of the soul. For the entering into the "perfect man," or something of this sort, denotes the "putting on" of his Self, not of an alien garment. Similarly the common saying about putting on indestructibility, of brilliance, of light, of life, or the like, after putting off the body often is figuratively meant for the liberation from death and does not presuppose any special garment which the Pneumatic receives instead of the body of death.

361   Also R. Reitzenstein, *Hellenistische Wundererzählungen* (1963, 2nd ed.), pp. 67-68, misunderstands the passage. Cf. Hipp. V, 19.21; V, 8.44; Pap. Berol. 8502 (Apocr. Joh.) 69.5-6 = Till, p. 179, *et passim.*

In my judgment, the explanation that for Paul those who die before the Parousia live in a state of nakedness, and that Paul feared this condition, an interpretation which is most recently represented by H. Grass, *Ostergeschehen und Osterberichte,* pp. 154 ff., 307-8, does not do justice to the text. It is also in total contradiction to the statement made, e.g., in I Thess. 4:13 ff. and Phil. 1:23, that death before the Parousia is in no wise to be feared.

In view of the religio-historical parallels alone the interpretation of "nakedness" given by D. W. Oostendorp, *Another Jesus,* pp. 71 ff., is utterly misleading. "Clothed" is said to be a Pauline figure for righteousness and salvation, and "naked" on the other hand a metaphor for unrighteousness and an unsaved condition. In II, 5:1 ff. Paul is allegedly speaking of Israel, which it is true already has many advantages, but now must also be clothed as well with the righteousness of Christ, in order not to forfeit salvation!

Parth. Gliedhymnen AR VIII, 4 = Colpe, p. 87: "I am clothed in a   362
garment of light"; Coptic Psalm-book = Allberry, pp. 50.24 ff., 83.
21 ff.; Act. Thom. 7; cf. E. Preuschen, *Zwei gnostische Hymnen* (1904),
pp. 14-15.

Cf. further Od. Sol. 11.11; 25.8 (but 8.9); Act. Thom. 111-12;   363
G. Widengren, *The Great Vohu Manah and the Apostle of God*
(1945), esp. pp. 35-36, 49 ff., 76 ff.; K. Rudolph, [2], pp. 181 ff.

Therein the widespread conception that the soul is surrounded by   364
celestial light or brilliance may lead from the idea of nakedness to that
of a particular celestial garment.

Cf. further H. Schwantes, pp. 85 ff. R. Bultmann ([1], p. 6) presumes   365
that with the polemic against nakedness, Paul had "taken up only the
negative aspect of the opposing view," that is, the desire to be freed
from the mortal body, so that the expectation of an immortal garment, a pneumatic body, is not ruled out by the Corinthian Gnostics.
This is possible, but not probable, especially since even in II, 12:2-3
the interest of the Corinthian heretics in the liberation from the σῶμα
becomes quite evident (see pp. 209 ff.).

D. Georgi would like even to draw from II, 5:1 the positive inference
that the Gnostics in Corinth affirm the existence of a celestial garment
([2], p. 92). The common ground, asserted by Paul in II, 5:1, in the
anticipation of a heavenly dwelling place refers to a common ground
with the Gnostics which is known to the apostle, according to Georgi.
But then the polemical remark in vss. 3-4 would be incomprehensible.
According to Georgi ([2], p. 95) of course II, 5:1-10 has "no clearly
polemical tendency." "Another conclusion is more probable: Paul
feels himself compelled by a new situation in Corinth to show how
close to him the Corinthian Gnostics are, in any case nearer than to
the *new* instigators of anti-Pauline agitation who now are coming in
from without and of whom II Cor. 3:1 is speaking." At this point in
our study there is no need for further establishment of my view that
both points—the double battlefront in the epistles to Corinth which
is presupposed here and the close proximity, asserted here, of the
Corinthian Gnostics to Pauline theology—are excluded (see further,
pp. 289 ff.). If Georgi is supporting his opinion about Paul's conscious
approach to the Gnostics in Corinth—who curse the crucified Jesus!—

in Epistle C on "the thoroughly positive use of the concept γνῶσις, phrases in common use among the Gnostics (3:18; 4:4 and 6:3; 3:17*b* and 5:16) ," the question would be what he would deduce, using this method, from such passages as I, 2:6-16; I, 14; Rom. 6:1 ff.; 8:2 ff.; Phil. 2:6 ff., etc., with respect to the community being addressed. Since the epistles to Corinth without exception address the community and warn against the false teachings, the assertion that the οἴδαμεν in II, 5:1 includes the Gnostic opponents moreover is quite wrong.

Georgi's curious exegesis becomes comprehensible only if one considers that according to Georgi, Epistle C, to which II, 5 belongs, is no longer directed against the Gnostics at all, but against the purported new opponents. Under this presupposition, under all circumstances the anti-Gnostic character of II, 5 must be denied.

366   See H. Windisch, pp. 372-73; A. v. Gall, *Basileia tou Theou,* pp. 325 ff.; Kautzsch, *Pseudepigraphen,* p. 447, and on Gr. Bar. 4; Asc. Jes. 10.9.

367   The relative independence of vss. 6-8 is correctly recognized by H. Windisch, p. 165, among others.

368   According to R. Bultmann ([1], p. 4) , 5:6 takes up the vs. 4:16 again. The "we" in 5:6 then would be the apostolic "we." This is not entirely ruled out, but it appears to me to be not very likely. This would not change much in the interpretation, for even in this case the apostolic existence in 5:6-10 would only be an example of the existence of Christians in general.

369   H. Windisch, *in loc.,* remarks on this, in substance correctly: "Herewith the basic idea of 4:7 ff., 16, that already in the present an inner life is being powerfully formed in us, which already holds within itself the conquest of death and the mystical union with the living Lord, is practically denied." In fact the "to be absent" is not understood dialectically as elsewhere in Paul. For our present passage we may say that Paul becomes "an apocalypticist to the enthusiasts and an enthusiast to the nomists, not in order to assert apocalypticism against enthusiasm and enthusiasm against nomism, but in order with all means to affirm the gospel as the word of the cross" (E. Jüngel, "Die Freiheit der Theologie," *Theol. Studien* 88 [1967]: 23) .

370   Cf. P. Hoffmann, pp. 335 ff.; also, p. 320: "The debate with the adversaries in Corinth shows . . . how the pure Hellenistic belief in im-

mortality just the same remained foreign to the apostle." The opposite
view is held by H. Koester, "Häretiker im Urchristentum als theologisches Problem," in E. Dinkler, ed., *Zeit und Geschichte* (1964), pp.
75-76.

Here the emphatic τοὺς γὰρ πάντας ἡμᾶς specifically has in view the   371
opponents who imagine themselves clear of such responsibility, as L. J.
Rückert has observed in his commentary on II Cor. (1837), *in loc.*
The φανερωθῆναι, unusual in this context, might possibly also refer,
as in vs. 11, to the favorite concept of the Corinthian Gnostics (see
pp. 190-91), who with their φανέρωσις claimed already to be at the
eschatological goal. Over against this, Paul states that the real φανέρωσις, i.e., the open confirmation in the presence of God's eschatological
judgment, is still in the future for everyone.

The sense is best translated without any more exact definition: 372
"Whether we stay at home or away from home," i.e., whether we know
ourselves to be perfected or not.

Cf. further Gal. 3:5.   373

E. Käsemann has seen this in essence correctly: "The doubt about   374
the presence of the apostolic signs casts suspicion on . . . Paul's pneu-
matic status" ([1], p. 35; cf. pp. 50-51). Of course by "apostolic signs"
Käsemann also understands miracles like the σημεῖα reported in the
Synoptic Gospels and in the book of Acts. But this understanding is
equally foreign to Paul and his opponents, as then conversely also the
Synoptic miracles are never meant to identify the miracle-workers as
Pneumatics.

Of course it is based upon the Jew's acquaintance with the inspired,   375
though not ecstatic but understandably worded discourse of God's
prophets; cf. D. Lührmann, pp. 36-37.

"The apostle chooses the designation common in the community.   376
Otherwise it would not be evident for what reason he particularly
mentioned the prophets," thus G. Heinrici, Meyer *Kommentar* V
(1896, 8th ed.) : 437.

In his analysis of the opponents' self-designations, D. Georgi ([1])   377
does not mention the title of prophet. This is explained by the restriction of his study to II Cor. On the other hand, he thinks that from

II, 11:23 διάκονος Χριστοῦ can be inferred as a self-designation of the Corinthian heretics, and II, 11:13 ἐργάτης. I am unable to agree with this; see pp. 207-8, esp. note 251.

378   S. Schulz's and D. Georgi's way of interpretation is approved in principle by D. Lührmann, pp. 46 ff., 55 ff. The interpretation of an anti-judaizing thrust is followed again by D. W. Oostendorp, pp. 35 ff. Quite unsatisfactory is the article by H. Ulonska, "Die Doxa des Mose," EvTheol 26 (1966) : 378 ff.

Properly critical of all such attempts are the expressions, among others, of W. C. van Unnik, "With Unveiled Face, An Exegesis of 2 Cor. 3,2-18," Novum Testamentum 6 (1963) : 153-69; H. Conzelmann in NTS 12 (1966) : 253-54; U. Luz, "Der alte und der neue Bund bei Paulus und im Hebräerbrief," EvTheol 27 (1967) : 324-25: "Most of all, the apostle's fighting his adversaries by glossing one of their texts would be utterly unconvincing to me. What would decisively distinguish him from his opponents, namely the assertion that the old covenant as a διακονία τοῦ θανάτου is inferior, is in fact not at all proved by Paul but is presupposed. Paul does not wage a polemic against Moses. Moreover, Gal. and II Cor. afford adequate examples of how one of Paul's polemics actually looks."

379   Similarly—though tentatively—H. Windisch, pp. 25-26.

380   W. Ellis, "Some Problems in the Corinthian Letters," Australian Biblical Review 14 (1966) : 33 ff.

381   That even this would be a very poor case is evident from the simple observation that in the Pauline usage, Χριστὸς κατὰ σάρκα cannot be any sort of "historical Jesus" whatsoever; see pp. 310 ff.

382   The passage which I missed is found in D. Georgi, [1], p. 15; thus his argument is self-contradictory. Moreover, the letters of recommendation could simply have attested the personal integrity of their bearers, as was customary and necessary in antiquity. Nothing can be inferred about their content, which by no means must have been known to Paul, from the fact that Paul skillfully uses them in polemical conflict upon given occasion.

383   On the criticism, cf. also E. Güttgemanns, p. 147, n. 29; pp. 285 ff. et passim; also in ZKG 77 (1966) : 126 ff.

Similarly J. M. Robinson in ZThK 62 (1965) : 336, feels prompted   384
to concede that one could "reckon altogether with a hidden continuity
in the Corinthian 'heresies.' " So then also D. Georgi must at least posit
for II, 5:1-10 the Gnostic opponents from I Cor. as Paul's partners in
conversation; cf. VuF, 1960, p. 95.

Similarly also J. M. Robinson, *Kerygma und historischer Jesus*   385
(1967, 2nd ed.), pp. 68-69; also in ZThK 62 (1965) : 326 ff., to be sure
with occasional criticism of Georgi's quite particularly unfounded
assertions; H. Koester in ZThK 65 (1968) : 197-98, according to whom
there were of course at the time of I Cor. still no "theological parties"
at all in Corinth (p. 195), "in spite of the fundamental theological
questions which are broached here" (p. 196) !

Yet see above, p. 78, n. 197. Recently J. Roloff (*Apostolat—Ver-*   386
kündigung—Kirche, p. 80) again describes Paul's opponents in II Cor.
as "representatives of a gnosticizing Judaism," but then must also
speak of the "heterogeneity of their self-understanding" (p. 81) and
refrain from adducing religio-historical parallels for this divided product of syncretism.

K. Rudolph in the *Sonderheft* 1963 of the WZUJ, p. 93: "The exis-   387
tence of a pre-Christian Gnostic tendency in sectarian Judaism thus
can no longer be denied."

Of course this again is the point of what H. Conzelmann indicates   388
concerning the Corinthian situation. He parries the question about
influences "from without" and proposes rather to understand the
situation in Corinth from questions like these: What ideas did the
Corinthian Christians bring with them into the community? How does
the Christian faith affect these? In what direction is their imported
thinking turned? and so on.

Pauline beginnings gradually form "what is later presented as 'Gnosticism,' that is, Gnosticism *in statu nascendi*. One may characterize
the Corinthians as Proto-Gnostics." Out of the Pauline credo of cross
and resurrection is developed the conviction that death is abolished.
"The faith is turned into the movement of the spiritual ascension with
the redeemer. This movement can be confirmed by means of the experiences—inaugurated in Corinth by Paul—of the Spirit in ecstasy,
which delivers the Pneumatic out of the world into heaven. Thus the
Spirit is no longer criterion and ἀρραβών, who sustains me as a believer
in the world and leads me here in a new walk of life. The experience

of the Spirit becomes the experience of self, and Christ becomes a cipher for the same. One can also be led in the same direction by the catchwords introduced by Paul, 'wisdom' and 'freedom.' In the sense of the pneumatic self-experience the liberty of faith is transposed into a world-view principle which is supposed to actualize the release of the Pneumatics from the world. All the phenomena which appear in I Cor. are explained in terms of this transformation of faith related to the word into the spiritual experience of self . . ." (pp. 30-31).

All this may be clear enough: in Corinth Paul is battling his own shadow. Gnosticism is syncretistic hyper-Paulinism, an acute hellenizing of Christianity. Pneumatic self-glorying and libertinism are rooted not least of all in Paul himself.

It appears to me beyond question that with all this one is actually fair neither to Paul nor to Gnosticism. A century of religio-historical research and of hermeneutical reflection is here too quickly thrust aside. Conzelmann writes: "The Corinthian position is not to be reconstructed on the basis of general religio-historical possibilities. Only what is to be inferred from the text is certain" (p. 29). In these words, what belongs together in the hermeneutical circle is represented as an antithesis. In my judgment the result is a religio-historical impossibility, in behalf of which Conzelmann improperly appeals to the text. Where does Paul indicate that he regards himself as engaged in battle with a misconceived interpretation of his gospel?

It is not accidental that in his view of the circumstances at the time of I Cor. Conzelmann must completely leave out of consideration the further course of Paul's correspondence with the Corinthian community; for the ecstatic Pneumatics and false apostles who are opposed in II Cor. undoubtedly have invaded the community from without. Conzelmann consistently ignores II Cor. without in any way informing the reader as to the reasons for this procedure which, methodologically speaking, is more than questionable. Precisely if the proto-Gnostics in Corinth developed the Pauline views into their own, this development would have to be evident and demonstrable in II Cor. in its further progress. Conzelmann however prefers to invoke Romans for the illumination of I Cor. (p. 16, *et passim*). There would be no objection to this only if the heuristic function of II Cor. did not at the same time remain wholly unnoticed.

389   In other words, it has to do with turning from the *service* of the visible to the *service* of the invisible, from *life* that arises out of what is tangible to *life* that comes from God.

"Thus the passage is effectively closed with the τῷ ἐγερθέντι: the last   390
word is left to life" (H. Windisch, p. 183); cf. also Rom. 4:25.

Of course it is in itself hardly conceivable that Paul could somehow   391
concede a pneumatic knowledge of Jesus to those who curse Jesus (I,
12:3) and have "another Jesus" (II, 11:4) than he has.

Like Georgi also J. M. Robinson, *Kerygma und historischer Jesus*   392
(1967, 2nd ed.), pp. 68-69; also in ZThK 62 (1965): 328. For G. Friedrich (in O. Michel, pp. 190-91) the Χριστὸς κατὰ σάρκα is the "historical Jesus," to whose teachings Paul's opponents appeal. D. W.
Oostendorp (pp. 54-55) revives F. C. Baur's explanation and connects
κατὰ σάρκα with the Jewish-nationalist conception of the Messiah of
Paul's opponents. According to P. Stuhlmacher, EvTheol 27 (1967):
383, n. 25, in II, 5:16 Paul "is refuting a view of Jesus as the crucified
deceiver of the Christians . . . , in other words, the same view which
had once led Paul himself in his persecution of the Christian community." For H. Flender, *Die Botschaft von der Herrschaft Gottes*
(1968), p. 72, the "Christ according to the flesh" is the "minister of circumcision," whose earthly mission limited to Israel only has been
superseded.

Agreement with the foregoing analysis of II, 5:16 is expressed, e.g.,   393
by U. Wilckens, *Offenbarung als Geschichte* (1963, 2nd ed.), p. 71,
n.; E. Güttgemanns, pp. 282 ff., with renewed detailed and, on the
whole, convincing justification; cf. G. Klein in ZThK 57 (1960): 278.

Even the switching of subject and predicate, as it is again most   394
recently proposed by P. Galetto ("Dominus autem spiritus est,"
Revista Biblica 5 [1957]: 245-81), would change nothing in this respect: the Spirit (subject) is the Lord.

W. Kramer (*Christos, Kyrios, Gottessohn*, AThANT 44 [1963]:   395
163 ff.) thinks that the identification of Kyrios and Spirit as a "bound-
ary saying" is possible. Paul *means* simply the close connection of the
Kyrios with the Pneuma." But with the catchword "Pneuma" Paul
refers back to vs. 6 and explains: "*The Kyrios belongs entirely to the
sphere of the Pneuma;* stated in other categories, he has his place entirely in the new covenant." But the reader could hardly understand
this unmediated reference back to vs. 6, particularly since the counterconcept γράμμα is lacking. And the wording of vs. 17a does not permit
us to quibble about the plain identification of κύριος and πνεῦμα.

396   Cf. W. Bousset, *Kyrios Christos* (ET, 1970), pp. 222 ff.

397   Cf. H. Conzelmann, *Outline of the Theology of the New Testament* (1969), p. 83: "The Spirit is the effective presence of the Lord." When Conzelmann (*ibid.*) states that the sentence ὁ κύριος τὸ πνεῦμά ἐστιν does not mean that "the Kyrios is a sort of fluid in which we are mystically immersed," we readily agree. But when he continues: ". . . it means, rather, in that particular context that the Lord is freedom," the problem is avoided. For it is in the following sentence that Paul first speaks of freedom. That he *previously* identifies κύριος and πνεῦμα calls for an explanation in itself.